# IN THE COUNTRY OF BROOKLYN

## Also by Peter Golenbock

Amazin': The Miraculous History of New York's Most Beloved Baseball Team

American Prince *with Tony Curtis*

Balls *with Graig Nettles*

Bats *with Davey Johnson*

The Bronx Zoo: The Astonishing Inside Story of the 1978 World Champion New York Yankees *with Sparky Lyle*

Bums: An Oral History of the Brooklyn Dodgers

Dynasty: The New York Yankees 1949–1964

The Forever Boys: The Bittersweet World of Major League Baseball as Seen Through the Eyes of the Men Who Played One More Time

Guidry *with Ron Guidry*

Idiot: Beating "The Curse" and Enjoying the Game of Life *with Johnny Damon*

Number 1 *with Billy Martin*

Red Sox Nation: An Unexpurgated History of the Red Sox

The Spirit of St. Louis: A History of the St. Louis Cardinals and Browns

Wild, High and Tight: The Life and Death of Billy Martin

Wrigleyville: A Magical History Tour of the Chicago Cubs

# IN THE COUNTRY OF BROOKLYN

## INSPIRATION TO THE WORLD

# PETER GOLENBOCK

WILLIAM MORROW
*An Imprint of* HarperCollins *Publishers*

HarperCollins books may be purchased for educational, business, or sales
promotional use. For information please write: Special Markets Department,
HarperCollins Publishers, 10 East 53rd Street, New York, NY 10022.

FIRST EDITION

*Designed by Janet M. Evans*
*Title spread photograph © Library of Congress*

Library of Congress Cataloging-in-Publication Data

Golenbock, Peter, 1946–
    In the country of Brooklyn : inspiration to the world / Peter Golenbock.
        p. cm.
    Includes bibliographical references.
    ISBN: 978-0-06-125381-2
    1. Brooklyn (New York, N.Y.)—Social life and customs—20th century.
2. Brooklyn (New York, N.Y.)—Social life and customs—21st century.
3. Brooklyn (New York, N.Y.)—Biography. 4. City and town life—
New York (State)—New York. 5. New York (N.Y.)—Social life and
customs—20th century. 7. New York (N.Y.)—Social life and customs—
21st century. 7. New York (N.Y.)—Biography. I. Title.

    F129.B7G65  2008
    974.7'23043—dc22                                2008007403

08  09  10  11  12  OV/RRD  10  9  8  7  6  5  4  3  2  1

*Professor Joe Dorinson was the first person I consulted after asking myself the question "Why did Brooklynites love Jackie Robinson when everyone else hated him?" With his help, I was able to answer that question, and I owe him a lot, and it is to him that I bow deeply. Also I wish to recognize the talents of Jules Tygiel, whose work has inspired all who love baseball, democracy, and freedom.*

# CONTENTS

INTRODUCTION *xi*

*Part One—The 1930s and 1940s* 1

1 ◆ Coney Island's Conscience—LADY DEBORAH AND GEORGE TILYOU *2*

2 ◆ Here Come the Jews *17*

3 ◆ Crushing the Jewish Troublemakers—THE PERSECUTION OF EMMA GOLDMAN *24*

4 ◆ Growing Up Jewish—IRA GLASSER *41*

5 ◆ A "One Hundred Percent Jewish" Childhood—SY DRESNER *51*

6 ◆ The Lincoln Brigade—ABE SMORODIN *61*

7 ◆ Victims of Rapp-Coudert—HENRY FONER *72*

8 ◆ On the Side of Labor—MARVIN MILLER *88*

9 ◆ The Roots of Racism—DOROTHY CHALLENOR BURNHAM *104*

10 ◆ Sports Editor of the *Daily Worker*—LESTER RODNEY *122*

11 ◆ The Negro Soldier Returns from the War—MONTE IRVIN *141*

12 ◆ The Jews Love Jackie—JOSEPH BOSKIN AND JOEL OPPENHEIMER *151*

13 ◆ Jackie Robinson's Place in History—IRA GLASSER *160*

14 ◆ The Accidental Rabbi—SY DRESNER *166*

*Part Two—The 1940s and 1950s* *177*

15 ◆ Victims of the Smith Act—STAN KANTER *178*

16 ◆ Victims of McCarthy—TERRY (TED) ROSENBAUM *203*

17 ◆ The Absurdity of McCarthyism—JOSEPH BOSKIN *219*

18 ◆ Fearing the Unknown—PETER MEINKE *225*

19 ◆ The Protestants Blend In—JUSTUS DOENECKE *235*

**20** ✦ Muslim Immigrants—DAVE RADENS   *246*

**21** ✦ Growing Up Greek in Red Hook—PETER SPANAKOS   *259*

**22** ✦ Here Come the Italians—CURTIS SLIWA   *277*

**23** ✦ Here Come the Irish—PETE HAMILL   *297*

**24** ✦ Windsor Terrace Memories—JOE FLAHERTY, BOBBY MCCARTHY,
AND BILL REDDY   *312*

**25** ✦ A Wild Child—JOHN FORD   *323*

**26** ✦ Son of Holocaust Survivors—HARRY SCHWEITZER   *337*

*Part Three—The 1950s and 1960s*   *347*

**27** ✦ For the Love of Billy Cox—JOHN MACKIE   *348*

**28** ✦ The Musical Genius of Lincoln High—NEIL SEDAKA   *362*

**29** ✦ The End of Race Music—BRUCE MORROW   *374*

**30** ✦ The Whites Discriminate—JOHN HOPE FRANKLIN   *391*

**31** ✦ The Move to the Burbs—IAN GRAD   *400*

**32** ✦ The Dodgers Flee West—BILL REDDY, IRVING RUDD, STAN KANTER,
AND PETE HAMILL   *413*

*Part Four—The 1960s and 1970s*   *423*

**33** ✦ Growing Up Black in the Hood—ROBERT CROSSON   *424*

**34** ✦ Cop on the Beat—JOHN MACKIE   *438*

**35** ✦ The Black Panther—CHARLES BARRON   *445*

**36** ✦ Here Come the Puerto Ricans—VICTOR ROBLES   *460*

**37** ✦ Ocean Hill–Brownsville—CLARENCE TAYLOR   *468*

**38** ✦ Going to School with the *Moolies*—CURTIS SLIWA   *480*

**39** ✦ Nothing Stays the Same—PETER SPANAKOS   *489*

**40** ✦ The Guardian Angels—CURTIS SLIWA   *495*

41 ✦ King of the Tra-la-las—NEIL SEDAKA  *507*

42 ✦ The Night the Lights Went Out. Again.—ABRAM HALL  *517*

*Part Five—The 1980s and 1990s*  *529*

43 ✦ Whites Move Back—HARRY SCHWEITZER  *530*

44 ✦ A Marine Guards the Peace—RICHARD GREEN  *535*

45 ✦ Shirley Chisholm's Boy—VICTOR ROBLES  *550*

46 ✦ Brighton Beach's Russian Jews—ALEC BROOK-KRASNY  *558*

47 ✦ The Battle for Sexual Freedom—RENEE CAFIERO  *569*

*Part Six—The Twenty-first Century*  *581*

48 ✦ The Echoes of 9/11—RICHARD PORTELLO  *582*

49 ✦ The Mural Painter—JANET BRAUN-REINITZ  *591*

50 ✦ The Councilman for Change—CHARLES BARRON  *603*

51 ✦ The Real Estate Boom—ABRAM HALL  *616*

52 ✦ Brooklyn's Cheerleader—MARTY MARKOWITZ  *621*

53 ✦ The Atlantic Yards—JIM STUCKEY  *635*

54 ✦ Remaking Coney Island—JOSEPH SITT  *649*

ACKNOWLEDGMENTS  *665*

BIBLIOGRAPHY  *667*

NOTES  *671*

## INTRODUCTION

THIS IS A RECOUNTING OF THE IMPORTANCE OF IMMIGRANTS TO THIS LAND, WITH the spotlight on those who escaped war, hunger, and deprivation to come to Brooklyn.

It is also the story of those whose bigotry and narrow-mindedness caused them to fight to keep out those who were different from them. I came to discover that those in power get to define who's a good guy and who's a bad guy, so American history marks as heroes politicians who were antidemocratic and anti-American while those who fought for freedom, for racial equality, and for social justice were labeled as enemies of the state, arrested, and imprisoned. I am hoping that *In the Country of Brooklyn* will allow the reader to take a second look at some of these "heroes" and "villains."

The Puritans, who came to America to escape religious persecution, set the standard. Conservatively Christian, the leaders like the Reverend Cotton Mather made the rules and set the punishments. Brooklyn, it turns out, was founded by a woman who left Salem to escape the Puritan madness.

Though the Puritan sect no longer exists in America, its conservative brethren still do, and if you study the history of bigotry, Christian ministers and their followers were at the forefront of the segregationist and isolationist movements. The Christian South justified segregation using quotes from the Bible. The Ku Klux Klan was a faith-based organization. The White Citizens Council was made up of devout churchgoing Christians.

As for the hatred of the Jews, most presidents in office in the first half of the twentieth century were anti-Semites or exhibited anti-Semitic tendencies in their private lives. Woodrow Wilson was an anti-Semite, Franklin Roosevelt knew about the Holocaust and did nothing to help the victims, and Harry Truman's wife, Bess, vowed never to allow a Jew to set foot in her house. Congress wasn't any more tolerant. In 1921 Congress passed a bill effectively stopping the flood of Jews into this country, which resulted in the deaths of millions of Jews who had no place to run to when Hitler started wiping them out in Europe less than a generation later.

The Irish and Italians also faced bigotry. Once in America, the Irish had to face bigotry from the WASPs. NO IRISH NEED APPLY signs were routine, but once the Irish organized politically, they became a powerful force unto themselves. The Italians kept to themselves at first, but with each generation became more assimilated.

The history of blacks in America is a whole different story. Blacks weren't barred from coming to America but rather were brought to America against their will. Once here, they were enslaved. After the Civil War, they were marginalized, prevented from getting an education and from earning a decent living. After the war, the whites in America used all their political and financial power to keep the blacks subservient. Even as late as 1947, blacks were down so far that the very idea that a black man would be allowed to play major league baseball was revolutionary.

As more and more Latinos came to America, they faced similar racist attitudes and made great strides with each generation. The last group fighting for their equal rights are the members of the gay community.

As you will see, as people become used to living with those of other cultures, tolerance grows and bigotry dies. As a result, every generation becomes less and less bigoted.

It has been estimated that by the year 2030 whites will no longer be the majority population of America. The ability and willingness of Americans to integrate the newcomers to this land will determine how we as a nation fare in the twenty-first century. Perhaps the experiences of the transformation of Brooklyn can be used as an example for the rest of America. While it's often said that "New York City is not America," one in seven Americans can trace their family back to Brooklyn. If your family came to America from another country, chances are pretty good your great-great-grandfather lived in Williamsburg, or Flatbush, or Bay Ridge, or Brighton Beach before moving on to other places.

The 70.61 square miles of Brooklyn include densely populated urban areas, suburban areas with beautiful private homes, public housing projects, and luxury high-rises, co-ops, and condos, and the type of building that will forever be associated with Brooklyn—the brownstone. There are beaches, swamps, city parks, state parks, and national parks, an army base, a former navy yard, a Revolutionary War battlefield, railroads, subways, highways, tunnels, bridges, churches, synagogues, mosques, a minor league baseball stadium, and nearly four hundred years of history.

In the 2000 census, Brooklynites numbered 2,465,326, living 34,916.64 to the square mile, compared to 79.56 to the square mile for the rest of the country. Demographically, Brooklynites were 41.2% white, 36.4% black or African-American, 19.8% Hispanic or Latino, and 7.5% Asian. And 4.3% were racially mixed. There are even Native Americans and Hawaiians living in Brooklyn!

In the twentieth century, Brooklyn went from farmland to suburb to thriving metropolis to the poster child for suburban flight, crime, urban decay, and drugs—and to the poster child for urban revival and gentrification. Brooklyn is booming again, real estate prices are out of sight, crime is down, and it's even become a tourist destination.

So, while the Brooklyn of today and tomorrow may almost be unrecognizable to the generations of Brooklyn's past, some things have remained as constants throughout Brooklyn's history. The biggest one, as I've indicated, is change. Brooklyn always seems to be reinventing itself. Like many urban areas, it struggled through the upheaval of the 1960s and 1970s. But unlike some other areas that had fallen on hard times—Detroit, Buffalo, and Camden come to mind—Brooklyn has risen from the ashes. And while that's not a unique phenomenon (the Bronx is on its way back, as is Newark, and Cleveland is already back), it's being done in a truly Brooklyn style. Just as in the old days, new money has come in, new immigrant groups have come in, and both pushed out the less fortunate. The Europeans came and pushed out the Native Americans. Then the descendants of the English and Dutch settlers were pushed out by the European immigrants of the 1800s—mainly the Germans and the Irish. The German immigrants in Williamsburg, in their turn, fled to Ridgewood and Glendale in Queens after the opening of the Williamsburg Bridge led to the influx of Jews from the overcrowded ghettos of the Lower East Side. Those same Jews and their children left for the suburbs in the 1950s, when the Puerto Ricans moved in. Then the Hasidic Jews came and lived in uneasy harmony with the Hispanics. And then came the artists, the Williamsburg hipsters who took over the old empty factories and the run-down apartment buildings and the dilapidated stores and made the 'Burg a cool destination—like

Manhattan's SoHo back in the 1970s. And when the artists and hipsters fixed up the buildings, it was time for the developers and the yuppies to come, and with them came the big glass luxury condos—pushing the artists out to Bushwick, and pushing out the remaining Hispanics and Hasidim who could not afford the rising rents. It's a story as old as Brooklyn itself.

# IN THE COUNTRY OF BROOKLYN

# PART ONE

# The 1930s and 1940s

Immigrants looking at the Statue of Liberty.

# CONEY ISLAND'S CONSCIENCE

LADY DEBORAH AND GEORGE TILYOU

CONEY ISLAND, A WILD, ISOLATED SPIT OF LAND ABUTTING AN out-of-the-way beach in the territory of New Amsterdam, was "discovered" in 1609 by Dutch explorer Henry Hudson, sailing his ship, the *Half Moon,* in a failed voyage to locate the riches of India. Hudson anchored his ship, went ashore, and made another discovery: people were already living there—the native Canarsee tribe.

In an attempt to make a good impression and to score some food, he traded knives and beads to members of the tribe for some corn and tobacco. The red men, whom Hudson called Indians even though India was half a world away, were savvy enough to realize that the coming of the white man did not bode well for their future, and while Hudson's men were fishing the next day, the Indians attacked, and petty officer John Coleman was pierced in the throat by a flint-tipped arrow and killed.

Some experts believe the area was named Coney Island in honor of Coleman, but those experts don't explain why it wasn't called Coleman Island. Others say it wasn't named until the early 1800s, after the Conyn family that lived there. Still others insist the name comes from *konijn kok,* Dutch for "rabbit hutch" or "breeding place for the rabbits"—or coneys—which were abundant there.

Though Hudson "discovered" the place, the municipality of Coney Island was not founded by the Dutch. It was started in the 1640s by an Englishwoman by the name of Deborah Moody. Born Deborah Dunch in London in 1586, she married Henry Moody, who was knighted, and so she became Lady Deborah. Six years after Sir Henry died in 1629, she was hauled in front of King Charles I's Star Chamber. She was accused of not being a good Christian, because she believed a person should be baptized not at birth but when the person is old enough to understand the meaning of the ceremony. To be accepted by the Anglican religious community, it wasn't enough just to be a Protestant. You had to be *their* type of Protestant. To do otherwise was to risk the wrath of God or, more accurately, the wrath of God's self-appointed representatives.

In her search for religious liberty, Lady Deborah fled England for the New World in 1640. Unfortunately for Lady Deborah, who was in her fifties, her cross-Atlantic journey landed her in the Massachusetts Bay Colony, where Puritan fire-breathers were just as unyielding.

Sixty percent of the Puritans who fled to the New World came from East Anglia. They had come from a poor, agricultural society, where they fought to tame the meager soil of the region. Because the Puritans conflicted with the Anglican creed, they were viewed as dangerous radicals, and they were persecuted by Anglican bishop William Laud, the Darth Vader of Puritan history.

When the twenty thousand or so Puritans settled in New England, they were defined by their strong religious beliefs. True believers who worked for the Glory of God, they were sure they had all the answers. They believed in the dignity of the individual, but saw order and discipline as "tough love."

The Puritans, similar to the Taliban today, were a joyless lot. Cotton Mather, the psychopath who was in charge, preached that having fun was sinful. His followers weren't allowed to sing, dance, or even celebrate Christmas. Those who defied the anti-Christmas decree "shall pay for every offense five shillings as a fine to the county."

Pessimistic by philosophy, the Puritans saw *everyone* as sinners. They were tough on themselves. They beat their kids. "Spare the rod, spoil the child" was their credo. Their punishments were cruel, if not draconian. If a child was a bed wetter, they made him eat a rat sandwich. The justification was their desire to get the devil out of the child. What they ended up with was a society of punishers and abusers.

They believed in the "right" behavior, and, with order as the key to the Puritan world, their concept of liberty was to persecute those who didn't toe the line.

By 1662 the Puritans almost died out, because the bar they set for membership was too high for most people to clear. The survivors became what we today call "Yankees," with most becoming nose-to-the-grindstone Presbyterians.

Lady Deborah, a headstrong woman who believed in freedom of speech and the freedom to follow whatever religious doctrine she wished, risked bringing down the wrath of the church elders when she announced that she didn't believe in the ritual of baptizing babies. Said Puritan leader John Endicott about Lady Moody: "She is a dangerous woeman [*sic*]."

Anyone who didn't follow the Puritan creed was subject to severe punishment, including the humiliation of being exhibited in stocks in the public square and being shunned. As history reminds us, the extreme religious intolerance that has reared its ugly head through American history had its low point in the British colony of Puritan Massachusetts when a dozen or so unfortunates from Salem, accused of being witches, were tied to stakes and burned to death. The persecutors cited a line in Exodus. According to God's will, "Thou shalt not suffer a witch to live."

This was America's first Reign of Terror. No one dared protest for fear of becoming the next one put to the devoted, righteous Christian judge's not-so-objective witch test. In one such test, the accused would have rocks tied to her feet. If she sank, she was "proved" to be innocent. Lady Deborah, who lived in Lynn, which was just down the road from Salem, again found herself facing the charge of not being a good Christian.

Probably because she was a baroness, her punishment was relatively light: excommunication. Though her friends begged her to stay, she decided she needed to live in a more tolerant society. She and her group of about forty Anabaptist followers headed south to find religious freedom, first traveling to Manhattan, where she was told by Dutch director general William Kieft that she could choose any area to settle from the unassigned lands of the West India Company. As she had heard, the Dutch proved to be much more tolerant and open-minded. Hoping to attract settlers, the Dutch were happy to accept anyone willing to work for the benefit of New Amsterdam.

Lady Deborah chose a way-out spot near the beach, where she and her followers could feel safe from the religious zealots. She settled in what was then the southwestern tip of Long Island, to be called Gravesend. The area, now in Brooklyn, encompasses Bensonhurst, Coney

Island, Brighton Beach, and Sheepshead Bay—the first settlement in the New World founded by a woman.

When she asked Director General Kieft if the area was safe from Indians, he said it was. But Kieft would turn out to be one of the first Brooklyn politicians who not only lied but also was a bit of a crook. Lady Deborah didn't know it, but Kieft, who felt underpaid, couldn't resist keeping presents meant for the Indians, and they retaliated by shooting arrows at Lady Deborah's log house. She considered returning to New England but decided against it when she was told she could only come back if she disavowed her dangerous religious ideas. For Lady Deborah, the hard-headed and hard-hearted Puritans were more dangerous than the arrow-laden redskins.

Lady Deborah was concerned that another outbreak of witch-hunting might occur—and it did, in 1799 in Virginia, with the rise of the Illuminati, a group of freemasons. Said Congregationalist minister Jedidiah Morse, who may have been the model for Senator Joe McCarthy years later, "I have now in my possession, complete and indubitable proof . . . an official, authenticated list of names, ages, places of nativity, professions, etc., of the officers and members of the society of Illuminati . . . instituted in Virginia, by the Grand Orient of France."

Her group moved inland until a stockade could be built, and when they returned for good in 1645, Lady Moody displayed an idealistic socialist bent. Under her orders, each of the forty settlers received an equal share of the sixteen-acre plot inside the fort, along with an equal amount of farmland outside it. At town meetings, everyone was encouraged to voice an opinion.

After she demanded from the Dutch governor the right of people to practice their religion as they saw fit on Gravesend, Kieft signed a document giving Lady Moody and the other residents the right of freedom of conscience and of self-government. When Peter Stuyvesant, who replaced Kieft, made public his dislike for the Quakers, an antiwar Protestant sect that arrived in 1657, Lady Moody invited them to Gravesend, and that year the first Quaker meeting in the colonies was held in her house.

Lady Moody also advocated the fair treatment of the local Indians, giving them grazing rights to the marshes. Her advocacy of tolerance would set an example for Brooklynites far into the future. She died in 1659, at age seventy-three.

THE TOWN OF GRAVESEND, WHICH WOULD LATER BE KNOWN AS CONEY ISLAND, WAS separate and independent from the rest of Brooklyn and rather typical of the time. There was a town center, and an outlying public park that belonged to all the townspeople. Remnants of that original settlement still remain where once a stockade surrounded the town, centered on Gravesend Neck Road and McDonald Avenue.

In August 1664 the British sent four warships. Four hundred men went ashore near Coney Island. The British declared a blockade, threatened to destroy the town, and demanded Stuyvesant surrender the port.

On September 8, 1664, the Dutch, outgunned, surrendered without firing a shot. Fifty-five years after Henry Hudson's discovery, Dutch rule was at an end.

Coney Island remained isolated and hard to reach on foot or horseback until 1829, when a private bridge was built across the creek that then separated it from the mainland. The men who built the bridge in 1829 also built the Coney Island House, intending to attract summer visitors. Among the luminaries who came were Washington Irving, Herman Melville, and the duo of P. T. Barnum and songbird Jenny Lind. Three of the more famous Civil War figures, Henry Clay, John C. Calhoun, and Daniel Webster, also visited. A small pier was built in 1846, which allowed excursion boats to land.

Coney Island continued to be a thorn in the side of the conservative Christian community as late as the 1850s. Sunday was supposed to be a day of rest, but Sunday excursions to the Coney Island beach to enjoy a day of swimming and dining out were common. The more devout Brooklyn churches, harking back to their Puritan roots, went so far as to threaten to ostracize parishioners who ventured on Sunday to Coney Island.

Nevertheless, Coney Island was becoming a premier tourist attraction. By the 1870s, every kind of conveyance was bringing visitors for fun in the sun. There were stagecoach lines, steam trains, horses and carriages, and even a short monorail, which ran for two years from Bensonhurst to its terminus at Coney Island. Excursion boats brought tourists across the bay. The payoff was a dinner of exotic, fresh seafood. This was an era before refrigeration, and seafood didn't travel very well. Lundy's restaurant, located then, as now, in Sheepshead Bay, provided one of the finest lobster dishes anywhere in the country.

*In the Country of*
**BROOKLYN**

By the 1880s the wealthy elite began building racetracks and hotels on Coney Island. Horse racing was illegal in the rest of New York State, but was allowed in Coney Island. Three tracks—the Sheepshead Bay racetrack, the Brighton Beach racetrack, and the Gravesend racetrack—all were built. The Coney Island Jockey Club was founded by wealthy socialites August Belmont, William R. Travers, and A. Wright Sanford, and among its judges were men on the A-list of American society: W. K. Vanderbilt, J. G. Lawrence, and J. H. Bradford.

Leonard Jerome, a flamboyant stock marker speculator and promoter, convinced state officials that their tracks should be allowed to operate, arguing that since the Coney Island racetracks were owned and operated by these elite millionaires, everyone would follow their example and keep the sport clean. "We will be the moral incentive," he told them. It didn't quite turn out that way, but it was a winning argument. By the beginning of the twentieth century, the top races would draw crowds of forty thousand spectators or more.

Austin Corbin, the president of the Long Island Rail Road, built a railroad line to get the horsey set to the tracks and built grand hotels to house them. Corbin built the Oriental Hotel and the Manhattan Beach Hotel, subsequently the home of the Coney Island Jockey Club, which ran the Sheepshead Bay racetrack. These were tracks for the elite, and during the off season, picnics and other events, such as military parades, were held there.

Ministers of the conservative Protestant churches, who saw gambling as a sin, complained that horse racing was attracting a rather unsavory crowd as hundreds of bookmakers handled $15 million in bets. Gambling was both big business and popular. After preachers complained in 1885 and again in 1886, William Engleman, the owner of the Brighton Beach track, was arrested and indicted on gambling charges. Each time, the jury refused to convict him.

The conservative ministers also were wary of their churchgoers taking trips to Coney Island because by the 1880s it had become an open and notorious den of sin: bars, gambling joints, cabarets where Mae West, daughter of a Coney Island cop, later tap-danced and belted out the song "My Mariooch-Maka-Da-Hoocha-Ma-Coocha," and where houses of prostitution proliferated. You could watch chorus girls lift their legs, and then you could talk one into a private dance if the price was right.

Because it was so far from central Brooklyn, Coney Island was a place that drew its share of criminals, outlaws, and escapees. All of these crooks put together, however, didn't fleece the populace nearly as badly as one politician/businessman by the name of John Young McKane. It was the era of William Marcy "Boss" Tweed and unchecked greed, when—like under the George W. Bush administration—the wealthy and connected had carte blanche to conduct their business any way they saw fit. The goal was to make as much money as possible at the expense of as many other people as possible. Morality was never an issue; only the final score mattered, and that was determined by how much money you made. Only the most corrupt were caught, including Tweed, the head of Tammany Hall, who, after being sentenced to prison, escaped. En route to the Caribbean and Spain, where he was rearrested, he first made a stop at Coney Island to see his buddy McKane.

McKane's political career began when he was elected Coney Island constable in 1868. He ran on a Big Business platform, charging that the farmers who ran the town—the descendants of Lady Deborah—didn't know much about business, that they needed a man who could raise revenues from leases on the town's common lands near the beach.

McKane was a man who didn't smoke or drink and who taught Sunday school at the Methodist Episcopal Church. But though he believed in Christianity, there was nothing Christian about him. For McKane, playing by the rules was for suckers. There were no rules. His goal was to use his political position to gain absolute power.

His climb to authoritarian rule was ingenious. A builder by trade, he became the town's supervisor, a position from which McKane snatched power in the community. Whoever held the position also was chairman of the board of health, town board, water board, and board of audit. He also had the power to nominate the justices of the peace. Once he became supervisor, McKane hatched his scheme to use his political position to make his private fortune by leasing the town's public property, "renting" these spaces to entrepreneurs who wanted to start businesses, and keeping the "rents"—payoffs—for himself.

If someone said, "I want to operate a bathhouse," McKane would give his blessing and his company would build it. If someone wanted to open a store, McKane would give his approval and build the store. At first, in order to attract more entrepreneurs, he kept the "rents" reasonable. Though the land on which he built was not his, he was able to control all of Coney Island before the townspeople realized what he was doing. By the time they did, it was too late.

By 1876 McKane had allied himself with some of the wealthiest, most influential businessmen in America, including LIRR honcho Austin Corbin, who was seeking public land on Manhattan Beach to build a hotel. McKane agreed to "sell" Corbin the land worth $100,000 for $1,500—a price approved by the town assessor, who was in McKane's pocket. The respectable farmers expressed their outrage that McKane was getting rich from his thievery, but when the vote came up to ratify the deal, Corbin packed the meeting with two hundred thugs armed with clubs. The sale of the property was approved.

McKane then got permission from his wealthy cronies in the legislature in Albany, in 1881, to set up his own police force. Though it was paid for with the payoffs made from his leases and licenses, McKane had the gall to proclaim that as chief of police he was serving at no salary.

Coney Island had become an authoritarian state. The town belonged to John McKane. What McKane said, went, whether it was legal or not. He made the rules and enforced them through his paid henchmen. McKane's permission was enough to operate any saloon, gambling house, or carnival concession, in return for his getting his cut. Under McKane, prostitutes, con-gamers—like three-card-monte artists—and land swindlers plied their trade. McKane's public philosophy was "If I don't see it, it doesn't exist."

The Society for the Suppression of Vice was formed for the purpose of ending the prostitution and closing down the racetracks. Anthony Comstock, the spokesman, revealed that the pool sellers—bookies—at the three racetracks took $15 million in illegal bets. Yet when the society scheduled a raid on the bookies, they were tipped off, and nothing incriminating was found.

The all-powerful McKane made a fortune, but then he got too greedy, raising the "rents" beyond reason. He was brought before the Brooklyn Common Council and charged with corruption. He would prove difficult to convict, because almost everyone in the town was beholden to him in some way and his political allies were powerful. Many were called to testify, but they either denied knowing anything, or lied for fear of retaliation. Only one man, Peter Tilyou, a successful real estate broker, dared to stand up and risk everything by telling the truth in court about McKane's corruption. Tilyou named every house of prostitution and gave their locations. He told of the misdeeds of McKane's justices and chief of police. He told of McKane's flagrant fraud of "selling" public land.

The committee doing the investigation for the assembly said that Coney Island was a "source of corruption and crime, disgraceful . . . and dangerous." It called McKane "an enemy, and not a friend, of the administration of justice." The recommendation was for Coney Island to be made a part of the city of Brooklyn and called for McKane's indictment, prompt prosecution, and his impeachment from office.

Because he was protected by Hugh McLaughlin, the powerful Democratic Brooklyn boss, nothing happened to McKane, as the committee's report was pigeonholed in Albany. Peter Tilyou, the whistle-blower, suffered for his stand. He had to retire from the real estate business, and his father would be stripped of his beach property and forced by McKane and his goons to leave town.

McKane would go on to become an important state and national political figure. Aligned with the powerful McLaughlin, he was even able to fix elections. Through intimidation and chicanery he was able to deliver an inordinate number of Democratic votes come election time. In 1884 his arm-twisting of the Coney Island populace provided Grover Cleveland enough of a margin to carry New York State by 1,200 votes and win the presidency.

In 1886 McKane, brimming with hubris, made a mistake. Biting the hand that fed him, he cavalierly backed a Republican assemblyman. McLaughlin demanded he resign from the Democratic state committee and from the board of supervisors.

Having switched sides to the Republicans, in 1888 McKane instructed the locals to vote straight Republican for presidential candidate Benjamin Harrison. Many of the voters' names were taken from the Greenwood and Washington cemeteries. New York's thirty-six electoral votes won Harrison the election. According to historian Jeffrey Stanton, this triumph of corruption was "McKane's finest hour."

McKane continued in power until 1893, when he again sought to fix a local election. In the past there had been one polling place, which he would pack with his armed supporters to scare away the opposition. Reformers were aware that although Coney Island had only 1,500 registered voters, McKane's people had submitted more than 6,218 voter names. In an attempt to stop the voter fraud, the reformers passed a new rule providing for six polling places, one for each district. The idea was to prevent McKane from directly overseeing the ballot boxes.

This was an election McKane knew he could not afford to lose, because if he did, the winners would surely make him and his supporters pay, and so he knew he had to be more resourceful and unscrupulous than ever. To get around the new law, McKane came up with an ingenious solution. He gerrymandered the districts in such a way that all six polling places were located inside Coney Island's town hall. Voters entered from six new doors cut out by McKane's employees. Once again McKane and his goons had a ringside seat inside town hall to make sure the election went his way.

Said McKane with a straight face, "The people of Gravesend must not be interfered with, but must be let alone to do their own voting in their own way."

When the reformers tried to enter the town hall to supervise the election, McKane had them arrested or tossed out. When he was handed an injunction to force him to let the reformers lawfully observe the election, he uttered the line "Injunctions don't go here." Several of the reformers were beaten unmercifully by McKane's police.

William Gaynor, the reform candidate for New York Supreme Court justice, was sure that McKane was stuffing the ballot box against him, and he sent his men to copy the registration lists. McKane's goons arrested them and threw them in jail, charging them with drunkenness and vagrancy.

McKane hollered to his thugs, "They're all drunk, take 'em away, take 'em all away and lock 'em up."

One reformer who was able to avoid arrest raced to the offices of the *Brooklyn Eagle* to give his account of what was happening. The wire services picked up the story, and McKane's quote, "Injunctions don't go here," was repeated all over America. Convinced he was invincible, McKane was unapologetic and unconcerned.

But this was to be the year of the reformers. The new mayor of Brooklyn was a reformer. The new state attorney general was a reformer. William Gaynor, who as a youngster had been on McKane's payroll, won his seat on the New York State Supreme Court despite McKane's fraudulent vote-counting in Coney Island, and the angry, righteous Gaynor came looking for payback. McKane and twenty of his henchmen were indicted for voter fraud in 1894. McKane's henchmen offered at least one juror a bribe of a house and land in exchange for a vote of innocent, but the jury was so outraged it came back with a guilty verdict. He was sentenced to six years of hard labor at Sing Sing. No one thought he'd serve it, but he did.

As McKane rode across the Brooklyn Bridge on his way to Grand Central Station for the train ride up the river, Peter Tilyou stood and cheered when the carriage went by. When questioned by reporters, Tilyou said, "This is my revenge. John Y. McKane is on his way to Sing Sing and Peter Tilyou is a poor but free man. Don't you bet he'd change places with me now?"

With McKane's reign at an end, a bill passed the New York State legislature that annexed Coney Island to Brooklyn. McKane, who allowed no visitors to see him during his years in jail, was released on April 30, 1898. After he suffered two strokes, he died in September of 1899.

Reformers also ultimately put an end to the racetracks. In 1908 a state law provided that the bookies would be liable for any and all debts at the tracks. When the bookies fled, the tracks died.

Though horse racing had died out, Coney Island still had its primary attractions, its four large amusement parks that had their heyday before the start of World War I.

The man who began the amusement-park craze in Coney Island was an adventurer by the name of Paul Boyton, who became famous for his swimming feats across Europe, South America, and in the United States. Boyton once donned a rubber flotation device and paddled 2,300 miles down the Mississippi.

In 1895 Boyton opened the first outdoor amusement park in the world at Coney Island—Sea Lion Park—which featured an aquatic toboggan slide and a two-passenger roller coaster that performed a loop-de-loop. It closed after wet and cloudy weather during the summer of 1902 kept the crowds away.

The second park, called Steeplechase Park, was built by Peter Tilyou's son George, who was able to start back up in business after his father's nemesis John Y. McKane went to jail. In 1893 George went to Chicago to see the World's Columbian Exposition. When he saw the giant steel wheel built by George Ferris, he decided to buy it. When the wheel was sold instead to the promoters of the Louisiana Purchase Exposition, he built a smaller version for himself and put it up on Coney Island. It quickly became a huge attraction. He added an aerial slide and the Double Dip Chute, and also added a very popular attraction, a ride for six customers at a time that felt like they were riding in a horse race—hence the name Steeplechase Park.

Tilyou continually searched for new attractions, and in 1901 he attended the Pan-American Exposition in Buffalo, bringing an attraction called A Trip to the Moon for the

1902 summer season. The ride was enclosed, impervious to the weather, and during that wet summer of 1902, 850,000 curiosity-seekers paid to ride A Trip to the Moon, saving Tilyou from bankruptcy. Tilyou was also one of the first to rent the newfangled bathing suits to customers. The only access to the beach was through the amusement parks, and he charged a dollar, which was a lot of money back then, to use his bathhouse and swim. Doctors of that time warned that swimming in the ocean would leach the salt out of a person's body, so Tilyou rented heavy woolen suits that went from the neck to the ankles to prevent that. Ministers of conservative Protestant churches were quick to point out that such public bathing was a sin, because it brought together men and women who were essentially swimming in their underwear.

The pool at Steeplechase Park. *Library of Congress*

The third amusement park built at Coney Island was called Luna Park. It was started by Frederick Thompson and Skip Dundy, the two men who owned the Trip to the Moon ride that George Tilyou had featured at Steeplechase Park. Thompson and Dundy bought Sea Lion Park from Paul Boyton, and opened Luna Park in 1903. They built a War of the Worlds building, put up more than a million lights at the entrance, and re-created an enemy siege on Fort Hamilton. A Twenty Thousand Leagues Under the Sea ride was featured in a third building. Ticket prices ranged from 25¢ for a handful of rides to $1.95 for admission to all rides.

In 1908 Thompson, an ingenious man, a predecessor to Walt Disney, re-created the epic battle of the Monitor and the Merrimac, and two years later he built A Trip to Mars by Airplane, where passengers felt like they were flying all the way to Mars. Thompson, like Disney, felt the need to keep his customers amused while they waited in the long lines to ride the rides, hiring clowns and elephants as diversions.

Dreamland. *Library of Congress*

But Thompson spent more than he made, and in 1912 he had to file for bankruptcy. He lost Luna Park to creditors. Barron Collier, the new owner, ran it until it went bankrupt in May of 1933, during the height of the Depression. New owners renovated the park, and it operated until August 12, 1944, when a major fire destroyed most of it. After another fire in May of 1949, the land became the site for a low-income housing development.

The fourth park, called Dreamland, was founded in 1904 by a politician, William Reynolds, a Republican state senator who had been accused of graft and other chicanery. Reynolds spent $3,500,000 building his park. The rides were mostly copied from other parks. The place had a carnival atmosphere because it was run by a former circus promoter. It boasted a tribute to the armed services, firefighters putting out a large blaze, and Midget City, where some hundred midgets performed at Lilliputian Village.

The Beacon Tower stood 375 feet tall in the middle of a lagoon. A steel pier jutted almost a half mile into the water, so excursion boats could dock. In 1906 Reynolds added a biblical show called *The End of the World,* in which the good people were seen going off to heaven while the wicked headed for hell.

On May 26, 1911, a disastrous fire erupted and burned the wooden buildings to the ground. There had been ten serious fires before this one. An early-morning fire had burned Steeplechase Park to the ground on July 28, 1907. Owner George Tilyou had no insurance and lost over a million dollars. But this fire was far worse. Workmen were repairing a leak with hot tar at a ride called Hell Gate, when suddenly there was an explosion. By the morning the entire fifteen-acre Dreamland Park was destroyed. The Iron Pier was a smoldering ruin. Little of it was insured. Twenty-five hundred jobs were lost. Reynolds never rebuilt, and the Golden Age of the Coney Island amusement park was over.

Though Coney Island amusement parks continued to operate after World War I, the craze lost some of its allure despite the construction of three of the most famous roller coasters ever to thrill the passengers. In 1925 the huge wooden Thunderbolt roller coaster opened, with its many twists and turns, followed the next year by another huge roller coaster, called the Tornado, and in 1927 by the Cyclone.

Perhaps the amusement-park craze cooled off due to the somber nature of the war. Perhaps it was because the world was becoming more sophisticated and ever more assessible as the automobile made travel easier. The wealthy—and, thanks to Henry Ford, even the middle class—could buy cars and sally forth across America. Air travel would not be far behind. In 1911, the year of the Dreamland fire and a year after the last racetrack was closed, an airplane pilot by the name of Calbraith Rogers took off from the deserted Sheepshead Bay track and flew

The aftermath of the Dreamland fire. *Library of Congress*

across the country to Long Beach, California. The first transcontinental flight lasted eighty days, because more often than not, when Rogers landed, he crashed. It would not be too long before planes would make the world a lot smaller.

Though the amusement-park craze had died down, by the end of the 1920s Coney Island would have more visitors than ever before. The change that swelled the crowds was the opening of the Coney Island beaches to the public in 1923. Until then visitors had to pay one of the amusement parks or a private bathhouse 25¢ during the week or 50¢ on weekends to gain access to the water. After the beaches were taken back by the city, there were Sundays in the late 1920s when more than a million visitors covered the long stretch of sand almost completely with blankets and bodies.

For the teeming immigrant poor who had flooded Brooklyn in a wave during the late nineteenth century, living in a hot apartment during a sweltering summer before the advent of air conditioning, Coney Island became the favorite destination. After the subway system reached Coney Island in 1920, anyone from the Bronx, Manhattan, and Queens within walking distance of the subway could pack a lunch and head there for a nickel—or two nickels if you had to transfer between the IRT and the BMT. And if you didn't have the nickel, you could collect enough glass bottles and turn them in at the local soda shop for a penny a piece, and off you'd go.

If you had an extra nickel, you could buy a hot dog at Nathan's, which opened on the corner of Surf and Stillwell Avenues in 1916. Nathan was Nathan Handwerker, an employee of Feltman's, the biggest hot dog seller on Coney Island. When the owner, Charles Feltman, raised the price of his hot dogs to a dime, legend has it that a local singing waiter, Eddie Cantor, and his pianist-accompanyist, Jimmy Durante, were so furious, they loaned Handwerker the $320 he needed to set up his stand to compete with Feltman. Nathan sold his hot dogs for the customary nickel, and it wasn't long before Nathan's hot dogs became so popular that the stand became a destination unto itself. Nathan, who apparently also had a good eye for beauty, hired as a waitress Clara Bow, who was discovered, while working there, by a film talent scout. She went to Hollywood and became the "It Girl" of silent-film fame.

Coney Island in the twentieth century drew from Brooklyn's immigrant melting pot, from the Jews, the Italians, the Irish, the Poles, and the Germans. The various groups came together and harmoniously shared the warm sand and the cool water. For that reason Coney Island—once called "Sodom by the Sea," while under the thumb of John Y. McKane—would become better known as the "Democracy by the Sea."

# HERE COME THE JEWS

THE FIRST JEWS TO COME TO AMERICA LANDED IN NEW AMsterdam in September of 1654. Twenty-three in number, they came from Brazil after the Portuguese recaptured the country and threw them out for refusing to become Christians. The fleeing Jewish refugees who followed also settled in Philadelphia; Newport, Rhode Island; Charleston, South Carolina; and Savannah, Georgia.

There were only five thousand Jews in the United States out of more than ten million Americans, until 1830, when a serious depression struck Europe, and anti-Semitism ran rampant.

Among the worst anti-Semites were the Lutherans, thanks to Martin Luther himself. Luther's primary beef was with the Catholic Church. He felt that worshippers should be free to think for themselves without being told by Rome what to do. In the 1500s he called the pope the Antichrist and later married a nun and fathered six children. He cursed the pope with his dying breath.

His revolution allowed art, literature, and philosophy to flourish, but upon his death, in 1546, religious warfare between Catholics and Protestants raged for the next 150 years.

As for the Jews, Luther at first was tolerant, figuring they hadn't converted because they hadn't heard the Gospel. But when he saw that efforts to convert them were futile, he became angry, and he began preaching that the Jews were evil and needed to be expelled from Germany. In his book *On the Jews and Their Lies,* he quoted from Matthew 12:34, where Jesus called the Jews "a brood of vipers and children of the devil."

Luther was particularly upset that certain laws that applied to Christians didn't apply to the Jews. Under German law, if a Christian committed blasphemy, he could be put to death. Not so a Jew. A Christian could be punished for charging high interest. Not so a Jew. When Luther began calling for the deaths of certain Jews, it was to bring those Jews under the same laws as the Christians. But after his death, the call for the death of Jews became a clarion call in Germany. Martin Luther's *On the Jews and Their Lies* became gospel for such men as the composer Richard Wagner, and Alfred Rosenberg, Hitler's Nazi Party ideologue. Anti-Semitism was so virulent in Germany over the centuries that it was an easy transition during World War II from talking about killing the Jews to actually carrying it out.

After the depression of 1830, thousands of Christian Germans opted to leave Germany, which wasn't yet a country but a collection of states, for America—the outflow was so great that even today, German-Americans comprise the single largest ethnic group in the United States. At the same time, the German rulers decided to blame their problems on the peaceable but clannish Jews. They passed laws prohibiting Jews from living in certain towns and from marrying. Those who could took the hint and left. These German Jews who came to the United States mostly moved West, settling along the Erie Canal and the Ohio and Mississippi Rivers. Jewish settlements sprang up in Cincinnati, St. Louis, Chicago, and other, smaller Midwest cities.

The wave of Jewish immigration swelled in the 1880s, after Czar Alexander II of Russia was assassinated on March 13, 1881, by a suicide bomber throwing handmade grenades while the czar was riding in his bulletproof carriage down the main streets of St. Petersburg, Russia. Alexander II had banned the Polish language, and Polish anarchists killed him.

When his son, Alexander III, took over, he decreed that Russia would have one language, one religion, and one nationality. He was determined to wipe liberal ideology from the country, and an important part of his plan was to rid the country of its Jews.

Alexander III continued a campaign of vicious anti-Semitism that had begun several years earlier, when in March 1879 nine Jews in the Caucasus were brought up on charges of having slain a Christian child and drunk his blood as part of the Passover ritual. Incensed by these false charges, ignorant Cossack peasants, stoked on vodka, attacked the residents of the

Jewish *shtetls* with knives, clubs, and axes, and burned down their houses. There were reports that the Cossack attackers tore the limbs off Jewish babies as their mothers watched. The Jews, whose greatest sin apparently was that they had not embraced Jesus almost two thousand years earlier, could not understand why they were being attacked. All they could do was flee—or die.

Under Alexander III anti-Semitism became a government-sponsored policy. Under his decrees, Russia's Jews were banned from her major cities, segregated into settlements, denied access to employment and education, and reduced to poverty by special taxes, fees, and bribes they were required to pay.

Between 1879 and 1882, more than a hundred thousand Russian Jewish families were reduced to "homeless beggary," and $80 million worth of property was destroyed. Because Jews in the Middle Ages were given last names using common German nouns or compound words like Berg (mountain), Silverberg, Goldberg, Bernstein, Wald (forest), some children were taken from their families on the grounds that their names had not been registered.

When the Jews of Moscow were expelled in 1891, the Jews without means were marched to a railway station fettered together in chains. They were put on railway carriages and locked in under military escort. On arrival in the region of southern Russia far from Russian cities, the captives were turned loose.

In 1891 the St. Petersburg synagogue was sold to speculators for 700,000 rubles. The final expulsion of the Jews from St. Petersburg came in June 1895.

Driven out of Russia, the Jews were refused entry by both Germany, which didn't want them, and Great Britain, which had its own problem with the restive Irish. America became their primary haven and refuge.

They traveled to America along two paths. One group walked or rode by horse east, across Russia, to Shanghai and then sailed on to San Francisco, and the other large group rode west by horse or trekked on foot to Bremen or Hamburg, Germany, or to Liverpool in England, and with little more than the shirts on their backs they rode in the dark hold of a ship on a voyage that could be smooth or extremely rocky and land in New York Harbor, where they were taken in or assisted by relatives or by philanthropic groups like the United Hebrew Charities of New York or the Hebrew Sheltering and Immigrant Aid Society. Also helping the Jews were the settlement houses, including the Educational Alliance, Henry

Street Settlement, and University Settlement, which provided services and educational activities for both adults and children.

A significant percentage of immigrants from countries like England, Italy, and Germany had always returned to their native lands after a period of time. Not so the Irish, who rarely went back. Their departures were called "American wakes," because they were as good as dead. And not so the Russian Jews, who had nothing to return to. Of the millions of Russian, Polish, and Ukranian Jewish families who fled from czarist persecution to the United States, very few ever went back.

Jews moved into Manhattan and Brooklyn in a steady stream. In 1897, for example, 937,000 Eastern European Jews immigrated to America; 1,776,883 came in 1907; and by 1917 the figure had risen to 3,388,951. Between 1880 and 1920, the American Jewish community grew from 250,000 to 3,500,000. Though they came from *shtetl*s, three-quarters of them settled in the large cities of the Northeast. In addition to flocking to the Lower East Side of Manhattan, many settled in large numbers in the Williamsburg, Borough Park, Bensonhurst, and Flatbush sections of Brooklyn.

Poet Emma Lazarus, who herself was a Jew, wrote the lines that can be seen at the base of the Statue of Liberty:

> *Give me your tired, your poor*
> *Your huddled masses yearning to breathe free*
> *The wretched refuse of your teeming shore*
> *Send these, the homeless, tempest-tost to me*
> *I lift my lamp beside the golden door.*

Many of the Jews who came from Eastern Europe were Orthodox, spoke Yiddish, and highly valued the study of the Torah in particular and learning and education in general. Many others who opted for a secular life adopted socialism as their new religion. Unlike the Puritans who came before them, few of the Jewish immigrants were farmers or unskilled laborers. Most were skilled workers, peddlers, small businessmen, and clerks, and a few were professionals. After the boom in ready-made clothing at the start of the twentieth century, at its height a million Jews plied their skills in the garment trade.

One story goes that the Russian Jews were scorned by the German Jews, who noted that many names of Russian Jews ended with "ki." They began calling the Russian Jews "kikes." Some Russian Jews, sensitive to the name-calling, changed their names to ones that sounded more German. Many of the snootier German Jews changed their names and became Episcopalians.

As early as 1870, the Christian leaders who lived in Brooklyn sounded the alarm about the "Jewish invasion." Leading the fight were Christian church leaders. An alarmist wrote in the Brooklyn church paper, *The Methodist*, "The misfortune of the race is that the whole of it persists in the trading life. The poorest insist on being merchants or financiers. An agricultural Jew is rare, and comparatively few addict themselves to honest handcrafts and artisans. It cannot be denied that these lower trading Jews are a species of social nuisance in every land to which they get access, and this means almost every land under heaven."

The garment trade was run by Jews working out of their tenement apartment sweatshops. *Library of Congress*

By 1895, the complaint was sounded that too many Eastern European immigrants were allowed to come to America. The Reverend A. H. MacLaurin, pastor of the Union Avenue Baptist Church of Brooklyn, was among the leaders in a movement to restrict immigration. He headed several meetings in which he urged Congress to pass a measure to allow only those immigrants with a "clean bill of health and good character."

He said, "This great influx of European paupers to our shores should command the attention of all lovers of American liberty and her institutions. Our fair and noble land has become the natural cesspool for the reception of the scum and sewerage of all Europe. The danger is that our American customs will be supplanted by foreign ideas and that our institutions will be overshadowed and finally overthrown."

The Immigration Building at Ellis Island. *Library of Congress*

After praising the English, the Scots, the Dutch, the Germans, the French Huguenots, and the Scandinavians who came to this country and fit right in, he said, "Look at the immigrants who besiege our shores today. We are crowded with the Italians, Poles, Russians, Slovaks, Bohemians, and mixed races of the Austrian provinces—people who have the smallest possible, if any, affinity to the people of America, and who do not assimilate and will not take up Americanism, and will not pull in with American institutions and be woven into the texture of American life. Where is the loyal patriot who is not alarmed by this lowest grade of illiterate, brutal and filthy—the scum of the nations of Europe—pouring into this country almost daily? These turbulent anarchists, communists, thieves, and lawbreakers in general, whose places made vacant in the land of their nativity is [*sic*] a thousand times more desirable than the creatures that filled them. From these lawless beings spring the leaders in riots, enemies of good government, anarchists, mafia, etc."

The Reverend MacLaurin was one of the first to broadcast the mantra that would be repeated often by Christians during the next century. He added, "Goodby [*sic*] to our American home, goodby to culture, music, books and plenty. I am not in favor of allowing any foreign element to come here and swallow or engulf America."

He urged that something must be done.

Nonetheless, an influx of Jews to Brooklyn and Manhattan continued, until in 1901 a headline in the *Brooklyn Eagle* asked, "Is America the Jews' Promised Land?" Asked the first sentence of the story, "Is America the promised land, pledged to the Jews, the chosen people of the Lord? Are the remarkable activity and seeming prosperity of this people to be considered as manifestations of the actual process of taking possession of their inheritance?"

Of the 1 million Jews who settled in the United States by the turn of the twentieth century, fully 300,000 had settled in the New York metropolitan area. By 1910 there were 1,252,000 Jews living in New York. There were more Jews living in Brooklyn than in any other city in the world.

· N° 3 ·

# CRUSHING THE JEWISH TROUBLEMAKERS

THE PERSECUTION OF EMMA GOLDMAN

THE JEWS WHO CAME FROM RUSSIA HATED DESPOTISM AND autocracy. After what they had suffered at the hands of the czar, it's not hard to understand why. The czar had thrown them out of the country after his Cossacks were allowed to run rampant in a campaign of murder, rape, and pillaging. It's no wonder many of the Russian Jews embraced such left-wing ideologies as socialism, championed by the German economist Karl Marx, which called for the decision-making powers of society to go to the workers, not the company owners; communism, which called for a classless, stateless society; and anarchism, which called for the abolition of all rulers, laws, and religious leaders.

The most visible anarchist in America at the turn of the twentieth century was a hard-boiled woman by the name of Emma Goldman. She had been born Jewish, in a *shtetl* in Russia, and when she was thirteen, her family moved to the city of St. Petersburg. Czar Alexander II had just been assassinated, and a wave of pogroms left her family in dire need. She had to leave school to work in a factory.

Even as a child, she insisted on making her own decisions. When she was fifteen, her father tried to marry her off, but she held steadfast and refused. She was sent to live with relatives in Rochester, New York, where she resided in a slum and worked in a sweatshop.

In Chicago, in 1886, protesters were holding a rally in support of the eight-hour workday when someone threw a bomb into the crowd.

Four men, who called themselves anarchists, denied being involved, and there was no substantive evidence to prove their guilt, but the judge convicted them anyway, just because they had said they were anarchists.

The incident, known as the Haymarket Riots, spurred Goldman to become an anarchist herself. She divorced her husband of ten months and moved to New York City in 1889. There she met Johann Most, a socialist who made Goldman his protégée. Her cause became the overthrow of the capitalist system. But, after a time, that no longer was her intent. Personal freedom became what interested her most, and she made spreading the gospel of anarchism her life's work.

As Emma Goldman defined it, anarchism was *not* a violent philosophy. She wanted to abolish laws, because, she argued, laws were used to benefit the rich and oppress the poor. In the battle between the wealthy corporations and the workers, she was on the side of the workers. Monopolists, she said, supported the government and robbed the poor. She also accused the church of taking, through the priests, from the poor what belonged to them. Her solution was to abolish religion.

Emma Goldman. *Library of Congress*

When asked how she operated, her answer was: moral law. When asked what that meant, she said, "Moral law obligates everyone not to do harm to the next one."

Her message carried no weight with the public or the press, who considered all anarchists bomb-throwers and a danger to society. As a result, despite her moral position, Emma Goldman—having been labeled an anarchist—was considered by corporate America and by right-wing politicians as a menace to American society. That notion became a fixture in everyone's mind during the Homestead Steel strike in 1892, after seven locked-out workers were killed by Pinkerton thugs hired by the steel company. Her lover and fellow anarchist, Alexander "Sasha" Berkman, sought revenge, and he shot and wounded Henry Clay Frick, the manager of the steel plant. Despite the fact that Goldman firmly believed that each person should act on his own and was horrified by what Berkman did, there were whispers—

although no evidence—that she had conspired with him to shoot Frick. Berkman was sentenced to twenty-two years in prison. He served fourteen.

A year later, Brooklyn tailors went on strike. In front of a crowd, Goldman told the unemployed that she had no problem if they stole whatever food they needed. For saying that, she was arrested in Philadelphia while attending a meeting of anarchists there. There is no doubt that what offended those in authority—besides her radical political activity—was that she was not only a rabble-rouser but an independent woman lacking stature and grace. And if that wasn't enough, she was a Jew.

In an echo of Puritan leader John Endicott's description of Lady Deborah Moody as a "dangerous woeman," Police Superintendent Byrne told the press, "Emma Goldman is a bad woman in many ways and her sway over ignorant anarchists is wonderful! She is more like a man than a woman in her mannerisms. She never loses an opportunity to incite ignorant Hebrews to rise against law and order. She is an immoral woman, too, and has been the mistress of a dozen prominent anarchists. We have a clear case against her, and I believe we shall rid the city of her for a long time."

For telling the starving to do what they had to do to survive, she was sentenced to a year in jail. Said the judge, "You are a woman above the ordinary intelligence, yet you have testified that you have no respect for our laws. There is no room for you in this community."

After she was released, she continued her lecturing, but the cause of anarchism was set back forever on September 7, 1901, when a self-proclaimed anarchist Leon Czolgosz, the son of Russian Poles, traveled to Buffalo, New York, where he shot President William McKinley with a .32 revolver. When he was arrested, Czolgosz said he got his idea to shoot McKinley from listening to one of Emma Goldman's speeches at a meeting in Cleveland.

Dr. M. A. Cohn, Brooklyn's most prominent anarchist, defended Goldman. His main argument was that she believed each person should take action independently. He said he didn't believe Czolgosz acted on behalf of any group of anarchists, "for it is absurd to think that we do our work that way. We do not select men to kill off the rulers. Our aim is to abolish government of man, but we do not hold meetings and designate men to accomplish our purpose by assassination. If we did that, we'd be in conflict with our own principles, for in making one of our number kill a ruler we would be taking away his freedom of action. I cease to be an anarchist when I request a brother anarchist to do something which will infringe upon his individual freedom, his individuality or his liberty." Cohn said he and Goldman believed in peaceful means to accomplish the annihilation of law and government.

Arrested in Chicago, Goldman disclaimed all knowledge of Czolgosz and his crime.

"I do not; I never advocated violence. I scarcely know the man," she said. She admitted having had a few words with him. She said when she heard what he had done, her reaction was, "You fool."

"I am an anarchist," she said, "a student of socialism, but nothing I ever said to Leon Czolgosz knowingly would have led him to do the act which startled everyone Friday. Am I accountable because some crackpot person put a wrong construction on my words? Leon Czolgosz, I am convinced, planned the deed unaided and entirely alone. There is no anarchist ring which would help him." She concluded, "[He] may have been inspired by me, but if he was, he took the wrong way of showing it."

After Goldman was arrested, she expected an attorney to arrive to bail her out. But the police dragnet had captured most of her anarchist friends, and she spent the next two weeks in jail.

The police, meanwhile, did everything they could to find evidence she was somehow involved. They tried to discover secret meetings at which she might have inspired Czolgosz. They failed.

Two men of the cloth, the Reverend Naylor of Washington, DC, and the Reverend Doctor T. De Witt Talmadge of Ocean Grove, New Jersey, called for the lynching of anarchists in retaliation for the president's death.

An editorial in one of the conservative Brooklyn papers, the *Independent,* criticized the left-wing newspapers that had derided McKinley for being in the pocket of political boss Mark Hanna, charging that their constant making fun of the president had contributed to his death.

"We have seen, in papers which this week are full of his praise and of denunciation of the assassination, day after day, pictures which represent him as an insignificant monkey-like dwarf, submissively led by an obese, dollar-marked figure representing the trusts of Senator Hanna. We have all seen those pictures, and have read the editorials to match them. But they are all of the same criminal character as the speeches of Emma Goldman. To them we must look for the accursed inspiration that struck down the President."

McKinley, a Republican president who was beholden to Big Business and held in little esteem by the public, was eulogized by Reverend D. B. James of the Central Presbyterian Church in Brooklyn. The Reverend James described McKinley as one of our nation's "greatest statesmen and one of the greatest minds this great country has ever produced.

"Like Lincoln, he had sensible Christian parents, and he was brought up on the Bible. His principles were founded on God's word. He had this foundation. He had a clear head, a sound and broad mind. . . . Mr. McKinley had plenty of ability, but not much cultivation, and yet an Austrian paper ranked him with Bismarck as a great leader, a man of ability and a statesman." He said McKinley was the most popular president ever, including George Washington.

"He was about as perfect a man as a man could be."

James too blamed the left-wing newspapers for McKinley's death. He called for a boycott of those papers. "The utterances of some of these papers have been as bad as those of Emma Goldman."

On September 24, 1901, Emma Goldman was cleared of all charges in the murder of President McKinley. She would remain a voice for the workers against Big Business for the next twenty years. During that time she championed women's suffrage and, along with Margaret Sanger, whose first clinic was opened in Brooklyn, advocated handing out birth control information and providing abortions to women.

Sanger's mother had become pregnant eighteen times. Eleven of her children, including Margaret, lived. Margaret saw that controlling pregnancy was the only way for immigrant women to get out of poverty. Some of these poor women were desperate enough to seek illegal abortions.

Sanger's first birth-control clinic—opened on October 16, 1916, in Brownsville, Brooklyn—charged five cents. She served five hundred women, when she was abruptly arrested and thrown in jail. It was an important event, contributing to the beginning of the women's movement in America.

Goldman not only approved of birth control, she also opposed America's entry into World War I. If ever there was a Jewish left-wing target running around America infuriating the right-wing white, male, Christian establishment, Emma Goldman was it.

The conservative Christians in the Congress sought to put a lid on Goldman and those like her with their radical ideas. In the name of a strengthened democracy, in 1917 Congress sought to curb them with the passage of the Sedition Act, a law that said if an immigrant was involved in immoral or criminal behavior or the espousal of radicalism within five years of entering the United States, he—or she—could be deported.

The next year, the U.S. government, using the Sedition Act, targeted the most popular left-wing causes. The Sedition Act outlawed the restriction of military recruiting, writing or publishing disloyal information, or expressing contempt for the government's actions or in any way speaking out against the war. Under the act, the government could deport anyone who questioned the rise of Big Business, encouraged the use of strikes, or objected to the war.

This legislation, which was clearly unconstitutional, was upheld by the conservative U.S. Supreme Court in the case of *Schenck v. United States* in 1919, with the unanimous opinion written by Justice Oliver Wendell Holmes Jr. Charles Schenck had been found guilty of passing out pamphlets against the war. In another case, Eugene Debs, an outspoken socialist leader, was found guilty of supporting socialism and of opposing the war, and he was sentenced to ten years in prison. The Supreme Court said such speech was not protected by the First Amendment. (Debs would later be pardoned by President Warren G. Harding.) One man, Herbert Warner, was sentenced to six months in jail for pointing to a picture of Lenin and saying, "There is what I consider one of the brainiest men in the world."

In Chicago, in 1919, eight members of the Chicago White Sox threw the World Series and were suspended for life by baseball commissioner Judge Kenesaw Mountain Landis, even though a court had found them innocent. The same year, that same Judge Landis sentenced Wisconsin congressman Victor Berger and several others to twenty years in prison for sedition, but the convictions were later overturned by the Supreme Court on a technicality.

It's hard to say how much of the backlash was anti-Semitism, but Albert Johnson, a Republican congressman from the state of Washington, gives us an idea. Johnson, the chairman of the House Committee on Immigration, argued that the country was being swamped by "abnormally twisted" and "unassimilable" Jews, who were "filthy, un-American," and "often dangerous in their habits."

The stated target of the Red Scare was not the Jews, however, but the Bolsheviks. When the Bolsheviks overthrew Czar Nicholas II in the spring of 1917, Americans approved. But when the Bolsheviks abolished private property, Americans—especially the conservatives and the wealthy—became horrified and afraid such a turn of events could happen in America. Rebellion seemed to boil up from the Russian Revolution of 1917, and with so many anti-czarist, left-leaning Jews fleeing Russia to live in the United States, the Christian right developed an anti-immigration fervor.

After World War I ended, the United States suffered through a depression, and many of those out of work were servicemen. There was a lot of talk about immigrants taking jobs from servicemen; from "Americans." The workers, who had taken over Mother Russia, became people to be feared, especially by Big Business and the U.S. establishment.

According to historian Joel Kovel, it was not just a fear felt by the admitted target of the Bolsheviks—the rich—but it was something deeper: the stream of venom was such that *all* Americans, not just those with something to lose, felt the fear and loathing. The elites transmitted fear to the populace "by arousing the dread of the dark outsider, whose symbol was assigned to Communism." The truth was, the real effect of communism on the United States has never been very great; it's been rather negligible. Communism never did capture the imagination of the public, and its American leaders never did have much influence. But communism was—and still is—the perfect vehicle "for bringing the demonizing mentality up to full speed." As intelligence expert Frank Donner explained it, "The great American nightmare of a foreign-hatched conspiracy had become a reality."

Hysteria arises when the people fear the *threat* to the powers that be. Rumors about the foreign-sounding Bolsheviks abounded. The most outlandish: their intention was to nationalize our women as well as our private property. They were going to "slaughter the bourgeoisie, capture their women, and sell them into sexual slavery." Though distorted and exaggerated, these rumors were believed as fact.

The anti-immigration hysteria was fed by Mrs. George Thatcher Guernsy, the president of the very Protestant Daughters of the American Revolution, founded in 1890 in an attempt to maintain the Christian identity and character of the nation, which they felt was being threatened. She said, "[Nothing] will save the life of this free Republic if these foreign leeches are not cut and cast out."

The Society of Mayflower Descendants, another group that didn't want anyone to forget how the nation was founded, was organized in December of 1894 in New York City by descendants of the Pilgrims to "preserve their memory, their records, their history, and all facts relating to them, their ancestors, and their posterity."

In 1919 the American Legion was founded, organized to fight "extremists" seeking to overthrow the government, and by the end of the year, had more than a million members.

The goal was to get rid of the immigrants and the radicals. We had just fought the Germans in World War I, and Karl Marx, the father of communism, was German *and Jewish.*

At the same time, there was the specter of rebellion by African-Americans. In 1919 race riots had left more than forty dead in Washington, DC. Who was responsible? The racists charged that it was "outside agitators" who were stirring up the blacks, as they were sure the blacks were incapable of raising their voices against injustice. Said the *New York Times,* "The worst of all despicable actions of the radicals is undermining the loyalty of the Negroes."

A. Mitchell Palmer. *Library of Congress*

The conservatives targeted resident aliens, those who had immigrated to the United States but who had not yet become citizens. They were the most vulnerable. They had no rights. They had no way to fight back even if the charges were untrue or unproven.

In 1919 President Woodrow Wilson, a straight-laced Presbyterian, authorized U.S. Attorney General A. Mitchell Palmer to arrest and deport foreign-born radicals. At a cabinet meeting, Wilson told him, "Palmer, do not let this country see Red."

Wilson distrusted the Jews, and that included Bernard Baruch, whom he had appointed chairman of the War Industries Board in 1916, giving him authority to mobilize industry and manpower. Baruch had made a fortune on Wall Street. Even so, Wilson had his right-hand man, Colonel Edward House, put spies on Baruch. Nothing suspicious, however, was discovered.

Palmer, who had presidential ambitions, had no name recognition. He needed a cause to jump-start his campaign, and his purge of the "radicals" made his face and name known all over the country. Palmer, who, like Richard Nixon fifty years later, was a militant Quaker, recklessly maintained that the Bolsheviks were planning to rise up and destroy the U.S. government "in one fell swoop." The charge was ludicrous, and he never produced any evidence to back it up. When asked to substantiate the charges, he replied that his information was confidential. His fear tactics and his raids were part of a pattern of postwar bigotry that affected all radical, religious, and ethnic minorities and set the tone for fear campaigns that would be repeated throughout the rest of the twentieth century. Fear overcame justice. Two anarchists of Italian descent, Nicola Sacco and Bartolomeo Vanzetti, were executed in 1927 for a murder they could not have committed, after spending nearly seven years on death row and despite clemency pleas from the pope. During this period, membership in the militantly racist Ku Klux Klan rose dramatically.

Palmer's campaign reflected the mood of the country. His sentiments melded with the anti-Semitic attitudes of such men as carmaker Henry Ford, who charged that Jewish settlement workers, social reformers, and public educators were ruining Christian America as they knew it. Ford and his sympathizers came from small towns in the middle of the country, conservative Protestants who wanted no part of a changing society. They didn't want unions. They didn't want justice for blacks. They didn't want Jews teaching their kids. They complained that the big cities were dens of radicalism and sexual immorality, where Jews and Bolsheviks were plotting to overthrow the government.

Ford, who wrote a column in the paper he owned, the *Dearborn Independent,* attacked all Jewish influences in the United States. After eight members of the Chicago White Sox were accused of throwing the 1919 World Series, the press reported that the two men who masterminded the fix were gambler and gangster Arnold Rothstein and former featherweight boxing champion Abe Attell—two Jews. Henry Ford published two articles in his paper in September of 1921, describing Rothstein and Attell as "Jewish dupes" who conned gentile "boobs." Ford accused Jews of trying to corrupt baseball and other "Anglo-Saxon institutions." He would argue that Jews were "the conscious enemies of all that Anglo-Saxons mean by civilization."

It was Henry Ford who, in his *Dearborn Independent,* first published the "Protocols of the Learned Elders of Zion" in 1920, the czarist forgery that charged Jews in Russia with killing Christian children and drinking their blood during Passover services. It also linked the Jews to International Communism and other evils. When Ford learned the book was a forgery, his retraction was half-hearted, but a decade later his partner in anti-Semitism,

Father Charles Coughlin, would cite "The Protocols of Zion" as proof the Jews intended a world conquest in an effort to destroy Christian civilization.

In April of 1919, a mail bomb went off in the home of Senator Thomas Hardwick of Georgia. The bomb blew off his maid's hands. Hardwick, who hailed from Atlanta, had urged a reduction of immigration as a way to keep Bolshevism out of America. A postal clerk in New York City, who read the newspaper account of the Hardwick bombing, discovered sixteen similar packages addressed to federal officials and capitalists, including J. P. Morgan, John D. Rockefeller, Supreme Court Justice Oliver Weldell Holmes Jr., and Attorney General A. Mitchell Palmer. The bombs were dismantled by the police.

Father Coughlin. *Library of Congress*

On June 2, 1919, a bomb went off outside A. Mitchell Palmer's home, blowing a man—probably the bomber—to oblivion. A pamphlet was found nearby, signed by a group calling themselves "The Anarchist Fighters." They threatened bloodshed.

Who was responsible? According to Palmer and the conservatives, the Bolsheviks were behind it. There may well have been a handful of dangerous criminals plotting evil, but rather than go after the handful of criminals behind the plot, he decided to mount a campaign against thousands of immigrants.

The overwhelming majority of the radical Jewish immigrants—anarchists, communists, and socialists, were peaceful. They were fighting for social justice, union boosters who wanted no more than to improve the conditions of the workers, men and women who wanted peace and not war. Under the Sedition Act of 1918, however, being against Big Business or against war was enough to get you deported even if you didn't do a thing.

Palmer was handed all the ammunition he needed by his youthful assistant, a fellow named John Edgar Hoover, a twenty-four-year-old from Washington, DC, who, in high school, was a top debater and the captain of his ROTC marching unit. Hoover began his public career working for the Library of Congress, and it was there that he discovered his passion for sifting and sorting through information. He attended George Washington Law School, where his mother was the unofficial "house mother." After law school, he used his family's contacts to get a job in the Justice Department. It was 1917, World War I was on, and

J. Edgar Hoover. *Library of Congress*

a government job guaranteed him a deferment. Though disdainful of anyone who campaigned for peace, Hoover never saw any irony in the fact that he had sought—and found—a way to avoid military service himself.

At Justice, Hoover was in charge of gathering intelligence in A. Mitchell Palmer's assault on alien "radicals." Hoover, who was an anti-Semite and a stone-cold racist his whole life, attacked his job with a vengeance. He began by infiltrating left-wing organizations. His idea was to do to subversives what they wanted to do to "decent society." And he did it with efficiency and thoroughness.

Before he was done, Hoover had compiled files of index cards on 450,000 Americans, every "radical" Hoover could think of, including Bolsheviks, socialists, communists, anarchists, homosexuals, Negroes, Negroes who were sexual deviants, as well as the friends, relatives, and coworkers of those radicals. Palmer was aided by a corps of volunteer citizen informers, called the American Protective League, whose task was to spy on and report the activities of their neighbors. When suspects were arrested, they hired lawyers, and Hoover added the names of their lawyers to his subversives index-card database.

Hoover's "evidence of radicalism" invariably was flimsy or nonexistent. Possession of radical literature or guilt by association was sufficient for Hoover. Palmer and his henchmen, doing away with probable cause when making an arrest, should have been viewed as the thugs they were, but with Hoover inciting the public with accusations that these alien radicals were plotting against democracy and Western civilization, the press duly recorded what he was saying and the public accepted the justification at face value. Hoover used the media for his propaganda purposes every bit as effectively as Hitler and Mussolini did later.

The first of A. Mitchell Palmer's raids took place in December of 1919. His announced solution was deportation. Even though:

- Most of the accused were American citizens

- The Justice Department had no authority to deport anyone

- It was not a federal crime to be a socialist, communist, or radical

Most of the six thousand foreign "radicals" were rounded up and arrested without warrants, and history would show that most were innocent of any crime and were not even connected to radical politics.

As the country metaphorically revisited the insane bloodlust of the Salem witch trials, the public cry arose: kick out the aliens anyway.

The most powerful voice for the government was J. Edgar Hoover, who with a straight face testified in front of Congress that they were all "avowed revolutionaries." He talked of their "sly and crafty eyes" and their "lopsided faces, sloping brows, and misshapen features," which marked them as "the unmistakable criminal type."

First to get shipped out were 249 mostly Russian-born defendants, including Emma Goldman and Alexander Berkman. Goldman had been sentenced to two years in prison and was deported after being found guilty of conspiring against the draft. In the deportation hearing, J. Edgar Hoover labeled Goldman "the Queen of the Reds" and America's "foremost advocate of free love," and he argued that she should be deported because she had inspired Leon Czolgosz to kill President McKinley. Nothing he said was factual, but the panel ordered her kicked out of the country anyway. In her final plea before she was deported, Goldman lamented the repressive climate in the United States, which, she said, made it indistinguishable from czarist Russia. Journalist H. L. Mencken commented more acerbically about the climate of the times: ". . . the Reds . . . were hailed by their supporters as innocents escaped from an asylum for the criminally insane."

Even though anarchist bombs had brought on the Palmer raids, they were used as an excuse to go after not only anarchists and Bolsheviks, but communists as well. In January of 1920, members and supporters of the Communist Party were Palmer's next targets. Rule 22 of the Immigration Act required that immigrants should be allowed to examine the warrants against them and be represented by counsel. The rules were suspended, as agents raided meeting halls and residences with little regard for due process. They seized literature, books, papers, and membership lists.

Bystanders were swept up in the hysteria. Eight hundred men were accused of being communists because they had attended a dance or a class at Detroit's Communist Party headquarters. They were arrested, held incommunicado, made to stay in the dark without food, bedding, or bathroom privileges for almost a week. Finally, 140 were arraigned, and when the press took their picture, they looked like the unkempt Bolshevik terrorists they were described as being.

A. Mitchell Palmer never got the nomination for president because he began to believe his own rhetoric. Palmer stoutly predicted that on May 1, 1920, there would be a communist revolution in the United States. His words created panic, but when his prediction turned out to be groundless, he was seen as the demagogue he had become.

After the hysteria died down, civil libertarians protested his unconstitutional actions so loudly that right-thinking people ultimately became angry and disgusted by his iron-fisted terror tactics. Louis Post, the assistant secretary of labor, began to reject most of Palmer's immigrant cases brought before him. On September 16, 1920, a bomb went off at the House of Morgan on Wall Street, killing thirty-eight people and injuring four hundred. Anarchists and communists were suspected, but the bomber was never caught. But the Red Scare had played itself out, and, as they should have done with the earlier bombings, the feds limited their activity to catching the criminals involved in the bombing.

As for J. Edgar Hoover, his career was just beginning. Under Presidents Wilson and Harding, Hoover had been the number two man in charge at the Bureau of Investigation, under William J. Burns, founder of his detective agency, but after Harding died in 1924 of a heart attack, Calvin Coolidge appointed Harlan Stone as attorney general, and Stone, the former Columbia Law School dean, fired Burns. On May 10, 1924, Stone hired Hoover as "top dog." It would not be long before the Federal Bureau of Investigation would become the personal fiefdom of J. Edgar Hoover, for the next half century.

Hoover and the conservatives learned one very important lesson from the Red Scare: even though much of their purge was unconstitutional and based on trumped-up charges, it was very effective. The Communist Party was forced to go underground. Antidemocratic repression was established as a precedent, union activity was scorned, and America again was made safer for Big Business.

The Red Scare also taught the conservatives a second, equally important lesson: if you want to ruin someone's reputation, you need only accuse him of being a communist. Wrote historian Joel Kovel, "From then on, the term Communist became linked with anyone who challenged the order of things from a progressive direction, and at the same time he became associated with the Jew who killed Christ and the howling savage at the gates."

Ordinary citizens also learned something from the Palmer raids: they could avoid being considered foreigners if they attacked their neighbor for being a communist. Fearing and hating the communists was proof you were a red-white-and-blue-blooded American.

The Palmer raids also resulted in the formation of the American Civil Liberties Union. The organization was founded by pacifist Roger Baldwin and other notable civil libertarians, such as Jane Addams, Felix Frankfurter, Clarence Darrow, and Upton Sinclair, all disgusted by the persecution of people for their political beliefs.

By then the country had decided it had its fill of European immigrants. The time had come to stop taking them. Between 1918 and 1921, almost a million and a half immigrants, mostly Jews and Italians, entered the United States, and this horde offended the Protestant Republican majority, who warned against the harmful effects of "abnormally twisted Jews . . . filthy, un-American, and often dangerous in their habits."

The country, moreover, was turning to mechanization, and the need for unskilled labor was shrinking. Companies no longer needed to risk hiring an immigrant worker with "radical ideas" like seeking social justice or wanting to establish labor unions so the working man could earn a fair wage.

Senator William P. Dillingham, a Republican from Vermont, was a man who held dear the rural, literate, Anglo-Saxon Protestant way of life. He had begun his career as a prosecuting attorney and later became Vermont's tax commissioner, and then was elected governor of the state in 1888.

Elected in 1900 to the Senate, Dillingham became chairman of the United States Immigration Commission. Spurred on by President Theodore Roosevelt, who was seeking "a solution to this immigration business," Dillingham mounted a campaign designed to stop the tide of Jews, Italians (Catholics), and Japanese coming to this country. He ordered a study of the 2 million public school children in 1908 and found that 42 percent of the students were native-born and 58 percent of them were foreign-born. According to Dillingham's study, the students who were the most "retarded" (meaning behind in class and studies) were the Polish Jews, at 66.9 percent. Second were the Italian kids, at 63.6 percent. The least retarded, said the study, were the children of British ancestry. Since it took time for the children of immigrants to learn a new language, the results were not surprising.

W. P. Dillingham. *Library of Congress*

Based on these "findings," Dillingham then proposed a bill that would limit annual immigration for each ethnic group to 5 percent of the number of foreign-born of that group in the 1910 census. The House cut the percentage from 5 to 3 percent, and President Warren Harding signed it into law in 1921.

For some conservatives in the Congress, this was still letting in too many Jews and Italians. They wanted the law to be even *stricter*. Henry Ford's lobbying, as well as that of violently anti-black, anti-Jewish, and anti-Catholic groups like the Ku Klux Klan, were able to spur Congress to virtually cut off the entry of Eastern European Jews and Italian Catholics in 1924.

The House proposed a bill similar to the 1921 bill that would use the 1890 census as its guide, before most of the foreign-born arrived. The Senate said no. Senator David Reed of Pennsylvania came up with a more effective but less obviously discriminatory solution. He said the bill should tie the number of immigrants allowed to come in from any given country to the percentage of that nationality as measured against the entire U.S. population. The rest of the Republican-led Congress agreed.

In May of 1924, the Reed proposal became law. Under a quota system that was put into effect based mostly on guesswork, the law, which was written by Congressman Albert Johnson of Washington, allowed the admission of about 150,000 immigrants each year. Under the bill, most of the immigrants allowed in would come from Great Britain and Germany.

The bill allowed 5,800 to come from Italy, 2,784 to come from Russia, and 307 from Greece. Most Asians were excluded, and no one was allowed in from Africa. The two groups not excluded were Mexicans and those from the Caribbean islands, who later would come in droves.

Three years after the bill was passed, Republican Congressman Albert Johnson, its author, wrote, "The United States is our land. We intend to maintain it so. The day of indiscriminate acceptance of all races has definitely ended."

The 1924 law, called the National Origins Act, reduced the immigration of Jews from a hundred thousand a year to about ten thousand. Had the law not been passed, a lot more Jews would have found refuge in the United States and survived the Holocaust. It's been estimated that in the fifteen years before World War II, 1,350,000 Jews would have been in America instead of ending up murdered by the Nazis in concentration camps.

In 1939 a bill was introduced in Congress to admit twenty thousand German-Jewish refugees under the age of fourteen. The bill was sponsored by Senator Robert F. Wagner, a liberal Democrat from New York, and Congresswoman Edith Rogers, a Republican from Massachusetts. News of German atrocities against Jews had reached the United States, and thousands of families responded with offers to adopt these children. The Quakers even offered to supervise resettlement procedures.

But anti-Semitism was so strong in Congress that the bill didn't even come up for a vote. A series of objections were raised, including the scarcity of jobs and not wanting to separate children from their parents. Secretary of State Cordell Hull, a Southern gentleman married to a Jewish woman, said it would set a bad precedent, and he complained about having to add more personnel and office space to do the job. President Franklin D. Roosevelt never said a word, never used the power of his office to pressure the newly conservative Congress.

Between the years 1933 and 1940, while half the quota for German immigrants went unused, more than 300,000 Jews who applied for visas were turned away.

On January 16, 1944, the staff of Secretary of the Treasury Henry Morgenthau, who was Jewish, prepared what was called "Report to the Secretary on the Acquiescence of This Government in the Murder of the Jews." Before the report was sent to President Roosevelt, the title was changed to "Personal Report to the President."

The first sentence of the report stated: "One of the greatest crimes in history, the slaughter of the Jewish people in Europe, is continuing unabated." The report was an indictment of American policy in general and of the State Department in particular. It attacked the visa policy, which kept the quota levels under the guise of national security. It charged that some officials, including Breckinridge Long, the U.S. State Department official in charge of European refugees, had deliberately failed to try to rescue the Jews. A plan for rescuing the Jews had been brought to Long, a protégé of Woodrow Wilson, and he had sat on it for eight months.

Six days later, Roosevelt issued an executive order creating the War Refugee Board, whose job was to rescue survivors and give them aid. But the board was not authorized to bring a single Jewish refugee to America, only to other countries.

In all, the board ended up helping exactly 987 refugees, mostly Jews from refugee camps in Italy.

Roosevelt's defenders say he was powerless, given the tenor of the times. Others are less charitable, looking to the words of his cousin Laura Delano, wife of Commissioner of Immigration and Naturalization James Houghteling. During the 1939 debate over the bill that would have brought twenty thousand Jewish children under the age of fourteen to America, sparing them from death under the Nazis, Laura Delano opined to her guests at a cocktail party that the "twenty thousand charming children would all too soon grow into twenty thousand ugly adults." Most of those twenty thousand Jewish children no doubt perished in the Holocaust.

# GROWING UP JEWISH

IRA GLASSER

COMPARED TO EUROPE, THERE WAS RELATIVELY LITTLE ANTI-Semitism in the United States in the eighteenth and nineteenth centuries. The first signs of open anti-Semitism appeared during the Civil War. It was a time of economic slump, political unrest, and frayed tempers. Jews were accused of profiteering, smuggling, black-marketeering, and draft-dodging. On December 17, 1862, General Ulysses Grant issued Executive Order No. 11, expelling all Jews from Kentucky, Tennessee, and Mississippi. President Abraham Lincoln countermanded it three days later, but Grant had made his position clear, although he would carry the Jewish vote in the 1868 election and name a number of Jews to high office.

In 1877 a Jewish banker Joseph Seligman was refused admission to the Grand Union Hotel in Saratoga Springs, New York. This signaled a new trend, excluding Jews (and blacks) from social contacts. This was true for resorts, social clubs, and private schools. The Protestant social elite saw the Jews as climbing too fast. They had to be kept in their place.

The rise of anti-Semitism came after the Great Migration from Russia. Stereotypes from religious, economic, political, and sociological prejudice ran rampant. Jews were seen as either clannish, international financiers or communists, greedy and cheap, and they were accused alternately of being too bookish, too aggressive, and also too withdrawn and introverted. For many, moreover, their greatest fault lay in the fact that they did not have classic W.A.S.P. good looks. Rather they were angular, with big noses. Opprobrium followed.

Eastern intellectuals like Henry Adams and Midwest farmer types like Ignatius Donnelly and carmaker Henry Ford saw the Jews as a symbol of their discontent. Among the reckless charges of the populist agitators was the one that the Jews controlled the banks. The Jewish bankers were taking the farmers' land. The Jews favored the gold standard. It was just such irrational hatred that spurred the Immigration Acts of 1921 and 1924.

Jewish children at school. *Library of Congress*

During the 1919–20 Red Scare, the deportation of Jewish radicals by A. Mitchell Palmer and J. Edgar Hoover solidified the image of the Jew as the Antichrist. The Ku Klux Klan, citing Scripture, made Jews a target. So did outspoken anti-Semites such as radio preacher and Nazi sympathizer Father Charles Coughlin, America Firster and Holocaust denier Gerald L. K. Smith, and Mississippi senator and white supremacist Theodore Bilbo. Universities, including those in the Ivy League, kept strict quotas on Jews. A 1944 poll showed that 24 percent of Americans believed Jews to be a menace to American society.

If there was one place that insulated Jews from anti-Semitism, it was the Jewish neighborhoods of Brooklyn. For many Jewish Brooklynites, anti-Semitism was something talked about in the newspapers but rarely felt, because everyone in Brooklyn, it seemed, was Jewish. (In neighborhoods close to Italian and Irish communities, Jewish kids often heard "Christ-killer" taunts from other kids.) And while most of the Jews who had immigrated to Brooklyn were uneducated because of the persecution and anti-Semitism in Russia, and had unskilled jobs, many of the men had tailoring experience, which elevated them to semi-skilled status and allowed them to rise on the socioeconomic ladder. The immigrants with no skills at least had escaped the pogroms. Despite the poverty, they were making more than they had been making in Russia. Their goals were modest: to have something to eat, to save some money, and to send their children to college. To that end, their sons and daughters were expected to study hard and live more prosperous lives. Sons were pushed by parents, who recounted their travails in Russia, to take advantage of this land of opportunity to become doctors or lawyers, and daughters were indoctrinated to marry doctors or lawyers.

At the same time, a small percentage of immigrant daughters chose to become independent. These ambitious women themselves became doctors and lawyers in New York City, and they would become leaders in the union, women's suffrage, and birth-control movements. These women limited the size of their families and made sure their daughters were as well educated as their sons.

Immigrants' sons also rebelled, mostly against the Orthodoxy. Boys would sit outside the synagogues hatless. The fathers, dressed in black, entered the synagogue crying real tears. To the fathers, these boys were lost souls, "lost to God, the family, and to Israel of old." As Lincoln Steffens observed, "Two thousand years of devotion, courage, and suffering for a cause were lost in a generation."

Ira Glasser, who one day would be a leading protector of the Constitution and the Bill of Rights through his work with the ACLU, remembers growing up in an all-Jewish milieu. Christians were the odd ones. Growing up, he knew Protestants, but virtually all of them were black.

**IRA GLASSER** "I was born on April 18, 1938, at Brooklyn Jewish Hospital. My dad was born on Rivington Street on the Lower East Side. His father came shortly after the turn of the last century from Eastern Poland or Western Russia, depending on the borders of the last war, when he was ten years old. He didn't speak English when he arrived, and left school early. My father didn't complete the fifth grade. My grandfather was a construction worker, a glazier, which is where our name comes from. He was one of four or five brothers, and my father was one of four or five brothers, and every single one of them was in the glass business. I was the oldest son of the oldest son, and it was something of a family scandal when I announced at age five that I was not going into glass.

"My father wasn't political. He was what I used to call a Vincent Impellitteri Democrat. He was a fierce union guy. Most of his working life he was an official of the glaziers' union, and for many years he was head of New York City Local 1087. There was nothing radical about him. My father's family read the *Daily News* and the *Journal-American.* I always thought growing up that he and most of the people in the construction union were racists. My father in his later years made a remarkable transformation. He worked with Ernie Green, one of the original Little Rock kids, who was then with the Department of Labor, to begin one of the first minority apprenticeship programs in the New York City construction unions. He was very proud of that. But it wasn't political or ideological. He just believed in fairness, in giving people chances. But [when I was] growing up, there was none of that from him. I got most of my politics from my mother's side of the family.

Ira Glasser and his father.
*Courtesy of Ira Glasser*

"My mother's father was an early organizer of the International Ladies Garment Workers Union, or the ILGWU. His politics weren't radical, and he ended up with the Liberal Party, which in those days was an anti-Communist rival of the American Labor Party, and my father and he always used to argue, in a friendly but passionate way, about the best route to progress for the working man.

"My father was very American. He wasn't religious. I don't think he was bar mitzvahed. He never went to shul. All that came from my mother's side. My father came out of a culture where there was strong-arming by the unions. He was a street guy. The story I heard about my paternal grandfather's early days had to do with guns and knives and hoodlums—that's what being an early organizer in the construction unions was often about. My father grew up in that milieu. He never spoke about it until he was in his eighties. To the day he died, at almost ninety, he carried around a blackjack in his car. He had had it since he was a young man. That was the kind of thing that outraged my mother. Her family, though also union activists, were more refined. My mother had a year of college, which was unusual for a woman. My father didn't seem to value education or culture. There was always tension around those differences. My mother's family liked my father, but I think they wondered who this guy was. My father never said three words to me until I was married. He was never mean to us, but it was awkward and difficult for him to relate to children. We never had a serious conversation until I was an adult and he knew who I was. The notion of me talking to my father was literally unthinkable. It wouldn't have occurred to me. It wouldn't have occurred to him. My mother, like many Jewish mothers, couldn't relate to you *unless* you were a child.

"At home we read *P.M.*, a left-wing newspaper, much farther to the left than the *New York Post* during the Jim Wechsler years. In order to maintain its independence, it took no advertising, which is why it finally went out of business in 1947 or 1948. Its editor in chief was Ralph Ingersoll, and during the years I was reading it, among the writers were Max Lerner, Murray Kempton, Wechsler, and I. F. Stone. This was as close to a serious, left-wing mass-circulation paper as there has ever been in New York, and it was a paper a lot of liberal Jews read.

Ira Glasser and his mother. *Courtesy of Ira Glasser*

"My maternal grandmother came from Russia, of course. Her husband came from Warsaw. She came over when she was twelve or thirteen, the oldest daughter of a family of seven kids. Her father came over first, got a job, and then she came over with the older kids, and then the mother came with the infants. So my grandmother was thirteen when she made that three-month journey of train and boats and steerage, arriving here in 1905. She lived two blocks from where I grew up in East Flatbush, and when I was eight, she was always terrified I would be crossing the intersection of Remsen Avenue, Linden Boulevard, and Kings Highway by myself. I used to tell her, 'You crossed half the world by your-self when you were my age.' She'd say, 'Yeah, but there was less traffic.'

"My grandfather on my mother's side was as close to a socialist as there was in my family. He was a liberal Democrat, and the argument in the household would be between the Liberal Party he liked and the Democratic candidate my father sup-ported. The story I had heard was that my grandfather was a cantor, very religious and very smart, had a great tenor voice, and he was one of the few Jews who got into the gymnasium [Polish high school] and was going to school. When he came here at age sixteen, he had to give up the educational track he was on, and he ended up working in the garment industry. He was one of the early union organizers with David Dubinsky, on those picket lines in the early days of the ILGWU. He spent his whole life as a union official.

"I lived on East 95th Street between Church Avenue and Willmohr Street. I suspect it is virtually unchanged, but Haitian or Dominican now. [That stretch of Church Avenue is also known as Bob Marley Boulevard.] At one point, the old shul was a Pen-tecostal church. Most of the buildings were four-family, two-story brick structures.

"My world was my block. When I walked from 95th Street to 93rd Street, where my grandparents lived, it was scary and ominous, because there were kids you didn't know. I used to joke you needed a passport to go to 94th Street. We're talking one block. It was scary, because what if you met some kids you didn't know? And these were Jewish kids. There were Catholic neighborhoods where people were Jew-haters and called you Christ-killers, but none of that ever happened to me. It was a totally Jewish area. I used to say, 'If I started from the stoop in front of my house and walked as far as I could walk in a day in any direction, I would never find anyone who wasn't white and Jewish.'

"There was one Christian family next door. A woman and her brother. I remem-ber what an oddity they were. [Whispering] '*They're Christian.*' I was supposedly growing up in this urbane and sophisticated New York City, but in reality, the way I grew up and most people grew up, it was the most parochial experience imaginable. I didn't learn that Jews and Catholics weren't the majority in this country until I was twenty-one and going to graduate school in Ohio. I remember asking, 'Who is the majority?' 'The Protestants.' I knew there were Protestants, but they were black. I knew that once a summer white Protestants went to some sort of gathering at Yankee Stadium, but I never saw them. Ironically, I ended up marrying a white Protestant, which was a very big thing for a Jewish boy to do in 1959. She always regarded herself as a minority, because she was. Even the Hasidic Jews I saw once in a while seemed weird and alien and other. The only blacks I ever saw, once in a while, was a janitor or a cleaning woman. I remember the first time I saw a black person. I was walking on my block with my mother. I couldn't have been more than five or six. A very dark-skinned man came walking over. He was delivering coal, and I was startled in the same way I was startled the first time I saw somebody on crutches or with cerebral palsy or in a wheelchair.

"I said to my mother, 'What is that?' Not *who* is that. And my mother was just totally matter-of-fact about it. She was passionate about these issues in a way my father was not. She said, 'Oh well, some people have different skin color the way some people have different eye color or hair color.'

"It was an astonishing moment. This was in 1943. I couldn't have been more than five, and it was not just the content of what she said but the matter-of-factness, because very often when liberal parents try to respond to questions like that, they are so anxious to impose a nonracial view on this kid, it becomes something important, like teaching the catechism. The elevation of their tone of urgency communicates more to the kids than the content of what they are saying. She's saying this is nothing, but her tone makes it sound like it's a *very big deal.*

"But my mother was very matter-of-fact about it. The whole idea of skin color being like eye color and having a kid perceive it that way was significant, that color was not connected in any important way to issues of character or intelligence or anything like that.

"In school many of the teachers were Irish Catholic. In the first grade I had a light-skinned black teacher named Mrs. Bush. That was very unusual. There were virtually no black teachers in the New York City public schools in those years, and there weren't many Jewish teachers either. The wave of the dominance of Jewish teachers in New York City didn't happen until a decade later.

"We were Orthodox. There was no Conservative or Reform. My mother kept a kosher house more out of respect for her parents than out of belief. I grew up with two sets of dishes, two sets of utensils—four sets, actually, because there were two separate sets for Passover. There was this transformation, like moving, where everything was cleared out and brought up from the basement for ten days, and then everything was brought back down. To this day, there are certain patterns of dishes, if I see them in an antique store I associate [them] with milk and not meat.

"All these memories have a Proustian quality. I never remember a time when I thought any of that made any sense. I just grew up that way. Just as apostate Catholics still have warm feelings about Christmas trees, I remember the Purim and Passover holidays with nothing but fondness and wistfulness and nostalgia and warmth, but I never remember a time when I had a belief system that supported it.

"They sent me to Hebrew school four days a week. I'd come home from school at three thirty, and Hebrew school went from four thirty to six thirty, and when you got home it was cold and dark. I used to play hookey a lot, because otherwise I would never play ball, which was my passion. I had to figure out how to deal with the truancy notices my mother would get from Hebrew school. I learned how to pick the mailbox lock and intercept them so she would never see them. But I also remember being impressed with the ridiculousness of the fact I was spending eight hours a week in Hebrew school, and they never taught me the language. They taught me to read phonetically. To this day I can open a Hebrew book and read it phonetically. Years later I used to say, 'They tested you in your reading of the *sidur* in Hebrew the same way they tested typists, which is to say they gave you two minutes with a stopwatch, and you read as many words as you could, and they subtracted the number of pronunciation mistakes you made from the number of words you read. Which was exactly how they tested typists. But I always marveled that you never knew what any of it meant. They never tried to teach you that, and it wasn't until years later that I realized it was intentional. They were training you to take your place in a ceremony with ritual. They were training you to attend shul, to take your place and be familiar with the service.

"Another thing I remember about shul: the women were always upstairs, and the boys, who were special, were downstairs. The genders were totally segregated, and that reinforced the gender roles, so you never came to see gender in the same way you were taught to see race. Which is why a lot of Jewish liberal men were more reflexively good on racial issues in the 1970s than they were on gender issues. Because they were raised with differential religious roles, they were slower to come to the gender-equality issues. I was the son who was going to go to college, and my sister was the daughter who would hopefully marry well. My struggles with 'What should I major in? Where should I go? What should I be?' were taken seriously. Nobody took that seriously with my sister. She went to college, but it was more like a finishing school. And all of that was derivative of the fact that the role differentiation was very rigid and very much reinforced by religion, and the way they taught you to take your place in the ritual. It was approximately the same thing the Catholics used to do with Latin. You learned Latin as part of the liturgy, but for me I found that distressingly meaningless. I went to junior high school at PS 252 in the neighborhood for about a year, and I was headed toward Tilden High School, when my parents in 1950 bought a house as part of that postwar-affluence move to the suburbs. That was the American Dream. They were going to buy a house in the country. Your own fence. Your own home. They moved me against my will, to my bitter objection, to what they told me was Long Island, but which I later discovered was Queens.

"In 1950 we moved to the town of Laurelton, Queens, near the border of Nassau County. For the first time in my life we were among the first wave of postwar Jewish families moving to a suburb which was not dominantly Jewish. There were still no blacks, but I'd go to school, and I would play basketball, football, softball with Italian kids and Episcopalians and Lutherans, which I hadn't known existed. We moved when I was twelve, and I lived there through [graduating from]

*Courtesy of Ira Glasser*

Queens College when I was twenty-one. During all those teenage years the social segregation within an entirely white community was extraordinary. I went to school with all these other people, Irish and Italian, Catholics and different kinds of Protestant faiths, and you were in class every day, and it was very cordial. I would spend entire weekends from dawn to dusk with these guys playing ball. They were my friends. But it wasn't until years later that I realized that although I played ball with Bob Laino and a kid named Ganzer and Bob Phleiger, who was Lutheran, never once after the game broke up did I go back to their homes, or they to mine. I have no idea where those guys lived. You always went back with a Jewish kid. I never dated nor did I know any Jew who dated a girl who wasn't Jewish. So there was ethnic and religious segregation within the apparently integrated community. Years later, when I was a different person, I remembered back: *Oh my God, that was astonishing.* It was never talked about. I'd sit on my porch with my Jewish friends, all Roosevelt Democrats— we all hated Joe McCarthy—and we were all good on race, although none of us had ever confronted it. We were nearly all Dodger fans. But we never once talked about how strange it was that we never went back to Bob Laino's house, that we didn't even know where he lived. We were guys who discussed everything, and we never discussed that. During my teenage years we spent hours talking about politics and philosophy, and what we were going to be and how we were going to change the world. We were social talkers and political talkers, but it never occurred to us."

# A "ONE HUNDRED PERCENT JEWISH" CHILDHOOD

SY DRESNER

JEWISH OFFSPRING DESPERATELY WANTED TO BLEND INTO THE American tapestry. They competed to be the best, becoming exemplary students, with hundreds of thousands going to college and leading prosperous lives until, by 1976, four out of five Jewish high schoolers were going to college. They were able to prove they were as American as anyone else by becoming involved with the local baseball teams—in New York City it was the Dodgers, or, for the rebels, the Giants and the Yankees. Because of the constant threat of persecution that hung over their heads, they held a deep interest in politics and social justice. Despite President Roosevelt's passivity about saving the European Jews from the Holocaust, his economic policies that helped bring the nation back from the Depression made him the overwhelming choice of Brooklyn's Jews.

Israel "Sy" Dresner, who would go on to become a rabbi and a figure in the civil rights movement, moved to Brooklyn from the Bronx in 1930, when he was a year old. He grew up in Borough Park, which, during his childhood, he says, was "one hundred percent Jewish." Until he went to New Utrecht High School, Dresner's view of the world, like Ira Glasser's, was ethnocentric. Up to age fifteen, he had met exactly one black person, and very few non-Jews. After he went to high school, he thought the rest of the population was Catholic, because half his high school was Jewish, half Italian. Living in Brooklyn, he didn't know Protestants even existed.

**SY DRESNER** "I was born on April 22, 1929, six months before the beginning of the Depression. Whenever my mother would get angry at me as a little kid—and as a little kid I was a *tsatzkala*—she would yell at me in Yiddish and blame me for the Depression, because it was a clear case of cause and effect.

"When she was seven years old, in 1913, my mother came from what Jewish history books refer to as Congress Poland, what Americans refer to as Russian Poland. It was the Poland of the czarist empire, a *shtetl* of about six thousand people called Austrovitz. *Shtot* in Yiddish means 'city,' and *el* in Yiddish means 'little,' so a *shtetl* is a little city, or a town. Until I was ten, I thought she was born in America, because she lied to me. You could not tell she was born abroad. She had a thick New York accent.

"My father, who was born in 1898, was twenty-one when he came to America from East Galicia, which was part of the Austro-Hungarian Empire. My father was born in a place that was smaller than a *shtetl*, what in Yiddish is called a *dorfel*. *Dorf* means 'village,' and *el* in Yiddish means 'little,' so a *dorfel* is a hamlet. My father's hamlet had nine hundred people, all Jewish, about a hundred who were related to him.

"My father's older brother Lazar, Uncle Louie, came to America in 1913, and my father would have come earlier, except for the breakout of World War I in 1914. The czarist Russian army captured the hamlet in late August of 1914, the first month of the war. Illiterate peasants made up the army, and many of them had no contact with Jews because Jews were prohibited from living in most of Russia. When the army captured a Jewish town, there would be semispontaneous pillaging, looting, and raping. These pogroms occurred hundreds of times as regions of Galicia and Bucovina fell.

"My father's sister, who was sixteen and a half, was raped by a Russian soldier, and she went into shock. There were no doctors, and she died the next day. The entire hamlet fled into the interior of the Hapsburg Empire, as did a half a million other Galicianer Jews. My father's family got within twelve and a half miles of Krakow, and they all wound up in a refugee camp in what today is Bohemia in the Czech Republic. After spending two and a half years there, he was drafted into the Austrian kaiser's [Franz Joseph—not to be confused with Kaiser Wilhelm of Germany] army.

"Most people don't know that, for the Jews, World War I was a disaster. Jews fought on both sides. More than half a million Jews lost their lives in World War I.

"My father was wounded on the Russian front. He was hit by shrapnel. He was sewed up badly, and thirty years later you could still see the bad stitches in his forehead. But it was lucky for him, because it got him out of the war.

"My parents met in America. It was an arranged marriage. When my father came in 1921, he was already close to twenty-nine, which was considered very old for a bachelor. He went to work for Uncle Louie, who had been in America eight years and owned a bar and grill on the Upper East Side of Manhattan. It was part of Yorkville, a German neighborhood. East 86th Street was lined with one oompah-band restaurant after another.

"My father had no education to speak of, not even a Jewish education, but he had a very high IQ.

"My mother didn't have much education either. She went for one year to Washington Irving High School in Manhattan, and then she dropped out. Her best friend was the daughter of Margareten, from Horowitz Margareten, a company that makes matzo and matzo meal, and my mother got a job in the factory when she was fifteen.

"They had two weddings, a civil wedding in New York, and a religious wedding in Montreal, because the Montreal part of the family couldn't leave Canada because they weren't Canadian citizens yet. They had come to America after 1924, after the second National Origins Act. The law was designed to keep out inferior people from Southern and Eastern Europe—Jews, Poles, Italians, Lithuanians, Czechs, Slovenes, etc.—from entering the United States, and if it hadn't been for those laws, a lot more Jews would have survived World War II, saved just by normal immigration.

"My parents were living in Yorkville with my uncle, and when I was six months old, they moved to the Bronx. The Depression had started, and in April 1930 my uncle kicked my father out of the bar and grill because things were already doing very badly.

"Six months later my uncle did help him get a deli in Brooklyn, in Flatbush, between Parkside Avenue and Ocean Avenue, and we moved to a little four-story building at 188 Parkside Avenue, about ten stores down from the deli, which was called Dresner's.

"It was a *goyishe* deli, a *traif* deli, because it was not in a Jewish neighborhood. My father had all sorts of terrible things in it, like liverwurst, pork, and ham, and we were not allowed to eat in the store because our home was kosher. On occasion, my father would slip me a cream cheese sandwich on a kaiser roll. He would make me swear not to tell my mother, who was super-kosher.

"My father became an American because of baseball. When he first came to this country in 1921, *the* team in New York was the Giants. The Yankees had not yet won a single pennant. The Dodgers had won two pennants, in 1916 and 1920, but lost in the World Series. By 1921 the Giants had already won six pennants.

"When my father worked for his brother in Manhattan, he would go to the Polo Grounds all the time. He got to know the game really well. He loved the game, and the only sports activity he ever did with me was to take me to the Parade Grounds, about a three-block walk from where we lived, to play catch.

"He had this phenomenal memory for numbers. He knew all the batting averages.

"In 1927 he went for his citizenship papers. He had been in the country six and a half years. My father got all dressed up with a bowler hat, a tie, a white shirt, and a suit, and he had to take a test on American history.

"To study for it, my father went to night school for exactly one session. He fell asleep during class because he worked a twelve-hour day. He never went back. He didn't know from nothing about American history.

"'How many states in America, Mr. Dresner?' My father answered, 'Eighteen,' which for Jews is a lucky number.

"'Who was the first president?' 'Warren Harding.' My father liked him, because his middle name was Gamaliel, a Talmudic rabbi.

"'What is the capital of the United States?'

"'New York.'

"My father got all the answers wrong, and every time he answered, he would take out his pocket watch and look at it. Finally, the interrogator said to my father, 'Mr. Dresner, why are you looking at your watch every two minutes? You've been waiting to become an American citizen six years. We can keep you waiting much longer.'

"My father, in his Yiddish accent, said, 'Your Honor, I don't mean to be disrespectful in any vey, but dese questions and answers are going on so long. In honor of my becoming an American citizen, I bought two tickets to the Giants-Cubs doubleheader at the Polo Grounds, and if you keep asking me dese kvestions, I'm going to miss most of the first game already, and the Giants are only two games behind. If they win the doubleheader and the Cardinals lose a doubleheader, they'll be tied for first place.'

Casey Stengel, left, managed the Brooklyn Dodgers from 1934 to 1936.
*AP Photo*

"At this point, the interrogator said, 'Mr. Dresner, you are a true American in every way, a lover of baseball, the national pastime. Citizenship granted.' It was a story my father told many times.

"After we moved to Flatbush, we would go to Ebbets Field maybe thirty games a year. Across the street from Dresner's was a big apartment building, six stories high, with an elevator, and the entire Brooklyn Dodger baseball team lived there, and they all ate at Dresner's. In 1933 I sat on Casey Stengel's lap. He was the manager. Babe Herman used to come in to eat all the time.

"We would get free tickets to any game we wanted, because the Dodgers were a terrible team. It was the 'Wait 'Til Next Year' era. They would inevitably finish in seventh or eighth.

"There was no night baseball, so the games started at three P.M. The games were quick. They were over in an hour and fifty minutes. You didn't have long commercial breaks between innings. There was no advertising, no television. You didn't have eight pitchers come into a game. A guy would start, and he'd finish.

"If it was a slow day and there wasn't much business, my father would close up the store at around two thirty P.M. He'd sweep up in five minutes, go to the front door, and switch the sign from OPEN TO CLOSED, and he'd lock the door.

"We would walk half a block to Flatbush Avenue and get on the streetcar. It was a nickel, and I was free because I was four years old. We'd go down to Empire Boulevard, alongside Prospect Park, and we'd get off and walk to Bedford Avenue and into Ebbets Field.

"We had free tickets, and it was almost like I was the mascot of the team. I even got into the dugout a couple of times. I knew all the Dodgers. They had a pitcher by the name of Van Lingle Mungo, who became famous because of a pop song by that name many years later. We had Luke 'Hot Potato' Hamlin. They had wonderful monikers for the players back then. I became a real *maven* in baseball.

"Still, we were Giants fans. I was four and a half in 1933 when my father took me to my first World Series against the Washington Senators. I was about seven when I learned to read my first box score, and I celebrated in 1936 when the Giants won the pennant again.

"My dad and I used to sit down the right field line right near the Giants' bullpen in the Polo Grounds. My father sat there because he liked the second-string catcher named Harry Danning. Harry was Jewish, and he and my father would schmooze in Yiddish all the time to each other.

"I was a *yeshiva bucher*. I didn't go to public elementary school. I started attending in 1935, and took the Thirteenth Avenue bus to get there. The first day my mother went with me, and after that I went by myself. I was five years, nine months old. She talked to the driver, who told her he'd be driving every day, and he promised to make sure I got off at the right stop.

"After a year at the yeshiva, my parents decided we would move closer to the school. Moving day was June 30, and we moved to Borough Park so I could walk to school. It was 1935, the middle of the Depression.

"My mother read the *Daily News* every day. The *News* was owned by Cissy Patterson, the sister of the owner of the *Chicago Tribune,* and it was anti-Roosevelt, anti–New Deal, and pro-Republican, but my mother didn't read the editorial page, and neither did most of the other 2 million readers, because my mother and most of the people who read the *Daily News* voted for Roosevelt. So did my father, who every day read a Yiddish newspaper *Der Tog,* a middle-class, pro-Zionist daily.

"Roosevelt came in on March 4, 1933, and he was reelected in a landslide. In 1936 he won every state but Maine and Vermont. There was a famous expression, 'As Maine votes, so votes the nation,' but at a victory dinner a couple weeks later, Jim Farley, the chairman of the Democratic National Committee, got up and said, 'As Maine goes, so goes Vermont.'

"My dad went bust in 1937. The New Deal improved employment greatly, but in 1937 there was the Roosevelt recession, and my father had huge debts, of around $2,800. He refused to go bankrupt, and it took him until 1944 to pay everyone off. He went to work for one of his distributors, Kings Beverages, delivering soda and soda water on commission.

"My father had to learn to drive, because the company gave him an old Model A with two doors and a rumble seat, and my mother wouldn't get into it during the daytime, because on each side was painted in white letters KINGS BEVERAGES, and she was embarrassed.

"I never went to camp during the summer, not once. Growing up, I never saw a Broadway play, though my dad would take me to Yiddish theater. Through reading the *Daily News* and the paper *P.M.,* I developed a keen interest in politics.

"The first election I was really involved in was the Roosevelt–Wendell Wilkie race in 1940. I read the *Daily News* every day, and in September they had a poll of various counties in New York State. It was a primitive poll. What they didn't understand was that people change their minds. By Yom Kippur, Wilkie was leading in the polls, and my father was distraught. My father was in such a state of depression, he was sitting in shul, glum. He and this old man with a white beard were talking in Yiddish, and my father was really depressed, and they were talking about the election, and my father said in Yiddish, 'Even the Jews are voting for Wilkie.' And the old man looked at my father, and he said in Yiddish, 'Don't worry. A Jew lives in *drei velt,* three worlds. He lives in *di velt,* this world. He lives in *yenna velt,* the other world, and he lives in Roose-*velt.*' My father started laughing, and it really did snap him out of his funk.

"And in 1940 Roosevelt ended up with 90 percent of the Jewish vote, and of course he won easily. It was normal, if you were Jewish, to be liberal. Jews were still poor, many were immigrants, and Jews were an oppressed group, the most oppressed group in the world.

FDR and Mayor LaGuardia. *Library of Congress*

"The country had a lot of anti-Semites in it. It was very prevalent in 1940. I was fully aware of the anti-Semitism of Father Coughlin and Henry Ford.

"I went to the yeshiva as far as the ninth grade. I had a scholarship to continue in the high school department of Yeshiva University, which was up in Washington Heights, but beginning two years before that, I had gone into rebellion against Orthodoxy, and I refused to go. I became an atheist. I was a smart fourteen-year-old kid who knows everything.

"I've always had a big mouth. I started studying Talmud when I was nine. They had a special class for smart kids, an hour a day with Rabbi Binimovich, an old man with a white beard, who had been the disciple of one of the great Talmudic scholars in Lithuania. As I got older, I started asking the wrong questions, and sometimes I would get a slap in the face.

"Say we were studying the kosher laws. I would say, 'When the three angels visited Abraham in the book of Genesis, Abraham served them milk and meat at the same time. How was it Abraham, the founder of our faith, was not kosher?' It was a provocative, subversive question, and Binimovich, who was no dope, knew it, and he slapped me across the face, and I was tired of it.

"Part of my dissatisfaction with Orthodoxy was not knowing there was any other kind of Judaism. It was not until after the World War II that the Conservative and

Reform movements became popular. Jews between the ages of eighteen and thirty-five in the army came into contact with Jewish chaplains, who were 99.3 percent Reform or Conservative, because the Orthodox were not able to serve in the army. They couldn't eat the food, because they were kosher, or they didn't know enough English, so all the Jewish chaplains were Reform or Conservative, and when these guys got out of the army in 1945 or 1946, they founded Reform or Conservative synagogues. They became the two massive movements in Jewish-American life.

"So I was getting slapped for asking the wrong questions, and Hitler and the war also were on my mind. It was October of 1942, and it looked like the Axis was going to win the war. The Wehrmacht was at the gates of Stalingrad. The Japanese had overrun everything under the sun, conquering the Philippines, Malaysia, the Dutch East Indies, most of New Guinea, and Burma. The American Navy had been destroyed at Pearl Harbor. The Germans had captured one country after another in Europe. We didn't know yet about the Holocaust, but we did know things were going very badly for the Jews. So I had all sorts of reasons for becoming an atheist. Plus I wanted to be sophisticated, advanced, modern.

"I had a friend, Gabey Bloom, with me at the yeshiva. His father had served in the Jewish Legions in World War I. It was a special unit the British had created, open only for Jews. General Allenby was the commander of their Middle East army fighting in Palestine. Gabey was richer than we were. He had a house with a porch, and he joined a Zionist group called Habonim, the Labor Zionist Youth Movement, that urged Jewish kids to go to Israel and live on a kibbutz, and because of Gabey, I joined as well.

"I entered public school in the tenth grade, in Brooklyn, at New Utrecht High School. Utrecht is a Dutch name. The New York City flag has orange in it, and the orange is for the House of Orange from

Sy Dressner. *Courtesy of Sy Dressner*

the Dutch days. I became the sports editor of the New Utrecht High School weekly paper, which was known as the NUHS [pronounced "news"]—we were very clever.

"New Utrecht had a great track team. We used to get into the finals every year in the old Madison Square Garden on 48th Street, where we always lost to a Catholic school called Bishop Laughlin. It was the only thing we were good at. Erasmus, our great enemy, would beat the shit out of us all the time in basketball and football.

"New Utrecht was half-Jewish and half-Italian. The school was in an Italian neighborhood, and we got to it on the BMT line. We got off at the 79th Street stop and walked half a block to the high school. Even though we were as numerous as they were, they controlled the neighborhood, so we had to watch our Ps and Qs, otherwise we'd get the shit beat out of us. We had family members of the Mafia in the school. Albert Anastasia was a famous mobster who was gunned down in a barbershop. An Anastasia kid was in my class.

"I ran for president of the GO, the student government. It was the war years, 1944, and there was a morning session that started at seven thirty and ended at noon, and an afternoon session that began at eleven and ended at three thirty. I ran against a kid named Delvecchio, and when the morning results came in, I was leading by 387 votes, and everyone was congratulating me. The girls were kissing me, and then the afternoon results started to come in, and my majority kept falling, and I lost by 6 votes.

"The morning session was juniors and seniors, which was overwhelmingly Jewish, because a lot of the Italian kids had dropped out to go to work or to join the army. The freshman and sophomore classes had a lot more Italians in them, and by the end of the day Delvecchio had more votes than we did. It was a clear-cut case of ethnic politics."

# THE LINCOLN BRIGADE

ABE SMORODIN

I T MADE SENSE THAT THE JEWS WOULD EMBRACE PHILOSOPHIES opposed to the czar. The czar, after all, had murdered, raped, and plundered them before kicking them out of Mother Russia. Among the antiauthoritarian philosophies many Russian Jews embraced was the brainchild of a German Jew by the name of Karl Marx. In 1848, Marx wrote his *Communist Manifesto* based on a core thesis: that in any society there is a war between the rich and the poor. In a capitalist society, he stated, the rich reap undue profits from the work of the laborers, and the hardworking laborers end up with very little to show for it.

To end what he considered the evil of capitalism, Marx had a solution. End private ownership. Let the laborers run the factories. He also advocated revolution. He urged the laborers to rise up and take over the government run by those in power and their rich businessmen friends. Marx scared the bejesus out of capitalists all over the world.

Though Marx wrote the *Communist Manifesto* in 1848, it wasn't until 1917 that the Russian workers and peasants acted on his words. Czar Nicholas II was a despot, certainly, but no better or worse than the czars before him. Russia was ill-equipped to fight in World War I. The bigger problem facing Russia was lack of food. There wasn't enough even for the army. Serious famine was looming.

The first major protest occurred in St. Petersburg on February 23,

1917, when 90,000 people gathered to demand bread. The next day, hundreds of thousands of people filled the streets, calling for the czar to abdicate. A day later, the entire city was on strike, and violence broke out. The czar called out the troops, but the soldiers mutinied. They refused to fire on the striking workers. When 150,000 soldiers joined the revolution, the czar was finished.

Vladimir Lenin took over and tried implementing Marx's ideas, such as the end of privatization. The result was a catastrophic economic collapse. The human equality and brotherhood that Marx was seeking failed to materialize as the nation sank into a dictatorship.

The Communist revolution, it turned out, was no panacea for the Russian workers. Emma Goldman, the anarchist who had been deported from America, went to live in Russia in 1920 and 1921, and she wrote a piece on the conditions there, titled "There Is No Communism in Russia." She reported that the Bolsheviks ran an authoritarian, centralized government. As for the factories and the tractors, she said, they weren't nationalized, as Marx theorized. They were taken by the government that controlled their use. Thus, she said, "there is no socialization either of land or of production and distribution. Everything is nationalized, it belongs to the government. There is nothing Communist about it."

As for a classless society, she said, "the very opposite is the case. Today the peasantry is entirely dispossessed of the land." She talked of a "vast Soviet bureaucracy which enjoys special privileges and almost unlimited authority over the masses, industrial and agricultural."

She concluded, "I think there is nothing more pernicious than to degrade a human being into a cog of a soulless machine, turn him into a serf, into a spy or the victim of a spy. There is nothing more corrupting than slavery and despotism."

Soon thereafter, Lenin died, and Joseph Stalin took over. Stalin enslaved the country. He started five-year plans—state-controlled programs for economic improvement, which stifled all individual initiative. Everyone obeyed orders, or else. Freedom died with the Russian Revolution as it sank into a totalitarian state. All criticism—and opposition—was eliminated. Stalin killed anyone thought to be a traitor. A paranoid despot, he saw traitors everywhere. To maintain control, Stalin killed an estimated 20 million people over twenty-five years.

But though Marxist Communism backfired in Russia, it did not prevent a core group of Americans from believing in and adopting Marx's ideals: a classless society, the end of the tyranny by the rich, and the end to fascism. These American Communists were advocating a revolution, but as loyal Americans they were not advocating Revolution. Marx may have called for the overthrow of the proletariat, but in America the Communists were calling for a social revolution—social equality, civil rights, and stronger unions. They were such staunch enemies of fascism, as practiced by the czar and later by Nazi Germany and Fascist Italy, that in 1936 thousands of men from the United States and Canada voluntarily and heroically went to Spain to fight for the legally elected Republican government after General Francisco Franco and his Fascists staged a military coup in what would become known as the Spanish Civil War. These men, who flocked to the Republic's cause, were by any definition American heroes who were fighting for democracy against evil despots. But because of politics, America—and England, France, and every other country that was scared to death of Hitler—chose to remain neutral. When these men refused to stand silently by, Americans calling themselves "patriots" branded these soldiers traitors. There should have been parades for these men who fought for the cause of democracy, after the survivors returned from Spain. Instead, there was silence.

Abe Smorodin was born in 1918 to Jewish parents who were founding members of the Communist Party back in the old country. His father came from Kharkov, in central Ukraine, and his mother was born in Belarus. They migrated to the United States looking for work. They had four sons, including Abe, who grew up poor but intellectually cultivated. Taught to fight fascism and capitalism and to embrace the forces fighting racism and poverty, when the Italian Fascists attacked Ethiopia and murdered thousands of innocents, he was horrified. When the Nazis supported Franco in the Spanish Civil War in 1936, he felt he no longer could sit back and watch another fascist leader take over without a fight. Though the United States was a democracy and the Spanish Republicans were trying to save their country from right-wing tyranny, the country refused to act. It had signed a nonaggression pact, and it was sticking to it. Smorodin, along with hundreds of other Brooklynites (they made up 10 percent of the 2,800 volunteers) joined what has become known as the Abraham Lincoln Brigade. Smorodin spent three years in Spain, fighting to free the country from Fascist tyranny. The war was bloody, and nine hundred men from his battalion, including his best friend, died, as the Republicans fought the Fascist army despite a marked disadvantage in manpower and firepower. Though Franco ended up winning the war, Smorodin was never prouder of the ideals he stood for than when he was fighting for Spain's freedom.

**ABE SMORODIN**   "My dad was in his early thirties when he came over from Russia. Dad had already had political jousts with the czar's police. I grew up in this kind of radical home.

"He landed first in Philadelphia. My father and mother were both interested in Yiddish as a language, and they proselytized all over Philadelphia, promoting Yiddish. They had shuls, which were after-school schools for Jewish children who wanted to learn Yiddish and some history of the Jewish people, and they were ardent about it, spending hours trying to set up these schools. For many years it was quite a popular movement among the fraternal Jewish organizations.

"My dad was really a menial kind of worker. In the '20s and '30s wallpaper was very popular. Everyone had it instead of paint. And my father wasn't even a wallpaper hanger. He was a wall scraper. In other words, he prepared the walls for the guy with talent who put on the wallpaper. He scraped away and filled in the holes with some plaster. He worked very hard. He was unemployed a lot. We were poor.

"We moved to Brooklyn six months after I was born, in 1918. You can be sure any time we moved, work was the motivation. My father had reached his mid-forties, which meant in those days he was practically out of the workforce. The alternative was to find a little business, a grocery store, a candy store, a little store that was prevalent in all the neighborhoods. He bought a grocery store.

"When you buy a grocery store in the middle of the Depression, and your customers are workers and a lot of unemployed workers, they come into the store and they want a loaf of bread and a dozen eggs and some butter, and they say, 'Put it on the tab.' And my father had no way in which to say no. Which eventually drove him into bankruptcy. He wasn't getting paid, and he could not make the store go. He couldn't exist. It was tough going.

"He then went looking for work. He worked in a garment shop. He worked various jobs. He did not have all the skills needed. It was very rough. There was no Medicare. It was very hard.

"I was a Dodger fan, but we didn't have enough money to get into the ballpark, so a bunch of us would go down to Bedford Avenue, and there were knotholes in the fence, and if you put your eyes close to it, you could see the outfielder's feet once in a while. There was a gas station across the street on Bedford Avenue, where fly balls flew. That's what I did. I waited to catch them. We didn't have television, but we had radio, and we had imagination.

"When I was growing up, we had a house in which everyone was socially conscious. We had lively conversations around the kitchen table. Our home had a lot of books, a lot of music on 78s, if you remember those old records, and we couldn't afford it, but once in a while we went to Lewisohn Stadium [on the CCNY campus at 136th Street and Amsterdam Avenue in Upper Manhattan], which doesn't exist anymore, to hear the philharmonic. When you got there, you paid 10¢, and they gave you a little cushion to sit on because it was all concrete.

"We lived in Williamsburg. There was a lower Williamsburg, which went down to the Williamsburg Bridge, and there was an upper Williamsburg, which was a little better off. We lived in lower Williamsburg, in a section which was not wholly Jewish. There were a lot of Irish and Italians, and we got along very well in those years.

"The area was divided by three elevated lines. Myrtle Avenue, Lexington Avenue, and Fulton Street were the three els that operated through our area. Under those els lived African-Americans, and only under those els. The rest of the neighborhood in between were Jewish people, and it held this pattern until World War II.

"I was a Young Communist, and on Sunday afternoon I was given an area to go sell the publication of the Young Communist League, which came out once a week. I was very bad at it, and I usually wound up in a movie theater. I saved my missionary work for some other time. We had dances and lectures in our hall on Tompkins Avenue, a place where we gathered, where we spent time looking at girls' T and A. We were young fellows.

"I went to Boys High School at the corner of Putnam and Marcy Avenues, that old, old building that had a steeple on it. I graduated in 1932. My folks insisted I try to go to college. I was accepted at Brooklyn College, which hadn't been built yet. At the time it consisted of three floors in a high-rise on Livingston Street downtown. I registered, and I went for half a term, but I couldn't stand going to school while seeing what the financial situation was at home. So I quit, and I worked at various two-bit jobs to help out. I'm reticent even to talk about this, because this is not understood by anybody today.

"If you want to know something about Brooklyn, I can tell you a lot of the Jewish residents lived in two areas, Williamsburg and Brownsville. This was where the core of the left wing of Brooklyn lived. Most of the volunteers who went to Spain came from Brooklyn. We used to compete, jokingly, to see which part of Brooklyn sent more guys to Spain.

"Part of the reason was we had more unemployment than anybody else! I shouldn't say that. It sounds demeaning, but it had something to do with it, and our antifascism had something to do with it, and also maybe our social lives weren't complete. But we did not go with a sense of adventure. There is nothing at all romantic about war. We knew going in that people get killed. But of all the areas in the country, nobody produced more Lincoln Brigade vets than these two areas of Brooklyn.

"The character of the war is correctly stated when you say 'the Spanish Civil War.' The country was split in half, as deeply as North and South in our country. One side wanted a republic, and the other side wanted a monarchy, wanted to retain the old Bourbon regime. We went to Spain because the Italian Fascists had sent a division into Spain, with all their arms, and they blockaded the ports along the Mediterranean. It was an intervention of the most shameless kind. And it was denounced at the League of Nations, mainly by the Russians. The Russian diplomat Maxim Litvinoff, a Jew, represented the only country of any size that protested the intervention.

"The United States had signed a nonintervention pact, and as a result refused to send men or arms in support of the Republicans, even though they were fighting for democracy.

"In those years the United States was under the thumb of British diplomacy. Lord Chamberlain was calling the shots, and he didn't want to take action because he was appeasing Hitler, who marched into Czechoslovakia unhindered, didn't get a peep from Chamberlain, and he also moved into the Rhineland, and the French didn't do anything about that, even though these were treaties Hitler was breaking from World War I.

"In the case of Spain, it was the Italians who sent over the foot soldiers. The Germans sent their *Stuka*s, their bombers, in great numbers, and that was a terrible thing. The Russians sent planes and troops to fight them, but they had to come from far away. You can hate Stalin—he was a psychopath—but he helped the Spanish Republic. The Russians lost thirteen merchant ships, sunk by German and Italian submarines. This was a silent war, never reported in the press. My wife, Rose, had two brothers, and one died in Spain, and the other died after his merchant marine vessel was sunk by a German sub on the way to Murmansk."

*Beginning in 1936, an international volunteer force of 35,000 men from fifty-two countries was recruited by the Comintern. Twenty-eight hundred Americans, many from Brooklyn and many from western Canada, volunteered to go to Spain to fight.*

**ABE SMORODIN**   "The Comintern was the moving body, but they had very little to do with us. We went for one reason—we were antifascists. Two years earlier, we had seen the Italian Air Force bomb Ethiopia in mass raids, so black people were the first people to feel the effect of the fascist air raids, and they died by the thousands. They had no way of fighting back, and we had no way of intervening, except to protest to the League of Nations.

"When Spain happened two years later, we were determined there would be no repeat of that. The left and the Communists swore, 'We are determined to fight the fascists wherever they appear.'

"On July 16, 1936, the fascists began an uprising against the Spanish Republic. The first international resistance came when four columns of French volunteers mobilized and marched to Madrid to fight them. A Fascist general by the name of Mola said that they had a 'fifth column' waiting to liberate the city. He was boasting. They didn't liberate it. They imprisoned it.

"After the French came on the scene, we mobilized fairly rapidly. We had lived in Brooklyn all our lives. I had never even gone to Bensonhurst, and here I was going to Spain. That was the situation for a lot of us. We would never have thought of making a trip like that.

"The only way to travel back then was to go by ocean liner. It was all arranged for us by the leaders of the Communist Party. The recruiting went on for a couple of years. We went third class, right next to the boilers.

"We landed in Paris, and when we arrived, the overwhelming majority of us gave our passports to the French Communists. For the underground fighting the Nazis, an American passport was worth its weight in gold. We gave them over a thousand

Abe Smorodin during the Spanish Civil War. *NYU Archive*

passports. I'm sure these passports saved a lot of lives. They were used all the way through World War II by the partisans [fighting] against fascism. I never regretted turning in my passport.

"When we arrived in Spain, we grouped in a little town called Tarancon, south of Madrid. We trained at an international base, did maneuvers, learned how to salute someone. We didn't know the most rudimentary things. Most of the other countries had conscription, taking old soldiers, forty-year-old guys who had even fought in World War I. We didn't know what side of a gun a bullet came out of. The Americans were total strangers to this. About 30 percent of the group were Jews. As I said, ours was the single largest national group.

"Another big group of longshoremen and seamen from Vancouver, Canada, made up a whole company. An immense majority of people, including 2,800 Americans, supported the loyalists internationally. There was very little support for Franco. We were organized into the Lincoln Battalion, and when enough came, they formed the Washington Battalion. After the battle of Brunete, so many men died that they joined both groups together to make up the Lincoln-Washington Battalion.

"I was in the MacKenzie-Papineau Battalion, a Canadian outfit. There were a lot of Americans in it. I was there at the birth, and I was there for the duration of the war.

"As proud as I was to be a Communist, I was never prouder than seeing men from all over the world with the same beliefs as mine, giving their lives in double and triple figures. It was awful. War is awful. Sherman was right.

"We were not without arms. We had artillery pieces that went back to World War I. You fired it, and two guys would fall down from the backlash. The gun would jump in the air.

"Because we were so highly motivated to fight fascism, we were used in every battle. They called on us to be shock troops. You can't hold it against the high command, but it was a little much. The casualties were just too high for a unit of our size to have nine hundred die. And virtually everybody else was wounded.

"I had a wound in the *pierna isquierda,* the left thigh. It was what the British called a 'blighty,' a flesh wound which would put them in the hospital between clean sheets for as long as they could get away with it. I was wounded, and I thought, 'Good, I'll have a stay in a hospital.' The doctor came, slapped on a Band-Aid, and he said, 'Take the next truck out.'

"I lost a lot of friends. I lost my best friend, Jack Freeman. He was a year ahead of me at Boys High, and he went on to college. His father was a union official in the Amalgamated Clothing Workers of America. He was with the Lincoln Brigade, and we were in the rear, next to them, and I asked Major Smith, a Canadian in charge, if I could go see Jack. He said okay, and I took a little walk, and I met Milt Wolf, the commander of the Lincolns. I told Milt I was going to see Jack. He said, 'Jack was killed.' It was a sunny day, and he was lying on a little spot, getting the sun, and there was artillery fire, and just a fragment of it pierced his brain. It was terrible. You can't respond.

"It all ended tragically. By 1939 things had gotten very, very desperate. Franco had cut the Republic in half below Valencia. In desperation, Prime Minister [Juan] Negrin announced over the radio that all foreign forces were to leave Spain. He demanded Franco do likewise with his German and Italian troops. Which was rhetoric. It was a bunch of baloney. Franco wasn't moving.

"We gathered to leave Spain in the town of Rapalo, at the foothills of the Pyrenees. The American consul from Barcelona came up to count us, and he demanded our passports. We gave him all kinds of excuses. 'My passport was in my back pocket, and I got hit in the ass.' It became evident to them they weren't going to get our passports. We were all American-born, so the government couldn't deny us a right to return to our country."

*For the rest of Abe Smorodin's life, nothing would compare to his days fighting the Fascists in Spain. When Abe returned to Brooklyn, he found that his father had bought a candy store on Utica Avenue. He married his sweetheart, Rose, and the two of them worked behind the counter grilling hamburgers and selling soda, cigarettes, and candy until his retirement.*

A Smorodin family gathering. *Courtesy of Abe Smorodin*

"Rose and I despised it," said Smorodin. "It was not my idea of how I wanted my life to go."

*That may have been the case, but Abe Smorodin, whose left-wing beliefs included a lifelong fight for integration and racial tolerance, proved himself to be a wonderful friend to his neighbors, including the African-American kids who lived there. When Martin Luther King Jr. was gunned down on April 4, 1968, riots broke out in black neighborhoods all over America, including Brooklyn. Amid the chaos and ruin, Smorodin's store wasn't touched.*

**ABE SMORODIN** "They knew I was always square with them. I never patronized them. I never cared that they were black, and they were my friends. When I sold them a candy bar, I would point out the evils of capitalism. I'd say, 'You're paying me a nickel for that candy bar. You know what it costs me? Three cents. I'm making two cents on your bar. You think that's right?'

"On the night Martin Luther King was killed, I was vacationing then, visiting my sister in L.A. I turned on the TV, and I saw black kids rampaging on Utica Avenue, and I'm thinking, *Geez, when I get home, I'm going to find the store in shambles.*

"I got home the next day, and I got up, and I usually opened the store before six in the morning, and it was still dark. I got off the bus taking me to the store, and I had all my fingers crossed, and I was looking at the storefronts with all the windows broken, and I got to my store, and there was a young black kid sitting on the newspaper stand.

"'Everything looks all right here,' I said.

"'We wouldn't let them touch your store,' he said.

"That was the kind of friends I had among the black kids.

"I'm eighty-nine years old, and I'll never be bored. You know why? Because I have a library card, a passion for music—I'll play WQXR—and a third thing: I live with a passion for politics."

*Abe Smorodin passed away on April 7, 2008. He was ninety-two years old. Only three dozen veterans of the Lincoln Brigade remain.*

Abe Smorodin and his wife visit a cathedral in Seville. During the Spanish Civil War Seville was controlled by the Franco forces. *Courtesy of Abe Smorodin*

# VICTIMS OF RAPP-COUDERT

HENRY FONER

ACCORDING TO THE BOOK OF EXODUS, AFTER MOSES LED the Jews out of Egypt and into freedom, he called his followers together to urge them to pass the story of their escape down to their children so the story would never be forgotten. Moses, it seemed, wanted his people to become a nation of educators.

And when Moses went up to Mount Sinai to receive the Word of God—the Ten Commandments—the Bible says that what he didn't write down, he kept in his head in order to pass it down to others, who were then instructed to pass it down to their children. Teaching history and tradition to others became so ingrained that education became the cornerstone of a Jewish upbringing.

When the people wanted to give Moses their highest honor, they called him "Moses our teacher." The honorific "rabbi" simply means "teacher."

Why did Jews care so much about education? Because time after time they were persecuted, and they figured out that for their children to reach their full potential despite all roadblocks thrown their way, they had to be educated. And it was this love of education that helped them survive even after years of pogroms and deportations.

In addition to a love of learning, these Jews, who had fled from czarist Russia, also shared a love of freedom and a hatred of authoritarianism. When the Depression hit, along with the rise of fascism in

Europe, many of these Jews joined the Communist Party. Opposed to capitalism and wanting to help those of the working class advance in society, by the mid-1920s the American Communists had replaced any interest in violence or regime change with a concern for social justice. They turned to building labor unions, protested black lynchings, and fought for better living conditions for the poor. By the late 1930s, a broad left-wing movement grew up around the Communist Party, though most who said they were communists did not belong to the party. They were communists with a small *c*. They sympathized with the party's goals, but did not want to submit to its discipline. There rose up dozens of organizations fighting for racial equality, freedom for Spain, unions, and social equality. Many Jews, who were communists with a small *c*, also were devoted to education and to teaching. Though uneducated, their parents insisted that the children study hard in order to live a better life. These offspring gained a love of learning that they wished fervently to pass on to others.

Among the sons of Russian immigrants to Brooklyn imbued with this love of learning and education were four remarkable brothers: Phil, Jack, Moe, and Henry Foner. The oldest, Phil and Jack, twins, became college professors at CCNY, who would later go on to write groundbreaking books on unions and civil rights. Moe was a college administrator. Henry, the surviving brother, began his career teaching high school.

Even though Hitler was the enemy, Russia an ally, and the American communists focused on stopping Nazi totalitarianism, in 1940 the New York State legislature appointed a committee to investigate teachers in New York City colleges and high schools. The committee, headed by two staunch conservatives, Republican state assemblyman Herbert Rapp from Genesee County (between Rochester and Buffalo) and Republican state senator Frederic Coudert from New York City's Upper East Side, more than anything else wanted to curb the influence of the Jewish teachers who had joined the Communist Party, and were determined to stop the anti–Jim Crow teachings of leftist professors. Some of the outrage was over the fact that CCNY had actually hired a black professor, Dr. Max Yergans, who was a member of the Communist Party. The argument that gained the conservatives their firmest footing was one that appealed to the religious contingent: because communism posits a state without religion, those who joined the Communist Party lacked the religious bona fides to teach. In other words, they didn't want these left-wing Jews preaching civil rights, equality, and rights of the poor to impressionable kids.

The conservative Christian legislators accused CCNY and Brooklyn College of tossing out any faculty member who was "not in accord with the Godless, material theories" of those running the school system. The loudest protests came from New York Archdiocese cardinal Francis Spellman, Episcopal bishop William Manning, Tammany Hall, and the Hearst newspapers—the *Daily Mirror* and the *New York Journal-American*.

Henry Foner on the steps of his home at 310 South 3rd Street in Williamsburg, after returning from his first day at school at PS 19 in September 1925. *Courtesy of Henry Foner*

It was a ridiculous, absurd argument taken from the Puritan New England handbook, but when fear rages, logic and democracy always suffer. When hundreds of teachers were fired—not for any treasonous act but solely because they had been Communists—the firings were upheld by the Supreme Court until 1957, when the Court finally ruled that such flimsy grounds for dismissal were unconstitutional.

By the time the Rapp-Coudert Committee completed its witch hunt, over eight hundred high school and college teachers had been targeted. All four Foner brothers were thrown out of teaching in 1941 by the second of the Red Scares, which sought to stop men fighting for civil rights, union rights, and social justice, by demonizing them as Communists.

Forty years later, CCNY held a ceremony apologizing to the victims of the Rapp-Coudert witch hunt, including Phil and Jack Foner. Henry Foner, to his credit, rolled with the punches and spent the rest of his life working for others as a union organizer.

Phil, Jack, Moe, and Henry Foner grew up in Williamsburg, sons of immigrant Russian-Polish Jews. Their father owned a horse and wagon in the 1920s, and he used it to deliver seltzer in glass bottles to customers around Brooklyn. He was successful enough that he was able to buy a share in a parking garage on the corner of Pearl Street downtown. In addition to cars, the garage held trucks from various companies. One of them was Brooklyn Edison, and through his connection to the company, Pop Foner was able to get twin sons Phil and Jack jobs turning on and off the street lights in Greenpoint, which adjoined Williamsburg. Each had a special key, and at five in the morning they would go on their respective routes and manually turn off the lights. Then at five at night, they would return and turn them on again.

Another customer was the Simmons Beautyrest Mattress Company, and the family joke was that occasionally a mattress would fall off the truck and land at 310 South Third Street, where they lived. Another customer was a candy company. The father would bring home some candy, which the kids thought tasted like soap, but their mother would tell them, "Listen, don't be so particular. We got it for nothing, so eat and enjoy it."

Clair Bee, the basketball coach at Long Island University, was another customer. Bee would give Pop Foner tickets to their home games, which in those days were played in the gym of the Brooklyn College of Pharmacy. Basketball was very big in Brooklyn, and in the 1920s and 1930s it was largely a Jewish sport. "Rip" Gerson, who played on the legendary St. John's Wonder Five, lived down the street from the Foners. His teammates on that team were all Jews—Mac Kinsbrunner, Matty Begovich, Mac Posnack, and Allie Shuckman. According to Henry Foner, the neighborhood joke was that Gerson would go to college carrying only a pair of basketball trunks under his arm. "We never found out if he ever went to class," said Foner.

Moe Foner, the middle brother, played basketball at Eastern District High School and went on to play at Brooklyn College. He had the distinction of playing against St. Francis in Brooklyn's very first game at Madison Square Garden.

Moe and Henry would go to the Prospect Hall in the Park Slope section to watch Brooklyn's professional basketball team, The Visitations. Among the stars who played for the visiting Trenton Tigers was Lou Spindell, a remarkable athlete who had played for City College from 1928 to 1930. Spindell and Henry Foner later would become active members of the teachers' union.

Henry Foner wasn't athletic, because as a child he suffered from rickets and had frail legs. Since he also had difficulty dancing, he became a saxophone player so at least he could play at the dances.

For the Foners, the focal point of the community was Public School 19. Like most Jewish immigrant families, his parents placed a great deal of emphasis on education and took great pride in their children's academic achievements. It was very important that their children go on to college, and there was more than one joke told about the desirability of their becoming either doctors *or* lawyers.

Eastern District High School, which all four Foner boys attended, had neither a football nor a baseball team, and as a result debate became a very important competitive activity. Evening debates at Eastern District High were events equivalent to football games at other high schools. The entire Foner family would turn out to hear Phil and Jack debate in the school auditorium. One of their opponents was Boys High School's Gus Tyler, who for years has written a column for the *Forward*. Back then his name was August Tilove, and he would go on to become education director and vice president of the ILGWU and a close associate of union leader David Dubinsky.

Henry, unable to play basketball like Moe, followed in Phil and Jack's footsteps and became captain of the Eastern District debate team. He also emulated his brothers by taking up a musical instrument, the alto saxophone.

The four Foners played together in a dance band. Along with Henry, Phil played alto sax, Jack drums, and Moe tenor sax. The boys had two cousins who were undertakers, and the cousins joined a number of community organizations where they became the social chairmen who arranged to hire the Foner band for their parties.

"For years we had steady work," says Henry Foner.

At the dances they played songs of the Depression, including "Brother, Can You Spare a Dime?" Another song had the lyrics

> *Here it is Monday*
> *And I've still got a dollar—*
> *So why should I holler*
> *When here it is Monday and I've still got a dollar.*

During the summer the Foner band traveled to the Catskills to work. For several summers Phil and Jack played at a hotel in Monticello, New York, called the Royalton House. Not only did they play at the dances, but, since the musicians at the smaller hotels also provided other entertainment, Phil and Jack did skits in front of the guests, and for those, they needed material.

During the off-season, brothers Moe and Henry would go to the Palace Theater at 47th Street and Broadway in Manhattan, where they would sit in the balcony and watch the routines performed by the Marx Brothers, Bob Hope, and Phil Baker. They would write down the jokes and pass them along to Phil and Jack to use over the summer.

Phil and Jack went to the prestigious City College, where they were outstanding students. They were so busy with their Edison Electric job, their music, and their studies that when Henry was twelve, they bought him an Underwood portable typewriter, brought it home, put it on the dining-room table, and told him, "Learn to type." Henry, a dutiful brother, typed many of their college papers. Later on Henry would go on to teach stenography and typewriting to high school students.

When the stock market crashed in 1929, the Foners weren't deeply affected, because their father had his seltzer route and his garage, and he hadn't speculated in the stock market.

"He hadn't bought stocks, so he didn't jump off the roof," said Henry Foner. "We did not lead fancy lives, but I was buying apples rather than selling them."

What Henry and his brothers *were* deeply affected by was the growing labor movement and their desire to fight against racial discrimination and Jim Crow. This was also a period when Adolf Hitler came to power, and the threat of fascism hung over the world. Phil and Jack were organizers of the College Teachers' Union after they became professors at City College. They were also active in another faculty organization, called the Anti-Fascist Association. In addition, they became members of the Communist Party.

"There were reasons so many Jews embraced this movement," said Henry Foner. "When I became active in the Furrier Union, I learned that the other leaders, Ben Gold, Sam Burt, and Irving Potash, came here as immigrants with backgrounds of activity in leftist movements back in the old country. Another aspect was the emphasis on education, which meant you had a growing intelligentsia among Jewish people, and I have found that educated people tend to be more liberal, more radical than the population as a whole. There were bitter differences between the communists and the socialists that were inherited. We never fully understood why this was. They even had their own newspapers—in the Jewish community there was the *Frei Height,* the communist newspaper, and the *Forward,* the socialist newspaper—but in both cases they had the same goal: social justice."

High school student Henry Foner also was an activist. In 1934 he took part in an annual peace strike conducted by the National Student League. He was on a committee that arranged for an outdoor rally outside Eastern District High School. The speaker that day was Joe Cohen, who later became Joseph Clark, a columnist for the *Daily Worker.* In the years before Hitler and the Spanish Civil War, the issue was a movement for peace. Henry Foner was part of the movement, which asked students to sign the Oxford Pledge that they would not join the ROTC or go to war.

When Foner entered CCNY in the fall of 1935, he immediately became involved in a student protest to save the job of Morris Schappes, a popular English teacher accused of using his teaching position to indoctrinate the students with leftist dogma. Apparently, the chairman of the English Department, a Professor Horne, had visited his class while Schappes was lecturing about the poet Percy Bysshe Shelley. He read the lines:

*Men of England—heirs of glory*
*Heroes of unwritten story*
*Nurselings of one mighty mother*
*Hopes of her and one another*
*Rise like lions out of slumber*
*In unvanquishable number.*
*Shake your chains to earth like dew,*
*For you are many, they are few.*

Horne—stupid, jealous, or vindictive—charged Schappes, who was one of the most popular professors on campus, with indoctrinating his class with radical ideas, and he was fired. Foner and several thousand students couldn't believe such a farce could take place at their prestigious school, and in protest they sat-in at the entrance hall of the main building. They sat for several hours, when the announcement came that the case was going to be reconsidered.

"Our protests had an effect, so we disassembled," said Henry Foner. Schappes's job was saved.

During the 1930s there were no black teachers at CCNY, and after a campaign by the students' Frederick Douglass Society and by the communists and progressives on the faculty, the college introduced its first course in Negro history and culture, and it appointed Dr. Max Yergans, a prominent black scholar, to teach it. The first time Dr. Yergans came into the faculty cafeteria, the white cafeteria workers refused to serve him. The Communist Party members and their allies had to mount another protest to get his meals served. None of this "subversive" activity escaped the notice of the conservatives on and off campus.

In defeating the attempt to fire accused Communist and Jew Morris Schappes and in hiring a black professor, Dr. Max Yergans, CCNY incurred the wrath of the Christian conservatives in the New York State legislature. The powerful conservative right had taken a big hit when the Depression made their Big Business Knows Best position much less legitimate. FDR upset the conservatives greatly with his New Deal, and in 1940 the labor movement was giving Big Business real trouble. There were

Philip, Moe, Jack, and Henry Foner in the summer of 1939.
*Courtesy of Henry Foner*

sit-down strikes in Flint, Michigan, at the GM plant. Truckers struck in the city of Minneapolis. The Congress of Industrial Organizations (CIO) and the leaders of the Communist Party worked together to organize. By the end of the 1940s the Communist Party had achieved major status in American intellectual and cultural life, and the conservatives no longer could stand by and watch the Jews, Communists, and blacks gain ground in their longtime WASP-controlled society.

They wanted life to go back to the way it was before the coming of the Jews and Franklin Roosevelt. Though Russia was still an ally, full-scale anti-Communist repression, through the Rapp-Coudert Committee of the New York State legislature, was being prepared for the purpose of political revenge and cultural rollback.

The final straw came when CCNY announced it intended to hire peace activist Bertrand

Russell onto its faculty. Though it was the conservatives who led the America First drive to keep America out of the war against the Nazis, somehow the conservatives were allowed to attack the leftists in the antiwar movement. For them, the thought of allowing Bertrand Russell, the leading figure of the antiwar movement, to teach at CCNY became too much.

**HENRY FONER**   "The story that went around was that the conservatives considered Russell an advocate of free love. But they were also opposed to his social ideas, his progressive outlook on life and on the problems we faced. I would refer to it as the reaction of reaction—reactionary people who can't contemplate the idea that change can be good for us. They were very uncomfortable with anything that challenged the status quo, particularly with respect to discrimination. My brother Phil was a target because his historical work was centered on labor and black history. Among his pioneering works was his uncovering the work of Frederick Douglass and publishing it."

*The targets were the Jewish teachers who had joined the Communist Party, and Max Yergan, the outspoken black professor who dared reveal that "the emperor had no clothes" by telling his students that slavery and peonage had not been abolished, but rather that racism was as bad as ever.*

*Yergan made a speech to defend himself before the Rapp-Coudert Committee, but its contents were kept secret. In response, the teachers' union paid for air time on radio station WMCA so that Yergan could be heard, but the Rapp-Coudert Committee twisted the arm of the head of the radio station to cancel his appearance.*

*Here is what the committee didn't want the public to hear: "I was dismissed because I was unwise enough to interest myself in community affairs. I was unwise enough to concern myself with the conditions under which children are being educated. Why are the schools in Harlem zoned so that Negro children are Jim-Crowed? Why must Negro children be schooled in fire traps? Why, in this richest country in the world, must our children be hungry because there is too much to eat? Why is it 90 percent of all schoolchildren have bad teeth?"*

*In 1940 such rhetoric—by a black man, no less—was considered downright subversive by conservatives, who were proponents of a segregated society and didn't want to hear criticism of the American way of life.*

*Within a year of the Rapp-Coudert Committee's appointment, over eight hundred public school teachers and college faculty members were targeted by the committee. The key informant at City College, William Canning, named more than fifty of his colleagues as members of the Communist Party, which was enough to get them fired. Under the Smith Act, no actual acts of subversion had to be proved. Membership in the Communist Party was deemed subversive by definition.*

*Canning's testimony was supported by two other witnesses—Annette Sherman Gottsegen and Oscar Zeichner. As a result of their testimony, more than fifty members of the City College faculty and staff—including Henry Foner's three brothers—were fired or compelled to resign. The charge against one of his brothers—Phil—was that he devoted "excessive attention to the role of blacks in American history." Defending the rights of blacks in 1940 was proof enough that you were up to no good. But Jews like Henry Foner felt that discrimination was wrong no matter who the victim, and he and many other liberal Jews sympathized.*

**HENRY FONER**   "My contacts with black people were players on the basketball teams that my brother Moe was playing against. Since I couldn't play, I was his satchel-carrier. I carried his bag when he went to play the away games for Brooklyn. I saw that Boys High had a black player named Wynn. And that was one of the first black people I saw. And I remember Dolly King. Clair Bee used to give me tickets, and I saw Dolly King play for LIU. I didn't have social contact with blacks.

"Another black who we rooted for was Joe Louis. The night that Louis fought Schmeling, during that period the Young Communist League was having a training school in the co-ops in the Bronx. At every YCL training school, you wrote songs. Songs were a very important part of our lives. So we had a song, which I've sung— David Margolick got me to come to his opening at the Brooklyn Library, and called on me to sing the song—'Just as Louis knocked the Nazi stuffings out of Max, we'll exterminate the vermin from the workers' backs. YCL.' The Louis-Schmeling fight was really a tremendous event in our lives at that time. The exciting thing about it, it was an event that united the Jews and the blacks, because anything that was counter to Hitler—and Schmeling was considered an ambassador from Hitler—was critical, and I don't have to tell you how the black people felt about Louis. My memory is reading and learning about celebrations all through Harlem that night. Yes, Louis played a very important role in that, and Lester Rodney and Bill Mardo did interviews with Louis in the *Daily Worker*, and later on, when I became involved in activities on behalf of Paul Robeson, I had occasion to do some studying and discovered when Louis was being interviewed he said he felt that Paul Robeson, who was a scholar at Rutgers and one of the outstanding performance artists, had done more to break down discrimination against blacks than anybody else.

"I had the thrill of meeting Paul Robeson. The Furriers' Union had a resort on White Lake. I was the educational director in 1949, the year of the Peekskill riot. Earlier that summer we invited Robeson to come and sing. I had the thrill of writing an introduction for him. I wrote a sketch, and it was sung to the tune of 'Old Man River': 'Here's Paul Robeson, our own Paul Robeson, he sure knows something, he don't fear nothin', he just keeps fighting, he keeps on fightin' for us. The people love him, the people need him, in every corner his name means freedom, he just keeps fighting, welcome Paul . . .'

"My brother Phil was very close to Robeson, because while he was teaching at City College, evening session, Robeson's mother-in-law attended the college and was a student of Phil's. She was very impressed when she heard Phil speak about Reconstruction, emphasizing its progressive character and giving the lie to those who vilified it as a period of chaos and anarchy as depicted in the film *Birth of a Nation*. Ms. Goode, Eslanda Robeson's mother, lived with the Robesons near the college on Hamilton Terrace, and she was so moved that she invited Phil to come over to their home. Phil did not know at the time that Eslanda was a descendant of the first black senator elected during the Reconstruction period. He visited the house, met Robeson, and the two remained close thereafter. When Robeson learned that Phil was preparing a collection of the writings and speeches of Frederick Douglass, he expressed an interest in making a commercial recording of them.

"The witch hunt came, and Ossie Davis ended up doing the reading. So there was a close relationship. Robeson was closely involved in the battle against the Rapp-Coudert Committee, and all the fights for academic freedom. He was closely associated with the teachers' union. There was a connection right through. Later on Phil edited a book, *Robeson Speaks,* which has all of his writings. It's the most complete collection of Robeson's writings."

*While most of the victims of Rapp-Coudert Committee never taught again, the only one who served jail time was Morris Schappes, who acknowledged membership in the Communist Party, but when pressed to name others, would only name those professors who had died fighting on the loyalist side against the fascists in the Spanish Civil War. He was charged with perjury and Judge Jonah Goldstein sentenced him to serve fourteen months in The Tombs.*

**HENRY FONER**   "Morris's case generated a good deal of support. There was a newspaper in Harlem at the time, published by Adam Clayton Powell, called the *People's Voice,* and I remember it carrying articles on the persecution of Schappes, [comparing it] with the struggle of black people.

"The main informant for the Rapp-Coudert Committee was Bill Canning, a professor at CCNY and a colleague of Jack's and Phil's who had been taken into our household when he didn't have a place to live. One of the things that enraged my father when he learned of Canning's betrayal of my brothers and me was the fact that when he didn't have money for eyeglasses, my father drove him to an optometrist on the East Side and paid for his glasses.

"Canning was Catholic, and the person who specialized in reaching out to Catholics who had been part of the left movement was Monsignor Fulton Sheehan. Canning became a disciple of Sheehan and when the Rapp-Coudert Committee came along, it provided him with an opportunity to curry favor with the committee and advance his career. Sheehan influenced other people I knew. Bella Dodd was a very outspoken legislative representative for the teachers' union, who became a devout Catholic and an informer as well.

"The Catholic Church was an important right-wing influence during this period. In the Spanish Civil War, the Catholic Church was a bitter enemy of the loyalist government and an avid supporter of General Franco. One of our most important efforts during this period was to lift the embargo on arms for the loyalist government, which had been imposed by the United States, Great Britain, and France as part of the so-called nonintervention policy. This was a mockery, because Franco had no trouble getting both arms and soldiers from Hitler and Mussolini.

"One of my early dramatic ideas on how the American Student Union should mobilize came at City College. The idea was to set up a large scale in the lobby, and on one side there was a sign that said EMBARGO and on the other side was another scale. We asked the students to sign postcards to call upon Roosevelt to lift the embargo. They signed them, and we put them in a pile, and as they multiplied—we collected thousands of them—the scale tilted. The pressure to lift the embargo became so great that for a time it was believed that President Roosevelt would bow to it, but it didn't work. The pressure of the Catholic Church prevented him from doing so. I shall never forget walking in Times Square one evening and reading on the Times Building's news streamer that the United States had definitely decided to keep the embargo in place. We knew then that the cause of the loyalists and Spanish democracy was doomed."

*It is remarkable that after all four Foner brothers—Phil, Jack, Moe, and Henry—lost their jobs as a result of the Rapp-Coudert Committee's assault on academic freedom, all of them were able to continue to contribute to the cause of civil and human rights, either on another campus or in the labor movement.*

**HENRY FONER**   "It was a terrible thing to lose our jobs, but the victims of Rapp-Coudert were very close-knit, so you didn't feel alone. When the attack first came, there was a good deal of support from the student body. One of Phil's students was the famous basketball player and coach, Red Holzman, and he participated in the protests against Phil's firing. One of Jack's former students wrote to the committee that he was a police officer who could recognize subversion, and that his classes with Jack had been the highlight of his collegiate career. There were fund-raising events for the Foner Defense Committee, and the comedians Sam Levenson and Irwin Corey performed at these events.

"At all the city colleges—CCNY, Brooklyn College, Hunter, and Queens College— they succeeded in getting rid of the best teachers. Frederick Ewen—who was a later victim of the McCarran Committee—has been acknowledged as one of academia's greatest scholars and was recently given an honorary degree posthumously by the college. His nephew, Herbert Kurz, a prominent insurance executive, has been influential in establishing the Ewen Foundation for Academic Freedom."

*Even though Henry Foner was just a student at CCNY at the time William Canning turned on the Foners, Canning's testimony would ultimately cost him a career in teaching. While serving as a high school substitute, Foner had passed the test that would enable him to get a regular teacher's license, but he was denied a license because of "insufficiently meritorious record." While he was teaching stenography and typewriting as a substitute at Samuel J. Tilden High School, he was inducted into the army in 1942. The school board held its decision on*

Mayor John Lindsay and Henry Foner in October 1969.
*Courtesy of Henry Foner*

*his fitness in abeyance, waiting to see whether he would survive the war, and when he did, bearing a Legion of Merit, the army's fourth highest award, he returned to teaching as a substitute at Prospect Heights High School for three years, in 1946, 1947, and 1948. From all accounts, he was a popular teacher, interspersing songs like "You're Just My Type" throughout his syllabus. When the state commissioner of education turned down his appeal, the board took away his substitute license, and a generation of students was denied the opportunity to learn from a gifted teacher.*

*Henry Foner was able to switch smoothly from teaching to union activism through the efforts of his brother Phil, who had undergone the same transformation. After Phil was fired from his teaching job at CCNY, he was hired as educational director of the Fur Floor Workers' Union, and after becoming acquainted with the union leaders, Phil was asked to write a history of the union. When Henry was denied his teacher's license in the fall of 1948, Phil got him an audience with union head Sam Burt, and Henry was hired as educational director of the Furriers' Joint Board, which represented the workers in the fur dressing and dyeing section of the industry.*

*In addition to his educational duties, Henry also took on the job of welfare director. When a worker was denied his unemployment insurance benefits, for example, a hearing would be held, and Henry would argue the case, almost always successfully. When the union welfare and pension funds became an important part of its life, Henry was appointed the supervisor of those funds as well, and when union president Sam Burt died suddenly in 1961, Henry was named the president of the joint board.*

*On October 26, 1981, the Board of Trustees of the City University of New York passed a resolution apologizing to the victims of the Rapp-Coudert Committee and pledging never to allow another such violation of academic freedom. The story of how it came about is worth telling.*

Henry Foner today. *Courtesy of Henry Foner*

**HENRY FONER** "In 1980, a ceremony was held at City College, where a plaque was laid honoring the three teachers and the students who had died fighting on the loyalist side against Franco in the Spanish Civil War. The event was arranged by Irving Adler, himself a victim of another witch-hunting apparatus—the New York State Feinberg Law—and one of the outstanding mathematicians in the world. My brother Phil was one of the speakers, and in the course of his remarks, he said that if the three teachers listed on the plaque had returned from Spain alive, they would have been fired by the Rapp-Coudert Committee.

"The acting president of the college at the time—Alice Chandler—was intrigued by this comment and she asked around to find out what Phil was talking about. College staff member Steve Lieberstein did the research, and Chandler was so moved that she shepherded a resolution that went through the faculty senate, calling for the administration to apologize for what happened to the victims of the Rapp-Coudert Committee and pledging never to let it happen again. The same resolution was presented to the Board of Trustees of the City University of New York (CUNY) and passed unanimously. Morris Schappes was invited to the session and he spoke about the historic significance of the board's action.

"What does this tell you? It tells you that when sanity takes over, an attempt is made to remedy the damage that is done. The lucky thing about our family was that even though we were all victims of that period, we all reestablished our lives and led fruitful and significant lives. Phil went on to teach at Lincoln University in Pennsylvania and Jack joined the faculty at Colby College in Maine. Both retired with high honors. Moe became the executive secretary of Local 1199, the Hospital Workers, during its period of phenomenal growth representing hospital and health-care workers, as well as the founder of the world-renowned cultural program Bread and Roses. As far as we were concerned, there was a happy ending, but not all the victims were so lucky."

## ON THE SIDE OF LABOR

MARVIN MILLER

**B**EFORE THE START OF THE AMERICAN LABOR MOVEMENT, there were no laws protecting workers, no labor boards to watch after their interests. They were at the mercy of the rich and powerful factory and company owners, who in many cases treated them with utter contempt. Low pay, long hours, horrible work conditions, and inhumane treatment were common. Workers who dared complain about conditions were fired.

When asked about the apparent unfairness of their policies, companies ignored the plight of the human beings toiling for them and focused instead on the benefits to their bottom lines. Hiring people for the lowest possible wage and charging high prices at their company store, they said, was "good business." Without government intervention, these owners would have been content to keep wages low perpetually.

In the 1880s, conditions in some factories were so onerous that the workers were willing to face the consequences of going on strike, which for them was the action of last resort. Only when the workers felt hopeless did they do something as desperate as risk their paycheck. At one carriage manufacturer in Rochester, New York, for instance, management locked up the water faucets in the sinks. When an employee wanted a drink of water, he had to go to the foreman, who unlocked the faucet, gave him a single cupful of water, and then locked the faucet again. Another rule dictated that if a worker was a minute late, he would not be allowed to work that day. These workers struck.

At one quarry in Massachusetts in 1879 the workers had to buy their goods at the company store, which charged outrageously high prices for necessities. No matter how frugal these workers were, they never got ahead. The workers had become peons to the quarry owner. Despairing that conditions would ever get better, these workers also went on strike. To strike literally could mean taking one's life in one's hands, as these companies hired thugs and goons to beat them and scabs to replace them. In addition to violence against the strikers, companies also used more subtle means to impede unions, such as blacklisting, company unions, legal tactics, and yellow-dog contracts, in which employees, if they wanted to be hired, had to sign a pledge not to join a union.

Among the best-known early strikes was the Great Railroad Strike of 1877, a strike over working conditions, low wages, and an antiunion stance that resulted in the deaths of twenty-two men. President Rutherford B. Hayes had to call out federal troops to quell the violence of the angry strikers and the resulting property damage. The strike failed, but it set a precedent: during the Pullman Palace Car Company strike of 1895, President Grover Cleveland called out federal troops. This strike also was broken, as was the strike by mine workers of John D. Rockefeller Jr.'s Colorado Fuel and Iron Company in 1903–04 and again in 1913. (It's interesting to note that as far back as 1877 strikers were being called communists by those opposing them.)

World War I brought something of a moratorium on strikes, but in 1919 two major strikes shook the country. Hundreds of unions struck in Seattle, and there was a police strike in Boston. The unrest made everyone nervous.

Conservatives and the Big Business interests they served blasted the unions for being un-American. Said the *Chicago Tribune,* "It is only a middling step from Petrograd to Seattle." The *Salt Lake City Tribune* commented, "Free speech has been carried to the point where it is an absolute menace." Added the *Washington Post,* "Silence the incendiary advocates of force . . . bring the law's hand down . . . DO IT NOW!" There was so much fear that the press announced its willingness to suspend the basic constitutional freedom of speech.

In New York, four hundred servicemen ransacked the socialist paper *The Call,* and beat up everyone inside. Six days later, Governor Al Smith signed a bill forbidding the display of red flags.

Most strikes didn't succeed because the workers did not have federal protection until 1932, when Franklin D. Roosevelt signed legislation to better their bargaining power against the biggest, toughest company-owners in the United States. His support of this legislation is still one of the reasons FDR's picture hangs on the walls of homes of many union members and a big reason why conservatives and wealthy business owners demonized him.

The first federal legislation to help workers unionize was the Norris–La Guardia Act of 1932. The act legalized union organizing and outlawed yellow-dog contracts. The National Industrial Recovery Act of 1933 gave employees the right to organize and bargain through their representatives. It outlawed forcing workers to join a company union. The third important piece of legislation was the National Labor Relations Act of 1935, which was passed to stop companies from bargaining unfairly. It created a National Labor Relations Board to oversee companies to make sure they complied.

Between May of 1933 and July of 1937 there were ten thousand strikes involving 5,600,000 workers.

By the start of World War II, the efforts of the American Federation of Labor (AFL) and the Congress of Industrial Organizations (CIO) substantially reduced the number of unorganized workers.

Only after the legitimacy of trade unions was accepted was there any chance for peaceful bargaining.

It was not a coincidence that Jews played an important part in the labor movement. Brothers like Phil, Jack, and Henry Foner, communists who hated the inequality between big companies and their workers, spent their whole lives fighting to get workers a fair shake. But you didn't have to be a communist or a socialist to believe in fairness for labor.

Marvin Miller, who rose to the top of the ranks of the Steelworkers' Union and then lent his skills to fighting for better wages and benefits for major league baseball players, was neither a communist nor a socialist, but after the crash of Wall Street in 1929, he saw how an economy with no safety net affected his father, and after graduating from college, he went to work for the New York State welfare department. The misery he saw moved him. An economist by trade, Miller spent most of his life working to improve workers' conditions. He worked for the Machinists' Union, the United Auto Workers, the Steelworkers—where he became the top economist and negotiator—and then he gained fame as the guiding force behind the Major League Players Association. His was a life spent fighting for the underdog against the powerful guys with the money. Almost never did he lose.

Marvin Miller was born in the Bronx on April 14, 1917. Less than a year after his birth, his father bought a house on East 19th Street between Avenues S and T in the Flatbush section of Brooklyn. His father, who worked in Manhattan on Division Street on the Lower East Side, not far from the Manhattan Bridge, sold expensive ladies' coats. During the Roaring Twenties, business boomed. His mother, an elementary school teacher in the New York City public school system all her life until she retired, was the disciplinarian of the family who taught young Marvin to read by age three. Three times he skipped grades, so by the time he entered James Madison High School in 1929, he was not yet twelve years old.

**MARVIN MILLER**  "My father came from Russia. He was brought here in 1883 by his father when he was about a year old. My father was one of ten children, all of whom were born a few blocks from where I live in Yorkville. We moved to East 19th Street in 1918, about two miles north of Sheepshead Bay, Manhattan Beach, and Brighton Beach. When I was a small boy, a good part of my block and the blocks around us were empty lots. We never lacked a place to play. There were even small farms on the street, one acre, two acres, sometimes larger fields, what they called truck farms, where vegetables were grown and sold. I remember tomatoes, radishes, pumpkins, cantaloupes, string beans, green peas, and lettuce. On my way to school sometimes I would steal tomatoes and eat them. The fields were open, and it was early, and no one was around. It got so sophisticated that friends and I would bring salt along with us.

"When we moved in, it was a predominantly Jewish neighborhood, but when I was young, a Catholic church was built on the corner, and what had been a series of empty lots soon were filled with new houses. Mostly Italian and Irish Catholic families moved in. But everybody got along. It was just a great, great neighborhood. In my memory, and my younger sister Thelma's as well, it was a very happy time.

"My father was a salesman of rather expensive ladies' coats. His bosses were Sheiman and Perler. The shop was on Division Street, which ran four or five blocks, and on both sides of the street were establishments all selling women's coats. Nothing else. He worked there all his life.

"My mother was a teacher. When my mother and father lived in the Bronx, she taught in Harlem, but after they moved to Flatbush, she transferred to a school in Coney Island. My mother was the strict one in the family. She had important standards, whether it was being a good student in school, never being allowed to cut school, never being allowed to say 'I don't feel well today. I don't want to go to school.' School was a central part of our lives. She was the one who taught me the rudiments of reading, and I would practice in the subways, reading the advertisements posted above the windows and reading them aloud, to the amusement, or annoyance, of the passengers.

"I entered elementary school when I was five and a half, and I promptly began skipping grades, which was not that unusual in New York City at that time. I skipped three grades, and I entered James Madison High School in 1929, a few months before I turned twelve.

"James Madison was a pretty special place. It just seemed to me that the kids were so bright. They seemed a lot brighter than the children I had gone to elementary school with. So many of them achieved later in life. Maybe that reinforced the whole thing.

"For one, I went to school with Marty Glickman, the sprinter, basketball player, and football player. Glickman was one of those athletes who never got the recognition he deserved. He went to the 1936 Olympics, and at the tryouts in 1935, he finished a tenth of a second behind Jesse Owens—as a high school student. He was kept from competing in the Olympics by Avery Brundage, who was a right-wing Nazi running the American Olympics team, because the Olympics were held in Berlin that year, and Brundage didn't want to embarrass Hitler, so Marty and another Jewish sprinter by the name of Sam Stoller were kept out.

"Growing up in the '30s, we were aware of what was going on in Europe. We were aware of the rampant anti-Semitism there, but I never felt it in Brooklyn. I'm sure there was some. But not in and around East 19th Street. That was a neighborhood where people got along, and almost never moved out. The only memory I have of moving trucks was people moving in when the new houses were being built. It was a most stable neighborhood, with all kinds of people eventually.

"There were candy stores on Avenue U, a shopping center, and candy stores on Kings Highway. We hung out mostly in the streets, and in the empty lots, and sometimes in our backyards, and sometimes on the front stoops. We played all kinds of games, from very simple stoopball to smashing a ball against a curb, to stickball in the streets, and after they were paved we roller-skated and played roller hockey. As we got older, when school was out during the summer, we would go to Brighton Beach where we swam and played hand tennis and handball.

"In Brighton Beach, Manhattan Beach, and eventually Oriental Beach—Coney Island generally—one-wall handball was the sport. There were hundreds of courts on those beaches. That was the center of one-wall handball in the United States. The national men's singles championships were always held at one of the beaches in Coney Island. When I went to college later in Ohio, I took up four-wall handball. I became the men's singles champion of Miami University.

"We had a radio in the house from the time I was five or six. They were not small portables, but great big RCA Victors. I listened not just to baseball, but to boxing as well. My father was a boxing fan. I remember listening to the two Dempsey-Tunney fights, one in 1926, the other in 1927. The Long Count was a *big* deal. When Dempsey lost that fight because he wouldn't go back to his corner, I lost a lot of picture cards in a bet. It was awful.

"The other boxer everyone admired was Joe Louis. We didn't live in an area where blacks lived, and there were no Negroes in our schools. Maybe one or two at Madison, but not many more. I grew up with parents who had great familiarity with black culture. Both came from the Lower East Side, and my mother had worked in Harlem.

"The story I like to tell: My mother would go off to school early, taking my sister with her. She went to the Coney Island school where my mother taught, and I'd be home with my father. When I started Madison, things were so crowded that they had two sessions. The upper classmen went to school from eight until one, and the freshman session went from one P.M. to six P.M. Brooklyn was becoming a bedroom community to Manhattan, plus the subway system was expanding, making Brooklyn accessible whether you were going to work in Manhattan or other parts of Brooklyn or Queens.

"My father didn't leave work until about midmorning, so he and I would be home together when the city sanitation truck would come by. The coal ashes from our furnace would have to be hauled up from the basement to the street, and twice a week a crew of three—usually a white driver and two black men who did the hauling—came and hauled the heavy ash cans from the street into the truck, emptying them, and putting them back. And on cold winter days, my father would invite the crew in, and he would serve them coffee and sometimes Four Roses whiskey so they could warm up and get a breather. I remember the comments I would hear from our neighbors who felt that was really not acceptable behavior, to invite black men, garbage men, ash men, in. And my father paid absolutely no attention to the neighbors. He had a kind of easy camaraderie with working people. It's one of the very nice memories I have.

"My parents were real theater fans, and I went with them to lots of plays. Before a play we would go to Gray's Drugstore just off Broadway about 43rd Street in Manhattan, where we could buy cut-rate tickets.

"My father would also take me to Dodger games on his day off from work. I was very excited, because by the time I went, I already was a fan. I followed their progress. I knew the names of the players. I already collected cards with their records on them that I bought in candy stores.

"By the time I was nine or ten, I talked my parents into letting me go to Ebbets Field on my own. It took some doing to convince them I could make it. I took the BMT subway at Avenue U, and a few stops later I got off at Prospect Park, and then I'd take the Franklin Avenue shuttle, one stop, and you'd be within three or four blocks of Ebbets Field."

*In September of 1929 the stock market crashed. As it was for so many Americans, the crash and the subsequent depression altered Marvin Miller's life in unimagined ways.*

**MARVIN MILLER**   "I remember the stock market crash mostly because I had an economics teacher at James Madison in my first semester there who predicted it. Starting in January of 1929, he would talk to us every day about it, like an obsession. He

WAREHOUSE Nº 5
E. F. KEATING C
PIPE, VALVES, FITTIN
Offices 452 WATER ST.
Phone ORCHARD 9700

A breadline at the base of the Brooklyn Bridge. *Library of Congress*

never let go of the subject. When it happened, I thought, *Wow, this guy knows more than I thought he knew!*

"The crash itself had very little impact on our family and the people we knew, but the aftermath, the enduring depression which went years, oh, that had a profound impact on our family and everybody else we knew. It was a terrible impact.

"In the case of my father, he had always been a good earner. Even when he was single and very young, he was a supersalesman, and he worked on both salary and commission. As a good salesman in a place with expensive merchandise, he made a lot of money.

"When the recession began and as it hit harder and harder, they began shortening the work year on Division Street. Traditionally he worked all year round with a two-week vacation, but then he got cut to forty weeks, then thirty weeks, and then twenty-six weeks, with no end in sight. It just kept going down and down, and it had all kinds of other effects. He was getting older as it went on, and he was being reminded he was a salesman and was expected to be attractive to women, because they were his customers, and I remember the pressure on him to dye his hair, which had become gray and almost white, so he could look younger. It was so undignified, and the impact on him you can just imagine. And I was aware of all this, even though we didn't discuss it directly.

"My mother never lost her job as a teacher, and teachers' salaries were pretty good. I can't say we had any real economic hardship, because we didn't. I can't say the same for our relatives. I had an uncle and an aunt who were close to my mother. My uncle had driven a Sheffield milk truck, got laid off, became a taxi driver, got laid off that, and so on. All through the Depression we had members of the family living with us. Sometimes for a few months, six months, different ones coming and going. It was a tough time. These were my formative years, and I was getting an education in what the economy was and what the problems were. I began to see neighbors—middle-class people with apparently secure jobs, professions, some lawyers, some businessmen—where I used to only see them on weekends, suddenly I would now see them all the time. They were unemployed, and some of them would sit down and talk with me. I remember accidentally running into a next-door neighbor in the subway station when I was going into Manhattan, and I asked him what he was doing so late in the morning. He was a very dignified and reticent man. He began to talk and talk about his problems, and he broke down. He said he did not think he would ever find another job.

"Looking back, even though we always had a car, had whatever was needed, I was becoming more and more aware of the problems of life. In January of 1933, I was not yet sixteen. It was my senior year, and at that tender age, I began to wonder, *Will I ever find a job?* I had no relatives who owned businesses where there could be employment opportunities. So my senior year, I began to cut classes with friends. My grades fell off. I didn't really get serious about college for a couple of years.

"I remember when I first got working papers and was looking for a summer job. I was sixteen. I went through the hopelessness of it. You had to maneuver just to get an application at an employment agency. They no longer gave out applications, because they had too few jobs and too many applicants. So you had to trick them into giving you an application. And I remember going through want ads and not seeing anything suitable. Yeah, I had my own profound depression about the future.

"When Franklin Roosevelt took office in March of 1933, my parents were quite enthusiastic. When the banks closed, my family was affected. They had accounts in the Bank of America. There was a bank holiday, but after a while they let you take out a few percentages, 4 percent, at a time. It would take a long time to get it all out. Plus there were the things your eyes told you. When I went to Manhattan, I would see bread lines in front of a church or a synagogue, people just shuffling along waiting for a meal handout, and you would see apple salesmen, selling them for a nickel apiece. If you took a good look, you'd see these people were not accustomed to doing that for a living. You could see it everywhere. And when I would visit my father at his place of work, we would go out for lunch and walk along the Bowery, which was right there, and oh, the people sleeping on the sidewalk, people just hanging out outside, clearly without work, most of them their clothing in tatters, all new sights in New York.

"During the two years after high school I took a few courses at night school at Brooklyn College, but never more than six credits a semester. I found some work in a local drugstore, first delivering pharmaceuticals by bicycle, and filling in as a short-order cook behind the counter of the drugstore. That kind of thing, and loafing. Sometimes in the early part of the day I'd look for a job, answering ads. But I wasn't really being too productive about anything.

"In the summer of 1934 I met a new friend, Seymour Simon, playing handball at Brighton Beach. His father, Philip Simon, was a prominent lawyer who later became a judge. Seymour said, 'Since you're not really involved with anything, what about considering going to St. John's in the fall?' I thought about it and decided okay. In September of 1934 I enrolled as a full-time student at St. John's in Brooklyn [the university didn't move to its Queens campus until the 1950s], but after a year I decided I didn't really want a pre-law course. I was disillusioned enough about education. I thought, *I'll be damned if I go through four years of this, and three years of law school afterward.* I was not going to do it.

"I had a distant cousin who lived in Yonkers, who was about to graduate from high school, and he had looked into colleges, and he told me about Miami University of Ohio, which he had visited. It was small, with about three thousand students, and he said the town of Oxford was delightful. It was a Land Grant university, which meant tuition and living costs were low. A full year's tuition for an Ohio resident was $80 a year. For an out-of-stater it was $130. Dormitory rent was $5 a month, and food was another $5 a month. I was turning my interest to teaching, and Miami had a very famous, well-thought-of school of education. My parents encouraged me. So in September of 1935 I enrolled at Miami and enjoyed the next two years there, but for a variety of reasons I decided to transfer back to New York for my senior year.

"One of the things that made me consider leaving Ohio was the lack of awareness of what was going on in the country by both the student body and the faculty. It was as if you were in a cocoon, and the rest of the world wasn't there. There was no sense of social justice. In places like City College and Brooklyn College, movements were arising—communism, socialism, Trotskyism—but not at Miami University. You have to understand, that was the center of Taft Republicanism. I went to NYU senior year, and NYU was a little more progressive, but wasn't all that different. You had to go to the public high schools and colleges, to Brooklyn and to City College to get a real contrast. There political ferment, awareness, and interest were great. This was New York. This was not Taft Ohio. You're talking about a population that consisted of very many who were either first- or second-generation Americans. If they weren't immigrants themselves, their parents and grandparents had a background in Europe. They had an awareness of discrimination, of anti-Semitism, and they had a working familiarity with socialist thought, communist thought, Trotskyist thought, and socialist-democratic thought, and while there was very little agreement among all these groups, they had one thing in common: they were all left-of-center political people. You just didn't find that in other places.

"I never did join one of these groups. I was still formulating a viewpoint, though I would certainly fit the description of left-of-center. Though I wasn't a member of the Communist Party, I did read the *Daily Worker*. People who weren't socialists read the socialist *Call*. I read the *Daily Worker* in part because of Lester Rodney, its sports editor. It was unlike a sports column you read today. I forget when I first picked up on his column, but I soon realized he was the only one writing about discrimination in baseball, and I was a dyed-in-the-wool baseball fan. It was through Rodney and his column that I began to realize a lot of things about baseball. He wrote part-and-parcel about what kind of industry it was, that this was a monopoly industry working on the edge of illegality.

"In 1940 I was working in Brooklyn for the welfare department when the Rapp-Coudert Committee began investigating professors at City College and Brooklyn College. It was in the news every day. Most of the damage they did to the college professors they descended on was reversed later. Some people got payments. Because the thing was McCarthyism, pure and simple. I didn't know any of them personally, but they were prominent teachers. I can remember the name of Frederick Ewen. He was an English teacher at Brooklyn [College]. He was subversive all right—he taught English.

"My job at the welfare department, which I began in April of 1940, was social investigator. I was to investigate applicants for what was then called home relief. I then had to service a caseload, which was supposed to be sixty families but was always nearer to eighty. They were on relief rolls and under the law you had to constantly keep in touch with them to make sure they weren't hiding employment, but also to make sure they were looking for jobs. And also, I had to service them—there were all kinds of illnesses.

"What was remarkable to me was how little the press and the public knew about these people—folks who had finally been reduced to applying for home relief. If you believed the press, they were all a bunch of lazy louts and welfare queens, and nothing could have been further from the truth. These were people who were so beaten down by economic adversity and by illness and by what they were required to do. When the WPA labor program started, all the men were required to accept placement as laborers, regardless of their physical condition. Most of the men on relief in East New York and Brownsville had been garment workers. They had been sedentary workers all their lives. And now, in middle age, they suddenly were supposed to work on road gangs, lifting big boulders and doing physical, manual labor. So they all got sick. It used to be an unfunny joke about how many hernia victims we had to refer to Beth Israel Hospital.

At right, Marvin Miller, 1947, with some of the workers he represented. *NYU Archive*

"During the three years I worked there I learned a lot. I can remember once walking toward an area where my clients were, when I saw a crowd of people standing around an entrance to an apartment house. I walked over, and the crowd, both white and black, were quietly standing there. In a minute or two I saw what the situation was: a sheriff and his deputies were evicting a family, and they were carrying furniture and personal belongings out of the apartment house and depositing them in the street. There was a fine rain coming down, so everything was getting soaked, and it was one miserable scene. Finally the family came out, and after the last piece of furniture was placed on the street, the sheriff and the deputies walked to the corner, turned the corner, and left. And like a rehearsed, choreographed scene, as soon as they were gone the people standing there began moving everything back. The solidarity of those people with each other that this represented was to be repeated I don't know how many times in the almost three years I was there. It was like an act. The sheriff and his deputies did what they had to do, and the neighbors did what they considered their job to be. These and similar incidents were a great education.

"After World War II began, I was classified 4-F. I had a birth injury to my right arm. I remained with the welfare department until November of 1942, when I went to the World Production Board in Washington. I was an economist by training, and I had taken a federal civil service exam, and I had apparently placed highly on what was called the Junior Professional Economics list. I was interviewed in New York by a former Queens College professor who was heading one of the World Production Board's divisions."

*The World Production Board had a specialized job. It was to determine the needs of domestic industry for the components important for war production. In other words, the job was to allocate steel, aluminum, rubber, and petroleum, and all the things needed in the war effort to the war agencies and the army, navy, and air force.*

**MARVIN MILLER** "And so I was in Washington when Branch Rickey signed Jackie Robinson to the Dodgers in 1946. The most knowledgeable sportswriters assumed Rickey had signed him to play for the Dodgers, and so there was some anticipation while he was playing in Montreal. The *New York Times* would run a box several times a week showing how Jersey City, the Giants Triple-A team, did and how Robinson did playing in Montreal.

"I had seen blacks playing baseball before. My father used to take me to Negro League games. I don't remember much. I was pretty small. But I remember blacks playing for the Bushwicks, a semipro team that played in Brooklyn. Through Lester Rodney I was following the progress of bringing up a black player to the big leagues.

"Robinson came up in April of 1947, and I got back to New York around June of that year. My memories of Robinson are that he was an exciting player. When you went to a game specifically to see him, as many people did, he didn't disappoint. He was so spectacular on the base paths, for example. If he could get on with a hit or a walk or hit by a pitch, an error, you were in for a show. He drove pitchers and catchers crazy. And he was just fun to watch. We were all rooting for the Dodgers, of course, but he added an element of fun.

Marvin Miller today. *AP Photo/Bebeto Matthews*

"Lots of people appreciated the significance of his integrating baseball, and not necessarily people who went to games. There were some there too, of course. Everywhere you talked to people, whether in the street, or listening to the games on the radio, or a public place, talking to people reading newspaper columns, all these people understood the social significance of what Jackie was doing.

"I must say just from reading about the way Robinson was being treated and the way the other clubs were slow to react to signing black players, my thoughts at the time were these: *Anyone who thinks discrimination has now ended is crazy.*

"I joined the Steelworkers' Union on March 1, 1950. I had several influences. My father had been a salesman who had been miserably treated as an employee. One day when I went down to visit him, to my surprise I found him on a picket line. The Retail-Wholesale Department Store employees were trying to organize all of Division Street, and the stores had gotten together and decided to adopt the strategy of refusing to recognize the card check signifying that the employees had picked the union. And that picket line I saw was the result.

"My mother was also a member, of the Teachers' Union. And when I got my first job with the federal government, with the Treasury Department in Washington, I joined the only union there, the American Federation of Government Employees. And that was at a pretty tender age, so I guess you could say we were a union family.

"I was not affected by Senator McCarthy. He didn't go after any of my friends that I know of. When Ed Murrow finally took out after him, I was in Pittsburgh, working for the Steelworkers' Union, and I exulted at Murrow's integrity and courage.

"I was involved at the time with negotiations with Alcoa, the aluminum company. You may have forgotten, but they were the sponsor for Ed Murrow's television program. Within a day or two of the Murrow program, I had an occasion to meet with people from Alcoa, and I was curious to see what their reaction was. This was, after all, an antiestablishment position that Murrow took. And to my amazement, there wasn't a single dissenting voice on the other side of the table. They all were in praise of Murrow."

*Miller would rise in the Steelworkers' Union until he reached the post of chief economist and head negotiator. On July 1, 1966, he left, to take over as head of the Major League Baseball Players Association. Back then, a baseball player made an average salary of $19,000 a year. By the time this Brooklyn boy retired in 1982, Miller had an undefeated record against the team owners, and the players' salaries had risen to an average of $240,000 a year. With the advent of free agency, the players today average more than $2,700,000 a year. Miller is not yet in baseball's Hall of Fame, but he will be in time. Few other figures have had such a powerful impact on the game.*

# THE ROOTS OF RACISM

DOROTHY CHALLENOR BURNHAM

IF THERE WAS A GROUP THE CHRISTIAN CONSERVATIVES HATED more than the Jews, it was the African-Americans or blacks—or, as they were called in the South before the civil rights movement made people watch their tongues, the niggers. They started out as slaves, captured in Africa and brought to America half-dead in the hold of fetid ships. They were sold as chattel in the slave markets of southern cities like New Orleans, Atlanta, Montgomery, and Savannah to Christian plantation owners, and northern ones like New York City and Boston to merchants and households as well as to farmers. Black families were split up, the individuals forced to work for their white masters for no money.

Early on, the liberals in the North wanted to end slavery, but the southern Christian conservatives, including Founding Fathers Presidents George Washington, Thomas Jefferson, James Madison, and James Monroe, were resolute in their desire to continue the practice. They felt the economic viability of their large plantations depended on it.

To back up the legitimacy of what they were doing, churchgoing slaveholders could quote Bible passages chapter and verse. The primary passage had to do with Noah and his three sons, whose descendants repopulated the earth. According to the way the Bible was interpreted, after the flood, Noah's son Ham, whose descendants were black Hamites, was cursed. Says the Bible, "Noah cursed Ham to be a slave to his brethren Japheth."

Since Japheth's lineage goes through Europe and the Caucasus Mountains, the interpreters of the Bible concluded that God meant for Ham's descendants to be slaves.

It's hard to imagine a person using religion to justify keeping another human being in bondage, but for hundreds of years the Christian right not only used their religion to justify slavery—after it was abolished, they used it to justify segregation.

It took a civil war, of course, to end the practice of slavery in America, and for more than two decades the North administered the southern states, allowing blacks to vote in over a hundred of their kind to the legislatures of North and South Carolina alone.

Then, in 1876, the nation's centennial election was held. Neither of the presidential candidates—Republican Rutherford B. Hayes and Democrat Samuel J. Tilden—had the votes to win. Hayes's people made Tilden's people an offer he couldn't refuse: if you throw your electoral college votes my way, I will withdraw the northern army from the three southern states still being occupied by northern troops: Florida, Louisiana, and South Carolina. Tilden agreed. Hayes became president, and for the first time since the end of the Civil War, the South completely controlled its future.

Immediately, the Southerners in those states did what the Southerners did in the other states after the withdrawal of federal troops: they threw out all the blacks that had been elected to office, and they passed laws making sure they would never return. Since slavery had been abolished by the Constitution, they could only do the next best thing: pass laws to make sure blacks ended up as badly off as when they were slaves.

As part of these Jim Crow laws, blacks were effectively banished from white society. They weren't allowed to eat in the same restaurants as whites, stay at the same hotels as whites, shop in the same stores as whites. They had to use separate bathroom facilities, go to separate schools—if blacks were allowed to go to school at all—drink from separate drinking fountains, and ride in separate train cars. Some cities even designated where blacks could and could not live and shop.

The poor white Southerners didn't know it, but they were being sold a bill of goods by the Southern aristocrats. No matter how badly off they were, they were told, they were still in better shape than the Negro.

Ku Klux Klan rally. *Library of Congress*

To make sure the Negroes kept their place, an organization called the Ku Klux Klan was founded. It was begun right after the Civil War by six former Confederate soldiers in Pulaski, Tennessee. The name *kuklux* was a form of *kuklos,* the Greek word for circle. These men rode horses through the countryside while draped in white sheets and pillowcase hoods. It wasn't long before it evolved into a multistate terrorist organization designed to frighten and kill emancipated slaves using lynching, shooting, burning, castration, pistol-whipping, and other forms of intimidation.

Membership in the Klan was restricted to those who believed in the strict interpretation of the Protestant Bible. To join, you had to swear that you believed in three Christian principles: the virgin birth of Jesus; the literal infallibility of the Bible; and the bodily resurrection of Christ. To enforce the notion that the Klan was a terrorist group fighting in the name of Christianity, it chose as its symbol the cross, and when it wished to show its power, the Klansmen would burn a large cross on the property of those they wished to intimidate. They were an army likened to crusaders, only their targets weren't the infidels but rather fellow Americans of the Catholic, Jewish, and black persuasion.

A primary task of the Klan was keeping blacks in their place.

In 1872, President Ulysses S. Grant went before the House and spelled out the aims of the Klan: "By force and terror, to prevent all political action not in accord with the views of the members, to deprive colored citizens of the right to bear arms and of the right of a free ballot, to suppress the schools in which colored children are taught, and to reduce the colored people to a condition closely allied to that of slavery." Through legal and military intervention, Grant seriously curtailed the Klan. After Hayes took office in 1877, it was once again free to roam the land in support of the white race.

Whites in the South between 1890 and 1910 did everything to make sure black leaders who spoke out against Jim Crow were silenced. Ida Wells was run out of Memphis for her outspoken opposition to lynching. After race riots in Atlanta in 1906, Jesse Max Barber, editor of *Voice of the Negro,* was given three choices: leave town, recant his opinions on the causes of the riots (that it was the whites' fault), or serve on a chain gang. He fled to Chicago.

What brought about a renewed resurgence of Ku Klux Klan activity was the movie *The Birth of a Nation,* which exploded onto the scene in 1915. In an age in which most movies cost a nickel, this one cost two dollars, and the lines stretched around the block in every city in which it appeared. More than 25 million tickets were sold.

Written and directed by D. W. Griffith, the movie portrayed the Klan as the protectors of America. Blacks during Reconstruction were the villains of the piece. Thomas Dixon, who wrote the novel upon which the film was based, went to visit President Woodrow Wilson, his college classmate. Wilson, a Virginian who had segregated the formerly integrated federal bureaucracy, said, "At last there had sprung into existence a great Ku Klux Klan, a veritable empire of the South, to protect the Southern country." He also is reported to have said about the movie, "My only regret is that it is all so terribly true." Wilson's feelings about Jews were so open and notorious that Eugene Debs, writing in the *Dearborn Independent,* called the president "the nation's premier anti-Semite."

A few days before the film opened in Atlanta, Colonel William Joseph Simmons climbed Stone Mountain, burned a cross, and announced the rebirth of the Klan. The Klan's message combined hyper-patriotism and moralistic Christianity with the disdain for elites, cities, and intellectuals, and a hatred for blacks, Jews, Catholics, and foreigners. By 1920 the Klan had 8 million members.

LeRoy Percy, a U.S. senator and a large landholder in the Mississippi Delta, who defeated the Klan in a local election in 1923 on a platform of decency, fairness, and humanity, blamed the Protestant Church for its proliferation. He wrote: "No class of American citizenship can escape responsibility to its duty as the protestant ministry. The repudiation of this sulking, cowardly, un-American, unChristian organization as the champion [of] Protestantism should have been instantaneous and wide spread and such a repudiation would have sounded its death knell . . . [but] the rank and file of the Baptist and Methodist ministry has either acquiesced in it or actively espoused it."

According to the Klan, the world was falling apart, but the Klan would make things right. Out of fear, the Klan enforced a conformity of hate. It was "us" against "them."

As John Barry described it, "The 'them' has often included not only an enemy above but also an enemy below. The enemy above was whoever was viewed as the boss . . . Wall Street, or Jews, or Washington; in the 1920s the enemy below was Catholics, immigrants, blacks, and political radicals."

Little had changed in the country by the 1940s. Both the Republicans and the Democrats were deathly afraid of losing the Southern bloc, so neither party dared voice any objection to the status quo. The people who were brazen enough to take up the cause of the Negro were mostly white, immigrant Jews—members of the Communist Party, which in 1924 proclaimed that "the Negro workers of this country are exploited and oppressed more ruthlessly than any other group." Negroes, with few exceptions, did not campaign to end Jim Crow. It was too dangerous. They could be tarred and feathered, or lynched. The Jews who suffered such treatment under the czar sympathized, and they banded together to see if they could help their black brethren get a fairer shake in American society.

In 1928 the Communist Party made twelve demands to end black oppression. One of them was ending race discrimination. Full social equality was another. Because the Palmer Raids and the Red Scare had been successful in marginalizing the Communists, few right-thinking Americans paid any attention. (Forty years later, segregationists in Congress read the Communist Party's platform into the Congressional Record in an attempt to undermine civil rights reform.)

That same year the Communist Party attempted to organize in Harlem. Their candidate was Richard Moore. The Communists had so little sway with the black community that Moore garnered exactly 296 votes.

In the 1930s there were two major trials that resulted in such obvious injustice against black defendants—the Scottsboro Boys and later Angelo Herndon—that America was embarrassed by public opinion around the world. The Scottsboro case marked the emergence of the Communist Party in Harlem more than any other event.

In that case, a group of twelve black boys riding a freight train were accused of driving a group of white boys off the train and then attacking two white girls. One of the girls cried rape and pointed out her attackers. The problem was that when the girls arrived at the station, they never said anything about being attacked. Doctors who examined them said that though the girls had had sex, they had seen no signs of injury or struggle. It was only after a group of vigilantes arrived to avenge the attack by the black youths on the white boys that the girls made their rape charges. The National Guard had to be called to prevent a lynching. The Communist Party made the Scottsboro case the focus of its antilynching campaign. The prosecutor announced he was seeking the death penalty for all the defendants. In his summation, the prosecutor said to the jury, "Show them that Alabama justice cannot be bought and sold with Jew money from New York . . ."

It didn't take long for the jury to agree to put the first defendant, Haywood Patterson, to death despite the lack of evidence. It was surely a legal lynching. Communist lawyers han-

The Scottsboro Boys. *Library of Congress*

dled the appeal. When the Supreme Court agreed to hear the appeal, the legitimacy of the Communist Party in America greatly increased.

The Communist Party led a powerful march on Washington on May 6, 1933. That month, Harlem congressman Adam Clayton Powell threw his support to the Communists. He said, "The day will come when being called a Communist will be the highest honor that can be paid an individual and that day is coming soon." In June of 1933 the jury verdict in the Patterson case was overturned, and a new trial ordered.

The next big case was that of Angelo Herndon, who was prosecuted because he was black, a union activist, and a member of the Communist Party. His father had died from "miner's pneumonia" when Angelo was nine. He saw that segregation was used by the Lexington, Alabama, mine in which he worked as a "cunning" device to keep the union out, and at seventeen he became a recruiter for the National Miners' Union. When members of the Communist Party came to talk to them, he was impressed.

"They believed that Negroes ought to have equal rights with whites. It all sounded okay to me . . ." he said.

In 1932, at age nineteen, he traveled from Cincinnati to Atlanta to become an organizer for the Communist-led Unemployed Council, mobilizing jobless workers, their wives, and children, who were literally starving to death while the Georgia authorities did nothing. Herndon was attempting to get the County Commissioners of Atlanta to pay $6,000 to whites and blacks for unemployment relief when he was arrested without a warrant by the Atlanta police on charges of being a vagrant and of "attempting to incite negroes [sic] to insurrection." The law he was accused of breaking was first passed in 1861, through the influence of slaveholders who were scared that their slaves might revolt after listening to Northern antislavery propaganda. The only penalty under the statute was death. The law was revised in 1871 to include all incitement to insurrection. No mention, of course, was made of slaves. It was aimed at the carpetbaggers who had taken over the South's governments. Herndon was never charged with any specific act. His crimes included attending public assemblies, persuading people to join the Communist Party, and circulating Communist literature.

Herndon was held in jail for six months. The fact that he had organized whites and blacks together was what really riled the racists in the prosecutor's office. The prosecutor sought the death penalty.

During his six months in jail awaiting trial, he was systematically starved.

He was represented at trial by Ben Davis, a black Harvard Law graduate and a member of the Communist Party, and a young white Atlanta lawyer by the name of A. W. Morrison. At trial the prosecutor told the jury, "This is not only a trial of Herndon, but of Lenin, Stalin, Trotsky, and Kerensky. As fast as the Communists come here we shall indict them and I shall demand the death penalty in every case."

Said the prosecutor about Herndon's championing of equal rights for blacks: "Stamp this thing out with a conviction." He asked for the death penalty, but the jury was "lenient" and he was sentenced to eighteen to twenty years on the chain gang.

The prosecution witnesses constantly referred to Herndon and other blacks as "niggers" and "darkies," over the objection of the defense. The judge clearly was hostile to Herndon. The literature in Herndon's room had been seized without a search warrant, but the judge allowed it into evidence anyway.

Because of the national and international publicity of the case, Atlanta suffered a black eye in the court of public opinion, and Herndon was released after a year in jail. He was greeted by six thousand supporters when he arrived by train from Georgia at New York's Pennsylvania Station.

In the 1930s many college students were looking to understand the Depression and why it happened, and because of the vacuum left by the Republican and Democratic Parties, which had no answers to explain why capitalism had failed them, they joined the CP's Southern Negro Youth Congress, another organization dedicated to civil rights and to the rights of workers to unionize. The Southern Negro Youth Congress supported the CIO's blue-collar organizing, established campus cooperatives and student labor unions, and campaigned against segregation in college area stores, services, recreational facilities, athletic teams, and in university admissions. It also sought to battle Jim Crow in the South.

The organization gained in strength until August of 1939, when Stalin entered into a pact with Hitler and Nazi Germany. When this happened, American Communists were left demoralized and confused. Nazi Germany had been the enemy. Fighting fascism always had been the primary goal. At the end of September of 1939, the Comintern ordered the American Communists to change their target—they were ordered to attack President Roosevelt so as to keep America out of the war. Some Communist leaders did this, which put them on the same side as the America Firsters like Joe Kennedy and Charles Lindbergh. A few American Communists went along, but most members became disgusted and dropped their membership. By 1940 the student movement in the Communist Party was about over. By the end of World War II, the CP had very little influence left. Russia was no longer an ally, and overnight it had become the enemy that had stolen our secrets and threatened our way of life. When the reprisals came, it was open season on anyone who had ever been a member of the party or one of its many organizations.

The civil rights work done by the Southern Negro Youth Congress, however, should not be forgotten. It was among the very first organized efforts to do something about Jim

Crow. It was also part of the campaign to force major league baseball to hire a black player.

Dorothy Challenor, who was born in 1915, was one of the pioneers of that movement. She grew up in Clinton Hill, a small neighborhood in north-central Brooklyn. East of Bedford-Stuyvesant, it was a community where blacks and whites lived in interracial harmony. A block from where Challenor lived, stately mansions lined Clinton Avenue, home of millionaires' row. Challenor's dad was a janitor and her mom cleaned houses for whites, but she never let her lack of means deter her from getting an education. When she began attending Brooklyn College in the mid-1930s, she met influential teachers who led her on a path of trying to change the world.

After the public trials of the Scottsboro Boys in 1931 and Angelo Herndon in 1932, Challenor became aware of how much worse Southern blacks had it than she did. She and fellow Brooklyn College students Edward and Augusta Strong helped form an organization called The American Youth Congress, a group dedicated to social justice and racial equality. After driving to New Orleans in 1938 to attend a conference of another group dedicated to civil rights, the Southern Negro Youth Congress, Dorothy learned firsthand the trials of traveling in the South while black.

Dorothy met and married Louis Burnham, and for the next seven years the two would live in Birmingham, Alabama, working with the unions of black steelworkers and black coal workers to pressure Southern political leaders to repeal the poll tax. When black veterans returned from World War II, she organized them to increase the pressure to repeal the oppressive measure. Alas, despite their efforts, Southern resistance remained steadfast.

One white who was moved by their efforts was Eleanor Roosevelt, who saw how hard the poor—and poor blacks in particular—were struggling to get a fair shake, and it is fair to suggest that planks of Franklin Roosevelt's New Deal came directly from the yearnings expressed by groups such as the Southern Negro Youth Congress. As a result, federal laws were passed preventing discrimination in housing and health care, and it was under Roosevelt that laws were passed calling for a minimum wage, social security, and the end of job discrimination.

By 1940, the establishment was ready to fight back, and it did so with a vengeance, under the Smith Act, which decreed that anyone who willfully advocates the overthrow of the U.S. government shall be imprisoned or fined. The bill was sponsored by Representative Howard W. Smith of Virginia, a racist Democrat who supported the poll tax and was a leader of the antilabor bloc of Congress. The bill was signed by President Roosevelt. What Roosevelt did not anticipate was that all prosecutors had to do was charge a defendant with being a Communist and then cite Karl Marx's desire to overthrow the government. The argument would be made that if Marx wanted revolution, then so did the defendant. Dozens of those charged under the Smith Act, who had done nothing but push for civil rights, social justice, or unions, were convicted. Worse, anyone accused of being a Communist was stained as being a traitor, when the truth was that many of the defendants were just the opposite: fighters for freedom, and lovers of a just America. The Supreme Court in 1957 would declare many convictions under the Smith Act unconstitutional. The smear campaign that was the hallmark of the 1950s McCarthy era also meant that anyone branded a "Communist" would disappear from history, no matter how important his or her work in helping to create a better world for workers, blacks, or the poor.

By 1953, the Southern Negro Youth Congress was out of business, as organizers were arrested, their families harassed, and donations dropped precipitously. Dorothy and Louis Burnham moved to Harlem, where he and Paul Robeson started *Freedom* magazine. Robeson, who was blacklisted and couldn't work, moved to Europe. Louis and Dorothy Burnham together continued their work until Louis's death in 1960. The saintly Dorothy Burnham, now ninety-three, who risked life and limb so that African-Americans could live in freedom, resides in anonymity in Brooklyn, still hoping for better days for the working class.

**DOROTHY BURNHAM** "My father was a shoemaker who grew up in Barbados, but the shoemakers' union in Brooklyn kept him from working at his trade because of racism, and so he became a janitor. He did work at the I. Miller shoe company off and on, but he was steadily employed as a janitor. My mother was a house worker and a factory worker.

"I grew up in the Clinton Hill area of Brooklyn. When I was growing up, the neighborhood was integrated. There were fairly well-off people living there, so the schools were good. I went to PS 11, and then I went to Girls High School on Nostrand Avenue. I had white friends and black friends. There was no obvious discrimination at school that I remember, though there were no black teachers in either elementary or high school, and sometimes the white kids were treated a little bit better than the black children. But it wasn't obvious.

"My mother knew one black teacher. My sister and some of her friends went to the Maxwell Training School for teachers, and there were two or three blacks in her class, and they didn't let them pass the oral exam because they spoke with a Southern accent, so there was discrimination in that way. When my sister graduated, it took her a while before she got a job teaching, but she finally did get a job.

"The segregation wasn't open, but the real estate companies wouldn't sell houses to black people in white neighborhoods in Brooklyn. There were expansive mansions on Clinton Avenue, a block from our apartment, and that was limited to white people. There were no blacks at all living on many streets. In 1935, when I was twenty, I remember a friend was married to a white man, and he went and got an apartment, and when they moved in, there was a big hullabaloo about it. We organized, and they had to let them stay, but right after that that apartment house became mostly black, because the white people started moving out.

"A number of the restaurants in Brooklyn wouldn't serve blacks, so there were places we couldn't go. One we could go into was Horn and Hardart. You put nickels in the slots and took your food. It was like the McDonald's of its day.

"I went to Brooklyn College because it was free. The average to get in was in the eighties, and my grades were good enough, and at that time there was a very small minority of black students. There were two or three black girls in my class, and we got together and organized a group and met fairly regularly. It was an opportunity for us to get together and talk.

"At Brooklyn College I met some teachers who were very much interested in changing the world. They were socialists and communists, and they talked about discrimination and poverty, and they explained what we had to do to end it, and they gave us reading materials, made me interested in changing the world.

"I learned about the Angelo Herndon case and what happened to him. And then there were the Scottsboro Boys, who were falsely accused of rape. There was a black woman a year ahead of me in school who started organizing support for the Scottsboro Boys. And then she introduced me to other people in the movement. The Scottsboro case made me understand the racism that was going on in the South. What moved me most into the movement was my hearing about the discrimination and the lynching of blacks in the South."

*While Dorothy was studying at Brooklyn College, in 1936 her friends Edward and Augusta Strong organized a civil rights group called The American Youth Congress, and another friend, James Jackson, organized another civil rights group that called themselves the Southern Negro Youth Congress (SNYC). A year later Dorothy was invited to attend SNYC's second annual national meeting in New Orleans.*

**DOROTHY BURNHAM** "I was living in Brooklyn at the time, and I and several friends of mine in the movement drove to New Orleans for the conference. It was the first time I had traveled South, the first time I saw open discrimination. I just remember we had to be very careful where we stopped. We could only stay at the black YWCAs or YMCAs. In Brooklyn there was a white YWCA and a separate black YWCA. The pool was at the white YWCA, and we could only swim in it once a week. Once we got South, we had to find the few black restaurants along the way."

*In 1940 Dorothy met Louis Burnham, an active member of the American Youth Congress and of the student movement at City College. He was a fiery orator on the street corners of Harlem, a man dedicated to ending discrimination wherever he saw it. They married in Brooklyn in 1941, just before he was asked to move to Birmingham, Alabama.*

**DOROTHY BURNHAM** "Louie ran for assemblyman on the Labor Party ticket. He talked mostly about discrimination, racism, and opportunities for working-class people. He attended a lot of street-corner meetings, and he would speak around Lenox Avenue, Seventh Avenue. In 1941 he was invited to replace Ed Strong as the executive secretary of the Southern Negro Youth Congress. Their primary task: getting blacks the vote.

"The poll tax was one of the ways the whites were able to keep people from voting, especially blacks, and there was resistance to what we were doing, because they wanted to exclude blacks from making decisions about what happened with their lives. Blacks couldn't vote, and as part of our campaign we fought for equal opportunity and the right to vote in a democracy.

"We would get letters from people threatening the offices of our organization. 'Stay away.' I don't remember actual threats to our lives. We were especially active getting the black coal miners and steel workers to help us organize in our fight to end the poll tax.

"It was a big struggle. I don't think they ever did do away with it. At that point they weren't quite ready, but it was the beginnings of the struggle in the South. And when the black soldiers came back from the war, Henry Mayfield tried to organize the veterans, but that didn't work either. The cops would push people away from campaigning or walking the picket lines. They'd come and arrest us.

"One of our members, Mildred McAdory, got on a bus one day, and she refused to move to the back of the bus—that was long before Rosa Parks—and they arrested her. When Rosa did it, there was enough backing to mount a campaign for her, thank goodness. They took Mildred off to jail, and we had to pay a fine, and they released her. She didn't have to serve any jail time. But her actions didn't have any further repercussions either.

"My husband, Louie, was eating in a restaurant with three white teachers from Talladega one time. It was a black restaurant, and occasionally whites would come over and eat in a black restaurant, but this time somebody gave the signal, because they were Southern Negro Youth Congress people, and the cops were alerted and arrested the four of them for eating together in a restaurant and took them to jail. They spent half the night in jail before they were let out. They had to go to trial, and they were fined.

"Louis was never beaten up, but some of our members picketing in New Orleans were beaten when they were arrested. New Orleans was rough. James Jackson went down to New Orleans to work with Raymond Tillman, who was organizing. Ray lived in New Orleans, and it became too dangerous, and both of them finally had to leave."

*In 1942 the Southern Negro Youth Congress invited Paul Robeson to sing at their meeting in Tuskegee, Alabama. What made the concert more notable than usual was that it was integrated.*

**DOROTHY BURNHAM** "Paul was a person very outspoken about civil rights. He refused to sing before segregated audiences. I remember one year Marion Anderson came to Birmingham, and she couldn't stay in a hotel. She stayed with a woman near us who had a rooming house, who entertained the black guests as they came through the city. Marion sang to an audience that was segregated, but Paul would not. He rarely performed in the South because of that. In Tuskegee, when he came and sang, the audience was integrated. When Glen Taylor, who ran for office with Henry Wallace, came to Birmingham to speak, we decided the audience would be integrated, and they arrested the minister of the church and my husband."

*Though their civil rights work may not have had much short-term effect in the South, what is clear, looking at history, is that their actions had an important effect on President Franklin Roosevelt and his New Deal.*

**DOROTHY BURNHAM** "Esther Jackson was James's wife, and I do know that she and some of the young members of SNYC once met with Eleanor Roosevelt. Eleanor was interested in the youth and the youth congress, and they met and discussed some of the items on the agenda of the youth organization. She saw there were organizations out there really struggling, and Franklin Roosevelt's actions in the areas of housing and health care were certainly in response to the pressure he was getting from these organizations. The unions, which were much stronger than they are today, also were able to apply pressure, and many of the unions supported the black movement.

"One of the campaigns I participated in in New York was to get baseball desegregated. I was involved in some of the marches to get black players into the league. We marched in New York. In Brooklyn I also campaigned on Fulton Street to get the Woolworth's store, which was in the middle of Bed-Stuy, to hire black salespeople. They had all white salespeople, didn't hire any blacks. Blacks were only working as cleaners in the department stores. A&S didn't even have a black elevator operator. So we campaigned in front of Woolworth's many, many months, and they finally gave in and started hiring black salespeople. At the same time, in Harlem, Adam Clayton Powell was leading the demonstrations on 125th Street against the Woolworth's there.

"As for Jackie signing with the Dodgers, any struggle we won was big. We could realize that if you struggled for something hard enough, you might be able to win a change in the system."

*Robinson's entry into baseball was one of the last successes of the Progressive Movement before the right-wingers in the government used the repressive and unconstitutional Smith Act to destroy anyone they wished who was connected in any way with the Communist Party. Though not a single one of the 140 defendants was ever found to have committed a single act against his country, the wording of the Smith Act enabled prosecutors to dismantle and scatter groups dedicated to social justice and racial equality.*

*After firing hundreds of college and high school teachers in New York City under the Rapp-Coudert Commission hearings and under the Feingold Law, the House Un-American Committee, under the Smith Act, prosecuted anyone who was a member of the Communist Party. Many civil rights and union activists were stopped cold. Some were jailed. Some*

Paul Robeson and Ben Davis.
*Library of Congress*

*went into hiding. Others fled the country. Illegal or not, the right-wingers used the Smith Act to end any effectiveness these people might have had. And all their dangerous, hard work for social justice and civil rights in hostile cities across the country has been forgotten or, worse, ignored.*

**DOROTHY BURNHAM**   "Many of the teachers who were prosecuted were people who had been active in forming the teachers' union, and in prosecuting them they tried to scare away other people and scare away business, and in that they were quite successful. I was friends with James Jackson, who had to hide, and with Claudia Jones, a very close friend who had to leave the country. It was really very hard to take. I attended some of those trials. It was difficult. McCarthyism was a really bad time. The best teachers I had at Brooklyn College were prosecuted and lost their jobs. The FBI followed us. They even followed my children to school. Our phone conversations were tapped. We had to be careful what we said on the phone, because we knew anything we said was being recorded. It was very difficult.

"Because of the continuing efforts of the FBI, the financial support for SNYC dwindled. Some of our advisors, who were college presidents and professors, were threatened, and they resigned, so it was difficult to keep the organization going. That's when we moved back to New York. Louie came back and worked on the Henry Wallace [1948 presidential] campaign. Louie and Paul Robeson then started *Freedom* magazine, and they got people in the movement to contribute to it. Paul wrote a weekly column, and Alice Childress and Lorraine Hansbury were contributors. It lasted a few years, but it was difficult to keep going because you had to continually fund-raise, and there were no automobile ads to pay for it. What I remember most about Paul was that in spite of the fact he was so famous, he was a very friendly and open person. He was very open and anxious to get to talk to people and get to know them. He and his wife, Essie, were really dedicated to changing conditions of black people in the United States, that's for sure.

"It surprises me that our civil rights work in the South has disappeared from the history books. I'm surprised at that, because many of the liberals bought into that, the idea that the Communist Party was completely negative, pushing for totalitarian government. I didn't know a single person who advocated the overthrow of the American government. They were advocating changes in racism and discrimination policies, to get equality, but certainly not to overthrow the government. I'm proud to say we did play a role nationally and internationally, because we were able to send people to conferences to talk about the segregation and racism in the South, so people could understand.

"I can't explain why no one talks about our work in the South, but my feeling is for the children of this generation and the coming generation, it's going to be very,

very difficult in terms of our getting all the things people need—housing, health care, and so forth. The poor and the working class are getting out of reach, and the organizations have been splintered. The trade unions have to be rebuilt, and you have the threat from globalization, which didn't exist before. The problems of people interested in change are very great.

"It's a different world, but it's not working in favor of the working class—yet."

## SPORTS EDITOR OF THE *DAILY WORKER*

LESTER RODNEY

Lester Rodney, who was born in 1911 ("a year before the *Titanic* went down") grew up in predominantly Jewish Bensonhurst and was a product of the Depression. His Jewish parents had not been immigrants. Both were born in New York City, his father in 1867, his mother in 1882. His father, who was in the garment industry, had been very successful through the boom of the 1920s. He owned a home, and like many high-rollers at the time, he had seen other men growing rich by investing heavily in the stock market, and he himself had taken a plunge, borrowing more and more to buy stocks as they spiraled up and up, until that disastrous October Tuesday in 1929 when the market suddenly crashed, leaving rich men broke and strong men broken. Unfettered capitalism had taken its toll, and for thinking men like Lester Rodney and millions of other disillusioned Americans, the crash and subsequent depression prompted them to question whether some other economic system might be better for the Average Working Man than the capitalist system that had failed them so badly.

While attending New York University, Rodney began reading the Communist newspaper, the *Daily Worker*. He saw that the Communists had interests that jibed with his own, especially when it came to civil rights. Rodney was born with the baseball gene, and he could not understand why blacks were barred from playing major league baseball. He figured if he could become the paper's sports editor, he could further the two causes he felt so strongly about. Before he was finished, Lester Rodney became one of the major moving forces behind the campaign to bring blacks to the major leagues.

**LESTER RODNEY**  "I grew up in Bensonhurst, a majority Jewish, with quite a few Italians, and a mix of German-Irish and Germans. There were no African-Americans, no blacks in our community. A Negro was an abstraction to me. I would sing mindlessly with the other kids the ditties, 'Oh, you dirty little nigger, does your mother know you're going out with her?' I think back. *Did I say that?* But it really had no meaning to us. It was an abstraction.

"The neighborhood was pretty much peaceful. At Halloween a bunch of Irish kids would fill their socks with chalk and come around, and we'd scuffle with them, but that was kids' stuff. It was a different time. We didn't have Little League. We had empty lots, and we cleared them of glass and rocks and created diamonds and played baseball. We played stickball in the streets.

"This was long before television. In fact, I remember when radio began. We got a big Atwater Kent box. My mother heard the music and threw open a window and put her head out one night and looked up and said, 'You mean somewhere

Lester Rodney, 1918, is the kid with the Buster Brown hair on the left. *Courtesy of Lester Rodney*

there's a band playing this music? And it comes through the air, not on wires? It comes through our windows?' The wonderment of this was an amazing thing.

"Of course, the thing about Brooklyn and sports was that everyone was a baseball fan. And most everyone was a Dodgers fan. It was far more truly a national pastime than now. There was no pro football league, no pro basketball league. It was unthinkable that people weren't Dodgers fans.

"In 1920, when I was nine years old, I skipped school early one October morning, got on my bicycle, and pedaled thirteen miles from Bensonhurst to Ebbets Field. The right center field exit gate on Bedford Avenue didn't quite reach the sidewalk. There were a few inches of space and room for six kids lying flat on their stomachs on the sidewalk there to peer underneath and watch the game—what we saw was the centerfielder, the second baseman, the pitcher, the catcher, and the umpire. I saw the first game of the 1920 World Series, Brooklyn against Cleveland. Stanley Covelesky, the spitball pitcher, started that day. He won three games for Cleveland. That was the series in which Bill Wambsganns made a triple play unassisted, and Elmer Smith hit a grand slam. It was a year after the Black Sox scandal, which I can't say lessened my enthusiasm for the game or my feelings about the Dodgers. I would say that was true of all the kids on the block.

Both blacks and whites lined up outside Ebbets Field to get in to see the 1920 World Series. *Library of Congress*

"In the 1920s we had a first baseman named Jacques Fornier. He was our cleanup hitter, though Zack Wheat was my favorite player. I'd go to the bleachers for 50¢, and before the game Zack Wheat would lean up against the barrier and chat with the kids in the bleachers. We'd say, 'How many hits today, Zack?' And he'd hold up two or three fingers. Wheat and Fornier batted third and fourth, and I remember one game with Philadelphia. Clarence Mitchell, a left-handed spitball pitcher, was leading 1-0 in the bottom of the ninth, two out, and Wheat singled, and Fornier hit one over the wall into Bedford Avenue to win it. That's the kind of game I remember.

"The Dodger manager was Wilbert Robinson, Uncle Robbie, a fat, jovial-looking guy. From reading the sports pages I knew he had been the pitching coach for New

York Giants' manager John McGraw. I read the sports pages. Teachers today ask, "How do you get kids to read?" The first things we read were the box scores and the stories of the baseball games. That's one way that many kids became interested in mastering reading. They say anything can start you reading, but for us it was baseball. It also introduced us to drama, the drama of the game and the tensions and great empty disappointments and how to cope with that. Baseball was so important a part of our young lives.

"We played all kinds of games in the streets, and I also played baseball on a sandlot that we made into a makeshift field. After high school I played more organized sandlot ball. I was nineteen and twenty, and we had a team, the 83rd Street Dodgers, which was managed by a former minor league player, Bill Renner. I played shortstop. We played against neighborhood teams, a team from Borough Park, for instance. We played on Sundays, and people would gather, and we'd pass the hat, and they'd put in loose change or dollar bills, and we'd use the money to buy balls and bats. It was a culture of baseball you don't find today.

Lester Rodney's father.
*Courtesy of Lester Rodney*

"My father was a silk salesman, and the Depression finished him, as it did many men at that time. We lost everything with the stock market crash, his job, our home. We had stocks on margin, and our home was mortgaged. Although we had a solid middle-class existence, it was just quickly wiped away. They had no idea of the social background of the Depression. All they knew was that the man is supposed to support his family, and they had failed their families. It just destroyed so many men, knocked their lives apart. My father was hit particularly hard. He had a stroke. And he was a Republican, by the way. I remember when Roosevelt was elected in 1932, the first year I voted, I didn't vote for him. He was a rich, aristocratic governor of New York. He developed later. In 1932 I voted for Hoover.

"I had gone to New Utrecht High School, where I earned a track scholarship to Syracuse. I ran the 880, the half-mile, the two-mile relay, and occasionally the mile. New Utrecht had the best track team in the city the four years I was there. I was a good long-distance runner, and after graduating in June of 1929 I was going to go to Syracuse, and then came the crash in October, so instead I went to NYU at night. I worked traditional Depression jobs. I was a stock clerk. I was a chauffeur for a rich family for a while. I drove two young girls to school and drove their parents around in a big Cadillac. I would take them to the Catskill Mountains to summer resorts. That was my first taste of Catskill Mountains luxury.

Lester Rodney's mother.
*Courtesy of Lester Rodney*

"I didn't have any class consciousness at the time. I was twenty. In fact, if I would pass a Communist Party rally on a street corner, I would say to myself, *Comes the revolution, ha ha ha.* Not vindictively. But once I started going to NYU, everybody there was part of the hubbub of 'ists.' You were either a communist, a socialist, a Trotskyite, or else you were pretty brain-dead. If you were on a college campus at that time and weren't questioning the workings of capitalism, you were pretty dull.

"The Wall Street crash would be a huge scandal today, like the Enron scandal, whose stock doubled and tripled through manipulation. What it was was unregulated capitalism, and it took Roosevelt to restore some order in the capitalist system.

"At NYU I joined the Young Communist League, because I thought the Russians had paved a new path. We were Americans who believed that socialism was a far more equitable way for our country to go, and Russia was the first country in the world to proclaim itself socialist. We rooted for them to show the world it worked. And in that process we put on self-inflicted blinders. We refused to see what was jammed in our face by Stalin, but that's all history.

"At NYU people in my class would ask me, 'Have you ever read the *Daily Worker*?' 'No, what's that?' When I got a hold of the paper, I found it was a stridently written paper that rubbed me the wrong way in some instances, but they had a weekly sports section. It talked about sports, but it had a down-the-nose attitude toward sports. By that time I had become more radicalized than I had realized, so I wrote a letter to the editor of the *Daily Worker*. I didn't even know his name. I wrote, 'Editor, *Daily Worker*.' I said, 'I've been reading your paper,' and I made suggestions. I said, 'You seem to have a standoffish feeling about sports,' which was part of the ideology, that sport dulls the worker, engages his interest, and lessens his class instincts. I suggested to him that young workers were people who loved sports, that they played ball in the streets, played ball in high school, and they were trade unionists, and he should appeal to people like that by covering sports, and covering it as though he liked it. I said, 'And you can still point out what's wrong with sports while you are doing it. There is no contradiction.'

"What was wrong with sports, with baseball, at the time was it was lily-white."

*After President Rutherford B. Hayes took office in 1877, segregation became so prevalent throughout the entire country that black baseball players were no longer allowed to play on the same team with whites. In 1883, Fleet Walker, an excellent catcher for Toledo in the major league American Association, was ordered off the field by Cap Anson, the captain of the Chicago White Stockings, before an exhibition game. The Toledo manager confronted Anson, and told him that the White Stockings would forfeit their portion of the gate receipts if he had to take Walker off the field. The color green apparently being more important than the color black, Anson relented. But within the next five years, Anson's actions would cause the major and minor leagues to institute a complete ban on black players, effectively keeping blacks off major and minor league fields for another sixty years.*

**LESTER RODNEY**  "I was called in by the editor, and he said, 'How would you like to do a little writing for the Sunday sports page?' I said, 'Sure.' I wrote articles about baseball. I talked about the love of the game and the beauty of a perfectly executed double play, and the camaraderie of the players. My column led to a poll of the readers as to whether they wanted a daily sports section, and to the surprise of some people and to the hostility of some of the party people, the vote was six to one in favor of starting a daily sports section. So I became the founding sports editor of the *Daily Worker* in September of 1936. My first big headline came during the 1936 World Series between the Yankees and the Giants. GIANT POWER THREATENS YANKS. I wrote it that way because someone kidded me by saying, 'If New York was playing Cincinnati, would you have said, YANKEE POWER THREATENS REDS?'

"To get accreditation to cover the games I had to prove I was actually covering baseball, and after a time I got my accreditation, and when I retired in 1957, I was voted an honorary lifetime membership in the Baseball Writers' Association. Which is usual, but not automatic. So I can get into any press box in the country now.

"One of the very first things I did was attend and cover the Negro League games. The Negro Leagues were not covered in the mainstream press, except perhaps a notice that the Kansas City Monarchs were playing the Baltimore Elite Giants at 3 P.M., but nothing about the fact that none of these players could play in the big leagues or even in the minor leagues of what was called Our National Pastime. If you go back to the great newspapers of our time in the mid-'30s, the *New York Times,* the *Washington Post,* the *Boston Globe,* you would find no editorials saying, 'What's going on here? This is America.'

"So I had a scoop. I had the story all to myself. One of the first points to make was that there were black players qualified to play in the big leagues. And who were they? I began running articles about Satchel Paige and Josh Gibson and others. I saw Josh Gibson play maybe twenty times, and I think he was the greatest catcher ever to put on a uniform. I agree with those who say Johnny Bench was the definitive big-league catcher, but Josh was at least as good as Bench defensively and maybe a little quicker popping out for a dribbler in front of the plate. Josh was catlike. Pitchers loved pitching to him, like he was in a rocking chair. At bat he was nothing less than a right-handed Babe Ruth. There can never be accurate records of all his home runs. They didn't keep statistics like the big leagues did and do. But back then I would go to ballparks, and people would say to me, 'He hit one into the third deck of Yankee Stadium, and it almost went out of the ballpark.' Josh was just remarkable. When I speak to a young audience, it's so hard to make them believe that halfway through the twentieth century, in the land of the free, a ball player who was qualified—or over-qualified—couldn't play because of the color of his skin. My granddaughter (a big Giants fan) lives in Santa Rosa. Imagine everybody knows how good Barry Bonds is, just like everyone knew how good Josh Gibson was, and yet he couldn't play?

"In 1937, my second year, I interviewed Burleigh Grimes, the manager of the Dodgers. I was on the field before the game, browsing around, and he knew me, and I said, 'Burleigh, how are things going?' He was sixth in an eight-team league. He didn't have much of a team. He said, 'I don't have to tell you, I need some pitching and some hitting.'

"I said, 'How would you like to put a Dodger uniform on Satchel Paige and Josh Gibson?' You'd have thought I had hit him over the head with a two-by-four.

"He said, 'Don't talk about that. You know better than that. That can never happen.'

"'Why not, Burleigh?' I said.

"'The trains; the hotels. It just won't happen.'

"'But do you know how good they are?' I asked.

"'Of course I do.'

"All baseball people knew.

"'Can I put that in my paper?' I asked him. 'Just a headline, I KNOW HOW GOOD THEY ARE AND THEY OUGHT TO BE IN THE BIG LEAGUES: GRIMES.

"'Oh no,' he said. 'I don't want to stick my neck out.'

"But a couple of years later Leo Durocher was the manager of the Dodgers, and he was a different kind of cat, confident. In 1939 he had a pennant-contending team evolving, and he said, 'Hell, yes, I'd sign them in a minute if I got the okay from the

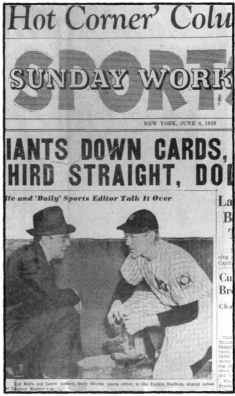

A page from the *Daily Worker* in 1939. Lester Rodney is interviewing Yankee third baseman Red Rolfe. *Courtesy of Lester Rodney*

big boys.' I printed it, and the institution in the person of Judge Landis dropped down on him. Yeah, Landis clamped down on him. But still the word got out, as part of this developing campaign.

"We saw that Judge Landis was probably the biggest roadblock to bringing blacks to the major leagues. He was a stone racist. Back then it was not that unusual even for a federal judge to be a racist, especially a Southerner.

"We called him on it. We said, 'It's up to you, Judge Landis.' He never responded to any of our questions. He would say, 'Go talk to the baseball owners. They don't want them. The ballplayers will never stand for it. Just forget it.'

"So one of the first things we tried to do was shoot down the notion that white players wouldn't stand for it. To prove that wrong, I collaborated with Wendell Smith, the sports editor of the *Pittsburgh Defender,* a black weekly. I would run his stories in my paper, and he would run my stories in his. The key year was 1939. After our campaign got under way, Smith really got into it, and he was a key factor. He was the guy who got Bill McKecknie, the manager of the Reds, to say, 'I know about twenty players in the Negro League who belong in the big leagues, and I'd like to have them on my team.' Bucky Walters and Johnny Vander Meer both said, 'I have no problem with black players wanting to play.'

"Every year I would send out telegrams to every big league owner, respectfully asking, 'Would you be in favor of accepting qualified Negro players?' And in 1939 William Benswanger, the owner of the Pirates, was the very first one to answer positively. He wrote, 'I see no reason why Negroes, just as they do in music and other things, shouldn't participate.' And Benswanger agreed to a trial of three Negro players, including a young Roy Campanella.

"The trial never took place. I'm sure pressure was put on Benswanger, but I have no hard evidence of that. But he gracefully backed out of it. But still, his agreeing to do it made a big splash. Wendell Smith and I both wrote it and played it up very big. It's an interesting 'What if?' Suppose Benswanger had been as bold as Branch Rickey and said, 'I'll take Campanella, and I'll take Satchel Paige, and I'll take Josh Gibson. Pittsburgh, the very center of Negro League ball with the Crawfords and the Homestead Grays, would have been the place, not Brooklyn. By Wendell Smith's estimation, six players on the Crawfords were possible major league all-stars. Pittsburgh could have won the next ten pennants, and Brooklyn wouldn't have.

"An important editor on the *Daily Worker* was a black man by the name of Benjamin Davis, who subsequently would be elected as the first Communist city councilman in New York. Ben was the editor of Negro affairs, as they called it. He had strong opinions, and he influenced the direction of the paper in many ways. Ben had been the attorney for Angelo Herndon, one of the more publicized civil rights cases in the 1930s. He was legally active too and a great guy.

One morning I was going to work, made the turn from University Place onto East 12th Street, walking toward the Building, as we called it, and Big Ben comes up behind me and gives me a big clap on the shoulder and throws his arm around me and says, 'Well, Lester, here it is in black and white.' That's the kind of guy he was, lighthearted about things like that, when some people weren't.

"Ben reinforced the campaign to end discrimination in baseball, actually mapping out the petition drive. He set up the picket lines at ball parks—we picketed at Ebbets Field, Yankee Stadium, and the Polo Grounds, but he made it clear that we were to make sure people understood we were not stopping them from going into the park. In the thirties, especially, that's what a picket line meant. But Ben, who was very sensitive about that point, said, 'Some people are not used to seeing blacks and whites together, let alone on a picket line. They may think it's just an angry attempt to keep people from attending the ball games.' So on the picket line, we would chant, 'Enjoy the game. Sign here to make the game democratic, a real American game.' This was his sensitive contribution.

"The picketing spread to other cities as well, like Cleveland and Detroit. At that time a Communist was actually running the United Auto Workers. It was just before Walter Reuther, who was a Socialist. Why? It was a result of who did all the organizing, the hard work on the ground. John L. Lewis admitted, kind of ruefully, that they needed the Communists in the rough situations. Ford sent goon squads to beat us up.

"I can remember in 1939 seeing Joe Louis fight Bob Pessner in Briggs Stadium in Detroit, and there was a big contingent of auto workers who had worked with Joe on the assembly line not too many years before that. They were mostly, but not all, black, and they were holding up signs saying, JOE WORKED WITH US.

"I met Joe Louis's mother then, and when another sportswriter, Lester Bromberg, who covered boxing for the *World Telegram,* a Scripps-Howard newspaper, heard I was going to see her, he asked if he could come along.

"He came, and he was fascinated. The other Lester asked her questions, but not a word appeared in his newspaper. I had a really good talk with her, and I ran a big story about what she thought about the cartoons showing Joe as a lazy beast and being a 'natural' fighter. She said, 'There was nothing natural. He used to come home from work at the auto plant and go to the fight club and train, and he could hardly keep his eyes open.' She particularly resented the characterization of her son as being some kind of animal."

*On December 7, 1941, the Japanese attacked Pearl Harbor, and Rodney was drafted in May of 1942.*

Lester Rodney in uniform during World War II. *Courtesy of Lester Rodney*

**LESTER RODNEY**  "After Bataan and Corrigedor, they crash-trained a bunch of us who had no medical training to be med techs. I had six months of intensive training without the niceties of bedfolding. You can learn an awful lot. We helped the doctors. We'd land, set up a field hospital, and treat the casualties. I was in the Pacific thirty-two months. I saw a lot. We patched up the wounded during the Sullivan Islands and most of the Philippines campaigns.

"When I was in the army, it would become known I was a Communist—a new CO would come in, and I discovered that the magic word 'sportswriter' inevitably trumped the word 'Communist.' He'd ask me, 'You mean you actually talked to Joe DiMaggio? Tell me about him.' A white Southern guy would say, 'I'm from Fulton County in Alabama; that's where Joe Louis's family came from.'

"During the war blacks were discriminated against, but as a medic I could do what I could. I remember one stormy, rainy night on the island of Mindanao in the Philippines. I was in charge of the ward. There was segregation, but segregation would break down in real-life situations. A white kid, bleeding from the shoulder, walking wounded, came in. I said, 'You take the bed next to that man.' 'That man' was black. The kid stiffened, and I looked at his dog tag, and it said BILOXI, and I was in a position to say to him, 'Listen, soldier, this isn't Biloxi, this is the United States of America army, and you take that bed right now or stand right there and bleed to death. You won't be treated.' He lay down. There was no great conversation, but I'm sure he learned a little something about his fellow humanity.

"When we got out, we were given the option of being sent to a medical school. They would factor in what we had learned and give us a crash course, and we could emerge as doctors, and the catch was we would have to spend at least three years in the army. Some of the guys I soldiered with did that. I was tempted, but I was a Communist, and I had strong feelings about going back to the *Daily Worker*. I also wanted to see the culmination of this campaign to integrate baseball.

"I came out of the army in December of 1945, and I took a little leave for R&R. We all did before we went back to work.

"I didn't begin to write sports immediately. I was too overwhelmed by the war. I began writing general articles, but by opening day of 1947, I was back as sports editor.

"In 1946 Branch Rickey of the Dodgers had signed Jackie Robinson to a minor league contract. He played for Montreal. The time was right for baseball to integrate. It was a short time after the war in which blacks bled and died the same as whites, which gave it the final impetus. Eleanor Roosevelt even spoke out. Not Franklin, Eleanor. Then there had been two big shipyards in Brooklyn, the Todd Shipyard and the other big one, the Brooklyn Navy Yard, where at first there was enforced integration. It was war production. They were churning out the liberty boats. You learned to sit next to a black. And Brooklyn had its fair share of New Deal radicals, more than its fair share. And it had a strong African-American population.

"Rickey was arrogant, self-promoting, and smarter than the other magnates, and he decided to take credit for what he saw would become inevitable. Sort of like Nixon going to China or Reagan and the fall of the East Berlin wall. But looking back, I give him high marks. I didn't at the time. You have to consider what his motivations were in the climate of the time. I have to admit from my vantage point today I would not be too harsh on Branch Rickey.

"The other man, one who has not been fully recognized for the role he played, was Bill Veeck, who owned the Cleveland Indians at the time. Rickey had brought in Jackie, and the other owners were hoping to seal it off with Brooklyn, and then it would die out. I heard verbal, anecdotal testimony where the owners said, 'We'll live with Robinson in Brooklyn and hold the line.'

"Seven weeks later Veeck brought in Larry Doby, so what he did was open up the American League at a time when the baseball establishment apparently thought they could hold the line. I heard stories, and I couldn't run them because I couldn't prove it, but I heard the stories, and what Veeck did was underrated, because he integrated the American League, and it helped break things wider open. He defied them. He really defied the establishment. He was that kind of guy. When I went to Cleveland in 1948 to cover the World Series against the Boston Braves, I went to Municipal Stadium, a big, rambling place, and Veeck said, 'Lester, I want to show you something.' He had established a babysitting service so women could drop their kids off when they wanted to see a game. He said, 'Of course, I want the money from Cleveland housewives who know they can come and get professional help for their kids. But this is what I wanted to show you particularly,' and he pointed, and there in that room were kids, both black and white, playing together. That's the kind of guy he was. He was a real *mensch*.

"After the country was integrated, one thing I noticed, some whites, especially northern whites, didn't know how to act with black guys. The same thing in baseball. Paul Richards, who was from Waxahachie, Texas, was a good catcher. He was managing the Chicago White Sox, and in the dressing room one day he pointed something out: 'You know, Les,' he said, 'we Southerners, once we get rid of the poison, are much more natural and at ease with the black guys than the Northerners.' It was a very interesting observation. And there was truth to that. Black and white kids in the South often grew up playing together until they were seven or eight. They lived close to each other and didn't know any better. It's like the song in *South Pacific* says, 'You have to be carefully taught when you're seven or eight to hate.' But Paul Richards, a Texan, made that observation, and I never would have had the wit to pose it that way—or even think it.

"I look back at 1947, when Jackie came in. People ask me, 'Was there a celebratory feeling? Did people have a sense of history when they went to the ballgame?' Not at the beginning. On that first day, April 15, a cloudy afternoon, there was no sign of a close, intimate relationship between Jackie and his teammates. You know Dixie Walker initiated a petition against Jackie. Bobby Bragan and Carl Furillo signed it, and so did a couple of others. The celebratory feeling only developed as Jackie became part of the team and things happened. Carl Furillo was the most dramatic example of Jackie's effect on people.

"Carl, who was a guy from a working-class family in Pennsylvania, at first said, 'I ain't gonna play with no niggers.' Six weeks later I came down to the field early to browse around before the game. Before taking infield, two players were warming up their arms along the sidelines before they threw hard, and here were number 6 and number 42 tossing back and forth. Furillo and Robinson. This was the guy who had said, 'I ain't playing with no niggers.' What happened? The abstraction wore off. Jackie was no longer 'The Negro.' He was a ballplayer and a better ballplayer than him, and that's all he knew. Furillo was a baseball person, and how do you measure superiority and inferiority with these guys? Can he play ball as well as me, or no? To complete the story, I'll leapfrog ahead to 1955, when the Dodgers beat the damn Yankees for the first time in the World Series. They had a big party at the old Bossert Hotel for the ballplayers and their wives and the baseball people and the writers. The borough was seething. There were tens of thousands of people outside. They put up wooden horses to hold back the crowd. The cars came with the ballplayers, and the ballplayers went inside—it was just a madhouse. I was in there when Jackie and Rachel arrived, and Carl Furillo jumped out of his chair and rushed over and hugged Jackie, and they were cheek-to-cheek, swaying, saying, 'We did it. We did it.' You tell that to kids today, and they say, 'Big deal. They do that in the NBA.' But back then it was really something.

"The kids today can't imagine what Jackie Robinson went through. Here's a guy who was a tough, scrappy, militant athlete at Pasadena City College and UCLA. Did you know he was a four-sport athlete? Did you know he averaged eleven yards a carry in his second year of football? White players who are set on playing big league baseball do not play football in college. There are very few exceptions. I remember Jackie Jensen. You don't want to bang your shoulders in scrimmages. Incidentally, the only part of Jackie's all-around game that was ordinary was his throwing arm. That's why they changed him from shortstop to second base. He made the throws when he had to. But you have to think those years of pounding playing college football might have had something to do with it.

"I've seen grainy films of his playing at UCLA. God, he looked just like Gale Sayers. He'd reversed his field, had blazing speed, incredible, plus in basketball he was the leading scorer in the Pac Eight for the two years he played. And he was the national champion in the running broad jump.

"The *San Francisco Chronicle* had a series of articles on the greatest all-around athlete of all time, and they never mentioned Jackie Robinson. Here was a guy who was good in four sports, and he came up to the big leagues at age twenty-eight. Babe Ruth came up at nineteen, Ted Williams at twenty, Mickey Mantle at nineteen, and Willie Mays at nineteen. Eight ripe years, and for him to do what he did and not consider him as the greatest all-around athlete? And he was a great tennis player. I saw him play a few times.

"Jackie was a guy who had been court-martialed at Fort Hood in Texas for refusing to go to the back of the bus that circled the fort. That's the kind of guy he was. Now he's asked by Rickey to suppress his very being. No matter what is said to him, he was not to fight back or even to glare back.

"I say to kids, 'Imagine Tiger Woods walking down the fairway with the other golfers, and along the way people are screaming vile things at him, and screaming to the white golfers, "How about Tiger and your wife tonight?" ' Unspeakable stuff that Jackie went through. And they come to the putting green and someone throws a black cat in front of Tiger Woods, and that happened to Jackie in Philadelphia with Ben Chapman standing and laughing in front of his dugout. As for the physical part, Jackie was hit by pitched balls at least three times as much as the next player in the National League.

"To suppress his own nature and to play the way he did—he was the first Rookie of the Year and they won the pennant—that has to be the most amazing and courageous feat in the history of American sports. I don't like ringing statements like that, but that absolutely has to be a fact. There never was any feat like that, and nothing even close. People ask me, 'What are the parallel things in sports today?' I say, 'There is nothing as blatant as that.'

"People don't remember, but it was incredible how short a time it took for Jackie to win everyone over. When he first came to Brooklyn, there was a little race-baiting in Brooklyn, but it was more hushed up. But on opening day with the cool reception—not an unfriendly reception—here he comes out, wearing that unfamiliar first baseman's glove, and I remember this thirteen-year-old white kid in the stands beneath me, and he piped out, 'Let's go, Jackie.' It was the first encouraging sign I saw. Before long, if somebody stood up and said, 'You lousy nigger,' he would have been isolated. Quickly Jackie was a recognized star. Especially in Brooklyn, where people would not have stood for that.

"Jackie and I got along. He was very proper and professional with me. I always had the feeling that Branch Rickey did not want him to fraternize too much with me, and Rachel, too, was afraid of having him linked with the Communist press. But I did get stories from him, chatted with him on the field about the game. I was much chummier with Roy Campanella. He didn't have restrictions placed on him like Jackie did. Campy didn't care.

"The impact of the Jackie Robinson Brooklyn Dodgers was amazing. Early in 1949, they broke camp in Florida, and as was the custom then, they would stop at minor league cities. Atlanta was one of them. This was going to be the first interracial game in the state of Georgia. The Dodgers had Campanella and Don Newcombe as well as Jackie. The Grand Kliegel of the Ku Klux Klan said, 'This game must never take place.' So there was an air of tension that night.

"Blacks poured in, not only from Atlanta, but from the suburbs and farms. The Atlanta Crackers, like all minor league ballparks in the South, had small, segregated stands, which quickly filled up, and the ballclub had to make a quick decision. Whether it was their sense of history or the sight of all these people waving green money we'll never know. What they did was put a rope around the outfield, foreshortening the field. There was also a crevassed right field wall where blacks climbed up. It was a sea of blacks out there when the Dodgers first emerged.

"A roar erupted from the black fans, and the second thing that happened was the booing and hissing from the white stands. And then a third thing happened: like in a movie, white men and women began standing up singly, hesitant at first, to differentiate themselves from the booers. Hundreds stood. Who were these people standing? They were people, men and women, weaned in the South on baseball at one of their mothers' breasts and sportsmanship on the other, and so for whatever reason, they wanted to differentiate themselves. It was total bedlam. The roaring and greeting and booing and hissing and then white people standing up. How do you miss the social impact of something like that? The Klan said, 'Never in Mobile. Never in Shreveport. Never in New Orleans.' And this happened in every one of those cities. That was the impact of the Dodgers.

"And nobody in the mainstream press wrote about it. People ask me, 'Do you mean all the sportswriters were racist?' Of course not. But that was the policy of the papers. If a sportswriter came in with a story about race, he'd get a quizzical look and a friendly pat. 'You know we don't fuss about this stuff.'

"If you go back to the great newspapers of our time in the mid-'30s, the *New York Times,* the *Washington Post,* the *Boston Globe,* you would find not a single editorial asking, 'This is America. What's going on here?' You'd find nothing about the fact that none of these great black players were allowed to play in the major leagues.

"I've never seen the electricity in any sports anywhere since that crowd in 1949 at Ebbets Field. I'd look down from the press box, and here was this raucous, thoroughly integrated crowd, good-natured, and what added to that was the fact that six main position players—Campanella, Hodges, Reese, Furillo, Robinson, and Snider—stayed with the team throughout the whole Jackie Robinson decade. It would be unthinkable today in the age of free agency. It was unthinkable then. Not only that, but they all identified with Brooklyn. Some of them lived there. They made their summer homes in Brooklyn. People in Bay Ridge still talk about where Pee Wee Reese lived."

*Lester Rodney, the sports editor of the* Daily Worker, *was the one reporter to ask the question: Why can't a black man play major league baseball? In his columns over and over he browbeat America and baseball into doing what was just, right, and fair.*

**LESTER RODNEY** "I was in a union position. By the way, the *Daily Worker* at the time had an impact well beyond its circulation, because of the nascent trade union movement. In his book, John L. Lewis reluctantly admitted that the Communists played a leading role. There were Communists in large unions like the United Automobile Workers and the Transport Workers Union. Young trade unionists and all the union leaders read the *Daily Worker*. And on May Day, May 1, we held an annual parade, and during our peak years in the 1930s half a million people paraded down Fifth Avenue. These were the years when Russia was still our ally, before the Great Opprobrium. I meet lots of people who say to me, 'I wasn't a Communist, but I was sympathetic.' These were the famed 'fellow travelers,' people who for

Lester Rodney today. *Courtesy of Lester Rodney*

whatever reason just didn't like party discipline, but they were with us, and many were in the trade unions. During these May Day parades we'd have teams in baseball uniforms from the big unions carrying signs that read, END JIM CROW IN BASEBALL. The *Daily Worker* had an impact far and wide.

"After McCarthy came in, they tried to say the Communists wanted to overthrow the American government, but that was nonsense. We wanted socialism. We wanted social justice. We didn't want to overthrow the government. There were fifteen thousand Communists on the record who served in the armed forces in the war, and many of them won outstanding commendations.

"When Joe McCarthy started his campaign and HUAC had its witch hunt, no one ever bothered me. Being a sportswriter, out in the open, shielded me from some of this, plus the main thing for HUAC and McCarthy was to unearth Communists in the professions and in Hollywood and government. You don't unearth someone who's working for the *Daily Worker*. So I escaped all of that."

*Lester Rodney retired in 1957, the same year the Dodgers fled for Los Angeles. By then, largely because of the Joe McCarthy witch hunt, membership in the Communist Party had fallen to under ten thousand, and the paper folded. Lester Rodney's impact on the game of baseball and civil rights, however, should never be forgotten.*

# THE NEGRO SOLDIER RETURNS FROM THE WAR

MONTE IRVIN

As we live through the first decade of the twenty-first century, it is hard to remember what life was like for blacks in the mid-1940s. Jack Foner, Henry Foner's older brother, wrote a book called *Blacks and the Military in American History.* In it Foner recounted the treatment of the more than a million black men and women who were inducted into the American armed forces, half of them overseas. The most shocking fact was that because of the racist policies in place at the time, 90 percent of those soldiers were not permitted to serve in combat units, but were used as laborers, building roads and bridges.

Wrote Foner, "The war provided a fascinating social laboratory in which to observe a nation's schizophrenic behavior when its professed ideals conflicted with its treatment of one-tenth of its citizenry."

Before Pearl Harbor, blacks who volunteered to serve were turned down, and those who wanted to work in defense plants were denied jobs. To limit the number of eligible blacks, the army had a literacy standard, fourth-grade reading and writing.

In July of 1940, 4,700 blacks volunteered to serve. Two hundred were accepted as mess attendants to be servants for white officers. In November, eighteen blacks on the USS *Philadelphia* complained to the *Pittsburgh Courier* that their work was limited to waiting on tables and making the beds of the white officers. Nine of the men had been placed in solitary confinement. The letter writers warned other blacks not to make the same mistake of becoming "seagoing bellhops, chambermaids, dishwashers, in other words mess attendants, the one and only rating any Negro can enlist under."

Three of the signees were thrown in prison. The others were discharged.

An editorial in the newspaper *P.M.* stated, "Negroes cannot help but feel that their country does not want them to defend it."

Black soldiers with Eleanor Roosevelt. *Library of Congress*

When the draft bill was passed on September 14, 1940, nothing was said about protecting blacks from discrimination. A. Philip Randolph, the founder and president of the Brotherhood of Sleeping Car Porters, and other black leaders met with government officials two weeks later to present a program to end discrimination. Secretary of War Henry Stimson voiced his opposition to the proposals. The army had millions of Southern white Christian inductees, and he didn't want to do anything to offend them. The Red Cross even refused to take blood from blacks, knowing how many whites would refuse it if they knew.

On October 9, 1940, Franklin Roosevelt announced changes. The armed services would draft blacks in proportion to the population. There would be three National Guard units of blacks, but the officers would be white. Blacks could fly and be eligible for Officers Candidate School. But the policy of segregation would remain, and the policy that prevented blacks from becoming officers also stood.

In January of 1941 a frustrated A. Philip Randolph announced that on July 1 there would be a march on Washington protesting how blacks were treated in the armed forces. To forestall the march, President Roosevelt issued an executive order banning discrimination in defense industries. The result was the placement of blacks in war industry jobs, but nothing changed in the military. Not even after the attack on Pearl Harbor.

Shortly after Pearl Harbor, a black college student declared, "The Army Jim Crows us. The Navy lets us serve only as messmen. The Red Cross refuses our blood. Employers and labor unions shut us out. Lynchings continue. We are disenfranchised, Jim Crowed, spat upon. What more could Hitler do than that?"

What led to an increase in the number of blacks accepted into the armed services were the increased manpower needs. In March 1942, the Army Air Forces began taking applications from black youths. A month later, under pressure from President Roosevelt, a limited number of blacks were accepted for general service. In the meantime, whites and their families were complaining that the military was taking them while they were turning down single black men. Beginning in June of 1943, inductees previously rejected for failing the literacy test were sent to Special Training Units in the army to learn to read and write. When they passed, they were sent to basic training. By 1945 over a million blacks had been inducted.

But once inducted, most black soldiers didn't fight. They were concentrated in the service sector, building roads, stevedoring, doing laundry, and fumigating. Even blacks who passed basic training with flying colors were shipped out to perform common labor.

Said one black at an air base, "It is not like being in a soldier camp. It is more like being in prison." Wrote a compassionate white soldier, "The Negroes are segregated from the minute they come into the camp . . . the whole picture is a very sad and ugly one. It looks, smells, and tastes like Fascism."

Suggestions were made over and over to integrate volunteer divisions. The War Department always said no, refusing to tamper with the established American way of life.

Southern whites more often than not were assigned to command the black troops. Wrote one black enlisted man about his superior officer, "His obvious dislike for Negroes seemed to be a prime qualification for his assignment with Negro troops." When black soldiers complained to the press, the army banned black newspapers in post libraries and from sale at the PXs.

Blacks who knew their rights and insisted on exercising them were threatened with court-martial. They were considered "bad Negroes," and they would be assigned the most unpleasant and humiliating tasks to break their spirit.

In the summer of 1943, the 92nd Cavalry Division, comprised of black troops, was broken up, and the men were assigned jobs unloading ships, repairing roads, and driving trucks. They were forbidden from writing home about it. Secretary of War Stimson defended the move, saying it was done in the name of efficiency. Said Stimson, "In that so many blacks were poorly educated, many of the Negro units accordingly have been unable to master efficiently the techniques of modern weapons." As though the white soldiers the army had taken were Rhodes scholars.

The black press called for Stimson's resignation. The Republicans immediately applied their spin, appealing to blacks to vote for them, saying this was a Roosevelt administration policy. The Democrats blamed the military.

The upshot was that the men were restored to combat duty. The 92nd arrived in Italy in 1944, and they won seven thousand medals. When morale of the division was investigated by *Newsweek,* the journalists discovered that it was extremely low among the troops. The black soldiers were convinced it was more important to the white cracker officers to make their life miserable than it was to win the war.

After the Battle of the Bulge, which led to great loss of life among American soldiers, the military had no choice but to retrain blacks in supply and service units to turn them into riflemen. The plan was for these men to fight on the line alongside whites on a fully integrated basis, but General Walter Bedell Smith, Eisenhower's chief of staff, said no. Blacks were instead organized into platoons to fight alongside white soldiers. But the policy of keeping whites and blacks separate was broken. Twenty-five hundred blacks fought along white soldiers across Germany to the end of the war.

Said Brigadier General Charles T. Lanham to the black volunteers, "I have never seen any soldiers who have performed better in combat than you."

Afterward the army took a poll of the white soldiers who had fought alongside them. Three out of four said their respect for the black soldiers had grown. The survey was classified and never made public. At the end of the war the blacks were returned to all-black units and discharged.

In the Army Air Forces, six hundred blacks, the Tuskegee Airmen, flew over Africa, France, Poland, Romania, and Germany. Operating as fighter escorts in two hundred missions, not one bomber was lost to enemy fighters. The black fliers were credited with shooting down 111 enemy planes in the air and 150 others on the ground.

Not a single black soldier received a Congressional Medal of Honor.

If treatment was rough for black soldiers, it was far worse for the few black officers, who were regularly abused and humiliated in the presence of their men by white unit commanders. Black officers were required to sit in the back row of an army theater while front seats were reserved for white officers and Italian prisoners. In Italy an officers' club was set up by black soldiers. When it was completed, black officers were barred from eating there.

In March 1945, black officers of the 477th Bomber Group, an all-black outfit at Freeman Field, Indiana, were refused service and threatened with arrest if they insisted on entering the clubhouse. The officers were required to sign an agreement that they would accept the segregation of the base. One hundred and one officers refused. It was an officers' club, and they insisted on using it. They all were arrested and held in prison for a month, when the War Department dismissed the charges. Numerous black officers had breakdowns. Many sought transfers and discharges.

When black soldiers in uniform returned to their hometowns, danger awaited. A black sergeant was killed in March 1943 by a city policeman on the streets of Little Rock, Arkansas.

Wrote a black sergeant from the China-Burma-India theater of operations, "I have a very clear idea of what we are *not* fighting for. We certainly are not fighting for the Four Freedoms."

Attorney General Francis Biddle warned Roosevelt in November of 1943, "The situation among the Negro voters is still serious. The greatest resentment comes from Negroes in the armed forces, particularly those who have been in southern camps, and they are writing home about it."

Shortly before the war ended, the War Department called upon Congress to pass a bill making it a federal offense to attack or assault men in uniform. The bill never passed.

In the summer of 1944 a directive was posted to ban segregation in theaters, post exchanges, and buses operating within army camps. The directive was ignored.

Change came only after the death of Secretary of the Navy William F. Knox on April 28, 1945. He was succeeded by James A. Forrestal of New York. The navy abandoned segregation of advanced training schools. Recruit training, though, remained segregated. Blacks were assigned to ships with whites, but they could only make up 10 percent of the crew.

In July 1945, at the Great Lakes Naval Station, two black companies were placed in the same battalion as four white companies. A black company won battalion honors.

In August 1945, Captain Richard Petty, who was in charge, moved to integrate the companies. They shared the same barracks and mess. Not long afterward, the mixed company named a black sailor as its "honor man."

Monte Irvin in the uniform of the armed services. *Courtesy of Monte Irvin*

Said Captain Charles Alonzo Bond, commandant of the service schools, "Segregation was an egregious error. It was un-American and inefficient—a waste of money and manpower."

But for most black soldiers, their experiences during World War II would color their way of looking at whites and at American society forever. Wrote James Baldwin, "The treatment accorded the Negro during the Second World War marks for me a turning point in the Negro's relation to America: to put it briefly, and somewhat too simply, a certain hope died, a certain respect for white Americans faded."

Jackie Robinson is justifiably celebrated as the first African-American to break the "color barrier" in major league baseball. But Robinson was Brooklyn Dodger general manager Branch Rickey's second choice for the job. His first pick was a mild-mannered outfielder for the Newark Giants, by the name of Montford Merrill "Monte" Irvin. He was born in Haleberg, Alabama, in 1919. Irvin's father was a sharecropper who migrated north in 1927 and settled in Orange, New Jersey, where son Monte became a four-sports star at Orange High School.

He attended Lincoln College for a year and a half, and in 1938, while still in college, played for the Newark Eagles of the Negro Leagues under the assumed name of Jimmy Nelson. When his father called him home to help the family out financially, he quit college in 1939 and joined the Eagles for good at age twenty.

When Jorge Pasqual, the owner of the Mexican League, offered him a significant raise over what the Eagles were paying him, $500 a month, he spent the 1942 season playing in Mexico. It was the best year of his life. For one season he was able to escape the brutal racism of America.

Then came the war, and he was drafted into the army, and those were the worst years of his life. Being black, he was humiliated and harassed by the white Southern officers.

Irvin was discharged from the army in September of 1945, and in October Clyde Sukeforth, Branch Rickey's scout for the Great Experiment, asked Monte Irvin to sign with the Brooklyn Dodgers, to be the first black player in baseball. Irvin, a bright, gentle man with extraordinary skill, who might well have become as lionized as Muhammad Ali, said no. The years in the military suffering under the abuse of cracker officers and a policy of neglect and abuse by the army had left him in no condition, either physically or mentally, to take on such a challenge. It was bad enough he had been away from the game for three years. But the three years of relentless torture he had endured from having to put up with racism in the army made it impossible for him to face yet another, more difficult struggle of black liberation. Feeling but a shell of himself, Irvin told Sukeforth that after he got back into shape and into the right frame of mind to play, he would call the Dodgers.

Irvin didn't call until 1949. By then Jackie Robinson had been in the National League two years, and with Roy Campanella, Don Newcombe, Larry Doby, and Satchel Paige joining major league teams, the presence of blacks was becoming more accepted. Irvin signed with the New York Giants and helped lead them to pennants in 1951 and 1954, and in 1973 he was elected to baseball's Hall of Fame. Today he lives in retirement in Houston, Texas. He is content. He gives Jackie Robinson all the credit in the world, and he has never looked back.

**MONTE IRVIN**    "I joined the Newark Eagles in Daytona Beach, Florida, in 1939. I was twenty years old. I learned how to play all positions. I was noted for my arm. I had an arm better than anybody. I hit to all fields, hit the long ball, and I could run.

"The Eagles played about 140 games a year. In 1942 I was making $150 a month. The head of Mexican baseball, Jorge Pasqual, sent me a telegram saying he'd give me a salary of $500 a month, and $250 a month for an apartment, if I agreed to come to Mexico.

"I showed the telegram to our owners, Abe and his wife Effa Manley, and they said, 'We can't match it.' I said, 'I'm only making $150. Just raise it to $200, and I'll stay.' He said, 'No, Monte, I have all these other stars to pay.' I said, 'Then I'm going to Mexico.'

"That was the best year of my life. I played right in Mexico City. I was the league's MVP, was among the home run leaders, hit .397, and had a wonderful time playing there. In Mexico, for the first time in my life, I felt really free. You could go anywhere, do anything, eat in any restaurant, go to any theater, just like anybody else, and it was wonderful.

"In 1942 the Negro League owners and the players took a poll, asking which player would be the perfect representative to play in the major leagues. They said I was the one to do it, the perfect representative. I was easy to get along with, and I had some talent.

"Then I went into the war, where I was treated very shabbily. I was with a black unit of engineers in England, France, and Belgium. More than anything else, we weren't treated well in the army. They wouldn't let us do this. We couldn't do that. The guys said, 'If they weren't going to give us a chance to perform, to reach our potential, why did they induct us into the army?'

"We had a lot of problems with our own soldiers and sailors. Other guys said, 'Maybe we're fighting the wrong enemy.'

"We trained at Camp Clayborne, in Louisiana. It wasn't a good situation. There was a black tank outfit at Camp Clayborne, and by the time they came off the field and took a shower, the PX had sold out of everything—no beer, no ice cream, no soda, no soft drinks. The men just got fed up. They got in their tanks and tore all the PXs down with their tanks. They had to send over to Mississippi to get an antitank outfit to stop them. Two weeks later they were shipped over to Africa to fight. They said, 'Damn, they should have done this many months ago.'

"All of our commanding officers were white. In England we had a Southerner who had no business being a company commander, and he made some remarks about no fraternization with whites, said we couldn't do this, couldn't do that. After he spoke, we had a company chaplain who got up and said, 'Men, you're members of the United States armed forces. You can do anything anybody else can do. I assure you, this company commander will be gone in two weeks.' And he was. He was replaced by a lieutenant, a black company commander. This was 1944 in England, in a little town called Red Roof in southern England.

"We didn't think we were ever going to get back home. We felt like we were thrown away. We built a few roads, and when the German prisoners started to come in, we guarded the prisoners. We said, 'It would have been better if they hadn't inducted us and just let us work in a defense plant.' They wouldn't let us do anything. We were just in the way. They were going to send us to the Pacific, but then after the bomb dropped, they sent everybody home.

"I got home on September 1, 1945, and in October I started playing right field for the Newark Eagles. I had been a .400 hitter before the war, and I became a .300 hitter after the war. I had lost three prime years. I hadn't played at all. The war had changed me mentally and physically.

"We played an all-star team in Brooklyn. Ralph Branca and Virgil Trucks struck out about eighteen of us. Trucks and I visit every year, and we talk about the old days. I won't say, the Good Old Days. The Old Days.

"Clyde Sukeforth, the scout for the Dodgers, had Campanella and me come over to the Brooklyn office in October of 1945. I signed with the Dodgers, but I told them I had had a tough time during the war. I said, 'I don't have the skills I used to, and I don't have the feel for the game I used to.' I told them I needed a little time to get my act together. They said, 'Okay, let us know when you're ready, and we'll bring you up.'

"In order to get back on track, Larry Doby and I went to Puerto Rico to play in the winter league. They gave us $500 a month. I was paid as high as $1,000 a month in the Negro Leagues.

"I didn't feel I was ready until I played in the Cuban Winter League in 1949. I called the Dodgers and told them I was ready. Meantime, the Eagles owner, Effa Manley, said, 'Mr. Rickey, you took Don Newcombe from our team. I'm not going to let you take Monte. You're going to have to give me at least $5,000.' So rather than get in a lawsuit, the Dodgers released me, and the Giants gave the Eagles $5,000 and picked up my contract. I didn't get a nickel of it. I asked for half, but Mrs. Manley said, 'No, I worked so hard to get this done. I'm going to split it between my lawyer and myself.' She took the $2,500 and bought a fur stole with it, and when I saw her twenty-five years later, she was still wearing that same fur stole.

The first all-black outfield——Monte, Willie Mays, and Hank Thompson. *Courtesy of Monte Irvin*

"On July 8, 1949, Hank Thompson and I reported to the New York Giants. Leo Durocher came over and introduced himself. And when everyone got dressed, he had a five-minute meeting. He said, 'I think these two fellows can help us make some money, win a pennant, win the World Series. I'm going to say one thing. I don't care what color you are. If you can play baseball, you can play on this club. That's all I'm going to say about color.'

"This was two years after Jackie. They had gotten used to seeing an African-American on the field. It wasn't a picnic. We heard the names. But we didn't have it as rough as he did."

# THE JEWS LOVE JACKIE

JOSEPH BOSKIN AND JOEL OPPENHEIMER

WHEN HE WAS FIVE YEARS OLD, JOSEPH BOSKIN AND HIS family moved from Williamsburg to Brighton Beach, in large part because his mother, a strong swimmer, wanted to live near the ocean. As he was growing up, Boskin, who later became a longtime professor of history at Boston University, was caught up in the political fervor of Brighton Beach, the heart and center of the radical movement in Brooklyn. Though he was barely a teenager, he was acutely aware of issues concerning social justice and civil rights, and the fact that the country—Brooklyn even—was segregated. At Abraham Lincoln High School, one of the largest high schools in the city, if not the country, there were but two black athletes in the entire school. Boskin, the sports editor of the school newspaper, highlighted their accomplishments by putting their pictures in the paper as often as he could. When Jackie Robinson came to play for the Brooklyn Dodgers in 1947, Boskin, and the thousands of other Jews who believed in social justice, were jubilant.

**JOSEPH BOSKIN** "My grandparents all came from Russia and settled in Williamsburg. My grandfather on my mother's side left because they were going to conscript him into the army. He departed, came to the United States, accumulated some money, and went back and got my grandmother.

Ebbets Field under construction, 1912. *Library of Congress*

"My father was one of nine children, which was unusual for a Jewish family. There were six boys and three girls, and all were independent-minded. A number became political radicals. Not my father. He became a minor hood.

"His name was Abraham Jay, but he was known as Brummie. From Abraham, the Hebrew is Avrum, and from Avrum you get Brum, and pretty soon you have Brummie. That's how he was known.

"He was a runner for the Jewish mafia, Murder Incorporated. He told me about it later in life. He used to carry guns. They elevated him to running numbers. Then during Prohibition he drove a hearse from New York to New Jersey, filled with booze. He made $75 a night, which was a lot of money.

"I met a number of them. There was Louie, Paul, and Bernie. I didn't know last names. He was in the lower ranks. Any person who drives a hearse is not a major player.

"He had to get out of the rackets because he had two babies quickly, and my mother insisted he leave, otherwise she would end up a widow. My father was devoted to my mother. He called her 'Queenie,' and he meant it.

"My mother was born Dihan Guyer. Every five or six years, when she got bored, she would decide to change her first name. She became Dora, Dina, and Diana. All starting with *D*.

"My mother was a crackerjack typist and stenographer. When she met my father in high school, and in 1927 decided to marry him, there was a great deal of wailing that went on in her family. They thought she was marrying beneath herself.

"My father became a plumber, and when the Depression hit, he was thrown out of work. He hustled for jobs. He was a master hustler, did all kinds of things. Eventually he and two of his friends took out across the country on a building program, going wherever the WPA had jobs.

"I lived in Williamsburg until I was five, and then my parents moved to Coney Island, and from there to Brighton Beach, two working-class neighborhoods where the rent wasn't very high. We lived a block and a half from the ocean. My mother loved to swim and wanted to be near the water, and she felt it would be healthy for the kids. She used to swim miles out into the ocean. She walked the boardwalk, did calisthenics, square dancing. What a blessing it was to live there.

"Brighton Beach was essentially Jewish, but it was essentially working-class, so you had a lot of tough guys around. Italians lived right across Sheepshead Bay and in Coney Island, so there were gangs. At the same time, because it was Jewish, the upward sense of mobility was huge, in terms of education. The students really vied against one another in school, even though they were at odds physically with each other. There was a sense of the value of education, which permeated the Jewish community.

"I can remember in the fifth grade at PS 225, there were thirty-five of us in the class. In their wisdom, the New York Board of Education numbered the classes according to ability and intelligence. So the number-one class, 5A1, was the smartest, and then the 2 class was the dumbest, and 3 came after 1, and 4 came after 2, and so on. And within the classes, they ranked everybody according to reading ability. Once you were locked into a class in the third grade, basically you stayed where you were.

"I was in the slow class, the dumb class. Truly the dumb class. For one, I was physically precocious, meaning I was very big for my age and very tough, very angry. I got into a lot of fights. I fought with kids in the neighborhood. There were a lot of tough kids who wanted to fight. You got in an argument over a call in a stoopball or punchball or stickball game, or someone would step on you when they shouldn't have, playing football, and you'd fight. I enjoyed it enormously.

"And I think I was just a slow learner. So they put me in the slow class, and that's where I stayed until high school, and then during my sophomore year I flunked half my classes, and so the dean called me in and said, 'If you flunk another class, I'm going to send you to trade school.'

"I was so humiliated and embarrassed I decided I'd better do something about it.

"Abraham Lincoln High School had over 5,500 students in it, so it was enormous. Once again, the competition was severe. And a substantial number of my teachers were radicals, because Brighton Beach was the center of radicalism in Brooklyn. Coney Island–Brighton Beach was the center of the Communist Party. The AYD, the American Youth for Democracy, was located there. The Folklore Movement was there. They were a group of people who were into folk singing and folk songs, and their music was closely tied to protesting inequality. The Zionist Movement had a center there, and the Socialist movement, which included the Socialist Party and Socialist Youth. I was a socialist. All of these groups had their headquarters near the corner of Brighton Beach and Coney Island avenues.

"Neither my father nor my mother had any political consciousness or awareness, but I did. I got it from the zeitgeist of the community. If you walked on the boardwalk, there were always a huge number of people making political arguments. It was astonishing how many people spoke on the boardwalk or on Surf Avenue over the nature of socialism and communism. My friends and I would argue all the time, and often I'd get taken apart because I didn't know much, didn't know as much as a lot of people knew, and that goaded a lot of us into reading in order to better ourselves in the arguments. I had teachers who were members of the CP who also directed us into certain kinds of reading, and gradually we became very good debaters.

"Some of the arguments were theoretical. Some were about Stalin and in particular his purges. That began when I was nine or ten years old, and the arguments got pretty severe. When Stalin signed the nonaggression pact with Hitler, the consternation was enormous. The arguments were fierce as to what it all meant. And then my friends would ask me, 'Why aren't you coming to more of the meetings? Why aren't you more rigorous and vigorous in your political stance?' At the same time we were trying to learn to live with women. We were trying to find our place not only in the political community but also we were laden with teenage issues. We found if you went to the Village, you found more girls who were more amenable. We also found they were part of the Folklore Movement and the Socialist Movement.

Professor Joseph Boskin. *Samuel Fuchs*

"Every now and then I read the *Daily Worker,* but I didn't find it interesting. I read the *New York Post,* the *Daily Compass, P.M.* I would say *P.M.* was my favorite newspaper. It was left. It had Mex Lerner and Markee Childs, wonderful columnists, and a host of others. It wasn't as dogmatic as the *Daily Worker.* Also I. F. Stone published a little magazine called *In Fact,* which was very popular.

"In 1940 I was aware the Rapp-Coudert Committee was going after college and high school teachers, but it didn't have much impact on my teachers at Abraham Lincoln. There were a couple of teachers who were members of the Communist Party. They didn't reveal it, but I knew. But they continued to teach the way they always taught. It wasn't until 1947–48 that the crackdown took place.

"As a boy I played all different sports. My sports were boxing and football. I was not very good in baseball. I was a good fielder, but not a very good hitter. I followed the Dodgers. I went to Dodger games, which I enjoyed immensely. I was well aware of the racism that existed in baseball, as I was of the racism that existed in the country. There was a civil rights movement in our high school that was very much a part of the whole folklore tradition, related to the folk songs of Woody Guthrie and others. And when World War II started, we became even more aware of how everything was segregated. We were aware of how badly the black troops were being treated during the war. It was common knowledge in my neighborhood. Absolutely.

"We grew up on Paul Robeson. I used to listen to his 'Ballad for Americans' in elementary school. The 'Ballad for Americans' is an entire operetta. It begins, 'In '76 the sky was red, thunder rumbling overhead. And old King George couldn't sleep in his bed . . .' This was the story of the American Revolution. Robeson sang it for about an hour and a half. 'On that Sunday morn old Uncle Sam was born . . .' It goes on like that. It's beautiful. My teachers would play it over and over in the fifth and sixth grade, and then they'd discuss Paul Robeson, which was very unusual, but this, after all, was Brighton Beach. We used to play it among ourselves. So we were aware of Paul Robeson.

"When I was in Abraham Lincoln High School, we were completely aware there were no blacks in the school. In fact, when one or two black players did show up, they were heralded as heroes. They were given first-class treatment. I was the sports editor of the student newspaper, the *Lincoln Log,* and I used to play it up. I would show photos of the black athletes to highlight them. One was on the track team, and one was on the football team. They lived right on the edge of Coney Island in a poorer neighborhood.

"And so when Branch Rickey signed Jackie Robinson to play for the Dodgers late in 1945, in my neighborhood all of the radicals were well aware of what it meant.

Robinson came up to Brooklyn in 1947, and I made a desperate attempt to contact him because I wanted to interview him for the paper. I placed a lot of calls to the Dodgers and made a nuisance of myself. Pretty soon they got to know who I was.

"I had played baseball in the Public School Athletic League, so I contacted them to help me. In Brighton Beach there were social athletic clubs, both boys and girls. We played in the PSAL league, and I was the captain of my team. So I called PSAL and asked them to help me in getting an interview with Jackie Robinson.

"Finally, I was granted an interview. It was all set. I was to meet him in the Dodger clubhouse before the game, an afternoon game. And it rained, and the game was rained out. When I got to Ebbets Field, no one was there. I never did get the chance to interview him. I had Regents exams to take—it was the end of the academic year—and then I had graduation. But I hustled my ass off to get that interview. And it rained. I didn't know what to do after that. I was thrown by it.

"But I got to watch him play many times. Jackie was exciting. He was an unbelievable player, as you know. Every time he got on base, there was always a rising excitement, because everyone knew he was going to try to steal. I was at Ebbets Field once when he stole home. Everyone went berserk. *Berserk!* They had to stop the game for a while.

"Jackie succeeded, and for a variety of reasons. Because of who he was and the way it was handled. It was handled very judiciously, and they lucked out with guys like Pee Wee Reese, whose behavior was exemplary. Whereas Dixie Walker refused to have anything to do with him and asked to be traded. And we turned off to people like Dixie Walker. I was there when he was booed. I was doing the booing. So we were all aware of how the lines were drawn racially.

"Brooklyn was a very complex community, so it isn't easy to talk about Robinson's effect on Brooklyn. You could go into the Italian community, because there was an affinity between Jews and Italians. The Irish community was hostile to blacks and hostile to him. We avoided going into it. Once or twice when I went into it, I could actually sense the palpable violence and antagonism that existed there. We got out very quickly.

"Once in a while we played the Irish baseball teams. We were ahead once in a game, and it must have been about the fifth or sixth inning, when one of our guys came over to the bench and said, 'Listen, they are talking about beating the shit out of us because we're winning. We got to start losing. We gotta get the hell out of here.'

"We were playing on their turf, and the only way we could get home was on the subways. There were no cars. You took the subway. He said, 'We're not going to make it if we win this game.' And we went out and lost, and we lost big, to make sure.

"So the impact of Jackie Robinson in Brooklyn was primarily among the Jews. He was embraced. There was an enormous amount of acceptance and pride, especially among the radicals, that someone from a minority had actually broken through. Not unlike following the only Jewish ballplayer in those days, on the Detroit Tigers, Hank Greenberg.

"This was a clear indication that social justice was a possibility."

*Jackie Robinson's first game as a Dodger was on April 15, 1947, against the Boston Braves. It was opening day at Ebbets Field. Jackie played first base.*

*The announced attendance was 26,623. Of those, 14,000 were black. In his first game, Robinson had earned his $5,000 salary.*

*That day, eighteen-year-old Joel Oppenheimer was working in his dad's leather goods store in midtown Manhattan. Joel was home from Cornell University for spring break.*

**JOEL OPPENHEIMER**   "There are two kinds of fathers in the world to work for. There's the kind who makes his kid the president of the firm, and there's the kind who is convinced that he must bend over backward not to show favoritism. Guess which type of father I had? Not that Dad was mean. He just didn't want the other employees to think his son was getting away with anything.

"On this particular day, I was sweeping the floor. It was about eleven in the morning, and Dad was standing behind the cash register up front. He called me over, and I assumed he had another errand for me to do. Instead, he asked me, 'If you could do anything in the world today, what would you like to do?' I was so stunned I couldn't answer. He said, 'Isn't there something you want to do?' 'You mean like going to the moon?' I said. 'No,' he said, 'something real.' I couldn't think of anything to say. He asked me, 'Wouldn't you like to be at Ebbets Field today?' And I couldn't believe my ears. Of course I wanted to go. I knew Jackie Robinson would be playing his first game, and I was astounded that, one, my father was even aware of Robinson, and two, aware that I would want to go.

"So off I went, and when I arrived in the grandstand it was standing room only. I remember standing behind third base in a thick crowd of people, and for the first time in my life I was in a crowd of blacks.

"For years we used to hear stories about this fantastic black pitcher who once was supposed to have struck out all the Yankees. We didn't know his name—Satchel Paige—but we had heard about all the great black ballplayers and how they weren't allowed to play, and so for me Jackie was all those guys rolled into one, and he was going to lead my Dodgers to glory.

"During the game Jackie made a good play in the field, at which point everyone was yelling, 'Jackie, Jackie, Jackie,' and I was yelling with them. And suddenly I realized that behind me someone was yelling, 'Yonkel, Yonkel, Yonkel,' which is Yiddish for Jackie. With great wonderment and pleasure, I realized that here was this little Jewish tailor—I always assumed he was a tailor—the only white face in a crowd of blacks aside from me, and he's yelling, 'Yonkel, Yonkel, Yonkel.' It was a very moving moment."

## JACKIE ROBINSON'S PLACE IN HISTORY

IRA GLASSER

**S**AY WHAT YOU WILL ABOUT BRANCH RICKEY'S MOTIVES FOR bringing Jackie Robinson to the Dodgers, the fact remains that not only did Robinson become a great player who led the Dodgers to National League pennants in 1947, 1949, 1952, 1953, 1955, and 1956, but the UCLA-educated Robinson was exactly the sort of role model that Rickey envisioned him to be. Kids, both white and black, wanted to *be* Jackie Robinson. Playing on the streets, the kids tried to run the bases like him, emulated his batting stance, holding their bat high like he did, and through the phenomenon of hero worship, they intuited that Jim Crow not only was evil, but that racism's premise that whites are better than blacks was a lie. It is safe to say that the American civil rights movement went into high gear with the coming of Jackie Robinson to Brooklyn.

**IRA GLASSER** "When I was a young boy growing up in Brooklyn, I was aware that no blacks were allowed to play major league baseball. Everybody I talked to who grew up in Brooklyn was aware of it. I was aware because my mother spoke of it, because it was a very big issue. She would say, 'It's outrageous.' My father was a little grumpier about it. My mother thought Jackie Robinson coming to the Dodgers was social justice. I can remember her saying, as Branch Rickey intended her to say, 'He's a college-educated man, and he speaks so well.' She bought into it. 'Why shouldn't a black man have a chance,' she said. 'This is America. What did we fight the war for?'

"My mother presented this to me in ways that made the racial situation in America a different version of anti-Semitism. What had happened to the Jews in Germany and what the blacks were suffering through in America were different examples of the *same* phenomenon.

"Years later, when people were talking about Norman Podhoretz and *Commentary* magazine, and how it had turned to the right, I said, 'There are two kinds of Jews politically and racially. If you grew up in Brooklyn the way I did, you were taught to believe that racial injustice was the same thing as anti-Semitism in Germany, that what led to the concentration camps was the same thing that led to slavery and Jim Crow justice, that they were all aspects of the same thing, and therefore, if you were a Jew, racial justice was your issue. That they were part of the same phenomenon, judging people on the basis of criteria that were out of their control and irrelevant to their character and abilities. Later that came to be embraced with the disabled and women and gays. But that was not explicit then.

"The other kind was what I came to call the Norman Podhoretz Jew, Jews who grew up and were taught and came to believe that of all the forms of discrimination, anti-Semitism was the first among equals, that it was something special and extraordinary, that there was nothing worse than the Holocaust, including slavery. And for those Jews, they grew up protecting themselves against the demands of blacks. So the race issues became competition instead. These were Jews who weren't for affirmative action, for example. These were Jews who opposed the blacks who wanted community control of their schools in Ocean Hill–Brownsville in the 1960s.

"During my early years at the ACLU, there were a bunch of Jewish lawyers around my age, who all shared the same sense of race and anti-Semitism as I did. And, with one exception, they were all Dodger fans. And they would tell you the same story. My love for Jackie Robinson wasn't just my private obsession, it turned out. We all discovered we all thought the same thing. And that's why I began to see it as a sociological and political phenomenon that was more serious than I first thought.

"The way I think it happened was this: my mother reacted to Robinson becoming the first black baseball player in the major leagues even though she wasn't a baseball fan. So where did I learn about Robinson and what he had to go through after he joined the Dodgers? I was nine when Robinson came up, and most of us didn't read the papers much. We were kids. And in those days sports columns weren't so-

Jackie Robinson. *Library of Congress*

ciological the way many of them are now, so you couldn't learn about it from that. There was no television. There was just radio, which we were glued to. We lived on the radio. And no question, Red Barber, the Dodger announcer, reported what was happening to Robinson. Not only did he teach us baseball, explaining the strategy of the bunt and the sacrifice fly and the stolen bases that announcers today often don't describe, but we knew what Robinson was going through because of Barber. We all remember—I've had this conversation with fifty different people. We knew the story about Rickey saying to Robinson, 'You have to turn the other cheek.' We knew that Robinson's fiery temper was under wraps the first two years. We knew about Ben Chapman and the Phillies and the way they threw a black cat onto the field and shouted racial epithets at him.

"Barber was from Mississippi, and he had a crisis of conscience as to whether he could stay the Dodger announcer. He wrote about how he gave up his racist attitudes to keep his job. I remember, when I was nine, learning from his broadcasts about Jim Crow segregation and public accommodations in hotels and restaurants. I learned that when Jackie and Campanella and Newcombe went on their road trips to St. Louis, they couldn't stay in the same hotels as the white players, couldn't eat at the same restaurants. That was the first time I learned about segregated public accommodations, and that was how I came to hate it.

"We were very connected, not just to the baseball part of it, but we all knew about Lena Horne, and we all listened to the Joe Louis fights and knew about the Louis–Max Schmeling fight. But there was no event that in 1947 was capable of communicating in a way that did not require a lot of book learning, a lot of explanation, no laws, no Supreme Court arguments, no Congressional debates, in an emotional way what was wrong with America and what had to be set right. And we ingested it. I say ingested, because it wasn't cognitive. It was visceral, and everybody I ever talked to who was within three or four years of my age who grew up in Brooklyn in those years, knew all the stories. And we didn't learn it because it was taught to us in the history books. It wasn't talked about in school. There were no television discussions. It wasn't because of Martin Luther King Jr. Most of it we learned in a general way from Red Barber, and it was important, because the Dodgers were our guys, and they were fucking with them. We would have hated it if they had done it to Duke Snider. I often joke that had I been a Yankees fan, I undoubtedly would have been a racist and would have had no sympathy for Robinson. I had a number of Yankee fan friends who deeply opposed racial subjugation, but what was a fact was that the Yankees were one of the last teams in the majors to have a black player, and that didn't come until nearly a decade after Robinson came into the league. So what young Dodger fans went through with Robinson *was* different. What was important to us was not the color of his skin. What was important to us was the color of his uniform.

"Cause and effect are funny things. Part of who you end up rooting for as a kid is accidental. But whatever caused me to be a Dodger fan, it reinforced all those feelings about Robinson and race, and without quite expecting it, all of us were suddenly thrown into the middle of this incredible experiment in civil rights, which was unprecedented. This was just one year after World War II ended. This was before Truman's order to desegregate the armed forces. This was eight years before Rosa Parks sat down on that bus. This was seven years before *Brown v. Board of Education*. As a nine-year-old boy who loved Jackie Robinson, I was confronted with this.

"On this team of heroes, there were many. But on that team all of us wanted to be like Jackie Robinson. I played a lot of serious fast-pitch softball into my forties, and my stance was always Robinson's. I copied it when I was twelve years old, holding the bat high, taking your right hand off the bat as the pitcher wound up, and brushing your right hand on your hip, the little nervous tic he had. We modeled the way we ran the bases from him.

"Once in the 1970s one of my kids asked me, 'Who today is like Robinson?' I said, 'To imagine Robinson dancing off third base, imagine the great Knicks basketball player Earl Monroe. No one had ever seen anything like that before, his fall-away slides, his hook slides, the way he would charge off third base, go way down the line, and come back. And he'd steal home. Kids today never saw anyone do that, because no one does it.

"The other thing that was significant about those years and that was visceral and entered our souls in a most effective way was Ebbets Field. In 1947 Ebbets Field was the only integrated public accommodation in America. It was an astonishing experience for a nine-year-old boy. I would go with a couple of friends, or by myself. My friend Donald Shack is ten years older than I am, and he remembers Ebbets Field as entirely white. I remember it as integrated. I remember going to Ebbets Field as a ten-year-old and sitting in the grandstands next to this guy who I thought of as old, but who might have been in his thirties, this burly black guy in an undershirt and a bowler hat, with a big cigar and a beer, and the two of us were sitting next to each other, and we were Dodger fans. If Furillo threw somebody out at third base, we were up punching each other in the arm, and if Robinson took second on a pop-up to short left field, we were hugging. There was no color there. But there was color everywhere. Where else in 1948 could a ten-year-old boy be sitting next to a black man in a comfortable, familiar way and in common cause? Embracing physically? Touching? And feeling natural and safe. And not being aware of it. Only years later did I realize, *Oh my God, what an incredible psychological experience in the kind of society we lived in in 1948!* And you learned early from watching Robinson and Campanella and Newcombe that what my mother said when I was five was true: that skin color was as meaningless as eye or hair color, that it said nothing about whether a man could steal second base or hit a baseball, and from there it was not hard for a kid to think ten years later that it also meant nothing as to whether a black man could teach mathematics or run for office, that it was not a quality that had any relationship to talent or character, and because Robinson was not just a talent, but a man of incredible character, the linkages that got established in an unconscious and visceral way for kids nine, ten, and eleven went way beyond the simple notions of 'A black man should have a chance.' The whole experience destroyed the mythologies that perpetuated racism.

"So the Robinson experiment was enormously underestimated—not only underestimated but unrecognized for decades as a value-driven impact on white kids at a time when America was segregated, even in a city like New York. As I said, where I lived, I could walk as far as I could walk in any direction and not find anyone who wasn't white or Jewish, but suddenly I'm sitting in Ebbets Field, and I'm identifying with the struggles of a black man for equal opportunity. I want to play like number 42. If I'm playing in an empty lot in

Ira Glasser, upper right, and friends in Cooperstown.
*Courtesy of Ira Glasser*

Brooklyn, I'm copying him. And what that meant for a nine- and ten-year-old kid, modeling yourself and identifying with him, that was unrecognized and underestimated as a force. And it tells you something about the way value education actually takes place. It had far more of an impact than the traditional highlights of the civil rights movement, starting with *Brown v. Board of Education*, Rosa Parks, and the Civil Rights Act of 1964."

# THE ACCIDENTAL RABBI

SY DRESNER

After Israel Dresner graduated from New Utrecht High School, he entered Brooklyn College in the fall of 1945, and, while a student there, he became a leader in Habonim, the Zionist organization that encouraged Jews everywhere to emigrate to Israel to work on a kibbutz. After Dresner got a master's degree at the University of Chicago, he traveled to Israel to meet his Habonim friends. Had he not been drafted into the U.S. Army during the Korean War, Dresner probably would have become an Israeli citizen.

In the army Dresner became the assistant to the Jewish chaplain on his army base. The experience led him to become a rabbi and later a noted figure in the American civil rights movement.

**SY DRESNER** "I got involved in politics when I entered Brooklyn College. The president was a guy whom many students considered authoritarian, and there were periodic rebellions against him. They had a balcony overlooking the central part of campus, and when he spoke to us from that balcony, we used to yell, 'Viva Il Duce.' He was a white Protestant from the Midwest, a very bright guy and by modern standards would be considered a liberal. Over the years everything has moved more to the right.

"I was associated with the left, but I never did join the student group called American Youths for Democracy, a pinko, fellow-travelish bunch that tried to get me to join. I wouldn't because they were non-Zionist, and for several years I had been involved in Habonim, which made me a super-Jew and a super-Zionist, even though I considered myself a socialist at the time. The AYD was a sort of Stalinist line in a much more American context. And remember, during the first twenty-nine years of Israel's existence, it was headed by the Socialist Party. My Jewishness and my Zionism was what kept me from the Stalinist tentacles.

Eleanor Roosevelt and Marion Anderson.
*Library of Congress*

"As I said, when I grew up, Jews voted for the liberal candidate for president 90 percent to 10 percent. Roosevelt got that in 1940 and again in 1944. Jews were still poor, there were many immigrants, and Jews were an oppressed group, the most oppressed group in the world. The Holocaust had occurred, so it was normal if you were Jewish to be liberal. There were no Jews to speak of living in the Southern or mountain states. The Jews lived in New York, Philadelphia, Boston, Chicago.

"It was normal to be pro–civil rights, even though it wasn't much of an issue. When I was nine, I remember, the Daughters of the American Revolution wouldn't let Marion Anderson sing. If the DAR excluded someone, we would have been against it even if she was white. We loved Eleanor Roosevelt. Franklin and Eleanor were worshipped by the Jewish community. Read *The Plot Against America* by Philip Roth. It's worth reading. He's the greatest living American novelist. Saul Bellow is dead. It's about the 1940 election, a counter-historical novel. He has the Republican Party nominating Charles A. Lindbergh for president, and he's right—had they nominated Lindbergh, he would have beaten Roosevelt that year. Roosevelt was running against the two-term tradition. 'What is he? Greater than George Washington?' And Lindbergh was the greatest single hero of all of American history. If Lindbergh had run and won, we would not have gotten involved in the war against the Nazis. Germany would have won the war. I don't think Germany could have conquered America, but America would have been a semi-fascist country. There would have been a Lindbergh kind of regime in America.

"While I was still at Brooklyn College, I became fiercely pro-Zionist. Jews had gone through a terrible period with the Nazis, were discriminated against, murdered in the Holocaust, and I felt certain that Jews needed their own homeland.

"In 1947 a ship called the *Exodus* sailed to Palestine with Jewish refugees, and the British government refused to let it dock. A group of eight of us from Habonim took the subway to the British Empire building at Rockefeller Center, and we sat down to block the main entrance in protest of what the British did. We had signs, DOWN WITH BRITISH IMPERIALISM, because the British were keeping the Jews from getting to Palestine. Most of the people were sympathetic, so they didn't try to step on us, just went to the side door of the building.

"The policemen were Irish, and the Irish hated the British, so even though they might have been anti-Semitic, they were very kind to us and tried to negotiate with us. They tried diplomacy, but after an hour we wouldn't give in. They issued an ultimatum: get up in fifteen minutes or face arrest. And they arrested us and took us to the police station. But none of us were even eighteen, so they released us to our parents.

"We had just gotten a phone. Until the war you couldn't get one, and after the war ended, there was a long list of applicants, and so we didn't get ours until 1947.

"My father was working. He didn't know about it. My mother had to get on the subway and schlep all the way to Manhattan. On the way home to Brooklyn, she was twisting my ear, yelling at me in Yiddish, *'A shonda for a Yiddishe bucha,'* a disgrace for a Jewish boy to be arrested. I was not booked, because the police were very kind and we were all minors, and they were all anti-British anyway. I didn't get arrested for real until June of 1961.

"I dropped out of Brooklyn College in 1948, and I went to the Habonim Institute. They were Zionists and *kibbutznicks,* but they were also anti-religious, religion being the opiate of the people, if you remember the quotation from the *Communist Manifesto.* Habonim was not quite in that category, but during that period I would sneak into a synagogue every once in a while and not tell my compatriots. I attended the institute from February of 1948 until the early part of June.

"Israel was born on May 15, 1948, and I remember the day very well. I marched around town that late afternoon and evening with my fellow students. There were eighteen of us, and we were living in Manhattan, and we walked by the Waldorf-Astoria. Next to the American flag flew the Zionist flag, the flag we know today as the flag of Israel with the blue Magen David and the white field, and as we walked by, I began to cry. This was six or seven P.M., right after Israel was proclaimed by the United Nations, and President Truman immediately gave it recognition.

"We went to a rally at Town Hall on 34th Street, and then we went to Times Square, and there were two huge hora circles surrounding the Times Building, blocking off all traffic. We were mostly kids, teenagers, young people. To form the inner circle there had to be a couple thousand kids, and double that for the outer circle.

"Right after the institute ended, I enrolled at the University of Chicago. The Habonim movement sent me there as an organizer. I had to take an exam and get in, and I had to get some money. Chicago was $500 a year, and that was an enormous sum. My father wasn't making more than $3,000 a year. But I got a scholarship and was admitted.

"The University of Chicago was founded by John D. Rockefeller in 1888. His plan was for the university to be great the moment it opened its doors. He gave $10 million, which today is about $3 billion, to create it. When it opened in 1892, its faculty included a young philosopher named John Dewey, and its economics department had a young economist named Thorstein Veblen. When I went there in 1948, it had six Nobel Prize winners on its faculty.

"I was there a couple years. I got my bachelor and master degrees. I wrote my master's thesis on Israel. It was on the historical development of the boundaries of modern Israel, about two hundred pages. I got my master's in 1950, and I came back to New York, and I was an organizer for Habonim in Crown Heights, where Eastern Parkway is, where the Lubavitcher Movement has its headquarters. Today Crown Heights is primarily black and Caribbean. In those days it was a 100 percent Jewish. After a year, I went on an *aliyah* to Israel. I washed dishes on a ship called the *Nellie* and got a free passage to England. After hitchhiking across Europe for six months, I became an immigrant to Israel in a kibbutz called Urim, in October of 1951. I sailed from Napoli on a little Israeli ship, and on the ship was Lena Horne, who was the first famous black I ever met or talked to. She was married to a Jewish guy with a beard, her second or third husband, older than she was. She was going to perform a concert in Israel, and she drank like a fish but never got drunk.

"I landed in Israel, and I hitchhiked around to see friends for a month before going to the kibbutz, where most of my friends were living. The kibbutz had been established three months before I arrived. It was in the northern Negev. In those days its main city, Beersheba, had nine hundred people. Today it has two hundred thousand. It was a little Wild West town, and it was there that I met Eleanor Roosevelt, who was visiting with Levi Eshkol, the minister of agriculture, who later became prime minister. She spotted us, and she waved us over to her, and she told us, 'I know you must be American. You're wearing dungarees.' It was the winter, and even in the Negev it gets cold.

"Then on May 8, 1952, I got a letter that began, 'Greetings. You are to report to Whitehall Street at 8 A.M. on May 8.' The Korean War had broken out. I asked myself, *Do I want to get killed in Korea or do I want to stay here?* In those days the kibbutz looked on itself as a New England meeting place. We had a meeting devoted to that question, and the vote was for me to stay. It was not a Jewish war the way World War II was a Jewish war. There was no reason to get killed on Pork Chop Hill. Why would I want to get killed in a *trayf* place?

"I decided to stay in Israel, when a few days later I received a letter from my uncle Joe, my mother's older brother, the only member of that side of the family who had any education. He had a law degree, even though he didn't go to college. The letter said, 'You owe America something. You went to college. You were the first member of your family.' It didn't convince me. Then he wrote a last paragraph that did. He said, 'I am now writing you not as your uncle, but as a lawyer. If you don't come back, you will not be able to attend your parents' funerals, because you will be arrested the second you land in America as a draft dodger during wartime.' *That* convinced me to go home and go into the U.S. Army.

"I missed the June induction date. I came home on the sister ship to the *Andrea Doria,* the *Italia.* I had to wait until July 8, 1952, to go in. I brought all sorts of X-rays showing I had a bad back, but I was inducted anyway. I was sent to a place called Camp Kilmer in New Jersey, named after Joyce Kilmer, the poet who wrote, 'Only God can make a tree.' He was killed in World War I in Château-Thierry in the Argonne. Camp Kilmer was also where the Army-McCarthy hearings were held several years later.

"I had to fill out a form. A corporal asked me, 'What is your profession?' I didn't have one. I wasn't competent to do anything, even though I had a master's degree. I had a liberal arts background. I tried to make up something that sounded professional.

"'I'm an economist,' I said.

"This corporal turned white, and he knocked on a door, came back, and told me, 'Report to the captain.' I stood before this guy seated behind a desk for what seemed like half an hour, and he said, 'Corporal Swanson tells me you're a communist.'

"'An *economist,*' I said. I started laughing, which was not the right thing to do. The captain was pissed off, but once we got it straightened out, he got to even like me a little bit, because, I'm convinced, he saved my life. I didn't go to Korea, I think, because of this guy.

"I was sent to Fort Dix for sixteen weeks of basic training. My MOS [Military Occupational Specialty] was infantry, but when I received my posting, I was sent to Finance School USA at Fort Benjamin Harrison, in Indiana. They put me in a class with fifty CPAs. I did well, because the army taught single-entry bookkeeping, and all the others had learned double-entry bookkeeping, so they had to unlearn a lot of what they knew in order to do well on the tests. I had no knowledge of accounting at all, so I learned it easily. Halfway through, it dawned on me: *The army is using this crazy system from the Dark Ages, and it isn't intelligent, isn't sensible, doesn't make sense, and that's why I am able to do so well.* I had been first or second in the class, but once I realized that, I dropped, finishing eighth.

"By finishing eighth, I got to become a finance instructor, which I felt was ridiculous. The army was round pegs in square holes. It was a very unintelligent system. But I ended up staying in Fort Benjamin Harrison, so I didn't have to get killed in Korea.

"I'm convinced life is mainly chance. It's like playing Russian roulette. Sometimes there's a blank, and sometimes you get shot in the head. I was one of the lucky ones.

"One day I was hitchhiking around the post when a car stopped to pick me up. The driver was a first lieutenant, and he started interrogating me. I'm slow, dense, and it finally dawned on me what he was trying to find out.

"He said, 'Soldier, are you Jewish?'

"I said, 'Yes, sir.'

"'I'm the new Jewish chaplain,' he said. 'I just got transferred here. I just rented a house off post. My wife and kids are coming.'

"He found out that not only was I Jewish, but I knew Yiddish and Hebrew, had been in Israel, had been a yeshiva graduate. He asked if I'd be his assistant. I said, 'Sure,' and I was transferred from Finance School USA, and he was the one who got me to apply to rabbinical school. I applied on an army typewriter.

"I went back to the University of Chicago for a year, and then I went to rabbinical school. I took the exams for both the conservative and reform schools and passed both exams. I decided to go to the conservative school, because I liked the tradition. It seemed more logical to me. When I came to register, Seymour Siegel, the provost, gave me two pledge forms to fill out. One was a pledge that I would eat kosher, not only the right food but I wouldn't eat in *trayf* restaurants. The second pledge was that I would observe the Sabbath—wouldn't turn on lights, wouldn't turn on the radio or the television, wouldn't open the refrigerator if the light went on, and wouldn't drive.

"I was willing to abide by both promises, but I was appalled by the idea of having to sign a pledge. This was 1954, and there were loyalty oaths in America at this time.

They were making schoolteachers and people who worked for the government sign them, pledging their loyalty. I said, 'This is horrendous. I'll give you my word, I will do this. But I think these pledges are terrible.'

"At the time, Seymour Siegel was a liberal. Later, he became a neoconservative, in the Nixon election of 1972. He teamed with Norman Podhoretz and those other characters who became neoconservatives. Siegal agreed with me, but he said, 'I work for the seminary, and these are the rules. Let me try to do something about it. Call me on Monday.'

"On Monday he said he couldn't change it. He said, 'They're convinced if they let you off the hook, all the other students will demand the same thing.' And that's how I ended up at the Reform Rabbinical Seminary—though, as it turned out, I was one of the rabbis who traditionalized the reform movement in small ways.

"I had two congregations, in Springfield, New Jersey, and then in Wayne, a little ways north of there. I always had two days of Rosh Hashanah in my synagogue, even though 98 percent of the Reform movement was one day. I wore a yarmulke and a tallith always, even though the great majority of the Reform rabbis don't. I had Shabbat morning as well as evening services. I had the holidays on the real day, not on the closest Sabbath. And I didn't personally eat *trayf.* I didn't eat pork products or shellfish. I gave it all up, even though I ate it in the army. And I pushed for these things in the reform movement."

*Even though Sy Dresner knew exactly one black person during his childhood in Flatbush, the stings of anti-Semitism caused him to make a commitment to the black community to help, in every way he could, end the bonds of segregation. A ubiquitous Jewish face in the civil rights movement, the voluble Dresner became the most-often arrested rabbi in American history.*

*He became involved in the civil rights movement from his pulpit. When Governor Orval Faubus tried to stop eight black students from entering Little Rock High School in 1957, Dresner spoke out against him. In the summer of 1961 he left his congregation in Springfield, New Jersey, and headed South to get arrested as part of the nonviolent civil rights movement.*

*He rode a Freedom Ride bus from Washington, DC, through the Carolinas. At the Raleigh-Durham airport he used the "colored" men's room. He drank from a "colored" water fountain.*

Sy Dressner walked over the Edmund Pettus Bridge with Martin Luther King Jr. on March 21, 1965. *AP Photo*

*Dresner was menaced by a man with a shotgun. Another man carried a long box and claimed a deadly rattlesnake was inside. Dresner was scared, but it never stopped him from exercising his conscience. He was jailed in Tallahassee for trying to integrate the lunch counter at the airport.*

*In 1962 Dresner visited Martin Luther King Jr. in jail in Birmingham, Alabama. For four days he stood by Dr. King's side. After returning home, Dresner was asked by Dr. King to bring a large group of clergy to Albany, Georgia, to protest segregation. Seventy-five came, and all were arrested. He took part in the March on Washington on August 28 and stood ten yards from Dr. King while the latter made his "I Have a Dream" speech.*

*In 1964 Dresner was arrested in St. Augustine, Florida. The Civil Rights Act had been introduced by President Kennedy, and in June of 1963 he had delivered an impassioned address to the nation, where he called upon Americans to end the hate.*

*Kennedy couldn't get it passed, and after he was killed, in the summer of 1964, Lyndon B. Johnson was working toward its passage. Dr. King asked Dresner to go to St. Augustine with a group of rabbis to protest against discrimination. A group of fifteen rabbis demonstrated with two hundred others and were arrested. The headlines caused the filibuster in the Senate to be broken, and the bill desegregating all public accommodations became law.*

*Dresner also accompanied Dr. King across the Pettis Bridge in Selma. A white Unitarian minister was murdered on the street that day.*

**SY DRESNER** "That night Dr. King and I were talking, and he told me he had been to his first Passover seder that year in Atlanta. The rabbi had a big reform congregation, and Dr. King said the rabbi had invited him to the seder, a gutsy thing for a rabbi to do in Atlanta in 1962. Dr. King didn't go through the back door, where the help came in. He went in through the front door.

"Dr. King described the seder to me. He said, 'A little kid stood up and asked some questions in

Portrait in suit and tie. *Courtesy of Si Dresner*

Hebrew and in English.' I imagine it was the rabbi's grandchild who was reading the Four Questions, the *feer kashas.* Dr. King said they then began reading from this book, the Haggadah, answering the questions.

"He said, 'And I remembered the first words after the boy asked the questions, which were, "We were slaves unto Pharaoh unto Egypt."' And he said to me, 'You Jews have not forgotten in over three thousand years you were slaves. You don't try to cover it up. You don't try to conceal it. You don't try to make yourselves descendants of royalty, of kings and queens. You're not unproud of the fact your ancestors were slaves who battled for freedom.' Dr. King said, 'We Negroes are doing exactly the same thing. We are not going to cover up our slave ancestry. It wasn't our fault. You don't blame the victim.'"

PART TWO

# The 1940s and 1950s

# VICTIMS OF THE SMITH ACT

STAN KANTER

The LAW THAT GAVE RISE TO THE PERSECUTIONS OF THE LEFT in the 1940s and the 1950s was written by an antilabor, segregationist congressman by the name of Howard W. Smith, a Democrat from Virginia. Formally titled the Alien Registration Act, but more widely called the Smith Act, it made it a federal offense for anyone to "knowingly or willfully advocate, abet, advise or teach the duty, necessity, desirability or propriety of overthrowing the Government of the United States or any State by force or violence, or for anyone to organize any association which teaches, advises or encourages such an overthrow, or for anyone to become a member of or to affiliate with any such association."

It was the first statute since the Alien and Sedition Acts of 1789 to make a crime out of advocating an idea.

The bill was signed into law by Franklin Roosevelt in 1940.

The first prosecution under the act was against Communist leaders in Minnesota who were advocating that the Teamsters strike for better wages. The Communist Party at the time was also campaigning to stay out of the war.

The evidence the prosecution used were readings from the *Communist Manifesto* as well as writings by Lenin and Trotsky. They also called two witnesses who said that a couple of the defendants had told anti-war soldiers to complain about the food and the living conditions.

On December 8, 1941, one day after fear gripped the country in the wake of the bombing of Pearl Harbor, the jury handed down its sentences. Twelve defendants got sixteen-month terms, and eleven others received a year in jail.

In 1944, there was another trial, this time in Washington, DC, of men accused of supporting the Nazis. Charles Lindbergh was not a defendant, and neither was Joe Kennedy, even though they were well-known Nazi sympathizers. But under the Smith Act, they could have been. After the prosecutors failed to come up with any evidence, a mistrial was declared and everyone went free. Freedom of speech won out this time around, but certainly not the next.

Howard W. Smith. *Library of Congress*

The framework for the House Un-American Activities Committee, with its platform for hunting out Communists in the 1950s had its beginnings in 1938 with the establishment of the Dies Committee. The sole function of this body was to "expose" threats to America's way of life. It was supported by liberals like Congressman Samuel Dickenson, who had become alarmed at the growth of the German Bund and of anti-Semitism. Its focus, however, always was anticommunism.

Representative Martin Dies Jr. of Texas originally supported the New Deal, but by the late 1930s he had become a vocal opponent of Franklin Roosevelt and the New Deal programs, as he had become obsessed with what he saw as the subversive threat from the left. He introduced to the House a resolution calling for a special committee to investigate "un-American propaganda" instigated by foreign countries. His intention was to investigate Communists, Socialists, Trotskyites, and those who were not members of those organizations but who held similar beliefs. On May 26, 1938, the House voted to establish the committee, and Dies became its chairman. His chief investigator was J. B. Matthews, publisher of Father Coughlin's anti-Semitism-laced book, *Social Justice*.

Dies wanted to go after those who were advocating change. But Dies had one unmovable roadblock in his way—Franklin Roosevelt, whose social reforms included welfare, taxation, and the WPA, and who drove the conservatives and especially the Christian right to hate everything he stood for. William Randolph Hearst, a fierce Roosevelt critic, called the president "Stalin Delano Roosevelt" for his "bastard taxation" program, which was "essentially Communism." As long as Roosevelt was alive, Dies and his committee would constantly be frustrated and blunted. But even Roosevelt couldn't stop them from wreaking some havoc.

Martin Dies. *Library of Congress*

The American Federation of Labor was battling the Congress of Industrial Organizations for control of labor unions. Dies's first witness was John Frey, the president of the Metal Trades Department of the AFL. Frey testified—without providing any evidence— that the CIO was filled with Communists. He identified as Communists 283 CIO organizers. Dies accepted his testimony, and headlines and firings followed.

The next witness, Walter Steele, a self-appointed "patriot," testified that there were Communists in the Boy Scouts and in the Camp Fire Girls. Reporters rushed to print the allegations, as ridiculous as they may have been. Again, those who were named were not accused of having *done* anything. It was accepted that just belonging to the Communist Party was enough to find one in the wrong.

The political nature of why Dies was doing what he was doing was highlighted when he went after the Federal Theater Project of the Works Project Association, which employed several thousand writers and actors. Dies hated that Roosevelt and his government were spending money on keeping artists and writers from starving. Dies, moreover, didn't like the kind of plays being staged. As far as Dies and his committee were concerned, any play with a social issue at its core was a "Communist play."

When the director Hallie Flanager was asked about an article she had written about the English playwright Christopher Marlowe, Congressman Joe Starnes ignorantly asked her,

"Is he a communist?" All across America there were howls of protest and derision. Nevertheless, the investigation was enough to kill the theater project.

Dies's House Un-American Activities Committee was scheduled to expire in 1938, but Dies petitioned to keep it going. The public was very supportive. All the while Dies accused President Roosevelt of refusing to pursue subversives.

In 1939 Dies went after an organization called the American League for Peace and Democracy. It had twenty thousand members, and it presented Dies with yet another opportunity to try to embarrass President Roosevelt.

When the offices of the ALPD were raided, on the list of members were Harold Ickes, the secretary of the interior, and Solicitor General Robert Jackson. The release of 560 names on the list created a firestorm. President Roosevelt condemned HUAC's action as a "sordid procedure."

Dies pushed to prosecute the organization, but Attorney General Francis Biddle said it hadn't broken any laws. Nevertheless, the notoriety caused the organization to dissolve.

In 1940 Dies began to investigate the Communist Party itself. It raided the party's office in Philadelphia and carried off documents. A U.S. district court judge, upset by the lawlessness and unconstitutionality of HUAC's action, ordered the investigators arrested. Dies accused the judge of protecting "agents of foreign dictators." Even though Dies pressed the campaign, the Communist Party officials, citing their rights under the constitution, refused to testify.

Under the law, Dies was obligated to go before the full House to ask for contempt citations. He ignored the law, and he got warrants without having the authority to do so. Dies brought the hearings to a close without further action.

Then in 1940 Congress passed the Smith Act. The bill passed the House by 382 to 4. The one country that heaped praise on Dies and HUAC was Nazi Germany. When Hitler invaded the Soviet Union on June 22, 1941, the Russians became our wartime allies, but Dies nevertheless viewed the Communists as a greater danger to our national security than the Nazis.

Pursuing his political agenda, Dies went after Vice President Henry Wallace. Then in 1941 he ordered the Justice Department to investigate more than a thousand federal employees accused of "subversive" activities. After all 1,121 were investigated, Attorney General Francis Biddle fired exactly 2. Dies, furious, accused Biddle of dereliction of duty.

Dies released yet another long list of federal employees to be investigated. One employee, William Pickets, who was black, was singled out, and the House moved to cut his salary. An uproar ensued. The resolution to cut his salary was killed.

When Roosevelt ran for a fourth term in 1944, Dies went after him again. He attacked Sidney Hillman, the chairman of the CIO Political Action Committee, a close advisor to FDR. The CIO PAC had been campaigning to defeat all the members sitting on HUAC. Dies said that this proved they were pro-Communist.

In 1945 Dies, in poor health, announced he would not seek reelection. But HUAC did not expire with his departure.

The man who saved HUAC was John Rankin, a racist from Mississippi. Using his knowledge of procedure, Rankin offered an amendment to make HUAC a permanent committee and also gave it broad investigative powers.

When FDR died on April 12, 1945, HUAC could start operating without its most powerful foe. In 1945 Rankin went after subversives in Hollywood. None of the victims was found guilty of anything. Those convicted were convicted either of contempt or perjury. Then, in November 1946, Republicans took control of both houses of Congress. One of the new members of HUAC was Richard Nixon of California.

One of the first actions of President Harry Truman was to ask Attorney General Tom Clark to make a list of subversive organizations. The list included any group for workers' rights and especially for civil rights. Said Jack O'Dell, a civil rights activist, "Every organization in Negro life which was attacking segregation per se was put on the subversive list."

In 1947 Truman warned the nation of the Cold War with the USSR. In a speech he said it was up to the United States to support "free peoples of the world in maintaining their freedom." His approach to international relations would be called the Truman Doctrine. The Communist threat now would be seen in global, apocalyptic terms. The Soviet Union was now our enemy, and anyone who in the past had supported the communist ideology was now suspected of being disloyal or subversive by definition.

On March 21, 1947, nine days after his Truman Doctrine speech, Truman signed an executive order creating a loyalty program for federal employees.

It was up to the FBI under J. Edgar Hoover to enforce the Truman Loyalty Program, which meant that Hoover now had carte blanche to repeat, if not improve, his performance during the Palmer Raids of 1919. The antiblack, antiunion Hoover was to become both the chief investigator and the mastermind of the Great Inquisition known as the McCarthy period. The "high priest of American anticommunism," Hoover was seen as a Christian soldier fighting for peace in America.

Hoover had taught Sunday school as a high school student. He became a lawyer through going to night school while working as a messenger at the Library of Congress. He was a file clerk at heart, but he had the power to conduct an inquisition. His FBI staff had limitless power. His domain was secret, and secrets. He used hearsay, rumor, snitching, backbiting, and innuendo. He was not above using blackmail, even against the nine presidents he served.

The great irony was that the one country that condoned such secrecy as practiced by its police was the Soviet Union, followed later by East Germany. When Attorney General Charles Bonaparte proposed a Bureau of Investigations in 1908, Congress turned down his request because it felt such a unit would create a "blow to freedom and to free institutions." A month after Congress adjourned, Bonaparte established the future FBI anyway. He was supported by President Theodore Roosevelt, who accused Congress of being soft on crime. The United States now had a secret police that rivaled the one of czarist Russia.

Said historian Richard Gid Powers, "All the institutions young Hoover joined—Sunday school, church, Central High—regarded themselves as defenses against the immigrant threat to the nation, hegemony, its character as all-but-officially Christian nation, and to the national leadership of the old-stock American."

This was as true in 1949 as it was in 1919. America after World War II was changing. Urbanization, increased social mobility, the rise of consumerism, a shift toward the emancipation of women and blacks and most of all the decomposition of traditional religious patterns—all of this scared the shit out of conservatives. For Hoover, the immigrant and the radical were part of what he saw as a larger pattern of lawlessness belonging to a modern world.

Hoover felt the ground under his feet moving, and he became scared. In the 1920s he had gone after Emma Goldman and her ilk, and it hurt his reputation in the eyes of the public. He then turned to gangsters like John Dillinger, Pretty Boy Floyd, and Baby Face Nelson, and with a savvy media campaign he became known as America's G-Man.

By the mid-1930s Hoover was famous, and after the death of Franklin Roosevelt, he would be unleashed by Harry Truman to go on the warpath against communists. Along the way he not only wiped out the Communist Party in America, he went after a generation of men and women devoted to social justice, the labor movement, and civil rights.

Hoover was a Red hunter in the same way the Puritans were witch hunters. Both were fueled by superpatriotism and fear. Hoover, a stone-cold racist, justified what he was doing by saying that if the FBI didn't do it, America's citizens would.

Hoover, who was both obsessive-compulsive and gay, began attacking the sexuality of Americans in the 1920s. He went after those who violated the Mann Act—people who crossed state lines to have sex. He said it was essential for the law to attack "the problem of vice in modern civilization," and he said he was not going to rest until America's cities were "completely cleaned up."

He talked about communists in sexual terms, calling them "lecherous enemies of American society." He often referred to the left wing as "intellectual debauchery," and warned his agents of the "depraved nature and moral looseness" of student radicals.

After civil-rights worker Viola Liuzzo was murdered, Hoover sent President Johnson a memo saying: "A Negro man was with Mrs. Liuzzo and reportedly sitting close to her." Due to the presence of a Negro with her, Hoover refused to investigate, feeling she deserved what she got.

Martin Luther King Jr. was his special target. Hoover called him a "tomcat with obsessive degenerate sexual urges." After King was assassinated, Hoover planted an item with columnist Jack Anderson, saying that James Earl Ray had been contracted to kill King by a white husband whose wife had borne King's child.

The average American did not really care very much about communists, but because Hoover was sexually tormented, he went after gays in the U.S. government, causing more homosexuals to be fired by the State Department than communists. He focused his efforts by displacing a whole range of dangers onto the one master signifier of communism. Thus he could blame on communism everything that wracked his twisted soul, using the power of his image as the "omniscient, incorruptible protector to convince others that the attack would bring security to all Americans."

Hoover may have had a twisted soul, but he needed a front man to conduct the witch hunt that he so desperately desired. That man appeared quite by accident on February 9, 1950, in Wheeling, West Virginia, at a meeting before the Ohio Country Women's Republican Club. During dinner the man, Joseph McCarthy, a senator from Wisconsin who had come into office in 1946, along with California senator Richard M. Nixon, was discussing with his cronies how he could revive his flagging political fortunes. When he got up to speak, he told the assemblage that "While I cannot take the time to name all of the men in the State Department who have been named as members of the Communist Party and members of a spy ring, I have here in my hand a list of 205 names . . ." McCarthy went on to say that the secretary of state had their names but allowed them to work anyway. In a similar speech in Salt Lake City the next day, he must have noticed a bottle of Heinz ketchup on the table, because to that assemblage he said he had a list of "57 communists in the State Department."

It was nonsense, of course. Hoover had told McCarthy that there were Russian spies in the State Department, but McCarthy didn't know who they were and had no way of uncovering them. As A. Mitchell Palmer had done in the 1920s, McCarthy merely assumed that anyone who had ever belonged to the Communist Party was subversive. It may have been a fishing expedition, but it was exactly what J. Edgar Hoover and wealthy conservative Christians such as oil moguls Clint Murchison, Hugh Roy Cullen, and H. L. Hunt wanted to hear. It was Hunt who once said, "Communism began in this country when the government took over the distribution of the mail." The oilmen were strident haters of all Franklin Roosevelt had stood for. Roosevelt, after all, put a cap on how much oil their companies could drill, and he and the Democrats were behind laws that forbade them from drilling sideways into neighboring oil fields, a shabby practice that had gone on for decades.

Once the media spread the word of what McCarthy was saying, it wasn't long before he in the Senate and the equally determined House Un-American Activities Committee launched the most far-reaching witch hunt since the Salem trials.

The McCarthy and HUAC rampage was fueled by fear, and there was no greater fear than of the Soviet Union after it tested its first atomic bomb in 1949. Stalin, once our ally, now had nuclear weapons. That year Mao took over in China, turned it Communist, and in 1950 the Korean War broke out. There was panic in the land. A ferocious repressiveness became the order of the day. Only a secure suburban home, populated by a nuclear family, Dad presiding, could provide protection against the outside agitators. It was an era when a lot of people built bomb shelters to house their family in case the worst occurred. And here was a U.S. senator saying that members of the State Department were card-carrying Commies who were out to destroy our way of life.

When it came to the communists, McCarthy was an opportunist and a demagogue, but J. Edgar Hoover was truly psychotic.

Once the Inquisition began, the important question was no longer whether you were a communist. Rather it became whether you were *not* an *anti*communist. If you dared criticize McCarthy, you became one of *them*. Throwing away the Constitution, the investigators employed snooping, accusing, and informing as they looked into civil service, unions, industry, universities, local school boards, and churches.

Sam Kanter organizes a union. *Courtesy of Stan Kanter*

Meanwhile, the Christian right was in its glory. It was hunting season, and all they had to do was accuse someone of being a communist, and he was a dead man. The truth had nothing to do with it. The FBI would come poking around, asking your neighbors about you, and before you knew it, your landlord wanted you out.

It became so nuts that the YWCA and the Girl Scouts were combed for Reds. But for the victims of this witch hunt, there was nothing funny about it as civil liberties were abused and jobs—and sometimes lives—were lost.

Stan Kanter, who was born in June of 1938, grew up poor in Brighton Beach, his father a union organizer for the American Labor Party, his mother a secretary at the Communist newspaper, the *Daily Worker*. As a boy, Kanter attended a constant string of biracial union rallies or meetings at home at night in an attempt to bring better pay and safer conditions for the working man. Another of their causes was the end of Jim Crow, in America in general and in baseball in particular.

In the early 1950s the witch hunt for Communists, launched by Senator Joseph McCarthy, began to claim its victims. Communist Party officials, fathers of Kanter's best friends, were jailed, accused under the Smith Act of undermining the U.S. government. Then one day

Stan's mother informed him that his father had "gone away," on the run from the FBI. His father hadn't really done anything more than organize unions, but under the Smith Act, he could be arrested, and he wasn't taking any chances. He went into hiding, returning several years later, after the evil era of madness had passed. Before the witch hunt was over, 6.6 million people had been investigated. Except for the Rosenbergs, not a single case of espionage was proven in court. But despite the failure to find subversion, the Red hunt gave the appearance that the government was riddled with spies. The lives of thousands of men and women, including the Kanters and their friends, whose singular desire was the betterment of the poor and powerless, were left in its wake in shambles.

**STAN KANTER** "When I was five, we moved from Manhattan to Brighton Beach. We lived in a condemned building. My father, who was often out of work, was a union organizer.

"Most of my young childhood memories were union meetings or rallies just about every night. My parents couldn't afford babysitters, and I was taken to these things. If I was home, it was because there was a meeting at the house, thirty people I didn't know, sitting around, talking.

"I was always taken to May Day parades, rallies, picket lines. As a little kid I was always walking around carrying picket signs.

"We really weren't communists. We didn't know about communism really until Joe McCarthy started talking about it. What my parents were were members of the American Labor Party. They believed in better working conditions, in

A young Stan Kanter pickets for peace.
*Courtesy of Stan Kanter*

workers' rights. My father organized unions for people who worked in factories, where there were fires every day, always unsanitary conditions. He went around trying to organize.

"They also believed in equality of the races. At the union meetings at our home, half the people who attended were black. We all read Lester Rodney in the *Daily Worker*. Rodney had been championing getting blacks into the major leagues ever since he began his column. My father was an avid reader of Lester Rodney, and it became his cause too. Integrating baseball was also a cause the American Labor Party was pushing, and my father would take petitions around and speak on street corners. When Robinson was playing for Montreal, he would say, 'We need Robinson in the major leagues.' He'd attend rallies. We couldn't have made phone calls. We didn't have a phone. There's a tremendous picture of my father and Jackie Robinson shaking hands on Jackie Robinson Day (September 23, 1947). He worked very hard to get Jackie into the major leagues, and so there was a picture of him shaking hands with Jackie at home plate.

Sam Kanter shakes hands with Jackie Robinson on Jackie Robinson Day, September 23, 1947. *Courtesy of Stan Kanter*

"When I was growing up, Brighton Beach was middle class. On one side is Manhattan Beach, which is ultra-wealthy. There were guards at every entrance and only doctors, lawyers, heads of corporations, and congressmen lived there. To the other side of Ocean Parkway was the Coney Island area, which was very poor, lower class, gangs and street fighting all the time, and in between was our Jewish middle-class area, very, very, very left-wing. The elementary school I went to, PS 253, had pictures of Paul Robeson hanging in the auditorium, and pictures of left-leaning author Howard Fast [he wrote *Spartacus*]. Kids would do reports on Fast's books. They used to hold mock presidential elections, and in 1948 Henry Wallace [who was nominated by the Progressive Party] won in our school over both Truman and Dewey.

"Almost no one I knew had a car. We played in the streets all the time, stickball, punchball, and we never had to worry about a car coming. There were mothers looking out the windows. None of the other mothers went to work. We'd come home from school and go down into the street and play ball. We had almost no interaction with girls. We didn't know from girls. The wealthy Manhattan Beach kids knew from girls, and the toughs who lived on the other side of us seemed to be hanging around with girls from the time they were nine years old.

"In the winter we played basketball at the after-school centers. We always got home at a respectable hour, when it was getting dark. Once a week we would be allowed to go to a neighborhood gym in the evening with a whole bunch of guys, and each mother approved. We had to go as a group to a home and say, 'Can Eugene come with us to the gym today?' 'Yes, if he's home by nine.' And you'd be back on time. That was the kind of neighborhood it was, wholesome and nice.

"For junior high school I had to go into Coney Island. Half that school was Jewish kids from Brighton, who were walking to the other side of the tracks, and the other half was Italian street gang–type kids, who lived there. We could only walk to school if we all walked together, like thirty of us. When we got within two blocks of the school, we ran just as fast as we could, because there were gangs waiting for us.

"We didn't have confrontations. You can't call them confrontations. You would call it getting beat up. These were tough street kids. They wanted to fight. They enjoyed a good fight, and they found out quickly they couldn't get a good fight out of us. Nobody would even punch back. We'd be crying and whimpering, so it didn't even pay for them to beat us up. Most of the time we were so pitiful, they didn't even bother. It wasn't like they could rob us. We didn't have any money. Nobody had lunch money. We had a little sandwich that they didn't want. After a while, they said, 'No point even harassing them anymore.' But we still had to be careful. We didn't dare go to school alone.

"I ended up becoming friends with some of these toughs. We played ball together in gym class, and they could see I was pretty good, and I ended up tutoring a couple of them, because I felt sorry for them, big galoots who were good athletes, but the math teacher would pick on them mercilessly, would really make fun of these Italian kids who knew from nothing and who liked the Jewish kids who knew the answers.

I would help them with their math during lunch hour, and in return they would protect me from the other kids. So it worked out very nicely. When I got to Lincoln High School, it was the same situation. I never really got beaten up, because some tough guy would come by and say, 'I know him. He's okay.'

"I was not religious. My parents were nonreligious. We were well aware we were Jewish. We were very interested in a Jewish ballplayer, a Jewish comedian, a Jewish singer. My friends had bar mitzvah lessons. I went to shul a half hour a day to learn Yiddish, but it barely took. We were not kosher. We all went to Nathan's to buy hot dogs. We could walk along the boardwalk to get there. My friends all ate them, whether they were kosher or not. But in their houses it had to be kosher. In those days the only restaurants were a Chinese, where we would eat chow mein, and a deli, where we could get a corned beef sandwich or frankfurters once in a while. Mothers made supper. I didn't know from going out to eat until I got married.

"On special occasions—somebody's birthday—we would go to Lundy's in Sheepshead Bay. We didn't have a car, but somebody always did, a relative, friends, somebody to get us there. Lundy's was a huge barn of a place, where they served shrimp and lobster. There was no maître d'. You got there on a Sunday afternoon, the only time people seemed to go, and you stood over the table. You'd hover over a table and say, 'It looks like they're almost done.' Every table had two or three families standing over who was eating, fighting. 'We're next. *We're* next. *We're* getting this table. Aren't you people done yet? Come on.'

"The people at the table would say, 'Get away. We're still eating.'

"The waiters, who barely spoke English, were mean and hostile. It was a very hot place. There was no air conditioning. I don't know why everybody loved to go there. But the food was good and inexpensive. You could get a lobster dinner for $3, with muffins and shrimp. It was a very special thing to go there.

"We moved many times in Brighton in those years. Basically, my parents could never pay the rent. Union organizing didn't pay practically anything. And my mother worked at the *Daily Worker* as a secretary, and most of the time she didn't get paid. We really had no money. They'd go seven or eight months without paying rent, and my father would just find another place and move a little closer to the ocean. At one point we lived with another family in a three-family house, and the guy who owned the house couldn't afford to keep it anymore, and he offered it to my father and the other family who we were friends with. He said, 'For a hundred dollars, you can have it.' But nobody knew from a hundred dollars. Today it's worth a million dollars.

"In that house we had two families living together in a one-family apartment. My parents had one bedroom. The other set of parents had the other bedroom. Two daughters from the other family slept in the living room. There was no bedroom for me, so I slept on the kitchen floor.

"I never resented it. I realized we were poor. I'm sure if my parents had money, we'd have lived better. I didn't know any different. Most of my friends didn't have any money. My friends' fathers got up in the morning, went to the train several blocks away, came home late at night, ate dinner, lay down on the couch, and took a nap. In the case of my parents, they went to meetings. I didn't know you were supposed to have money.

"We went to the movies on Saturday to see a film that took place in Hollywood—a fantasyland. It had no relation to us. There were two movie theaters in Brighton Beach, the Oceana and the Tuxedo, where you could get in for a nickel. They had double features and cartoons and shorts and newsreels and we'd get there about noon and stay right through the double feature. We went for the serials, and the deal was if you went to the first eleven, you got into the twelfth for free if you kept all the stubs. I would always get sick on the eleventh week. You could never hear the films, because there were hundreds of kids screaming in the theater. One week we went to see *Go Man Go!*, the story of the Harlem Globetrotters. The other picture was *Seven Brides for Seven Brothers*. We said, 'Do we have to sit through this so we can see *Go Man Go!* again?'

"And we all got captivated. All these big studs were saying, 'This picture isn't half bad.'

"There was one other movie theater, called the Lakeland, which we called 'the Dumps,' because you could get in for about 2¢. The seats were all broken, and it smelled of urine. It was awful.

"There were two theaters in Coney Island, the Loews and the RKO, which were a little fancier. They were 20¢. That's where the pictures came to first, but two weeks later they'd be at the Oceana and the Tuxedo. We knew to wait."

*More than for any other attraction, Kanter's great passion was for his beloved Brooklyn Dodgers.*

**STAN KANTER**  "Before Jackie Robinson was Pete Reiser, who they said would have been better than Mickey Mantle. His first year he led the league in hitting. But he kept crashing into walls. He came out of the hospital with a concussion, couldn't even walk, and Leo Durocher sent him up, and they deliberately walked him, even though he couldn't lift his arms. Pete was on the team Robinson's first year, and the two of them were just spectacular on the base paths.

"I remember the first time I saw Jackie Robinson play. I couldn't believe any athlete could be that exciting. Did you ever see him in his early days?

"Pete Reiser would be on third base, and Robinson would be on first, and Robinson would deliberately leave the base, and they'd have to throw over, pay attention to him, and he'd stay in the rundown until Reiser could score—and most of the time he got out of it. It was phenomenal watching him.

"And Robinson would steal home. Whoever saw anyone steal home? I always got taken to Pirates games, because Ralph Kiner, who hit home runs, was a big attraction. I saw the Cubs with Hank Sauer and Frankie Baumholtz, and the Giants, who had big, lumbering guys. Robinson was the first real runner.

"I loved Duke Snider. He had the most graceful swing I ever saw. We liked to watch him miss as much as connect with the ball, because his whole body wound up, an amazing swing. He was also a graceful outfielder, climbing the fences.

"Snider was a terrifically nice person, and in left field a lot of times we had Cal Abrams, who was Jewish, so you really cared about him.

"There was a TV show before the games called *The Knothole Gang*. They would have three kids out in the field trying out. A Dodger would hit balls to them, and then pick which kid was the best. No matter what Dodger was there, he was so nice and friendly and wholesome. You could admire any one of these guys and say, 'I would like him to be my father or pal.' There wasn't one who was arrogant or stupid. Now you watch interviews with ballplayers and you say, 'My God, I wouldn't want to be in a car with this guy for ten minutes.' Every Dodger seemed so nice, and if you ever saw one of them outside the ballpark and asked for an autograph, it was the same thing. 'Hi kid, how are you doing?' 'How are you doing, Duke?' They always smiled. They were always nice. Cox was a little bit sullen and withdrawn, and Furillo wasn't a great outspoken guy, but Reese, Hodges, Snider, Abrams, and Campanella were nice, warm people, and most of them lived in the neighborhood. You knew that Gil Hodges lived on Bedford Avenue. People saw the players shopping for groceries, working a part-time job at a gas station. In those days they weren't multimillionaires, above the

Stan Kanter listens to Red Barber on the radio. *Courtesy of Stan Kanter*

fans. They were just nice people who were terrific athletes living in the neighborhood. This was a team you could really root for. The Yankees, of course, were U.S. Steel. We hated them.

"During the World Series, when I was in elementary school, we sat in the classroom, and they piped in the game over the loudspeaker. Whenever the Dodgers were in the World Series, which was about every year from 1947 to 1957—we missed 1948, 1950, 1951, and 1954—we'd sit in class and listen to the games, and then at three o'clock, when the bell rang, we'd go, 'Oooh, we're missing a pitch.' You'd leave school and walk home. Dodger games were always on the radio, and as we walked home from school, we'd hear it coming out of every window. It was early October, still pretty warm, and there was no air conditioning in those days. People had their windows open. When you got home, you listened to the end of the game.

"I was home by the time Bobby Thomson hit that home run in the final game of the 1951 season. The Thomson home run was not a happy thing. I remember all of us walking out into the street and sitting on stoops quietly, nobody talking. It was sad.

"I didn't blame Ralph Branca. Not at all. No. This was a team you rooted *for*. Nobody ever felt anything negative, not that I know of. None of my friends. We never thought anything negative about anything the Dodgers did. Losing to the Giants that day wasn't so terrible. Although the Giants were our rivals, they were a National League team, and they played fair. See, the Yankees weren't and didn't. Every year at the end of the year the Yankees would wrap up their pennant with a month to go, because there was no competition in the American League. The Dodgers were fighting the Giants, the Cardinals, the Phillies, and they'd go down to the last day, and they'd enter the World Series with their pitching staff spent. One year they started Joe Black, a relief pitcher, in the first game, because no starters were available. The Yankees would be rested for three weeks. They'd have their rotation in order. They would buy National League stars, pick up terrific players, to help them in the Series. They bought Ewell Blackwell, Johnny Mize, Enos Slaughter. Their payroll was always much higher, and these guys would make a difference in the World Series.

"The Giants were like the Dodgers. We didn't want to lose to them, but I loved Willie Mays, a tremendous player. Stan Musial was an all-time favorite, even though he was an opponent. I liked Richie Ashburn and Robin Roberts from the Philly team. I didn't feel bad losing to those guys. The Yankees, who were an all-white team, were the one team I could never root for. I rooted against them—always. I didn't feel horrible if the Giants, Phils, or Cards would win. It was just the Yankees. I knew they were going to the World Series. So I didn't feel horrible about Thomson. If you re-member, the slogan in Brooklyn was, 'Wait 'Til Next Year.'

"My mother worked at the *Daily Worker*, which was not a mainstream newspa-per. It was the paper of the Communist Party. In those days there were twelve daily newspapers in New York City. Most of the kids read the *Daily News* and the *Daily Mirror*. There was also the *Times*, the *Post*, the *Journal-American*—which was always right-wing, the *Herald Tribune*, and the *Sun*, plus the *Compass*, the *Brooklyn Eagle*—plenty of newspapers. Those papers, which were owned by capitalists, were always attacking unions, attacking the *Daily Worker*, attacking anything that was leftist. If workers went out on strike, every editorial in the city supported the corporations, and the workers were thrown in jail. The *Daily Worker* was the one paper saying, 'No, the workers are right. They deserve raises and better working conditions.' It was in the best interest of the other papers to give a black eye to the *Daily Worker,* badmouth it all the time. It wasn't a crusade, but if you were a reader of the other papers, you would come across the line 'that left-wing rag, the *Daily Worker,*' and people were just going to have a negative opinion of it, which was so hard to understand. When I became a teacher, I noticed that every black teacher I worked with read the *Daily News*. I said, 'All of their editorials are antiblack. Why do you read this paper?' They said, 'I know. I know. I like the sports section. My mother likes it.' It was hard to understand. They should have been reading the *Daily Worker* instead. I have friends who are teachers today, who vote Republican, and I say, 'You're so interested in health care, and the Republicans are doing everything to destroy health care. Why do you vote for them?' And they turn a deaf ear.

Sally Kanter was a secretary at the *Daily Worker. Courtesy of Stan Kanter*

"So the *Daily Worker* was not a paper you wanted people to know you had in your house, even before McCarthyism came in. My mother would get Knicks tickets under the basket for me and my friends from Lester Rodney, the *Daily Worker*'s terrific sports reporter. My friends would have been appalled to know how I was getting them. Since I kept getting Knicks tickets from Lester Rodney, I told him once, 'I'd like to cover the games.' I wrote one up, and he printed it in his column. He just wrote, 'By Stan.' But I couldn't tell any of my friends I had written a column in the *Daily Worker*. I was shocked the next day when one of my teachers came over to me and said, 'I saw your column in the newspaper. I'm very impressed.' I thought, *There's a teacher in my school who reads the* Daily Worker*! I can't believe that.* But none of my friends ever knew. Nobody knew. Years later my closest friend, Ernie Brod, was on the *Columbia Spectator*, and he was assigned to do a story about something happening at the *Daily Worker*, and he called, and my mother answered the phone. He said, 'This is Ernie Brod from *Columbia*,' and she almost blurted out, 'This is Sally Kanter. How are you, Ernie?' It would have been quite a shock to him. I never let my friends in the neighborhood know.

"None of my friends from Brighton ever knew from blacks. There was one kid in our elementary school, Michael Gordon, who was black. So they didn't know from black people. But every summer I went to interracial camps."

*Kanter was sent by his parents to a union-sponsored summer camp in upstate New York's Catskills Mountains on White Lake, called Wo-chi-ca, which was shorthand for Workers' Children's Camp. The ideology dictated that since children were the future leaders, summer camp would be a perfect place to instill in them core values. The goal was to prepare these children to be leaders in the fight for peace, civil rights, and social justice. To the townspeople, these kids were dangerous Commies and subject to attacks. In an attempt to lower the animosity, the name of the camp was changed from Wo-chi-ca to the less-threatening Wyandotte.*

**STAN KANTER**    "I went there for two weeks for several summers. The first year I went there I was put in a bunk with several kids whose fathers were the first Smith Act victims. Bill Gerson's father was Sy Gerson. There was Fred Jerome and Pete Berry, and half of the fourteen kids in my bunk were black, and I became friends with them.

"When I first went to camp there, I was shocked at how much more my camp friends knew than my neighborhood friends. Most of the kids in the neighborhood had never been out of Brooklyn. They might have been to Manhattan once in their lifetime to see a show. Most of these kids from camp lived in Manhattan, and they had been all over, to California, to Canada, even to Europe, and they knew about everything. They read newspapers and magazines I had never heard of. They were so much smarter. They were really bright, won awards, went to Cooper Union or Columbia. They were really bright because they had grown up reading. My friends who I met in camp knew about everything that went on in the world.

"During my teens I led a double life in the afternoons. I had my neighborhood friends, and every once in a while I'd get on the train and go to Manhattan, and meet my camp friends. The group was called the Young Communists, but we weren't Communists. It was the Labor Party youth group.

"I would have to come home to the neighborhood and really tone it down. A teacher would ask some questions about Russia, and I would know everything going on in Russia, but if you seemed too knowledgeable, it would be, 'What are you, a communist or something?' So I had to be careful in school, even in having conversations with them. I couldn't seem too knowledgeable. 'How do you know all this stuff?'

"Later on I worked as a busboy at a place called Camp Unity, which was run by the labor unions but which had the reputation of being a communist camp. A lot of the blacklisted actors worked up there on the entertainment staff. Pete Seeger was the resident folk singer. My friend Bill couldn't stand him, because he used to hold his concerts on the basketball court when we wanted to shoot baskets. We had constant battles with him.

"Paul Robeson was always at the camp. The Peekskill event [where he was pelted with rocks by "patriots"] was really big in our family. My father had gone up there and gotten pelted with stones. Most of the people who met in our house had been there, and they had rocks thrown at them, and their car windows were smashed. At the camp Robeson would sing "Old Man River," and songs by the Weavers, who used to perform there. They were such nice people. They cared about people. They cared about the workers. They cared about equal rights for people. Women's rights. Medical insurance for people. And for them to be blacklisted . . . they were such good guys. It was a pleasure to listen to them.

"Hesch Bernardi [actor Herschel Bernardi, who was blacklisted in the 1950s] was a wonderful person. I was a kid, and he was a grown entertainer, but he knew the busboys and waiters weren't getting much to eat, and he'd say, 'Come to the canteen. I'll buy you a sandwich.' Lorraine Hansbury, who wrote *Raisin in the Sun,* was on the staff. Lionel Stander with that gruff voice and Les Pyne were there too as was a guy named Paul Draper, who was the best tap dancer I ever saw.

"It was at the camp that I was introduced to jazz, which wasn't popular in my neighborhood. Back home everyone listened to Perry Como and Eddie Fisher, but at the camp there were black entertainers, great jazz musicians, and these guys would play all day long, rehearse for hours. I fell in love with the trumpet. Jazz concerts were held almost every night. They were terrific. And then I would go back to my neighborhood, where kids didn't know from anything.

"'Where were you?'

"'At the camp.'

"It was during my junior high years that we started getting visits from the FBI. My parents would be out working during the day, and every once in a while the doorbell would ring, and two FBI men would be there asking questions.

"'What time will your father be home?' I was told never to answer anything. 'I don't know. I don't know. I don't know.' My father would come home, and I'd tell him, 'Two FBI guys were here.' 'Did you tell them anything?' 'No. All I said was, "I don't know."' 'Why did you tell them that?' Whatever I said, he would say, 'Why did you tell them that?'

"We got this every few days, and they would interview neighbors in the building, and this was another reason we would have to move, because the landlord would say, 'The FBI guys keep coming here and bothering me, and they say you're a communist. Why am I allowing you to live here?'

"The landlords were sympathetic, because they were working-class Jewish people, but after a while they would start to get scared. I wasn't privy to all the conversations, but I gather they would say to my parents, 'Listen, I really don't need this anymore. See if you can find another place.'

"I didn't care. I figured, *If you have to find another place, you move.* And we were moving in the same neighborhood. I kept the same friends. It wasn't like I was living in a beautiful room in a beautiful house to begin with. All we had were books, which most people didn't have, and we always took the books.

"I attended Lincoln High School, which was probably the best high school in the city. We had an incredible teaching staff. They were the top teachers in their field, and they kept winning citywide awards. Joseph Heller came out of there, and Arthur

Miller. Our senior class president, Louie Gossett, was appearing on Broadway in *Take a Giant Step.* Neil Sedaka had been a classmate since we were in the second grade. I'm probably the only kid who never beat up Neil Sedaka. They'd say, 'Let's beat up Neil.' I'd say, 'What are you going to beat up Neil for?' Neil Diamond was a classmate. The principal of Lincoln was very interested in theater, and they would put on shows! Our star basketball player was Mark Reiner, who we thought was one of the greatest players of all time, but he went to North Carolina as the only Jewish ballplayer, faced anti-Semitism, quit the team, went to NYU, and was never the same. Our football team won the city championship, and many of them were all-city players, but none of them became famous. They didn't go to the pros. They were Jewish. They used football to get into college, to pursue their studies. I graduated in 1956.

"Around the beginning of my high school years, McCarthyism started to take flight, and it became a very unpleasant situation, because you couldn't even say the word 'Russia' in a classroom. 'Does anyone know where Russia is?' If you raised your hand, everyone said, 'He must be a Commie. He must be a Commie.' Russia was a dirty word. To us, it was the Soviet Union.

"Once McCarthy started appearing on TV, talking about Communists infiltrating the government, the army, the country, things got worse. When the first Smith Act trial was held, twelve defendants were accused of conspiring to stage a violent overthrow of the government. As I said, a number of these men were my friends' fathers. One of them, Fred Jerome's father, was a little rabbi scholar type, a man who never raised his voice, who wouldn't step on an ant. If a fly came and someone said, 'Swat that fly,' he'd say, 'No no, you don't kill things. You don't hurt things.' They were all that way. I'm thinking, *The violent overthrow of the country by these people?*

"The one who wasn't like that, Sy Gerson, was a big, strapping guy, a war hero, an athlete, who ran for office and got elected to the city council. His campaign was, 'Peace, prosperity, and a pennant for the Dodgers.' Sy was cut loose from the other eleven because he had been a war hero. Bill Gerson and Fred Jerome were my closest friends, and their fathers were on trial. After school, I'd take off and go down to Foley Square in Lower Manhattan and watch the Smith Act trials. It was amazing, watching the prosecutor point at these people saying, 'They are trying to overthrow the government by violent means.' I would look at them and think, *All they know from is how to read.* They were such quiet little types.

"After they were put in jail, they started to have hearings in Hollywood. People all over were being thrown into jail, including a distinguished teacher from my sixth-grade class. Everyone wanted to be in his class. One day he suddenly disappeared. I asked, 'Where's Mr. Lipschitz?' 'He isn't coming into work anymore.' I found out afterward he had been arrested after he was asked to give names, and he wouldn't. Suddenly people were disappearing all over the place.

"I can't say my father felt any pressure about losing his job when McCarthyism heated up, because he never really had a good job, and we never had much money. The union wasn't going to get rid of him, because he was working for practically nothing. The *Daily Worker* wasn't going to get rid of my mother. They weren't going to lose their friends, because their friends were other left-wingers. Although friends started to disappear. They would go into hiding. I do remember one of my uncles wouldn't come over because he didn't like my parents' politics. So life didn't change much—until my father didn't come home one day.

"My mother said, 'Dad has to go into hiding. They are arresting people, and for his own good, he has to disappear.' The fathers of my close friends were in jail. Suddenly I didn't see some of the left-wing fathers of my other friends. Mothers began running the houses. At this point my grandmother came to live with us. My mother was out working, and my grandmother did the cooking, if you call it cooking. Reheating leftovers was more like it. I was older, and I had to take care of my younger sister, walk her to school and pick her up after school and get an after-school job, because we needed money in the house.

"I wanted to be president of NBC, but I couldn't get that one so I worked in a candy store, in grocery stores, delivering, stocking groceries, crummy, low-paying jobs. I had to deliver milk cartons to school. We used to get free milk, little, teeny cartons of milk, which would sit all day in school until milk time, at which point the containers were all warm and the wax would drip into the milk. I carried these huge cartons to the school, a five- or six-block walk, because we didn't have bikes or cars.

"I never kept the money. They were very low-paying jobs, and I gave the money to my parents. When I had a summer job, working as a counselor or busboy, the arrangement was to mail the money home to my parents. We lived on allowances, and the highest I ever got was a quarter a week. But what did I need? A notebook every year. My parents took me to buy clothing and sneakers. Books we had in the house, and I went to the public library all the time. I didn't buy records. We didn't have that in those days. So I didn't need much money, just some school supplies, and it was the same for all my friends, which is why we weren't dating. We didn't have the money to spend on girls.

Sam Kanter. *Courtesy of Stan Kanter*

"We didn't know we were poor, because there were poorer kids in Coney Island. You would walk through there and see really broken-down hovels. We lived what we considered a middle-class life. We were living in two-family houses as opposed to tenements. It didn't seem bad.

"During the time my dad was away, anywhere between three to five years—I'm really bad with time—I didn't see him more than a half dozen times. It was like out of a movie. I would be given instructions what to do: we'd get on a train at the Brighton Beach station, get on the express train, get off at the next stop at Sheepshead Bay, and both the express and local would be standing there on opposite sides of the platform. We would stay on the platform until the last second, and we'd hop on the local. We kept changing cars all the way to Manhattan, making sure no one was following us. We'd take a bus somewhere, get off where they told us, wait on a corner, and someone would pick us up in a car and drive us somewhere. I have no idea where. Seemed to us like upstate New York.

"We would get out, and another car would take us somewhere remote in the country. My father would walk out of the woods, give us a hug, and say, 'How is everything?' We'd talk to him for two minutes, and a car would come and pick him up. It seemed ridiculous.

"When I was working at the camp, once or twice we made the same arrangement. Someone would say, 'Come with me. Get in the car.' And he'd drive somewhere up a hill and around winding roads, and I'd get out, and another car would come and take me. I'd get out, and my father would come out of another car, and we'd talk for a few minutes.

Stan Kanter today. *Courtesy of Stan Kanter*

"I found out years later that in the last year of his hiding he was staying with very wealthy friends on Bedford Avenue and Avenue M. I had once babysat there. I loved it, because that house had beautiful rooms and beautiful Heritage books. The kid would watch television, and I could watch too. While my dad was living in this millionaire's house, we were living in Coney Island in a slum, a fifth-floor walk-up, the only white people on our block, because we couldn't afford Brighton anymore. Before that, he never told me where he was living. He was on the move a lot, just to keep from getting arrested. During that period the FBI kept coming to the house. 'Have you heard from your father?' It's conceivable they never would have arrested him. I don't think he was that important a person. But he didn't want to take the chance. Same thing with several of my other friends' fathers. They didn't want to take the chance, and they went into hiding.

"Things started to get better when McCarthy was finally revealed to be the fraud he turned out to be. I watched while Edward R. Murrow challenged him, and then at the army hearings, Joseph Welsh, the army lawyer, went after McCarthy, exposing him, and that brought tears to everyone's eyes.

"To me and a lot of people, McCarthy really was evil. I had been a great fan of John Garfield. *Body and Soul* had been on the Million Dollar Movie, on Channel 9 in New York. They showed the same movie every night for seven nights. I watched that every night. It was a sensational movie, and McCarthy drove Garfield to his death. He wrecked a lot of lives."

# VICTIMS OF MCCARTHY

TERRY (TED) ROSENBAUM

**W**HEN YOU TALLY THE DAMAGE INFLICTED BY JOSEPH MCCARTHY and HUAC, you could argue that compared to the 20 million Russians Stalin killed, the purge victims in America got off easy: a few foreign-born socialists were deported, Julius and Ethel Rosenberg were put to death, about 150 people went to prison for a year, two years at the most, and perhaps 10,000 others lost their jobs.

As in 1940, when the Rapp-Coudert Committee targeted Jewish teachers, ten years later HUAC came back for a second shot at them. Never mind that this was supposed to be a nation that cherished academic freedom or that someone's political activity away from the classroom should have had nothing to do with his ability to teach. The way Joe McCarthy and HUAC witch hunters defined it, anyone who had been a member of the Communist Party or who refused to testify before his committee had surrendered the right to teach.

The Senate tried to stop McCarthy in June of 1950, after his scattershot charges about Communists in the State Department. Congressman Millard Tydings issued a report on his charges, calling McCarthy a "fraud and a hoax on the Senate." But McCarthy, before seeing the report, undermined the findings by saying any such report would be a "disgrace to the Senate, a green light for the Reds." When McCarthy pushed on, making more undocumented charges, he was backed by the Christian right and by Republicans wanting to give

President Harry Truman and the Democrats a black eye. In the next Senate election, Democrat Millard Tydings was beaten in Maryland. The winner, John Butler, had received a potful of money from McCarthy's rich oilmen backers. As part of the campaign, Butler's henchmen displayed a doctored photo of Tydings standing with Earl Browder, the former head of the Communist Party. Karl Rove would have been proud.

McCarthy never let up. Every day he demanded Truman be impeached and Secretary of State Dean Acheson be fired. For the next four years McCarthy poisoned America's air, turning this country into everything he said he feared. The only person who could have stopped him, Dwight Eisenhower, Truman's successor, decided for political reasons it was best to remain quiet, a mistake he would later regret.

What was notable was that before the Communist witch hunts began, many of the teachers who were later fired—teachers who had been teaching for years—had never been accused of recruiting students or teaching the party line. Most had been active Communists in the past, but after they realized that Stalin was a monster and that the Soviet Union held no panacea, their pro-Communist political activity had waned. None of that mattered to HUAC or to Senator McCarthy, whose boldness seemed to grow along with his notoriety.

Most of the firings came after a target exercised his Fifth Amendment right against self-incrimination. With the nation gripped in fear of Soviet domination, the courts allowed the Wisconsin demagogue to suspend constitutional protections.

The ordeal usually came in two stages. First a representative from an official agency, such as a school superintendent, would investigate, followed by a hearing in front of McCarthy. Splitting the job made it easier for the school superintendent to shun responsibility for a person's dismissal. He could rationalize his actions by saying that McCarthy had ordered the firing.

Once someone was fired, the victim stayed fired. The victim's name remained on a blacklist that everyone denied existed, and getting another job in the field—or even in another line of work—became almost impossible.

Terry (Ted) Rosenbaum, whose mission in life was to teach high school students the joy of learning, was one of the victims of McCarthyism. He was fired in April 1954, and he would not be vindicated until 1972, when the United States Supreme Court ruled that a person could not be fired for taking the Fifth Amendment. Rosenbaum would get benefits and his pension for the years he taught, but he could never again get back what he had lost: his life's work. He became a fund-raiser for the Educational Alliance for a children's hospital on Long Island. To his everlasting credit, Ted Rosenbaum found a way to do good for others, despite his ordeal.

Ted Rosenbaum was born with the given name Terry in the Brownsville section of Brooklyn on February 7, 1918. His father, a baker who came from Poland, arrived at Ellis Island at the beginning of the twentieth century, in the wave of Eastern European Jewish immigrants. He met his wife in Brooklyn, and they had three children. Spurred by their mother, Terry and his siblings all had top grades in high school, and all graduated from college. Terry's goal in life was to teach American history, and he was well on his way to a brilliant career, when his civic activities on behalf of black citizens attracted McCarthy's attention.

The incident that put him directly in McCarthy's gun sight occurred in Brooklyn in 1951, when Henry Fields, a black man driving carelessly, scraped a parked car. The owner of the parked car, furious, summoned the police, who chased Fields five blocks in a squad car and after cornering him ordered him out of the car. Fields turned, and, without provocation, the policeman shot him three times in the back.

The blacks were furious and threatened to riot. Rosenbaum, a popular community leader who four times had run for assemblyman on the American Labor Party ticket, was known for his connections to the black community. In the early morning, he went to the police station to help ease tensions.

Not long afterward the superintendent of the New York City public schools called Rosenbaum in for a meeting, and so did Senator Joseph McCarthy. There had been complaints about his behavior. When Rosenbaum asked what he had done, he was asked, "Are you a member of the Communist Party?" Rosenbaum wasn't, in fact, but his knowledge that the Constitution protected him from having to answer such a question emboldened him. He told the superintendent it was none of his, or anyone else's, business. When he was called in personally by Joseph McCarthy, he told the senator from Wisconsin the same thing.

Rosenbaum's license to teach was revoked, and he would have to wait eighteen years before the Supreme Court ruled that his job—and all those people whose jobs had been taken away after Smith Act convictions—had been taken from him illegally and unconstitutionally.

Unable to find work of any kind, Terry Rosenbaum changed his name from Terry to Theodore, and he spent the rest of his life raising money for charitable organizations. In addition to his livelihood, the loss was also borne by the hundreds of high school students denied the opportunity to learn from his inspired instruction.

Nettie and Abe Rosenbaum married in 1916 and lived their entire lives in Brownsville, Brooklyn. *Courtesy of Ted Rosenbaum*

**TED ROSENBAUM** "My father left Poland because life for Jews was made unbearable there. He was discriminated against in all sorts of ways. The jobs he could hold were limited. His income was limited. He was a baker who worked very hard, but he made a bare living. He told me about the pogroms, where Cossacks would ride into his town and murder Jews. Life was very uncomfortable there. Every time he thought about his past, tears would come to his eyes.

"His brother had come to Brooklyn a couple years before, and he came too, and he had a tough job earning a living. He finally got a job as a baker, and he met my mother through mutual friends who knew my mother's family. They were introduced, and they got married.

"My mother also was Jewish, but she was not an immigrant. Like so many other Jewish mothers and fathers, but mostly mothers, she made sure her children were going to get an education. That was their way to liberation. 'You have to get good marks,' was all we heard.

"I was the oldest of three children. I have a younger brother and sister. All three of us graduated from college, because she was on our backs every single hour of every day. I can never forget it. One day when I was in the fifth grade I came home, and I said, 'Mommy, I got a ninety-eight on my report card.' She looked at me, and she said, 'What happened to those other two points?'

"I went on to get a master's degree at Columbia; my brother, Lloyd, became a professor at MIT [Lloyd, denied employment as a professor because of anti-Semitism, changed his name to Lloyd Rodwin. He went on to become the chairman of the Urban Studies program at MIT], and my sister graduated Brooklyn College and also had a career working for various businesses. She was very competent.

"Brownsville was a poor, poor working-class area. It was 85 percent Jewish and 15 percent black. The main shopping street was Pitkin Avenue. On both sides of the street there were stores: shoe stores, clothing stores, candy stores, restaurants. On weekends all the working people came there to shop and eat, and on certain streets pushcart peddlers sold all kinds of things. It was very rich culturally.

"There were synagogues all over the place. We did not belong to the synagogue. My father and mother were atheists, and I was too.

"We played punchball and stickball and handball in the playgrounds, and basketball. We played stickball in the streets, using broom handles for bats. We were rabid Brooklyn Dodger fans even though we couldn't afford to go to Ebbets Field.

Twenty-eight year old Terry Rosenbaum and his parents, Abraham and Nettie. *Courtesy of Ted Rosenbaum*

"I went to Samuel J. Tilden High School. It was a good school located just outside of Brownsville. Fortunately I was able to walk there, because it was not easy for us to pay for buses. I graduated in 1932. I was young—fifteen. My mother was always on my back, and I skipped several grades. From one point it was good for me, but from another, I was always the youngest, youngest, youngest in the class, and it made life socially more difficult.

"I was three years younger than the other students when I enrolled at City College. In my day CCNY was the top of the pyramid. The school had a terrific reputation, and getting in was something. I got on the subway every morning, and I rode for an hour and ten minutes to get from Brownsville to the 137th Street station in Manhattan. And I'd return home the same day. I did my studying on the train. I was a big guy with long legs, and people would trip over my legs while I studied.

"I wasn't involved in any politics there. I went to classes, and after school I worked at the Thom McAn shoe store on Pitkin Avenue. We were a poor family. I didn't have much spare time.

"After I graduated from CCNY, I went to Columbia University, where I got a master's degree in history. My goal was to be a teacher of American history in the New York City high schools. Which I did. I loved teaching.

"You had to search around for placement until you got your teacher's license, and my first job was in the East New York Vocational School. I walked in there, and I'll never forget, the kids' attitude was: *I'm learning auto mechanics and similar trades, why do I need this?*

"They even said it to me. One kid told me, 'My mudda sent me here to loin a trade. Why are you giving me this goddamn history?'

"It wasn't one or two kids. It was in general. And it devastated me. I had just come out of college, and I was going to be a teacher, make young people interested in American history, and then this. I can't tell you how devastated I was.

"I was there about two weeks, and I thought, *I have to make a decision. I have to prove to these kids that learning American history is vital to their future.*

"I took a week off and prepared a series of lesson plans, the title of which was 'Why History Is as Important to Me as My Trade.'

"I came into class, and I said to the class, 'I'm going to be a lawyer for the defense, defending my subject.' And for a week I gave them lessons. I gave them simple concepts. I said, 'You're an auto mechanic. There's a depression, and you can't earn a living. Or you don't have money to buy things. Or your job is menaced. Your wages go down.' Or, 'You say to yourself, "Why do I care about the farm problem?" Because farmers, when they're poor, they can't buy, and when they can't buy, your job is menaced. Or you get lower wages.'

"I went down a whole list of things, and at the end of the week I turned to them, and I said, 'You're the jury now. I gave you my case. How do you feel about this? Am I right or am I wrong?'

"Some of the kids were crying. 'I didn't realize,' they said. It was the greatest thrill of my life. A couple of years later [April 14, 1953], one of those kids was a sergeant in the army in Europe, and the *New York Sun* had pages on education, and my former student wrote a letter and in it he said, 'I had a teacher, Terry Rosenbaum, who taught me American history. He made me understand why it's important (I get tears when I talk about it), so I always wanted to join the army, because I felt as though it was my duty as an American. There is one thing Mr. Rosenbaum made us learn, and that was the heart of the Declaration of Independence. I'll always remember it, as long as I live.'

"I taught for close to a year, and then I transferred to Samuel J. Tilden High School, where I had been a student. It was a very special feeling to work there. I taught there for eleven years.

"I loved teaching. I loved teaching history. I must say I was very popular with my students. They could feel my interest in history and my enthusiasm and my willingness to interact with the students, getting their opinions. Those were fruitful years, except they didn't last too long."

*Rejected by the army because of bad ears, Terry Rosenbaum did his patriotic duty by raising money for the war effort. Away from the classroom, he also became an active member of his community. His first civic act was to expose a New York City patrolman who was distributing anti-Semitic literature. He then became chairman of the Brownsville CIO Community Council and the legislative director of the Brownsville Neighborhood Council. He was also cochairman of the Brownsville Red Cross Drive.*

*He joined the American Labor Party because, he says, it was the only party at the time interested in the health and welfare of poor working folk. It worked on campaigns relating to rent control, minimum wage, more library facilities, and better working conditions, and in 1944 he was asked to run for the New York State Assembly.*

**TED ROSENBAUM** "The American Labor Party was pretty strong in Brownsville. I liked what it was doing, and I became active. Various members of organizations, both Jewish and black, came to me and asked me to run for the assembly, which was the farthest thing from my mind. At first I wasn't sure if I should do it when they asked me to run, but it occurred to me that one of the best ways to promote the issues, rent control, price control, discrimination, was to get active in politics, so I agreed to run. I felt so strongly about the issues in those days with the war on. Working-class people were taking an awful licking, so I became a candidate, and I ran four times.

"The American Labor Party was the only party interested in helping the working class. The Republicans, just like today, were just reactionary. The Democrats were supposed to be the liberals, but when it came to action on issues—better schools, discrimination—they did much better than the Republicans, but in terms of real action in the community, they did nothing of consequence.

"Helping in my community is what turned me on. I worked very closely with the black community, with black leaders like Justice Hubert Delaney, who was a justice of the domestic relations court, and with dozens of black ministers. The black community needed jobs. They needed tenant rent controls and rights. Many of them were unfairly evicted. Our party represented not only the blacks, but poor whites as well, but we especially fought for black rights. I don't want to exaggerate our influence, but at the time Jackie Robinson came to the Dodgers, we had helped create an atmosphere of tolerance in Brooklyn.

"I had no expectation of winning but at least it gave us an opportunity to raise the issues and verbalize them and bring them before the public and debate them, and that was something I relished, because it was our way of getting our issues on the public agenda.

"It was part of the movement generally in those years to liberalize the Democratic Party, and in that sense it was successful. If we hadn't raised the issues, no one would have. That's why a third party can serve a useful function, so long as it doesn't help the most reactionary people get and keep power.

"The only American Labor Party candidate ever to win was Vito Marcantonio [New York State congressman from East Harlem, 1935–37, 1939–51] in Manhattan. What a guy! He thought very highly of me. I did very well, and two years later, in 1948, I ran, and the Democratic candidate, Alfred Lama, was so scared because I was quite popular, that they got the Republican Party and the Liberal Party to endorse him. He had three lines on the ballot to my one line."

*He sings:*

> *Terry Rosenbaum, ALP,*
> *Cast your vote for democracy.*
> *There's a man in this community,*
> *Who fights for victory, unity.*
> *Send him up to Albany!*
> *Vote for Terry Rosenbaum.*

*Rosenbaum's life proceeded as planned until a fateful day in 1951, when in the middle of the night he was called to go down to the police station to help quell a disturbance.*

**TED ROSENBAUM** "My wife and I had attended a family gathering in New Jersey. We went to bed, and I was awakened at one in the morning by a phone call from Max Gilgoff, a teacher colleague of mine who worked with me in the American Labor Party. What a guy!"

*Gilgoff, like Rosenbaum, was a teacher and a community activist. Gilgoff was chairman of the East Flatbush Child Care Center, which he organized to help working mothers during the war. Gilgoff and Rosenbaum together had organized a community service to help people who had landlord and welfare problems.*

**TED ROSENBAUM** "He called to say there was a near riot in Brownsville. A twenty-six-year-old black father of four had been shot and killed by a cop. He was driving and apparently turned the corner and nicked a parked car in front of a grocery store and kept going. The owner of the car came out and called a cop, who was nearby, and the cop chased him in his police car five blocks, and with people sitting out on their stoops in the street—in those days that was their way of getting sunlight and fresh air—the cop swung in front of Henry Fields's car, backed up, got out of the car, pulled a gun, and ordered him out of the car. Fields was so shocked when he saw the cop with the gun, he turned away, and the cop shot him three times in the back and killed him.

"It hit the press the next day, and the black community went nuts, as you can understand. That's why the black community besieged the police department that night, and why my friend called me, because he knew I was well respected by the ministers. I went to see what I could do to pacify the situation. I ran down there at two in the morning, and it was really a hell of a scene. I led delegations to the police department and to the mayor of the city of New York, protesting against this terrible thing. We didn't want this incident to serve as a role model for other cops.

Terry Rosenbaum presented a challah to Paul Robeson. Robeson campaigned for Rosenbaum when he ran for the New York State assembly in 1948.

*Courtesy of Ted Rosenbaum*

"Not long afterward I got a letter from Dr. William Jansen, the superintendent of the board of education of New York, to come down to his office. He had gotten reports I was doing terrible things in the community.

"I came down, and after he asked me a few questions about the Fields case, I told him, 'Look, I am a teacher of American history. You're a superintendent of schools. One of our obligations is to teach our students the value of democracy and to practice what we preach. That's exactly what I did in this horrible incident. And you're calling me in?'

"'I got letters of protest,' he said.

"'From whom did you get them?' I asked.

"'Are you a member of the Communist Party?' he asked."

*Rosenbaum was not, but so what if he was? The question offended him greatly.*

**TED ROSENBAUM**    "I said, 'You called me down about the Fields case. Here's your letter. Why are you asking me if I'm a Communist? What does my political position have to do with anything? I'm not answering such an unconstitutional, illegitimate question.'"

*He was told to expect another letter. It came in November of 1953, and this time he was ordered to appear before Senator Joseph P. McCarthy, who was on a witch hunt to oust suspected Communists he contended were plotting to overthrow the government from such disparate places as the federal government, Hollywood, and the army. His target at the time Rosenbaum was called was army personnel at Fort Monmouth in New Jersey. In that Rosenbaum had never been an employee of the federal government, he was perplexed as to why McCarthy, who stood for everything Rosenbaum abhorred, was calling on him to testify.*

**TED ROSENBAUM**    "McCarthy voted against almost every law that would benefit the average American: housing, schools, hospitals, laws against discrimination. He has opposed the truce in Korea. He was supported by almost every anti-Semitic and anti-Negro group—who have made him their hero. He has sabotaged the Bill of Rights more than anyone in our history. So you see that McCarthyism hurts all the American people. Therefore, like Hitler, to scare people, he calls anyone who disagrees with him either Communist, pro-Communist, a tool of the Communists, or a 'Fifth Amendment Communist.'"

*At the time Rosenbaum was called, McCarthy was holding hearings in New York on the army. Rosenbaum said to himself, I was never a member of the army. What the hell does he have to do with the board of education?*

**TED ROSENBAUM**    "I was called down to McCarthy's special hearing room at Foley Square in Manhattan, where he and Roy Cohn, his henchman, conducted an inquisition. You can imagine how horrifying this was. I got myself a lawyer, who advised me, 'The best, smartest thing you can do is keep your mouth shut. If you answer one of his questions, you'll have to answer them all. Not that you have anything to hide. But he has no right to cross-question you.'"

*Before McCarthy could question him, Rosenbaum felt the need to give the senator a history lesson. He said, "The Fifth Amendment was written into the Bill of Rights by real patriots to protect innocent people from public officials. Taking the Fifth Amendment does not mean a person is guilty of any wrongdoing. It compels government officials to obey the principle that a person is innocent until proven guilty." Rosenbaum said he had committed no illegal acts, either in or out of the classroom.*

Senator Joseph McCarthy and his wife.
*Library of Congress*

**TED ROSENBAUM** "Sure enough, he asked me, 'Are you a member of the Communist Party?' I gritted my teeth. Oh boy, was I fuming. I said, 'You called me down here because presumably I did something wrong. What did I do wrong?'

"He cited me for contempt. We went up and back, and when it came to it, I refused to answer. Before I left the session, I had sixteen citations for contempt, and it killed me, because I would have liked to have told him off. But my lawyer looked at me, warning me to keep quiet, and when I walked out of that room I figured I'd be going to jail for the next ten years. I came home, and my wife and I were petrified."

*When it became known that Rosenbaum and Gilgoff were being investigated and might be fired as teachers, a petition to retain them was signed by Justice Delaney; Lindsay White, past chairman of the NAACP; Rabbi Louis Gross, the editor of the* Jewish Examiner, *and more than fifty ministers, rabbis, and other community leaders—both white and black. Said the petition, "Their threatened dismissal would be a victory for McCarthyism in our schools, and a threat to our democratic institutions."*

*Wrote Justice Delaney, "The public should become aroused and concerned about the sincerity of purpose of a Board of Education which goes easy on a May Quinn, who admittedly spreads anti-Negro and anti-Semitic poison in her classroom, which on the other hand, it tries to pin the red label on teachers who fight to keep alive in their community the spirit of the Bill of Rights."*

*An editorial on November 23, 1951, in the* Jewish Examiner *said, "Instead of injecting the red issue into a clear and shocking case of injustice, the Board of Education should have publicly commended the two teachers for their social conscience and courageous initiative in coming to the aid of a Negro family."*

*The pleas fell on deaf ears.*

*On April 30, 1954, Rosenbaum was fired from his teaching job and blacklisted.*

**TED ROSENBAUM**    "I was dismissed by the New York City Board of Education because I had refused to answer questions posed by a federal authority. And I was kept from teaching for eighteen years! In those days, the atmosphere, I can't tell you, was so horrible. I couldn't get a job anywhere, and I was Phi Beta Kappa and I had a wonderful record as a teacher.

"A friend of mine, Herbert Kurz, head of the Presidential Insurance Company, offered me a job. He said, 'How about working for me? You'll make a wonderful insurance agent.'

"'Who the hell wants to be an insurance agent?' I said. But in desperation I succumbed to him, and I filed an application with the state superintendent to sell insurance with Herb's recommendation attached. A week later he got a call from the state superintendent.

"'Do you know this guy?'

"'Yes, I do.'

"'Tell him he has no chance. I am sending out my response today.'

"That was the atmosphere in those days. So I didn't get the job. It wasn't until

1972, when an outfit called the U.S. Supreme Court ruled that a public employee may not be lawfully dismissed under section 903 of the New York City charter under circumstances that infringe upon his constitutional privilege against self-incrimination. At the end of that year the New York City Board of Education amended its by-laws to reinstate all employees like me, who had been dismissed under section 903, and in December of 1972 I was reinstated, and in 1976 I was granted the annual retirement allowance from the New York State teachers' retirement system, based on my twelve years of service. That included health benefits, which I am receiving to this day.

"Unable to get work, I decided to change my name. Terry was an unusual name, and so I changed it to Theodore, which is my name today. Ted Rosenbaum. And I pursued another career, that of a fund-raiser. I was hired by the Educational Alliance on the Lower East Side, the second-largest settlement house in America next to Hull House in Chicago. It was formed at the end of the nineteenth century, and it provided housing to immigrants, to some of the greatest names in Jewish history, entertainers like Eddie Cantor, George Jessel, and Sam Grosz.

"When I started, my goal was to raise a couple million dollars, to double the size of the facility. You don't raise that much money by knocking on doors and getting nickels and dimes. No, you have to go for the big bucks.

"I began researching the board of trustees of the Alliance, whom they knew, when one of the guards outside came over and said, 'Mr. Rosenbaum, I got to tell you a story you might find helpful. For years a big limousine would pull up, and out of it came a man, a very dignified man, evidently very well-to-do, and he'd come in, walk to the lobby, and then walk into the auditorium, where he'd sit down for a couple of hours without saying a word. And then he'd leave. Year after year.'

"You didn't have to be much of a brain to figure out who the man was. First, he had a big limousine and he had money. Second of all, he must have been emotionally involved to come back year after year. I figured, I'd better find out who knows him and get an interview with him. The mystery man, it turned out, was David Sarnoff, the founder of RCA.

"I went to see him, and I told him who I was and what I was doing. I said, 'Tell me. What made you come up year after year and sit in the back of the auditorium?'

"Tears came to his eyes. He said, 'My father was an immigrant.' (He was this powerhouse, and I can see him crying now.) He said, 'I sold newspapers outside the Alliance to earn a few pennies for my family, and one day they called me in and said, 'Would you like to be in a play we're putting on?' Sarnoff said, 'I was scared stiff, but I couldn't say no. I was afraid they wouldn't let me stand outside selling newspapers. So I joined the play. I had one line: "Cleanliness is next to Godliness."' And he said, 'I was on the stage with the other kids, and I forgot my line!'

"I told him of our plans, to extend the Alliance facility to make it possible for hundreds of new immigrants to stay. And he gave half a million bucks to start with, and he got friends of his to kick in several million bucks more. And that was how I started my career in fundraising."

Ted (nee Terry) and Beth Rosenbaum celebrate their 50th wedding anniversary in 2001. *Courtesy of Ted Rosenbaum*

*Rosenbaum's next job was working for the Long Island Jewish Hillside Medical Center. They had heard about Rosenbaum's success, and they wanted him to head the effort to build the first regional children's hospital, covering forty-three communities in Queens and Long Island. Each local hospital treated children, but none had the expertise or the equipment to treat the most seriously ill cases.*

**TED ROSENBAUM** "I don't have to tell you, knowing my background, how excited I was to be part of building a children's regional hospital. I took the job, and I worked there eighteen years, and in 1983 it was opened and dedicated by Governor Mario Cuomo."

*In 1990 Rosenbaum moved to Leisure World, the largest retirement community in the state of California. He is one of eighteen thousand residents. When he arrived, other members of the community began talking about setting up an organization for universal health care. It was an issue right up his alley, as he describes it.*

**TED ROSENBAUM**   "I became their political consultant, and then their president, and for the last seventeen years I've been working on that project. There is now a bill in the state legislature called the Senator Kuehl bill SB-840, which passed the Senate and is now being processed through the California assembly. It has to go through a couple more committees, but at this point, with the political mess taking place, I doubt that Governor Schwarzenegger will sign it, because of the tax implications. And we'll need a two-thirds vote to override his veto.

"We have 6 million uninsured people in California alone, and over 15 million underinsured. This issue turns me on, even at age ninety-plus. I'm up to my goddamned ears."

# THE ABSURDITY OF MCCARTHYISM

JOSEPH BOSKIN

FOR RIGHT-WINGERS LIKE JOSEPH MCCARTHY, YOU DIDN'T have to be a Communist to be accused of being a disloyal American. You could also be a socialist, a philosophy that wasn't so tied into the Soviet Union, but one which posited that we'd all be better off if certain powerful industries were better-controlled by the government. Franklin Roosevelt was the one president who understood the benefits of letting the government control certain functions that formerly had been left in private hands: he began Social Security, a socialistic program that guarantees every American some income in their later years; he began a system of welfare that kept the poorest Americans from starving; and he initiated legislation that controlled corporate greed, calling for a minimum wage, better working conditions, a curbing of monopolies, environmental protection, and higher taxes for richer Americans. All these programs were anathema to McCarthy and his wealthy conservative friends. (These were the programs dismantled by George W. Bush.)

The socialists believed that their message of civil rights and social justice was ethical. Joseph McCarthy—another in the tradition of Christian Puritans—pursued tactics that were contemptible, if not unconstitutional, to stop them. Be that as it may, McCarthy had the power of Congress behind him, and during the first half of the 1950s he planted the fear of prosecution into anyone who had ever gone to a meeting of any radical group.

Joseph Boskin, who as a youth felt strongly about the rightness of socialism, saw the effect McCarthyism had on America.

**JOSEPH BOSKIN**   "The radical community began to pull in badly with the start of the Smith Act prosecutions and then HUAC's and McCarthy's hearings in the late 1940s. The radical teachers and professors became much more conservative in their lectures and in their behavior and criticism. They were not as open or as blatant as they were before. A great fear came into existence.

"There was a debate over how we should handle the loyalty oath, whether to sign or not. I was confronted with this when I was drafted for the Korean War. You had to sign a loyalty oath. There were two parts to it. The first part says, 'Are you now or have you ever been a member of . . .' and then they list about 270 subversive organizations in the United States, ranging from the Lower Slobovian Marching Band to the CP to the Socialist Party.

"Organizations you couldn't possibly imagine were on the list. And you had to indicate whether you had actually been a member at any time. If you put down yes, tried to be honest about it, you were taken away and put in a very 'safe' area, away from everyone else, and then you were constantly monitored. Then you were haunted for the rest of your career in the army, and after you got out, the FBI followed you and monitored you.

"If you put down that you were a member of the Abraham Lincoln Brigade, you had your phones tapped, your mail confiscated, and so on.

"But if you lied and put down that you never had been a member of anything, they didn't follow up on it. So the question was, should you be honest or dishonest? How to deal with it became a serious question for a lot of my friends.

"Two of my friends told me what happened to them after they answered yes on the army questionnaire. It was deplorable. And for no reason. None of us were radical in the sense that we believed in the overthrow of the government. Most of my friends were evolutionary socialists. They believed with Erich Fromm, who extolled independent thought and the use of reason to establish moral values, that there was a close relationship between socialism and ethics.

"There was no doubt in my mind what I was going to do: I said no. Of course not. I wasn't going to give in to this kind of nonsense and also be harassed for the rest of my life. It was crazy. We knew it was nonsense."

*The irony was that Joseph Boskin, the onetime socialist, who had to lie to escape harassment from the government, wound up in a top-secret army outfit. Said Boskin, "At the time the United States was ringing the Soviet Union with air force bases. I was assigned to the Transportation Arctic Group, a scientific expeditionary force that went to Thule, Greenland, to see if we could find a feasible route across the polar ice cap on the other side of Greenland to build a B-52 base closer to the Soviet Union. But you couldn't do that. It was impossible. Besides, shortly afterward, missiles came into existence, and they rendered the B-52 bombers obsolete. Thule became a missile base." After the war ended, Boskin went to the State University of New York at Oswego. It was there that he discovered what he wanted to do for the rest of his life: teach.*

**JOSEPH BOSKIN** "I was blessed with a roommate in college who had the most insatiable curiosity of anyone I ever knew. His name was Mel Bernstein. He was also from Brooklyn. We roomed together in college for three years.

"His art form was the question. He was always moved by the question itself, and he taught me the whole beauty of the question itself. We took a lot of classes together, and before we'd go to class, we would arm ourselves with questions for the professor. Which we then sat down and asked.

"We had one young professor in sociology, and we would come to class and pepper him with questions. One day he said, 'Enough. Enough. You two guys. Are you roommates?'

"We said, 'Yes.'

"He said, 'Now it makes sense. You, Bernstein, you're the most pessimistic young man I've ever met. You're truly cynical. I want you to get a book'—it was a book on altruism—'and I want you to report back to the class. An oral report.' He added, 'And you, Boskin, you're one of the most optimistic persons I've ever met. You need a dose of cynicism. I want you to read Sigmund Freud's *Civilization and Its Discontents*. And I want you to report to class.'

"We went to the library, got out the books, and I started reading. I was nineteen years old. I had never read Sigmund Freud in my life.

"It wasn't easy reading. I couldn't get past the first two pages. I didn't know what *thanatos* or *eros* meant. I had the dictionary next to me, and I was looking up all the words.

"'I'll never make it,' I told my roommate. 'I don't understand any of this.'

"'Continue reading,' he said.

David Schine, Roy Cohn, and Joseph McCarthy.
*Library of Congress*

"I read the book three times. I finally had it memorized. And then I drew up a flow chart, and I gave a full lecture before the class and answered questions.

"I was blown away by the experience. Blown away. I never realized what it meant to be a professor. That was my epiphany. From that day on I knew what I wanted to do for the rest of my life.

"My big debate was whether to become a sociologist or a historian. I don't know why, but I opted for history. I became a social historian."

*Boskin's first job was at the University of Iowa. He went from there to the University of Southern California, and then to Boston University. He has also been a visiting professor at UCLA and the University of California at San Diego.*

*Boskin managed to avoid getting ensnared by the evil web of McCarthyism. He was one of the lucky ones. Unlike Teddy Rosenbaum, he got to fulfill his lifelong dream of becoming a teacher.*

*As a footnote, after Martin Luther King Jr. was assassinated in 1968, there was rioting in the black sections of many cities, including Baltimore. One of Joseph Boskin's uncles was an optometrist who had several offices, including one in Baltimore's black community. When the riots took place, his brother took a copy of a book Joseph had written, titled* Urban Racial Violence in the Twentieth Century. *He put it up in the window with a big sign:* MY NEPHEW. *His office was spared.*

The McCarthy era came to an end because McCarthy's legal assistant Roy Cohn had become infatuated with his friend David Schine, who was drafted, and after failing to get him a commission, Cohn did everything he could to make sure the object of his affection lived like a king at Fort Monmouth, New Jersey, where he was stationed. When Cohn's unseemly behavior was revealed, McCarthy, trying to protect Cohn, then decided to investigate whether there were subversives at Fort Monmouth. The whole thing smacked of blackmail.

During the hearings McCarthy attacked Fort Monmouth's commanding officer, General Ralph Zwicker— who had led a key regiment at the Battle of the Bulge—for allowing a dentist to get an honorable discharge even though he had refused to answer questions about his being a member of a "subversive organization." McCarthy tried to humiliate Zwicker, a close friend of President Eisenhower, by accusing Zwicker of protecting a Russian spy. The charge was absurd.

On March 3, 1954, Edward R. Murrow did his show *See It Now.* He showed clips of McCarthy terrorizing witnesses. He showed him patronizing the president. At the end, he intoned, "The actions of the junior senator from Wisconsin have caused alarm and dismay amongst our allies abroad and given considerable comfort to our

Edward R. Murrow. *Library of Congress*

enemies. And whose fault is that? Not really his. He didn't create the situation of fear. He merely exploited it, and rather successfully. Cassius was right. The fault, dear Brutus, is not in our stars but in ourselves. Good night—and good luck."

Then the White House released a memo revealing how McCarthy and Cohn had been demanding favors for David Schine. Forty-four counts of improper behavior were listed.

The next day McCarthy went after Robert Stevens, secretary of defense. At a hearing about the Cohn-Schine affair, Joseph Welsh, a trial lawyer from Boston, represented the army. When McCarthy charged that Welsh had hired a Communist attorney as an assistant, and named him, Welsh turned to McCarthy and said, "Let us not assassinate this lad further, senator. You have done enough. Have you no sense of decency, sir, at long last? Have you left no sense of decency?"

When Welsh was finished, the room broke into thunderous applause. It was all caught on TV. McCarthy had become a liability to the Republicans and even to the cause of anti-Communism.

On June 17, 1954, after thirty-six days of testimony, the army hearings were recessed. Said Arkansas senator John McClelland, the Democrat who'd led the walkout of the hearings, "I think this will be recognized and long remembered as one of the most disgraceful episodes in the history of our government."

When the fall election was fought, Vice President Richard Nixon used McCarthy's tactics and methods to tar Democratic opponents from sea to shining sea with charges of being soft on communism. The Democrats won both houses of Congress anyway.

On December 2, 1954, McCarthy was censured by the Senate, sixty-seven votes to twenty-two. He was finished. Eisenhower put the senator's name on the list of people never to invite to state dinners. Worse, reporters stopped writing about him, even when he called press conferences.

Joe McCarthy had two and a half years to live. He died on May 2, 1957, of acute hepatitic infection. Though he had hepatitis, he wouldn't stop drinking, and the combination killed him. But the conservatives have never stopped defending, even praising him. He is a hero to Ann Coulter. Said an editorial in the *Fort Worth Southern Conservative,* "Joe McCarthy was slowly tortured to death by the pimps of the Kremlin."

After all the hearings, with so many of the accused losing their jobs, McCarthy never uncovered one single subversive. Instead he just smeared innocent people with impunity. He brought with him names, documents, and statistics, even though most of them were phony. Said historian David Oshinski, "He understood intuitively that force, action, and virility were essential prerequisites for a Red-hunting crusade."

# FEARING THE UNKNOWN

PETER MEINKE

I T HAS BEEN SAID THAT ONE IN SEVEN AMERICANS CAN TRACE their families to having once lived in Brooklyn. It is equally true that those who have left it have never forgotten it. This is certainly the case with Peter Meinke, a poet and retired professor of English at Eckerd College in St. Petersburg, Florida. Meinke, who was born in Midwood Hospital in Flatbush in 1932, was removed from the Brooklyn streets the week before he was to enroll at James Madison High School in the fall of 1946. Meinke's father was of German origin, and he didn't like what was happening to the neighborhood. Italians were moving in, and he had fears that Brooklyn no longer would be safe. It was a precursor to what would happen all over Brooklyn and many other American cities during the next decade. Because Mr. Meinke owned an automobile, he had mobility that allowed him to travel across the Hudson River to buy a house in bucolic New Jersey. Son Peter, one of the country's revered poets, was crestfallen, but he never forgot from whence he came.

**PETER MEINKE**   "My father's father, Harry Christian Meinke, came over as a young boy in the late nineteenth century from Hanover, Germany. His mother had died in childbirth, and he had a relative who was a fisherman in Sheepshead Bay back when it wasn't a golf course, and my father came by boat to

Brooklyn. He was a big guy, about six foot one, a husky fellow. He was one of the few family members without a Brooklyn accent. He did not say, 'Shut the daw.' He taught himself that.

"He was a very strict patriarch who ruled the family. He was a cigar-smoking man, and whenever one of us would light up a cigarette, he'd say, 'Throw out those stinkaroos.'

"After I became engaged to Jeanne [his wife of many years], I had to introduce her to Grandpa. He lived on Flatlands Avenue, near Nostrand. I forgot to tell Jeanne that Grandpa hated cigarettes.

"In those days we all smoked. We sat down at the table. I had seven aunts from my mother's side of the family, and they all were there. Jeanne was a little nervous, and she lit up a cigarette. There was silence around the table. Grandpa looked at her and bellowed, 'Put out that stinkeroo.' Jeanne put it out, shaking, when he threw a cigar at her. He said, 'If you're going to smoke, smoke a real smoke.' Even though she had never smoked a cigar before, Jeanne took her fork, jammed it into the cigar, lit it up, put it in her mouth, and there was smoke everywhere. You couldn't even see Jeanne. From the silence, Grandpa turned to me and said, 'She's all right.' And everybody applauded.

"Grandpa worked most of his life. After he stopped being a fisherman, he became a night watchman in a factory, so he stayed up all night for a long time. He was a blue-collar worker who spoke perfect English, and he was very political, right-wing and pro-German, and he would argue with the rest of the members of the family, who were very much against Germany and Hitler. The vehemence of the arguments was very scary for a child. This was before the beginning of World War II, when no one knew what Hitler had done. After we went into the war, Grandpa finally came around, but for a long time there were raging arguments.

"Whenever we'd visit, we would go into the house, the kids would start running around, and my aunt Marge would make Manhattans for the men, who'd give the cherries to the kids. The men would light up cigars, and they'd all sit around talking politics, little of which we understood. I do know they hated Roosevelt. They thought he was an aristocrat, and they didn't trust him. He was never mentioned by name. He was always 'That man.' My father's side of the family tended to be Republican. My mother's side was different.

"Grandpa would pay us to sing German songs at Christmas. Once the war started, my father forbade us to practice them. When Grandpa asked for his songs, we told him they weren't allowed. 'You are German,' he would shout. 'Sing.'

"Though he was a tough guy, he had that sentimental German streak. He gave me a poster called a *Schnitzelbank,* and it had pictures, and I would point to the pictures and sing, *'Ist das nicht ein Schnitzelbank?'* And then he'd answer, *'Ja, das ist ein Schnitzelbank.'* He said to me, 'One day you should go to Germany,' and I said I would, not knowing it wouldn't be long before I would be going into the army. He had married and had two children—my father and my aunt Marge—but his wife, a small, chubby woman, died when we were very young. He'd talk about his wife, and he would burst into tears. I remember being very touched, thinking how complicated older people were. Here was the boss of the family, crying.

"I liked him very much. He didn't complain. He was not sympathetic about anyone complaining about anything. He wanted people to work hard, and he would give us boring lectures to that effect.

"He had a lot of bad traits. He was prejudiced in all kinds of ways. The worst thing he would say—and this is terrible—we'd settle down and make the Manhattans, and we'd ask him, 'How is everything, Grandpa?' And he would say, 'Ah, the Jews and the guineas are ruining the world.' We would just look. No one would argue.

"Years later I went to college as a freshman at Hamilton College, and my roommate and best friend was Carmen Bufania. No one looked more Italian. His parents were divorced, so I said, 'Why don't you come home and have Thanksgiving with us?' Then I remembered the dinner would be at my grandfather's house in Brooklyn. I said, 'Carmen, I hope it doesn't bother you, but whenever I ask Grandpa how things are, he says, "Ah, the Jews and the guineas are ruining the world."' Carmen said, 'I'm from Newark. Is there going to be a lot of food?'

"Carmen and I arrived, and we sat down, and the Manhattans came out, and Grandpa was in his big chair. My father said to him, 'Well, Dad, how are things?' And Grandpa looked at this swarthy kid sitting next to me, thought for a second, and said, 'Ah, the Jews are ruining the world.' Carmen and I clinked glasses.

"No one ever said to me, 'Don't play with anyone,' but prejudice was in the background. It was also clear that the adults were more prejudiced than the kids.

"My father, who was born in 1906, wasn't a big guy, but he was a good athlete. He grew up in Brooklyn, went to Manual Training High School, where he was on the swimming and basketball teams. He never went to college, never even thought about college. It was not in the language of the family. It was a blue-collar family, and it was not what our people did in the 1940s. After high school, he worked for a company, Conklin Brass & Copper, selling metal products. He began as a stock boy, and he worked himself up until toward the end of the war—there were not many men around—he was promoted to salesman. He worked hard for Conklin, and eventually became a manufacturer's rep selling metal products all around New Jersey.

Peter Meinke's grandparents, Catherine and Harry. *Courtesy of Peter Meinke*

"He met my mother coaching a girls' basketball team in a church league. They were the same age. My mother, who was of Irish descent, went to Erasmus. She was a good student, straight A's. My father didn't read books. My mother won the Latin prize. Back in those days you could become a teacher with a high school education and a few extra courses. She went to Cornell one summer, and became a teacher in the elementary schools in Brooklyn. When she first became a teacher, a girl in class kept staring at her, and when she looked back, this girl removed her eyeball—she had a glass eye—and my mother fainted.

"My mother was a very gifted pianist, and if she had come from a different family, she might have gone on to study music. She could play by ear. She had perfect pitch, which is very rare. She took lessons and became a piano teacher as well. But she could have been a really good pianist.

"My mother's father was a disappointed Irishman, an alcoholic Irishman, who could also sit down at the piano and play without ever having studied it. But he was a postman, and he felt he was undervalued in America, so unlike the Germans, who felt everything was good, he was disappointed in his life and drank and died early, so I didn't know him very well.

"We all went to the Lutheran church, a German kind of church. There was a secular feel in our house. We never prayed. We never said grace. I was never religious, but I never objected to church. The family never talked about religion, and to me it was both social and literary. I liked the stories. They had a big, heavy volume of Bible tales illustrated by Doré, very intricate illustrations, many of them featuring naked ladies, including the picture of the flood where all these naked women were hanging on, and I would pore through this, fascinated. There were also a lot of battle scenes from the Bible. I looked on religion as sensational stories that were scary, violent, and sexy, so I didn't object to religion, because it was kind of interesting.

"We lived at 1851 East 32nd Street, between Avenues R and S, a German-Irish neighborhood. We weren't far from Red Hook, which was a tough Irish section, with a lot of bars. I didn't go there but my father did. We had a lot of German stores, German-Jewish stores also. Ebinger's bakery was where we got our bread. There were Irish bars, bars named Kelly's. There were few Italians. I never heard of pizza. There were no blacks. There were Germans, Irish, English, and Welsh, that kind of mixture.

"I liked living there very much. My neighborhood was a row of brick houses, attached twelve in a row, separated by alleys. You didn't want to have the house at the end of the alley, because the kids liked to play ball against it. Each house had a little stoop in the front and a little, teeny lawn the size of a couple of couches. In the back there were small backyards, with tiny gardens, which during the war we called Victory Gardens. Instead of flowers, we grew Swiss chard, peas, food, and we ate it. We even grew grapes, and we made grape jelly—in Brooklyn.

"I walked to school, PS 122. We had bullies. The bullies were Irish. The Kelly brothers. When I was young I got smallpox, and all of a sudden I was blind, truly blind, so from the time I was five I had to wear thick glasses. I used to break them, because I was embarrassed, and all the time I would walk with them in my hands because the kids would tease me when I wore them. 'Four eyes,' they would taunt. I would get into fights, and they'd break. Eventually I got used to wearing them all the time.

Peter and sister Pat in front of 1851 E. 32nd Street, Brooklyn, in 1938. *Courtesy of Peter Meinke*

"I learned to avoid the Kelly brothers, who were just mean. One time they stole my hat. They tried to get my glasses, but I was kind of speedy. They often would chase me around, but would have to settle for someone slower.

"I was an early reader, and the Kelly brothers were pretty dumb, and one of them couldn't read. One day, for some reason, I read the comics to one of the Kelly brothers, and this eventually gave me a kind of immunity. I was the guy who read the comics to the Kelly brothers. And they would get *great* comics. I remember *Sheena, Queen of the Jungle*. I would read with great animation, and they loved it, and they'd be yelling 'Freakin'-A,' and so when I came home, my mother would say, 'Would you like some potatoes?' I'd say, 'Freakin'-A,' and my father would get up and grab me, and I was truly an ignorant child. I'd say, 'What's wrong with "Freakin'-A"'? I didn't know what it stood for. 'Never say that word again.' How bad could it be? It was what the Kelly brothers always said.

"I remember one incident that had a bearing on our idea of fair play. I knew the Kellys were terrible people, and one day a Kelly brother picked on me a little bit, gave me a shove, and there was this boy, whose name I never knew, an older boy but not much older, fairly big, dressed neatly with a white shirt, curly-haired, and after the Kelly brother shoved me, this kid went over and decked him. I feel tears when I think about it today. As I stood pressed against the wall, all by himself he whacked a couple of them, and after they ran off, he said, 'You okay, kid?' I said, 'Yeah.' Now and then in that school people got their comeuppance.

"I discovered I was reasonably coordinated, and I started playing on teams out in the streets, and fair play really held forth. I joined the Police Athletic League, which organized leagues, softball teams, touch-football teams, and best of all we got free bleacher tickets at Ebbets Field, and we went a lot. I was a great fan. I liked Dolph Camilli, Pete Reiser, who hurt himself running into outfield walls, Pee Wee Reese, and I liked Dixie Walker a lot. We listened to all the games on the radio. I had all these aunts, all of whom lived in Brooklyn, a big Welsh-Irish family, and they all were baseball fans. I loved Red Barber. We also got free tickets for the New York Rovers at Madison Square Garden at night. My dad would take me to the hockey games. [The Rovers played in the Eastern Amateur Hockey League from 1935 to 1952.]

Courtesy of Peter Meinke

"Taking the subway was very exotic, and eventually I learned to do it by myself. I took piano lessons in Bay Ridge, and I learned the Nostrand Avenue trolley and the IRT and others. We went to Coney Island in big groups, and I rode the Cyclone over and over. We used to lie down in the Tunnel, where you went into the park at the entrance, and tumble all over, and we didn't ever want to get out. We ate the hot dogs at Nathan's.

"We would spend a lot of time in Marine Park, roller-skating, playing ball. My dad played handball there. And my dad was getting heavy already. He got fat fairly early on. But he was a good athlete, and every once in a while he would team up with the boxer 'Two Ton' Tony Galento, and when they played doubles, there appeared to be about a thousand pounds of men out there. [Galento gave a famous interview to a reporter before his 1939 bout with Joe Louis at Yankee Stadium, where he claimed he'd 'Moida da bum.' He lost to Louis in four rounds.]

To us little kids the players looked like elephants clashing in the jungle, and they would sweat and yell and tell jokes. Handball was big, but I never liked it. I have smallish hands, and it hurt my hands, and I was better at baseball and other sports.

"For a long time my grandfather had his shack on Sheepshead Bay, and we would go there and have dinner parties. The kids would put bacon or chicken necks on a line, and we'd catch our own crabs, or we'd go out in a rowboat and catch sheepshead, porgies, fluke, flounder, and there were a lot of eels in those days.

"We would also go to Riis Park, over the bridge near where the Naval Air Station [Floyd Bennett Field] was. On the way there was an empty warehouse, a circular building, and my father would see it and he'd say, 'This is where the Gallo brothers and the Mob made hootch and had their headquarters,' and he'd tell me gangster stories. Every once in a while there'd be a gangland slaying, and I think that was one of the reasons my father wanted to get out of Brooklyn. Even though my two closest friends were Eddie Martini and Bobby Pepitone, he associated Italians with the Mob. The Italians were moving closer, and to him they were scary.

"My father would say, 'The neighborhood is getting tough.' He wasn't sure it was a good place to bring up kids. I would argue with him. I didn't feel the neighborhood was scary. I didn't want to leave Brooklyn. I thought it was an exciting place, a rich place for a boy to grow up. So much was happening all the time. Stores were opening. Buildings were being built. The cost of the movies at the Quentin Road theater was 11¢. Sardi's, the restaurant, wasn't expensive. We went on special occasions. I even liked the idea of there being bullies, as long as they were under control. This was grade school, and I liked it. I was good at school without having to do any homework. Even then I wrote little poems. I published an East 32nd Street newspaper, kid stuff, with gossip and my poems, and I printed it out. I dragged my feet whenever my father talked about moving.

"I can't say the war affected me very much. I was interested in it, but not the horror of it. I collected war cards that showed Germans and Japanese cutting babies in half. I looked at maps, and I kept charts of the battles, like the Battle of the Bulge. I didn't get too emotionally involved, because none of our family was in it. In fact, our family prospered during the war. Most of the men were gone, and my dad kept getting promotions, and he was able to save up enough money to buy a house in New Jersey. My mother was teaching school. They were making enough money that we even had a black nanny. It was not unusual in those days for a blue-collar family to have a nanny. She babysat me and my sister. I remember she was nice. I'm sorry to say I have no pictures of her.

Peter Meinke, a professor at Davidson College, 1989. *Courtesy of Peter Meinke*

"The last couple of years I lived in Brooklyn we had a car, and my parents began to go out to New Jersey. I went occasionally to see some trees, some farms, and somewhere along the line they met a friend who had bought a house in Mountain Lakes, and we went out to look at it, and we bought this big stucco house for $10,000. That was 1946, and now it's worth over a million dollars. I can remember my father took me over to James Madison High School, and I would have started there, but during that first week of school, we moved to New Jersey. Instead I went to Mountain Lakes High School. It was so small all the grades were in the same school. I was terribly disappointed."

*But Peter Meinke's dad achieved his purpose, at least in his own mind. In son Peter's class of fifty kids, only one was Italian, Emily Leone, who became one of the school's cheerleaders.*

"She's the only Italian I can remember," said Meinke.

*And though Meinke moved from his Flatlands row house to his large two-story house in New Joisey sixty years ago, it was the little house in Brooklyn that has never ventured far from the poet's mind's eye.*

## THE HOUSE

*Let us say there is an ideal realm*
*Whose spires and minarets send endless light*
*above white avenues of maple, elm,*
*unlighted by the grinding worm of change.*
*Below this, or inside, the real world*
*shifts its shoulders in its struggle*
*to be born, to grow toward possibility.*
*Cities flash and shudder in the sun, whole forests*
*disappear beneath the blade, and everywhere*
*some inchling of a tree is pushing*
*its pale question, some family plants and hammers*
*in the shadow of a slanting roof.*
*In the middle of this second world,*
*near Flatlands Avenue in Brooklyn,*
*my father and my grandfather bought*
*with banging hearts and hesitant hands*
*and minuscule downpayment, a skinny,*
*dark, three-stories house, brick stoop*
*in front, small yard in back;*
*and through its heavy door our vivid aunts*
*and uncles thrust their demanding way*
*in a tumbling stream of family and friends,*
*dogs, cats, parakeets, and turtle. Unlike*
*the condominium of today—now*
*towering in its place—this was a house*
*that could be called a house, passionate*
*and painful, splintered forever in this mix*
*of orbiting atoms, mortar and memory,*
*story, stone, and blood.*

*In the Country of*
**BROOKLYN**

# THE PROTESTANTS BLEND IN

JUSTUS DOENECKE

**M**ANY OF THE EARLIEST GERMANS WHO CAME TO AMERICA went to Philadelphia. They scared the locals sufficiently that in 1729 the Pennsylvania legislature tried to place a duty of five shillings on each foreigner coming to the colony. The governor refused to sign it. The Germans were craftsmen and farmers, but they were reviled by such men as Benjamin Franklin for insisting on speaking German, going to German churches, and reading German newspapers.

In 1845 there was a potato blight in Germany, and there was famine, and after the German states began a revolt in 1848, over 430,000 Germans came to America between 1850 and 1860. Most of them went to the Midwest, where they were shunned for being drinkers who desecrated the Sabbath, for being Catholic, and for speaking German. In 1890 the states of Wisconsin and Illinois passed laws saying kids had to be taught in English.

Although the exodus pretty much stopped by 1895, during World War I the loyalty of all Germans was questioned, and suddenly hamburgers became Salisbury steaks, frankfurters became hot dogs, and German newspapers started publishing in English instead of German.

The non-Jewish Germans, who were mostly conservatives, set up the first kindergartens. "Silent Night" is a German hymn. Santa Claus was a German invention, and so are the Easter bunny and Easter eggs.

During World War I, when Germany became the enemy, President Woodrow Wilson, once the president of Princeton, exploited the country's fears by warning that hidden enemies were undermining the nation. George Creel, who was to Wilson what Karl Rove became to George W. Bush, created a hysteria. "True Americans" started going after German-Americans. Near St. Louis, a German-American defended Germany in an argument. A mob stripped him naked, wrapped him in an American flag, dragged him through the streets, and lynched him.

German American Bund parade. *Library of Congress*

During World War II some fifty thousand German-Americans belonged to the German Bund, an organization sympathetic to the Nazis, but most Germans were loyal to America.

In Brooklyn in the 1950s, Protestants were in the minority, and their presence was further fragmented because of the many denominations that competed for church membership in the borough. In Flatbush alone, within a two-mile radius, there was St. Mark's Methodist Church, Baptist Church of the Redeemer, Flatbush Tomkins Congregational Church, and All Souls Universalist Church. By the 1960s, the German population had pretty much blended in and disappeared along with many of the other Protestant sects in Brooklyn.

Justus Doenicke lived in Flatbush, the son of German immigrants, a group that assimilated into America's mythical melting pot faster than any other ethnic group. He grew up attending the local Baptist church on Cortelyou Road and Ocean Avenue.

His father, a talented estimator in the family's construction business, made a lot of money building Catholic churches in Queens, earning enough to vacation in Europe every summer. A conservative, the father subscribed to the *New York Journal-American,* the most right-wing of New York's daily newspapers, and before the war he even donated a few bucks to the America First organization.

The son, Justus, who grew up with wealth and privilege, went to the Jesuit-based Poly Prep, one of the elite prep schools for well-to-do Brooklyn WASPs. He went to college at Colgate, earned an advanced degree at Princeton, and went on to become a professor at the New College in Sarasota, Florida. His specialty became the study of right-wing organizations—the Liberty League, America First, and the German Bund.

**JUSTUS DOENECKE**  "I was born in the Brooklyn Hospital on March 5, 1938. My grandfather came from a German village near Kassel, called Helmarshausen, around 1870 just before or during the Franco-Prussian War. The village, which was owned by the Hanoverians, is not found on a lot of maps. The family occupation in Germany was *mauer*, which means 'bricklayer,' but it can also mean 'builder.' In Germany his name was David Eustus Dönnaka, and he came over with his brother Arthur. When he came to America, immigration officials changed his name to Justus David, got rid of the umlaut in Dönnaka, and spelled it Doenecke.

"My grandfather and his brother married two sisters, who were born and raised in the United States. My grandmother had no German accent at all. Their name was Kappel. They were called Free Methodists. She went to a finishing school called Roberts Wesleyan Seminary in Rochester.

"I don't know why my grandfather settled in Brooklyn, except that every large American city had a German section. He settled in the old downtown on Bedford Avenue, where he attended the Lutheran church.

"He and his brother may have started in bricklaying, but they were bright enough to organize their own company, Justus C. Doenecke and Sons, at 66 Court Street in Brooklyn. From about 1890 to the 1930s they did quite well. After World War I they hired an employee, Joe Fogerty, who had an in with the Roman Catholic archdiocese. Queens County was beginning to attract massive numbers of ethnics—Italians, Germans, Irish, and various Slavic groups. When an area was developed, it wanted its own Catholic church and Catholic school, and through this Fogerty, my grandfather obtained a lot of contracts for building them.

"My father joined the firm, and his skill was that of estimator. He was the guy who looked at the blueprints and all the books of the subcontractors and their prices and then figured out how much to bid for the job. This was before calculators and computers. He would come home at night, and the dining table would be covered with blueprints and yellow legal pads. He would do the math in his head.

"The company folded up during the Depression. I frankly think they lived too high on the hog. It was my grandfather and his two sons, my father and my uncle Arthur, and during the '20s they were wealthy enough that one of them would be vacationing in Europe while the other two did the business. They took turns that way, and it caught up with them.

"After the family firm folded, my father during World War II worked for the Brooklyn Navy Yard. Then he worked for a company called Pfeifer until 1951, and then he went to work for a construction firm called Gens-Jarboe. The company dissolved around 1964. He had inherited money from his mother, so he just retired.

"My father met my mother when he was in his thirties. My mom's father, Rule Fairly Smith, was the city editor of the *New York World,* which was Pulitzer's paper. He was very much a newspaper man. He grew up in Bangor, Maine, and briefly attended Harvard Law School. I assume he settled in Brooklyn because New York was the center of the newspaper business. He stayed with the *World* until it dissolved about 1931. According to my mother, when Joseph Pulitzer died, the Pulitzer boys bled the paper for all the money they could get out of it, and then sold it to Roy Howard and the *New York Telegram.* My grandfather's wife was Ellen Cyr, who wrote the Cyr primers for children.

"My father went to Dartmouth College for two years. He was class of 1916. His parents encouraged him to drop out to go into their business. His nickname at college was Dutch, meaning Deutsch. If he had a religion, it was Dartmouth. He had an unreal loyalty and expectation about it. He wanted the school to remain the way it was in 1914. When they built the Hopkins Center on the Dartmouth Green, he said, 'That destroys the architecture of the school.'

"My father always hated Roosevelt and the New Deal. That was his politics. He was a LaFollette Progressive who then became very right-wing. His feeling was that labor was too assertive, and he also bitched about taxes. He thought Roosevelt had conspired to get us into World War II and also that he had sold out the country at Yalta. His was the standard right-wing, prototype Birchite line.

"My father gave to America First. He'd send them a dollar for the cause. A dollar in those days is like $10 to $15 today. The committee was organized in the fall of 1940. Between 1940 and the start of World War I he sent them maybe $3. These were a coalition of people who often agreed on little else but the war.

"Its original name was the Emergency Committee to Defend America First, and it was organized to fight the Lend-Lease legislation sponsored by the Roosevelt administration.

"Since Britain was in debt and couldn't pay for arms, Roosevelt wanted to lend them or lease them the arms, and they were supposed to pay us back in kind.

"The argument of the America Firsters was: 'We need this ourselves. We shouldn't be giving it away now. We're on a limb and sawing it off. Britain well could go under and then where are we?'

"The next issue was convoys, because once you give permission for the United States to send tanks and uniforms and airplanes to Britain, how are we going to transport this stuff? The British ships were getting sunk by U-boats. The question became: should the United States convoy this material ourselves? This resulted in quite a heated fight in Congress. It was only voted through about a month before the Japanese attacked Pearl Harbor. Once Pearl Harbor was attacked, America First dissolved in three days. It dissolved for good, and everyone scattered, though the people who supported it in Congress stayed around until the Eightieth Congress, which fought the Truman administration, and on into the early part of the Eisenhower administration.

"Two of our presidents contributed to America First, including Gerald Ford, who was an assistant football coach and law student at Yale, and John Kennedy, who gave $100. He gave it as a surrogate for his father, Joe. When I read the internal correspondence of America First, they all said that Joe Kennedy was a notorious cheapskate; that he was trying to cover his ass with the Roosevelt administration. [Joe Kennedy was the U.S. ambassador to Britain before the war.] They had no respect for him, found him to be an expedient man.

"People tend to forget, because of the liberal nature of the way Brooklyn voted, that within any large city were people who were very, very right-wing. Not too far from us Father Coughlin had support in Brooklyn. If you were a reactionary Catholic, you got the *Brooklyn Tablet,* which was edited by the Scanlon brothers. It represented the Cardinal Spellman wing of the Church.

"We were Protestants. My father was confirmed in the Lutheran church, and my mother was Baptist, and I grew up going to the Baptist church on Cortelyou Road and Ocean Avenue. They were very doctrinal people. My father'd say, 'If you lead a good life, you'll go to heaven.' In fact, the old man Doenecke, my uncle, just before he died, was asked, 'Have you made your peace with God?' He said, 'I have come to believe in nothing.' But these were not deep people. It's not like they were mulling over this stuff.

"My father got his news mainly from the most right-wing of New York papers, the *Journal-American,* which had two columnists he absolutely worshipped. One was Westbrook Pegler and the other was George Sokolsky, and he thought those two men were great sages. He would quote them like scripture. When people would say to me, 'What newspaper do you get?' I was embarrassed. My mother would say, 'Always tell them it's for Pegler.'

"We Protestants were very much in the minority. One day each spring there was a parade called the Anniversary Day Parade, which was to celebrate Sunday school in the Protestant churches. If it weren't for the Jews in the scout troops—the Cub Scouts and the Boy Scouts had a lot of Jews—you wouldn't have had much of a parade. And the longer I lived there, the numbers got smaller and smaller.

"We lived on Ocean and Caton Avenues in Flatbush. We were right near the Parade Grounds, which was an extension of Prospect Park. As a kid, I played the usual games, stickball and stoopball. We collected bubblegum cards, and we went to the movies a lot. We had seven different movie theaters within walking distance. We went to the RKO Kenmore the most, but also Loews Kings, and the Astor, which had foreign films or films that were coming back after being out of circulation two or three years. If we ever missed a movie, my mother would say, 'We'll see it when it comes back to the Astor.'

"As a kid I always rooted for the Dodgers. That was tribal. I enjoyed going to Ebbets Field. I found watching the fans interesting. To go to the games was being part of an amateur sociology class. There were a lot of drunks, and yelling all the time.

"I remember when Jackie Robinson came up, my parents didn't care at all. It was fine with them. Their attitude was somewhere between 'It's not nice' to not giving a damn. They never went to a single game in their lives. They ignored sports.

"I remember Robinson. He was fast and a little heavy. He gave the impression of being strong with all the weight he was carrying. We took them all for granted. I knew who they were and what they were doing.

"My mother knew Kate O'Malley, the wife of the owner of the Dodgers. There was a garden club in Flatbush, and Mrs. O'Malley was active in it. She evidently had lost her vocal chords and had trouble speaking. She would talk in a whisper. She was a great gardener. Mrs. O'Malley loved orchids. She offered my mother tickets to go to the games, but my mother had absolutely no interest. I would have had to explain baseball to her to get her to go. As I said, my father never went to a game in his life.

"I would denounce O'Malley because he moved the Dodgers to California, but my mother would defend her friend. 'Kate O'Malley is such a lovely woman.'

"Sometimes we'd go to New York. I remember going to Madison Square Garden to watch Clair Bee and LIU and their great star, Sherman White. They all got nailed in a basketball scandal in 1951, which made a lot of headlines. They weren't throwing games. They were manipulating point spreads. A lot of local schools were involved.

"What I remember most about Flatbush was the lack of grass. It was apartment buildings. We were basically cliff-dwellers. You look out the window, and there was nothing but sidewalks for blocks upon blocks. I didn't have the youth a lot of suburban kids did, because of that. I wasn't out mowing the lawn or having a cookout or getting your license when you were sixteen. You didn't ride bicycles in the neighborhood. In a way you were more sophisticated and streetwise, but in a way you had your own provincialism and naivete.

"We lived across the street from the Church Avenue station on the BMT Brighton line, called the D train. My father worked in Manhattan, so he'd take the subway every day, and he'd get up very early in the morning to beat the crowd so he could get a seat.

"The area was predominantly Jewish with maybe 40 percent a general mix of gentiles. No blacks at all. The Irish kept themselves separated. They would go to the Catholic schools.

"The only reason I knew any Irish kids was that for two summers I went to camp in Friendship, Maine, owned by a man by the name of John Duda. During the year he ran a Boys Club, and he would take us out to Prospect Park, and most of my friends from that club were either from St. Xavier parish or from St. Angelo Hall school.

"For my elementary education I went to Berkeley Institute on Lincoln Place near Grand Army Plaza, about three blocks from my home. It was a girls' school but it took boys up to the sixth grade.

"Beginning in the seventh grade, I went to a school called Poly Prep. Broadly speaking, it's in Bay Ridge, overlooking the Narrows. It was a country day school, very much college preparatory. It was ethnically half-Jewish, half-gentile. About 20 to 30 percent of the gentiles were Anglos, but you had Italians, Syrians, Scandinavians, and Greeks, some of the dominant ethnic groups of Bay Ridge.

"The Protestants and the Catholics very much had a parallel system. Those upper-class Christians who were Protestants went to Poly Prep, and those Christians who were Roman Catholic would go to Brooklyn Prep, which was Jesuit, and it was a feeder school for Jesuit colleges. Very seldom did someone from Brooklyn Prep go to a secular college. It was a straight route from primary school through to a Catholic university. Holy Cross was the big one. Holy Cross was almost an alumni group for Brooklyn Prep and for Loyola School in Manhattan. Also Fordham. Not so much Georgetown, which at the time was a play school for Latin American rich kids.

"If you went to a more Diocesan college, you'd go to St. John's or St. Francis. These were run in office buildings. These colleges supplied a lot of lower-echelon white-collar people, civil servants—that layer of society. If you wanted a profession or an upper-echelon business, you'd go to Holy Cross, Fordham, or Georgetown.

"Daniel Kelly, my best friend growing up, went to Brooklyn Prep. Kelly wanted to go to Yale, and they wanted him to go to Holy Cross. The brothers of Brooklyn

Prep told him, 'We're not going to write you a recommendation. You're going on your own.'

"He said, 'The heck with you people. I'm going to Yale if I can get in.' And he went. That was bucking the system.

"When I attended my cousin's graduation from Loyola School in Manhattan, the priest who gave the commencement address was Father Arthur McRatty. He shook my hand in the reception line. I was obviously a college student, and he asked me where I was going to college.

"'I go to Colgate,' I said.

"He said, 'You're one of those who couldn't get into Holy Cross or Georgetown.'

"It was a really diplomatic remark. People talk about the good old days, the world of our fathers. This is the world of our fathers.

"Poly Prep was a rather small school, about 450 students in all. It was quite competitive athletically within a league that involved St. Paul's School on Long Island; Adelphi Academy; Riverdale, up in the Bronx; Horace Mann School; and a school called Trinity. They pretentiously called themselves 'the Ivy League.'

"At Poly Prep you were either a brain or a jock, and I was neither, though I got through life all right. You were expected to be extremely able in one of those categories. I was always in the second quarter of my class, and my senior year I lettered in track.

"We had some well-known alumni. Arthur Levitt, the head of the stock exchange, went to Poly Prep. His father was comptroller of the city. There is a very successful Wall Street lawyer named Daniel Pollack. He takes on a lot of heavy cases that are argued before the Supreme Court. Myles Behrens is an excellent eye doctor and surgeon and medical scholar. And Kenneth Duberstein was with the Reagan entourage. He was several years behind me. Also James Fluge, who's been for several years the assistant to Teddy Kennedy.

"What was remarkable was the tremendous assimilation among the Germans. It started in the twenty years between World War I and II. Once there were several German-language newspapers in New York, but after World War I, there were pressures to enforce assimilation and to avoid using German in conversation. There was a curbing of the teaching of the German language.

"By World War II only one German paper, the *Staats-Zeitung,* remained. It was owned by the Ridder family. The company later became Knight-Ridder. The paper was becoming minuscule. Very few people—mainly the lower middle class—read it. By the start of World War II, there was no German community. It had folded up. Intermarriage really took hold by the second generation. I don't think one of my father's cousins or brothers married another German-American. The thing pretty much dissolved as far as ethnic identity. We didn't go to Yorkville [Manhattan's Upper East Side]. My father never went to Luchow's [an old-time German restaurant on 14th Street near Union Square that hung on until 1982]. I didn't know any German at all until I had to take doctoral qualifying exams when I went to graduate school.

"When I started at Poly Prep in 1950, German was one of the four languages taught. It was French, Latin, Spanish, and German. You take Spanish because it's easy. You take French because there's a culture. You take Latin because you had to take it in the eighth grade, and you said, 'Hell, I might as well continue with it.' And that's why you took those languages. It wasn't ethnic identity or any deep choices of any kind. We didn't give a whole lot of thought to any of this. Within three years the German was dropped, never to be recovered, and the German teacher ended up teaching biology. There was a lack of interest.

"In the beginning Flatbush was really farmland, and when it started being developed, houses came, and the houses were replaced by apartments, and you had all these Protestant denominations, each setting up its own church. Within two square miles you had Episcopal, Lutheran, Christian Science, Methodist, and Presbyterian.

"By the 1950s a lot of these parishes couldn't support themselves. They didn't have enough money or enough old people to keep things going, when any logical planner would say, 'You have to merge these congregations into one large one.' And they could have done that. The major Protestant ones, who wouldn't have argued too much over doctrine—Methodist, Presbyterian, Congregationalist, Disciples of Christ—could have federated, though the Baptists would not have joined any other and the Episcopalians would have remained apart. They were sacramentally oriented and saw themselves as Catholic as well as Protestant. It would have defied canon law for the Episcopalians to federate. But the others—if you wanted a church as healthy as one of the major synagogues, or the Roman Catholic Church, they should have gotten together.

"They actually did that in the summer to give the ministers a vacation. Five or six of these churches would join together and meet one week at St. Mark's Methodist this Sunday, and next Sunday at Baptist Church of the Redeemer, and the next Sunday at the Flatbush Tomkins Congregational Church, All Souls Universalist. If they were able to do it for the summer, they could have done it for good. But they didn't.

"When I went back to Brooklyn about five years ago, they all had become black churches. The Baptist church I went to is Haitian now. I could tell because the service was in French. I also found some of the movie theaters had become black gospel temples.

"My neighborhood turned black between 1960 and 1970. The whites went to the suburbs. Long Island was the logical place, or New Jersey. Whether the whites left first or whether the blacks moved in first depended on the area. Maybe on the block.

Justus Doenecke today. *Courtesy of Justus Doenecke*

"When I was a boy, the merchants along Flatbush Avenue, the main commercial street, were 70 percent Jewish. By 1970 I would ride down the street and notice that they had been replaced by Asians. Except for a few elderly people, the Jews were gone."

# MUSLIM IMMIGRANTS

DAVE RADENS

The Jewish immigrants from eastern Europe who settled in Brooklyn in great numbers were most influential in the early part of the 1950s. But Jews were not the only immigrants who came from Eastern Europe at the turn of the twentieth century.

Dave Radens, who grew up in mostly Jewish Williamsburg, was the son of Muslim immigrants, although in those days the spelling used was Moslem. His father, whose given name was Radlinsky, was a Lithuanian Tartar in the fur trade, who, as a teen, walked east from Vilna across Russia and China, then got on a ship and crossed the Pacific Ocean to the New World, settling first in Ontario, Canada, and then in Brooklyn, where he helped make mink coats and helped organize the Fur and Leather Workers Union.

As a teenager, Radens developed a keen interest in the printing business. When his dad forbade him to go to college to study it and ordered him to get a job, the boy, with the help of a friend's father, ran away from home and enrolled at the Rochester Institute of Technology. After fighting in Korea, he returned to RIT, where he completed his BA and met his wife, Margaret, a Jew. When his mother refused to consent to the marriage, the couple defied her. His mother boycotted the wedding and cut him out of her life as though he had died. She is still alive, and it is going on forty-eight years that they have not seen each other. She has never seen his grown children.

**DAVE RADENS**   "My father was the first generation to come over to this country. He was born in Vilna, Lithuania. The border of that country was like a rubber band. Sometimes it was Russia, sometimes it was Lithuania, and at one time it was even Poland.

"I was raised in the Moslem church. In the early days the Moslems took great chunks of Europe. We were descendants of the Tartars. You talk about persecution. All the male members of my father's family, except my father, had their trigger fingers chopped off. Members of the family began fleeing to America, settling in Brooklyn, and in the late 1800s his father arranged for him to escape, and he and six or eight others headed east, largely walking across Asia. At one point, they were in a Mongolian village, and they were surrounded, and the Chinese took all the males and inducted them into the army. My father served in the Chinese army for a while, and he was one of two who snuck off in the dark of night, and the route they took from there got all muddy and confused, but he lost track of the other and never saw him again. He eventually wound up in Ontario, Canada, where he was hired to work in a coal mine in the town of Timmons.

Dave Radens on a pony, 1941.
*Courtesy of Dave Radens*

"While he was in Canada, he contacted the imam of the Lithuanian mosque in Brooklyn, and he made the trip down. When he arrived, the families thought he was a gold miner—they had misunderstood him when he said he was *coal* miner, and the legend was that he was pictured as a very wealthy man, and so the elders paraded their daughters in front of him, and he was attracted to my mother, and when his visa was up he returned to Canada. He communicated with my mother's family, and a marriage was arranged. Dad came down, and they got married in Brooklyn, and he took her back to Canada. I was conceived in 1935, and my grandmother wanted me born stateside, so in her eighth month my mother got on the train, came to the States, and I was born in Kings County Hospital, and as soon as I was able to travel I went back to Canada.

"We stayed until I was four, and we returned when my father wanted to return to his relatives. One of the Mos (we called Moslems 'Mos') had a decent job in a dairy, and offered my dad a job pasteurizing milk. The rest of my father's relatives in Brooklyn were dirt farmers, very poor. Other members of this Mo community were in the fur industry, and my dad's family was highly regarded in that field. Dad's family were skilled craftspeople—tanners of minks. He was what they called a flesher, and that meant removing the meat from the hides. It was considered a skilled position in that industry. Between fleshing and the actual tanning of the animals, there was a chemical process that removed the skin, and he knew the secret of the formula that had been passed down from generation to generation. Dad did it, his father did it, and his father's father did it, and so did my younger brother.

"When he did his work, he put up a curtain so no one could watch him, and part of the secret was to dump half the chemicals, because they weren't part of the process but part of keeping the thing a secret. There were other formulas, but not one was ever able to produce as fine a mink as his formula.

"My father was involved with the founding of the Fur and Leather Workers Union, which at first was part of the Meat Packers Union. In the process scabs were brought in, and they would bust up union meetings with baseball bats and lead pipes, and my dad would come home with his head all bandaged up. There were a lot of beat-up heads. The goons would come in and break up union-organizing meetings, and there'd be bloodshed, frequently and regularly.

"The stories I heard were pretty brutal. There was a large population of Lithuanians down around Coney Island, and they were hired to bust the union. My dad would try meeting with them, and my mother was petrified. I remember her being in a frenetic state. I can remember ten men with their right hands cut off by the union busters. If you don't have a hand, you can't work. My mother wondered, *Are they going to get him? Is he going to lose his hand?* But he had the secret to the formula, and they wanted it—they also knew if they cleaved him, they would never get it. They tried bribing him to get it—but he didn't give in because he knew the fur-and-leather guys depended on him heavily.

"His union activity led to his becoming a member of the Communist Party, which represented the working people. Back then they were still arguing about the forty-hour workweek. They were talking about social security, all the things my dad thought were right and proper. When my mother's brothers got wind of this, they didn't like it. They called him 'that damn Lithuanian.' Even though they were all Lithuanians. They thought my dad was some kind of Commie, not American. They felt it was un-American.

"It was a knee-jerk reaction, but deeply, strongly felt. They were the ones who were going to benefit from my dad's union activity, but the owners kept telling them that the result would be that they were going to lose their jobs.

"We built up the union, and it was strong until the 1950s, when the Puerto Ricans got in big-time and spearheaded a movement that the old guard felt was a sellout. Because they had no jobs, they were willing to settle for less. They wouldn't go out on strike. They wouldn't support the union, and eventually the union was virtually dissolved. They sold out. They were bought out. And in the 1960s my dad's formulas were duplicated in China, and it was all downhill from there. My dad retired in the 1970s, and he was in his nineties when he died.

"What I remember about Williamsburg were all the shuls. A shul is a small chapel, smaller than a synagogue. There were tiny shuls in storefronts. There'd be three shuls on a block, and each had differences with the others.

"There were a lot of Hasidim in our part of Williamsburg. They wore skullcaps and talliths and they had curly hair and beards. My grandmother, who lived a walk from where we lived, made dear friends with them. I knew all those kids. We were good friends.

"Yiddish was the dominant language. My grandmother even spoke Yiddish. That's what was spoken in the stores. Where else were we going to shop? Where do we buy our chicken, and butter, and groceries? So she learned Yiddish in Williamsburg. My wife's family is Jewish from Westchester, and they didn't know Yiddish. When they heard this Moslem woman speaking Yiddish, they were blown away.

"What the Hasidim couldn't understand was how we got so close with the mafioso. They were different, and so they had nothing to do with them, and the Italians had nothing to do with the Hasidim. Our involvement was largely due to sheer accident. Our neighborhood was chopped up into blocks. From Marcy Avenue to Union Avenue, Graham Avenue, Manhattan Avenue, was Yiddish. East of there, toward Flatbush, was Italian Catholic. St. Catherine's Cathedral was huge. The building we lived in was owned by a goombah, a man named Provatera, the local godfather. He owned several buildings, several factories, the local Cadillac dealership, the local pool hall, owned a lot of stuff.

"He would send his nephew Frank, who looked like one of the mobsters from an Al Pacino movie, to collect the rent. He had a thick Italian accent. One day my father discovered a pair of legs sticking out from under the bushes, and there was Frankie Provatera, lying with his eye slashed. A rival gang had attacked him. My dad took him to the hospital, and that put us in real good stead. They were forever grateful. Frank's son Dominick and I became close friends, and I would dip into the goombah's wine cellar and get smashed.

"I was golden. I would eat at their home. There were seven-course meals seven nights a week. I mean feasts. They served every kind of fowl—partridge, hen, duck, chicken—steaks like you couldn't believe, pastas, a full seven-course meal—soup, salad, dessert—every night.

"Lena, the *goombah*'s nephew's wife, and her daughter, Gracie, did all the cooking. Gracie was allowed to go to the movies with my mother Wednesday nights and collect dishes. In those days just before the war it was two for a nickel to get into the movies, and you'd get a free dish. Gracie was joyous that her mother would let her go to the movies with my mother and bring home those dishes.

"I had to walk through that very heavy mafioso neighborhood to get to Junior High School 49. When the Hasidim kids walked there, the Italian kids would beat them up. I didn't carry a zip knife, but I did carry knuckles. You ripped the handle off a certain kind of garbage can, and they made perfect metal knuckles, and I would hide the knuckles under the front stoop. There was a special brick that would come out of the wall of the stoop cellar, and I would hide my knuckles there. Any time I left the house, the first thing I did was to go under the stoop and get out my knuckles. And I used them. You had to. I was part of a small group of boys who were always together. There was Sam Setzer, who was Jewish; myself, the Mo; Billy Hasstler, who was Protestant; Tony Virella, who was Italian Catholic; and another kid, named Phil. We were together constantly, liked each other, got along real well. We were tall, physically large, and no one would mess with us.

"The six of us played a lot of handball at a housing project in a public park nearby. They had handball walls, and the six of us were good to the point where the local bookies would come by on Sunday afternoons, and we would draw straws from the parkie's broom to see how we'd be broken up into teams, and the bookies would set the odds, and they'd bet *big* money, $100 a game, on the outcome. They'd supply us with pizza and soda. It was great fun. Other kids tried to get into the games, but the bookies would decide who would play and who they would back.

"We lived a full life, even though we didn't have much money. When my dad first came to Brooklyn, he was bringing in $5 a week. We were poor. We lived a roller-skate away from Ebbets Field, but I never saw a game. It was 50¢ to sit in the bleachers, and I couldn't afford it. I would roller-skate to Ebbets Field with a lot of other kids, and we'd stand outside the outfield fence and wait for a baseball to be hit over, and that we would fight for.

"That didn't stop us from rooting for the Dodgers. When Jackie Robinson joined the team in 1947, he was adored. There were no black people in our community, zero, none, but everyone rooted for the black heroes. Joe Louis was a great hero. When he fought, it was on the radio, and everybody listened. You didn't have to be in your own apartment. It reverberated through the building. And when Robinson played, you could hear it on the radio. Everybody was tuned to it.

"They rooted for Louis and Robinson because they were underdogs, and they considered themselves underdogs.

"The movies, as I said, were two for a nickel. Some kids got 2¢, and some kids got 3¢, and the kids with 2¢ would line up against the wall, and the kids with 3¢ would come strutting by and flick a finger at you, and you'd go in with that guy. Except for the six of us—we went to the movies together.

"When we could get the 2¢ or 3¢, we'd start off at ten in the morning, and there were serials—*Captain Marvel, Captain Midnight, Zorro,* and *Gene Autry.* You'd be there four or five hours continuously.

"On Friday nights we went to services at the mosque, which was on Powell Street, right around the corner from Metropolitan Avenue, on the border of Flatbush and Greenpoint. My mother and father weren't really all that religious. Well, yes and no. Except for my father, who was president of the church society, these were illiterate people. During Friday night services the people could sing songs from the Koran because they trained themselves to recognize symbols in the book, but they didn't know what it meant. It was Arabic, and these people didn't speak Arabic. They spoke Lithuanian. We would sing these songs, and I would ask my dad, 'What does this mean?' He could read Lithuanian and English, but not Arabic, and he asked me if I really wanted to know. I said, 'Yeah, I'm curious.' And he took it upon himself to go to the United Nations and he hunted around and found an Egyptian who was totally fascinated by this Tartar/Mongol/Lithuanian/Moslem sect, and he came and taught us Arabic at Friday-night school.

"And what we discovered was that this group, which had no idea what they were reading, had been using as a wedding ceremony a sultan talking about monitoring horse trades. What they were using as a funeral service, one of the most revered services of any faith, was the sultan admonishing his people to grow watermelons.

"When word got out, my dad was in trouble. Ooh, he was in big trouble with the church elders. They were ready to throw him out, but the kids said, 'We wanted to know, and now we know. We don't have to change it. As long as we feel the same about the music, that's all that matters.'

"For a while there was a panic, but it eventually subsided, and things went on as before. They kept the same songs.

"I was a top student. My mother made certain of that, though in fact and in deed, there was an element of cruelty in it. One time I brought home a C in penmanship on my report card, and that was not acceptable, and she took a cast-iron skillet and beat the daylights out of me, and I was hospitalized several times as a kid. I skipped grades twice, and I started college at sixteen. At the time, the educational system was such that there were so many totally illiterate kids who had to learn English as a second language that if you knew your ABCs, you were practically skipped. So it was not that big a deal.

"When it came time for me to go to high school, I wanted to go to Boys High, which was an academic high school, but my father wouldn't hear of it. After school I worked in the corner print shop as a delivery boy and as a printer's devil—I would distribute type, which was hand-set. And you would have to put the type back in the cases. I got interested in it, and so I went to the New York School of Printing [now known as the High School of Graphic Communication Arts] in Manhattan, right around the corner from Macy's. One of my teachers took an interest in me and said I could go further, and he introduced me to the idea of the Rochester Institute of Technology, one of two colleges—Carnegie Tech was the other one—that specialized in printing-plant management.

Dave's parents, brother, and sister. *Courtesy of Dave Radens*

"When I told my father about RIT, he said, 'No way. You get a job.' I said, 'I think I can make it in college and build a career.' He wouldn't hear of it.

"I had another friend, Vinny Costello, whose father was a longshoreman. Vinny's dad would get us work chits. Most people had to give a percentage of their pay to get them. But Vinny and his father knew I was trying to save enough money to run away and go to college, so he gave me the chits and countersigned a secret savings account for me. I saved up about $3,000 for tuition and living expenses, and I went off to college. My parents were beside themselves.

"I went to school full-time days and worked full-time nights, and I loved it. I slept two hours a night. I was doing it my way, and it was wonderful. I loved every minute of it. But after two years I got a bit tired, and after earning my associate's degree, I volunteered for the draft. I went down to the draft board, and they said, 'Sorry, we met our quota. We can't take you.' And guess what happened? The Korean

War broke out. I went back to the draft board and said, 'Let me out.' This time they said, 'No can do. We got your name. We got your number.' After meeting their quota three more times, they finally got me, and I went to Korea in the fall of 1950.

"They made me a medic because I was big and strong, and I could carry the equipment. As a medic, you were supposed to wear the cross on your helmet and on your arm, and you were not supposed to carry a weapon. Even so, I killed more people than you know the first names of.

"The weapon in Korea was the M-1 rifle, a big, heavy, cannon-like rifle that could shoot a thousand yards accurately. Which was totally useless in Korea. When the hordes came over the hilltops, you wanted an automatic weapon. You didn't want to aim. You wanted to spray. And because I was a medic, in charge of bandaging their asses, the outfits I was attached to made sure I had an automatic weapon. To be sure, they wanted to keep me alive.

"It was something, to see the hordes come charging over a hill at you. Some of them didn't even carry a stick. They would try to overrun you and slit throats and stab you and beat you up. Our guys were very demoralized. It was wicked.

"The soldiers would get off the ships at the big landing base at Inchon. And talk about cold. That place was cold. Civilians would be throwing rocks at us. Not because they hated us; because they were jealous. We had socks, and we had food, and they had nothing.

"One afternoon our troops were out on a mine-clearing detail, and every time they went, a medic had to go along. The kid next to me stepped on a mine, blew off one of his legs, and I got it tied off, got him on a chopper, evacuated him, and the next thing I knew, I woke up in the hospital with a cast from my armpit to my knee. And I had no left knee. I was hit by the shrapnel that hit him. And I didn't even know it. Fear and adrenaline make you tough.

"Later I watched the movie and television show *M*A*S*H*. That was a mockery. They made the Korean War out to be a Sunday-afternoon tea party. It was sacrilege. A lot of guys died, and those guys on TV basically were having a party.

"The strangest group I was ever exposed to was the Greek troops in Korea. They were insane. Those guys were notorious. In the middle of it all, there was a Greek celebration, the equivalent of the French Bastille Day. They had roast pigs on spits and a bottle of ouzo for every person who was invited. You drank and sang and danced until you fell. This was a whole brigade, and they arranged with the Turks to guard their perimeter so they could have this party.

"The Greeks and the Turks were enemies, but not in Korea. It was insanity. People are crazy. We still are. When the hell are we ever going to learn? Advance of progress? We just learn to kill more people in a single stroke. It peeves me still, and I grit my teeth. We know more about the other side of the planet Mars than we do about what happens in our own country. People are starving here, and we're putting rocks from the moon in our laboratories. What craziness. How are historians going to write about this?

Dave in uniform. *Courtesy of Dave Radens*

"'Cause the Korean War was the most misunderstood war. We hear a whole lot about the Vietnam War. Well, the Korean War was even crazier. We didn't know what the hell we were doing there, or why we were there. We knew these were hungry, starving people who would slit your throat for a pair of socks. We knew it and felt it and didn't want to be there. But we didn't know enough to rebel. Civil disobedience wasn't fashionable until Vietnam.

"Three times I got busted from corporal down to private. Because I was a medic, I had two guys from the Korean military—what they called KATUSA, which was an acronym for Korean Attached to the U.S. Army—basically they were litter-bearers. These two guys would tell me horror stories. These people were so destitute and primitive. The way they heated their houses, they would dig a shaft under the house and would feed weeds into a fire at the bottom of the shaft, and the smoke would come up in the cottage, and the wind would blow hot ashes up into the thatched roves and set the whole village on fire. Women and children burned literally to a crisp. There was also a lot of sickness among the populace. The KATUSAs asked me if I could help their people. Sure, why not?

"I would get penicillin by the truckload, a-deuce-and-a-half-ton loads, and I distributed it as best as I could to the sick civilians. Well, the IG got wind of this and examined and explored and talked to countless people and discovered I was not selling it. If I had been selling it, I'd still be in jail. But he found I was giving it away to the natives, and he called me into his office.

Dave and his wife in mid-1960s.
*Courtesy of Dave Radens*

"There were three levels of court-martial. The lowest level was to be busted to private and given a pass, a little leave, a vacation. I got this three times.

"The second time I was called to a scene where a half-ton truck filled with troops was hit by mortar, and a lieutenant colonel was ordering his men to load up the injured into jeeps—and by moving them, he was killing them.

"I yelled out, 'Don't touch them. Keep your hands off them. You're not helping them. You're killing them.' The lieutenant colonel was embarrassed, and he said I didn't follow military procedure and I wasn't courteous. But when the adrenaline starts to flow, you don't know what you're doing or saying. So I got called in front of the inspector general again, and he said, 'Private Radens? Another pass back to the trenches.' The whole scene was nuts.

"Then came New Year's Eve of 1952. The army would only guarantee your health for eighteen months, and I was in month fifteen, and the way it worked for clap, if you got clap three times, it was an automatic bust. And I was supposed to write up any officer who came in with the clap. Well, if an officer came into my hooch with a bottle of whiskey tucked into his trousers, I'd give him the penicillin—again, I didn't sell it—and I wouldn't report him. I put together a hoard of about sixty quarts of whiskey, and I had me a New Year's Eve party. I invited everyone I knew, and we had us a party, I want to tell you. Everything was on the up and up. Anyone assigned to guard duty took his shift. Human lives were at stake, and we knew that. And we got smashed. And word got out, and I again went before the colonel—the same guy—and I was made private again and got my pass and went off, and that was that. I once again was promoted to corporal, and I got out of the army in 1952.

"I had received a Purple Heart for bravery, and on the ship on the way home I threw it overboard. We all threw our medals overboard. Big batches of us got up on deck. The prize emblem for an infantryman is his rifle on a blue shield, about half an inch high and three inches long. If it's on a white shield, it means you never saw combat. But we had combat infantryman badges and Purple Hearts and whatever else we had, and we threw them overboard. Some of the men on the ship snickered and called us Commies and Pinkos, but all I could think was, *Poor bastards, they don't know any better.*

Dave and his wife today. *Courtesy of Dave Radens*

"After I came home, I returned to the Rochester Institute of Technology, and I earned my bachelor's degree. I also met Marge, and we decided to get married. She was Jewish, from Westchester, and by that time my parents had moved to the Brighton Beach area in Coney Island.

"I phoned my mother, and told her we were coming to visit. My dad insisted we be guests in their house. My home was more kosher than Marge's house, and it was the first and only time my mother served pork chops.

"She did it to give offense. I was totally surprised, and I laughed. It was so petty and beside the point. I knew my dad wasn't aware of what she was doing. I felt hurt for him. But my mother refused to go to our wedding, and I never saw her again. My father would come to visit us in Riverdale under the guise of going to union meetings. Once I even smuggled him off when we lived in New Hampshire, under the guise of going to a weekend union meeting. Even my grandmother, my mother's mother, would come to visit. But I had defied my mother, and this was above and beyond. My mother saw herself as the keeper of the faith of Islam, and I was marrying a Jew. To show you the extent of my mother's alienation, I was not allowed to go to my father's funeral. Or my grandmother's. My mother doesn't know my children. My sister came of age and was quite talented musically. She got a scholarship to Juilliard. My mother was dead-set against that. I cooked up a deal with my father where my sister left home and came and lived with Marge and me and went to Juilliard. And she eventually wound up with the Moonies."

# GROWING UP GREEK IN RED HOOK

PETER SPANAKOS

THERE WAS NO CENTRAL GREEK COMMUNITY IN BROOKLYN IN the 1950s. Most of the Greeks who came to New York City were drawn to the Chelsea section of Manhattan, from West 20th Street up to the 40s, or to the Astoria section of Queens. Petros Spanakos and his twin brother, Nikos, were Brooklynites most of their lives because their father, who emigrated from rural Sparta in 1914, opened a restaurant in Red Hook, a hardscrabble, rundown area of Brooklyn that could have been right out of the movie *On the Waterfront*.

The village of Roode Hoek was settled by the Dutch in 1636. It is named for the red clay soil and because it's a point of land that projects into the East River. (*Hoek* means "point," not the English "hook.") The subway doesn't go to Red Hook. And when master builder Robert Moses built the Brooklyn-Queens Expressway and Gowanus Expressway, it effectively cut off the neighborhood from the rest of Brooklyn. To get there you have to take a bus or drive a car. A home to fishermen and longshoremen, Red Hook was always a tough, tough neighborhood.

The Spanakos twins, who were small at about five foot four, one hundred pounds, learned to survive on the mean streets of Red Hook by becoming talented street fighters. Spartan mothers who sent their sons into battle had a saying, "Come back with your shield or on it." The Spanakos twins were small, but ferocious in battle.

In 1952 they began their formal training in the New York City Parks Department gym in Red Hook. They then moved to the PAL 76th Precinct gym. Their goal was to fight in the 1956 Olympics. Despite the threat from muggers, they would get up at five thirty in the morning to run around the equestrian paths of Prospect Park.

Peter won his first Golden Gloves competition in 1955. That was also the year the Dodgers finally won the World Series.

"Nick and I were in the papers, on TV, and the newsreels, and it was very exciting," said Spanakos. "That summer I knew the Dodgers were winning, and when they won the World Series, people were drinking, and cars were honking, and I said to my mother, 'What the hell happened?'

"She said, 'The Brooklyn Dodgers won.'

"I said, 'Won what?' I didn't realize all the involvement."

Between 1955 and 1964 Peter was undefeated in Golden Gloves competition, winning ten titles from New York City to Seattle. (Nick won seven titles.) During his reign, Peter became a ring favorite of a neighbor, gangster "Crazy Joe" Gallo. Through his boxing, Spanakos got to know many of the Mafia kingpins, including Sammy (the Bull) Gravano, a hit man whose testimony sent John Gotti to jail.

Peter and Nick were talented enough to try out for the 1960 United States Olympic boxing team. Nick, who fought at 126 pounds, made it. Peter, who boxed at 118 pounds, was one fight away from going to Rome. Though he was way ahead on points, the fight was stopped because of a head cut.

That year, during tryouts for the Pan American Games, he roomed with a sixteen-year-old heavyweight boxer from Louisville, Kentucky, by the name of Cassius Clay. According to Spanakos, even though Clay announced to all he was the GOAT—the "greatest of all time"— Clay was "the last boxer on the team anyone would have picked for stardom."

Spanakos went on to Brooklyn Law School, where one of his professors was Senator Joe McCarthy's assistant Roy Cohn. Hating the law profession, Spanakos chose a career in education. After graduation, Spanakos taught in some of the toughest schools in Brooklyn.

**PETER SPANAKOS**  "My father and mother came from Mani, which is Sparta in Greece. Their part of Greece was rural. The land wasn't arable, so they had to travel.

They were merchants, and there were pirates who were basically illiterate killers. The Greeks were persecuted by the Turks. Of course there was poverty. If you were middle-income, why would you leave to go to the boondocks of America?

"In Greece they had famine, and combining that with persecution and poverty, my dad came over at sixteen in 1914. Like most Greeks, he settled in Chelsea in Manhattan, and took a job as a baker working for German people. Most Greeks who came to New York wound up making chocolate, making cigarettes, or working in flower shops and restaurants. My father got a job working as a busboy and waiter in a restaurant.

"They were Laconians, and my father was very Spartan, with its history of being a culture of warriors and men of honor. In their day, in Greece, there were honor killings and vendettas, and it continued when they came to America. If someone hurt your sister or family, you had to do the right thing.

"My father never spoke about these things, but relatives said he was an honorable man who did honorable things. My father was not someone you fooled around with.

"Greeks love to gamble, and before he married my mother, my father got into gambling, was very good at it, and he ran a gambling game in Manhattan. In the 1920s he had a big house on 28th Street called Greek Town USA. He made quite a bit of money. He had a Packard—the Cadillac of its day—and a chauffeur. At one point he was very wealthy. You didn't fool around with my father. You paid your debts. He was very strict about people keeping their word. His whole contract was a handshake. And God help you if you broke your handshake. He carried this code with him his whole life.

"When my father met my mother, he knew she was from his part of Greece, and that appealed to him, because they were very parochial, and your part of Greece had the best women, the best men. But he wasn't allowed to date her.

"My mother told her mother, 'This man is coming. I don't know him, but he sounds interesting.' My grandmother didn't like him, but she didn't know why she didn't like him. She showed her strong disapproval when she touched her tongue to the roof of her mouth. She had 'heard something' but she didn't know what she heard.

"'I like him,' my mother said. Every day she kept on her mother for about a week, and when my mother wouldn't bow, my grandmother said, 'You're going to marry this bum?' My mother said yes. My grandmother threw her out of the house.

"My father was very clever. In those days you had to offer a dowry. You had to pay what the woman was worth: a few cattle, a few buildings, a few sheep, whatever. He told my grandmother, 'I will take you to Cavanaugh's,' which was the best restaurant in Manhattan, 'and I will pay for the wedding.' My mother's mother started to like him.

"My mother made my father promise to give up the gambling game, because she was afraid he'd get killed, and he went into the restaurant business. He opened up in Red Hook in 1928. It was called the Paramount Food Shop, and its motto was, 'Eat With the Elite'—tongue-in-cheek, because the only ones who ate there were the gangsters, longshoremen, and truck drivers.

"The big thing in a Greek family was to have boys, called *dufekes,* guns. The more boys you had, the more honor. My parents had eight boys in ten years. My father was a *very* honorable man.

"I and my identical twin brother, Nick, were born at Polyclinic Hospital near the old Madison Square Garden on 50th Street and Eighth Avenue on July 26, 1938. We were the first identical twins born in that hospital. Nick came first. The birth certificate says by eighteen minutes. My mother says fifteen. Nick was the sixth son. I was the seventh.

"My father was very generous and concerned about people. A lot of Greeks, when they jumped ship or came off the boat, would come to our restaurant, and my father would give them $5 or $10 and wish them well. They helped each other, and if a guy had a problem, they'd call Congressman John J. Rooney, a powerhouse in the '30s and '40s. Rooney was elected for thirty years. He was the chairman of the subcommittee on appropriations, so J. Edgar Hoover was terrified of him.

"One time my father was visited by the FBI. They came into the restaurant, and they twisted his arm way high up and handcuffed him, and my mother got very upset, because she didn't know why they were doing this. She spoke English better than my father. She asked why they were handcuffing him.

"'Listen, you greaseball,' the FBI man said to him, 'you've got gangsters eating here, Italian gangsters.'

"'I don't know who is a gangster,' my mother said. 'They pay their bill like everybody else. Why are you blaming us?'

"'Shut up. We're tired of you greaseballs and guineas. You're all alike.'

"She got on the phone and called Congressman Rooney, and by the time my father arrived at the police station, they were apologizing, terrified because Rooney had called up Hoover. They brought him back and apologized and left him alone after that.

"To the Irish cops and FBI agents, the Greeks and Italians were just greaseballs, hoodlums, and gangsters. They spoke a foreign language, had another religion. The WASPs stepped all over them.

"Years later I belonged to the New York Athletic Club, which at that time was anti-Jewish and antiblack. When the WASPs were running it, the New York Athletic Club had signs: EMPLOYEES WANTED. IRISH NEED NOT APPLY. When the Irish took it over, they didn't want Italians. When the Italians and Irish came over, they didn't want Greeks. There was a hierarchy, and later on it became the Jews and the blacks who weren't wanted. In typical American style, thank God they integrated.

"Red Hook used to be very anti-Semitic. I remember one day the Irish and the Italians were beating up this old Jewish guy with a beard. My father left the restaurant, and he said, 'Leave him alone.'

"They said, 'Hey Greek, hey schmuck, we're doing what we want.'

"My father took out his carving knife from under his apron, and he said, 'My English isn't very good,' but when they saw the knife they knew exactly what he meant, and they stopped hitting the Jewish guy.

"My father said to him, 'Keep your mouth shut. Get in the back in the family booth. Wait till these guys leave.' After a few hours, my father gave him a few bucks and told him to be careful. Unfortunately, Red Hook was very anti-Semitic.

"With eight sons in the family, there were always issues of bullying and getting your parents' attention, and getting hand-me-down clothes. My older brothers would bully my twin brother and me. Fortunately, where we lived, there were a lot of venues for sports. We played soccer, baseball, and basketball, and there were three boxing gyms within walking distance. It was pre-television, and we didn't have TV, the computer, and video games. We were blessed, very grateful we could play sports all year long on the streets.

"Even though we couldn't play baseball, in the mid-'50s my twin brother and I got to be on the *Knothole Gang.* Three of us, Jerry Becklemeister, Nick, and I were on TV before the Dodger game. We were trying out for shortstop. Pee Wee Reese was the Dodger who rolled ground balls to us, and we'd scoop them up and throw them back. Pee Wee threw me the ball five times, and twice it went through my legs. Then I heard a kid say, 'That's Jackie Robinson.' I wasn't a baseball fan, so I didn't know what the hell was going on, but the other kids sure were in awe of Jackie and Pee Wee.

"In those days if you went on *Happy Felton's Knothole Gang,* they gave you a professional baseball glove. You couldn't go to the store and buy a professional glove. A year later I sold it to a kid named Pepitone. It didn't mean anything to me.

"My parents didn't allow us to just hang out. Maybe at the local candy store. My father was afraid of all the neighborhood bars that catered to the Irish and Italians. He didn't even want us going near those places. He didn't even want us doing sports. He hated boxing. We used to have to sneak into the gym.

"I can remember how hostile it was between the whites and the blacks in Red Hook. The projects weren't built until the 1940s, and the first black family to move in was the Greens. The story I heard was that the first time they swam in the Red Hook pool, a humongous municipal pool, the whites started to drown them, and when they went in the Clinton Theater on Clinton Street, the whites threw them off the balcony.

"I was on a boxing team in the early 1950s, and we had Italians and blacks on the team. There was always tension between them. The Italians would say to me, 'If we get jumped, you have to help us because you're a team member.'

"I'd say, 'I don't help the whites. I don't help the blacks. Do what I do. Mind your own business.'

"One of the Italians would say to me, 'The *mulignans* are going to get theirs.'

"I'd say, 'Listen, guys, that's not my game. Do what you want, but I won't get involved.' And it helped my brother and me with both groups, and it kept us from getting locked up.

"The Irish cops were the ones we feared the most. We were fourteen years old in 1953, and we were out on the street playing a game called Skeets and Bananas. Our group that day had some of my boxing friends, white kids and some black kids. The way the game was played, everybody froze, and the first one who moved, everyone would move in and punch him all about the body, beat him up. You didn't hit anyone in the face. One of the Irish kids flinched, and five or six of us, including a couple of the black kids, started punching him when four plainclothes cops wearing Hawaiian shirts showed up. One of them had a gun, and he was yelling to the other guy, 'Show your badge. Show your badge.' They slammed us against the wall, patted us down. My twin brother had a handkerchief full of mucus with a tiny penknife in it. The cop found it, and he put it in Nick's face, and he said, 'We know what's going on here. We have blacks and whites fighting. What are you doing with this knife?'

"Nick said, 'I clean my nails with it.'

"He smacked my brother in the head, and they told everybody to go their separate ways. The cops were very conscious of gang wars and people getting killed. The cops were Irish, and they didn't like Italians, and then the Irish and Italians got together, and they didn't like the blacks. In those days, the 1950s, they used to beat the shit out of the kids. It was unbelievable what they would do. As I said, the kids feared the cops more than anybody else.

"The cop would say, 'If I catch you doing anything, I'm going to beat the shit out of you.' And they did exactly that. 'You fucking guineas get off the corner.' 'I told you once, I told you twice . . .' 'I'll lose my size-nine shoe up your ass.'

"There was nothing you could do. You couldn't rat on the cop. If you went to the precinct and said, 'The cop beat me up,' you got another beating.

"At the same time there was a lot of corruption in the police force. Everybody, the bookmakers, worked hand in hand with each other. One day my friend who owned the corner candy store said to me, 'Don't come in tomorrow.'

"'Why?'

"'Because I'm being arrested.' For bookmaking. They had to make an arrest, and it was his turn to do it. There was *a lot* of corruption.

"A lot of my friends didn't make it. They wound up with a gun in their hand, or a spike, and they ended up in jail. Nick and I were lucky that we stayed away from drugs, stayed away from crime. Our parents were the reason for that.

"My mother would feed us in the restaurant under our six-family house, and then I'd go out and play and come home and eat and go out and play and come home and go out and play, until school started, and then I was forced to do my studying, because my father didn't want me to be 'like the other bums in the neighborhood.' Because of our father, six of us went to law school, and four of us graduated. It didn't matter. It wasn't good enough. He was still embarrassed, because the Jews and the Greeks were the same: if you weren't a doctor, you were a bum. We weren't doctors, so he considered us bums.

"He wouldn't settle for less. It made us strive harder. So we had high expectations. When my older brothers were thinking of dropping out of high school, my father would say, 'Over my dead body,' and he meant it. Parental expectations were very forceful. Sometimes I think my father and mother still rule from the grave.

"My mother was a phenomenal woman. In 1962 she was Mother of the Year of New York State, and she was runner-up in the Mother of the Year USA contest. In 1964 she became Greek-American Mother of the Year of the whole country.

"She was interesting. When she was thirteen or fourteen, her father took her out of school, and she worked in a restaurant. Her father was afraid if she stayed in school, she'd 'end up like the Polish girls,' who were thought to be loose. God forbid she wouldn't be a virgin when she got married.

"In those days you had to be married according to what the parents wanted. If you intermarried, it could ruin a family. Today the Muslims have honor killings. If a girl is going out with someone else, they will kill her, and in their tradition it's okay. It's only in America where the killers are arrested and locked up. It's still happening today.

"My wife was a guidance counselor in junior high school, and the Muslim girls were being married off at a young age, because the parents wanted to make sure they were still virgins.

"I can remember much later I was running a rough school in the Bronx. The black kids were hitting on this Muslim girl. She was beautiful. I took her aside, and I said, 'If your father found out these guys were hitting on you, even though you were keeping them away, he would kill you. You understand that? I'm not telling you what you should or shouldn't do, but you have to understand your father.' The Albanian Muslims were killers. They didn't fool around. They had their own sections of the Bronx, and they ran them. During that war in Yugoslavia, Albanian-Americans were going on their own to fight with the troops.

Peter and Nick Spanakos, Golden Glove champions in 1960. *Courtesy of Peter Spanakos*

"We worry about the perils of assimilation, but traditions, mores, customs, they continue.

"When I was growing up, there was no Greek community in Brooklyn. We were the only Greek family, and because my twin brother and I were small, everybody tried to kick our ass. I learned how to street-fight, and when I was fourteen I went into the gym, and it took me a few years to go from a first-class street fighter to a first-class boxer.

"Since we lived in Red Hook, we went to PS 27, grades one through eight, which at one point was the worst school in the city. It was terrible. World War II was still on, and there were munitions shops around, and second-graders would come into the school carrying guns. My brother and I were always in separate classes, and we were always getting beaten up by Irish and Italian gang members. They would chase us, and so the school would let us out ten minutes early so I wouldn't have to run the gauntlet going the four or five blocks back home.

"My mother felt we weren't learning, so from the fourth through seventh grade, we took the train from Brooklyn and traveled an hour and a quarter to the South

Bronx to go to a Greek school. That was a very Hispanic neighborhood, and we had to walk three blocks to the subway, and the Hispanics would beat the hell out of us. This time the principal of the parochial school let us out twenty minutes early to avoid getting beaten up. After a while these beatings reinforced my thinking, *This is crazy. I better learn how to fight.*

"As I got older, my father didn't mind me boxing locally, because I kept telling him, 'Papa, we don't have any money. My one-way ticket out of Red Hook is to get a college boxing scholarship.' He didn't think it was possible, but I did that.

"I won the local Golden Gloves championships ten times. In 1955 I won twice in one night at Madison Square Garden, and then I trained for a week, and now I'm to fight in the nationals, and my father said, 'You can't go. I won't let you out of school.'

"The principal and the dean called my father. 'Let him go. He's honoring the school.' My father said, 'No, I'm the father. He's not old enough.'

"The same thing happened the next year. I won the New York State AAU, and I and my twin brother were supposed to go to Boston, and my father called up Sam Levine, the head of the AAU, now USA Boxing, and he said, 'I'm their father. They're not going.'

"When I got on the scale, Sam pulled me aside and said, 'I don't want to embarrass you, but your father says you can't fight tonight, and if you win you can't go to Boston anyway.'

"I talked Sam into letting me fight that night, and I fought and won, but of course I couldn't go to Boston, and it cost me another national title.

"He was my father. He meant well. He decided what was the best thing to do. He was concerned about my health. He was concerned about our getting punchy. He knew Jerry the Greek, the trainer for Jack Dempsey, and my father knew all the gamblers, and he'd tell us, 'Boxing is a dirty game, corrupt.' Of course, I didn't think he knew what he was talking about. There is an axiom in boxing, 'The only thing square about boxing is the ring.' My father knew a lot more than I gave him credit for.

"It was only after he died in '58 that I was able to go on to the nationals.

"Even though I didn't live in Bay Ridge, I went to Fort Hamilton High School.

My mother saw to that. When I went to Greek school in the seventh grade, I studied English in the morning and Greek in the afternoon, and my mother saw that I was falling behind in grammar, and in math, and she wanted me in a school that concentrated more on English.

"Back then there was de facto segregation in the school system. You were assigned by neighborhoods. The kids from Red Hook went to high school at Manual, now called John Jay, on Seventh Avenue in Park Slope. That was a war zone. My mother didn't want Nick and me going there. She said, 'I'm going to give you a phony address and you'll go to Bay Ridge, the feeder school for Fort Hamilton High School. Bay Ridge Junior High was an upper- and middle-income school. There were no Greeks. There were Scandinavian girls: Olson, Johnson, Lawson. We had dances. These girls were tall, and I was short and I can remember how for forty-five minutes their boobs would bang on my head when I'd dance with them.

"One of my coaches asked me, 'Peter, why are you always rubbing your head after these dance sessions?'

"I said, 'I get a delicious headache because those boobs keep bouncing on my head.' It was a good school. I learned a lot. And I went to Fort Hamilton High School, which is located on 84th Street and Shore Road, a very, very chic neighborhood. It's right off the Narrows. Fort Hamilton in the 1700s was on the Brooklyn side, and Fort Wadsworth was on the Staten Island side, and all boats had to pass between them on the way to New York Harbor. In World War II we hung up submarine nets to protect the harbor from the Germans. In the 1700s Bay Ridge was called Yellow Hook, because it had yellow clay. Red Hook had red clay. In the 1840s there was an outbreak of typhoid fever, and they changed the name from Yellow Hook to Bay Ridge, because you were on top of the bay and could see the ridges.

"I was the senior class president of Fort Hamilton High School. My cousin was my campaign manager. There were very few Greeks in the school, but somehow we worked it out. It was 1956, and from reading about my boxing exploits in the *Daily News,* which covered the Golden Gloves very well, the principal discovered that Nick and I lived on Court Street in Red Hook, not in Bay Ridge. He called us down to the office to kick us out of school.

"We sat down and he said, 'I have perused your records, and you don't make any trouble. I should throw you out, but I'm not going to.' So we were able to finish the year and graduate.

"One of the neighborhood guys who was a fan of mine when I boxed was Joey Gallo. Joey lived on President Street a few blocks away. We met when I was in high school. My brother and I were walking down the street dressed in jackets and ties one evening, and Gallo said something like, 'Look at those faggots.' Which was dumb. I took it as an insult, and I went over and hit him. My brother faced off with one of his brothers.

"There were five Gallo brothers, and the next day they came down in a gang the four blocks to my house. Waiting for them were my neighbors, my closest friends, the Pepitones and the Monfortes.

"'What's going on?' one of the Monforte brothers asked the Gallos.

"'We've come to kick those twin Greeks in the ass,' Joey said.

"'I wouldn't do that,' the Monfortes said. 'They have six brothers, and they box every day in the gym. You're fooling around with the wrong people. And if you come here, you have the Pepitones and the Monfortes to worry about.'

"Later on Joey Gallo became one of my big boxing fans. I was fighting in the gym, and he took out his gun and started shooting it in the air. 'Go Pete! Go Pete!' I turned to see what was going on, and the other guy kept hitting me, and the cops came. They didn't arrest him. They just took away his gun and threw him out of the gym.

"Joey was nuts. Joey had a lion with no teeth in his basement. Someone knocked up his niece, so he grabbed the kid who did it by the scruff of his neck and took him to St. Mary's Church on Court Street.

"'You're going to marry her,' he said.

"Gallo was a known mob guy by this time. The kid said, 'I don't give a shit who you are. I'm not marrying her.'

"Joey brought the kid to his house, opened up the basement door, and there was Leo the lion, growling away. The kid said, 'Okay, I'll marry her.'

"The next day they took him to the church to get married, and just before the start of the ceremony, the kid told the priest, 'I'm not getting married.' Gallo went up to him, and he told him the same thing. Joey said, 'Okay, remember Leo the lion? I'm going to feed you to him.'

"The kid said, 'Don't do that.' And the kid got married.

"Joey went to prison, and in prison he turned gay. After he got out, whenever a thirteen- or fourteen-year-old boy turned up missing, one of the first places they checked was to see if Joey Gallo had him.

"When Joey went to prison, he had quite a mob of black guys. He was offering them buttonships. Joey had some of his black guys shoot and kill Joseph Colombo on the reviewing stand during the Columbus Day parade.

"Joey and his bodyguard, who was called Peter the Greek, and Punchy Liano went to Little Italy for dinner, and Colombo's men went into the restaurant [Umberto's Clam House on Mulberry Street] and killed Joey and injured Peter the Greek. I can remember a good friend of mine, Tony Di, wanted to go in with Gallo. I told him, 'Tony, don't. You're going to wind up with a cement kimono.' Tony was a boxer. He had a pushed-in face and a pushed-in nose, but it wasn't because of boxing. When he was twelve, he fell down a fourteen-foot sewer and landed on his face. His dream was to be one of Frank Sinatra's bodyguards. He used to hang out at Jilly Rizzo's restaurant waiting to be discovered so he could wind up on Sinatra's payroll.

"One day Tony disappeared. Thirty years later Tony's body was dug out of a canal. He was wearing cement boots.

"Heroin came in big in Red Hook even before Bedford-Stuyvesant and the black areas. You get a runny nose with heroin. I can remember when I was talking to guys, they kept rubbing their noses. Their eyes would look bleary. Their veins were shot. This was around 1950, and I realize now it was because of heroin.

"The guys who were selling it were making so much money, the mobsters' kids started to get involved, and so the Mafia don, Carlo Gambino, made a rule that you couldn't sell heroin, because they couldn't trust heroin addicts, and because they didn't want their kids involved.

"Gambino put out the rule, 'No heroin.'

"And John Gotti broke the rule, because there was so much money to be made.

In order not to be killed, Gotti killed the boss of Staten Island, Paul Castellano, and then after Gotti put out a contract on him, Bully Gravano, his underboss, turned on John Gotti. His testimony put Gotti away for life. Bully Gravano was a big boxing fan. He used to take boxing lessons downtown Brooklyn.

"Bully was a real character, small but wide-built. He came into my school once when I was a teacher in Bensonhurst. He was like a cartoon. Some black kids were insulting his daughter. He got out of his white Cadillac. He said to the dean, 'Any fucking niggers follow my daughter, and I will burn down the whole fucking school.'

"The dean came up to me and said, 'Peter, who is that?'

"I said, 'That's Bully Gravano. He's an up-and-coming gangster. You better be careful, because he means it.'

"Bully Gravano admitted to nineteen murders that the Feds excused just to get Bully to turn on Gotti. The government even let him keep all his money. He went out to Arizona, and because he's such a schmuck, he got involved in drugs. The guy didn't need the money. It made no sense. When it gets into your blood, I guess you can't get out. They took his son down, and they took him down.

"My brother and I each got boxing scholarships to college. I went to college my first year at Wisconsin. My brother went to Albertson College, a small school in Caldwell, Idaho. My sophomore year I joined him. College boxing was very boring. It wasn't competitive. As a pro you did body punching, infighting. College boxing discouraged you from hitting hard. As long as you hit him, it was fine. I was raised to be a pro, so you hit him and you wanted to make sure he went down. The coaches had a problem with that, but we had a lot of fun in college. We learned a lot, and it was important to cut our ties to Red Hook. We learned different values. They lived differently, thought differently, in Idaho. We were absorbing the basic Western culture.

"In the summer of 1959 I traveled to Madison, Wisconsin, trying to make the United States Pan American Games team. The Pan American Games are held every four years, one year before the Olympics. The teams that compete are from North and South America. My roommate was a sixteen-year-old by the name of Cassius

Clay. He was a kid from Louisville, Kentucky, shooting off his mouth, rapping and rhyming away. The more he talked, the more I was sure he was full of shit. He was afraid of his own shadow, but the kid could fight. He would tell everybody he was a GOAT, which stood for 'the greatest of all time.'

"'The greatest of all time?' I said. 'You're nuts.'

"Cassius said, 'You're a Greek GOAT, the Greek greatest of all time.' We started to laugh, and we got to be friends.

"In training camp the other fighters, guys who were older, mature men from the armed services, figured out Cassius was a virgin, and one of them said, 'Cassius, when you fuck a girl, do you fuck her in the first hole or the second hole?' I was the unofficial captain of the team. Cassius looked at me, and I said, 'I'm not getting into this.'

"'The second one,' he said.

"'You're not fucking her,' they said. 'You're cornballing her.'

The Spanakos brothers, left, with 16-year-old Cassius Clay, right, at the 1960 National Golden Gloves championships.

*Courtesy of Peter Spanakos*

"Cassius was so arrogant and obnoxious, they would jump on him all the time. He alienated everyone so much a couple of the guys wanted to beat him up. He would say, 'I'm going to knock you on your ass. I'm the world's greatest.' And he could go on all day long with this. The other guys were four, five years older, marines and air force men. I would tell them, 'Leave the kid alone.'

"One time, Cassius's coach back in Louisville, Captain Joe Martin of the police, the man who really started him off, sent him $5 by Western Union.

"He said, 'Greek, what is this?'

"I said, 'It's a money order, and you have to endorse it.'

"'What's that mean?'

"'You have to sign it on the back, and take it to the PX, and they'll give you money.'

"He waved the check in front of the other boxers and said, 'Oh man, I just got me $50,000.'

"As they all dived for the check, he put it in his pocket. They're *hondling* and heckling, and they got him down to $5,000. The other boxers came to me. I said, 'It's his business. Leave him alone.' He was always blowing up facts and figures.

"Bobby Foster, who later on became world light heavyweight champion, knocked out Cassius in the gym, which was unusual with the big gloves they were using.

"Cassius lost in his final match against Amos Johnson, a good marine fighter. The reason he lost was that in the afternoon we all went for dinner, and the NCAA served fish. I was the unofficial captain of the team, and I said, 'I like steak, and it's too early for us to eat.' And I walked out, and six of the other fighters walked out with me.

"Cassius, a really poor kid out of Louisville, stayed, and he saw seven plates of fish in front of him, and he decided to eat all of it. And he ate seven desserts. That night he fought, and every time Johnson hit him in the belly, Cassius ran to the ropes and went to throw up. I felt so sorry for him. He had lost, and I hoped he learned a lesson that when your eyes are bigger than your stomach, you can't indulge like that.

"In 1960 Cassius and I won a string of Golden Gloves titles. I didn't make the Olympic team, but my brother and he did. They went to Rome, settled into their quarters, and Cassius calls up Nick and says, 'Nick, you have to try this water fountain!'

"'What are you talking about, Cassius?' Nick said. 'We're in Rome in the Olympic dorms. What's so great about the water fountain?' Nick comes in, and he sees Cassius drinking out of the bidet.

"Nick said, 'Cassius, that's a bidet.'

"'What's a bidet?'

"Nick said, 'Don't worry. It won't hurt you.'

"When the coaches and I looked around and asked ourselves which of these guys were going to be not only number one in the country, but world champion, no one ever picked Cassius. The only one who picked him was himself. 'Cause he did everything wrong, but for him it came out right.

"Clay was a good guy but he had a problem with dyslexia. I would help him write his letters home. I never thought he'd make it, but he did very well for himself. It goes to show you don't always know what makes for success. Is it IQ? Nature? Nurture? He became one of the most famous people in the world.

"My brother and I were managed by Cus D'Amato, who also managed Floyd Patterson. Cus asked me, 'Pete, call Cassius.' He wanted to represent him. Cassius said to me, 'Pete, I have a group here in Louisville. They gave me $10,000, and I'm going to stay with them. With Cus, I'm just going to wind up as Floyd Patterson's sparring partner.' I told Cus he wasn't interested. I thought to myself, *This kid is not dumb. He's right.* I was amazed he was so perceptive. He could read situations better than most people.

"Later on, after they took his title away for not wanting to serve in Vietnam, he joined with his muse, Elijah Muhammad, the head of the Muslims [Nation of Islam]. Elijah was about five feet tall, and he was screwing all the young girls, impregnating five or six of them, and that was when Malcolm X went to Mecca and found out what being a Muslim really meant. When he came back, he was a threat to Elijah Muhammad, who had these guys with purple hats and fruits of Islam on them, his personal bodyguards, all recruited from jails, and two of them killed Malcolm X right on the stage of Audubon Hall right near Columbia University. The Muslims went into Malcolm X's home and kicked out his wife and kids. The guy who took over his house was Louis Farrakhan. Then he moved to Chicago. Farrakhan has a Rolls-Royce for every day of the week. Farrakhan took over the organization after Elijah Muhammad died.

"I called Cassius, now Muhammad Ali, up recently. His attention span is limited, but he still has his cognizance and his sense of humor. He said, 'Pete, can I ask you a question?' I said sure. He said, 'Did you grow any?'

"In 1960 I was a senior in college. I had to win my final fight to go to the Olympics in Rome. I fought a boxer by the name of Charlie Brown, who I had already beaten. I had sebaceous cysts on my head, and during the fight Brown hit me on the head, and I started to bleed.

"I told the ref, 'It's okay,' but he stopped it.

"He said, 'Peter, I know you're winning big, but I have to stop it.'

"I said, 'Why?'

"He said, 'If you get blood in your eyes, you go blind.'

"I said, 'Wait a minute. Do you really believe that?' A lot of guys in boxing did, but there is no such thing as going blind from blood in your eye.

"I said, 'You just cost me a shot at the Olympic team.'

"Again, the stupidity of boxing.

"In '64 I went again, and I lost in the trials. But then I was a senior in law school. Nick made the finals. He was the All-Army champion. But they didn't pick him."

Both Peter and Nick turned pro. They were represented by Cus D'Amato. Each lost his first fight. Each left boxing. Their education would allow them to make a living with their minds rather than their fists.

# HERE COME THE ITALIANS

CURTIS SLIWA

ITALY WAS A TERRIBLE PLACE TO LIVE DURING MOST OF THE eighteenth century. Only a third of the land was cultivated. People were poor. Food was scarce. Few homes were heated. The country was run by the autocratic Hapsburgs, a ruling elite that owned most of Italy's wealth, and they paid very low wages. Moreover, little money was spent on education for the masses, and most people were illiterate. Upward mobility was rare. And no one could leave, because the Hapsburgs made emigration illegal.

In 1871, when Italy's reunification was more or less complete and the various states had formed themselves into a nation, the ruling class imposed a brutal tax on the workers. Italians started to leave, but most went to other European countries, and many of those returned. Many of the emigrants who left toward the end of the nineteenth century went to South America, mostly to Brazil and Argentina.

The flood of Italians to the United States began in 1891 and continued until immigration was halted by the Congress in 1917. Four million Italians came to America between 1890 and 1920. Family members would come over, then write home letters glowing with promises of low taxes, plenty of work, and freedom. Some towns in Calabria and the Basilicata lost as much as 20 percent of their population.

*La familia*—the family—provided Italians with protection, assistance, and friendship. Italians defined themselves by the part of Italy they came from. They came as Venetians, Calabrians, Neapolitans, and Sicilians. They settled where their former neighbors lived. Italian immigrants did not feel isolated, rarely became public charges, and rarely suffered from alcoholism or from mental illness.

Another reason they banded together was that they were Catholic, and the American Puritans were hostile to them because of their darker skin and their religion. The Protestants didn't want them living next door.

The wealthier northern Italians tended to move west, as far as California, where they raised grapes and made wine. The poorer southern Italians stayed in New York and other eastern cities, replacing the Irish on work gangs, building subways, skyscrapers, and fixing streets. Italian women joined the garment industry.

Library of Congress

Life for the new Italian immigrants was hard. They worked long hours for little pay. They were targets of both the police and the mafiosi who preyed on them.

Though the Italians and the Irish had the Catholic Church in common, the Irish were prejudiced against the Italians because they weren't orthodox enough. The Irish were contemptuous of the Italians' love of processions during which they carried around tall statues of their favorite saints. For their part, the Italians felt the Irish too puritanical and cold. The Italians also were contemptuous of the Irish always hitting up their parishioners for money.

The worst of anti-Italian feeling came in 1920, during the Sacco and Vanzetti trial. Sixteen witnesses swore the two men were miles from where the murder in question took place, but they were convicted anyway. The jury foremen called them "dagos." There were whispers that they were anarchists. In the midst of A. Mitchell Palmer's Red Scare, they were given the death penalty. Like the Salem witch trials, it was a travesty.

In 1917, the Congress passed legislation demanding that immigrants be literate. A yearly quota was established at six thousand, and it remained that way until 1965.

Because most immigrants from southern Italy came from a farming background, they were suspicious of the public schools. Moreover, first-generation Italians wanted their children to go to work for the good of the family. They had a saying, "Don't make your children better than we were." As late as 1960, only 6 percent of students at City College had Italian names.

The second generation was tired of hearing how life was in the old country. They sent their kids to school, adopted a different manner of dress, became more American.

Curtis Sliwa, the founder of the Guardian Angels, was the son of a strict merchant seaman of Polish ancestry and a doting mother of Italian descent. As a child, he grew up in Canarsie in the home of his maternal grandparents. In the Italian culture, the youngest child took care of the parents in their old age, and so, in 1959, when Curtis was five, the Sliwas moved in with the rest of the Bianchino clan so his mom could watch over them. With his father away most of the year, young Curtis, the only male child, was the *mamaluke* in the family. He could do no wrong in the eyes of his kin. On the street he learned from the *gavones* who populated Canarsie and the Jewish kids with whom he went to school. Growing up in a Roman Catholic household, more than anything, he learned that selflessness and sacrifice would bring him closer to God.

**CURTIS SLIWA**   "I was born in Brooklyn Hospital in downtown Brooklyn on March 26, 1954. It was Dr. Duckman who slapped my *tuchas* and caused me to start jaw-boning for the very first time, and I haven't stopped since.

"I was eleven pounds, eight ounces, born to Frances Sliwa, a little Italian-American woman. I was heavy, and I had slanted eyes, so the medical staff assumed I couldn't be her baby after they saw my father, Chester, with his blond hair and blue eyes, and my mother with her dark hair and dark eyes. They said, 'Neither of you have Asian features. This can't be your kid.' It took twenty-four hours to straighten it out.

"Ironically, Dr. Duckman's son became a judge who actually got defrocked and thrown off the bench in Kings County for caring more about a convict being able to take care of his dog—that's why he released him and let him go home—than about the woman he was stalking who he wanted to kill. So guess what he did? When he got let out of jail, he went and killed the girlfriend. A tremendous bloodline there.

Curtis Sliwa as a young boy with his mother and sister. *Courtesy of Curtis Sliwa*

"My dad, the oldest of four boys, was born on the South Side of Chicago. My grandfather Anton and my grandmother Wanda were both born and raised in Poland. They met in Chicago, which had a huge Polish enclave.

"My mother was the thirteenth and last child in her family, and the only one born in America. Her parents, Fidele and Nicoletta Bianchino, were from Bari, Italy. Fedele could not read or write, but my grandmother was very learned, very educated. They were an odd couple.

"They came here after World War I. Fedele served in the Italian army in the Alps. He had volunteered as an English interpreter, even though he didn't speak a word of English. Anything to avoid being hung or shot by the Austrians or the Hungarians. His attitude was, 'You need an English interpreter? I want to learn English. I want to go to America.' He couldn't read or write. He survived the war, and he was living in poverty. He said, 'Let me go to America. I'll see if the streets are really paved in gold.'

"He came to Brooklyn and went back, and he said, 'It's a hell of a lot better than living in a mud hut with twelve kids and a horse.' And the horse had the most room. As my grandfather said to his kids about the horse, 'He makes money. You cost me money.'

"He arranged for the whole family to come to America. His cousin Lemesta, who owned a funeral parlor, was going to vouch for him. But Fidele told him he only had four kids. So when Lemesta arrived at Ellis Island, he was taken by surprise when he saw Fidele, Nicoletta, and he counts one, two, three, four, five, six, seven, eight, nine, ten, eleven, twelve kids, and he sees that she's pregnant with my mother.

"Lemesta said to the customs official, 'I never saw that man before in my life.' Remember, if you sponsored someone, you had to be responsible for him. If they couldn't make it on their own, there was no welfare, no social services. You had to pay their bills. So Lemesta freaked.

"My grandfather went nuts, and they quarantined him on Ellis Island. He eventually was able to contact another cousin who took them in. If not, the whole family would have been shipped back. My uncle Leonard had a mastoid ear infection. Eventually he would die of it, but they wouldn't let him in. My aunt Mary had a cough, and she was terrified they would think it was whooping cough. She had heard the horror stories about not passing the physical. Even if you had lice, that was it. Back you went.

"My grandparents had a tough survival, but they always reveled in how many failures they had had to endure before the ultimate success—from getting their first apartment, a cold-water flat on Skillman Street and Myrtle Avenue in the heart of Fort Greene.

"Fedele had told the landlady, 'We have just five kids.' Because five was the limit.

"'If I see any more kids, Mr. Bianchino, out you go.' So every day he would have the younger kids wait in the school yard of the public school on Kent Avenue until it was very dark and then he would wagon-train them into the apartment. Good weather, bad weather, they would have to wait until the landlady went to sleep.

"One night she must have had agita, no Brioschi, and there she was, eagle-eyed, and she started counting, 'Seven, eight, nine, ten . . .' After Grandpa got them all into the apartment, she knocked on the door. She came in and said, *'Esci fuori da questa casa.'* Which means, 'Get out of this house.' And that was it. There were no social services, no shelters. They took what little they had, and out in the street they went.

"Nowadays, you tell a story like that, and you lie on a couch watching Oprah, and she explains why you're dysfunctional, why you can't seem to have a relationship, why you became a dope fiend, and there's my grandparents and my uncles and aunts telling their story, busting their buttons and britches with pride, saying, 'Yeah, it was cold. We had nowhere to go, but we all pulled together, and we walked for hours until eventually we found a place to stay.'

"They walked all the way out toward Canarsie, which is a long haul. Canarsie was God's country back then, because the farther you went east, you would start hitting undeveloped areas, fields and lots, old farms still, and to my grandfather, this was nirvana. He felt like Lewis and Clark of Brooklyn. He said, 'I'm going to save my money, and I'm gonna buy a house in Canarsie.' People would look at him and say, 'Canarsie?'

"Canarsie was known for three things: the dump; a mini–Coney Island called the Golden Gate, right by Jamaica Bay; and a red-light district. Back near Paerdegat Bay were the houses of ill repute built on poles stuck in the water, the shanty shacks, and people like Mae West and others would perform in the jazz clubs, because jazz was considered the evil music, the cultural debaucher of the time. You'd drink at the gin mill and try to saddle up with a lady, and then go from the hooch mill to the brothel. That was what would attract people to Canarsie. It was out of the way, out of sight, out of mind. But the rest of Canarsie was like the *Little House on the Prairie,* undeveloped land, and eventually my grandfather saved his nickels, dimes, and pennies working a variety of manual-labor jobs, and he bought his house on Remsen Avenue.

"Back then a traditional Italian household would always be occupied by the extended family. Aunts, cousins, nieces, nephews—this was a huge family in the Bianchino compound, where my grandfather would work in the dirt-rock garden. No grass. No concrete. Italians were known for that. Just dirt, rocks, tomato plants, fig trees, parsley, and *basilico* [basil], and that was heaven, a slice of the old country.

"The extended family would contribute to the family's welfare. My grandmother Nicolette was a seamstress. She would do piecework at home while she raised the kids.

"My grandfather would wake up in the wee hours of the morning and go to work as a manual laborer, a pick-and-shoveler, to dig. He said, 'We were the bottom of the ethnic food chain, guineas, wops, and dagos.' And it was worse if, like him, you couldn't read or write. If they needed an extra body, he was hired, but they would go through the other ethnics first. The Italians were like the Puerto Ricans later on. Most times he didn't get picked, so he would have to walk all the way back. He would have to find a piece of cardboard to put in his shoe where the leather wore out. Because he didn't have the nickel for the trolley. So he walked miles, just to shape up, to be told most times, 'Go home.'

"My grandfather would be out from sundown to sundown, literally dark to dark, six days a week, shaping up. My mom would say, 'I wonder who that man on Sundays is,' because she was the youngest, and she'd usually be asleep when he came home. If he didn't hustle, the family would have starved. As I said, there was no food stamp program, no welfare. He never held a regular job until he was in his eighties.

"When we moved in with him in 1959, he was eighty-one and I was five. They had started building subdivisions in Canarsie, and he was hired as a night watchman, a job he took super-seriously.

"Back then there were many organized-crime families in Canarsie. That was their burial ground. The *gavones,* the *shadrools,* the muscleheads with muscles between both ears, the up-and-coming *cugines,* would earn their stripes by developing their track record of being able to steal and earn, and the way they would do that was by going to these work sites late at night and stealing materials.

"The job of the typical night watchman was to make sure they didn't get greedy, to make sure their skim wasn't excessive. Not my grandfather. He would say, 'What do you mean, skim? What do you mean, vig? What do you mean, percentage? Not on my watch. I was hired to see that nobody steals. That means *nobody* steals.'

"My grandfather hated the Cosa Nostra, the Black Hand. Sometimes I would go with him on his route checking the different sites. He realized he couldn't cover the entire enormous area of subdivisions, so he would set up booby traps. He used nails and broken glass. He dug holes the thieves would fall into. And he would catch them and turn them over to the cops, and this was considered *disgracia.* When he had information, he'd say, *'Juan yowan,'* meaning 'Come with me.' And he'd go to the 69th Precinct and demand to speak to a detective. This was not the police depart-

Curtis Sliwa's maternal grandparents,
Fedele and Nicoletta Bianchino.
*Courtesy of Curtis Sliwa*

ment of Rudy Giuliani. This was a police department that had been corrupted, that had links to organized crime, and the cops would turn around and tell the old-timers, who I call the Geriatric Psychotic Espresso Killers of Organized Crime, with the pinkie rings, that this crazy old man was ratting out their nephews as they were trying to earn their stripes. So they would approach him, sometimes in my company.

"'Hey Pops, who do you think you are, the FBI—Forever Busting Italians?'

"'Old man, you know the custom from the old country. You be swimming with the fishes in Jamaica Bay. You gotta big mouth.'

"'This is my job,' he would say. 'If the boss doesn't like the way I do my job, he's gonna fire me. I'm paid to make sure nobody steals, and that means you, your cousins, your nieces, your nephews, my sons, my daughters. Nobody steals.'

"He wouldn't bend, would not fold like a cheap camera. He stood resolute.

"They acted like they were going to whack him, but they didn't, because he was eighty-one. They treated him like you would your crazy uncle on gatherings, Thanksgiving, or Christmas. They would say, 'The old man is *oobatz,* he's *meshuggener,* he's *tetched.*' To punish him, they exiled him from the boccie court, where all the old-timers would come together and network, talk, exchange stories from the old country. Because he was such an in-your-face anti–organized crime guy, they wouldn't associate with him, wouldn't let him around them. He basically had to exist as a loner.

"There was him and me, and when he began developing cataracts and hardening of the arteries, I got him a big dog, part German shepherd, part Great Dane, to protect him. The name of the dog was Butkus. After the football player Dick Butkus, because he would tackle people. If you got too near the old man, Butkus would take you down. And Butkus was *huge.* In Italy my grandfather had had a hunting dog called German, named after Germany, and he would go out with the dog and shoot pigeons for the family meal. Pigeon soup was considered a delicacy in Italy. In America you'd say, 'Are you out of your mind? Eating a flying rat?' But in Italy it was considered a delicacy. He'd go hunting all day with German and come back with one or two pigeons.

"My grandfather was starting to have his senior moments, and so he would think Butkus was German, and he'd think he was going out hunting on the streets of Canarsie. He would see the pigeons, and he'd aim his phantom rifle. Butkus would look at him like, *This guy really is* oobatz.

"My mom, who lived at home with my grandparents, went to Tilden High School, the same high school that produced Al 'Slim Shady' Sharpton years later, and a host of others, including Willie Randolph, who was the manager of the Mets. It was a very good school, and she did fairly well and went into clerical work. She started working in an office in Manhattan before World War II, and she met my dad, a merchant seaman.

"My dad went to Lane Tech in Chicago, but he was the oldest son, and because of the Depression he had to go to work. He sailed flatboats down the Mississippi. Once at the port of New Orleans, he was able to sail on banana barges to Central America in order to make more money to send home, and eventually he worked on cargo ships, which prepared him for World War II. He went to Officers' Candidate School with the merchant marine. They sent him to a training facility where Kingsborough Community College is now. He would have to row out into the middle of Jamaica Bay in the winter, and they would throw him over, and he'd have to survive. This was in preparation for the Liberty fleet, where they knew ships would go down in the North Sea in the Atlantic, and you'd perish in a matter of minutes because of exposure, so they were trying to prepare them.

"My dad was an excellent swimmer. The idea was to stay afloat, swim, avoid the riptide, avoid the currents.

Chester Sliwa. *Courtesy of Curtis Sliwa*

Frances Sliwa. *Courtesy of Curtis Sliwa*

He was assigned to a ship berthed out of Brooklyn, and networking in Manhattan he met my mom. They got married in St. Patrick's Cathedral right before the war, and when the war started, he got shipped out.

"He was a second mate, and he'd be on watch at night with all the lights out, knowing that as soon as they left the Port of Brooklyn and went through the straights of Verrazano out past Coney Island, the German wolfpack would be waiting. They would start with a convoy of sixty-five ships, and the subs would start picking them off one by one, and by the time they arrived in England, they'd be lucky if thirty-eight made it. It was night, and there was nothing you could do. His boat was never hit, but he had a lot of close calls. Toward the end of the war, after Germany had given in, he went to the Pacific until Japan surrendered, and he continued to sail right through the Korean War.

"When I was a boy, my dad was away eight months of the year, sometimes ten. Back then if you went into a port, it took days to unload and load. He would go from port to port in the Middle East and then to Asia and then to California and through the Panama Canal and down to Argentina.

"My dad being away affected me in only the most positive way. Others would say, 'My dad was away. I didn't have a male role model.' I was the only boy in an Italian household, and I became a *mamaluke*. To your mom and your aunts you could do no wrong. The girls would grow up like they were living in a convent. They had a curfew. If guys looked at them the wrong way, your cousin would hit them so hard their mothers would feel the vibration. They were under constant observation. Guys? We had the freedom to do whatever we wanted. And I was never wrong in the eyes of my grandmother, my mom, or my aunts. Like I said, I was a *mamaluke,* the king, the prince, the *jambeen*. My dad wasn't of the Italian culture. He was more brusque. Along with four brothers, he had grown up with all men in his family, other than his mother, so it was a totally different energy. It was great to have him home a few months of the year, because he was great at telling stories and painting pictures of all these unbelievable ports of call. He would say, 'You could see the powerful Nile sweeping down and seeing all the crops growing and the Egyptians in their ancient boats, and yet a modern city, Cairo, but you also had to watch out for Ali Baba and the forty thieves, 'cause merchant seamen were considered easy prey.'

"He would say, 'A merchant seaman was the most despised pariah. It was thought, *Lock up your women. They're drunks, thieves, crooks; they have syphilis, and scurvy*—but, he told me, 'We were the most avid readers, because that's all we could do on our off time.' There was no radio or TV on the ship. They read books. So he would bring home with him a treasure trove of 25¢ classic books. They were the most learned. They would write great prose, but the minute they hit shore, the cops were out looking to bust them. Everyone was fearful of the seamen, though they were just hardworking guys who came from all over to sail. He would also explain the different ethnic groups, because we lived in a melting pot, New York City.

"I grew up around a lot of mobsters in Canarsie. My grandfather, who wouldn't be bullied by them, would say, 'Look at these men. They sit on the steps all day. They eyeball the working man, the man who goes back and forth to work, who opens and closes his store. They scheme all day, thinking, 'How am I going to take that guy's money without ever having to work a day in my life?'

"My grandfather said to me, 'You shake their hands, and their hands are soft. 'Cause even though they act tough, they never worked a hard day in their life.' So I would be walking through the neighborhood, and you would see exactly what my grandfather described. And worse. These older men would take under their wing young, impressionable teenagers, many of whom I played ball with, associated with, and I could see them eating up their minds with negative propaganda. They could dazzle the young people with their talk about chasing skirts, hanging out, carousing.

"They would say to the kids, 'What are you going to get from a book? You a freakin' moron? You gonna collect ten trillion Green Stamps so you can buy a toaster? You can own the store that sells the toasters. You're just not out front. You're protecting the man's business.'

"And I would say to the kids, 'Who are we protecting it from? We are protecting them from us. We're protecting the guy's store from us, so we don't burn it down or don't break his window. What are you, some kind of moron?'

"And the answer would come back, 'If we don't do it, the guys on the other block will.'

"That's how it would start. They might say, 'You look like a bright kid. Didn't you ever want to go joyriding in a car?' The kid would say, 'We've done that.' The old man would say, 'Why just joyride? The car is valuable. For parts.' They start talking economics, supply and demand. 'If there's a demand, say for a Lincoln Town Car, you joyride the car, you bring it to the chop shop, and you get money. It's not that hard to do. You've already taken the car. Bring it in and you make some moola.'

"When they started out, my friends like Joseph Testa, Anthony Senter, they were pretty boys, real Italian stallions, lover boys. Over time the Old-Timers would work on them, and they would change. One vicious predator, Roy DeMeo, was a total psychotic killer. He didn't live in Canarsie, but he would come to Canarsie at the Amoco Station across from South Shore High School, and he would hang out, and he'd get these kids to come there, and they'd start stealing cars, get money for parts, and he'd be infecting their minds. Before long, he had a crew of created psychotic killers. There were no doubts in my mind Roy DeMeo's furniture upstairs was arranged in the wrong rooms.

"As they were reaching their late teens, early twenties, I couldn't even recognize them. For instance, when Joseph Testa was a little kid, we were playing with a slingshot. We would go to the open fields, the lots where some people dumped debris, and we would shoot at blackbirds and rats. Naturally we couldn't hit the broad side of a barn. But this time Testa pulled the slingshot back with a rock in it, and he hit a sparrow in a tree, and the bird fell down, and it was flapping around, and the kid started crying like somebody had turned on a faucet. This was no hard-core, stone-cold killer. So how does that person ten years later become impervious to any human sentimentality? Was he born that way? No, but Roy DeMeo and the other Old-Timers kept feeding it. And Roy DeMeo and his crew went on to become the most vicious killing crew, hired out by John Gotti Sr. and others to do their dastardly deeds.

"Years later we found out what they were doing. They would meet at the Gemini Lounge on Troy Avenue in East Flatbush, just outside Canarsie, or they would meet at the Veterans & Friends Social Club, a main hangout in that same section of Brooklyn, and there were other gin mills where they'd hang out some. But in this den of doom and gloom, the Gemini Lounge, they would get the contract to kill guys, and they became so proficient, it became a slaughterhouse.

"They'd get contracts, lure their victims to the Gemini Lounge, and they'd have girls there, drink, have a good time, and then they would lure the victims into the back area, and they'd stab them. They perfected the art of draining the body of blood. They'd hang them upside down in the bathroom, drain the body of blood, chop up the body parts, package it for disposal in plastic sheets, and have a private carter pick up the plastic bags, and they'd be dumped in the Spring Creek dump along the Belt Parkway. Or the body would be put in a barrel, filled with concrete, and dumped in Jamaica Bay. Occasionally, they didn't put enough concrete in, and the barrel would surface, and the NYPD would have another murder case. Guys suddenly would be missing in action, off the street, boom, gone.

"DeMeo used to be referred to as the Murder Machine. The Gambino guys were terrified of him, because he was a total psychotic. One day in the 1980s he was found in the back of his car, shot multiple times.

"There are guys I'm having trouble with today who come out of the Gotti wing of the Gambino crime family. I grew up with Little Nick Corozzo, who is now underboss and the titular head of the Gambino crime family. No one wants to be labeled the don, because they fall fast and furious under indictment. So Little Nick is the titular head, and his brother JoJo is the consigliere. And JoJo's son Joseph is a criminal defense attorney who has represented his father. That's intimidating, because you are not going to want to be cooperating with the government when Joseph Corozzo is the lawyer.

"Little Nick's father was Big Nick Corozzo. Little Nick-Nick and I used to play stickball together when we were about eight years old. This one day I was batting, and there must have been a tornado behind me, because I hit the Spaldeen with the sawed-off stick from my grandmother's broom, and it had to have gone two and a half sewers, which was like a miracle. There was a strong gust of wind, and I lifted the ball, and it hit the windshield of this all-red Cadillac Eldorado with the top down and the little dice in the front and the Italian horns, the cornu with the crown on it.

"This well-dressed guy was sitting on the stoop talking with this Old-Timer, who may have been sixty. The Old-Timer was smoking the Italian stinker. The ball bounced off the car, and the guy in the suit, who was in his twenties, grabbed the ball, walked up to us, and he had an ominous look. He stared at us, and we were frostbitten from the tips of our noses to the tips of our toes.

"'Whose fucking ball is this?' he asks. Our reaction was 'Ubabubbabubbabubba.' We were barely able to speak. He pulled out a switchblade knife, sliced the ball in front of us as if he were slicing an apple, and he said, 'The next person who hits a ball anywhere near my car I will gut out like a pig.' And he used the term *schifosa,* which is a word you would never say in public. It's a nasty, nasty word.

"We were terrified. We went all the way down the block so we would have had to hit the ball five sewers to hit that red Eldorado. I was seven or eight. We were shaking. And Nick Corozzo grew up to be an out-of-control, psychotic killer.

"This was the 1960s, early 1970s, and the city itself was beginning to change. The Old-Timers were getting kids into the traditional rackets, like stealing cars, but now the Old-Timers are having them trafficking in drugs: speed, cocaine. They'd get hyped up, really on edge. They were taking bathtub crank, methamphetamines, cocaine powder. Those drugs gave them a feeling of invincibility. They thought they could take on the world. But they also had drugs like Quaaludes and downers to lure the young ladies and break down their inhibitions. Man, if you had those, these girls couldn't get enough of them. That was like candy to them. So one minute they might be playing stickball with me, playing street games, and they were also getting to be a little bit of wise guys, getting into a little bit of trouble. They were getting JD cards—juvenile delinquent cards—from the coppers, and don't forget, at the time almost all the cops were Irish. We called them O'Hares or O'Haras.

"Meantime, most of the troublemakers were Italian kids. Jewish kids in that neighborhood were studying Torah, were in the library, were doing extra-credit reports. Occasionally one of them would become psychotic and want to be a wise guy, and since the Italians and the Jews got along, they'd adopt him. They'd say, 'You're going to be our accountant when you get older. You being a Jew, who knows? You may be on the parole board when we're looking at twenty-five years to life.'

"But that kid was the rarity.

"Most people would say that life becomes better for them as they mature, get older, acquire wealth, equity, and are able to make decisions. I would go back in an instant, without hesitation, to the ages of six to twelve. I wish every kid could have had an opportunity to grow up in a place like Canarsie, Brooklyn. The neighborhood was, for me, nirvana.

"First of all, if you were Roman Catholic, you identified by what parish you belonged to. There were three in Canarsie; Our Lady of Miracles was mine. It was called OLM, and if you were a hard-core Roman Catholic you went to OLM or to Holy Family. These were the traditional parishes, called old-school parishes. OLM still had the Latin Mass, and when they shook the incense during the service, they'd shake the thing so thick you'd have to wear a gas mask not to pass out. We're talking hard-to-the-core Roman Catholic service. Whereas the New Jack parish, St. Jude's, which had just opened up and had no credibility, was artsy-fartsy, practicing with the Peter, Paul, and Mary folk Mass. And it was in English, not Latin.

"The other thing you identified your neighborhood by was the candy store/luncheonette. My cousin Lenny 'Beans' Bianchino's dad, Uncle Ralph, owned the local luncheonette, and we would visit his mother, Aunt Sylvia, there. She was behind the counter, and she would smoke unfiltered Chesterfields nonstop like a chimney, and she had a raspy voice. We used to call her the Chesterfield Queen.

"One day she was bending over, using elbow grease to Ajax the counter, getting it to shine, when I saw the Star of David, what I called the Ben Hur symbol, drop out of her blouse. I thought, *Oh, my God.* I said, 'Lenny, your mother. What's with the Ben Hur symbol?'

"'My mother is Jewish,' Lenny said. I couldn't believe it. We thought we'd be excommunicated if there was a Jew in our family. Her maiden name was Rosen. She was from Brownsville. At that time a Catholic was not supposed to marry a Jew, or vice versa, so it had to be very rough. Lenny wasn't raised very religiously, either Catholic or Jew, but I couldn't help but think, *Lenny is going to be excommunicated. The Flying Nun is going to come down, and that's it, buddy. No chance for you. Straight to hell without an asbestos suit.* You can imagine the shock for me!

"But being in the luncheonette became the identity for your slice of the neighborhood. The guy behind the counter was usually a World War II vet, a guy named Sam or Louie. You would see his World War II picture behind him. He was a corporal at Guadalcanal, and he had a Japanese flag as a souvenir. He'd say, 'Those nips. Those krauts. We taught them.' In those days I couldn't wait to read the comic *Sgt. Fury and the Howling Commandos*. It was so politically incorrect. They would never allow a comic like that nowadays.

"The person behind the counter took pride in how he made the egg cream. It was a science. The first thing you learned as a little kid was, 'There is no egg in egg cream.' I wanted to know, 'Why do they call it an egg cream?'

"'You ask too many questions. Just drink it.'

"The secret of the egg cream is the chocolate syrup, the glass being chilled appropriately, a chilled spoon, a long spoon, and the seltzer being *spritzed* in at the right level, and then naturally the wrist action where you're beating the chocolate syrup and the seltzer to get that fizz.

"People prided themselves on how they made their egg cream. They were so proud that it wouldn't foam over. They always had the proper texture, and naturally you had to have a salted pretzel rod—always so fresh—that came in one of those little canisters.

"The other thing we tried to do was bamboozle some pure Coca-Cola syrup, because we didn't know it, but this was a drug: a little cocaine action. It was *so* good. You didn't become addicted, but it was so sweet, so good, that you had to come up with a reason—a ruse—to get some. 'My mom says I'm coming down with strep throat.' Or 'I have a stomachache.' He was a combination soda jerk/pharmacist. If you were sick, your mom would send you down for it. 'I have strep throat.'

"'You have a lot of strep throats.'

"'Yeah, and the doctor said they have to take my tonsils out.' And he would buy it! Oh, it was *so* good. They only gave you a little bit.

"As for going to the movies, we went to the Canarsie Theater on Avenue L. The theaters were magnificent, with organ pipes and fine carpet and gargoyles. The Canarsie Theater wasn't the most magnificent in Brooklyn—no way, those were along

Flatbush Avenue—but for a local theater, everyone knew it. [It was gutted and turned into a banquet hall in 2004.]

"The big day was Saturday, matinee day. You went early, about ten o'clock, and you didn't get out until two or three. You got to watch a few cartoons, and they would show a picture, and then they'd have a raffle—you could win a Big Chief Schwinn bike, dolls, a pancake mitt. I never won—and then they'd show another picture. The first flick was always better than the second flick. Before they invented day care, the movies on Saturday was it. The cost was a nickel, cheap.

"I was trained by Lenny 'Beans' Bianchino. I was the young guy, the shrimp. I had to earn my stripes. Every time I was there, about halfway through the movie, he'd say, 'Curtis, there are ten of our friends outside. When I tap you on the shoulder, you're going to act like you're going back to buy some Jujubes or some Good and Plenty, and you look for the exit sign, and you break through, open the door, let the other guys in, and keep running.'

"Lenny's friends were waiting, and once I let them in, they would run in all different directions, because the blue-haired matron with the white gloves and the K-Light flashlight knew someone was bum-rushing the door once she saw the light pierce the darkness.

"The matron was like a track star. They hid, but she had radar with night vision built in. If she caught someone she knew hadn't paid, she'd grab him by the nape of the neck and the next thing you'd see, she'd be kicking them outside.

Chester Sliwa in his sailor suit. *Courtesy of Curtis Sliwa*

"Lenny's friends would hide in the men's room, because a woman walking into the men's room was not good. She'd have to come in real quick and leave, so if you could stand on the porcelain palace, she'd look under the door and leave, and when they started the next show, you could run out and watch the movie.

"Sometimes we would go to Coney Island, but I preferred Rockaway Playland.

We had a '54 Ford station wagon with wood-paneled sides and white-wall tires. My dad came out of the Midwest, and he believed in Fords. The Italian side of the family said, 'Ford? Ugh. The worst.' They wanted GM. But Ford was a fixture in our house, and Mom would load us into the car, my older sister Alita, my younger sister Marie, and myself, and sometimes my friends, and she'd say, 'We're not going to Coney Island. It's too crowded. You can never get on the rides you want, because you have to wait on the better ones, and the water is not the cleanest in the world. We're going out to Rockaway Playland.'

"We were so excited. We'd take the Belt Parkway to Cross Bay Boulevard. On the way we'd stop at Aunt Mary's in Howard Beach. We'd continue on Cross Bay Boulevard and pass Broad Channel, an island that separated the Rockaways from Howard Beach, and then you made a right, and you were at the Irish Riviera.

"You knew you were in Rockaway Beach because all the kids had freckles. No Italian kid had freckles. Maybe a mole. Never a freckle. But all the Irish kids had freckles, and every girl was named Colleen. They had blond hair, blue eyes. You would fall in love with the Colleens.

"Rockaway Playland had a roller coaster, had a Ferris wheel, had everything Coney Island had but was smaller and less crowded, and the beach was better. Rockaway Beach was on the Atlantic Ocean, not sheltered like Coney Island, so the waves were better.

"You couldn't bring food onto the beach. The only ones who were permitted to sell food were the guys in the safari hats and the shorts selling Bungalow Bars, which was like a Klondike bar. It would melt in your mouth. They looked like they were on Mutual of Omaha's *Wild Kingdom*.

"If you walked on the boardwalk, you'd better have a T-shirt on, or the O'Haras were going to cite you, and if you weren't respectful, they would give you a wooden shampoo—hit you with their nightstick, billy club, blackjack, or truncheon. Oh yeah. 'Cause the Irish Riviera was their turf. You're an Italian guy? Or you don't look Irish? You don't have freckles? Their attitude was, 'You're lucky you're here.'

"We played all sorts of street games. The Italian kids competed in a game we called stretch. This was the ultimate test of total manhood. It was the predecessor of chickity-out, when you finally got a hot rod, and you'd race and come close to the other car, and the first one to veer away lost.

"In stretch you'd take a switchblade and throw it in the dirt. You put your foot right there, and the next guy would take the switchblade and throw it next to the foot as close as possible. The question is: Are you going to keep your foot there? How close does the knife come? It's the ultimate test. And sometimes a guy would have to go to the emergency ward of Brookdale Hospital, because he wasn't going to move his foot, and the other guy's aim needed a little straightening out. Right into your foot!

"Some guys would just close their eyes. When they'd hear the click and the blade would go in the ground, they knew it hadn't hit their foot, and they could open their eyes like they were tough guys. 'You closed your eyes, punk. You're supposed to stare.' Oh, it was great.

"I was taught the game by my uncle Ralphie's son, my cousin Lenny 'Beans' Bianchino, who was four foot eight, eighty pounds soaking wet. Lenny was so short he had a Napoleonic complex. He would challenge all the big guys, even though they were going to turn him into a speed bump.

"'Don't go up to that guy,' I'd say to Lenny.

"'No,' he'd say. 'Nobody treats me like that.' And they'd pick him up and slam him down on his head. But he was tough. And Lenny loved baseball. We didn't have Rawlings or Spalding gloves. We had the pancake mitt that was made in Formosa, aka Taiwan. You didn't want to show it, because it didn't have a brand name, and it didn't have a signature, like Bobby Richardson of the Yankees or Rod Kanehl of the Mets. It only had that tag: Formosa. Everyone knew it was *cheap,* so you kept it tucked under your wing. The glove was bigger than Lenny was, but to make a good pocket, he'd take a hard ball, and then he'd take 22,000 rubber bands, and he'd tighten the ball up inside the glove so it made a pocket, and then he'd put the glove in the freezer.

"'What are you doing, Lenny?' I asked him.

"'This makes a pocket,' he said.

"We'd go to sleep at night after talking with my uncle Ralph, who was a degenerate gambler. At ten o'clock he would walk down to the local candy store and get the night-owl edition of the *Daily News* so he would have the racing form for the next day. It would also have the pari-mutuel results from that day, so you knew whose numbers won. So if you were playing the numbers, the bookie couldn't rip you off, because you knew the right numbers from the night. At night there would be lines. Sometimes more people bought the night edition of the *News* than the paper in the morning.

"We'd go to sleep. The glove would be in the freezer overnight, and we'd wake up the next morning to go out to the fields and play hardball. He took the glove from the freezer, and it was like a rock, and he let it thaw out, and damn if it wasn't a perfect pocket! It had such a perfect pocket the ball would just cuddle into it and not fall out. And he had oils. He put 10W-40 on it, and he'd work it, massage it. That glove was like an appendage, an extension of him. It became his personality, and he was very good with it.

"Lenny was three years older than I was, and it was he who taught me how to survive in the streets without being a sucker. He was in Little League, and I was there watching, and another kid came over and said to me, 'Can I borrow your bicycle? I'm just going to ride it around the block. I'll bring it right back.' I was willing, but Lenny, who was in the on-deck circle, saw this, and he came running over with the bat, and he said to the kid, 'I'll knock your head off.'

"'No, Lenny, I just wanted to take it for a ride.'

"'You're trying to steal that bike. That's my cousin. If you steal his bike, I will come for you.'

"'No problem, Lenny.'

"The guy was twice Lenny's size, but Lenny just didn't take shit from nobody. Lenny had this fearlessness he had developed. He was like my mentor, and I learned from him. I was able to accept what I felt was necessary and discard some of the other stuff that was over the top."

# HERE COME THE IRISH

PETE HAMILL

**L**ONG BEFORE THE JEWS LANDED IN AMERICA IN LARGE NUM-bers, the Protestant majority was threatened by the immigration of the Irish. Their feud went back to merry old England, where the Protestants worshipped God first, Oliver Cromwell second, and William of Orange third. Cromwell was loved because he drove out the "treasonous, idol-worshipping, priest-ridden" Catholics. When the Catholics staged a comeback in 1690, William of Orange defeated them at the Battle of the Boyne.

The Protestants banned the practice of Catholicism, so the Catholics had to worship in secret. The Protestants considered them to be spies of Satan, and felt it was God's demand that they convert them to the freedoms and liberties of Protestantism by any means necessary.

In the 1700s the English passed what were known as the Penal Laws. No Catholic could hold public office. No Catholic could study science or go to a foreign university. No Catholic could buy or even lease land. No Catholic could take a land dispute to court. If a Catholic had been a landowner before the passage of the Penal Laws, he could not leave it to his oldest son. He had to divide it among his children, ensuring poverty within three generations.

Among the most draconian of the Penal Laws was the one that stated that no Catholic could own a horse worth more than 5 pounds. Any Protestant could look at a Catholic's horse, say it was worth

6 pounds, or 60 pounds, or 600 pounds, and he could take it from him on the spot. The Catholic had no right to protest in court. Said Pete Hamill in his novel *Forever,* "In a country of great horses and fine horsemen, the intention was clear: to humiliate Catholic men and break their hearts."

Samuel F. B. Morse.
*Library of Congress*

The enmity between the two groups was just as intense in America. There was a lot the Protestant Americans didn't like about the Catholics: the Protestants saw the Catholics as clannish and intemperate. The Irish were in the habit of sending money back home, and so their loyalty was questioned. Worst of all, they practiced the Catholic religion, and Protestants were convinced Catholic monarchies and the Church in Rome were conspiring to undermine the American Revolution and the Protestant Reformation by sending immigrants to the United States.

How deep was the Protestant hatred of the Irish? Samuel F. B. Morse, the inventor of the telegraph, wrote a book, published in 1835, in which he said of the Irish:

"How is it possible that foreign turbulence imported by shiploads, that riot and ignorance in hundreds of thousands of human priest-controlled machines should suddenly be thrown into our society and not produce turbulence and excess? Can one throw mud into pure water and not disturb its clearness?"

The Irish insisted the initials F. B. in Morse's name stood for "fucking bigot."

More than a 100,000 illiterate Irish emigrated to the United States during the years 1843 and 1846, after the potato crop failed and it became a question of life or death. Most landed in Boston, because the fare was cheaper than it was to go to New York City, but large numbers of Irish immigrants nevertheless settled in the Five Points section of Lower Manhattan.

Protestants wondered whether Irish parents who refused to send their children to public schools could be good Americans. At the same time the Protestants gave the Irish good reason not to send their kids to the public schools. In the 1840s, textbooks would disparage them, and their children would be made to sing Protestant hymns and read from Protestant Bibles in public schools. Why should the Irish immigrants' children have to be subjected to that?

There were anti-Catholic riots in Boston and Philadelphia in the 1830s and 1840s. Protestant mobs attacked Catholic churches. They attacked men they suspected of being Catholic in the street, with cudgels. In the 1850s the Protestants formed an anti-Catholic political party called the Know-Nothings. It was a secret Protestant fraternal organization—the Order of the Star-Spangled Banner—you had to be born a white Protestant to join and you took an oath to resist "the insidious policies of the Church of Rome and all other foreign influences." When any question was asked about the organization, members were instructed to say, "I know nothing."

In two years the organization had a million members. In 1856 the Know-Nothing Party, which had by then changed its name to the American Party, received nearly 900,000 votes out of 4 million, but its presidential candidate, Millard Fillmore, carried only the state of Maryland. Fillmore had been elected vice president on the Whig ticket with Zachary Taylor and assumed the presidency upon Taylor's death in 1850. He did not receive the nomination of the Whigs in 1852. The party had largely faded away by 1860.

Anti-Catholic fervor returned during the Panic of 1893, a time of financial depression. Over time the Irish not only made up the bulk of New York City's police and firefighters, but they banded together, organizing politically, and they took control of urban governments, whenever possible, to guarantee their rights. In New York they took over Tammany Hall, which controlled city politics until 1960.

Another significant Irish influx into Brooklyn came after the opening of the Brooklyn Bridge in 1883. This time they came in droves from Manhattan, as the Irish walked across the big bridge and settled in South Brooklyn, neighborhoods now called Park Slope and Windsor Terrace. Pete Hamill, the renowned journalist and author, grew up in Park Slope long before the area got its name.

**PETE HAMILL**   "I was born in Brooklyn, in Bay Ridge, in 1935. When I was young, we moved to what is now called Park Slope by the real estate people. Nobody had fancy names back then. We called it 'the neighborhood.' We lived in three places. The first was right up near Prospect Park, a beautiful street with trees, and then we moved to a place right next to a factory, and that wasn't so beautiful, and the third was a tenement on Seventh Avenue.

"My father came to America from Belfast, Ireland, in 1923. He was twenty. He was a young guy in Sinn Féin. The British and the Catholics in Ireland were in a war like the Sunnis and the Shia in Iraq. The British Protestants organized pogroms. Mobs would go into Catholic areas and burn houses, and the Catholic toughs, who were protecting what was their little privilege, fought back.

"The Protestants, for example, got all the decent jobs at the shipyards. The *Titanic* was built in Belfast, and one of the myths of Belfast was, 'The *Titanic* hit the iceberg because they didn't employ Catholics. God wanted to give them a good shot.' So the deck was stacked against the Irish Catholics, particularly the men, especially if you piled up any sort of record of being in Sinn Féin.

"Michael Collins was the Irish leader, and when he was killed that year [1922], there was nobody left who was going to free them, and my father decided he better go. He had two older brothers who were already in America, so they were able to get him jobs. He came through Boston, which was the cheap ticket, and he came over with a guy by the name of Red Dorrian, who ended up running a very successful Manhattan bar, Dorrian's Red Hand. They arrived in Brooklyn on July 4, 1923.

"He hated the British. I'd say to him, 'You know, that Shakespeare was a pretty good writer.' He said, 'Yeah, but did you hear about the Sepoy Mutiny in India where the British shoved people into cannons and fired them?' The British were like the Japanese. The farther they got away from home, the more savage they became.

"My father lost his leg playing soccer in the immigrant leagues in the twenties. He had played in Ireland, and when he got here, he played all over, from Brooklyn to the Bronx. There was an Irish team, a German team, a British team, and a Jewish team called the House of David. He got kicked, and they didn't have penicillin, and gangrene set in. They sawed off his leg, so he did not go into the war.

"My father got a job in Brooklyn, and so he settled in Brooklyn. I'm sure he got the job through the Tammany organization. He was a clerk at one of the big grocery chains, Roulston's, whose headquarters were down by the Gowanus Canal, so some of the logic of our moves was to live closer to Roulston's. He had only gone through eighth grade, but he had good handwriting. He worked until the outbreak of the war, and then he went to work nights in a war plant in Bush Terminal. He worked on making bomb sights.

"My father went to Mass, but religion wasn't a big deal to him. My mother was more religious because it gave her a certain kind of consolation. And she was better educated. Somehow she finished high school in Belfast. For a woman to do that was astonishing, because more of the girls went off at fifteen to work in the linen mills. And for a Catholic woman to get an education—it was hard to believe.

"My mother was born in 1910, and she had come to America before World War I. Her father had been an engineer with what they called the Great White Fleet, the British fleet that went to Central America and Panama. When she was born, her father decided it was time to live on land, and he didn't want to live in Belfast, because of the religious strife. That was one of the reasons he and his brothers had gone to sea. Nobody at sea asked any of those questions. It was free.

"I was born in '35, so the war started when I was six, and for kids my age comic books were the biggest thing. Captain America was always doing battle with a guy by the name of the Red Skull, who was a dirty, rotten, filthy, stinkin' Nazi. He'd be sabotaging places, and I always worried he would sabotage Bush Terminal and my father. I was young and impressionable.

"And then after the war there was a lull where nobody could get work. All the war plants were closing. We thought our having to go to war was over. They didn't realize this was just the beginning of the United States as a permanent warrior nation. Dad finally got a job in a factory across the street from where we lived at 378 Seventh Avenue between 11th and 12th Streets. Across the street on the corner of 12th Street and Seventh Avenue was the Ansonia Clock Factory Building, once the biggest factory in Brooklyn in the nineteenth century. Now it's co-ops. My dad worked in a place called Globe Lighting in an assembly line, making fluorescent lights. So we had fluorescent lights in most of the rooms in our apartment. It turned everybody blue, the worst-looking thing you ever saw. To give you an idea how old these buildings were, we had old gas-lamp sconces on the walls from the time of gas lighting. They had been sealed up.

"The area that is now called South Slope is reasonably intact physically. A number of buildings burned down over the years, but there were no urban renewal projects. Basically the neighborhood was blue-collar. It was a good place to grow up. It was only a couple blocks from Prospect Park, and you could go to the park and walk across. You would see all the tribes of Brooklyn, the Jewish tribe, the Italian tribe, the Irish tribe, crossing the park to go to the ballgame at Ebbets Field. And after Jackie Robinson, finally, the black tribe. They finally got a seat at the table.

"One of the great benefits of my dad working at Globe Lighting was he got into the union, Local 3 of the International Brotherhood of Electrical Workers, Harry Van Arsdale president. So the family was obviously pro-union. The union gave people like that—as we will give the Mexicans, if they ever get legal—a chance to live a life with dignity. And of course they were Democrats.

"In the kitchen of our apartment at 378 Seventh Avenue, top floor right, were two pictures: the Sacred Heart of Jesus over the door and Franklin D. Roosevelt. I grew up with this vague impression that God must have liked Roosevelt—compared to the fucking dope we have who sounds like Tonto.

"The building had six apartments, and they were all working-class, either Irish or Italians. Right across the hall were the Caputos. Other Italian families were scattered about. It wasn't exclusively Irish. The Jews were fading. There had been more Jews there, but after the war the Jews tended to take advantage of the GI Bill educational benefits, whereas the Irish, by and large, took the VA mortgages and moved to Long Island.

"It was not white flight. There were no blacks yet. The black migration didn't start until the 1950s. There were a few Puerto Ricans around. A fighter by the name of LuLu Perez lived right up the block. He fought a famous fight against Willie Pep, which Willie dumped, the last time Willie fought in Madison Square Garden. The people in the neighborhood would yell at LuLu, 'You couldn't whip Willie Pep on the best day of your life.' It was sad. LuLu Perez wasn't in on the fix. He was a pretty good fighter. Everyone knew it was fixed, because Willie was such a bad actor. There's a film of it, and you can see Willie shaking, trying to get an Academy Award in the second round.

"Within that neighborhood were different class levels. The closer you lived to the park, the better off you were. The people living in the brownstones were doing better than those living in the tenements. And there were brick houses around the corner from the tenements. Jimmy Breslin's famous line: 'He can't be a crook. He lives in a house.' And scattered in and out were buildings that were slummy.

"I went to Holy Name School. Holy Name was on Prospect Avenue, and Gil Hodges lived on that block while he was playing. I saw him a couple of times. The thing about growing up in Brooklyn, you didn't ask people for autographs. You weren't going to demean yourself. But you'd say, 'Good morning,' or 'How are you?'

"I never asked my parents why they sent me to Catholic school, but I'm sure it was because the education level was higher. I ended up at a very good high school called Regis, a Jesuit school on 84th Street and Park Avenue in Manhattan. It took three trains to get there. At the time there were no Jesuit high schools in Brooklyn. There were two in Manhattan, Regis and Xavier, which was a semi-military school.

"The Jesuit schools are famous for creating atheists. I still stay in touch with some of the guys I went to high school with. They are all lawyers, and one of them is in the CIA. I once ran into him in Saigon, and then I realized what he was doing there. And it was a very good school for a young writer, an apprentice writer who didn't even think he was going to be a writer at the time. We were taught Latin, and I took a year of German.

"I never graduated. I went there for two years, freshman and sophomore years, and then I went to work at the Brooklyn Navy Yard.

"I quit for a number of reasons. One, there were money problems at home. Two, I found parts of school—Latin—really tedious. I had other ambitions. I could draw pretty well, and I wanted to be a comic-book artist. I was trying to get laid. How would I talk Latin to a girl from the neighborhood? All kinds of things were overlapping, but part of it was I wanted to get on with my life. And I had never met a single person who had gone to the university. It was common all over the neighborhood to drop out of high school and help support your family, until you had one of your own. And when I lived at home, I was the oldest of six. When I was seventeen, I went to work in the sheet metal shop at the navy yard.

"My mother was very upset by this, because it had been so hard for her to complete high school. 'How can you do this?' But my father didn't care one way or the other. He only went through the eighth grade. I had already surpassed him. But the fact was, nobody ever went to the university.

"I had to take an exam to work in the navy yard. The Jesuits had taught me how to pass exams. I worked in Shop 17 as an apprentice. And the way it worked—a wonderful idea for working-class kids—you worked for four weeks and then you went to school for a week, so there was still more schooling, though most of it was for their purposes. I had to read blueprints, so there was some math. You didn't get much exploration of Caesar's Gallic Wars, but it was pretty good, and the great value to people like me was it taught me how to work, how to get up in the morning and get on the train and get there on time and do work I didn't like, take it or leave it. I didn't like it, but I didn't hate it.

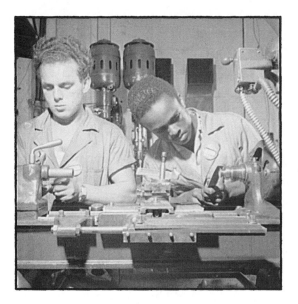

Blacks and whites worked side by side in the machine shop at the Brooklyn Navy Yard. *Library of Congress*

"The basic work that was going on was the conversion of aircraft carriers to jets. Because there was so much vibration from the jet fighters, they had to redo the top couple of decks and that meant we had to take the flight decks apart. It was one of the best jobs I ever had. I worked with a black burner who used an acetylene torch to cut out the old bulkheads. You could never make a clean cut with one of those torches, so I would come along with a twenty-five-pound sledgehammer and smash the hammer down on the wall. I would step over that one and move onto the next one.

"The majority of the people at the navy yard were like the majority of the people in Brooklyn—Irish. I met people there who knew my father when he was playing soccer. But there were black faces all around the place.

"It was federal civil service, so it was integrated. There were black students in the apprentice program. Truman had integrated the armed services, and the navy was supposed to be integrated, but it really wasn't. It was still segregated by jobs. If you were black, you would make a great cook, but you would not make an airplane mechanic.

"But before the integration of the armed services, before anybody, there was Jackie Robinson. We didn't learn humanity from our first experience working with a black person in Brooklyn, because we had Robinson. And by then, we had Roy Campanella and Don Newcombe.

"I worked in the navy yard in 1951, and at night I went to the School of Visual Arts on 23rd Street and Second Avenue in Manhattan, which was originally called the Cartoonists and Illustrators School. I studied with a guy by the name of Burne Hogarth, who had been an artist on *Tarzan*. He was a wonderful teacher. I'd finish at the navy yard at four and then try to go home and change clothes, but if I couldn't, I took the subway and went to 23rd Street, and there was a library across the street, and I could sit there and doze until class began at seven. I was making forty dollars a week, so I didn't have much to spare, but it was great. I had a sense of what an art school was.

"I had a wonderful teacher by the name of Tom McMahon, who saw that I had some kind of talent and let me write whatever I wanted to write instead of 'My Trip to Albany.' That was a terrific thing—a piece of luck. He had read everything, and he pushed me in certain ways. I read Katherine Anne Porter's short stories for the first time. I read Dos Passos.

"I worked at the navy yard for a year, when I realized I had fucked up stupidly by dropping out of high school. I thought if I went into the navy proper, I could take the high school equivalency exam while I was in there and be eligible for the GI Bill. And that's what I did.

"I did well in the navy in everything but manual labor. I would not have been a good airplane mechanic. They made me a storekeeper, and I learned how to type, which was invaluable in a future occupation, and they sent me to Norman, Oklahoma, for a couple months for some kind of advanced training. And then the Korean

War ended, and everything froze. I ended up in Pensacola, Florida, where there were seven hundred Baptist churches and one bookstore. But at the base was a great library, and there I first read Hemingway, Fitzgerald, people like that.

"While I was in the navy, I met a guy from Marietta, Georgia, Henry Whiddon, who was a painter in civilian life. He would paint in the back of my storeroom, and my passion began to change from comics to painting. I thought I could be a painter.

"I was twenty years old when I got out, and because of the GI Bill, I could go to any university I wanted to, as long as it was government-approved. I wanted to go to Paris. In 1951 I had seen the movie *American in Paris,* with Gene Kelly. He was a Mick, and he was painting, and he had Leslie Caron, and I wanted to go there, but I couldn't afford it. Even then, in 1955, what I got from the GI Bill after the Korean War was $110 a month, and out of that you had to pay tuition, rent, and food. I had been working since I was sixteen, and I didn't want to have to go to school and take some job as a waiter too.

"This is how everybody's thinking had changed from what the soldiers coming out of World War II did and what those of us coming out of Korea did with the GI Bill. It was only a matter of a half a generation.

"It wasn't just Ted Williams who had to go back into the armed services. Korea was five years after we were all dancing in the streets on VJ-Day. And guys from the neighborhood got killed, because that's the kind of neighborhood that fought both wars. They didn't profit from them. They fought them. It has to be stressed, not just in Brooklyn, but all over: what ended in the summer of 1945 was a fifteen-year period of deprivation, which included the Depression. The guys who didn't have work in 1934 or 1935 found work with a rifle in their hand, and when the war was over, they just wanted to marry the girl they left behind and have a home with a backyard.

"By the time of my generation, there was a shift to get an education rather than to buy a house in the suburbs.

"Reality had sunk in. *This is the ultimate boredom.* You needed a car and gasoline. It was hard. So rather than use the GI Bill to move, which is what we did after World War II, we felt the important thing was to get educated, and then you could make some dough. My brother Tom was two years younger than me, and he went to City College with Colin Powell, and he went off to Northwestern and got a master's degree in engineering.

"I went to Mexico City. Henry Whiddon, the painter I knew, had heard about Mexico City College. It had a very good arts school, and it was acceptable to the GI Bill. And it was a great place to be, because you had the typical mixture of young dopes—Ohio Staters going for the summer, who went down to Mexico to drink—and there were guys who had been in the Battle of the Bulge.

"We took courses in Spanish and English. When I arrived in Mexico City, all I could say in Spanish was, 'Hello,' and 'Good morning.' You wanted to take Spanish because you were living there. And one of the accidental benefits of learning a foreign language is that you really learn about your own language, which is why all classical education includes Latin or French or both. The Latin helped me with the Spanish, so I learned fairly quickly how to talk my way out of things, like if I walked into the wrong cantina. And Mexico City College had a very good writing instructor by the name of Ted Robins. He was good in terms of pushing us to do more than just show up. It was a great decision to go there; between the vowels of Mexico and the consonants of New York, I could get a sentence out of myself.

"While I was still in New York I had seen reproductions of the Mexican muralists José Clemente Orozco and Diego Rivera. After I began to think about becoming a painter, I went to see their actual work, and the one thing reproductions don't show you is their scale. They are gigantic, overwhelming, and if you're a kid, like I was—intimidating. In certain ways they turned me off to painting, and my instincts went to writing. When you come from Brooklyn, you're never in love with the grandiose. Your neighbors won't let you.

"I was more and more interested in narrative. I wanted to say, 'This happened, and this happened, and as a result, this happened,' but I couldn't figure out how to tell a narrative with paint. And at the time the attempt to do so was sneered at. To art critics there was nothing worse than Norman Rockwell, who told stories in paintings. It took a long time for people to realize he was valuable. So writing more and more began to interest me, and you write the way your heroes wrote, so I wrote like

Hemingway and Fitzgerald. My teacher at the Cartoonists and Illustrators School, Burne Hogarth, said, 'There are four stages for every artist. Imitate, emulate, equal, and surpass.' I wrote it down at the time, and I tell that to students now. So in the beginning it was all imitation, and somewhere in there I discovered James T. Farrell and Studs Lonigan, and there I began to see that I didn't have to write about bull-fighters. There were subjects right up the block in Brooklyn to write about. And then I discovered the Beats. When I got home from Mexico in 1957, I had read the first book in English by Carlos Fuentes, and in 1958 I read an excerpt of *On the Road* in *The Paris Review*. It was in *The Paris Review* that I read Philip Roth for the first time. So I read this excerpt from *On the Road* about Kerouac being on a bus going into Mexico, and I had taken the same bus trip. And then the novel came out the follow-ing year, and I was living in the East Village then, and these guys were living all around the place. The first time I ever saw Kerouac, he looked like Frank Gifford, a big, handsome guy dressed like a lumberjack. Too self-conscious, if you came from Brooklyn.

"In a way all of it went back to Brooklyn. I was shaped by it, but when I think back about the important things, one was the unleashing of this amazing optimism that was in working-class Brooklyn after the war, and it was underpinned by the GI Bill. The optimism said, 'This is America. You can be anything you want to be.' And that meant everything. You could be a doctor or a lawyer—or, if you were really lucky, a sportswriter: you could go to the games for free and get paid for it. All those possibilities were there. And it was a very rich time in the newspaper business. You picked up a paper, and there, writing about sports, were Red Smith, Jimmy Cannon, Frank Graham, W. C. Heinz, Willard Mullins's cartoons. It was like a feast, a very high level of work. It was no accident they called them sportswriters, not sports reporters. So all of that was feeding into discovering literature without a teacher. I'm convinced now that all education is self-education, that every decent writer is an auto-didact. But I didn't know any of that then.

"You look at the sheer accidence of life, and I think emotionally of the optimism at the end of the war, the GI Bill that said, 'You can do it,' and I think of Robinson. We didn't have a phrase like 'role model,' but that's what he was. We knew from reading the papers what he was going through, particularly the first year when Chapman and the Phillies, the fucking assholes, taunted him and threw a black cat out onto the field. And you thought, *If he can put up with that crap without exploding, so can we.* So it began to shift so you didn't fight at the drop of a hat, didn't have to prove what a tough guy you were every waking hour. And yet there was a toughness around that was also different from what you have now. The real tough guys never talked tough. They *were* tough, and everybody knew it. They weren't going around showing what tough guys they were, like Dick Cheney and those other pricks who couldn't punch their way out of a schoolyard.

"All those things made me understand other things, made me understand the other immigrants, made me understand what people had overcome without self-pity. That was a key thing too. I never heard my father curse his fate at having lost his leg. A couple times he slapped the wooden leg—he couldn't express himself very well, but that was a Belfast Irish thing as well as Catholic. Seamus Heaney has a poem about Northern Irish style called 'Whatever You Say, Say Nothing.' There was a great holding back about the most intimate things. I never heard him say, 'I could have been a contender.' And it doesn't mean he didn't feel it, but he wasn't going to say it to his kids. And my mother had this other sense of time, which was not that things would get better tomorrow. She wasn't naive. But they will be better the day after tomorrow. There was a sense that there was a future tense, that you were going somewhere, that each life had a narrative, and we—the Americans—were the lucky ones. We didn't have to put up with the kind of bullshit that mutilated some of these people in the old country, wherever the old country was, be it Calabria, Sicily, Poland, or Belfast. It was going to be better, and those promises that America gave those people were kept. It wasn't some right-wing bullshit. The right-wingers were the ones who tried to prevent it.

"Everybody's story is different, but I bet most of them would have a similar pattern. While I was in the navy, I saw the movie *Roman Holiday,* with Gregory Peck and Eddie Albert. Peck is a newspaperman in Rome. He has an apartment where the bed folds up in the wall, like in a Marx Brothers' movie. He never seems to work. He rides around on a Vespa all over Rome, and he's got Audrey Hepburn, and that was the other formation of another way to live a life. The movies gave these visions of possible lives to the young.

"On June 1, 1960, I began at the *New York Post*. The *Post* was my favorite paper, because it had stood up to Joe McCarthy, stood up to Walter Winchell. They did a twenty-three-part series that basically ended Winchell's career. Every day they had a sidebar box, right out of Winchell, called 'Winchell's Wrongos.' 'FDR will *not* run for a third term.' It was wicked and awful, but great fun. And a great corrective.

"Jimmy Wechsler had brought out a book called *Reflections of an Angry Middle-aged Editor,* a terrible title, but I read it. One of the chapters was on journalism, and I wrote him a letter. I asked, 'How do you expect to keep the vitality of newspapers in New York when you're getting all these reporters who go to the Columbia School of Journalism and then go to work on the paper, who have never lived in New York?'

"He sent me a note, 'Thank you for writing. Have you ever thought about becoming a newspaperman?' And I had. I called him and we had lunch, and by the time we finished he offered me a tryout. They kept me on the tryout for the legal extent they could under the guild contract, which was three months. It was June, and they did a lot of tryouts then because they had a lot of people going on vacation. After the three months, they asked for an extension, and the guild gave them one more month, and then they hired me full-time.

"In between I was being taught how to do this. I had not gone to journalism school. I didn't even know how to slug a story. I didn't know how to do anything, but I had these amazingly good editors. The assistant night city editor was Ed Kosner, who was younger than I was and later went on to *Newsweek, Esquire,* and the *Daily News*. He took pity on this dumb *goy* in the corner. Other people were there, particularly Paul Sann, who I didn't see until he came in at six in the morning, but he was the real ball-breaker who made me into a newspaperman. He was amazingly smart. He might have graduated from high school, but barely. They were proving a point with me, that you could make anybody into a newspaperman. If you had the passion, it didn't matter whether you went to journalism school.

"Ike Gellis was the sports editor, and he was fun. There were a lot of wonderful drifters who would come in and out, guys would get drunk, throw a typewriter out the window, move down to the *Journal-American*. It was the end of the Bohemian culture that newspapers had. Once you get to 1970, the newspapermen were getting paid what they deserved, and then they became suburbanites. Back then, the wife would throw the guy out, and he'd end up at the Hotel Earle in Washington Square with the alto sax players. It was a wonderful time.

"There were seminars every morning at the Page One Bar, where everybody'd go at eight o'clock and wait for the paper to come out at nine. All the older guys would go through the paper and turn to you and say, 'You can't write a fucking lead like that. For Christ's sake, this is the way.' It was apprenticeship like at the navy yard, an apprenticeship like Leonardo at Barrochio's studio, learning how to paint an eyelash.

"Again I was lucky. Had I gone to the *Times,* which also had its Bohemian element, I might have gotten stuck in school sports for four years instead of covering three stories a night and writing captions in between. It was a great, great school, and I tell the kids at NYU, 'Whatever you do, get a job on a daily paper somewhere. Even if you want to work on *The New Yorker,* start on a daily and become fearless at the typewriter.'"

## WINDSOR TERRACE MEMORIES

JOE FLAHERTY, BOBBY MCCARTHY, AND BILL REDDY

BY THE MID-TWENTIETH CENTURY, THE SONS AND DAUGHTERS of Irish immigrants fit into American society easily and quickly. The one Irish institution that they brought to America was the village tavern, where people got together to exchange ideas and information and to down a brew or two. In Irish neighborhoods the corner saloon was often the most important ethnic institution—a place where men came to meet and talk of the old country, women, jobs, and the Dodgers.

Windsor Terrace was a typical Brooklyn neighborhood, a small Irish enclave to the south and west of Ebbets Field. It is a neighborhood that exists today only in the mind, but to those lucky enough to have grown up there, it is as real now as it was then.

Joe Flaherty, a journalist and author, passed away in 1985. When he talked of his childhood in Brooklyn, his face would soften, and he would become a little kid again.

**JOE FLAHERTY**   "When I think of my boyhood growing up in Brooklyn, I think of the magic of the streets. Whenever my saintly mother gets mad at me, she says, 'Joseph, you were nothing but a street kid anyway.' But hell, we all were. At that time the street was the center of neighborhood culture. The streets thrived. They weren't dangerous. Strangers couldn't walk onto your block and muck around, because so many people were playing in the streets at all hours. The only time anyone got hurt was when someone got hit with a stickball bat or fell out of a tree.

"When you walked out of your house, you would walk right into a stickball game, and if you didn't have enough players for stickball, you played 'catch a fly and you're up,' which was one guy at bat, the rest of you down the street, and if you caught a fly off his bat, you got to hit. On ground balls, you had to roll the ball in and hit the bat in such a way that the ball would hit the bat and jump away before the batter could catch it [so the batter would lose his turn at bat]. And if you only had two people, you would draw a batter's box against the wall, and you pitched to the other guy. On the wall behind the pitcher there were marks indicating single, double, triple, home run. Football didn't mean anything. Football was just another device to get broads. If there was a game, the football was just a rolled-up newspaper tied with a string. The game would be two-hand touch, and one of the great pass patterns of the day was, 'Go down to the left, cut behind the blue Chevy, and I'll hit you.'

"I remember, in the neighborhood where we lived, every house had a cement stoop, which was six or seven steps, off of which we played a game called 'single, double, triple, home run.' You put two guys in the outfield, playing across a gutter in the street. One of the guys would stand in the gutter, just off the curb, and the other would stand farther out. You would wind up and throw the ball against the stoop and try to hit the point of the step. If you could do that, the ball would really go, on a line drive.

"If not, you'd try to ricochet it from the bottom step, have it hit the riser above, and you'd get a long drive out across the street. If the ball bounced once before you caught it, it was a single. Two bounces, a double; three bounces, a triple; and four bounces or more, a home run. And if you hit the opposite wall across the street, that was also a home run, unless of course you caught the ball off the wall, in which case it was an out.

"And guys could play the wall as well as Carl Furillo. We even knew the bounces off the fire escape. The ball would be dangling up in the fire escape, and the outfielder would be running to the spot where he figured the ball would come down, and while we were playing, the older men in the neighborhood would sit out with their growlers of beer and watch the games, and these games would be echoing all over the streets. Cheers would be coming out from the different stoops. And the men would spend their evenings sitting on their stoops in their strapped undershirts, and women would be together on a different stoop, gabbing, and the radio would be blaring Red Barber and the Dodger game, and when it got dark, the kids began playing ring-a-levio or 'kick the can' or 'three feet to Germany,' all the exotic games that disappeared with the emergence of the automobile.

"I remember mothers constantly yelling out windows for their kids to come in, and the kids would never come. Whenever a mother called, the other kids would tell her that her son was on the opposite team playing ring-a-levio and was hiding and that as soon as we found him and captured him, he'd come. We'd tell her, 'It isn't his fault he's late for supper. He's been hiding for half an hour.' So we always had an edge. The mothers didn't particularly believe it, but they couldn't beat their kids with a clear conscience, so usually they didn't.

"There was no such thing as walking into the house and saying, 'I'm bored.' After the stickball and the stoopball, around nine at night we used to stand under the street lamps and have games of 'fly.' We'd throw high flies to each other, and you could see a glimpse of the ball coming down in the lights, and it was good practice. When we got a little older, at the end of the night, when everything was dead and you were exhausted and there was no more running left in your legs, no more peg left in your arm, we'd go inside and play seven-card stud for pennies or for picture cards. Believe me, if we had had the stamina, we would have stayed out there around the clock.

"Sunday was the day when there was always a stickball game, with one street challenging another. The kids would bet a quarter a man, or, if it was a big game, a half a dollar. That was big money in those days. The men on the block usually chipped in and supplied the Spaldeens. The bats were broom handles, not the aberrations they have now—the manufactured stickball bats, which shows you something about America's lack of self-reliance around the globe, considering that a kid now goes out and buys a stickball bat made in China—we used to get old brooms from the women on the block, burn the straw off, and get pliers and take the wires and nails out.

"I played on a team called the Dwarfs. My older brother played on the team, and there was a great outfielder Joe Barberi, and the fastest guy on the team was Frankie Ramirez, who everyone lovingly called 'Frankie the Spic.' The Dwarfs had wonderful blue-and-yellow velvet jackets, and DWARFS written across the back. In front of the breast was a dwarf, and each of the players had the name of one of Disney's dwarves. I wore glasses, so I was called Doc.

"And what was so wonderful was that in our world of street games, no one was excluded. Even if you were the worst schlub in the world, nobody said, 'You can't play.' There was no Little League mentality. There was always a spot in right field where nobody hit the ball, or if someone did hit it there, it would be an event like the sinking of the *Titanic,* but at least you were in the game, and you got your lick up at bat. Maybe you were the last one picked, but by God, you got picked.

"There was no such thing as parental interference. When I think of my boyhood, I never think of parents. Parents came strictly as observers, and they tried to be as meticulous as possible about cheering good plays, regardless of which side made them. I remember my father, who died young, if ever there was a show of temper— and my brother Billy had some temper—my father would take him right off the field and hop him in the ass and send him into the house for being a bad sport. There was none of that parental pressure you see today, because all the fathers knew each other and were friends. They met in the same bars, and they went to the same church—all blue-collar workers, and there was little of that silly one-upmanship.

"Back in those days, the Italians and Irish people didn't refer to their neighborhood by name but by which church you went to. Today the neighborhood is called Park Slope by the nouveau riche. In those days, when someone asked where you came from, you said, 'Holy Name,' or 'Immaculate Heart of Mary,' which in Brooklyn was always known as 'Our Lady of Perpetual Help.' And you never went to Manhattan. Manhattan was always referred to as 'the city,' and it was always said with a certain dread. Manhattan was where in the bars they served you bottled beer, where you never knew the price and you always thought you were getting bilked.

"Prospect Avenue was the main thoroughfare, where the bars and markets were, and all the shopkeepers were Dodger fans. It was impossible to go into a store with the *Daily News* under your arm without talking baseball. People just constantly talked baseball, arguing. They lived and breathed with the Dodgers.

"There were centers, like Jerry's Hardware Store, and Jerry had a guy working for him, Bill Reddy, probably the greatest Dodger fan who ever lived, knew everything there was to know about the Dodgers, and I would go in there and *shpritz* and break balls, spend hours arguing baseball while Bill and Jerry waited on customers. Back and forth about the games we'd argue. Jerry's Hardware Store was the place to go and talk baseball.

"And the idea of walking through Prospect Park to see a rare night game at Ebbets Field—you felt like F. Scott Fitzgerald first seeing the ivory towers of New York. You would walk around the lake on a balmy summer's evening, and fathers and sons, hundreds of kids, would be chattering, talking, walking along, and then you would get to within perhaps two hundred yards of the ballpark, and from the horizon the rim of lights of Ebbets Field would become visible, and you'd keep walking, and all of a sudden the sky would be lit up. My God, it was like the Emerald City, and as you got closer, you'd pick up your pace, and you'd give your tickets and go charging inside."

**BOBBY MCCARTHY**  "I lived in Windsor Terrace. It was just a little area really, with Greenwood Cemetery on one side, Prospect Park on the other. When the Prospect Expressway was built, it cut our neighborhood in half. There wasn't a store on Prospect Avenue that was ever broken into.

"There were a lot of cop fights with the Irish drinkers who got a couple beers in them and thought they were King Kong, but never any burglaries or robberies, and never a rape. It was almost like a little hick town in a big city.

"Everyone thought their neighborhood was the best. Other neighborhoods were Crown Heights, Flatbush, and Red Hook, where the tough kids were. The rich kids were from Bay Ridge. They went to bed with pajamas on. Canarsie was sand dunes in those days. Bedford-Stuyvesant you didn't know too much about because it was all black. You didn't know black people in those days. There was Borough Park, Bensonhurst, Coney Island. We used to hitch on the McDonald Avenue trolley to Coney Island and go down there with a dollar. The rides were 15¢.

Windsor Terrace in the 1950s. *Brian Merlis Collection—Brooklynpix.com*

"I didn't play sports as much as some of the other guys. I often preferred to go to the movies. We went to the Venus Theater, which was better known as 'The Itch.' It had its own characters who ran the place. Mom Cosgriff wore a white dress—she looked like a nurse—and she was there to monitor the kids with her flashlight. Then you had Teddy Bentbelly, he was a hunchback, and Crazy John, who sold the candy for a penny apiece.

"Broken ones you got two-fers. The lowest price for the Venus I can remember was 13¢ for a kid, 17¢ for an adult, and on Saturday you went and watched six cartoons, a series like *Don Winslow of the Navy* or *Tarzan* adventures, and then Abbott and Costello. I lived at the Venus Theater.

"Kids would line up to go in on Saturday, and the line would go all the way down to Jerry Fine's Hardware Store, and you would spend the whole day at the movies. When they were over, you were supposed to leave, and so you'd crawl under the seats to get away from Mom Cosgriff so you could watch it all over again without paying. And that's why we called it 'The Itch,' because when you got home, you had bugs crawling all over you from all the candy getting thrown on the floor.

"Kids would play handball against the side of the Venus, and the manager would come out and chase them, because you could hear the thump of the ball bouncing against the wall while you were watching the picture. And when Zorro became popular, everyone ran into Jerry Fine's and bought dowel sticks, and you dueled with them, and Jerry didn't even up the price, which is what you could do these days. It was the same price, as if Zorro wasn't there. And then something else would come along, Flash Gordon or Davy Crockett, and then something else.

"And because Irish people lived there, there were several bars in Windsor Terrace. There was McDevitt's, the Terrace, Ulmer's, Harold's, and Behan's. McDevitt was a hunchback, a bent-over guy, a great guy, and he had little doghouses on the walls, and the patrons had their names on the doghouses. And if you were in the doghouse with your wife because you spent too many hours in the bar, he'd put your wooden dog in the doghouse.

"But there was only one Behan's. It was the place you went, where the elite met to drink. Jimmy and Margaret Behan owned it, and inside were all the old Damon Runyon characters: Mom Schultz, Mrs. Hughes, Kate McCarthy. The women would go to the twelve-thirty Mass, listen to the service, and then right up to the bar they would go, and their baby carriages would be lined up outside.

"The biggest thing was to get a ticket on the Friday Night Fights. The fight was at Madison Square Garden, but in every bar in Brooklyn you could go in and get a ticket for a dollar, and you'd bet who was going to win and in what round. You picked it out of a hat. Seventh-round Zale or fifth-round LaMotta. And if you didn't have a ticket on the fight, it wasn't a good fight.

"And if you won, you won $20. But the winner would always end up putting the $20 on the bar, and Behan would end up with the money. Behan won the fight every time! And when the Friday Night Fights was over, then everyone would start drinking seriously, and we'd have our own Friday night fights. They were held about three o'clock in the morning."

**BILL REDDY**     "Let me tell you what kind of place Behan's was. I was working at the hardware store when we got a call from Behan that he needed a new lock put on the front door. Over I go.

"'What's the matter with the old lock?' I asked.

"'Ah, Billy me boy,' Jimmy said, drunk as a skunk behind the bar, 'I forgot my keys this morning, and I had to break the goddamn lock to get in.'

"So I start to install a new lock, and while I'm working, Jimmy arbitrarily decides that he doesn't want booths in the place anymore. He's yelling, 'These booths take up too much goddamn room. I'm going to get rid of them,' and he carries the first one out into the street.

"He comes back in and gets the second one and carries that one out, and while he goes in for the third one, Joe Comiskey, who was the first mop at Behan's, sees the booths out on the sidewalk, and Joe carries the first one back in and puts it back. Meanwhile, Jimmy carries the third one out as Joe is carrying the second one back in, and now Jimmy is carrying the first one back out again. In the meantime I'm at the front door trying to put the lock in. Shut the door. Open the door. Shut the door. Open the door. Finally I said, 'Listen, Jimmy, for Christ's sake, you have to either leave the door open or leave it shut. I'll never get this lock in.' He says, 'Have a drink and don't worry about how long it takes.' And out he goes with number one again as Comiskey is carrying back number four. This goes on for about two and a half hours! Finally Jimmy turns to me and says, 'Bill, there's something I've got to tell you.' I say, 'What, Jimmy?' He says, 'I'm exhausted. I've never been so tired in all my days. I never knew I had so many booths in this place. No wonder it's so crowded in here!'

"And with that he went behind the bar, Joe carried the last booth back in, I put the lock in, and everyone was happy.

"This neighborhood has so many stories, had so many characters. Roundy was a guy who had a wonderful talent. He would go up into Prospect Park, up into the hills, and he would howl like a wolf, and in about five minutes every animal in the zoo would be howling, and the zoo would sound like a Tarzan movie. The elephants would be trumpeting, the lions would be growling, the tigers would be roaring, and the keeper would be running wild. He wouldn't know what in the world was the matter with the animals. And up on the hill, there would be Roundy, going, 'Oooo oooooo.'

Bill Reddy of Windsor Terrace.

"One warm summer night Roundy got drunk, and he and a couple of buddies decided they wanted to cool off, and they jumped into the seal tank and had a swim with the seals. The seals, of course, didn't quite know what to make of it, but they loved any new toy to nudge around and bang up against. Roundy and them got bruised up a bit, but they had a good swim.

"I remember the day Owney Fox, the neighborhood peddler, came through the neighborhood naked. It was bitter cold. I was opening the hardware store, and here comes Owney running down Prospect Avenue with only an undershirt on. Nothing else. The milkman was coming out of his truck to deliver the milk to the delicatessen, and he ran back into the milk truck and shut the door. A woman opened her front door on Prospect Street, saw Owney, screamed, and ran back into the house. Everyone was running away from him, and I was running after him trying to stop him. I was screaming, 'Owney, where are you going?' But he never answered me. Down he went past Greenwood Avenue. By this time a police car came up, and that was the last I saw of Owney for a while.

"Owney once was a policeman, and one morning he brought his horse into the hardware store. I thought Jerry the owner was going to die.

"Jerry climbed up onto the counter. 'What the hell are you doing? Get him out of here,' Jerry was screaming.

"'What's the matter?' Owney said. 'He's just come in for a visit.' At that point the horse plopped all over the floor. I had to get a shovel and shovel it out. I hit the horse a whack with the shovel. I was going to hit Owney next. 'Get out of here,' I screamed.

"'Ah,' he says, 'you guys got no sense of humor.'

"We called Banty Diner 'Banty' because he was about as tall as a banty rooster. He was a character the likes of which you'll never see again. Banty used to have odd jobs. In the spring he sold horse manure. He had a little pony cart that he rented, and a pony. And he'd shovel as much horse manure as the pony could make and the pony cart could carry, and he'd ride through the streets shouting, 'Hoorrrrrsse shiiiiitttt. Get your hoooorrsssse shit here. Guaranteed fresh.' And he'd sell it for 50¢ for a couple of loads to the people who had gardens. Around Easter time he would sell flowers. In between, he'd ask everyone he knew to 'lend' him a couple quarters. He'd say, 'You're a fine fellow. Can you spare a half? I want to get a drink.' And you would never refuse Banty.

"One time Banty was selling flowers around Prospect Avenue outside of McNulty's bar, and he was selling hyacinths that looked like no other flowers I had ever seen. Half the leaves looked like goats had been eating on them. As far as his lilies were concerned, the only way you knew they were lilies was by the sign on them. And a woman came over and started looking at the flowers, and he said to her, 'Pick out any one you like.'

"She said, 'How much is this one?' He said, 'Three dollars, for the pot and all.' She said, 'Three dollars? It looks like an old weed. You're a robber. I wouldn't give you fifty cents for it.'

"Banty looked at her and screamed, 'Before I sell it for fifty cents, I'll throw it out into the gutter.'

"She said, 'That's where it belongs.'

"He said, 'Take your fifty cents and shove it up'n your arse.' And he threw it past her head out into the gutter. And then he started throwing them all out there, and with every one he threw, his cursing became worse. And the woman was screaming that he was throwing the plants at her. The next thing I know, here comes the police, and there went Banty, wagon and all, down to Parkville Station. I didn't see him for a couple of weeks.

"In the neighborhood we had a guy by the name of Eddie Decker. Eddie was a carny man, a con man from the word go. One night he decided he needed a few bucks, and he stood behind a tree waiting for his chance on Vanderbilt Avenue. In his own neighborhood, mind you. Finally, he hears footsteps coming, and he jumps out from behind the tree, and screams, 'Hand over your money,' and grabs my wife's cousin, Willie Crane, who's known Eddie all his life. Willie says, 'For Christ's sake, Eddie, what the hell are you doing?' Eddie says, 'It just goes to show that I'm a loser all the way. My first stickup, and I got a guy with no money.'

"Even the cops were crazy. Jack Harrison was the local cop on the beat, and one day as Willie Crane was walking along Vanderbilt Avenue, coming home, Harrison came running down the street hollering to someone to 'Stop that man. Stop that man.' And Willie, who's wondering what's going on, started to run. Harrison was drunk as a skunk, and he chased Willie into his house. Willie ran into the hallway, and Harrison followed him. Willie said, 'What the hell are you trying to do? Everyone in the neighborhood is watching.' Harrison said, 'Yeah, but we had a fine run, Willie, didn't we?'

"It was always something."

# A WILD CHILD

JOHN FORD

IRELAND ALWAYS WAS AN IMPOVERISHED COUNTRY BECAUSE THE English Protestant majority, which ran the country, made certain it stayed that way through its laws, which not only prevented industrialization but barred Catholics from owning land, reducing the bulk of the Irish to peasant status. They could only rent, and between 1740 and 1840 the rents continued to rise until they had to sell their wheat crop to pay the rent, leaving the Irish Catholics to live on a diet of potatoes.

England, whose aristocracy historically treated the Irish little better than the czar in Russia had treated the Jews, passed a law in 1838 that shifted its responsibility to care for the poor from the government to the landlords, who figured out it was better for them economically to kick out their tenants and switch to sheep and cattle grazing. When a tenant couldn't pay rent, he was evicted.

Between 1845 and 1847 the Irish potato crop failed, and almost half the Catholic population either died or left. Most—half a million—went to America, only to find that the Protestants who hated them in England also hated them in America. It was not uncommon to see NINA (NO IRISH NEED APPLY) signs in shop windows.

The Irish in America worked menial jobs. Three out of four Irishmen were unskilled laborers.

The Irish were only accepted after the influx of Jews, Slavs, and

Italians, as hostility shifted to the newer immigrants. At the turn of the twentieth century, the Irish became cops and firemen, lawyers and politicians. The Irish political boss would ask, "What do the people want?" And he would do his best to provide it, whether he was honest or crooked. Thus the Irish were able to lift themselves up through politics—much to the Protestant majority's disgust.

Many of the Irish who lived in Brooklyn were rough-hewn, tough guys who lived hard, drank hard, and fought hard as they scratched out a livelihood. John Ford, a kid who grew up on the streets of Flatbush, started out in a gang, but maturity and the army provided him with a route to middle-class respectability.

On September 31, 1939, Michael Ford, a sailor, jumped 250 feet off the deck of the Brooklyn Bridge into the East River, swam to shore, walked into a South Street saloon, and ordered a drink. The article in the *New York Times* the next day went on to say that he had a laceration of his left leg, which he dismissed as nothing, and that he was then taken to Bellevue Hospital to have his head examined.

John Ford, Michael's son, a Brooklynite most of his life, said that his dad and his dad's five brothers were roustabouts, guys just trying to make a living.

John, who was born in 1934, was something of a hard-ass himself. A member of a small gang called the Irish Dukes, John Ford and his buddies spent their childhoods drinking, making mischief, and getting into fights. After skipping school almost every day for two years, he dropped out of Boys High School in the eleventh grade, but after serving in the navy during the Korean War, John Ford took advantage of the GI Bill and went to college at night while working for the phone company and running a bar he owned in Flatbush. He got his associate's degree from Brooklyn College and his BA from Pace College—after first getting a diploma from the school of hard knocks.

**JOHN FORD**   "I can't tell you much about my father's father, Simon Ford, except that he was born in County Cork, and he left Ireland because the Black and Tans [Royal Irish Constabulary Reserve Force] were after him. The rumors were he was fighting the British. He went over to London, got a job on the ships, and then he jumped ship in New York harbor and swam ashore. For the rest of his life occasionally he would disappear because he would get this inkling the Black and Tans were after him.

"My mother's parents came from Heidelberg, Germany. She came by herself when she was sixteen. In them days you had to have a sponsor, and she went to live with her cousin. She was a domestic servant most of her life.

"They settled in what they now call Bedford-Stuyvesant, but we always called it the Ninth Ward. Nobody ever called it Bedford-Stuyvesant. I didn't hear it called that until it became infamous, if you know what I'm saying.

"I was seven when the war started. My father went off to war, and my mother was working upstate New York, so I lived with my grandparents. They lived above a glass store. The building had three stories. They had five children in the war. In them days you used to put stars in the window, and a Gold Star was put up when my uncle Junie was killed.

"My father was born about 1916. Before the war he just knocked around. He worked on the docks. He was a bartender. Whatever work he could pick up. It was the Depression, and he told me he would shovel snow working for the WPA. He would sign up on one side of Prospect Park and start shoveling snow, and when the boss turned his back, he'd run across to the other side of the park, sign up there, and start shoveling snow. Running back and forth, he got paid twice.

"One of the jobs he had was the head waiter for the Bluebird Casino in Coney Island, in the days when it was bustling. During lunchtime he told me he would give the wealthy-looking customers the dinner menu, which was twice as much as the lunch menu, and pocket the difference.

"He was friends with Milo the Mule-faced Boy, who had the ugliest face you'd ever want to see. After Milo quit and ran across the street to join the competition, he became Milo the Dog-faced Boy. Milo lived in my neighborhood. He even had a girlfriend.

"My father was an amazing man. He never got past the third grade in school but from a third-grade education he became an officer in the navy. They wanted to make him a captain but he didn't feel he had the writing skills, and when he came out, he went into the MSTS, Military Sea Transportation Service, which used to bring the troops back and forth from Korea. He was a chief steward on the USS *Muir*, which meant he was the guy who fed everybody. He was in charge of the whole thing.

"I showed you the article in the *New York Times* about the time my dad jumped off the Brooklyn Bridge. The headline of that article was 'Tipsy Sailor Leaps.' His version was that he wasn't drunk, that he was sitting in a bar with his friends, and his bookie was in there, and they were talking about betting.

"The guy said, 'If I bet you $100 you wouldn't jump off the Brooklyn Bridge, would you do it?'

The Reinhold wedding. Ford's parents are seated in front. His father once jumped off the Brooklyn Bridge and lived to tell about it. *Courtesy of John Ford*

"'Sure,' he said, so off they went. They got in a cab, drove halfway over the bridge, and bing, he jumped over. He said he tied a towel around his crotch. He lived, but the guy never paid him. He said, 'I don't pay off on bets like that.'

"It's a wonder my father and his five brothers didn't wind up in the river or get their legs broken. One was badder than the other, roustabouts, guys just trying to make a living.

"Mostly my father was working the ships. He used to have this big, long coat with seven or eight pockets. He would come home all filled up with whatever he could take. He was offered a job on the docks as a checker, which was a big job, but checkers were tied to the Mob, so he turned it down. He figured he'd wind up in jail, because the guys with the bent noses don't take the rap. He does.

"The last job he had before he retired was working as the chief oiler of the presses of the *New York Times*. He went around oiling things. They liked him so much they gave him a management title.

"I have no idea how my father and mother met. She was a German Protestant, and he was an Irish Catholic, which didn't sit well in them days. My father was the patriarch of the clan, so they didn't mess too much when he was around, but she was never treated as one of the group, nor did she want to be part of that group, because they were hard-drinking, tough people, and she was a gentle person.

"I was born in September of 1934 in Bedford-Stuyvesant. I was baptized in the St. Peter Klaver Church. My parents were separated when I was a kid, and I didn't meet my father until I was seven years old. I lived in East Flatbush with my mother. The area was all-white. The dividing line in Brooklyn was Bergen Street. Blacks never went past it.

"I belonged to a gang called the Irish Dukes. We had ten guys. It wasn't huge, but it was big enough. We would sell chance books for a quarter so we could buy our jackets and put IRISH DUKES on the back. We used to fist-fight with the Garfield Boys and the Park Slope Boys. They'd come down in a mob and nail a couple of us. Wasn't anything personal. Some of them guys were my friends. But if you didn't know how to fight, you were in deep shit. Everybody was in the same boat. Everybody thought that was the way you were supposed to live.

"I remember when Jackie Robinson came up to the Dodgers in '47. The Irish were pissed off. When the blacks came to Ebbets Field, they didn't flock there. They came tentatively. In those days everybody was a 'nigger.' They asked, 'Who's going to sit next to all these niggers?' That's the way the people thought in them days.

"When I was a kid, Dixie Walker was my favorite player, but they got rid of him because he was the biggest racist on the club. That's why they traded him. He wouldn't play with Robinson. Dixie was the People's Choice. That was our man. But I loved all the Dodgers. They were all super players. Any one of them was an all-star. Our motto was, 'Wait 'Til Next Year.' We were loyal fans. I loved the Dodgers.

"I was going to Boys High, which was in a black neighborhood, and I had become friends with a black kid by the name of Hughie DeShan, and we were such good friends that Hughie used to come and swim off the piers with us. We even made Hughie an honorary Irish Duke. He used to come to our dances on Sunday night at St. Teresa's. He was the only black guy there. He used to do the Hucklebuck, and those white girls would go apeshit. At the same time we were calling them 'niggers.' Because you didn't know any better.

"There were a good number of blacks at Boys High. If you went to the bathroom, you had to fight your way out. One time after school I fought this one black kid—another friend—and two hundred people stood around and watched. After the fight was over, we were still friends. But you had to fight. You didn't back down. I never backed down in my life. That's the way it was.

"So the people in the bars where I hung out—the Irish and Italians—were upset when Robinson came to the Dodgers. They were really outraged. But when he started playing, when they saw what kind of player he was and how he conducted himself, he was our hero. If he had done half the shit these black players do today, they would have found him dead someplace. He was the only one, and we would have gotten rid of him and that would have been the end of the experiment. That's just the way it was. The element I hung around with was not the intelligentsia. We were just knock-around saloon guys. But when Rickey picked him, he picked the right man.

"My father, an uncle, and another guy ran a parking lot outside Ebbets Field right next to a bar that was behind left field on the corner of Montgomery and Sullivan Streets. As kids, we used to sell the Dodgers scorecard and the *Brooklyn Eagle.* Then we sold *Who's Who in Baseball,* and then we worked for a guy who gave us a board with buttons, hats, bats, and pennants, and we'd sell them, and he'd give us a cut. Pretty soon we figured out, 'Screw him,' and we made our own boards. We went down to Chinatown, and we'd get buttons with the team name or a player like Robinson or Newcombe, and we'd buy a row of ribbons and put a ribbon on each button, and we'd buy miniature bats, pennants, and we sold them ourselves. If we were too near the stadium, sometimes a cop would chase us, so we'd go down near the subway on Flatbush Avenue, which was right near Hugh Casey's bar. Remember Hugh Casey? He was the original relief pitcher. I heard he blew his brains out.

"My father knew the traveling secretary of the Dodgers, Bert something, and he used to let me get into the game through the press gate at the rotunda at Ebbets Field. If I got caught doing something wrong, my father made me work the parking lot. One day I snuck into a warehouse across from our house on Park Place. My buddies and I went in through the skylight, and we robbed the place of pencils and other shit.

Somehow my father knew it was me, so my punishment was I had to go to the parking lot every day while the Dodgers were in town and help park cars.

"In '53 my father and I decided we'd make some money scalping World Series tickets, so we paid people $20 to get on line and get us tickets. You were only allowed a couple tickets apiece, and I spent $200 buying tickets for the sixth and seventh games of the series, and wouldn't you know the Yankees won it in five games, and the series never did come back to Brooklyn. And I was going to use that $200 to get married.

"As a young boy I went to St. Teresa's, a parochial school, and in them days the nuns didn't screw around with you. They'd hit you on the hands, smack you on the head. If you missed church on Sunday, you better have a note. If you were absent, you had to be half-dead. They made you toe the line.

John Ford at his first communion from St. Teresa's, 9th Ward, Brooklyn. *Courtesy of John Ford*

"The better days of my life were spent down in Sheepshead Bay, where the fishing boats used to pull in. Piers stuck out into the bay, and every gang had its own pier. The Pier 9 Boys were from Sheepshead Bay. The Garfield Boys were from South Brooklyn. We had our pier. We didn't have a name for it. It was just ours.

"When we were thirteen, fourteen, fifteen, we would dive for coins. People used to go down and buy fish off the boats, and others would stroll along Sheepshead Bay, and they'd throw money into the water, and we'd dive down and stick the coins in our mouths. We could be treading water for a half hour.

"We used to go into the Brooklyn Botanical Gardens and swim there naked. People would stroll by, and here were these raggedy-assed kids, and the cops would chase us up the back. We used to sneak into Girls Commercial School and swim in their pool. There were so many things we did. When we were fourteen, fifteen, we would drink Five Star muscatel. It cost 35¢ a pint. We would give the 35¢ to one of the crazy Smitty brothers—they supposedly hung a black guy from a lamppost one time—and he would buy the Five Star, and we would give him a couple of swigs, and then we'd finish off the rest, and we'd stagger home. Nobody thought it was odd. It sounds like the Dead End Kids, but we were living it, and we didn't even know it. My mother was working, and my father was working. I never went home to a house with anybody in it. I was a latchkey kid, but I never felt neglected. You just went your own way. I used to go over to my friend Johnny Ryan's house, and his mother would let us smoke. We were nine or ten. She used to get us cigarettes. We'd go into the basement of her house and crawl into the basement of the adjacent grocery store, and we'd steal eggs and bring them back to her.

"During that time, around 1947, 1948, there was a polio epidemic, and they closed the beaches at Coney Island and Riis Park. We always thought we were immune to polio, because there were sewer pipes near where we swam, and shit came floating out of there. None of us got polio, but two of the Irish Dukes got MS.

"Nobody had any money. Of course not. We put oilcloth in our shoes after the big hole came. We never paid for transportation. We all hung off the back of the streetcars. We'd open up the back window, and everybody would crawl in. We never paid on the subway. We used to go down to Park Place in Brooklyn, go up a girder, cross another girder, come up under the station, go upstairs, and take the train to Sheepshead Bay. Coming back we went in the back, crawled up a girder, climbed over a fence, walked along the fence, jumped up onto the station platform, and caught the train home. We never paid—nah. The trolleys were 3¢ with a penny transfer, but we still hung on to the back.

"We didn't pay to go to the movies either. There were two movie theaters, the Savoy and the Lincoln, which were right next to each other on Bedford Avenue. The Savoy had first-run movies and the Lincoln second-run. The only way you could get into the Lincoln was to have one guy pay, and then he would open the side door and everyone would run into the place. To get into the Savoy, we would go next-door and open the cellar door, go down into the cellar, and we'd crawl out and come out into the bathroom of the theater. We'd go in the back, climb up stairs, and wind up on the roof, and from the roof we could go into the balcony. The problem was the balcony was for adults only. We'd get on our bellies and wiggle, like a snake, and if they saw us, we'd run away and hide.

"I didn't like school. I used to come in late every day for a year and a half. If you were marked absent, they would send a card home. I would show up every day, but I'd skip seven classes. I would get seven cut cards a day. I had no interest. You'd have figured after six months they'd have wised up. As it was, a group of five or six of us would come in late every day, and we'd go up to Jackson's Pool Room and shoot pool. Boys High was in the black section of town, and if the people there saw the teacher coming into the pool room to check it out, they'd hide us in the back. We would go to the movies downtown or play basketball at Girls Commercial. That's how I spent my teen years.

"When I was sixteen, I hung out at a dangerous place called the Snake Pit, on St. Mark's Avenue. We were kids, but we had draft cards that said we were thirty-five, and as long as we had a draft card, nobody gave a shit. The Snake Pit was just down from Bergen Street, so we used to have black guys come in there, but they were our buddies. One time a gang came in there after the Irish Dukes, and there were only two of us there, my friend Pete and I. These two giant black guys, our friends, said to us, 'You stay over there.' They said to the gang, 'Let's go outside, boys.' And then they went outside and beat the shit out of the two gang members. We sat there drinking our beers when they came back in and said, 'That's it, guys.'

"I had friends who became gangsters. My cousin's husband, a cop, tried to screw with my friend Andy Jukakis, and Andy sliced the side of his head with a knife. Later they found Andy dead in a lot. There was this guy Tommy Cronin, who we called T-Cro. He had his own gang. He died when he went into a back room and blew his brains out. Then there was Charlie, my really good friend. We hung around a lot and we could have gone either way.

"Charlie, who was a nasty son of a bitch, traveled with a gun. I can remember being in a bar on Flatbush Avenue when Charlie walked in. He said to the bartender, 'I want you to leave.' The bartender said, 'What do you mean?' Charlie said, 'If you don't get out of here in five minutes, I'm going to kill you.' The guy left, and Charlie went behind the bar and served free drinks to everybody. I left before the cops came.

"We used to play in our Friday-night card game. We played at this guy's house, and come to find out he was queer—that's what we called them in them days—and Charlie murdered the guy. He beat him to death.

"Charlie was sent to Rikers Island, from where he and a few others escaped. They swam across the East River to LaGuardia Airport. He then tried to hold up this doctor's office in Bay Ridge, and he got shot. They sent him back to Rikers, and again he escaped, but this time he didn't make it. They found him floating in the Narrows. That was the end of Charlie.

"I was in so many tight spots that I don't even like to talk about them. I could have gone either way. It doesn't take much to take the wrong turn, and once you make that turn, it's hard to go back. The navy saved my ass to a certain extent. Having a family, going to school. And again, my father. He was my hero in life. I was the only guy in our family who ever went to college and graduated. He was so proud of that fact that I *had* to graduate.

"When I was seventeen, in 1951, I was walking down Franklin Avenue with my friend Joey Preston, when he said, 'I'm going to join the navy.' Joey had three brothers in the navy already. I said, 'I'll go with you.' But we had to wait until February for Joey to turn seventeen. And my father had to sign for me. What the hell? It was better than the half-assed job I had working in a stationery store.

"Joey and I went in. The Korean War was still on. Joey got sick, so we didn't graduate boot camp together. I went to radio school, and I was assigned to the USS *Ross,* a destroyer out of Norfolk, and I spent my entire military career on that ship. We were never shot at. We took a world cruise. We started in Norfolk, went past Florida, went through the Panama Canal, came back around the Suez Canal, and visited many, many countries. We were relief for the Seventh Fleet.

"About the time we showed up in Korea the armistice was signed. I can remember going up the Yalu River. The captain did this either because we earned an extra ribbon or just to be there.

"One day an officer said to me, 'John, I see you don't have a high school diploma. Would you like to take a test?' I sat and took that test, and I did very well, and when I got out of the service, they had passed the GI Bill, which was the savior for this country in a lot of ways. A lot of people went to school because of it. I said, 'Let me try this and see what happens.'

John Ford at the Albion Hotel in Asbury Park, New Jersey. *Courtesy of John Ford*

"I was working for the New York Telephone Company during the day, and I went to Brooklyn College at night, so I got half-pay, plus they were paying me $9 a credit to go. And I kept going until I got an associate's degree. I had to find a college that would recognize my credits from Brooklyn College, and Pace University down on the Bowery was recommended to me, and after seven and a half years of night school, I got my BA degree.

"One reason I did it was I had a family to support. My wife had had six kids in nine years, and I needed a better-paying job. I thought I could make some extra money, so while I was doing all of this, my father and I bought a bar on Nostrand Avenue and Clarkson called Ford's Bar. I owned it for a year and a half, but I didn't make any money. I was afraid if I didn't sell it, I'd end up in jail. Fuggedaboutit.

"One time this guy was giving me a hard time, and we went outside, and we were rolling on the ground and I was smacking him in the head, when a bus came by and almost ran over his head.

"I was behind the bar on Fridays, and these local guys, who would eventually wind up in prison, came in, and they were sitting there when this black guy walked in. The bar was right down the street from Kings County Hospital, which had a lot of black employees. When he came in, everyone treated him with respect, didn't say anything, but then he said to me, 'I'd like to buy these guys a drink.'

"Those guys were not interested in him buying them a drink, and I told him so.

"'Why, is it because I'm black?' he asked.

"I said, 'It has nothing to do with your being black. The guys don't feel like having a drink.'

"So he pulled out a knife. We backed him out the front door, and about eight or nine of us ran down the block after the son of a bitch, and we caught him, and down he went, and one guy kicked him in the head. One of the other guys suggested taking the guy down to Sheepshead Bay and throwing him in the river.

"I said, 'Stop. No no no.'

"One of the guys, Peter Lawler, said, 'I'll wait here and tell the cops he pulled a knife on us. We'll get him locked up. We'll do it legal.'

"I said, 'Good.' They would have killed the guy.

"We went back to the bar, and the cops locked both the black guy and Lawler up. We had to get him a lawyer.

"Three weeks later Lawler was in the bar, and three big black guys walked in. My uncle was behind the bar. One of the black guys says, 'My little brother was in here a couple weeks ago when somebody beat him up.'

"I thought, *Holy Geez*. My uncle, who was a tough son of a bitch, would have dropped two of them. And there sat Lawler at the end of the bar. I said to him, 'Shut up. You keep quiet.' I went outside, crossed the street, and phoned the cops.

"I went back to the bar and told my wife to get out and go back to the car. Eventually the three black guys left and started to walk away when this crazy bastard Lawler went outside, picked up a garbage can, and started running after them.

"'Are you guys looking for me?' he said.

"I locked the bar door.

"Two months later Lawler came in. I was behind the bar. He was pissed at me for locking the bar. I said, 'Pete, are you crazy? You went after them guys with a garbage can. What do you expect me to do? I couldn't have done shit.'

"He threw his keys at me, and he leaped over the bar at me. I got him around the neck, and I wrestled him to the ground, and his head hit the ground, missing the step going into the back room by half an inch. It would have cracked his skull open and killed him. I told him, 'Don't ever come in this place again.'

"This was what life was like in Brooklyn. Just growing up there was an adventure. But we didn't know it was an adventure. It's only as you look back and say, 'Look at all the crazy shit we did.'"

*After John Ford got out of the navy in 1955, his parents decided it was time to move out of their apartment in the Ninth Ward (Bedford-Stuyvesant). The economy was booming. People were finding work. Levittown on Long Island was opening, and people for the first time had an opportunity to move out of their small apartments and move into single-family homes with grass and gardens and two-car garages. John Ford, unlike many who moved to the suburbs, didn't want to leave Brooklyn. He had saved $75 a month from his navy pay, and his family and his parents moved into a two-family home in Flatbush.*

John Ford today. *Courtesy of John Ford*

**JOHN FORD** "My father was working. My mother was working. I was working. If you had an opportunity to buy a house—it was unheard of—so we did.

"When we owned that two-family house, Flatbush was a really nice neighborhood. There was a housing project there, but it was middle-income, mostly white, a good place. There were seven buildings, and Mayor Lindsay bought them and made them into subsidized housing. Little by little, poor blacks moved in there, and the place went to hell in a hand basket, just went down the tubes. I don't know if people panicked. They probably did, and then they started leaving Flatbush. And I was like the last guy to leave. I told myself, *I'm not leaving here.* But my kids were going to parochial school at St. Edmonds, and they started having problems. There was crime. They were getting hassled. Bikes were stolen. I then said, 'I gotta get out of here.'

"The blacks who first moved in were hard-working people, because now they were getting a chance to buy houses of their own, which was unheard of in their era. First the poor whites bought them, and then the blacks. But when blacks started selling to blacks, that was like the plague. The housing values started going down, and I said, 'I better get out of here while I can get something.'

"I moved down near Sheepshead Bay. I bought a house on Avenue U. I held on to that house until around 1990, when I sold it to Asians. I was separated at the time, and I decided to move to Florida.

"I wouldn't have traded Brooklyn for the world. I'm glad my kids grew up there. All my kids are college graduates and successful people. One of them is a millionaire."

# SON OF HOLOCAUST SURVIVORS

HARRY SCHWEITZER

THE CONGRESS STEMMED THE FLOW OF EASTERN EUROPEAN immigrants in 1924. As a result, about 1.5 million Jews who would have come to the United States perished in the Holocaust. After World War II, approximately 330,000 Jews who survived forced marches and death camps were put in displaced persons camps in Germany to await relocation. Their families had been annihilated, their property confiscated, their communities destroyed. Having survived the war, Polish Jews still faced physical violence from their neighbors. They had no home to go home to. The Soviet Union had demanded that all displaced persons be returned to their country of origin, but those Jews who came from Russia faced imprisonment, torture, and even death, and, so, many of them had no intention of going back.

Unfortunately for the displaced Jews, even after the Holocaust there was no cry from any of the allied nations to help them. Britain didn't want them; neither did France or the United States, where few members of Congress felt a responsibility to allow the survivors into America. One of the fears expressed was that the Jewish refugees would be receptive to Communism. The Jews, it became obvious, needed a homeland. But because of British policy, they weren't allowed to emigrate to Palestine.

The Zionists among the DPs wanted to go to Palestine. The anti-Zionists and those who were neutral on the subject wanted to come to

The Bergen-Belsen concentration camp after liberation. Zionist organizers tried to get survivors to emigrate to what was then called Palestine. *Courtesy of Harry Schweitzer*

the United States. President Truman, a haberdasher from Missouri, a former bag man for the Kansas City mob, was an unlikely proponent for Jewish emigration to both Israel and the United States. The strong anti-immigration sentiment in Congress in the country tied his hands.

DESPITE THE PRESSURES, ON DECEMBER 22, 1945, Truman issued a presidential order that DPs, especially orphans, receive preference within existing U.S. immigration quotas. Since the quota was still thirteen thousand Eastern Europeans a year, it didn't amount to much. But what the order did was make it possible for Jews who didn't have relatives to sponsor them to enter the United States on group affidavits. Groups like the United Jewish Charities could be the sponsor. All they had to do was pay the $60 fee for their passage.

There was pressure to allow many more Eastern Europeans to come to America. The American Jewish Committee and the American Council for Judaism argued that since America had failed to fill its quotas for Jews during the 1930s and 1940s, a large number of refugees could come in without threatening the economy. Congressman William Stratton, an Illinois Republican, proposed a bill to bring 400,000 refugees—300,000 Christians and 100,000 Jews—to America using that same argument. Considering that the United States had housed 400,000 German prisoners of war, it was hard to argue against it. But these arguments could not compel Truman to act. A Gallup poll taken in the spring of 1947 showed that 60 percent of Americans were opposed to bringing the displaced persons to America.

The refusal to allow the displaced persons to come to America was one of the key factors in the creation of the state of Israel.

After the end of the war, Joseph Schweitzer and Mania Snopkowska were freed by the British from the Bergen-Belsen concentration camp. It was said that he was "the last man standing." She had typhus and was at death's door. They were moved to a camp for displaced persons in Zeilsheim, Germany. Enclosed with barbed wire, it was overcrowded and dirty, and yet, after they were given medical treatment, somehow they survived. All the while, they waited for word that they would be allowed to come to America. It didn't come for four interminable years. During their long sojourn in the camp they met, courted, married, and had a son, Harry. In 1951 the Schweitzer family flew to America. After a short stay in Manhattan, they moved to Bensonhurst, Brooklyn, to begin their lives in their new home.

**HARRY SCHWEITZER** "My dad was born in Chorzow, Poland. He was sixteen when the war broke out. In those days being Jewish in Poland was no cakewalk. He went to a gymnasium that was segregated for Jewish kids. There were constant fights with the Polish kids. One of the slurs often thrown at him, my father told me, was 'Jew, go back to Palestine.'

"Before the Nazis took over Poland, my grandfather took my father and his brother to Lodz, where he and his sons worked for the Russians. They all were fluent in Polish and German, and they actually went to school to learn Russian. When the Nazis took over, they went to work for the Wehrmacht. My father and his brother were in provisioning, getting bedding. The commandant took a shine to my father because of his fluency in German, and so he and my uncle were able to maintain themselves for a while.

"The three of them managed to stay in Lodz for three years of the war until 1942, when my grandfather went to the Russian front, and my father and uncle went back to Chorzow.

Harry Schweitzer's parents, Joseph Schweitzer and Mania Snopkowska, on the day they got their marriage license. *Courtesy of Harry Schweitzer*

"They went by train, and they were rounded up by the Nazis and sent off to work camps. They were in a number of different camps: Dora, which was not far from Peenemunde, where they made rockets. They were in Nordhausen, and they went to smaller camps. When they were at a work camp called Bunzlau, the commandant took a liking to my uncle. He was his boot black, his shoe shine boy, and although he was Wehrmacht, he was never Gestapo, and he attempted to keep his people in his camp together, and he did it for several years, until he was relieved of his command, which coincided with the end of the war for the Nazis. So the end result was when the Nazis started losing the war, they started retrenching back to Germany, and they moved the surviving Jews back into camps in Germany, and my father and my uncle wound up in Bergen-Belsen for six months, where they were liberated, and the story from my uncle and people who knew my father was he was the last man standing.

"It was luck, he said, because when my father and uncle were in Lodz working for the Russians, they had been inoculated for typhus, which wiped out much of the population of the camps before the liberation. The inoculations saved them.

"My father's father actually survived the war under the Russians and was repatriated. My father had posted a notice that he was looking for his father, 'Looking for such and such person . . . ,' and they were going to meet, and my grandfather died on the train on the way. Can you imagine? They were never able to determine his cause of death. He was on the way to the reunion.

"My mother's story is more tragic. She came from a large city—by Polish standards—by the name of Zawiercie. My mother was the oldest of three. She had two siblings, a younger brother and sister. Zawiercie, being a relatively large city, was ghettoized, and they had a *yid-marat* who managed the affairs of the Jewish quarter.

"My mother told me this story. She wasn't able to tell me until 1985. It was very difficult for my mother to tell it. One morning the Nazis came. They had all the fifteen- and sixteen-year-olds assemble in the square. They were rounding them up, and my mother went. Her father took her there, and from what I gather her father was trying to keep them from taking her, and my mother told me he was surrounded and beaten around the head by the Nazis. And he wound up going on the transport. The rest of the family was left behind.

"She was the only survivor. The rest perished at Auschwitz. My brothers are named after her siblings.

"My mother went to a work camp called Neusalz. She worked at slave labor, making something for the German war effort. She was young enough, able to sustain herself. At the end of the war there was a forced march back to Germany. They had called a halt, and my mother and her friend Leah slept in a barn. When they awoke, they found that the column had left.

"Instead of fleeing, they chased after them and rejoined the column, because they were so inured to the fear. They had two enemies, the Nazis and the Poles, and they were afraid if they escaped and were discovered by the Poles, they would be killed. My mother said they actually felt safer within the transport. So my mother wound up at Bergen-Belsen for three or four months, where many died, and she was on her deathbed with typhus when in April of 1945 the British tanks came through the trees, and they knew they would be saved.

"A lot of people died that day because their saviors didn't know how to treat them. You've seen pictures of what they looked like. Skeletons. They fed them, and many died. My mother managed to survive. My father managed to survive. And, independently, they both wound up in the same DP camp in Zeilsheim. Somehow they managed to get together through friends.

"Zeilsheim was a suburb of Frankfurt. They got married in 1946. Though my mother had difficulty giving birth, as was to be expected, I was born in Frankfurt in 1950, and then, in 1951, through the Hebrew Immigrant Aid Society, we came to this country.

"When we arrived, we were given shelter on Irving Place in Manhattan. My father was a smoker at the time—I think everybody was. I remember he left my mother and me in the house for ten or twenty minutes, went out for a smoke, walked the street, and he couldn't believe how free he felt.

"My father had been involved in the black market in Germany, which was common, dealing in coffee and cigarettes. Some people came here with a lot of money. My father's means were much more modest. My father was a plumber by trade. He had done a little bit of plumbing before the war, when he was fifteen, and he learned the rest here. He became a union member, and he was a union plumber for his life. My mother was a housewife.

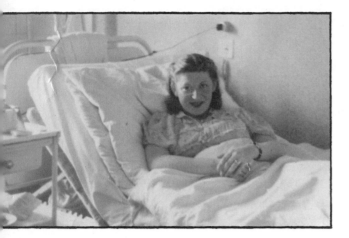

Mania Schweitzer gave birth to Harry in a German hospital.
*Courtesy of Harry Schweitzer*

"A lot of the DPs were relocated based on their connections with people they knew who were already here. People who came with a lot of money went to Forest Hills in Queens. Rego Park had a fair amount of DPs. And Brownsville, Brooklyn, had a very large DP population.

"My father went to Brownsville because he didn't have a lot of money. He was offered the job of superintendent of an apartment house. It was a two-bedroom apartment, rent-free. My mother also helped him out, which she hated. Eventually the building hired another super, and my father joined the union, got himself started, and made money, $65, $70 a week, which was fine for those days.

"We lived at 26 Bay 25th Street right by the el. It was called the West End line. We had the first floor of the apartment house. The neighborhood was Jewish and Italian. On the side of the block where we lived there were two apartments that had many, many Jewish people in them, and the rest were big one-family homes—not much land, but a lot of room, and they were owned by Italians. The Jews and Italians got along. Half my friends were Italian, and half were Jewish. There was one block of black families on Eighteenth Avenue and Bath Avenue that had been there since the Revolutionary War. And that was it.

"The streets were our kingdom. Everything revolved around the streets. There were no play dates.

"I don't know if it was born out of the concentration camp experience, but my parents were very protective with their kids. I have two younger brothers. We're still close. It was brought to me very early that the oldest brother had a responsibility to set an example for the others.

"The notion of extended family was not part of my upbringing. We had no relatives. Our extended family was all the fellow survivors my parents knew. But there was an arrogance built into that, and this was privately expressed: *We survived*. And in the early days there was also a malevolence attached to surviving, because within the Jewish community the survivors were quite suspect. *What did you do to survive?* My father would say, 'The best of us went up in smoke.' He had major guilt. He would reminisce about this kid who he knew, or that one, and a pathos would come over him. He would say, 'This one died . . .' And it was very difficult for him to talk about his parents or other relatives. But they did manage to become *Americanshe*: American-born Jewish people. They had a lot of friends. My mother was very popular. When I was a kid, my mother would be on the phone for hours. Friends would be calling her. She would field phone calls every ten or fifteen minutes. Her card game was the big thing. My parents loved to play pinochle, and my father loved to play poker. Typically on Friday nights my parents went to card games.

Harry Schweitzer's fifth birthday party, in Bensonhurst. *Courtesy of Harry Schweitzer*

"We didn't have much money. We never traveled a lot. We didn't have a lot of family. There was the five of us. And that brought home to me clearly that we depended on each other.

"To tell you the truth it was a very nice existence in Bensonhurst. The candy store where my father got his cigarettes, Benson & Hedges, was on the corner of Twentieth Avenue and 85th Street. It was called either Moe's or Irving's. When I got old enough he would give me money. 'Go get me a pack of cigarettes.' We got our candy there. Candy was cheap. We got bubble gum two for a penny. I was an incessant nosher. We had a deli two stores down, the Hy Tulip deli on 86th Street by the Twentieth Avenue stop by the el. We would get two franks with mustard and sauerkraut and a knish, my favorite thing.

"We would go there after we played ball in Cropsey Park, a big park with ball-fields and grassy areas and playgrounds. We played softball and baseball. And we would go all the time to Lenny's Pizza, which, if you recall the opening scene of *Saturday Night Fever,* the soundtrack starts up and you see John Tavolta's feet going right into Lenny's Pizza. It was the most delicious pizza. It was two blocks from our apartment. We were there all the time.

"We had a Chinese restaurant we liked. My mother's English wasn't very good. My father, being involved in the black market, learned English quickly. My mother did not. Beverly Jonas, one of our neighbors, brought home Chinese food one day. She said in Yiddish, 'Try it.' My mother liked it, and she asked, 'Where did you get this?' Beverly said, 'You get it at the Chinks. Go across the street under the el.'

"My mother went in and asked for *Chinks,* and she got thrown out immediately. She couldn't figure it out, until someone told her why, and my mother was upset, because she knew how smart she was, and she didn't like people laughing at her. We thought it was quite funny. She found out not to ask for *Chinks* anymore.

"Even though I was only five or six, I was a Dodger fan. We had an appliance store, like Save Mart, on the corner of Eightieth Avenue and 85th Street, right opposite the candy store. In the window they had a big television—big was twenty-seven inches—and they were broadcasting the World Series. There were twenty gazillion people standing around watching, and my father, all five foot three inches of him, put me on his shoulders. My father wasn't a baseball fan at all. He couldn't understand the game.

"When the Dodgers left after the 1957 season, there was a lot of white flight, but not in Bensonhurst. Nobody I know moved away. Nobody. I'm thinking about all my friends. They didn't move. And they may still be there.

"In 1962 my parents looked to move out of Brooklyn. My father was doing relatively well in plumbing. He made a foray into building houses. They started looking in Forest Hills, the mecca. But my father could not afford a one-family house. Even then a one-family house in Forest Hills was $30,000, and that was out of his reach.

But he had friends who had survived the war who lived in Flatlands. It had been the Canarsie dumps, and it was being built up on landfill. So in 1962 we moved to Flatlands. My father bought a two-family house in a Jewish neighborhood. Meyer Levin Junior High was a bus ride away. Meyer Levin was a decorated flyer from the New York area who died in a bombing mission over Europe in World War II. It had been Junior High School 285.

The Schweitzers on the day Harry's mother went blond.
*Courtesy of Harry Schweitzer*

"I went there for two years. I was in an accelerated program, did three years in two, and I applied for high school at Brooklyn Tech, a specialized high school, and got in, much to the surprise of my parents. It was all boys. It was in downtown Brooklyn, Fort Greene. I graduated in 1967.

"Brooklyn Tech was the quintessential cosmopolitan school. The other specialized schools were Bronx High School of Science, the High School of Music and Art in Manhattan, and Stuyvesant in Manhattan.

"The neighborhood around the school was dangerous. Recently I went to a reunion with my daughter. We live in Park Slope, and we walked, and I started laughing. She asked why. I said, 'Because I'm walking here.' Back then you wouldn't be caught dead in that neighborhood walking after three o'clock in the afternoon. The danger came from the underclass of white toughs hanging around the school looking for trouble, and from black kids who lived in the projects not too far away. These kids had nothing to do.

"Brooklyn Tech, unlike most high schools, only had one session. Everyone was through by one thirty, and everybody left promptly, unless you were on a team or in the band. I don't want to overemphasize the danger. It wasn't that terrible, but you had to be careful.

"I was always liberal. I remember watching the debates in 1960 between Richard Nixon and John Kennedy and hating Nixon. I couldn't vote until I was twenty-one, the 1972 election. I worked for George McGovern, and the Jewish people in Brooklyn didn't like McGovern very much. Because he was not pro-Israel. Nixon had a legacy of right or wrong—and, in my mind, wrong—but he had Henry Kissinger, and the Republicans were very strong on Israel and on defense. And so at a certain point a lot of Jews became Republicans.

"I worked for McGovern during that election. They stuck me in Boro Park, an ultraconservative bastion, to campaign. The Hasidim, who are ultraconservative, lived there. I worked my butt off, but it was like trying to push against the tide. It wasn't going to happen. They called me all sorts of funny names. Even though I was walking around with a yarmulke on, they were saying I wasn't a Jew. I used to laugh. I said, 'You guys will get yours at some point.'

"I was at McGovern headquarters in Brooklyn the night we lost dramatically. But I have always stayed very Democratic, very liberal. On a national basis, I have never pulled that lever for anyone but Democrats."

# The 1950s
# and 1960s

# FOR THE LOVE OF BILLY COX

JOHN MACKIE

**F**OR BROOKLYNITES WHO LOVED THEIR DODGERS, THE YEARS between 1947 and 1957 were magical. Six of those seasons Dem Bums won the National League pennant, and during most of this period the Dodger stars remained constants in their lives. Jackie Robinson, Duke Snider, Roy Campanella, Pee Wee Reese, Carl Furillo, Gil Hodges, Don Newcombe, Clem Labine, and Carl Erskine were the bullworks of the dynasty.

For John Lawrence Mackie, who grew up in Sheepshead Bay, the player he admired most was the third baseman, Billy Cox. In 1949, when he was five, Mackie developed polio. After he lost the use of his legs, he was treated by an Australian nurse by the name of Sister Kenny, who came to the United States prescribing a polio treatment that has been scoffed at by mainstream doctors and by history. But according to Mackie, Sister Kenny's treatments enabled him to walk again, and when he left the Jersey City Medical Center under his own power, a reporter from the *Brooklyn Eagle* interviewed him. When asked what he wanted to be when he grew up, Mackie told the reporter he wanted to be "the third baseman for the Dodgers, like Billy Cox." A correspondence between Mackie and Cox resulted. Mackie, who is now sixty-two, has never forgotten his childhood hero.

Cox left Brooklyn at the end of the 1954 season, but Mackie's love for the Dodgers continued. Baseball in Brooklyn during that era was as important to the residents as breathing the very air itself. It was the glue that held the borough together.

**JOHN MACKIE** "I was born on April 28, 1944, in St. Peter's Hospital in Brooklyn. My grandfather Percival Mackie, who they called Percy, came from Scotland. He was a mechanic, a guy who grew up around horse carts, who eventually became an automobile mechanic. I don't believe the man ever had a Social Security card or ever paid a nickel of Social Security. For years he operated a shop in his backyard. He got up in the morning and walked out to the shop and fixed neighbors' cars. He got ten bucks here, five bucks there, and that's how he made his way through life.

"He lived in Sheepshead Bay in a little house on East 15th Street, right off Avenue U and diagonally across from the old 61st Precinct. The Mackies were famous for noisy parties, and the cops would come over and tell them to quiet things down, and of course, they would never leave. They would become part of the crowd.

"My mother's maiden name was Hawke. She was English and Irish. Her mother's maiden name was Sullivan. Her parents were born in the United States, but their parents were born in Ireland and England. I don't know why they came. I guess because they wanted a better life.

"My parents met in Yonkers in the 1940s. My mother was living with her first husband, and my father was operating a bus company there. They got together, and they got married in Hoboken, New Jersey, and they settled in the Midwood section of Brooklyn on Ocean Avenue between K and L. We lived in a place called the Ocean Castle, an austere-looking apartment house with small courtyards. I can remember trolley cars going past the door.

"In 1949 there was a Brooklyn polio epidemic. The epidemic spread throughout the New York metropolitan area, but people were very parochial in those days. Things only happened in Brooklyn. There was no place else. Anyway, I contracted polio.

"I couldn't walk. I had weakness of the limbs. Our family doctor got me admitted to the Roosevelt Hospital in Manhattan, and I lay in bed for two weeks and did nothing, because they didn't know what to do. Salk had not yet come out with his vaccine, and even if he had, it was already too late for people who had contracted it.

"Polio was a mystery to physicians. However, an Australian nurse by the name of Sister Elizabeth Kenny found a way to treat polio and she brought her methods to the United States. She was given one whole floor at the Jersey City Medical Center. Though she was deemed a quack by the medical profession, she had wonderful results with her methods, and eventually she became state-of-the-art.

"Her argument was, 'If you don't do anything with these limbs, they will atrophy further and waste away to the point where they won't be able to do anything.' So she

Boy standing on table being examined by Sister Kenny. *Library of Congress*

would take wool, thick army blankets, cut them into long strips, put them in a barber towel machine, and heat them very hot, and then she'd wrap the limb with them, go up and down the leg to relax the tissues inside the leg, and then manipulate the leg.

"I can remember as a kid lying in a room with a big, bright light, and all these orderlies would be manipulating my limbs, making my legs work, bending my back, doing all these contortions with me to keep the limbs and muscles from atrophying. It was absolute agony. I remember screaming. It was as if I was in a torture chamber.

"I was there for several months. And then one day I woke up, and I was able to walk. I remember the first day I could run up and down the ward. I was cured. It was amazing. I was cured!

"I was released on Christmas Eve, and as a human-interest story, a reporter from the *Brooklyn Eagle* showed up and wrote an article with the headline 'Boy Receives Wonderful Gift for Christmas.' There was a picture of me being carried out of the hospital in my dad's arms. The reporter said to me, 'What do you want to be when you grow up?' I told him, 'I want to play third base for the Brooklyn Dodgers, just like Billy Cox.'

"I received a baseball in the mail signed by the entire 1950 Dodger team. Everybody signed the ball. Cox sent it to me with a little letter. My father got back to him, and from that point forward I would get a Christmas card from Billy and Anne Cox and their kids from Harrisburg, Pennsylvania. This correspondence continued until 1954, when he left baseball. In the spring of 1955 he failed to show up at the Cleveland Indians training camp. Al Rosen broke his pinkie, and the Indians, who had just gone to the World Series, needed a third baseman. They traded with the Baltimore Orioles for Cox and Gene Woodling, and Woodling showed up, and Cox never did. He went on a two-week bender, just vaporized, and he was out of baseball.

"Everyone had been amazed that I had been cured. My family was poor. There was no way we could have paid any amount of money to Sister Kenny, but my father wanted to thank her for what she had done. My father, who ran a Studebaker agency in Sheepshead Bay, drove a Studebaker all over Brooklyn and sold raffle tickets for a month, until one day I picked the winner out of a hat. Some guy won a brand-new Studebaker, and all the proceeds went to the Sister Kenny Foundation. In 1946 a motion picture was made about Sister Kenny. Rosalind Russell played the lead. [Russell was nominated for an Academy Award for Best Actress for *Sister Kenny*.]

Dodger third baseman Billy Cox, hero to young John Mackie. *Courtesy of Peter Golenbock*

"We lived in Midwood until about 1951, when we moved briefly to a little town called Valley Stream, on Long Island. My parents were no longer living together, and I lived with my mother and my sister. Then in 1953 we moved back to Brooklyn, to Sheepshead Bay, a little apartment in the basement of my older sister's house. Her husband, a New York City fireman, had bought a home right off Emmons Avenue and they were glad to get the rent. My father, who didn't live with us, paid. I was so glad to be back in Brooklyn! That's what I identified with as a kid.

"Sheepshead Bay was the home of a large fishing fleet. Any number of piers ran along Emmons Avenue. Dozens of charter fishing boats operated from there.

"We swam in those waters, much to my mother's chagrin. If she would have found out, she would have killed me, because she thought I would contract polio again because of the terrible polluted waters. I didn't care. I swam in those waters, and we would fish, scoop up blue-claw crabs, bring them home and enjoy them.

"I went to elementary school at PS 52, which was on Nostrand and Voorhees avenues. The area was a mix of everything. I played with the Leuci kids, five or six houses down. The Melillos were across the street from me. The kids I played the most with were the Weilguses, Stanley and Lenny. They lived in a house adjacent to the service road of the Belt Parkway. We would paint a little box on the side of that house and play stickball, which was the street game of Brooklyn, and it was a home run if you could hit it over the Belt Parkway. I can't tell you how many Spaldeens we lost.

"The Leuci family was interesting. Pasqual Leuci lived in a house that had a garage in the back. His father was an ice man. His truck would come along the street at night, and he'd park it. He had this big old wooden-body truck with the ice chutes on the side. He must have been the last ice man to cometh.

"And the old man didn't speak English. He was truly from the other side. I'd go over on Sunday afternoon to the family gatherings. The mother and the aunts would be stirring this big pot of sauce. The wine would be flowing, and the old man would be plucking a mandolin, playing Italian music.

"The garage in the back was never used to house an automobile. It had a big wooden vat in the middle of it. The whole backyard was one big grape arbor. They took the grapes when they matured and brought them in, and they did the tarantella on the grapes with their feet in this big, wooden tub and made their own wine.

"The Weilgus family also was interesting. I was like a surrogate part of their family. I would go with them on evening rides out to the Rockaways, and maybe we'd stop and get an ice cream someplace. I learned an awful lot about Jews. I learned their songs. I remember being at a seder, and I wore a yarmulke. I knew the Hanukkah song. It went, 'Hanukkah, Hanukkah, da da da da, top spins round, candle burns da da da da, it's Hanukkah today, da da da da.' In the shower I can do it better.

"At PS 52 most of the kids had names like Goldstein and Kammer. It was mostly a Jewish neighborhood because of an apartment complex built along Nostrand Avenue near Avenues X, Y, and Z, which became populated with Jews. I don't recall Protestants.

"I went to St. Mark's Church on Avenue X and Ocean Avenue. I was a very religious little boy. Even though I was a public school kid, I would get up every morning at some ungodly hour, like five in the morning, and I'd get on my bicycle and pedal all the way to St. Mark's and attend a six A.M. mass.

"I was enthralled by the whole idea of religion and the sense that this was a good thing. I was so involved in the idea of the church that at one time I even considered growing up and becoming a priest. Then, when I was ten or eleven, I didn't go anymore. My interest dwindled, and I would only attend Mass on Sunday."

John Gilbert Mackie and his two children, John and Patricia, Brighton Beach, circa 1951. *Courtesy of John Mackie*

*The main religion for Mackie and many of the Brooklyn kids at that time was the Brooklyn Dodgers.*

**JOHN MACKIE**   "Although my father and mother were estranged for as long as I can remember—my father didn't live with us for most of my life—on Sundays he would come and visit my sister Patty and me, and take us out, and he would take us to Ebbets Field to a Dodgers game. He would bribe the ticket taker in the booth, give him an extra $10 to make sure he got us seats right on the third base line near Billy Cox. When I became ten and eleven, I would go to games by myself. I'd catch the subway from Sheepshead Bay and take it all the way down to the Prospect Park station and walk over to Ebbets Field.

"At one time one of their sponsors was Borden's, and if you collected ten Fudgsicle wrappers or Dixie Cup lids, they would send you back a ticket to Elsie's Grandstand. There was a pharmacy around the corner, called Littman's. People would go in there and buy Borden's ice cream, and as they walked away, they would throw the wrappers on the sidewalk or flip them in the trash can, and I would loiter in the area and collect all of the wrappers and lids and send them in. I even made a little business out of it. I would sell the tickets I couldn't use to the kids in the neighborhood.

"When I went to the games, I would try to get autographs from the players. It was difficult. I knew where the players' entrance was, but it was always crowded with people. If you saw one of the players a block away where they parked their car in one of the lots, they were reluctant to stop and sign for you, because that would cause a crowd to collect, and they'd have to stand there for twenty minutes. So what I did, I bought 2¢ postcards and addressed them to myself. I would wait for these guys and catch them as they parked their car either before or after the game, and I'd simply hand them the postcard. They'd put it in their pocket and keep moving. Then the next day in the clubhouse, they'd sign it themselves and in some cases other guys would sign it too, and they'd drop it in the mail. I had a number of autographs. I even got Willie Mays that way.

"I can remember the day I met Sandy Koufax. It was back in '56. The Dodgers played the Milwaukee Braves in a double-header, and Sandy started one of the games. In '56 he wasn't *the* Sandy Koufax we all came to know. He was a young, promising pitcher with an amazing fastball, and he would have been great if he could have controlled it. But you never knew where this thing was going.

"He proceeded to get his teeth kicked in in the first two innings, and after the game I did my usual thing, hanging out near the parking lots, trying to catch the players and give them one of my postcards.

"I walked behind the right-field fence of Ebbets Field where there was an automobile dealership on the other side of Bedford Avenue. I could see Koufax walking toward a car. I trotted up to him. I was the only kid. There was no one else around. He let himself into this big, clumsy Jaguar sedan. I said, 'Sandy, can I have an autograph?'

"I had the postcard in my hand. He looked at me with a look of scorn, derision, and anger, and he taught me words I had never heard in my life, words I know now very well, but I had never, ever heard them before. If he could have bitten my head off, he would have. He drove away, and I stood there just totally deflated. My mouth hung open for the next ten minutes. I thought, *What the hell just happened here?* That was a rude awakening after thinking all ballplayers were these wonderful, terrific guys.

"What I remember most about Jackie Robinson was how strong he was. The Dodgers were playing the Pittsburgh Pirates on a hot Sunday afternoon. There was no worse heat than the confines of Ebbets Field. Jackie came to bat with several runners on base, and I remember him turning on a pitch. He was wearing one of those wool uniforms they wore, and he was soaking wet, and when he turned, I could see the sinews of his arms and forearms, and the moisture and sweat when he made contact with the ball, and he hit a rope into the left-field seats. It was a line-drive home run, and it seemed like the ball never started to fall, just went over the third baseman's head and stayed on a string straight into the seats. What a poke! And I thought to myself, *My God, how incredibly strong this guy must be.*

John Mackie in his Brooklyn Dodger
uniform, the summer of 1952.
*Courtesy of John Mackie*

"Jackie was the tail that wagged the dog in that Dodger organization. He kind of got what he wanted. For whatever reasons, he was pretty indulged. Billy Cox years later told me he was traded from the Dodgers because of problems he had with Jackie.

"Every spring training the Dodgers would be trying somebody else at third, trying to find a replacement for Cox. One year it was Don Hoak. Another year it was Don Zimmer. He was like Rodney Dangerfield. He didn't get no respect. But once the season started, Cox was back at third, and he played the season, and he was considered one of the best third basemen ever to play the game.

"In '53 Junior Gilliam came up, and Robinson wanted to move to third so Junior could play second. Then Jackie wanted to play left field. But Cox was the yo-yo. Whatever was going to happen, he was the odd man out. And Billy resented it terribly. He thought he was a better third baseman than anything Robinson could have hoped for.

"Also manager Charlie Dressen didn't like Cox, because Billy liked to drink. Cox and Preacher Roe, the Dodger pitcher, were pals. They roomed together, and they refused to fly. When the team would fly to Boston or to Chicago, they would sit on the train and drink beer from here to Boston or here to Chicago, and Cox would spill himself out of the train when they pulled into the city. Preacher Roe told me that Cox played third one day when he was totally loaded, and he said, 'I never saw a man play third base so great.'

"In Brooklyn Cox and Roe and many of the Dodgers stayed at the St. George's Hotel. There was a circular staircase that led from the upper level down to the main floor of the hotel, and that's where the bar was, so when Cox and Roe would be sitting there at the bar having a beer, they knew if Charlie Dressen caught them there'd be hell to pay. They got the bartenders to put up gypsy curtains along the entrance to hide that area of the bar from the stairwell so Dressen couldn't see them as he was coming down the stairs.

"They had an early-warning system, and when they were alerted Dressen was coming, they'd hide out until he passed through the lobby and went about his business.

"The Dodgers were my whole life. This was a sense of pride. I always looked at things deeper than my friends did. I said to myself, *What are the odds of being born in this world where countless billions of people have been born, lived their lives, and died in abject misery, poverty, and disease, and how lucky can I be to be born in the United States of America AND in Brooklyn?*

"There was this belief that this was God's country, the promised land. This was the greatest place in the world to be. You wouldn't trade it for Beverly Hills. My thought was, *How lucky I am to be living here.*

"The Dodgers were part of this grand scheme. They would validate the belief about this being the greatest place in the world, because every year the Dodgers either won the National League pennant or would come close, and of course there was that annual playing of our nemesis, the New York Yankees. It was the poor people of Brooklyn versus the rich guys from New York. We had this need to show them we could beat them, that their wearing fancy pinstripes didn't mean a thing to us. We were a better team. True, for a lot of years we didn't beat them, and you'd be saddened by it, but the attitude always was, 'Wait 'Til Next Year.' Somehow Brooklyn people found a way to rationalize the losses, and the next year the campaign would start all over again. It was a whole new ballgame, a new fight, a new battle, as we kicked and scratched and clawed to win a pennant so we could get back into the World Series against the Damn Yankees again.

"I can remember in '51 when Bobby Thomson hit that home run off Ralph Branca to win the pennant. We had a TV. I was watching the game. I remember watching a dejected Billy Cox turn and walk hunched over toward centerfield, 'cause the clubhouse was in centerfield. Billy knew it was all over. No point hanging around.

"That was heartbreaking, because Cox indirectly was responsible. You say, *If only certain things had happened.* In the middle of the season the Dodgers were twelve games ahead of the Giants. How does a team close a gap like that? But they did. The Giants got hot and won enough to force a playoff.

"But in the middle of the season there was a game against the Giants, and Cox was on third base, and another Dodger hit a long drive out to the outfield, which should have scored him easily, but Willie Mays caught the ball and threw Cox out at home. No one could believe it, because Cox was fast. Cox assumed he could coolbreeze it home, and he didn't make it. And because of that play, the Giants won that game. Had Cox kicked it into gear and scored, that '51 playoff never would have happened. IF. The biggest word in the English language.

"We finally won a World Series from the Yankees in 1955. It was another shootout at the OK Corral. The people of Brooklyn were so yearning to win a World Series against these Yankees. We listened to each game on the radio. No one went anywhere unless they had a radio connected to them, in their hand or in the car or in their ear at the beach or on a bus. No matter where you were, you could walk down the street and hear the game out windows or cars roaring by. You could hear Red Barber or Vince Scully doing the play-by-play. Everybody was so attuned to it. Each game came and went, and the Dodgers hung on, and in the seventh game this kid Podres, this new guy, was really an unknown factor. He was a young ballplayer.

"We were winning the game late by the score of 2-0. We thought we were in good shape, that we had a shot. And with runners on first and second, Yogila [Yogi Berra] came up. We called him Yogila. Yogila, that number 8, and he swung at a ridiculous pitch, as he always did, and he hit a ball down the left field line, and we thought, *There is no way this ball is going to be caught. It's going to drop in and score runners, and there goes another one.* But streaking across the outfield was this guy Sandy Amoros, number 15. He was left-handed, so he wore his glove on his right hand, which helped him catch the ball, because he streaked into the corner, stuck his right hand out, and good Lord, he caught the ball. He turned, wheeled, and fired the ball back to the infield, we got a double play, and that stemmed the rally and was the death knell for the Yankees.

"Horns began blowing along the Belt Parkway. Cars were going down the service road and along Emmons Avenue with their headlights on, horns blowing, cheering, carrying on. Sheepshead Bay was relatively quiet, but I know in other areas of Brooklyn it was all-out lunacy.

"Beating the Yankees was an absolute high, one of those moments in life when you look forward to something, after every year you meet with disappointment after disappointment, and finally you achieve this thing that is so important to you. When you're eleven years old and this happens, it is unbelievable, as if you had hit the lottery. Nothing better could have happened.

"We won the pennant again in 1956, but there was a lot of talk of Walter O'Malley wanting a new ballpark. O'Malley seemed to think Ebbets Field was poorly situated. He said because the neighborhood was changing from white to black, people were reluctant to go there and attendance was falling, though I don't believe that. O'Malley was seeing the likelihood of this eventually becoming the case. Only O'Malley knows his motives, and God only knows, but he wanted a bigger stadium with more seats. The bottom line is always the dollar sign.

"When we heard the Dodgers might leave, you thought, *Where there's smoke, there's fire,* but you hoped it would be resolved. Surely the Dodgers would never leave Brooklyn.

"Then it was announced in August of 1957 that the Dodgers were going to Los Angeles. Gil Hodges made the last out at Ebbets Field. And that was it. That was the end of an era. The Dodgers were gone, and not only that, but Roy Campanella got himself creamed in his station wagon on his way home in Long Island, and he broke his neck and turned into a paraplegic. That was very sad, heartbreaking. He never played in Los Angeles.

"In the spring of '58 life in Brooklyn was dismal without the Dodgers. There just was no electricity in the air. The Dodgers became a tough subject. It was an unpleasant topic. Some people were angry, and others hung on, were still Dodgers fans, but generally speaking, the thrill was gone.

"One weekend in 1971 I decided I was going to play detective and look up Billy Cox. I was a New York City cop, and all I had was an envelope with a return address on it that I had gotten from Cox on a Christmas card back in 1953. It had a Harrisburg, Pennsylvania, address. A friend of mine and his wife, and me and my wife got into my friend's brand-new Thunderbird, and off we went to Harrisburg. We found the address, and it was in the middle of a black ghetto. I thought, *No way Cox lives here. It's been twenty years. How do I find this guy?*

"I rode around the neighborhood and came upon a fire station. There were a couple of old white men sitting in wooden chairs, leaning back, chewing the rug with one another. I pulled the T-bird into the fire station driveway. I walked up and said, 'I'm looking for a fellow who used to live in this neighborhood. Billy Cox.'

"They said they didn't know any Billy Cox.

"I said, 'He used to play third base for the Dodgers.'

"'Oh,' one of them said, 'you mean Bill Cox. I don't know where he is. I heard he moved up to Newport'—which was twenty miles north of Harrisburg—'but I do know where his sister Daisy lives.' She lived around the corner.

"I went to a row house, knocked on the front door, and inside I could see a Baltimore Orioles game on the television and a woman ironing brassieres.

"I told her who I was and who I was looking for and why.

"'Come in,' she said. 'Want a beer?'

"'No thanks,' I said.

"She said, 'Today is Sunday, so he's tending bar at the Loyal Order of the Owls in Newport.' She gave me directions.

John Mackie and Clem Labine.
*Courtesy of John Mackie*

"It was a red-hot day, a hundred degrees. We got there, and my friend and I knocked on the first of two doors like speakeasys had. Our wives had to stay behind in the car. Men only. We couldn't get in because the county was dry on Sunday, and the only way you can drink is if you belong to a private club, and in Newport, Pennsylvania, the only private club in the town was the Royal Order of the Owls.

"A member finally came by, and when they opened the door for him, I was able to tell the guy at the door what I wanted. He let me in. Inside, Billy Cox was standing at a pinball machine. The balls were banging, and the machine was ding, ding, dinging, and here was a short, balding man with a big potbelly. He wasn't that lean, thin fella anymore.

"I walked over to the machine, and I said, 'I don't know if you remember, but back in the '50s when you were with Brooklyn, there was a kid who started a friendship with you because he wanted to play third base for the Brooklyn Dodgers just like Billy Cox. You sent him Christmas cards, autographed balls, and got him into the park.'

"He turned and looked at me, in the face and up and down, and he said, 'You look pretty healthy now, Larry.'

"Larry was my name when I was five. I was born John Lawrence Mackie, but my mother wanted me to be called Larry. I couldn't stand the name Larry, and when I was twelve I started calling myself John.

"Billy said, 'I have to go to the bar. I start working in five minutes. You guys got time to stick around?'

"Our wives went to the local hotel in Newport and got themselves established. We sat there at the bar, and Billy got me blown out of my shoes. We sat and talked to him and his cousin Gummy, who used to travel with Billy on the road with the Dodgers.

"We had a great reunion. Cox was a very reticent man and a strange guy, but he treated my friend and me like royalty that day. A number of years later I read that Billy Cox had died of cancer."

# THE MUSICAL GENIUS OF LINCOLN HIGH

NEIL SEDAKA

IN ADDITION TO THE DODGERS, THERE WAS ANOTHER ELEMENT that unified 1950s Brooklyn—its youth, at least—and that was rock and roll. The teenage musical genre crept upon the country slowly, because the early rock-and-roll records were by black musicians, and the white radio stations at first refused to play them. Slowly but surely, though, this new music, this exciting, sexy, moving music began to penetrate the psyche of Brooklyn's teens, and in the middle part of the 1950s there was a cultural revolution with kids on America's street corners forming singing groups and harmonizing. These kids were bored by their parents' music. The bland "How Much Is That Doggie in the Window" by Patti Page was soon replaced by Elvis "the Pelvis" Presley's "Hound Dog" and "Don't Be Cruel," as adults became horrified over their kids' embrace of a seemingly sybaritic, sex-filled culture influenced by this new music called rock and roll.

Brooklyn, which has played a part in every American cultural revolution, contributed greatly to this one. From the beginning of the twentieth century, Brooklyn's sons and daughters have helped form American popular music—it was the birthplace of George and Ira Gershwin, Eubie Blake, Betty Carter, Aaron Copland, Neil Diamond, Arlo Guthrie, Lena Horne, Wolfman Jack, Nora Jones, Julius LaRosa, Steve Lawrence, Robert Merrill, Harry Nilsson, Noel Pointer Sr., Martha Raye, Buddy Rich, Max Roach, Roger Sessions, Beverly

Sills, Connie Stevens, Barbra Streisand, Richard Tucker, Ben Vereen, Randy Weston, and other talented composers, musicians, and singers too numerous to mention.

Among the Brooklyn kids who made it big in the pop music biz over the years were Johnny Maestro and the Brooklyn Bridge, Neil Diamond, Carole King, Harry Chapin, Pat Benatar, the Beastie Boys, Barry Manilow, Lou Reed, and rap artists the Fat Boys, and Busta Rhymes. Rapper Jay-Z has become one of the most successful musicians/businessmen in music history.

Among the most talented and least likely pop stars to come from Brooklyn was a scrawny, diffident kid from Brighton Beach by the name of Neil Sedaka.

A self-admitted mama's boy, Sedaka was heading for a career as a classical pianist when one afternoon there was a knock at his door. Sedaka, then thirteen, was surprised to find standing there a chubby schoolmate three years his senior. The boy, Howard Greenfield, suggested that they write pop songs together. Sedaka demurred, but Greenfield insisted, and it's a good thing for us he did, because the team of Sedaka and Greenfield wrote some of the signature songs of early rock and roll, including such standards as "Stupid Cupid," "Oh! Carol," "Happy Birthday Sweet Sixteen," "Calendar Girl," and "Breaking Up Is Hard to Do."

Neil Sedaka, his big sister, Ronnie, and their parents. *Courtesy of Neil Sedaka Music*

Sedaka was born in Brighton Beach in 1939. His father's parents, Sephardic Jews, had come from Istanbul, Turkey, around 1910. At home they spoke Ladino—a mixture of mostly old Castilian Spanish and Hebrew—sort of the Sephardic equivalent of Yiddish. His mother's parents were born in New York City.

His mom and dad met at a dance on Ocean Parkway. His dad was driving for a taxi company in Manhattan, and he was well-off enough to own a car. He drove his car to the dance. Said Sedaka, "My mother was very poor, and the thing to do was get married, and when she saw the car she was very impressed. They dated awhile. She said, 'I don't love him, but I will learn to love him.' Which she did."

During his early childhood, Sedaka lived with his mom and dad, grandmother and grandfather, sister Ronnie, and his father's five sisters—eleven relatives living in a two-bedroom, one-bath apartment in Brighton Beach. It may have been crowded, but looking back, Sedaka didn't mind at all.

Young Neil and Ronnie Sedaka.
*Courtesy of Neil Sedaka Music*

**NEIL SEDAKA** "I had a blessed childhood. It was a loving, close family. They were wonderful people. I was raised by all those women. I was catered to, pampered.

"One by one my aunts got married, and my grandfather died when I was three. Eventually it was just my mother and father, my sister Ronnie and me. Ronnie and I were very close. She was eighteen months older and was my hero all my life. A wonderful girl. Scholastically, she was at the top. She was a cheerleader and beautiful and popular, and I was not."

*When Neil was eight, he was in the third grade at PS 253 in Brighton Beach. One day Neil's music teacher sent a note home saying she thought the boy had musical talent. His mother took a job and bought him a secondhand upright piano for $500. He began taking music lessons. After a year the teacher told his mother, "He's too gifted. I can't teach him anymore." At age nine he got a scholarship for the prep school of Juilliard in Manhattan, where he studied under the tutelage of Edgar Roberts.*

*Growing up, Sedaka lived at 3260 Coney Island Avenue between Brighton Beach Avenue and the boardwalk. Today that corner has been named Neil Sedaka Way.*

"The Brooklyn neighborhood was wonderful," says Sedaka. "I had three movie theaters to choose from, the Lakeland, the Tuxedo, and the Oceana. The Lakeland had rats under your feet. The Tuxedo was on Ocean Parkway and was a little classier. The Oceana, which I could walk to, was the main one. It was 21¢, and I always had money to go, and I saw the newsreel and the serial, Hopalong Cassidy or Roy Rogers, and after the movie we went to Ziemar's, which was a delicatessen. Nathan's, in Coney Island, was too far to walk. And I was afraid to go on the roller coaster until I was fifteen years old. That year my sister, Ronnie, went on the Cyclone, and she teased me. She said, 'You can't take it. You'll lose your breath. You're going to faint.' I got up the courage, and I became a roller-coaster freak. I went on the Cyclone, the Thunderbolt, the Tornado, the L. A. Thompson, and the Bobsled, all five of them."

*Since he was a toddler, music was always a big part of Sedaka's life.*

**NEIL SEDAKA** "I wouldn't eat as an infant unless music was playing. There was an immediate response when I heard music. And then, when I was three or four, my mother and I went to a record shop on Kings Highway. Don't ask me the name of the record. We had a seventy-eight record player. When I got home, I ran to the record player, slipped and fell, and it broke into a million pieces. We went back and bought another copy, and I played it to death.

"The only time I can remember listening to the radio was the Yiddish program on Sunday, *The Sunday Simcha*. My next recollection was at age eleven or twelve, listening to Martin Bloch's *Make-believe Ballroom*. My aunt Molly bought me *placas* 'records' in Span-

It's Neil's birthday. *Courtesy of Neil Sedaka Music*

ish). She bought me songs I had heard on *Make-believe Ballroom*: Johnny Ray, Patti Page, Les Paul and Mary Ford, Rosemary Clooney. I tried playing by ear but did it poorly. I could play the melody in the right hand with one finger, but I could not play the left hand. We would go on family picnics, and we would bring kazoos. We'd get on the city bus going to Prospect Park, and on the bus I'd play the kazoo and the family would sing all these Jewish songs, *'Shani de la Vuna'* and *'Bei Mir Bis Du Schoen.'*

The hit songwriter-to-be.
*Courtesy of Neil Sedaka Music*

"I had begun taking piano lessons from Murray Newman, a private teacher from Brighton Beach, when I was eight, but I was too lazy to read the notes. Then when I was nine I started with Edgar Roberts at Juilliard Prep, and I began practicing five hours a day, starting with the Béla Bartók *Mikrokosmos* pieces, which were for children. At Juilliard I had to read, because Bartók was atonal, dissonant. My mother was so proud. She called Aunt Frieda, Aunt Minny, and Uncle Joey to come hear me play. I sat at my piano at home and played the *Mikrokosmos* of Bartók, and my uncle Joey whispered to my mother, 'Eleanor, he makes so many mistakes.' Because he was used to hearing tonal music, things with melody, and this was all dissonance. He didn't understand it at all.

"But it hurt my feelings, and I went back to Edgar Rogers, and I said, 'This is great, but I need some melody. I need to play Schumann, Chopin, and some Bach.' I learned how to read music, and I learned a varied repertoire."

*Though the Sedakas weren't religious, Neil's father took him to the Sephardic temple on high holidays. When he was twelve, there was a question whether he'd be bar mitzvahed, because by then he was practicing the piano five hours a day, and he didn't have time to go to Hebrew school. Sedaka's mother, a persuasive woman who usually got her way, went to the rabbi of Temple Beth El, and begged, pleaded, and cried for him to allow her son to study for six months so he could get bar mitzvahed. The rabbi didn't stand a chance.*

**NEIL SEDAKA**   "My father was very thrifty, very tight. Being only a taxi driver, he was very poor. But my mother wanted me to have a beautiful bar mitzvah, and she took various jobs, a saleslady at Abraham & Straus department store, and she made me a beautiful bar mitzvah, a big doing at Rosoff's, which was in Manhattan. When I sang for the bar mitzvah, the cantors all went to my mother and said, 'He should be a cantor. He has a beautiful voice.'"

*Sedaka attended PS 253 from first to sixth grade, and then he graduated to PS 225, a seventh-and eighth-grade school at Oceanview Avenue and Brighton 13th Street. He had to follow his sister, Ronnie, an A student who was one grade ahead, and when he began a class, the teachers would say, "Are you Ronnie Sedaka's brother? You've got big shoes to fill."*

**NEIL SEDAKA**   "Of course, I couldn't. I had a seventy-five average. Because I practiced piano most of the time. And I was not a hit in school. I wasn't a jock. I couldn't play ball. I was afraid to hurt my hands. And I walked like a girl, because I emulated my sister, and I was made fun of. So I was an outcast. I had girl friends. There were four or five girl friends who lived in my building, and we jumped rope and played potsy [also known as hopscotch]. The kids would pick on me, and Ronnie would fight my battles. Ronnie did everything for me.

"It was terribly hurtful. That's when I decided, *I'm going to be something, and I'm going to be recognized.*"

*Sedaka was thirteen years old in 1952, when he started to write pop songs. On October 11, 1952—Sedaka remembers the exact date—Howie Greenfield, a sixteen-year-old self-styled poet, came to his door. They lived in the same building, and Greenfield's mother, Ella, had heard Neil practicing classical music in the mess hall at the Kenmore Lake Hotel at Livingston Manor in the Catskills while he was vacationing with his parents.*

**NEIL SEDAKA**   "I had never liked him. We called him 'Fat Howie,' 'cause he was obese, and he was three and a half years older, which was a big difference in age. I remember my sister giggling, 'It's Fat Howie at the door.'

"I said, 'What do you want?'"

"He said, 'My mother heard you playing, and I'm a lyricist and a poet, and I'd like to write songs.'"

"I said, 'Write songs? I'm studying to be a concert pianist.'"

"But he convinced me to write a song. And I was so enamored that I could write a song. Howie had a WebCor wire recorder, and we wrote the song 'My Life's Devotion,' and I sang it in a high soprano male voice, a terrible song. I called it a ruptured rhumba. Probably something I had heard in a Xavier Cugat movie. It was terrible. It went, 'My life is madness, it's sadness, it burns with desire, I'm yearning, just burning, my soul is on fire. Here I'm a slave, and you're just a sire of love.' Pretty bad. Ronnie laughed and said, 'Oh, you're wasting your time.' My mother said, 'This is a disgrace. You're a pianist. You're going to be a concert pianist.' But Howie snuck up every day when my mother was shopping, and we wrote a song every day for the first six months.

Neil Sedaka and Howie Greenfield.
*Courtesy of Neil Sedaka Music*

"Our songs weren't very good, but we were improving. My sister still laughed. She said, 'There are millions of people writing songs. You'll never make it.'

"But after I met Howard, I started to pick up pop music and play the pop songs on the piano fairly well, and I could dance too. I was a very good social dancer with the girls I grew up with. I began to get invited to the parties to play and dance."

*When Sedaka was fifteen, he enrolled at Abraham Lincoln High School. In the beginning he was ashamed of his singing voice, because it was a high-pitched soprano, and so he limited his performing to playing the piano for the Class Night shows. He also played the piano for the drama club's musicals such as* Oklahoma!, Carousel, *and* Finian's Rainbow. *Though he didn't get on the stage, classmates would sing Sedaka-Greenfield songs at the Friday-night talent shows. Francine Schneider sang the Sedaka-Greenfield song "Jungle," which began, "Jungle, love is a jungle. I'm lost in the rapture capturing the thrill of romance." Says Sedaka, "It was terrible."*

*In 1954, his sophomore year, Sedaka was sitting in teacher Molly Goldberg's math class. He said to himself,* I want to start a rock-and-roll group. *Sitting around him in class were Hank Medress, Cynthia Zolatin, Eddie Rapkin, and Jay Siegel, a boy with a beautiful falsetto voice. Sedaka could hear Siegel singing under his breath in math class. School ended at two thirty, and he then had to take the subway to Juilliard to practice the piano. After practice he would invite his four classmates to his home, and they would sing Sedaka-Greenfield songs and also the current doo-wop hits like "Earth Angel," "Ship of Love," and "The Closer You Are." At first Sedaka called the group The Linc-tones, from Lincoln High School, but he then changed the name of the group to The Tokens, because the group took the BMT to sing at sock hops. The group didn't get paid much, but the sock hops gave Sedaka his first taste of being on the stage in front of a crowd. The Tokens also sang at bar mitzvahs and weddings, and they made a TV appearance on Ted Steele's dance program on WOR (Channel 9).*

*Sedaka's profile was growing. He and Greenfield wrote a dance tune called "Mister Moon." It was sexy and a little raunchy, and after they performed it during the school's talent shows, principal Abraham Lass ordered them not to play it during the second show. But the students signed a petition saying they wanted to hear Neil "Mister Moon" Sedaka play the song again, and the principal relented.*

**NEIL SEDAKA**  "The adults didn't like the new music. To them it was juvenile-delinquent music. There was a sweet shop across the street from the school, and in the first half of the shop were the well-dressed, nicer kids, and in the back was the jukebox with the kids with the duck's-ass hairdos and the jeans. And they smoked tobacco.

"I was allowed in the back of the sweet shop because I was a hit with 'Mister Moon,' a slow, grinding, fish tempo. It was raunchy, and the kids went wild. They would say, 'Let Mister Moon in the back.' It was a big deal for me."

*In addition to being a rock-and-roll hit, he was also one of the top high school classical musicians in the city of New York. WQXR, the classical music station, held a contest, and Ben Goldman, the music teacher at Abraham Lincoln High School, submitted Sedaka's name. He played the piano at an audition in Manhattan in front of three of the most-respected classical musicians of the day, Abram Chasins, Arthur Rubinstein, and Jascha Heifetz.*

**NEIL SEDAKA** "I had already done some concerts on Saturday mornings at Juilliard Prep. Because every Saturday you had to play. So I was used to doing it. But I was frightened. I knew who my judges would be. I vomited before I went on, but I made it.

"There were five winners, and I was one of the five. I played the 'Reflets dans l'eau' by Debussy, Prokofiev's 'Third Piano Sonata,' and Bach's 'Prelude Fugue.' I was chosen to play on the radio, and my teacher taped it on a wire recorder."

*As accomplished as he was playing classical music, as a rock-and-roller he was becoming famous around town.*

*During his senior year, Cynthia Zalatin's mother knew a music publisher who set up an audition for The Tokens to play for Morty Kraft, a producer for Melba Records. Kraft had produced a hit song, "Alone," for a group called the Shepherd Sisters.*

**NEIL SEDAKA** "It was very exciting. We ran through a song Howie and I wrote, called 'I Love My Baby.' I sang the lead. And it got local play on Peter Tripp's Top Forty record show in New York. I'll never forget listening to the radio and hearing us singing 'I Love My Baby' on the radio. It was a thrill of a lifetime."

*Where Sedaka was really making his mark was as a side musician. Ahmet Ertegun and Jerry Wexler, the geniuses behind Atlantic Records, loved the way he played piano. So did singing idol Bobby Darin. Sedaka was the pianist on Darin's breakout hit "Dream Lover." On the B side, a ballad called "Bull Moose," he played a solo.*

*At age eighteen, Sedaka was forced to choose between his dual careers. He could either finish his education at Juilliard, or he could set off into a career of rock and roll. The race was on. The unanswered question was whether Sedaka and Greenfield would be able to sell any of their songs.*

*One afternoon Sedaka traveled to 1650 Broadway to see record producers Hill and Raines to try to peddle a song he and Greenfield had written, called "Stupid Cupid." The song was rejected, but while he was there he ran into one of his classmates at Abraham Lincoln High School by the name of Mort Shuman. The talented Shuman had performed in* Finian's Rainbow *at Lincoln High while Sedaka was in the pit playing the piano, and knew his talent. Shuman would go on to write rock-and-roll songs with the renowned songwriter Doc Pomus, including "Save the Last Dance for Me" by the Drifters and three of Elvis Presley's hit songs, "Viva Las Vegas," "Little Sister," and "Surrender."*

*After the turndown, Shuman told Sedaka, "Aldon Music is on the fourth floor. They are new, and they might be interested." Aldon Music, which stood for partners Al Nevins and Don Kirshner, had opened only a few days before.*

Neil, Howie Greenfield, and Connie Francis.
*Courtesy of Neil Sedaka Music*

**NEIL SEDAKA** "I went and played eight or nine songs, including 'Stupid Cupid,' and they said, 'We will sign you to a songwriting contract. But you and Howie have to bring your mothers in.' Because we were underage. Ella Greenfield and Eleanor Sedaka came in, and they signed the songwriting contract, and we got $25 a week.

"Donny said, 'We know Connie Francis. We'll drive you to her home in Haddonfield, New Jersey.' I was on top of the world. Connie had the number one single in the country, 'Who's Sorry Now.'

"We waited for Connie to come out of her beauty salon. She was having her hair done. Then we went to her home. I played all my best ballads, because I thought she'd follow 'Who's Sorry Now' with another ballad. She was on the phone in the kitchen as I was singing my little heart out. She was not interested.

"I whispered to Howie, 'I'm going to play "Stupid Cupid."'

"He said, 'It's not for her. We promised it to the Shepherd Sisters.' I had played it for them a couple weeks before and had verbally committed it to them.

"I said, 'I don't give a damn. She's Connie Francis. I'm going to sing "Stupid Cupid."'

"I did eight bars, and she said, 'Stop, that's my next record.' Because she loved Jo Anne Campbell, and Jo Anne Campbell was this raunchy little sexy thing with a gorgeous body who sang songs like 'Stupid Cupid.' And Connie wanted to change her pace.

"Morty Kraft produced 'Stupid Cupid' for Connie, and I played the piano with all the glissandos at the end. During the glissandos my thumbnail broke, and I bled all over the piano, but that was a small thing compared to Connie Francis singing our song.

"It came out in the summer of 1958, and it went to Peter Tripp's number fourteen, and on the *Billboard* chart it also went to number fourteen. I was thrilled. As a kid I used to buy seventy-eights and cross out the name of the writer and singer and write my name down to see how it looked on the record. Yeah, I had a lot of drive, a lot of chutzpah."

*Weekends in 1958 Sedaka was hired to perform at the Esther Manor Hotel in the Catskills. In addition to performing Sedaka-Greenfield songs with his singing group, the Nordinells—Norm, David, and Neil—he also played piano for singer Billy Eckstein and for Gregory Hines, who was with his act Hines and Dad. He also got to perform along with comedians Totie Fields and Jackie Mason, who was the hotel's social director.*

*The nineteen-year-old Sedaka also met the love of his life. Esther Strasberg, the Esther of the Esther Manor Hotel, was the owner, and her daughter Leba, who was sixteen, was working behind the desk.*

**NEIL SEDAKA**   "I saw her, and I said to myself, 'I'm going to marry that girl. It was like the *Dirty Dancing* movie. Of course, I thought she was a Catskill Mountain heiress, and boy, was I in for a shock. Because it was a summer resort, and they didn't make much money.

"I told Leba I was a songwriter. She said, 'I never heard of anybody who was a songwriter.' I said, 'I have a hit on the radio called 'Stupid Cupid.' That week she went to study hall at school and heard 'Stupid Cupid' on the radio. She said to me, 'You're not lying. I heard it on the radio.' Her mother wasn't thrilled. To her mother, every Jewish girl should marry a doctor or a lawyer, and I was a singer and songwriter. This was very strange, very foreign to them. But her father liked me. She and I dated for three years, got married in 1962, and our daughter, Dara, was born in 1963 and son, Mark, in 1966."

*After Sedaka began writing songs for Aldon Music in the Brill Building at 1650 Broadway, he brought in his former girl friend, Carole Klein, who changed her name to Carole King and subsequently wrote and performed the album* Tapestry, *the biggest-selling album of all time until* Thriller *by Michael Jackson.*

*After Sedaka sold "Stupid Cupid" and several other songs, he told Al Nevins and Don Kirshner he wanted to perform his own songs. Nevins had been in a group called The Three Sons that sang the hit "Twilight Time." They had recorded for RCA, and so Nevins brought Sedaka to Steve Schol, the RCA producer who had bought Elvis Presley's contract from Sun Records.*

*Sedaka auditioned his song "The Diary," and he was signed by RCA records on the spot. Sedaka appeared on Dick Clark's popular afternoon television show* American Bandstand, *as well as local TV shows in Baltimore, Washington, and New York. "The Diary" sold 500,000 copies.*

Says Sedaka, "I showed those football players at Lincoln High School that I was going to be a star."

# THE END OF RACE MUSIC

BRUCE MORROW

**W**HEN ROCK AND ROLL BROKE ACROSS AMERICA IN THE mid-1950s, white parents were aghast. Part of the outrage was a concern—no, a fear—that rock-and-rollers like Jerry Lee Lewis, Eddie Cochrane, and Elvis Presley were inciting their sons and especially their fresh-faced daughters to become looser sexually. The parents may not have known it, but the term "rock and roll" for years had been a slang black term for the sex act. The teen generation was ready to *get it on*.

There was an even bigger fear racing across pre–Civil Rights Act white America among the adults of the Dwight Eisenhower generation: "race" music. Racists were furious that glib and popular white disc jockeys like Alan "Moondog" Freed, Murray the K, and Bruce Morrow were disregarding society's unwritten code by allowing black acts like the Moonglows, the Crows, Fats Domino, Bo Diddley, Laverne Baker, Ray Charles, and the dangerous Chuck Berry, among others, to poison America's airwaves over the radio with their sensuous, exciting sound.

These disc jockeys—true, though rarely recognized, civil rights pioneers—were outraged that white artists like Pat Boone could cover (and tone down) a song by a more talented, black artist like Fats Domino or Ivory Joe Hunter and far outsell him, and they were determined to do something about the perceived injustice. They were also convinced that black music was what swayed the audience, moved the audience most, that the best rock-and-roll recordings were coming directly from the rhythm and blues and gospel sounds of the black community. And so, as often as they could, these DJs played these black artists over the airwaves. And when these black acts began appearing on TV with Dick Clark on *American Bandstand,* and black children danced together on the same floor with whites as millions of teenagers at home looked on in envy, one could argue convincingly that, like Jackie Robinson playing with the Dodgers, performers like Domino, Diddley, Charles, Baker, and Berry, and the black groups of the day—the Moonglows, the Charms, the Crows—along with Clark and the radio DJs who played their music, helped break down racial barriers and make America less intolerant and prejudiced.

With Dick Clark. *Courtesy of Bruce Morrow*

Freed, a Jew, was the true pioneer. He despaired of the way black artists were ignored by the white media, and though under threats of being fired, he deliberately, defiantly kept exposing America to these black artists, first in Cleveland and then in the biggest market of all, New York City. In both places his station kept attracting more and more listeners until the owners finally had to admit: "He's making us a lot of money. Let's leave him alone." Murray "the K" Kaufman and Bruce Morrow also were instrumental this way.

Of the three groundbreaking disc jockeys, only the Brooklyn-born-and-bred Morrow survives. In fact, fifty years since Bruce Meyerowitz from James Madison High School burst upon the scene as a young radio personality on WINS in New York, he is still going strong as a featured performer for Sirius satellite radio. Cousin Brucie was an important part of the lives of several generations of metropolitan New York listeners. Teens may not have seen eye to eye with their parents, but they always had a sympathetic cousin they could turn to in the evening. And he never failed us. We owe him a lot.

**BRUCE MORROW** "I tell people on the air I was born in Lubbock, Texas, but that's only my dream, because I loved Buddy Holly. I was actually born in Flatbush, Brooklyn. I'm a 100 percent Brooklyn kid."

*He was born Bruce Meyerowitz on October 13, 1935. He never knew his father's parents. He thinks they came from Russia. His mom's parents were Austrian immigrants named Platzman.*

**BRUCE MORROW** "My grandmother said they were not happy over there. They wanted to find the streets paved with gold. They wanted to get themselves a new opportunity in life."

*Meyerowitz's father designed and manufactured children's clothing. He called his company The Shop, employing forty workers. The firm designed hats and coats and manufactured them for other designers.*
*Though Jewish, the Meyerowitzes weren't very religious.*

**BRUCE MORROW** "They had an awareness of Judaism, but didn't really follow the faith. I was brought up to be very free in my thinking, and I really thank them for that. It really opened my vistas quite a bit, not being stuck in the past—which is okay if that's what you want, but I preferred—and I brought up my children the same way—to be free, to be proud of my heritage but not to be stuck to the rules.

"My parents were like that too, very open, never prejudiced. We were never taught that somebody's skin color or religion made them inferior. I was brought up by my parents to believe in good and evil. If somebody did evil, he was a bad guy. But I try to believe there is good in everybody, and I still believe that to this day. I look for the good in people."

*Meyerowitz grew up in Flatbush on East 26th Street between Avenues V and W. The neighborhood was Jewish, Irish, and Italian. The kids had territorial wars, he said, but they were not fought because of religion.*

**BRUCE MORROW**   "We had what I call the Lot Wars. A lot was an empty field, and in Brooklyn in those days we had lots of lots. Our parents used to pack us off in the morning, give us an old Hellman's mayonnaise jar filled with water, a wax paper–wrapped sandwich—peanut butter and jelly or cream cheese and jelly and white bread—trying to kill us, I guess—and a couple of chocolate cookies my mother baked but always burned on the bottom, and they'd say, 'Go.' Nobody had any fears anything would happen. The worst was we'd come home bleeding a little, but that was after playing a game of war. We'd hurl dirt bombs at each other, the 26th Street guys on one side, the 29th Street guys on the other. A dirt bomb would hit the ground and explode and throw dirt in your eyes, and they'd come and tag you.

"On the block itself we'd play ring-a-levio. I was a three-sewer man in punchball. That's 150 feet. We'd play king and stoopball. The street became our entire theater. It was the arena.

"I used to go to Saltzman's soda shop, which was right near my school, PS 206 on Gravesend Neck Road and East 21st Street. My favorite theater was the Mayfair on Avenue U and Coney Island Avenue, because it was walkable. We used to go there and stop in the deli, have a couple of hot dogs and a knish. We'd blow 25¢ doing that and another 25¢ to get into the movies, and for 5¢ we'd buy Good & Plentys so we could throw them at the matron. She was the disciplinarian, and when she'd walk up and down the aisle with her flashlight, as soon as she got past us, generally we threw the black ones and the pink ones at her, trying to hit her in the head, and we'd eat the white ones.

"As a child I grew up wanting to become a doctor. All my life I wanted to study gynecology. But my childhood was also deeply affected by the radio.

"I can remember a day in April in 1945. I was ten years old. I left PS 206 and walked the few blocks along the park near Bedford Avenue and Avenue V to my home. I had to be home by three thirty, so we had a little time to goof off, to go to the park or to Saltzman's, to flirt, play around, tease the girls.

"My mother usually had milk and cookies for me when I got home. On this day

I saw my mother on the porch across the street with Mrs. Flick and Mrs. Bloom and a few of these other very strong Brooklyn women, and they looked very upset. I got closer, and I saw them listening to a radio that was in the window, with the windows open. It was warm, and they were listening, and they were crying.

"I got very scared. My mother was crying, and these strong women who I knew were bawling hysterically. I was used to listening to the radio—ours was a little Bakelite box that said Philco on it—once in a while. It was magic, but I never realized it was informational, that it could have such an effect on humanity. Out of the radio came, 'Ladies and gentlemen, the President of the United States Franklin Roosevelt passed into eternity this morning.'

"And I couldn't understand why my mother wasn't home getting my milk and cookies ready. Or getting dinner ready. What could have been so important? But from that day on I became extremely interested in that little black box, that magic box called radio. It's my first recollection of wanting to get into that box.

"Like all kids, I would hide behind the console and make believe I was on the radio. I used to announce. I would take a newspaper or comic book, and I loved to do different voices. Friends would come in, and sometimes they would sing or play an instrument, and we would make believe we were doing radio shows.

"PS 206 went from kindergarten through eighth grade, and we went right from there to high school. The makeup was mixed: black kids, Jewish kids, and Italian kids. Very few Asians, and now it's 60 percent Asian in that area. It was a terrific school, because it was a real mixture of different ethnic and religious people, which I think is an essential asset to growing up. Putting a kid in a school with the same background economically, educationally, religiously is cheating the kids. And it's cheating the parents too.

"This was a great time in our lives. Nobody was afraid. Nobody was bringing guns to school. Nobody feared for their kids not coming home. Nobody had to worry about anything. It made growing up so pleasurable, so relaxed. It was easy, and you were able to develop skills. You didn't have to worry about anything else. My friends were mixed, and nobody fought. You'd be together, play the Lot Wars, touch football, but you weren't abusing or hurting anybody else.

"We were brought up to respect people. I was very lucky to be brought up in Brooklyn at that time, 'cause Brooklyn is very different today."

*He was first encouraged to use his oratory powers by PS 206 English teacher Elizabeth Frielisher.*

**BRUCE MORROW**   "You have to understand, I was very shy in class. I used to dread being called on. I wasn't a brilliant student. I did my work, but I didn't want to stand up in class. But Mrs. Frielisher made me read a poem in front of a microphone, and it sounded pretty good. And then I started doing announcements in school. That was my start.

"We used to have hygiene plays at PS 206. In those days we weren't allowed to have sex education, because no one was allowed to use the word S-E-X. So it was called hygiene. In those days hygiene meant we learned how to wash under our arms, change our underwear, and brush our teeth. So we were really being prepared for the world. That's why my generation is so screwed up. All we knew how to do was change our underwear and brush our teeth.

"There was an audition for the hygiene play to be shown in the auditorium, so I auditioned, and surprisingly to me, I passed, and I became an ugly tooth with a big cavity. I sang a song about how my mommy never told me to brush my teeth. And when I got out on stage, something happened to my body. I came out, and it was like somebody turned up the brightness. I was on that stage, and I was *liking* it. The inner me came out.

"When I was in the eighth grade, Mrs. Frielisher submitted me to the All-City Radio Workshop. It was a group of young people with instructors, professionals, which met at Brooklyn Tech High School that houses the studio and transmitter of WNYE-FM. Instead of taking regular English classes, we took courses in broadcasting. I did this for three years. I had my own radio show, and by the time I went to high school, I was feeling like a pretty big hot shot."

*After graduating from PS 206, Meyerowitz went to James Madison High School on Bedford Avenue between Quentin Road and Avenue P. By that time his father had made some serious money in the clothing business, and he moved his family into an upper-class neighborhood on East 29th Street between Quentin Road and Avenue P. Madison High was only a few blocks away.*

*When he got to high school, the kids knew him from hearing him on the radio, and his classmates asked him to perform in the Class Sing. Gone was his shyness about appearing in public. He played Goobah the Caveman and sang a parody of "Kisses Sweeter than Wine" by Jimmy Rogers. He was a big hit, and his class won the Sing.*

*It was in high school that he changed his name from Meyerowitz to Morrow.*

**BRUCE MORROW** "In those days you couldn't have an ethnic or religious name. You couldn't be Italian or Jewish. You could be Irish. Irish was a common denominator. So I had to get rid of the name Meyerowitz.

"I was going out with a young woman named Paula, who lived all the way up in the Fort Tryon Park area. Paula and I were going to the Drama Workshop. I was learning how to dance.

"One night I was up at Paula's house. Paula was extremely talented, and her mother was a kind of pushy stage mom. Her mother said to me that night, 'If you're going on the stage you can't have the name Bruce Meyerowitz. Let me pick you a name.' I said, 'Sure. But it has to start with the letter *M.*' I don't remember why. Some kind of Jewish tradition? I don't know.

"She pulled out the Manhattan phone book. She flipped through it and said, 'Tell me when to stop.' I said, 'Stop.' My name could have ended up being McGillicuddy or Morony or McCarthy. She put her finger down, went to the left and down and said, 'Morrow. That's it. Bruce Morrow.' And that's how I got my name."

*Morrow graduated from high school in 1953 and attended Brooklyn College for six months. He didn't want to go, but his parents enticed him with a new Ford convertible if he'd enroll. Six months later, after skipping more classes than not, he dropped out. For the next six months he bummed around town with his friends.*

*A friend then told him that New York University was talking about starting a radio station but didn't know how to begin.*

**BRUCE MORROW**   "I knew radio was going to be my life's work. I went and interviewed for Professor Irving Falk. Right away he took a liking to me, saw something in me. He saw I was a go-getter, and for the first two years of my college career I built the radio station at New York University. It was as though they were waiting for me to come. They needed a student who had Brooklyn balls. I got the money to start it. I strung the wires outside the windows.

"Let me tell you about Brooklyn. Brooklyn gives you a backbone, and when you show somebody from Brooklyn an opening, a light, and the person believes it's the right way to go, get out of his or her way. Nothing can stop them. They have a tremendous spirit. Brooklyn gives you a tremendous spirit. I am so proud of it, I can't tell you. And I know I am as successful as I am today because of growing up in Brooklyn.

"I called the dean of the school. He never did give me an appointment, and I got fed up, so I walked into his office. It was snowing and wet out, and I was wearing galoshes, and I trudged sludge onto his brand-new carpet. He freaked. He looked up at me with eyes the size of silver dollars and said, 'What do you want?'

"I said, 'My name is Bruce Morrow, and I'm here to get some money so I can build a radio station.'

"He said, 'You got it. Get out.' He was furious with me. He gave me $28, and with that money I bought wire and speakers and a little Dynavox phonograph. I put it all together. I put speakers in the lounges all over NYU with the cable I bought, I strung all the wire, and we were on the air. We had a radio station. It aired in all the dorms and lounges at NYU."

*Morrow was at NYU when the rock-and-roll revolution broke over the country. Like teenagers everywhere, to him the popular music of the day—"Old Cape Cod," "How Much Is That Doggie in the Window," "Wayward Wind"—was just a bunch of tired acts. When Bill Haley & His Comets sang "Rock Around the Clock," a new day in pop music had dawned. Morrow listened closely as the music for his generation began to change.*

**BRUCE MORROW**   "On the radio in those days was a gentleman by the name of Martin Block. He hosted a show called *Make Believe Ballroom,* and on Saturday morning he had *The Hit Parade.* As '54 and '55 came around, little by little something called rock and roll started to be heard. Rhythm and blues and vocal harmony started creeping in along with Perry Como and Patti Page and the Crewcuts, which to me was ad nauseam. 'Cause it was bland, monotone, boring, nothing new, but it was very safe. It was our parents' music. That music only lasted a decade, thank God. By the way, even though it was my parents' music, I know every single lyric of every single song. I know all the Perry Como songs. 'Hot diggety, dog diggety, oh what you do to me . . .' Little by little rock and roll started sneaking in. You heard Bill Haley & His Comets, then Elvis Presley came around, and we heard harmony, what they call doo-wop, which combined gospel, rhythm and blues, soul, and a little rock and roll.

"And suddenly black music, what we knew as 'race music' in those days—a disgrace on this nation of ours—I'm talking 1953, 1954, when the black records would be kept in a certain area of the store. And it was Perry Como and Pat Boone who covered the black artists, and they were the ones who got the air play. This was a very interesting time. Things were starting to change.

"I would go to the record store and buy records. I loved records. I bought the black artists like Bo Diddley. I realized that this was where the *real* music was. The Chords did 'Sh-Boom,' not the Crewcuts, though the Crewcuts outsold them twenty to one. I went to the store and bought the Gladiolas, and I found Laverne Baker and Ivory Joe Hunter, people like that, and I realized then that their music was being suppressed. I couldn't understand why. It was a matter of finance and money, and then suddenly the record industry, especially the independents, found out there was a market for black musicians, and they started exposing it, and little by little they got some air play.

"By the time I got on the radio, it was no longer called 'race music.' It was being integrated perfectly in the play. Because when Alan Freed started his radio career in Cleveland as Moondog, they were trying to stop him from playing all this black music. They didn't think there was any market for it.

"As a youngster I didn't realize this was an issue, but by 1955, 1956 I knew. And our parents were frightened when they heard Elvis Presley and then saw him. It was like the devil's doing. According to the parents, if you watched or listened to him, you would grow hair on your hand. Our religious, education, and political leaders took advantage of this, and they had themselves something to scream about, to yell on the pulpit about, which was absolutely ridiculous. Meanwhile, behind the scenes, some of these religious leaders were abusing little kids.

"In '57 Jerry Lee Lewis came out with 'Great Balls of Fire' and 'Whole Lotta Shaking Going On,' great stuff, and by then Alan Freed had come to New York. They give him credit for coining the phrase 'rock and roll,' but I think that is not true. Alan Freed borrowed the phrase, because 'rock and roll' is an old black slang expression for the sex act. You can go back to the '30s to find that. But Freed adopted it.

"Chuck Berry sang about rock and roll. There were great performers, and music helped heal a lot of the racial tensions in this land of ours, because suddenly we were listening to records by black artists, and soloists, and realizing, *Hey they are just like we are.* Whites who listened to them and liked their music became less racist.

"For years black groups like the Ink Spots and the Mills Brothers had huge white audiences, but they weren't allowed to sleep in the same hotels as whites. This happened in the early 1950s to people like Bo Diddley and Chuck Berry. They would come into town to entertain, and they had to sleep in black hotels. Very sad. So rock and roll, I really believe, had a lot to do with racial healing. That's been my thesis all my life."

*When Morrow graduated from NYU in 1957, he sent out demo tapes. Even though he had never been far from home in Flatbush, he knew he wanted to work in a warm climate, and he sent the tapes to Florida, Arizona, and Bermuda.*

**BRUCE MORROW** "It was kind of scary. I had never left the nest, my Brooklyn. I didn't know what lay ahead. I was so protected, I didn't know there were some ugly things in this world.

"I sent out ten demos. Eight general managers said, 'Go into your father's business.' One guy called me from Panama City and wanted to hire me. I called my father, and he picked up the phone. My dad was always at my side, and I miss him terribly.

"He said, 'What's the job?' The man said, 'He'll work at the radio station, be on the air, sell some time four hours a day, and for the other four hours he'll work in my other business.' The pay was $75 a week. I had to start the next week. My father asked, 'What's the other business?' The man said, 'A car wash.' We turned him down.

"Two days later I got a call from Bermuda, which was like the Magic Kingdom, millions of miles away, though it was really only ninety minutes by air off the coast of North Carolina. It was a foreign country, beautiful, an adventure for a young guy.

"I spent a year there, had the greatest time. Changed my life. Bermuda was settled by what they call the Forty Families. They left England to escape religious persecution. They were on the way to Virginia, and on the way their ship under the flag of Colonel Bermudiatis was shipwrecked on this twenty-mile-square reef. They got there, and they started practicing their own brand of persecution and religious dysfunction, though I have to stress that today things have changed. But this was 1958.

"Ken Bolton, the treasurer of radio station ZBM, took me around Hamilton, and I found a boardinghouse owned by a Mrs. McGuire. She loved me. Loved me. I started dating her daughter, and she was happy as heck about that.

"She was a lady who liked to drink, and one night she said to me, 'One thing about Bermuda that is great. We don't have any Jews here.'

"'Mrs. McGuire,' I said to her, 'why do you say that?'

"She said, 'You know how they are.' The same bullshit.

"I had the nerve to say, 'Mrs. McGuire. I'm Jewish.'

"She looked at me, drunk as a skunk, and said, 'Oh, you're not Jewish.'

"I said, 'Why do you say that?'

"'You don't act or look like them.'

"Her daughter apologized, but I moved out. I never talked to her after that.

"I remember going to the movies, and blacks weren't allowed to sit upstairs in the balcony. Orientals came from China, but Bermuda only let men in, not women. They were crazy.

"I used to do a show on the radio called *Search Party*. I used to have black kids and white kids dancing. It got to the point where I would get threatening phone calls that I better watch myself on the way home, that they were going to kill me.

"It was a ten-minute walk from the station to my home, and every time a palm tree would sway at night, I'd jump a million miles. I used to carry a lead pipe with me.

"I left Bermuda in an interesting way. A black church burned down, and they couldn't raise the money to rebuild it, and nobody would help them. If you're not Church of England in Bermuda, you're dead.

"I held a big dance. I hired a big warehouse in Hamilton Harbor, and I threw a dance. I raised the money, and they rebuilt their church, and after that it was suggested that I leave. 'Cause they didn't like that I was so friendly with black people.

"So I left Bermuda, but I learned about life there. In Bermuda they used to call me 'the Hammer,' because they never heard anyone talk like I did. See, I sounded like the music. I was very early with that. Alan Freed, who was my mentor, was the first one. He had that cacophony. He sounded like a rhythmic machine gun. Alan Freed used to pound on a big telephone book to the music. Rock and roll is a feeling, an emotion. You feel the music, a huge amount of energy. I still have that today.

"So it was time to go home, and I was getting tired. You don't like getting threatened, and so I went back home to Flatbush, and I started looking for a job. I met somebody who helped me get a producer's job at WINS. The DJs at WINS were on strike, and when the union pulls out the air staff, management walks in. Since I was hired as a producer, I was part of management. I wasn't a scab. I wouldn't have done that. When I was at NYU, WPAT in Paterson went on strike, and they came and offered me a job. I could have gone on the air, but I wouldn't take it. I wouldn't cross the picket line.

"I had all this airtime experience, so by the time the WINS strike was over, I had made quite an inroad, because I had my sound. I didn't sound like the other executives. I sounded like I was having a good time. So they hired me as the staff announcer."

*Morrow joined one of the great lineups of radio history. Among his colleagues were Murray the K, Tom O'Brien, Jack Lacy, Stan Z. Burns, and Al "Jazzbeaux" Collins from the Purple Grotto. This was the heyday of Top Forty radio.*

**BRUCE MORROW** "Top Forty radio started in the Midwest. A man named McClelland, who owned a radio station, took his program director to a bar every night, and they noticed that the customers were playing the same records on the jukebox over and over again. They started counting, and they counted forty different records, and that was the birth of Top Forty radio, as simple as that. People plunked their nickels into the same music over and over, and they kept score, and it became very obvious. And it spread all over the country."

*Bruce Morrow was making a name for himself at WINS, but he was looking for a handle, a name, that would stick in the minds of his listeners the way Alan Freed had called himself Moondog back in Cleveland, the way Murray Kaufman called himself Murray the K. Morrow found his handle quite by accident one night at work.*

**BRUCE MORROW** "One night a security guard came into my studio. He said, 'There's a lady who would like to see you.' I said, 'Absolutely.' He opened the door, and this white-haired lady, tiny in stature, walked in, and I motioned for her to sit down next to me. I said, 'I'll be with you in a moment.'

"I put a record on. I said, 'What can I do for you?'

"She said to me, 'Do you believe we're all related?' As soon as she said that, I thought, *I'm going to get hit up for money.* Because when I looked at her, I could see she wasn't a rock-and-roll fan. And because I'm a Brooklyn kid, I know.

"I said, 'Yes ma'am, I do believe we're all related.'

"She said to me, 'Well then, cousin, I'm broke. Can you lend me 50¢?'

"She had a sparkle and a beautiful smile, and I said, 'Sure cousin, here's 50¢.' I was cheap. I should have given her a buck. I didn't know all I was going to get out of those 50¢.

"She said, 'Thank you, cousin,' and she left.

"During the rest of the show I didn't give it a thought, but that night, as I went home to Brooklyn, I was in the middle of the Brooklyn-Battery Tunnel, and a light went on in my head. I repeated, 'Cousin, lend me 50¢. Cousin. Cousin.' And I said, 'Jesus, that's it. Cousin Brucie.'

"The next morning I called Mel Leeds, the program director. Don't forget, I was very young, very low on the totem pole. I said, 'Mel, I got my schtick. I want to be called "Cousin Brucie."'

"He said, 'That's the corniest, stupidest thing I ever heard in my life. You think this is Morgantown, West Virginia? You think this is Cheesequake?' He named tiny hamlets.

"He was glaring at me, but I felt he was testing me to see how sincere I was. I was a kid, but I garnered up all my energy, and I said, 'Mr. Leeds, I'm a New Yorker, and you're not. There's nobody cornier than New Yorkers. Corny is like going to your cousin's house and playing with his best toys'—because my cousins always had better toys than I had.

"He said, 'Good point. I'll tell you what you do. You try it tonight. But don't overdo it. Because if you overdo it and you're wrong, I'm going to fire your ass.'

"He scared the shit out of me. I went on the air. As Brooklyn Brucie, if someone says to me, 'Try it,' you don't tell him to do it without going full-speed ahead. I don't think a breath came out of my mouth that night without the word 'cousin' in the sentence. I cousined them, cousined the cousins.

"The next morning Mel Leeds called and ordered me to come to the office. He pretended he was going to fire me, and then he opened his desk drawer and showed me hundreds of telegrams. He said, 'We're putting you under a seven-year contract.' Cousin Brucie was born."

*In the fifty years of Morrow's career, the highlight came in 1964, when The Beatles came to America. By then popular music had become tired. It needed a shot of adrenaline. In England, groups devoured the likes of Chuck Berry, the Everly Brothers, and Jerry Lee Lewis, and began making their own sound. When in early 1964 the song "I Want to Hold Your Hand" hit it big on American radio, eyebrows went up. Who were these guys? When The Beatles arrived at Idlewild Airport on Pan Am flight 101, Bruce Morrow was there to witness the beginning of Beatlemania.*

**BRUCE MORROW** "Let me tell you how crazy it got. They get to the airport. I'm stationed there with our news director to broadcast their arrival. The place was going wild, really controlled mayhem. A few hundred kids were on the tarmac, and thousands more were up on the roof. The police controlled it pretty well, but it was enough to allow for some good pictures and to start the hype. And believe me, Beatlemania was hyped. Because most of us geniuses thought it would last six months. And we also knew that radio had gotten very boring, and we could use something to continue the action. Little did we know The Beatles were going to change the entire face of the culture.

Cousin Brucie interviews the Beatles in 1964. *Courtesy of Bruce Morrow*

"They walked down off the plane, and they had their first press conference. A makeshift press area was put up in the Pan Am lounge, and the boys were very scared. They didn't know what was going to happen here, even though they had had great success in Europe. This was the big time, the Big Apple, and they were in the United States where the streets were paved with diamonds. When they were looking down from the plane window onto the city, Paul McCartney said to John Lennon, 'I don't see any diamonds. Where are the diamonds you were telling me about?'

"Their timing couldn't have been better. Their PR guy, Brian Epstein, would not bring them over here until they had a number one record in the States. 'I Want to Hold Your Hand' hit very quickly, so they were coming over as conquering heroes, the first of this onslaught of British groups that we knew about.

"So they were at this press conference, and they were very nervous, and if you remember that conference, they were very snippy. They were acting like wise guys. But they were scared, really scared, and the press was after them. You have to remember the press at that time—and they were inundated with press—really represented Mom and Dad. So the questions were pitchforks. 'When are you going to cut your hair?' That kind of garbage. The reporters didn't understand the cultural importance of this group. Nobody really did. But once they arrived, we knew something was going on. It was crazy.

"And I was asked by Sid Bernstein, the promoter of the Beatles' concert at Shea Stadium, to host the show with Ed Sullivan. Now, Ed Sullivan was the very first one to expose The Beatles on national television. And Ed Sullivan didn't know The Beatles from salmon croquettes. Ed Sullivan didn't know whether he was alive or not. He didn't know if he was uptown or downtown.

"There's a great story: Ed Sullivan called Walter Cronkite and asked him if he ever heard of this group in England called The Beatles. Walter said, 'No.' And then Walter said, 'Wait a minute.' And he called over to his daughter, who was sixteen, 'Did you ever hear of The Beatles?' And Ed could hear the kid screaming on the phone. The kid went crazy because she was listening to them on the Cousin Brucie show, and all the tabloids and teenage papers had spreads on them. So Walter said, 'Ed, I'll put my daughter on the phone. If you put them on your show, she gets two seats.'

"She was at that show and was prominently displayed in the audience. And that's how Ed Sullivan found out who The Beatles were and booked them.

"Fifty million people watched that show that night, and I'll tell you where I was: I was outside the theater. ABC asked me to cover this thing. The streets were full like New Year's Eve on Broadway, and they piped out the sound. And the place was wild. I was outside, where it was exciting, because I was with the people that night.

"I was involved right from the beginning, playing the music and talking to them and doing interviews and having them on my shows. As a result, I was asked to introduce them at their Shea Stadium show.

"Shea Stadium was jammed. The feeling was there was going to be a disaster. I was in the dugout with them and Ed Sullivan, and John Lennon said to me, 'Cousin, this looks very serious.' I said, 'It is.' He said, 'Can anything happen?' I said, 'No, don't worry about it.'

"I don't know if you've ever been in a crowd where you could feel its power. This crowd had this power. Con Ed could have turned off their generators, and the energy from the Shea Stadium crowd that day could have turned the dynamos. You felt it in your gut, your belly. It vibrated in your chest. The sound was amazing. You could feel the electricity, and the boys were very scared.

"Sullivan and I were to introduce The Beatles. I introduced Sullivan, and he and I introduced The Beatles. We walked up to the stage like it was a scaffold. Sullivan was in front of me, and he turned and said to me, 'Cousin Brucie, this can be very dangerous, can't it?' I said, 'Yes, Ed, very dangerous.' He said, 'What do we do?' I said, 'Pray.' He turned back, and he very slowly walked onto the stage, scared stiff. I

Cousin Brucie today.
*Courtesy of Bruce Morrow*

wasn't exactly ready to dance the polka either. It was a frightening thing. I worried there would be an avalanche of people. There was such pent-up emotion, people could have been killed. Eighty percent of the audience was fifteen-, sixteen-year-old girls.

"Anyway, we introduced them, and the place went—I mean, forget it. I have never heard a sound like that in my life.

"Nobody heard their performance. You heard, 'Yeah, yeah, yeah' once in a while and some percussion, but that was about it. They couldn't hear themselves. It didn't matter if they didn't sing at all. They just had to move and play. But what they didn't understand—none of us did—was that the kids weren't there just to hear them sing. They have records. They have radio. They were there to share space. They wanted to be able to say they were with The Beatles live. That's all that counted. It was a sociological event.

"While they were singing, the police commissioner came over to me with a couple of his men and asked if I would walk with them to help calm down the kids. There was chicken wire all over the place to keep back the crowds. They did everything they could to maintain order. I walked around, skirting the infield to the sides of the seats, talking to the kids. The cops showed terrific restraint. NYPD earned their badges that day. Because nobody got hurt. Nobody died. It was a phenomenal event. I have never experienced anything so electric, so dangerous, so exciting as I did with Beatlemania that evening at Shea Stadium."

# THE WHITES DISCRIMINATE

JOHN HOPE FRANKLIN

**T**HE TEN YEARS THAT JACKIE ROBINSON STARRED FOR THE Dodgers opened a lot of eyes in a lot of different ways: to the existence of stifling racism in America, to the fact that White Supremacy was a myth created by those who designed such a system to make sure they would never have to prove themselves as worthy as blacks; to the fact that the men and women who were being discriminated against had a lot to offer this country.

Yet at the same time it was remarkable how little race relations had changed in America, even though Jackie Robinson, Roy Campanella, and Don Newcombe and other black teammates proved their worth by helping the Brooklyn Dodgers win six pennants and a world championship. As late as 1957—ten years after Robinson's arrival in Brooklyn—the Boston Red Sox had not signed a single black player, and the Jim Crow system in the South had not changed one bit, proving that hanging on to bigotry for many was more important than winning games or playing fair. Having kept their thumbs on the blacks for so long, many whites in America were deathly afraid that if they let go, the blacks might retaliate. They clung to the old system as though their very lives depended upon it.

In 1954, seven years after Robinson's first appearance in a Dodger uniform, the United States Supreme Court ruled that having separate-but-equal schools was wrong. But for years after that, little integration would take place as whites sought to establish parochial or private schools to avoid having to mix races.

History will also remember that those same Brooklynites who had embraced Jackie Robinson as a ballplayer refused to accept other blacks in their white-only neighborhoods.

In general, whites feared and disdained blacks moving in. White working-class home-owners viewed the prospect of Negro neighbors as a catastrophe equal to the loss of their homes. Restrictive covenants and a refusal to sell to blacks kept them out of the wealthiest neighborhoods.

A public opinion poll taken in Chicago in 1921 reflected whites' stereotypical racist feelings about blacks even thirty-five years later: they were minimally educatable, emotional, lacking moral standards, sexual, prone to sex crimes, larcenous, and malodorous. Whites were afraid these newcomers would not be able to adapt, that overcrowding would threaten the city's health. One worry was an epidemic of contagious disease. Another was that they would bring rampant crime.

Blacks were considered disorganized, lacking orphanages, day-care centers, old-age homes, clinics, public baths, and relief stations. To be fair, many blacks refused to take advantage of social services because of the discrimination they constantly faced. Many were reluctant to go to white hospitals, for example.

In 1956—almost ten years after Robinson joined the Dodgers—America's preeminent black historian, John Hope Franklin, left Howard University to become the head of Brooklyn College's history department. Franklin was the first black professor to be hired by a major white college anywhere in America. After living on Eastern Parkway in a mixed neighborhood, Professor Franklin determined that he wanted to live closer to the university. The problem, he would soon discover, was that Brooklyn College sat amid a lily-white neighborhood. What he would experience was enough to make any grown man cry.

The sophisticated and urbane Franklin was in Rome, Italy, in the summer of 1955, attending a historical society conference when he was met and befriended by three Brooklyn College historians. After he read his paper "The Frontier in American History," he was taken out to dinner by the three professors. He had no idea they were on a scouting mission to find a new department head and that his name was at the top of the list. The Brooklyn College history professors had formed two opposing camps, and so the president of the college decided the new head should come from outside the college.

In December of 1955 Franklin was scheduled to read another paper at a meeting of the American Historical Association in Washington, DC, and when he took the lectern, he noticed his three Brooklyn College buddies sitting in the front row. After his speech, one of them asked if he and some other Brooklyn College professors could come over to Franklin's house, where Franklin was throwing a party for friends. Franklin was a little put off at having to add seven people to his guest list, but he felt he had no choice.

John Hope Franklin and his wife, Aurelia, show off their son, Whit, who was four months old.
*Courtesy of John Hope Franklin*

A few days later Franklin received a letter from one of those professors. The letter asked if he would be interested in coming to Brooklyn College.

"I could not believe it," said Franklin, who was sure he was destined to spend the rest of his life at Howard University, the glass ceiling for black professors. "The ceiling had just been raised to the sky. I had nothing to lose, so I figured I'd just go for it."

Franklin visited Brooklyn College and met President Harry Gideonse, an outspoken anti-Communist heading a school with many left-leaning professors. The political split among the members of the history department was one reason Gideonse had felt the need to pick a department head from outside the college. Franklin also met members of the administration and reacquainted himself with the history professors he had met in Rome.

"I went back to Washington, and I could not believe that they were seriously interested in me," said Franklin. "I thought it might be a maneuver to get somebody else they really wanted. I just couldn't believe they wanted me."

He had a solid basis for skepticism. There were five black members of the Brooklyn College faculty, but none was a full professor. In fact, there were no black full professors anywhere in white America academia.

The next letter he received from Brooklyn College was a shocker: it said that the history department had voted to recommend him for full professor and *head of the department.*

"It's impossible to visualize in today's climate and appreciate the spectacular nature of the offer," says Franklin. "This was in 1956. I just couldn't believe it. I could *not* believe it. My wife, Aurelia, and I had difficulty putting our arms around it, but we said yes."

The next day Franklin received a call from the education editor of the *New York Times.* He said, "Professor Franklin, tomorrow morning you are going to be elected by the Board of Higher Education of the City of New York to be professor and chairman of the history department at Brooklyn College. It's confidential, but I have my way of knowing." He added, "It will be known around the world tomorrow, and I'd like to ask you a few questions to get my story accurate." Franklin agreed to be interviewed.

As a result, Franklin found out that the Board of Higher Education was going to meet the next morning at eleven thirty, and he was nervous and anxious.

The house at 1885 New York Avenue that John Hope Franklin and his wife bought. *Courtesy of John Hope Franklin*

His first class at Howard University met the next day at eight in the morning, and in the middle of it the door swung open and a colleague held up the *New York Times* and said, "Look. You're on the front page." The headline read NEGRO EDUCATOR CHOSEN TO HEAD DEPARTMENT IN BROOKLYN COLLEGE, and that broke up the class.

Word spread throughout the campus, and when reporters from the *Washington Post* and some local papers arrived on campus, Franklin was taken to a special room and was interviewed by one reporter after another.

Franklin moved to Brooklyn in the summer of 1956, renting an apartment on Eastern Parkway, a racially mixed neighborhood. An Egyptian merchant marine who was married to "an American Negro woman" owned the apartment building. The plan was to live there until Franklin could examine all the neighborhoods and decide where he wanted to buy a home and live permanently. The neighborhood he fixed on was right around the Brooklyn College campus. Franklin began his search for his dream house.

**JOHN HOPE FRANKLIN**   "I saw houses being advertised in the newspaper. My wife and I went to real estate brokers, and when we told them the house we wanted to see, they always had some excuse that the house was sold or they had a contract on it. So, they said, there was no point going to see it because it was already gone. This happened every day.

"After several weeks of this, I knew I was getting the runaround. I knew there was something wrong with the real estate dealers. They weren't showing me any houses. I wasn't sure how to proceed. I had hired Murray Gross, a Jewish lawyer whose office was right around the corner on Nostrand Avenue. I told him I was going to look for a house myself, not through an agent. He said, 'That might be a good idea.'

"I didn't tell anyone I was a professor at Brooklyn College. I was a human being looking for a home. I didn't announce my credentials. I didn't think that was necessary. If it took that to get me a house near Brooklyn College, I wasn't interested in getting it.

"We saw houses in the paper, advertised by the owners. Perhaps they didn't want to give a broker a commission. We saw a number of houses, but even then they would say, 'The house has been sold.' Or 'There's a contract on it. Give us your name and address, and if it falls through, we'll call you.' In other words, 'We'll call you. Don't call us.' We never got a call from any of these people.

"Most of them didn't even let us see the house. A few of them showed us.

"Then one Saturday morning—I never will forget—it was the fall of 1957 and we saw an advertisement for a house on New York Avenue that really sounded interesting.

"I called the owner, and he said, 'What are you doing?' I said, 'Nothing.' He said, 'Come on down here.' I got my wife and six-year-old son, Whit, and we got in the car. We went to the house, and you could see that the owner and another man who turned out to be his brother were sitting in the kitchen drinking—alcohol.

"The owner came to the door, and he said, 'Did you just call me?' I said, 'Yes.' I could see him go back into the kitchen and pour himself another drink. He came back and he said, 'Well, come in.' My wife, my son, and I did.

"He began by saying, 'This is the living room,' and at some point this man decided he better promote his house. He began to push it, telling me how much he had spent on the fireplace, on the windows, the floors. He was really promoting the house by the time we got to the kitchen. We went all through it, and he told me how much he had invested and that if we bought the house we could have the washing machine and the dryer.

"I told him we liked it but we would have to think about it.

"He asked, 'When can I have an answer?'

"I said, 'In a week or two. I have to go to Oklahoma, because my father isn't well.'

"He said, 'If you are really interested, I will take it off the market.'

"I said, 'I don't think you should do that.'

"We came back from Tulsa, and by this time he was calling me, wanting to know if I wanted to buy it.

"I said, 'I think we do.'

"The next thing, I went to see Murray Gross, my lawyer, and I told him we had found a house we were interested in buying, but that I would have to see about finding the money to buy it. It wasn't a lot of money. The house cost less than $10,000.

"Murray said, 'Do you have any insurance?'

"I said, 'Yes.'

"'With whom?'

"'The New York Life Insurance Company.'"

"He said, 'Your problems are over, because the New York Life Insurance Company has set aside $100,000,000 for its customers to buy homes, so you don't have to worry.' He said, 'Who's your insurance agent?' I gave him the name.

"The next morning my insurance agent called me. He said, 'I don't want you to misunderstand this, but we've done a lot for you people.' I said, 'I don't know what you're talking about.' He said, 'You want to borrow money from the company. But we can't lend you the money to buy the house you want because it's fifteen blocks away from where blacks live, and you will be jumping blocks, and therefore we can't do that. If you want to buy a house in a black neighborhood, we can let you have the money.'

"I said, 'You're passing judgment on where I can live, and I don't think you have any business doing that. So as of now, you can consider my insurance with you canceled. I'm not going to patronize a company that doesn't have enough regard for me to lend me the money when you have those millions of dollars set aside for your customers. I'm either your customer or I'm not. You can scratch my name from your list.'

"I called Murray and told him about it, and two weeks later Murray called and said, 'I've got your money.'

"I said, 'Where did you get it?'

"'South Brooklyn Savings Bank.' He didn't tell me his father was on the board and that's how he got the money. It wasn't until I left Brooklyn College that Murray pulled out a big correspondence file showing me that every bank in New York City had turned me down, and that he had gotten the money from the bank where his father was on the board!

Talking with several of his Brooklyn College students on campus in 1963. *Courtesy of John Hope Franklin*

"I bought the house, and then I moved in—tried to move in. New York Avenue was a narrow two-way street, and the moving van was so wide that if it was double-parked, no one could get past it. We wanted to get it up to the curb, and so the driver went next door to our house to ask the man if he would move his car, and the man said no. My next-door neighbor, whose name was Feminello, refused to let the moving van onto the curb. We had to wait until later in the morning, when people left for work.

"We moved in and settled in that day, but I could see the neighborhood was very hostile to our presence. The first clue was the man who wouldn't let the van park. And across the street, people were standing, like at a fire, looking at us. We could see

John Hope Franklin marches toward Montgomery, Alabama, in April 1965. *Courtesy of John Hope Franklin*

the disdain and hostility on their faces. That night we felt quite alone—isolated—in our house.

"After a while there was a thaw. My next-door neighbors, the Feminellos, warmed considerably. How can you share a driveway and not? It took a while, several months. I was in the news. I was on radio and television. People are awed by television personalities. But I continued to get anonymous calls at night from people: 'You think you're somebody. You just wait. You're nothing.' I wasn't scared. I wasn't going to give them the satisfaction of knowing I was being intimidated by them.

"But I saw evidence that the neighbors were warming up. Two old ladies who lived three doors down began to wave and smile at us through the window. Turned out they belonged to the Kings Highway Methodist Church, a white church, and they told their minister about us, and he came to call on us and invited us to his church. So that ice was broken. We went, and most people seemed to be cordial and welcomed us.

"Our biggest ordeal was my son, who was in primary school. The children were okay. It was their parents who were hostile to him. He was seven, eight, and they taunted him on the street. He would ride his bicycle, and they would shout at him and make him fall off. He'd come home from school frightened.

"My wife, Aurelia, had two degrees in library science. She had resigned her job in Washington and was to take a job in New York, but she decided she needed to leave her career to take care of him. She never worked again.

"We went to Hawaii when I was teaching a summer course at the University of Hawaii, and Whit learned what it meant to be free. He didn't have any problems there. The little boy next door was the same age as he, and they'd go out and play, and he wouldn't be harassed. So when it was time to go back to Brooklyn, Whit screamed bloody murder. He didn't want to go back. When I think about it even now, it almost makes me weep.

"The dean begged me to take a job, and I was tempted, but the reason I didn't stay in Hawaii—you know how far it is to the mainland? I had taught at Harvard, Cornell, Wisconsin, and California-Berkeley, and none of them even thought about offering me a job. But I realized I would be *way* out of the mainstream had I stayed in Hawaii. Hawaii was halfway around the world. I had sent out a reading list in January, and the books, which came by ship, hadn't arrived in June! I couldn't stay.

"So my boy screamed bloody murder about going back to Brooklyn, and it was just awful. When he was weeping, I was weeping.

"We spent another five years in Brooklyn. By this time things had cooled off. People don't retain their hostility over time. They can't remain hostile forever.

"Then in 1963 it was announced in the *New York Times* I was going to the University of Chicago. Everybody knew I was leaving, and the neighbors all wanted me to know they had a cousin or a sister-in-law or brother-in-law who wanted our house.

"I said, 'Oh no. It's already sold.' I wanted them to think I was selling it to another black person. I was lying through my teeth, though I did try, but I couldn't find anyone who wanted to buy it who had the money, and I didn't want to give it away, and so it wasn't until a few weeks before we moved to Chicago that I sold it to a white family."

## THE MOVE TO THE BURBS

IAN GRAD

By the mid-1950s moving out of the city to a house with a grassy lawn and a two-car garage had become part of the American Dream. With excellent trains running from Grand Central Station and Penn Station in Manhattan and newfound prosperity making cars more affordable, suddenly the residents of Brooklyn were eyeing fresh places to live, not only on the newly subdivided farms and potato fields of Long Island but in the suburbs of Westchester, Connecticut, and New Jersey as well. Arthur Levitt had built a huge community of single-family houses at affordable prices on Long Island. The Brooklyn apartments were aging. Children were going off to college and leaving the nest. This was not white flight. Whites were not fleeing from anything—yet. That would come later. Rather, people were beginning to migrate out of Brooklyn because they were seeking to escape the city's heat and concrete, to own their own lawns and backyards, to get their slice of the American Dream. Also, there was money to be made in the suburbs. The story of Henry Grad is typical of a Brooklynite who left for the greener pastures of the suburbs.

Henry Grad's father, Isaac, left Russia before the turn of the twentieth century, but only made it as far as England. The family name wasn't always Grad, however. As the story goes, it was either Stivian or Simeonov. When Isaac, who worked in the fur business in Moscow, went to work in the countryside either as a trapper or skinner, his rural coworkers nicknamed him "Townie." The Old Russian word for "Townie"—or "city"—is "grad" (think of Lening*rad*, Stalin*grad*). When he came to London, Grad was the name he adopted. He had four children with his first wife, who died. He remarried: a Latvian woman named Leah Salaway, and had five more children. Henry, born April 7, 1899, in Mile End Old Town—the East End slums—was the youngest of the nine. After World War I, where he spent time in the Royal Flying Corps and Royal Air Force as a wireless operator for the fifty-second Squadron in such places as Auxi-le-Château (near Amiens) and Escaudoeuvres (near Cambrai) in France, he joined the British merchant navy as a wireless operator. After sailing around the world, he came to Brooklyn to visit his sole American relative, his half-sister Millie from his father's first marriage. Millie had married Austrian immigrant Louis Katz, who had five kids from his first wife, Dora Tannenbaum, who had since passed away, and four with his second wife, Millie. Living in the house with Henry's half-sister Millie was Louis's daughter Anna, from his first marriage. Millie was her stepmother. In 1921 Henry married Anna. His half-sister now also became his mother-in-law, and his brother-in-law also became his father-in-law!

During their courtship, Anna Katz told Henry she wanted to marry a professional man. He studied for two years at the Brooklyn College of Pharmacy. The job of a pharmacist, it turned out, required him to work sixteen hours a day, seven days a week. Had he stayed in the radio business, he'd have been far better off. In 1921, that was going to become a booming industry, especially with the advent of commercial broadcasting the following year.

Henry Grad in front of his drugstore at the corner of Franklin and Union Streets, 1929. *Courtesy of Ian Grad*

Anna Grad. *Courtesy of Ian Grad*

Instead, he opened a drugstore on the corner of Franklin Avenue and Union Street in Crown Heights. When the Depression hit, it went under. Unable to pay his bills or find work, he went back to Hendon, England, to live in his brother Jimmy's house and work in his brother-in-law's fur-dying business—a dirty, smelly job. Six months later his wife and six-year-old son Ian went to live with him. After seven months in England, Anna demanded they return to Brooklyn. Son Ian remembers.

Young Ian Grad checks out his tricycle in front of his father's store, 1929. *Courtesy of Ian Grad*

**IAN GRAD** "My mother said, 'We gotta go back to the States. I can't stand it here.' Because compared to the United States, living in England was like going back in time. They didn't have central heating. They had fireplaces, and in the wintertime the house would be freezing. You'd have to warm up the sheets with hot coals before you got into bed. And she didn't like living in someone else's house, being second fiddle instead of being the lady of the house.

"So we came back to Brooklyn in October 1932 and rented a furnished room on Rochester Avenue, a few blocks from Eastern Parkway. My dad got a job with the New York City welfare department as a home investigator.

"My father wasn't political. He hated the extremes on both sides. In the early 1930s you took whatever job you could get. He had to go around and visit the homes of the people on welfare to make sure they were doing what they were supposed to be doing to get free money from the city. He was paid $20 a week, and that's a little hard to support a family, even at those days' prices. My mother also got a job, as a bookkeeper, to make ends meet.

"After we moved to Crown Heights, around 1934 or 1935, my father began moonlighting as a pharmacist in addition to his city job, and as time went on, we became a little more affluent, because my mother began working as a trainer of insurance salesmen for a big insurance company. She also played the piano and violin and had a good singing voice, and she had taught music when I was little. Her mother, who died when she was young, had been a performer on the Yiddish stage in New York.

"We lived in an overall Jewish neighborhood. As a matter of fact, in the 1930s practically all of Brooklyn, it seemed, was Jewish. There were houses set up as synagogues and storefronts set up as synagogues, and regular buildings which were actually synagogues. As a kid, I didn't pay much attention to religion. However, my parents, who were not very religious, decided that I should get a Jewish education, so they sent me to a yeshiva near my home, and I used to go there in the evenings, and there was a modern American woman teaching this stuff. The next year the class for my grade was going to be too late in the evening and my parents didn't want me out at that hour, so they sent me a couple blocks down to a small synagogue run by a rabbi with a black hat and a long beard, and I took one look at him, and I said, 'This is not where I come from.' I didn't relate to this old-fashioned stuff. That turned me off to the whole religious business.

"As I got older and started studying science, astronomy, and engineering, I said, 'This whole business about a belief in God is a lot of hokum. There ain't no such animal.' I can remember years later riding on an airplane, and who sits next to me but a young Catholic priest, and he tried to start a conversation with me about religion, and I turned to him and said, 'You know, you guys got it all wrong. God did not create man in his own image. It was the other way around. Man created God in his own image.' And that was the end of the conversation. He left me alone after that.

"The Dodgers were an important part of our lives. I couldn't afford to go to too many games. We didn't have much money, but as a teenager I only lived three blocks from Ebbets Field on Montgomery Street between Nostrand and Rogers Avenues. You walked straight down the block and got right to Ebbets Field. When I went to the games, I would pay $1.65 and sit in the grandstand and watch a doubleheader from behind the catcher in back of the screen. When I first started going, the Dodgers couldn't hit the side of a barn and couldn't field. We had Jack Winsett, a tall, skinny guy. When he struck out, he would wind himself up like he was going to screw himself into the ground. And I can remember another guy, Joe Stripp, and in 1939 Leo

Durocher came in as our manager. It was just nice to be at the ballgame. We had crazy characters there, the Dodger Sym-Phony, Hilda Chester with her cowbell.

"Before we went to England we lived on Union Street off Franklin Avenue. There was a trolley car that ran up our block, and in the summer I would stand on the corner at my father's drugstore watching the people coming home from the ballgame. As they rode by in the open-air trolley cars, they would throw out their ticket stubs, and we would walk around and pick them up, and I had a whole collection of them. They were nice to look at. As I got older we collected baseball cards. We pitched them, flipped them, playing heads and tails. I was pretty good at that. Years later, my wife, Janice, who was into flea markets and collectibles, would say, 'Why didn't you save those things? They'd have been worth a fortune today!' Who knew what was going to happen fifty years later?

The captain of the Boys High tennis team plays on one of Brooklyn's many courts in the late 1930s. *Courtesy of Ian Grad*

"I went to Boys High. I was half a block from the trolley car that ran up Nostrand Avenue and took me there for a nickel. In ten minutes I'd be at school. In nice weather, I'd walk home.

"I started high school in 1939. Boys High was in Bedford-Stuyvesant, a black neighborhood, so they had some black kids. We had a mix of kids from other Brooklyn neighborhoods, and for the most part everyone got along. I do recall one time Donnie Workman, a fierce fighter from our neighborhood who went to school with me, got in a fight with a black kid who was much bigger than him, and Donnie beat the crap out of him, so this guy pulled a knife and slashed Donnie's coat. But I never had any problem with anybody in the school. I was an academic and an athlete.

"Boys High was a very high-level academic school. Norman Mailer graduated from there the year before I started. I never knew about him until he wrote *The*

*Naked and the Dead,* and I read it. The great jazz drummer Max Roach was in the class ahead of me. It was the high school equivalent of what City College was in those days, a school with a very high academic standing. And I got a better education than if I had gone to a coed school like Erasmus, because I didn't have any distractions with girls.

"I was the captain of the tennis team there. There were a lot of tennis courts in Brooklyn back then. I used to belong to the Mammoth Tennis Club, which ran from New York Avenue to Albany Avenue and from Winthrop Street to Clarkson Avenue, opposite Kings County Hospital. Before the war, they had fifty courts and it only cost $15 a year to play there. After the war, they only had twenty-four courts. By the time I moved to Long Island, it was down to twelve courts, and it cost $100 a year to play. Eventually the land was used to build the Downstate Medical Center.

"My senior year I won the Rensselaer Medal for excellence in math and science. I was thinking of applying to Rensselaer Polytechnic Institute, so I asked my advisor, 'Do you think I could get a merit scholarship there?' He said, 'Don't waste your time. They will never give it to you because you're Jewish.' He told me straight out.

"My father wanted me to become a dentist. I said to him, 'I'm not standing, looking into open mouths all day and inhaling bad breath. No, that's not for me.' And I wasn't going to be a pharmacist, because I saw the hell his life was. I knew I wouldn't become a lawyer, from looking at other kids in my class who had the gift of gab. They could stand up and talk, and nothing bothered them. And I wasn't interested in medicine. I wasn't going to be a doctor, even though in all the middle-class Jewish families, a doctor was *the* big thing. Mothers always wanted their daughters to marry a doctor.

"I graduated from Boys High in January 1943. The war was still on. I was seventeen, and when I turned eighteen I would be subject to the draft. I had to make a decision. Should I go to college? Should I do something that would get me a better position in the service? I didn't want to get sucked in as a draftee and become a regular foot soldier.

"We had a family friend, Al Rogers, who, when I was sixteen, gave me a summer job in his machine shop, making fifteen bucks a week. He was doing subcontracting work for the war effort, and I was learning how to use the equipment rather than doing much work. I decided to go to engineering school at Rensselaer even if I couldn't get a scholarship. And I wasn't awarded that scholarship. The first year my parents had to pay my room and board, which was $1,200 a year.

ROTC cadet Ian Grad and his mother.
*Courtesy of Ian Grad*

"In the meantime, I interviewed for the navy V-1 training program. The officer who interviewed me asked why I was interested in joining the program, but I didn't give him the red-white-and-blue, patriotic, fight-for-your-country answer he was looking for.

"A smart man only makes a mistake once. After I entered RPI, I interviewed for its naval ROTC program. Two hundred students applied. Only twenty-five were accepted. This time I gave them a good story. I talked about how my father had been in the British merchant marine and how I wanted to carry on the family tradition, and me being technically oriented, this was the best way for me to serve my country.

"So they accepted me and another Jewish kid, Benjamin Ward. Neither of us had Jewish-sounding names. The other twenty-three were Christians."

*In July 1943, the ROTC at RPI was activated to full-time duty. The cadets wore uniforms, and the government paid them $25 a month. In July 1944, Grad and his fellow cadets were assigned to a Canadian corvette, and in convoy they went to the Guantanamo, Cuba, naval base. In danger of being sunk by U-boats lurking along the East Coast, they fired ash-can depth charges off the back of the ship.*

*On the way back they were caught up in a fierce hurricane near Cape Hatteras. During the hurricane, Grad had duty in the crow's nest, watching for the enemy. As the ship bobbed around like a cork in the middle of nowhere, Grad, dressed in his slicker, couldn't see a foot in front of him.*

"This was the first leg of my nonwar experience," he said.

*In July 1945, he was assigned to a minesweeper guarding New York Harbor. He was nineteen, and the highlight of the tour was a night of liberty in Times Square, going to a dime-a-dance parlor. The war ended before he graduated.*

*In the summer of 1946, Grad was transferred to an Italian ocean liner that had been captured in the port of Cristóbal on the Atlantic side of the Panama Canal. The ship, the SS* Conte Biancamano, *was stripped down and refitted into a troop ship, the USS* Hermitage, *that could transport seven thousand men. Grad sailed to Guam to fetch a load of troops waiting to come home. After the return, he was transferred to a ship that was scheduled to sail to the Bikini Atoll to observe the testing of the hydrogen bomb. Several days before he was due to sail, Grad got orders to go back to New York, where he was discharged.*

"As Rocky Graziano, one of my neighbors, used to say, 'Somebody up there likes me,'" says Grad.

*Still only twenty, Grad returned to Brooklyn to live with his parents in Flatbush. In 1941, before he left for college, they had moved into a brand-new apartment on Hawthorne Street between Rogers and Bedford Avenues. As his mother, Anna, said, it was easier to move than get the apartment painted. Soon after returning, Grad sought to turn his engineering degree into a paying job.*

*New York City during the summers could be unbearable with the combination of fetid heat off the sidewalks and high humidity. Without air-conditioning, Brooklynites would sleep on the rooftops and fire escapes, and even on park benches. Brooklyn's Jews fled their apartments to the Catskills and Poconos. With the end of the war, relief from the heat was on the way across America in the form of air-conditioning. The innovation would transform America. Ian Grad would be part of the transformation.*

**IAN GRAD** "I wanted to go into the air-conditioning business. Before the war, the only buildings that were air-conditioned were movie theaters and the textile mills of

South Carolina. That's where Willis Carrier got his start: in the textile mills, to climate-control the yarn so it didn't stretch."

*In 1946, Grad landed a job in a contracting firm that required him to go to the Carrier Engineering School in Syracuse for six weeks. While training there, his class was actually taught one day by Willis Carrier, the founder of the Carrier company and the man credited with inventing air-conditioning.*

**IAN GRAD**    "I finished the course, came back to Brooklyn, and I worked in the office designing air-conditioning systems for banks, retail stores, drugstores, and shoe stores. I did the Brooks Brothers store on Madison Avenue and 44th Street—my duct work still runs down the middle of the store today. I even did the nightclub of the Pierre Hotel, crawling around in the ceilings to see where we could run ducts. One time I saw Peter Lawford standing out front waiting for a cab."

*For his next job he designed air-conditioning systems for many of the Broadway theaters along 45th and 46th Streets. While he was installing the system for the Bijou movie theater, he saw* The Red Shoes *six times.*

*Ian Grad had accumulated enough money with his parents to buy a house in what was then considered "the country." His father had been working in a pharmacy on Avenue P in Brooklyn, and then after the war he bought a pharmacy on Woodhaven Boulevard in Rego Park, Queens, with his business partner Nat Kupor. In 1954 they bought a second one in Lindenhurst on Long Island.*

**IAN GRAD**    "We bought a house in Seaford, Long Island, in 1954. When I was working for Thermodyne Air Conditioning in the late '40s, I had said to the chief engineer, 'Where do you live?'

"He said, 'Massapequa, out on Long Island.'

"I said, 'Where the hell is that? I never heard of it.' I went to look on a map, and I thought, *This guy has got to be nuts. He travels all the way from there to get into the city?*

"Eight years later I was living in the next town."

*Moving to the suburbs wasn't all it was cracked up to be.*

**IAN GRAD**  "The first day was kind of horrendous. We get there, and the contractor who built the house had never cleaned his construction stuff from the garage. So the house was not really in move-in condition. And the first night we were living there, there was a huge rainstorm—a hurricane. I got up the next morning, and went down to the ground level—it was a split-level house—and the whole thing had two or three inches of water all over the floor. The wind had driven the rain through the foundation wall, which wasn't properly waterproofed. I grabbed every towel we had to try to soak up all the water. And the first thing that went through my mind was, 'What kind of a mess did we get ourselves into?'

"Our house was not the only one this had happened to. It was a totally new development, with all new houses. Eventually the contractor came around and sprayed waterproofing on the outside of the house. It never happened again, but that was some introduction to the suburbs, after having lived in an apartment building on an upper floor my entire life. This was quite an experience. Fortunately, since we had just moved in, there wasn't any furniture in the room.

"Before we moved, when I was working in Long Island City in the Paragon Oil Building, I would drive up past the Brooklyn Navy Yard, and park on the street. It took me about thirty, forty-five minutes door-to-door. When I moved to the suburbs, I first had to drive to the Long Island Rail Road station, which was about two miles away. I would pick up one of my coworkers, who lived in another development in Seaford, on the way to the station. We would take the railroad to Hunters Point, which was right across the street from the building where we were working. It was an hour and twenty minutes door-to-door, and we had to change trains at Jamaica.

"So here we were, in a house, and we had to do all this stuff we never had to do before—like landscaping. Every two minutes I was running to the hardware store to buy all kinds of tools, which I still have today. There were salesmen coming around to sell us things—plantings, shades, blinds, trees, etc. A lot of it seemed like a big scam. We really had to learn all about which nurseries to go to, which catalogs to order seeds from. We had to plant in the front, in the back, shrubbery around the house, add a fence to separate our property from our neighbors'. Money was flying out of the house—we were constantly spending on all of this.

"We bought the house because my father and Nat had bought a store in Lindenhurst and he would run that one, and Nat would run the store in Rego Park. Unfortunately, the Lindenhurst store was not successful, and after a couple of years they wound up selling it.

"My mother wasn't working at the time, so she stayed home and became the gardener. She seemed to enjoy it. In the back we planted tomatoes and strawberries, and indoor plants like begonias. We all kind of got into this horticultural mode when we got out there.

"We'd make the rounds of the local nurseries. We'd pick out something and take it home. We had all these books about how to plant properly. I remember planting a blue spruce tree—maybe it was about three feet tall. It had a big root ball with earth packed in it, and it was heavy as anything. I really hurt my back handling that tree. I went back around thirty years after I had lived there, to see the house, and that little tree had grown taller than the roof!

"I also did a lot of work around the house, fixing things up. The ground floor rec room was always cold, because the floor was just a concrete slab. I put in an insulated wood floor, laying down sleepers, and of course that concrete slab wasn't level. What a job to get that right. And then I laid a plywood floor with vinyl asbestos tile on top of it! Let me tell you, it was no fun working on your hands and knees like that. We really could have used a Home Depot back then—we had to run around to a million different stores.

"In 1957, I got a job up in Hartford, Connecticut, but when the company opened a Manhattan office, I moved back to Long Island. Now I was commuting into Penn Station. It was still about an hour and twenty minutes, though. That year I met my wife, who was living in Kew Gardens Hills in Queens. We got married in November 1958, and moved to Forest Hills. Now I only had a half-hour subway ride to Manhattan. The next year, my parents sold the house and moved to Rego Park.

"All in all, living in the suburbs was interesting in the beginning, because I was a handy guy, and I got to do all these things that I had never done before. But after a while, it all got to be a drag, and the commute was awful. On my way home, the train was a local, and it stopped at every town on the South Shore. By the time I got home, I was beat. Also, as a single guy, I kind of felt like a fish out of water. Everyone out there was married and had kids already."

*After Grad left behind family members in Brooklyn, black families moved into their neighborhood, and his uncles and cousins witnessed the very beginnings of the "white flight" that began in earnest in the late 1950s.*

**IAN GRAD** "When I was going to high school, the black population lived on the north side of Fulton Street. And as all the white middle class moved out to the suburbs, the blacks were becoming more affluent, and now they had someplace to move to. Brooklyn today has a large black population."

*After Ian Grad married Janice Schapiro (who grew up in East New York and Brighton Beach), and moved to Forest Hills, they raised their family. Their son Doug is the editor of this book. Henry Grad eventually retired to Margate, Florida. In 1979 he returned to college to take an organic chemistry course to get his Florida state pharmacy license so that he could do a little part-time work now and then, becoming, at eighty, the oldest college student in the state. He passed, of course. Henry lived there until 1987, when he died at age eighty-eight.*

*Ian Grad still lives in Forest Hills. Over the course of a nearly sixty-year career as an engineer, he was the project designer and manager for mechanical engineering work at the Jacob Javits*

Ian Grad and Janice Schapiro, the summer before they married. *Courtesy of Ian Grad*

Ian Grad today, re-creating his years as a straphanger at the Transit Museum.

*Courtesy of Doug Grad*

*Convention Center in Manhattan, the National Gallery of Art East Building in Washington, DC, and the Boston Museum of Fine Arts—all designed by architect I. M. Pei, as well as the United Airlines Terminal at O'Hare Airport in Chicago. He also designed the original air-conditioning system for the Museum of Modern Art in the 1950s, was the mechanical engineering consultant at Trump Tower for ten years, and was involved in the construction phase of the Ellis Island Immigration Museum.*

*Doug Grad got married in 1995, and a year later, he and his wife, Kim, announced that they were going to move from their one-bedroom rental apartment in Forest Hills and buy a co-op apartment in Brooklyn. When he heard that, Ian couldn't believe it. "You're moving where?" he said. "To Brooklyn? Why? We left there!" The last time he'd been to Brooklyn was in 1980, when he saw sad and depressing sights—graffiti, garbage on the streets, drug dealers—a far cry from what he'd remembered. But a lot had changed in the ensuing sixteen years, and Doug, whose Brooklyn roots run deep, returned to the ancestral home in 1996. Doug and Kim and their two kids—the fourth generation of Grads to live in Brooklyn—live in Park Slope.*

# THE DODGERS FLEE WEST

BILL REDDY, IRVING RUDD, STAN KANTER, AND PETE HAMILL

JACKIE ROBINSON WAS THE FINAL BROOKLYN DODGER BATTER in the last game of the 1956 World Series. He struck out. He was thirty-seven years old, had battered knees, and after the 1957 season, in which he fought with manager Walter Alston, he decided he was going to retire. He sold his exclusive story to *LOOK* magazine for $50,000. But he neglected to tell general manager Buzzie Bavasi of his plans, and a few days before the article was to appear, Bavasi traded him to the New York Giants for Dick Littlefield and $30,000. Robinson was in a bind. The Giants were offering him $60,000 to play, more than the Dodgers had ever paid him. The pressure was to keep playing, but what about the article saying he was quitting?

Bavasi told reporters that, in his opinion, Robinson's retirement article had been a ploy to wrest more money from the Giants. To be accused of greed by Bavasi—and, by implication, his boss Walter O'Malley, himself an avaricious man—was too much for Robinson to bear. He went through with his retirement. Robinson, the player who broke the color barrier, had been signed by Branch Rickey, a man O'Malley resented for doing so. O'Malley had even tried taking credit for it. But Rickey was gone, and Robinson's retirement drew little comment from O'Malley, even though Robinson had led the Dodgers to six National League pennants and one World Series. Instead of cheers, he was leaving amid controversy. Play for the Giants? Robinson just couldn't bring himself to do it. How could Bavasi and O'Malley even *ask* him to do such a thing?

What nobody knew was that Walter O'Malley was looking to the future. In 1953 the Boston Braves moved to Milwaukee. O'Malley couldn't help notice that County Stadium sat 43,000 fans—10,000 more than Ebbets Field—and featured 10,000 parking spaces for automobiles. Ebbets Field had fewer than a thousand.

Said O'Malley, "How long can we continue to compete on an even basis with a team that can

Walter O'Malley, left, discusses subscription TV in the 1950s, years ahead of its time. *Library of Congress*

outdraw us two to one and outpark us almost fifteen to one, which pays its park a token figure, and pays no city or real estate tax? If they take in twice as many dollars, they'll eventually be able to buy better talent. Then they'll be the winners, not us." The Braves had won the 1957 and 1958 National League pennants, and the 1958 World Series.

O'Malley had been talking about building a new ballpark even before he took over as Dodgers president in 1950. The Yankees packed 75,000 fans into their games. The Giants drew 56,000 at the Polo Grounds. Ebbets Field sat only 33,000. He wanted a new 55,000-seat stadium in order to compete. Every year between 1950 and 1957 attendance topped 1 million, second-best in the league. But O'Malley kept insisting the Dodgers weren't making money.

And there was something else O'Malley noticed. The white fans who had moved to the suburbs were not going to Dodgers games anymore. Said sports reporter Harold Rosenthal, "The people who were buying season tickets, the furniture companies in Jamaica, Queens, and the manufacturers on Long Island couldn't give their tickets away to customers because it was too difficult to get there."

Black fans were going to the games, but they were not united with the white fans. The black fans tended to root for the black players, even those not on the Dodgers.

**BILL REDDY** "After we did the big job in '55, the talk of the Dodgers moving was rampant all over the borough. Nobody wanted to believe it, but deep in your heart you knew it was true. The white families were moving out of Brooklyn, and they were the backbone of Ebbets Field. We didn't have enough blacks to replace them. We had a lot of Jamaicans and West Indians coming in who didn't appreciate baseball as we did. They were cricket players. And until the Hispanics could find jobs and get enough money to go out to Ebbets Field, they didn't have hard-core baseball fans. They would hang out at the Parade Grounds, where they could see free baseball. Attendance did fall.

"But I think O'Malley planned it that way. He didn't push for attendance like MacPhail and Rickey, where Red Barber would be talking on the radio, 'Hey, we're close to a million.' And everybody in Brooklyn was running out to go again to make sure they made it.

"O'Malley wasn't pushing for the big attendance. He didn't want it. He wanted to justify his move to California. And I think he had that in the works long, long before the first inkling was let out to the public."

THE HINTS HE WAS LEAVING BEGAN DURING THE 1955 SEASON. HE COMPLAINED THAT the area around Ebbets Field was a "bad neighborhood" and that after a night game you better get the hell out of there fast. During mid-season O'Malley announced that seven Dodger games would be played in Jersey City the following season. He wanted a new stadium, and soon.

In 1956, O'Malley stepped up the pressure on the city to build a new ballpark for the team. He wanted it built over the tracks of the Long Island Rail Road at the Atlantic Yards near downtown Brooklyn. Robert Moses, who had the last word on such a move, said no. Moses said the new stadium should be built in Flushing, Queens. O'Malley didn't want it there. He wanted it in Brooklyn. It was an impasse that would not be broken.

During the 1956 World Series one of O'Malley's guests was Kenneth Hahn, a member of the Los Angles Board of Supervisors. O'Malley had contacted him. He told Hahn he was looking to move.

After the Series, the newspapers revealed that the city of Los Angeles was prepared to offer O'Malley a sweetheart deal if he moved his team to the West Coast. How could O'Malley do this to his loyal fans? Irving Rudd was the director of public relations for the Dodgers. He had watched O'Malley closely and knew exactly how he could do this.

**IRVING RUDD**   "Sentiment meant nothing. Everything was business. It was a winter's night, and I was alone with him in his office, and I don't know why, but he let his hair down with me. I was confiding in him that I was having trouble with a man who had once done me a big favor. But lately he had become a real pain, and though I didn't want to seem ungrateful, I really didn't want to have anything to do with him anymore."

*O'Malley told Rudd he was having the same problem with an old friend, George McLaughlin, without whom he would not have been an owner of the Dodgers, but that he no longer consulted with the man.*

**IRVING RUDD**   "'So in the future, Irving,' O'Malley said, 'you'll find that it's great to have loyal friendships from the past, but sometimes you have to cut the cord to seek new horizons, and you can't be tied down by the past.'

"And he did feel badly about it, and yet, fuck it, on to Los Angeles, if you know what I mean."

*In the summer of 1957 O'Malley announced the Dodgers were leaving at the end of the season. The final game at Ebbets Field was played on September 24, 1957. Fewer than seven thousand fans came out to watch the Dodgers beat the Pittsburgh Pirates, 3-0. Gil Hodges was the last Dodger batter, and he struck out. After the game Gladys Gooding, the organist, played "May the Good Lord Bless and Keep You," but before she could finish, a recording of the Dodgers theme song blared on the loudspeaker.*

*Oh, follow the Dodgers*
*Follow the Dodgers around*
*The infield, the outfield*
*The catcher and that fellow on the mound.*

*Oh, the fans will come a-running*
*When the Dodgers go a-gunning*
*For the pennants that they're fighting for today.*

*The Dodgers keep swinging*
*And the fans will keep singing*
*Follow the Dodgers, hooray!*

*There's a baseball club in Brooklyn*
*The team they call "Dem Bums"*
*But keep your eyes right on them*
*And watch for hits and runs.*

*When the final line faded out, Gooding began to play "Auld Lang Syne." Amid tears, fans were looting the park and destroying the field. In Brooklyn they were called "Dem Bums," but the editor of one of the Los Angeles papers vowed that "Dem Bums" would never appear in his newspaper. These would be a more serious Dodgers.*

*When the Dodgers left, the borough lost the one passion people had in common. It also lost its national presence. Brooklyn would fade into becoming just another bedroom community.*

**STAN KANTER**    "The end of the golden era for Brooklyn came in 1957, when the Dodgers announced they were leaving Brooklyn. The Dodgers had played games in Jersey City, and attendance was dwindling, but it still came as an enormous shock. There's a quote in *Bums,* where Pete Hamill says the three greatest villains in history are Hitler, Stalin, and Walter O'Malley. I still feel that way. To me, O'Malley is up there with Hitler. This was a greedy guy who destroyed a borough, and the borough has never been the same since. It used to be such a good feeling where you could walk through the streets and listen to the Dodger games coming out of the windows. You could meet the toughest thug, who might be ready to beat you up, and you'd say, 'Did you see the Dodger game today?' Suddenly, you're pals. No longer. It just wasn't the same place.

"After they moved, I watched the Los Angeles Dodger scores, because I wanted to know how Hodges and Snider and Pee Wee were doing, but my heart wasn't in it. You just couldn't care about them, and to this day I root against anything from Los Angeles. You just can't shake these habits. I don't have a team."

*The departure of the Dodgers may have been Brooklyn's most tragic loss, but it wasn't the only one. Pete Hamill, who grew up in Park Slope in the 1940s, experienced not only the loss of his beloved Dodgers, but the demise of the* Brooklyn Eagle *and the closing of the Brooklyn Navy Yard and many of the factories that had hired his dad and his dad's generation. The widespread injection of heroin into New York City's subculture didn't help either.*

**PETE HAMILL**   "There were four events starting in the mid-1950s that really shook Brooklyn to its core. The first was the closing of the *Brooklyn Eagle* in 1955. I wasn't around for that, because I was in the navy. But for most of my life, getting the *Eagle,* which would arrive in the afternoon, was part of the rhythm of the day.

"The *Eagle* was a broadsheet. In its early history it was conservative, but not right-wing. It wasn't anti-immigrant. I don't know whether it supported Roosevelt or not, because we read it for the sports. They covered the farm teams of the Dodgers. So we heard about Robinson in the *Eagle* in 1946 because he was playing in Montreal. That year he came down and played against Jersey City.

"We read about guys who never made it. There was a player named Maynard DeWitt, who stole sixty bases one year in the minors. We said, 'Oh man, wait till this guy comes.' Of course, he couldn't bunt for a base hit.

"The *Eagle* had a very good sports writer by the name of Tommy Holmes and an older guy named Harold C. Burr. We would read the sports, and I would read the comics, and the *Eagle* would cover the neighborhoods of Brooklyn. Reporters would cover Bensonhurst, Midwood, all these places, so you got a sense that there was a Brooklyn beyond where you lived. It gave you a sense of being part of a place that was more than just the Dodgers and was certainly different from the William Bendix stereotypical Brooklynite. I thought we sounded like Red Barber. That was the voice of Brooklyn. We weren't dees, dems, and dose guys. There were people like that, but they weren't the only people. My parents didn't talk like that. They didn't even have strong Irish accents, because they were from cities. The thick Irish accent came from the countryside.

"A newspaper is like a plaza in South America, a zocalo where at one table they talk about soccer, and at another table about politics, and the next one women, and sometimes all at once. So no matter where you lived in Brooklyn, there was something in the paper about you. Not you specifically, but your part of Brooklyn.

"There were funny things in it. People would read the obituaries as an apartment guide. 'So-and-so died at 21 East 3rd Street.' This was after the war, when there was a shortage of housing, and immediately you'd think, *If some guy would only die, we could move someplace.* There were grifters who were still around from the Depression, and they would read the obits and show up at the wake. 'Ah, geez, Lenny was a wonderful fucking guy.' He'd eat the free food and drink and leave. He had never met the guy in his life.

"When the *Eagle* folded, the presses were bought up and shipped off to Ecuador. The function of the *Eagle* was never picked up by other papers. The *Post* picked up the *Bronx Home News,* but they never covered Brooklyn. And that was too bad.

"The second great loss to the borough was the Dodgers. It was not that the Dodgers were a baseball team, but that they were an *excellent* baseball team. They were a team built on all sorts of urban values. They were not perfect. They never had a great pitching staff, but they made it up in other ways, with the engine of Robinson. There were Furillo fans and Gil Hodges fans, because Gil was nice to everyone as he passed through the neighborhood to go to Ebbets Field. And they loved Duke Snider. They also loved Willie Mays, though they never quite connected with Mantle. It was Snider, Mays, and Mantle. It was like Christianity, Judaism, and Islam fighting over the same city, Jerusalem. And on a much higher level, because it's more important to argue over who's the best center fielder than whether God exists. We spent our time standing on street corners, not sitting and watching television, so there would be theological debates. A guy comes to me and tells me, 'Kill your son to prove you love me.' I'd say, 'Fuck you. Who are you?' Abraham and Isaac didn't work in Brooklyn. Nor did 'turn the other cheek.' But there was a kind of rough intelligence I remember. People might not have been as well-educated as they could have or should have been, but they were smart.

"Heroin began to hit the white neighborhoods while I was in the navy in 1955. When I came back, heroin was there, and people started dying. Seventeenth Street, between Eighth and Ninth Avenues, had always been a kind of alcoholic street. Public drunks would roister around, but in the '60s it became a pretty big junkie street.

"It became dangerous. If a guy staggered drunk out of Ratigans on Seventh Avenue, the cop was not going to lock him up. He'd take him home and stick him at the door, and he might make it to the second floor and fall asleep. But junkies, they didn't care. They would come to your house and rob your mother. It was a terrible thing when that began to happen. And it was the beginning of the end for the Mob, like in *Goodfellas*. Once the children of these Italian drug dealers began using, then they had no bench. They had a bunch of *gavones* standing in front of places they couldn't keep up. They were third-generation immigrants and second-generation hoodlums, and they were like the Hearsts: the farther you got away from the old man in generations, the more incompetent they were.

"And the fourth blow was the closing of the Brooklyn Navy Yard around 1966. Robert McNamara was the guy who closed it down, but before that it was closing in stages. I had a cousin David who worked there, and to protect his pension he ended up having to go to Philadelphia for a couple years, because the navy moved a lot of the functions to the Philadelphia Navy Yard.

"When I was working there, there were seventy thousand jobs. Through the Korean War they were working three shifts. It was a madhouse then just trying to get on the subway to get home. All those bars along Sands Street and down that way were all booming, because a shift would end at four, another ended at midnight, and during lunch break the guys would run over and have a couple of whiskeys and head back. That many jobs was like having three Ford plants in your town, and when it closed, that was the end of the blue-collar era, because other factories were closing as well.

"The world of factories is basically gone. I don't know whether it's better now or not. I'm not against gentrification, because it's better than junkies.

"Part of why the factories closed was they fled first to the South, where there were no unions and it was cheaper to run. We had unions in New York, and that's why people got a reasonably decent pay and pensions in addition to social security. But they went to the South first, and some of them just went out of business, because whatever they were making died. And then came outsourcing. Forty years ago companies started moving to Mexico and other countries. They tried setting up deals in Puerto Rico, where they paid no taxes for ten years, but then as soon as they had to pay taxes, they left there too.

"These were the key events: the closing of the *Eagle,* the Dodgers moving, heroin, and the closing of the Navy Yard and the factories, which led to a decline of the city."

CORE members walking down Fort Hamilton Parkway en route to the March on Washington.

*Library of Congress*

PART FOUR

# The 1960s and 1970s

# GROWING UP BLACK IN THE HOOD

ROBERT CROSSON

SOUTHERN BLACKS FACED DISCRIMINATION IN ALL PARTS OF their lives. The economic deprivation was most pronounced. Kept from most jobs, a few were teachers, though schools for blacks were few. Some ran funeral parlors, and some were ministers. The great majority of Southern blacks were farmers, most of whom fed their families but had little money left over. During the 1910s those farmers faced the incursion of the boll weevil, which entered the United States from Mexico in 1892 and devastated the cotton crops of Louisiana, Mississippi, and Alabama. Because both black and white cotton farmers secured loans on future crops, loans became scarce, and times became hard.

Then the Mississippi River flooded in 1912 and 1913, followed by drought the next year and torrential downpours the year after that. The dissatisfaction of the Southern blacks grew, but most felt they could not relocate until alternative jobs became available.

Other blacks felt so persecuted they migrated north anyway. Some Southern counties were driving blacks out in the same manner that Czar Alexander II drove the Jews out of Russia's central cities. In 1917, 2,500 blacks were forced out of two Georgia counties, and whites, led by the Ku Klux Klan, drove all blacks from Carroll County, Mississippi.

For most blacks, the discrimination they faced was enough of a reason to leave.

Before World War I, the Southern blacks who couldn't stand their treatment any longer headed for New York, Philadelphia, and Chicago, but the jobs they found were among the most menial and low-paying. Booker T. Washington's advice was to "stick to the farm."

Things changed when World War I began. Suddenly Northern factories needed labor. The war had stopped the steady flow of European immigrants. With millions of white males overseas, the factories began hiring white women and black Southerners, who no longer saw any future living in the South.

Approximately half a million blacks fled the South during World War I, and a million more followed in the 1920s. New York City's black population ballooned from 91,709 in 1910 to 152,467 in 1920. After they arrived, few went back.

Southern whites, who had done everything in their power to make sure the blacks were "docile," were shocked at the Great Migration. They refused to believe that their racism was the

Library of Congress

reason the blacks were leaving. They blamed labor agents hired by the Northern factories for luring them with free train tickets. Even after the whites succeeded in running the labor agents out of the South, whites continued to blame them, saying the agents were luring them by mail.

Fearing the loss of their cheap labor, in some cities whites then tried to forcibly prevent the blacks from leaving. In Macon, Georgia, police evicted several hundred migrating blacks after they entered the railroad station. Outside Americus, Georgia, police entered a train and arrested fifty blacks heading north. At Summit, Mississippi, police closed the railroad station. Hattiesburg, Mississippi, police kept blacks from the ticket windows and arrested any black who tried to board the train without a ticket. The police of Greensville, Mississippi, would go into trains and drag out blacks trying to leave—to little or no effect. All this did was reinforce in the minds of the blacks that the South was no place to live. In Jackson, Mississippi, so many blacks had left that two main streets were virtually deserted. In Greenville, Mississippi, two hundred homes had been abandoned by migrants. In Perry County, Mississippi, the black school had to close because the teacher had left for Chicago. Black businessmen often were left with few customers. Barbers, pastors, and insurance salesmen headed north, following their customers.

Whites were stuck. There was discussion in various Southern newspapers that one way to keep blacks in the South was to raise their standard of living, but employers argued that if they raised wages, blacks would use the extra money to buy a train ticket out of town.

Beginning in the 1940s Southern blacks left home in a stream and headed for Northern urban areas, mostly in the West and the Northeast. One reason was that Southern cotton farmers were buying tractors and other mechanical farming implements, reducing economic possibilities for black workers.

When poor blacks moved into Brooklyn, most settled in the ghettos in either Brownsville or Bedford-Stuyvesant. Segregation, it turned out, would be no less prevalent in Brooklyn than it had been in the South.

Brownsville, which was ringed by the neighborhoods of Bedford-Stuyvesant, Bushwick, East New York, Canarsie, East Flatbush, and Crown Heights, once was home to thousands of poor Jews. It was the site of Margaret Sanger's first birth-control clinic in 1916, and the home of Murder, Inc. in the 1930s. A real estate developer, Charles S. Brown, had tried to market the area as a middle-class suburb, but failed, and in 1887 a group of real estate speculators built tenements. They were hoping residents from the Lower East Side of Manhattan would move there. Two years later the Fulton Street Line of the Kings County Elevated Railway reached Brownsville, and by 1899 reformer Jacob Riis, author of *How the Other Half Lives,* declared Brownsville to be "a nasty little slum."

After World War II, the Jews who once lived there began to move out, and at first they were replaced by the black middle class. The poor followed, and once the tenements had too many poor people in them, and the landlord no longer was able to keep up the building, there would be overcrowding, and the black middle class would leave. What remained were poor black families, many headed by single mothers. Crime grew rampant; gangs and drugs flourished.

If you were a young black living in Brownsville, you lived in danger every day of your life. You faced danger from predatory criminals, from white thugs intent on keeping you away from their neighborhoods, from black thugs, and from the police. If you were a black youth growing up in the 1960s in Brownsville, you were lucky to reach adulthood.

Robert Crosson, whose parents had left the Carolinas to come to Brooklyn, was born in Kings County Hospital in 1953 and grew up in Brownsville during an era when blacks faced trouble at home from crushing poverty, drugs, and gang violence and had to withstand abuse from whites any time they left the black ghetto. Crosson's father, a sergeant in the army and an expert in hand-to-hand combat, taught the boy martial arts at a young age. It was this skill that enabled him to survive the mean streets of his youth. Today Crosson is one of the top martial artists in the world. In a life filled with racism and ugly incidents, he is remarkably free of bitterness. He is also lucky to be alive.

**ROBERT CROSSON** "My father became a sergeant in the army, which was a hard thing for a black man to accomplish. He was in Okinawa, and he learned hand-to-hand fighting in the service. He didn't talk much about the racism he encountered. He tried to shelter me from it. One time I was with him in upstate New York, and I had to go to the bathroom, and we went inside a restaurant. They told us we had to go around to the back. But I saw the bathroom inside the restaurant, and I said, 'Why can't we use that one, Dad?'

"He said, 'No, we have to use the one in the back. That's the special one for us.'

"My mom died when I was thirteen. I know a lot about her as a mom, but not much about her background. I don't even know how Mom and Dad met. When I was a boy, Brownsville was a rough place. I witnessed a guy getting stabbed. I saw someone get his throat slashed right in front of me. I actually saw a guy get thrown off a roof. I saw the driver of a car intentionally hit a guy walking on the street. I saw police

Robert Crosson's father in his army days. *Courtesy of Robert Crosson*

brutality. We had gangs around. Back when *West Side Story* was popular, there were the Roman Lords. Later there were the Jolly Stompers. There was a white gang, the Clarkson Avenue Boys, out of East New York into Flatbush, a white area. If you crossed that border line, you were in trouble. For a young black male, if you went into a white area, whether it was Canarsie or Flatbush or Brighton Beach, that was a no-no.

"When I was eight years old, my sister lived in Cypress Hills, Queens. Cypress Hills, which was a pretty decent area compared to Brownsville, is on the border line between East New York and Queens. I was visiting my sister, and I went to the store to get a paper and a slice of pizza. I walked outside, and I was approached by two white youths who were about fifteen. One of them smacked the pizza out of my hand. I looked at him, thinking, *What is this about?*

"One of them said, 'What are you doing on white boys' turf?' I thought, *White boys' turf?* I had never experienced any racism up to this point.

"I said, 'What do you mean?' The kid punched me. Then they pushed me down, took the little money I had, and started kicking me. Since I knew martial arts even then, I was just blocking. I was more amazed than anything else. I thought, *What the heck is this about? Why are they hitting me? I don't even know these guys.*

"A white gentleman jumped out of his car and hollered at them, and they ran. I ran home and got my brother, who was about eleven, and he came back with his bat looking for them. We didn't see the guys. But I said to myself, 'I'm going to train, and I'm never going to let anyone take advantage of me like that again.' That's when I really started to step up my martial arts training."

*When Crosson was in the fifth and sixth grades, he was bused from Brownsville to PS 225 in Brighton Beach. At age ten he couldn't quite figure out why for the life of him he had to get up early in the morning and take a bus to what seemed like the ends of the earth to go to school with white kids who hated him.*

**ROBERT CROSSON**     "I never understood that. I had to take a bus to school in Brighton Beach. That was another adventure. I got called 'nigger' there by the white students. I thought, *What is this nigger thing?* It was crazy. I haven't thought about this in a long time. Some of this stuff you have to put behind you.

"One time a teacher—a white teacher—asked me and two white students to come up to the blackboard and work up a math problem. We came up, and I did the problem, and she said, 'That's wrong.' The other kids got the same answer, and she said to them, 'That's correct.' I said, 'How could mine be wrong and theirs right when we got the same answer?'

"She said, 'You didn't do it the way I said to do it.'

"'But I got the answer.'

"'Don't talk back.'

"I got in trouble for that. I got put in detention.

"Racism was high in Brighton Beach, a totally white area made up of Italians and Jews. I made sure I caught the bus. I didn't want to be out there any longer than I had to be. I wouldn't hang out, wouldn't walk around the neighborhood.

"After PS 225, I went to Somers Junior High School, and then I went to James Madison High. The '60s was a time when racism was at its peak. Madison was in Midwood, an Italian neighborhood. I would be waiting for the bus, and a gang of whites would pull up in a car with chains and knives, and I would outrun them or outmaneuver them to get away. I used to get tired of running, but there were eight guys with knives and chains, and who was going to protect me? It was every man for himself. I couldn't go to a white cop and ask him to protect me against the white guys chasing me. The thing was, if someone was around, they'd [the white toughs] be cool, but if they saw me or two or three of us walking by, they had the advantage because they had cars and we didn't. Also, they lived around there. They'd be sitting on their stoops, and we'd walk by, and we'd hear, 'Hey, we got some niggers in the neighborhood here.'

"The odd thing, it never caused me to hate white folk. I never took on the racism thing. I would think, *Those are a bunch of crazy people*. For a while I was paranoid. Any time I would see a group of white guys, automatically I would assume they were coming after me. I had my guard up. If you got mugged by black youths, the next time you saw them, you'd think, *I'd better be careful.*

"I couldn't go to Coney Island to buy a hot dog at Nathan's. Forget it. I couldn't afford a hot dog, never mind go there. It was just crazy. One time I went to visit a friend, a white friend, who lived in a Coney Island housing project that was predominantly white. He was white, but his half-brother was black. They were pretty cool.

"I went to see him, and everything was cool, and as we were coming out of the building, a gang of white guys were standing there, and there was no way to get around them. Before you knew it, they started with the racist slurs, 'niggers,' and somebody threw something, but my friend was with me, and it didn't turn into anything. If he hadn't been there, it could have turned out a lot worse.

"In May of 1968, when I was fifteen, Martin Luther King was assassinated. There was rioting in the streets of Brownsville. They were turning over cars, burning and looting. It was like a nightmare. Police were on horseback looking like giant monsters because they had on all this riot gear, gas masks.

"I ran out of my building in an attempt to cross the street to visit a friend, and as I did that, someone snatched me by the collar. I looked back, and it was a cop standing there wearing all this gear. He had a big stick, and he started to swing it at me, and he was going to hit me in the head. That cop was getting ready to bust my head open—when I ducked. Otherwise I think he would have killed me. I really do.

"I made a little move, tried to pull away the best I could do, and he lost his balance and fell backward, and I took off.

"I saw him get up to chase after me, and I ran into a backyard and climbed up on a garage roof. Muddy water and leaves were trapped on the roof, and I lay down in that water, and I felt like I was in Vietnam. The helicopters were flying overhead with their spotlights shining. I could swear they were looking for me. You heard sirens. You heard the sound of horses, and people screaming.

"I'm telling you, it was crazy. I was afraid to come down off that roof, but I thought, *If I stay up here, the helicopters are going to search me out, and that'll be it.*

"I jumped off the roof, went around the yard, ran back across the street to my house, and went upstairs. I was trembling, because I was thinking, *Any moment they are going to knock on my door.* Which someone did. Thank God it was my upstairs neighbor.

"It's a wonder I survived it all. I think it was pretty much by the grace of God. He had his hand on me. He had a purpose for me at an early age.

"Unfortunately one of my brothers got involved with the drugs and became an addict. My cousin, the same thing.

"My brother was a bright and very innovative guy. He used to act. He sang, danced, and he also was a great artist. He could make anybody laugh. He could have been another Eddie Murphy.

"I tried to do everything my brother did. He went to Somers Junior High School, and so did I. He was on the track team. I joined the track team. He got involved in the talent show. I did too. He got involved in swimming. I became a lifeguard.

"But the negative peer pressure got to him. Some of his friends were experimenting, smoking cigarettes, and then smoking got to be boring, so they drank a little beer, drank a little wine. Then the wine wasn't doing the trick, and they tried a little reefer. Just experimenting. My brother and my cousin were bright, but they succumbed to the peer pressure.

"I don't know all of what they did. Maybe pills, but heroin was the thing back then. Heroin spread through Harlem and through Brownsville and Bed-Stuy, and they fell prey to that.

"I used to hang out with them, but something inside me said, 'That's a path you don't want to go down.' I had a strong resistance. I never really liked smoking and drinking. It was like God said to me, 'You can't follow that path. You gotta stick to this martial arts thing.'

"My whole childhood, I never really had anyone to talk to. After my mother died when I was thirteen, I went through posttraumatic syndrome. I had a lot of stress. It made it really hard for me to function at school.

"And when my mother died, that took a lot out of my father. Then three of his sisters died, and his brother died. So many people died, and I never realized the impact it had on him. He had had a few heart attacks. He had been a longshoreman on the piers in Brooklyn, but he had a heart attack at a young age and had to go on disability.

"I dropped out of school when I was sixteen so I could help make ends meet. I worked as a security guard in a factory. I worked at a White Castle. It was really tough times for my father, and I did what I could to help him.

"We're only becoming aware now why there is so much illness in the black community. We didn't know the effect of high blood pressure. Diabetes. We didn't know the effect of eating pork and salty foods and saturated fatty foods. We didn't have the medical care we have today. Still today, if you're poor, you're going to die younger. You won't get the proper care. Back then, they had no idea about prostate cancer. Today they have a cure, but today it still plagues the black community.

"Before my mother died, I didn't know we were poor, even though we were on welfare and our clothes were raggedy. But when my mother passed, that's when I realized we were poor, 'cause after that we had to live in some really bad places.

"We moved to Bristol Street in Brownsville between Blake and Dumont, a slum apartment that was dangerous and rat-infested. People got mugged quite a bit. One time I was coming up the stairs just as my father was leaving the apartment. Two guys grabbed him, trying to yoke him. They didn't see me because their backs were turned. As one grabbed him, the other was reaching into his pockets.

"Before I got up there, my father kicked the guy in the face with a front kick. The guy hit his head. I almost felt sorry for him. My father did something to the other guy and popped his finger out of its socket. He was screaming like no tomorrow. We didn't even call the cops. They took off.

"In the morning I would leave the apartment carrying at least four rocks, because it was a good morning if there was less than four rats in the hallway as you were leaving. That was my target practice. A lot of the surrounding buildings were torn down or abandoned, and that brought rats and roaches. We had no light outside our building at night. If you didn't know where the missing steps were, you could fall through the stairs.

"Living there was an adventure, but it was home. You either learned how to fight, or you stayed in the house, and I never was one to stay in the house.

"Mike Tyson was raised right around the corner. I knew Mike when he was small. I knew Riddick Bowe, the boxer, when he was a little guy. John Salley, the basketball player, lived there and went to Canarsie High School. I never saw any white people living there.

"It became about surviving, fighting against drugs, against the poverty, against the crime. One day a drug dealer approached me to carry a package. I said, 'Nah, I don't want to have nothing to do with that.' He then tried to get me to protect him. He pulled out a big bankroll. I had maybe 70¢ in my pocket, and I was hungry as hell. He said, 'If you watch my back, I'll take care of you.' He knew of my reputation through my martial arts. The gangs knew me. I wouldn't do it, even though I was starving. I couldn't.

"All I can say is, and I say it over and over, it was God's will, because He gave me the strength to do it. I really don't know how. I was depressed, but I somehow had a belief that things would get better. I saw how my brother and cousins and some of my friends fell victim to the drugs, the crime, the streets. A lot of my friends were arrested. Some were killed. It was just crazy. One guy—his name was Joe—was doing a drug transaction, and he messed with the money of one of the drug dealers, and they took him out. Another friend, Gary, used to steal cars. He tried to rob a milk truck, but they caught him.

"When I was sixteen, I was walking down the street, and I heard pop, pop, pop, pop, pop, and I ducked, and I turned around, and three or four feet behind me a guy fell to the ground, shot. The shooter tucked the gun in his shirt and started running.

"Another time I saw a guy walk up to another guy with a knife and slice his throat. But for all that I saw and experienced, I came out pretty good.

"One of the good times I remember in Brownsville, I was walking near this little park on Pitkin Avenue, and I noticed a white man speaking, and a bunch of people gathered round. I wondered, *Who is he?* I pushed through the crowd, went up to him, and he grabbed me. He was talking, and I saw TV cameras, and I was thinking, *Okay, I'm going to be on TV.*

"He said to me, 'What's your name, young man?'

"I said, 'My name is Robert.'

"He said, 'That's nice. You're going to be someone one day. I can feel your energy. You're going to be somebody who's going to make a great contribution to society.'

"Then he said, 'Robert, that's a nice name. That's my name.'

Robert F. Kennedy visits a playground in Bedford-Stuyvesant in 1966.

*Library of Congress*

"I went home and told my mother about what had happened, and then I saw him on TV. It was Robert Kennedy.

"I remember the suit he had on, the tie, even looked at his shoes. I had such a nice feeling about him, and that changed my thoughts too. *You know, not all white people are bad.*"

*Maybe not, but for a black teenager growing up in a racist society, trouble can lurk just around any corner. The presumption, whether on the street or in school, is if there's an altercation with a white kid, it's the black kid's fault. Especially if trouble arrives in the form of the white captain of the football team.*

**ROBERT CROSSON**   "I attended Madison High School, and the football team dominated the whole school. I was walking in the hall, and the captain of the team intentionally hit me on the knee with his helmet.

"I was new. I said, 'Listen, man. You know you hit me with your helmet on purpose.'

"He turned around. He said, 'You got a fucking problem?'

"I said, 'At least you could say, "Excuse me." Say something.' I was trying to be nice.

"He dropped his helmet, and he ran at me to tackle me. Well, that was a mistake. I had a black belt by then, was pretty accomplished. When he ran at me, I sidestepped him, and he fell and scraped his face. I weighed 160. He weighed 210. He was more embarrassed than hurt. Some girls were there, watching.

"He picked up his helmet and tried to hit me with it. I didn't understand that. I said, 'I don't want any trouble. I'm sorry. I didn't mean to trip you.'

"The other football players were laughing at him, and that just ticked him off. He came at me again, swinging. I ran, but he thought I was running away from him. I stepped onto a banister, and when he tried to grab me, I kicked him right in the face, busted him open. When he fell, I jumped on him and started whaling on him.

"His guys moved toward me. At that point I thought, *They are going to try to kill*

Robert Crosson worked for many years as a school security guard—shown here with Gregory Hines.
*Courtesy of Robert Crosson*

Crosson has done some security work for celebrities on the side, shown here with Jay-Z.
*Courtesy of Robert Crosson*

*me.* I had him in a choke, was hitting him, when the principal came out. It looked like I was beating up the guy, so I got expelled. They kicked me out of school.

"I went to Alexander Hamilton, which was more of a black and Hispanic school. But my mind wasn't into school. I was trying to function, but my depression made it hard. Even though the racism was crazy then, I didn't think much about it. Later on, I realized what racism was, that it existed, thought about some of the things that happened, but I always thought about Dr. King and how he preached nonviolence and school integration. At the time I didn't have an understanding of what was going on, but later on I did. I say to myself, 'Whew. I made it through that?'

"The martial arts is the reason I've been able to stay out of trouble and continue my journey. Today I hold twenty martial arts titles. I have won over three thousand awards and trophies. I've won world titles in Venezuela, Columbia, Panama, Trinidad, and Canada. The only thing: there is no money. Just trophies and belts.

"When I was seventeen, my jujitsu instructor for years, Dr. Moses Powell, took me with him to the Caribbean to do demonstrations with him, and that changed my life. We traveled to Antigua, Trinidad, Grenada, Barbados, St. Lucia, Dominique, St. Vincent, and some other small islands.

"I met Dr. Powell when I was eleven. I trained with him and his top assistant, Little John Davis, a legend in the martial arts, one of the top fighters in the world. Chuck Norris became famous, but Little John could beat him. I knew Chuck Norris back in the day, when he was competing in New York. He was going to form a traveling fighting team, and I was going to become part of it, but it never came off.

"Today I teach about 110 students at my school. I also teach another 200 youngsters at a school in my church, St. Paul's Community Baptist Church.

"For thirty years I have worked for the Board of Education with the Division of School Safety. I was at Somers Junior High School for nine years, and then I became a district security guard, and I worked at different schools in District 18.

"At one of the schools where I worked, South Shore [High School], I witnessed a race riot. I was walking through the lunchroom, and a black kid and a white kid were arguing, and then two or three, and then a bunch of white kids versus a bunch of black kids, and they started throwing food, and people were getting beat up. The riot squad had to come in.

Crosson is a multiple-time world-champion jujitsu practitioner, and the high-flying owner of a dojo in Canarsie.
*Courtesy of Robert Crosson*

"These days things have gotten better. Students seem to be getting along much better now. There are still problems, but we are learning to get along."

## COP ON THE BEAT

JOHN MACKIE

**B**EDFORD-STUYVESANT IS THE SECOND-LARGEST BLACK COMmunity in America after Chicago's South Side. In 1838, eleven years after the end of slavery in New York State, John Weeks bought a plot of land in central Brooklyn. Weeksville quickly became a safe haven for Southern blacks fleeing slavery and racial hatred. The seven-block area of Weeksville had more black property owners than many large cities, and by the 1860s it had its own schools, churches, and an orphanage. PS 83 in Weeksville became the first public school in America to integrate its teaching staff. Urbanization after 1930 blended Weeksville into surrounding communities until its origins have been all but erased.

Though Bed-Stuy was all black as far back as 1833, it didn't have a black elected official until 1948 when Bertram Baker was elected councilman.

By the time the A train reached Bed-Stuy in 1936, there were 65,000 blacks living there. In 1939 the Bedford-Stuyvesant Slum Clearance Project was announced. Real estate developers were outraged at the name. What resulted was the Kingsborough housing project, the first of many housing projects in the area.

After World War II, Southern blacks and Caribbean Hispanics flooded into Bed-Stuy. In the 1950s the black population almost doubled.

Blacks and Hispanics spread to Williamsburg, Brownsville, East New York, Bushwick, East Flatbush, and Crown Heights. All these areas now were considered part of Bed-Stuy by banks and insurance companies.

The Bed-Stuy Restoration, funded with millions of federal funds and promoted by Robert Kennedy, fixed up 3,700 homes within a ten-block area. It also underwrote home mortgages and built a community center and job-training center.

While the exquisite Victorian and Queen Anne–style brownstones routinely sell for over a million dollars now, in the 1960s Bedford-Stuyvesant was one rough neighborhood. Things got particularly hot when in the evening of April 4, 1968, Martin Luther King Jr. was murdered. John Mackie, the kid who wanted to

Martin Luther King Jr. and Mayor Wagner. *Library of Congress*

play third base like Billy Cox, had been accepted into the police academy shortly before. He was partway through the training program when King was gunned down outside his motel room in Memphis. Brooklyn became a powder keg, and Mackie was assigned the job of patrolling dangerous Bedford-Stuyvesant on a regular basis. It was a scary time for cops. This was under the administration of Mayor John Lindsay, who, the police felt, was too lenient when it came to blacks. It was also a time when the Black Panthers and the anti–Vietnam War advocates were stirring up trouble. For a white cop patrolling Bed-Stuy, danger lurked around every corner.

**JOHN MACKIE**  "As a boy I had had dreams of being a ballplayer. But when you're twenty-one years old and you're married and have a child, now you have to put bread on the table and pay the rent. The fantasies had to go away. My first job was working in a handkerchief factory in Lindenhurst. It was owned by a guy named Barasch, the brother of Jack Barry, the game-show host. I worked there for a dollar an hour, and after a week or so I couldn't stand it, so I quit, and I decided to join the navy. When my father got wind of it, he took me to work with him at a Lincoln-Mercury agency in Queens, where he was service manager. I wasn't making enough money, and when the owner refused to put me in the union, I read there was going to be a test for the police department, and I sent for it. First I had to go back and get my GED in order to qualify for the job, and I did that, and I took the test and got a very high mark, and I was in the first group to be called off that list.

"I reported to the police academy with four hundred other guys on February 9, 1968. We lined up, and they handed each of us a New York City police department shield, swore us in, and there I was.

"Less than two months later, Dr. King was shot. We were in the academy, looking forward to nine months of training. We were wearing our stupid gray rookie uniforms, learning the applicable laws and how to fire a gun. The class was so large it was taught in two sections. The first was eight in the morning to four in the afternoon. I was in the section that went from four in the afternoon to midnight, and I was sitting in the classroom on April 4 when somebody came in and announced that Martin Luther King had been assassinated. We all were sitting around looking at each other, wondering, *What does that mean to us?* They said, 'We're going to put you guys out on the street. There are some problems in Brooklyn.' Rioting had started.

"We piled into a couple of Transit Authority buses parked outside the academy, and off we went. We went to the 77th Precinct in the Bedford-Stuyvesant area of Brooklyn. While I was in the stationhouse, I could hear the sirens outside. Fires were starting. You looked outside, and you could see the smoke rising. Looting was beginning. Shots were being fired. Chaos was under way. Trash was flying, junk coming from the roofs, fires started, sheer madness, unlike the Brooklyn I had known as a kid. I had grown up in sleepy little Sheepshead Bay, and here I was in one of the major ghettos of New York, Bedford-Stuyvesant, during a full-blown riot.

"A few days before, our instructor, Lieutenant Fiore, said, 'You are going to be in a radio car, and you'll get an assignment: "Man on the corner and shots fired.

Respond.'" He said, 'Cops and firemen are different from everyone else. When the building is on fire, everyone else is running out. Cops and firemen are running in. When a guy in a building is shooting people with a gun, everyone is running out, and it's the cops' jobs to run in. Know that this will eventually happen to you.'

"It was no time that they took us from reserve status and put us in radio cars. I was teamed up with a veteran who had worked a long, long time. We were responding to assignments, and all the while fire trucks from Queens and other parts of the city were racing around trying to deal with the fire problem. The dispatchers couldn't give the jobs out fast enough. It was madness. I was green behind the ears in this squad car, and the job came over the radio to go to a location on Atlantic Avenue: 'Man with a gun. Shots fired. Units respond.' We turned our lights and the siren on, and off we went, full-bent, to the location. When we got there, the man was gone, but there were crowds in the street, and it was madness.

"I don't know what the police can do in a situation like that. Probably nothing. You are trying to keep the situation under wraps, doing whatever you can do, but basically it was out of control.

"We worked twelve hours on, twelve hours off for a number of weeks. The rioting did not subside, but

Rookie police officer John Mackie in September 1968, after a long, hot summer of unrest following the assassinations of MLK and RFK.
*Courtesy of John Mackie*

then after a week it tapered off, but for the entire summer of 1968 the city was a powder keg. The black ghetto areas were set to ignite for whatever reason or no reason. That was the beginning of all kinds of bad times for New York City.

"At the same time there was the antiwar activity going on. I was assigned to Columbia University, where there were demonstrations and civil disobedience and rioting. I was with the Tactical Patrol Force, which was going to go in and clear the campus of student protesters.

"The guy running the show was Sanford Garelick, the chief of detectives. We were lined up in ranks outside Amsterdam Avenue, waiting, while students were sitting on the walls yelling obscenities at us, telling us what our mothers were home doing. It was really nasty, and they just didn't stop. Around four in the morning after a lot of the press had gone home, hundreds of students began marching toward us. Garelick warned them to stay back, not to advance any further as we stood at attention looking like the British Army.

"Here came the students, yelling and screaming and throwing junk and garbage and bottles at us, and when the gap tightened, Garelick raised his bullhorn and said, 'Okay men,' and he walked away. That's when all holy hell broke loose. It became a riot of cops and students. And it was crazy. Kids got their heads bashed in. They had people dressed in white suits carrying stretchers. They were ready. They expected this to happen. It was a sad night. It was stupidity to the tenth power in all corners.

"John Lindsay was the mayor. The cops generally didn't like Lindsay. They thought of him as a sissy. John Vliet Lindsay, a guy who came from money. They thought of him as a guy who lived a charmed life and now was going to tell all the working people how to live. Cops felt he gave away the store to all the people who were screaming: the blacks, the Hispanics, and the gays, all the minorities who thought they were disenfranchised or perhaps even were. They had Lindsay's ear.

"It seemed like he did everything he could do to deemphasize the police department. In fact, he was the one who made us change from the blue-black uniform shirts. He thought we looked too much like the Gestapo. He personally saw to it we wore light blue shirts. So Lindsay was a wimp as far as the cops were concerned. He was not in the police's favor.

"We were kept out on duty that entire summer. I worked foot patrol in the Tactical Police Force. One night my post was the Black Panther Party headquarters, right on Nostrand Avenue, and it was surreal. I was the only white face within sight. As you walked along the sidewalk, every other store was a record store, and they all had their outdoor speakers playing the latest Gladys Knight tunes, or the Temptations, but they weren't in unison. At a thousand decibels, all this music provided a crazy background sound for the hectic activity that was happening on the street before you. It was like a busy ant farm. It was just crazy.

"The Black Panthers were the boys at the top of the heap. They were aligned with SDS—Students for a Democratic Society—and SNCC, another civil rights group, and all the muckamucks of these organizations would come and go through the night, and the Panthers would have armed bodyguards wearing black berets. I was fresh out of the police academy, and here I was, standing there like a target, while throughout the city cops were being ambushed, shot, fired on from rooftops. I could get popped any minute. Here I was from six at night until two in the morning, and here I was going to stay.

"You better believe I was scared. I wasn't shaking in my boots, but I was well aware of what could happen. The funny thing was that in spending my summer around that, I became hardened to the job. I became far more at ease on the street. I ceased having fear. Very rapidly I matured on the job as a street cop. I then never wanted to be anything but a street cop. That summer made a better cop out of me.

"Just like Billy Cox. His cousin Gummy told me Billy played town ball as a kid on slag heaps from coal mines. The infield surface was like a big chunk of peanut brittle with lumps and clumps and junk all over the field. The ball would make three or four moves before it got to him, and Cox learned to play third on that kind of field, so when he got to the billiard cloth of a major league field it was so much easier.

"I was a street cop for seventeen years, when I was injured badly in a car crash. We were working what we call a buy-and-bust. It was low-level chicken-shit pot stuff on the street, but this is what they wanted, and this was what we had to give them.

"We got descriptions, and now we're going to the location, driving a dark sedan, an unmarked car, but we weren't racing. We were driving along Pitkin Avenue, when a woman coming from a side street missed a stop sign, went through, and crashed into my side. I was the passenger, and I wound up in the hospital with back and neck injuries.

"I was never restored to full duty, and so I was surveyed out of the department. I got my pension, was treated nice, but I was out of the job I loved with all my heart. I was meant for that job. And I was a rising star.

"I retired to the Asheville, North Carolina, area, where, with my brother, I built my own house out of logs. I went to work for a local sheriff, but when I started getting a lot of the credit for how well the sheriff's department was being run, he started getting nervous, and I finally quit.

"I decided I would move to Vero Beach [Florida], where I could be with my Dodgers during spring training. Unfortunately I couldn't get a decent job, and I fell into a terrible depression. I had lost my identity. I decided to go home and write with a view to becoming published, and I wrote for ten years before I got a whiff."

*Mackie's first book, police thriller* Manhattan South, *was published by New American Library in 2003, followed by* Manhattan North, East Side, *and* West Side. *He has written 65,000 words of a new novel. Billy Cox would have been proud.*

# THE BLACK PANTHER

CHARLES BARRON

THE BLACKS WHO REMAINED IN THE SOUTH WERE SUBJECTED to racism and police brutality every day. It was part of their lives. In 1964 a young man from Lowndes County in Alabama decided he had had enough, and he organized the Lowndes County Freedom Organization. The emblem that that man, Stokely Carmichael, chose to represent his organization was the black panther, described as a vicious animal that never bothers anyone, but when cornered, takes no prisoners.

Bobby Seale and Huey Newton took Carmichael's symbol and formed the Black Panther Party. Begun in Oakland, California, initially the group was set up to give its members some solidarity in the fight against police brutality and racism. Its goal was freedom, full employment, decent housing, quality education for their children, the end to police brutality, putting black people in juries, and getting reparations for their days as slaves.

The group arranged medical clinics and provided free food to poor black schoolchildren. Before long the Black Panthers were feeding ten thousand children before they went off to school.

The Black Panther Party began taking its cues from Malcolm X, a spokesman and symbolic leader of the Nation of Islam in New York. The white press portrayed Malcolm as a hate-monger who was evil in his hatred. But to black youths, Malcolm was a more important figure than even Martin Luther King Jr., because Malcolm, who generated pride and self-reliance, focused on the problems of the ghetto and on black self-denial. To whites, Malcolm was the antithesis of Dr. King. To blacks, Malcolm X belonged beside Dr. King as a hero.

The Black Panthers preached black solidarity. Whites were not allowed to join the organization. The Black Panthers argued that blacks had to arm themselves if they wanted to be safe from the police. That black men would stand up and fight for their rights scared the bejesus out of local police in cities where the Panthers organized. They put a scare into J. Edgar Hoover and the FBI.

When Richard Nixon was elected president in 1968, he had run on a platform that included two themes: a hatred for Supreme Court Justice Earl Warren and a charge that Democrats were "soft on Communism." Upon his election, he began a campaign to harass political radicals, a campaign that was ongoing until the very day he was finally forced to resign in disgrace in 1974. During this period Nixon ordered the IRS to hound his enemies, and as a result the IRS collected dossiers on ten thousand individuals and organizations including the Black Panthers, SNCC, and Students for a Democratic Society. Nixon also compiled a list of personal enemies including Senators Ted Kennedy and Ed Muskie, New York mayor John Lindsay, singer Barbra Streisand, actor Paul Newman, Pete Hamill of the *New York Post,* and the always-dangerous Gregory Peck, Tony Randall, Joe Namath, and Carol Channing!

Under Nixon, J. Edgar Hoover was given a free rein to do his dirty work. With the death of Martin Luther King Jr., Hoover called the Panthers "the greatest threat to the internal security of the country." In November of 1968 he ordered the FBI to use counterintelligence methods to wreck the Panthers, including the use of infiltrators to stir up trouble and spy on the group.

In the middle of the night of May 25, 1971, the FBI invaded the Chicago home of the Black Panther Party. Fred Hampton and Mark Clark were killed. Those left alive were arrested and charged with attempted murder of the police. But evidence showed that the police had fired one hundred bullets at the Panthers, while the Panthers had fired just once. Later it was also revealed that Hampton's bodyguard, William O'Neal, had been an FBI agent-provocateur, who had delivered the floor plan to the FBI days before the raid.

Over six years, twenty-four Panthers were killed in shoot-outs with the police.

In 1971 a dispute arose between Eldridge Cleaver and Huey Newton over the direction the group should take. Newton wanted to renounce violence. Cleaver, who fled into exile, didn't.

To show how popular the Panthers were in the black communities, in 1973 Bobby Seale ran for mayor of Oakland and finished second with 40 percent of the vote.

Charles Barron, now a New York City councilman representing the East New York section of Brooklyn, had been an angry black teenager who felt he didn't fit into white society. He lived in the projects, and what he learned was how hard it was to escape from poverty and institutional racism. At school he resented that most of the teachers were white, and though he was a bright kid, he lost interest and dropped out of high school to become involved in "the movement." A member of the Black Panthers, Barron suffered with the deaths of his fellow Panthers killed by the FBI and police in shoot-outs. He watched as J. Edgar Hoover and the FBI infiltrated his organization, bringing chaos and paranoia. When the East Coast Panthers, led by Eldridge Cleaver, got into a dispute with the West Coast Panthers, led by Huey Newton, over what direction the organization would take—violence versus education—Barron left the Panthers to get his GED and to go to college. And what an education he got! As a youngster he felt the slings and arrows coming from white society, but it wasn't until he became educated that he fully understood that for African-Americans, learning history, language, and religion from a Eurocentric perspective could be destructive and self-defeating.

**CHARLES BARRON** "I grew up on the Lower East Side in the Lillian Wald Projects on Avenue D and 6th Street. You had to really compete with each other whether it was sports or how you dress. When people are growing up oppressed, you often have to put a front on your poverty by buying expensive clothing. I used to buy tailor-made pants, waistcoats, and leather fronts when I had my little jobs in the summer.

"One issue you had to deal with living in the projects was dealing with the police, particularly the housing police. It was always a tense relationship, though not nearly as bad as it is today. Then an officer at least would take you up to your parents and let them know what you're doing. You don't get anything like that now, especially with the black police officers. Though we also had some who were mean and abusive.

"But you also had to worry about the drugs and the gangs, and you had to worry about people coming in to exploit you for your labor. There were all kinds of schemes, multilevel marketing schemes, and you didn't know what was real and what wasn't. Knowing we were trying to get out of poverty, they were wanting you to invest, making you promises.

"There were a lot of people who just gave up hope, got on drugs, went to drinking alcohol, and had difficulty. People don't understand the conditions of oppression and how much hopelessness it brings.

"A lot of the elected officials were white. You didn't see any hope. Unless you were a boxer or an athlete, you didn't see any way out. A few might go to school and get through that way, but the masses of our people were—and are—suffering.

"I was lucky to have a job. I was very personable, likeable. Even when people didn't like my politics, they still liked me. I worked as a sorter for the post office, and that was big money back then. The people who worked for the Youth Poverty programs were making $38.63 a week. My post office job was very boring, but I was making a couple hundred dollars a week.

"There was discrimination in the U.S. Post Office just as there is in every institution in America. Most of the blacks had the lower jobs, the mail-sorting jobs. It was like the Rocky Mountains: the higher up you went in the post office, the whiter it got. Matter of fact, most of the time I worked there, I was an eighty-nine-day employee. If you worked ninety days, they had to pay you benefits. So they signed you up for eighty-nine days, fired you, and then you would have to re-up.

"I said, 'I want to be like the rest of them so I can get some health benefits.'

"They said, 'We don't have openings for that.'

"But in our neighborhood, unemployment was very high, so whatever job you got was good, and a post office job was very good.

"When I was fifteen, sixteen years old, I started to read books on my own seriously. I read *The Last Days of the Congo,* by Patrice Lumumba. That really turned me around. I was taken by his courage and sincerity and his tenacity to stand up to such powerful opposition—the Belgians. I was reading this book, staring at the pictures of his face, seeing this serious look of determination. I was, *Wow*. And I connected it to the discrimination I saw happening in New York, and the courage of Malcolm X to stand up, and I was seeing what my father was going through.

"My father had been in the merchant marine, and he was working for a place called Canadian Furs in mid-Manhattan. He did some stock work, some interior decorating, but he never made much money, $80 a week, chump change. I remember when I was seventeen, with tears in his eyes he told me, 'Son, don't you ever kiss the white man's ass.' To me it meant he had to sweep floors, had to buckle down for them. It meant he couldn't be the man he really wanted to be. And it led to my father drinking more than he should have—to his not always bringing all the money home, and this led to my father and mother separating.

"You might say they separated because of his drinking, but I would say it was because of oppression. Society would say drinking. I would say because of racism and oppression.

"Do we focus on the symptoms of oppression and say those are the root causes of a broken family or do we focus on the root causes of a broken family? Both are issues. There is truth to both. I don't think you should let society off the hook. I could say, 'I don't care how poor you are or how much racism there is, get over it, get around it, and work hard. You gotta work harder and stop using racism as an excuse.' Nope. I don't agree. The masses of our people are not making it even though 90 percent of our people want jobs and work hard. Why? Because structural racism, institutional racism, sexist, gender discrimination, and exploitation monopolism—capitalism—has created a class problem in the American society that creates poverty.

"From reading Patrice Lumumba and Malcolm X and being influenced by the Nation of Islam and the Black Panthers—and getting back to my dad—I saw how the system was tearing him down. And this was a strong man. There were times I didn't even know he and my mother were having arguments. There was a time I didn't know we were impoverished and oppressed. We as a family had a wholesome life. For the most part, my mother took care of my four brothers and sisters and myself.

"I went to Brandeis High School and transferred to Seward Park High School, but I never finished. I got caught up in the street life in the neighborhood, playing hooky, getting high, smoking reefer, hanging out with girls, not interested in school. As I gained consciousness, I saw there were too many white teachers, too much white curriculum, all our heroes were white, all the pictures on the walls of the school were white. Not enough was said about me and who I was and my struggles in life. So I lacked interest. I didn't see myself in school. I said, 'This is not for me. This is designed for someone else.'

"Each year I tried to get it together. The teachers all said, 'You're very bright, very intelligent.' But it just couldn't draw my interest. That's why I can understand what our black youth is going through, because I've been there. I can talk to them now and try to make them understand something I didn't understand until a little later, and that is, no matter what's going on there, this is a credential-oriented society, and you can get the truth somewhere else, but give them what they need for you to pass. You can speak the truth and still be disciplined to do your homework, pass the classes.

"What I did was say to myself, 'I'm not dealing with this. I'm going to seek the truth and join the movement, the struggle, the Panthers.' This was 1968. The Panthers had come into existence in 1964 in Oakland, started by Huey Newton and Bobby Seale.

"I lived on the Lower East Side, and two Panthers, Mark Holder and Tony Martin, who actually lived in the projects with me, came along selling the Black Panther paper. I used to argue with them, fuck with them. I said, 'You talk about your revolution. It's not making sense. If you were revolutionaries, why would you have an office in Harlem with a big picture of a black panther? That's why there's all the shoot-outs.'

"They said, 'Why don't you just come up to Harlem and see.'

"I went, and I remember seeing a lot of free clothing in front of the Panther office. And then they showed me where they fed children breakfast for free. I met some of the people in the office, and I went to a few of the educational classes they had, and what impressed me most was their ability to do so much with so little.

"I was an angry, young black man, and you have to channel that anger in a positive way, so I started organizing block parties, just to get people doing something positive together, shut the street down and let the children have some activities in the street. They'd ride their bikes up and down the street and not have to worry about cars. People who had things to sell could sell them in the street. People would cook food and make donations, and at night they'd play music and have dance contests. It was something positive, better than sitting there doing nothing.

"And I made a little community newsletter. 'So-and-so got into college.' 'This one got straight A's on his report card.' There was so much negativity around. I was trying to build their self-esteem.

"I was becoming culturally conscious, and I started wearing a dashiki, had a big Afro. I was really caught up in it. American is our citizenship, our legal identity, but we are African people who were brought to the Caribbean and to the Americas, and that doesn't take away from our Africanness.

"When it came to the police, there was some hostility. It was a scary thing to be on the subway selling my Panther paper. I'd stand on the train with another guy. I had a big Afro, black leather jacket, 'Free Huey' buttons all over me, and fifty Black Panther papers in my hand, combat boots with black dungarees or corduroys, a blue shirt, walking up and down the subway and walking past cops. I'd say, 'Get your Black Panther paper. Don't forget your Black Panther paper. Power to the people. Buy your Black Panther paper.'

"The cops would stop us from time to time, and they'd say, 'No solicitation. You have to take that out of here.' But I never had any real confrontation with the police.

"But it was a scary thing when you saw in the newspaper, 'Black Panther shot and killed,' or 'beaten and brutalized.' Here I was, letting everyone know I'm a Black Panther, walking the street, and there was a time when the police and the Panthers were having shoot-outs across the nation, and Panthers were dying or being jailed, and the rhetoric was scaring the system more than our actions.

"The government engaged in war. You had the New York 21 who were arrested— Afeni Shakur (Tupac's mother) and many of the others were charged with conspiracy to blow up the New York Botanical Gardens and Macy's. It was a bunch of crap, trumped-up charges. Eventually they beat the charges, but it took a year or two of their lives and hundreds of thousands of dollars to defend them. Some of them jumped bail.

Eldridge Cleaver. *Library of Congress*

"There was also the New Haven 8, and the San Francisco 6. All over the country the movement was raising money for legal defense. 'Free Angela Davis. Free Huey Newton.' Huey Newton was arrested for a shoot-out in Oakland.

"While all of this was going on, I was just a teenager in the party, not in the leadership, which was a good thing, because had I emerged as a leader then, we would not be talking. I would either be dead or in jail.

"J. Edgar Hoover said, 'The Black Panther Party is the most dangerous party to the internal security of America and should be neutralized,' meaning eliminated. Once that was put out there, thirty-three Panthers were killed, including Fred Hampton and Mark Clark—in their sleep, in Chicago. Then the Panthers were infiltrated by the FBI. Informants would join the Panthers and tell the FBI all about our plans, and they'd lead you to do something so you'd get arrested and busted. In California they changed the laws regarding the right to bear arms. Under the second amendment, we had that right as long as the gun was unloaded and exposed. That's why when you see pictures of the Panthers, the bullets are on their chests, showing the gun is empty. And then they changed the law so they could now confiscate all weapons, and that led to shoot-outs, and when the dust cleared, across the country twelve police were killed, but more than thirty Panthers were killed and many others ended up in prison.

"J. Edgar Hoover had done this with Marcus Garvey in the 1920s. With Hoover, it didn't matter whether you were Martin Luther King or Huey Newton, whether you said, 'Turn the other cheek, love your neighbor, be nonviolent' or whether we said, 'By any means necessary, an eye for an eye, a tooth for a tooth.' Any black organizational leader who stood up to the system was going to die or get character-assassinated or lose his freedom. There was no right way to fight this system under J. Edgar Hoover, and even to this day it doesn't matter what you say. If you stand up to the white power, you are a threat. Under McCarthy it was Communism. Now the new word is 'terrorism.' It's all part of the same deal. Before there was J. Edgar Hoover, and now we have the PATRIOT Act. Under Reagan we had a COINTELPRO type of program with the FBI, a similar kind of repressive legislation or policy or institution to suppress any kind of movement that might occur in this country. Under the PATRIOT Act you have to watch the library books you're reading.

"When I was twenty, in the early 1970s, the internal conflict of the Panthers got me out of there. Here we had the system coming down on us, arresting people, killing people, and we were being infiltrated, and on top of that, Huey Newton on the West Coast and Eldridge Cleaver on the East Coast got into an internal conflict over which direction the party should go in. Eldridge was more into militarism and going to war. Huey was into survival programs, political education, being involved in electoral politics. Bobby Seale ran for mayor. Erica Brown ran for assembly. Huey ran for Congress. Eldridge himself ran for president on the Fear and Freedom Party ticket. But the individual internal conflicts led to violence. Because of the infiltration by the FBI, everyone was accusing everyone else of being an agent, and the party started to purge people, and in the end Panthers were killing Panthers, and I said to myself, 'This is not making sense.' Because it was a scary thing to be walking down the street in my Panther uniform, especially after the Black Liberation Movement started, and cops started dying, and they were looking for Panthers. And here I am. And cops were killed on the Lower East Side. They were looking for Twyman Myers, who they eventually found and killed. Twyman Myers put fear in the police. They accused him of killing policemen, but here's the thing: did he? Not every Panther they accused of killing people was killing people.

"Around this time, one of the most troubling times in my life came when they turned the draft into a lottery in 1970. I was totally politically conscious. I was in the movement, twenty years old, and I was *not* going to war.

"I always found it interesting when I was learning my political history that everybody America hated were my heroes. I thought Ho Chi Minh, who was for his people, was a hero. The United States was for the dictator of the South. I thought Kim Il Sung in Korea was fighting to keep from splitting his country. The administration liked the guy in the South. They liked Marcos in the Philippines and Pinochet in Chile. I liked Salvador Allende, the duly elected Socialist president. The government backed Papa Doc and Baby Doc Duvalier [in Haiti], and Batista in Cuba, all right-wing dictators. I liked Castro and Che Guevara. I said to myself, 'Man, my country is on the wrong side of history and is creating a lot of divisiveness around the world.' I said to myself, 'I am not going into this racist army and fighting for America. That's just not happening. What am I going to do? Am I going to run away? Go to jail? Go to Canada? How am I going to beat this?'

"I thought of doing what Rap Brown did, act crazy when you go to see the psychiatrist. 'I need to go to this war because I'm a revolutionary and I want to learn how to shoot guns.'

"Fortunately for me, my lottery number was 263, and the cutoff was 125. I'll never forget those numbers, because it was one of the most traumatic times of my life.

"And right after that, in 1971, the Attica prison riot hit. The prisoners were asking for better living conditions, a right to education, and an end to the brutality by the jailers. They weren't saying, 'Free us.' They were saying, 'We want more humane treatment and some more respect.'

"What disturbed me so much was Governor Nelson Rockefeller's decision to go in there and just murder all of those people. I talked to William Kunstler, the Panther lawyer, about it. He was negotiating, and the state was about to give in—the prisoners were going to get some of their demands met, when Rockefeller sent his men in to just murder everybody. They tried to say the prisoners slit the necks of the hostages, but not one hostage's neck was slit. Not one. All of them died from the firing of the state.

"That they could just go in like that and destroy everybody just rocked my world. Kunstler had tried to negotiate, and Rockefeller went in there and murdered everybody—hostages and prisoners alike. To me, how could the government actually do that when there were negotiations going on? What were the prisoners demanding? Better food and more books in the library. And to be murdered because of that? I was very depressed, and Kunstler said that was the most depressing moment in his life too.

"When that happened I was in the college adapter program, going to New York City Community College on Jay Street and Borough Hall in Brooklyn and getting my associate's degree. I wanted to work with youth and get into social work programs. I majored in sociology and minored in elementary education.

"In 1972 I went to work at the Willa Hargrove Mental Health Clinic in Bedford-Stuyvesant in Brooklyn. I became the youth director of their summer camp and their after-school program.

"Working in a mental health clinic was deep. I started reading about black psychology, and I studied linguistics and learned a lot about Ebonics.

"I would see black children walk in, and if the diagnosis was schizophrenia or hyperactivity, the answer was always to give them chemotherapy, Ritalin, or Melperone. We had black clinicians who were using Eurocentric treatment and Eurocentric analysis and diagnosis and prognosis.

"I used to argue with them. I'd say, 'No, they don't need chemotherapy. You need to visit their families, get to know them, get to know more about their history.' But the black clinicians were not culturally black. That's why it's not enough to say, 'He's the first black this or that.' Look at Clarence Thomas, a [Supreme Court] judge, or Condoleezza Rice, she's the secretary of state. But can you say they're black? Hello! And it's the same thing in every field.

"Every black clinician should be required to know about the black experience in America. How can you treat black children if you're not aware of the social and interpersonal impact of racism on a child? I don't see how you can do that.

"I'd say to them, 'You need to take a course in black history so you understand.'

"Not every black child is angry. A lot of people say to me, 'Why are you so angry?' First of all, I have no problem being angry. Even the Bible says, 'Anger, but sin not.' But what is considered as hyperactivity or other diagnoses is really our black culture.

It isn't a sickness or an illness; it is misunderstood. As an example, the school environment and the curriculum isn't geared for the black child. All the studies to prepare classrooms are for the white, middle-class child.

"There is no understanding of this. Everything is geared to the white, middle-class child. In society, what is dressing for success? A shirt and tie?

"What is the language, standard English? No. Proper English, because Americans are messing up the King's English.

"It's how you walk, how you talk, how you think. You basically have to turn white to make it. Quote, unquote.

"Whoever has the power imposes their value system. If you're out of power, whatever your culture is, it's not going to be the standard. That's why you wear a shirt and tie, because unless you do, you're not going to get hired.

"When I was six years old, my mother made me wear a shirt and tie for my class picture. After that, I have never worn a shirt and tie in my life. I wear Nehru suits and collarless suits. I have them made, and once in a while, when they come back in style, I gather them up.

"I can't go in to a job interview and say, 'What your name be?' Which is a fine way to speak. But it's not acceptable. If I have power, and you speak the way you speak, I would be able to say to you, 'You're not going to get this job unless you learn some Ebonics'—the opposite of what happens to us.

"Look at rap music and the way whites react to it. This is what we're up against. And the esteem questions—I know people in college, brilliant black men and women who think they speak badly. They won't raise their hands and ask questions, because they haven't 'learned how to speak.'

"And it's the same with religion. After I got my associate's degree, I went to Hunter College in 1976. It took me twelve years to get a four-year degree because I was in and out, working at the mental health clinic, spending a lot of time in the movement, and it was during this time that I met the Reverend Herbert Daughtry, my closest friend and pastor. His church is the House of the Lord Pentacostal Church at 415 Atlantic Avenue in Brooklyn, between Bond and Nevin.

"In 1981 I moved to Bedford-Stuyvesant on Lewis between Putnam and Madison, and I've lived there ever since. I found a beautiful brownstone for reasonable rent right around the corner from the Willa Hargrove Mental Health Clinic. It wasn't far from Reverend Daughtry's church, and it was there that he unwrapped for me the European contamination of Christianity and presented its African and its revolutionary essence.

"The Panther movement had given me my politics and some of my culture. I would sometimes go listen to Louis Farrakhan and the Nation of Islam up on 116th Street in Harlem, and some of his people were trying to recruit me as well, but I just couldn't get with their lack of involvement in the political struggle. They were more institution-builders, but I did like their morality. *Don't get high. Clean up yourself. Learn how to eat right. Respect your women. Stand up.* That was good. They employed people and cleaned up brothers coming out of prison, but I just couldn't get with Islam and the lack of political involvement in the struggle.

"When I joined Reverend Daughtry, he was extremely political, very African-centered with the religion. Because all my life I had thought Christianity was a white man's religion, but Reverend Daughtry showed me that the origin of all major religions came out of Africa, whether it was Judaism, Christianity, Islam, or African traditional religions, and that Jesus Christ himself was black, that in the Bible it says he had 'hair of lamb's wool, feet of burnt brass.' When they described Jesus in visions, he was always black. And the areas he dwelt in—the Garden of Eden was down near the Euphrates River in Ethiopia, and I began to say, 'This is not a white man's religion.'

"The white man brought the Bible to Africa, gave the Bible to the African, and took his land. Missionaries came and pronounced us heathens.

"The white Baptist ministers for a century used the Bible to justify slavery, but you don't throw out the baby with the bathwater. What you have to do is reinterpret Scriptures, and the particular passage relating to this is the curse of Ham.

"According to the Bible, Noah's three sons, Ham, Japheth, and Shem, repopulated the earth. The lineage of Shem was the lineage of Jesus Christ. Shem had Tora, and Tora had Abraham, and he had Isaac, and Jacob had the twelve tribes, and out of the House of Judah came Jesus.

"But Ham meant black and warm, and the Hamites migrated to Africa, and that's why the whites who knew that Ham was black said that after the flood, when Noah was naked and drunk in the vineyard, his two brothers Japheth and Shem walked backward and put a cloth over him. Ham looked on his father in his nakedness, and the Bible said that Ham was cursed because of that. And that is where the whites got 'the curse of Ham.' Therefore black Hamites who went to Africa were cursed to be slaves.

"The Bible said, 'Curse ye, Ham.' The Bible also said, 'Noah cursed Ham to be a slave to his brethren Japheth.' And if you look at Japheth's lineage, it goes to Europe, through the Celtics, the Germanics, and the Caucasian Mountains—that's where you get Caucasian—and Ham's lineage goes to Africa, so they concluded that Ham should be a slave to Japheth.

"But read the Scriptures further, and you'll see that first of all, God didn't curse Ham. Noah did. So you have to question the validity of a curse from someone who's drunk in the vineyard, even if it is Noah.

"It's a great irony that the whites used the Bible to enslave blacks, but that's what they did. What we had to do in the black theology movement was change the tone. Reverend Daughtry, and A. Rod Gilmore, Cornell West, the Reverend Albert Cleeves, they began to unwrap the European contamination of Christianity and reinterpret the Bible.

"When they started to use religion, at first it was liberating. That's why during slavery it was against the law for blacks to read, let alone read the Bible. If it was brainwashing and making us docile, why did they forbid us reading it?

"You could die for reading the Bible, because they knew liberation was in that Bible. They knew that when Harriet Tubman read the Bible she had to be free. When minister Nat Turner read the Bible, he had to be free. Because the Bible was liberating. It was a liberating gospel.

"When the whites saw how liberating it was, they reinterpreted it. 'Love your enemy.' 'The curse of Ham. You're supposed to be our slaves.' They reinterpreted everything. Jesus became white. They made white pictures of Jesus all over the place. White supremacy took over the Bible.

"The Ku Klux Klan burned crosses, and they were religious people, and they justified it by saying, 'These people are cursed.' How could you come out of church and get your family and enjoy a lynching? What a contradiction! And they could do that because they were convinced that we were cursed people that had to be destroyed—or enslaved. People can only do that if they are convinced this is the right thing to do.

"So when you get to the 1960s, it was exciting when you get Martin Luther King, and Minister Malcolm X, and Reverend Herbert Daughtry, and Reverend Albert Cleeves all saying, 'No, no, that is not what Christianity is all about. It's not a white man's religion. You're not cursed. Jesus was not white. He's black.'

"So first you get a revival of Christianity, and it's the same Christian Bible that the slaves were not allowed to read, and then the whites reinterpret it so they can use it as a tool of enslavement, and then you get the '60s, where we revived it so we could get back to its original intent."

# HERE COME THE PUERTO RICANS

VICTOR ROBLES

THERE WERE ONLY 500 PUERTO RICANS LIVING IN NEW YORK City in 1910. By 1940 there were 70,000. Puerto Rico, a little island east of Cuba, was an American territory, so its people could move freely within the United States—legally skirting the immigration quotas. When poverty and overpopulation hit there, after 1945 the largest number of immigrants came from Puerto Rico—often coming to join relatives and find a *better* job. Low-cost airplane service from San Juan to New York City beginning in 1946 contributed to the deluge. By 1960 Puerto Ricans made up 10 percent of New York City's population. By 1964, 700,000 Puerto Ricans had come to New York, and Spanish had become the city's second language.

Like the Jews, Irish, and Italians before them, the new immigrants were stereotyped as neighborhood wreckers, criminals, and a burden on the public. Poor when they arrived, most of them were forced to move into old brownstones and tenements that were in a hopeless state of disrepair. When the heroin epidemic struck New York between 1964 and 1968, almost a quarter of the addicts were Puerto Ricans. In 1968 almost half the Puerto Ricans, most of whom lived in Spanish Harlem, Bedford-Stuyvesant, and Williamsburg, lived below the poverty level.

Puerto Rican children in the public schools faced terrible discrimination. Those entering kindergarten spoke little English. Many were embarrassed to speak it badly, so they chose not to speak it at all. Worse, guidance counselors put the Puerto Rican children in slow classes or assigned them to technical high schools. Like the blacks, many found the school experience frustrating and dropped out.

Victor Robles, who grew up poor in Williamsburg, was one of the large group of Puerto Ricans who should have gone on to college but because of cultural barriers and racial prejudice was directed on a path toward vocational school. Had he not been a good politician, Robles in all probability would have had far more limited economic and social opportunities.

As it turned out, he was a talented social activist in his community, and he was taken under wing first by New York Supreme Court Justice Gilbert Ramirez and then by U.S. Congresswoman Shirley Chisholm. At Chisholm's urging, he ran for the New York State Assembly and served for six years from 1978 to 1984. Robles went on to serve on the New York City Council for seventeen years from 1985 to 2001, when term limits forced him to give up his post. Since 2001 Robles has served as the city clerk.

**VICTOR ROBLES**  "I was born in Fajardo, Puerto Rico, in 1945. I migrated to New York City in 1947. My father's name was Felix Robles, but I knew very little about him, because my mother brought my brother Antonio and me here as a single parent.

"I went to Puerto Rico for the first time at my father's death, when I was nineteen, and I never could understand how anyone could leave such a beautiful island. But unfortunately, salaries even today are not like you find here. And there were jobs in New York, so New York was *the place* for Puerto Ricans to come for a better life. Not because they wanted to leave Puerto Rico. And nobody told them they had to confront the winter in New York, which they don't have in Puerto Rico. And they had to confront discrimination, because we didn't speak English.

"My mother's mother—her husband died and she remarried—she came to New York, bought a house in Spanish Harlem in 1947, and she convinced her daughter to bring her two kids and come live with her. In 1950 my grandmother and mother bought a house in East Williamsburg in Brooklyn, and I have lived in Brooklyn ever since, on Seigel Street between Manhattan Avenue and Graham Avenue, which was changed to the Avenue of Puerto Rico.

"When I first came, it was a Jewish community. We were the only Puerto Rican family within twenty blocks. Today there are Dominicans, Mexicans, Puerto Ricans, and Hasidim, which we didn't have many of back then.

"I had never seen anyone with sideburns like that before. We used to refer to the Hasidim as penguins, because they were dressed all in black with fur hats. As I grew up I found that those hats, made of real fur, could cost as much as $12,000. I say that because when we were growing up, kids will be kids. The Hispanic kids didn't understand the Hasidic religion or their culture, and the Hasidic kids were very meek and religious, and the Hispanic kids used to slap them and take away their hats.

"In those days we had gangs. We had the Ellery Bops and the Quintos, who today are called the Young Lords. Ellery Street is in Bedford-Stuyvesant, out by the Pfizer plant, and those kids lived there. That was the gang of the day, and they were dangerous. They didn't have a formal education—these kids, unfortunately, dropped out of school. I had friends who ended up running in these gangs. They got addicted to drugs. I was very fortunate, because I was more afraid of my mother and what she would do to me than whether my friends wouldn't call me.

"I'm not a smoker, and I'll tell you why. Like everything else with your friends, the temptation was there. One day I took a pack of Marlboro cigarettes. Remember the cowboy, the Marlboro Man? I went into the bathroom to smoke a cigarette. With my grandmother, who we lived with, you could go to the bathroom, but if you were in there longer than she thought the norm, she would start banging. And here I was, smoking. I flushed the cigarette, and I tried to get the smoke out, but when she opened the door, she smelled it.

"She took the entire pack of cigarettes, and she made me smoke them! I will never . . . After that, whenever I smelled the smoke, I wanted to puke.

"And it was done out of love.

"I only met my father once before he died. He had come to New York from Puerto Rico, a one-day visit. I came home from school, and I sat next to my mother on the sofa, and as my father turned, I saw he had a bald spot on the back of his head, and I said innocently, 'Look Mom, Pop has a bald spot.'

"I got a slap across my face.

"I said, 'What did you do that for?'

"She said, 'That's your father. Respect him.' So all I knew about my father was when I met him I got slapped. In those days that was discipline in a good way. Today you get locked up.

"I can't emphasize enough, now that my grandmother, grandfather, and mother are gone, I really believe I could not be where I am today without three things: my family, the faith, and their always cultivating in me that 'you were born with God's gift to be whatever you want to be, and if you fail, it's because you failed yourself, not because God didn't give you a brain.' I gotta tell you, I succeeded because of that upbringing.

"We attended a church called Most Holy Trinity, a German church, which is still there about five blocks from where we lived. [The church dates back to 1841, and the cornerstone of the current building was laid in 1882.] I was an altar boy. My brother, Tony, before he moved to Puerto Rico, worked in the rectory. Whenever he couldn't make it I would fill in for him.

"The Germans built it, and when we started going there, the Mass was in German. We didn't have a Spanish Mass until later, after Latinos started moving into the neighborhood. I was there for twenty-five years. Now we also have a Polish Mass, because we have Polish people from Greenpoint moving in. The census in the late 1970s indicated that Puerto Ricans were a majority in the neighborhood. In the last census it was the Dominicans. This census shows more Puerto Ricans. The next census will show a Dominican majority, because the Puerto Ricans are moving down to Orlando, Florida.

"After we moved into the neighborhood, we saw that it was changing, that a lot of whites were moving out. We did not see it that they were fleeing from us. My parents all the time told me about America, about the respect and love for the opportunities that America offered us, so you could not be a radical or be anti-American in their house, because they were very appreciative of America. My brother and I are veterans. He went to Vietnam. At that time President Johnson did not allow two brothers to serve in Vietnam at the same time, so I went to Korea. And so my family is for God and country. You respect God and always appreciate what this country has offered you. So when the whites moved, I saw that this was what America is all about: you work hard, you study, go to school, and that opens up avenues for you to go wherever you want to go. They were leaving for a better life. So I did not see it as they were running away from us.

"Like today, most of the third-generation Puerto Ricans who became professionals don't live in the city of New York. They live in Long Island, Connecticut, those places the whites moved in the 1950s and 1960s. It's not black and white, Jews and gentiles, Protestant and Catholic. I look at it that this is America. And America and capitalism say, 'If you work hard, study, respect and have faith in God, you can make it.' And when you make it, they don't expect you to stay poor. It's like the Jeffersons on TV, moving up to the East Side. That's America. Even a black man can move up.

"In Williamsburg we always had tensions between Jews and Hispanics, especially after the Hasidim began moving in in large numbers. Today it's not the Jews displacing us but yippies, dippies, artists, what-have-you.

"Our culture is a very happy one, with hugging and kissing, and the family. The Hasidim seemed strange and different, but after living there awhile I began to see, understand, and know the cultural differences. Because of my family and my faith, and people around me who showed me by example, I did not look at the Hasidic community as a threat. I was close to the Sodder family, husband and wife, son Bobby and daughter Anna. They had a fruit stand, and I used to spend time with them and help them out. On Friday they invited me up to their house for Shabbat. Once you get to know people, you realize we are all God's children underneath the skin. We all have blood. If I need blood, am I going to ask you if you are Jewish or not?

"Children learn what they see and hear, and that begins in the house. Kindness and understanding must be nourished, and you go to school and you come back home, and I better do my homework before running from the house. I didn't dare go outside and play without first getting permission from my grandmother."

*After going to PS 41, Robles graduated to Intermediate School 49, an all-boys school in Williamsburg on Graham Avenue. When Eleanor Roosevelt visited I.S. 49 in 1957 to read* John Brown's Body *to the students, Victor was chosen from a school of six hundred to escort the former first lady around the school.*

**VICTOR ROBLES**   "I mean to know I was walking the first lady of the country—that was it. Here I am, a Puerto Rican, and I'm walking the first lady of the land! In Puerto Rico, let me tell you, they love Franklin Roosevelt. You talk to my grandmother and grandfather about Franklin Roosevelt, forget about it! It was the greatest thing for them and for my mother that I was chosen to escort her."

*At I.S. 49 Robles was so trusted by the administration that he was given the key to the school. One night the parents attending a Parents Association meeting couldn't get in because the custodian forgot to open the school. The parents called the principal, and the principal told them, "Where's Victor? Tell Victor to open up. He has a key." That's how much he was trusted.*

*Nevertheless, at school Victor felt the sting of racism. The teacher who treated him most harshly at I.S. 49, he says, was black.*

**VICTOR ROBLES** "God is good. Don't get mad. Get even. I had a black teacher who was the biggest racist I could have. Every time she caught me speaking Spanish in class, she deducted five points in my English class. At the end of the term she gave me a 40, and I walked around for almost an hour, crying, wondering how I was going to face my mother and explain it.

"After I came home and explained it to my mother, she said, 'I'm going to school tomorrow, and if you're lying to me, I'm going to slap you in front of your class.' She came in, and the teacher showed her I had a 96, but I got a 40 because I constantly spoke Spanish in class. 'Well,' my mother said to her, 'let me tell you something. I carried him for nine months, not you, and I don't care what you want or how you feel. We are Americans, and we have given our lives for this country. I want you to know that my son will be somebody because I demand it. If he listens to you, he'll be on welfare the rest of his life.'

"The principal ended up apologizing, and I got my 96. My mother would not take no for an answer. And when I became a state assemblyman, this teacher, who had become the principal of a Bedford-Stuyvesant school in my district, invited me to be the commencement speaker.

"So when you ask what motivated me, I could have ended up as one of those Young Lords or a Black Panther, but I was taught by my mother that God gave me a brain, and you use your brain and your talent. And when you beat them at their own game, they will always respect you.

"Yes, every Puerto Rican faced prejudice. Everybody knows that for a fact. They won't say it, but that's a fact. When you have people telling you to your face, 'Spic, go home,' what does that mean?

"But I also want to be fair. I really believe that was said to me because they did not understand me, my culture, and where I came from. Again, my faith taught me something. I learned that evil triumphs when good men and women do nothing. So while I paint a rosy picture, I did not let racism or prejudice stop me from getting where I am. And at the same time I refused to give in to racism. On the south side of Williamsburg there were three public housing developments which were 90 percent Hasidim, and then a change in the law called for Hispanic residents. I would say, 'The Hasidim have the same right for housing that we have. Show me where they violate the law or if they have received favoritism, and I will stand up with you. But you cannot get me to say I will not support a Hasid to get into public housing if that Hasid is poor.' I used to be crucified in the Spanish media.

"Brooklyn is known as the borough of churches. That is not a cliché. It's a fact. There is no other place where you have more churches than Brooklyn. But it was my house that taught me what Christianity is all about. *Do unto others as you would have others do unto you.* That was not taught in the schools. That was taught in my house. Because my house also went to church. My poor grandmother read the Bible. She didn't sit on street corners and wave the Bible. My grandmother and mother were very religious people.

"Every Saturday at four o'clock I was in the church confessing, because my mother said, 'You cannot receive communion unless you go to confession.' Every Sunday at nine was a children's Mass. I was in Mass. Today my nephew—my sister's oldest son—lives with me, and he knows that on Sunday, wherever we are, we go for one hour to give thanks to almighty God. Even if we're on vacation.

"And every Thanksgiving and Christmas, I will be at the senior center. For Thanksgiving, I arrive at five in the morning. I'm in the kitchen cutting turkey. I've been doing it for thirty years, and that's my way of thanking almighty God for my blessings and thanking the people who elected me for thirty years. I go back to that foundation, which was in the house. Today parents will always find excuses why their kids will not succeed: it's the teachers. And I'm not saying the system is perfect. In my day my mother went to the Parents Association meetings. She went to the school board meetings. Today parents have their excuses.

"I went to Eli Whitney Vocational High School [now known as Harry Van Arsdale High School] and majored in carpentry, cabinet-making. I never used it. In those times it was rare when you graduated from high school. As long as I graduated, my mother was satisfied. In those days the Puerto Rican girls didn't even graduate from junior high school. They had to drop out of school to be in the house, cooking and cleaning. In those days if your son or daughter reached high school, that was like getting a college diploma."

N° 37

# OCEAN HILL–BROWNSVILLE

CLARENCE TAYLOR

**W**HEN DR. KENNETH CLARK STUDIED BLACK STUDENTS IN 1954, he determined that racist attitudes brought on by segregation caused white teachers to lower their expectations for the black students who were seen to have limited futures. According to Clark, the New York City public school system "was guilty of depriving black and Puerto Rican children of the ability to compete successfully with others."

Clark's finding embarrassed the New York City Board of Education. Toward the end of 1955, Mayor Robert Wagner pledged to do something about it. But ten years later, nothing had changed.

When Clarence Taylor entered the seventh grade in 1965, the teachers at I.S. 211 placed him and twenty-five other black students in class level 7-19, with 7-1 being the top whites-only class. After 7-1 came 7-2 and then 7-3, and if you keep going until you get to 7-19 you can understand the extent of the racism when you consider that Taylor today is a professor of history at Baruch College.

As Dr. Clark found, the system caused many black and Puerto Rican youngsters to become discouraged and to drop out of school. Taylor, however, took a different path. He made up his mind to work hard so he could get into a better class the following year.

Taylor's plight was common. In a school where the I.S. 211 student body was racially mixed, the teachers—with one exception—

were all white, and when the classes were assigned, the teachers almost invariably assigned the best classes to the white kids, and assigned the blacks and Puerto Rican students to the classes for the slowest kids. It was just such stereotyping that led black activists to call for local community control of the public schools.

A large part of the racial problem in the schools was that the school board, afraid to anger the white parents, refused to do anything about school segregation. The clash between the black parents and the white teachers became inevitable. When the white Jewish teachers went on strike, those blacks advocating community control were losers. The repercussions are being felt today.

**CLARENCE TAYLOR**   "I was born in Brooklyn in 1952 in Kings County Hospital. My father's parents were landowners in Alabama, one of the few in the South. So they were farmers. My mother's family came from Augusta, Georgia. They were day workers, and they died when I was very young.

"My father, Clarence Taylor Sr., was born in 1930. He grew up on the farm, which was just outside Birmingham, Alabama. He left home when he was fifteen. He was part of the migration in the 1940s.

"He left because of a family dispute. He had twelve brothers and sisters. He and his brother, my uncle Melvin, got into a bad fight. My father threw a brick at him, hitting him in the eye, and Melvin lost the eye. My grandmother, who was incensed, either beat him or he escaped before she could. My father decided to leave and go north. And when he did, he came to Brooklyn, because an older sister, my aunt Mary, lived there. She had left to escape the cruelty of the South and because of the opportunities of the North, and so did other relatives. None of them ever talked about how bad things were.

"They all came to Brownsville. My father got a job working for a florist. He lived with his sister Mary for a while, but then he became very friendly with a couple from Jamaica, and they took him in as a son. He was trying to make ends meet delivering flowers, and then he took up boxing. He tried to make the grade as a light heavyweight, but he didn't make much of a living at it.

"My father was eighteen and my mother was sixteen when they met. Her maiden

Brownsville was always a poor neighborhood, even more so when the Jews moved out and the blacks moved in.
*Brian Merlis Collection—Brooklynpix.com*

name was Mamie Robinson, and she came to Brooklyn in the late 1940s, after her parents died. She came to stay with an older sister. She also came looking for better opportunities. My parents met at the Berean Missionary Baptist Church, one of the well-known black churches in the community. She went to Alexander Hamilton Vocational High School. She was the one who talked my dad out of boxing.

"He then drove a yellow cab. He drove all over the city. He worked for a company. Eventually, when I was thirteen, he passed the New York City bus driver's test, and he became a bus driver for the Transit Authority. When I was in high school, he got his high school equivalency diploma, and he went to New York Community College and became a Realtor. Before he died, he owned three buildings, one in Bedford-Stuyvesant and two in Brownsville. He rented them out as apartments. He did very well.

"Neither of my parents was involved in the civil rights movement, though my mother was a big fan of Martin Luther King. I can remember the day John Kennedy was killed, how hysterical she became. She wailed, 'What are we going to do?' I was just a kid. They paid attention to the civil rights movement, but they weren't part of it. When I became politically active, my father was not happy with me.

"I grew up in the Breukelen Housing Projects in the East New York section of Brooklyn. There were ten or twelve seven-story buildings. [There are now thirty buildings, either three or seven stories tall, housing over four thousand people.] We lived there for a while. It was for lower-income folks, but people who made more money, like my parents, were able to hide their money, fudge their W-2s. It was not a slum. It was well kept. They had maintenance service to make sure it was clean.

"The area was mixed. It wasn't a segregated housing project. The dominant group was blacks and Latinos, but there were white families living right next to us, an Italian-American family, and we got along very well.

"I began elementary school in 1959. I went to PS 260 on Williams Avenue. It was within walking distance. There was one black teacher. There were no problems, except the usual kid stuff with kids getting into fights. It was safe. I walked home. Of course, there were neighborhood bullies. There was one kid by the name of Floyd. He constantly picked on me, called me names. Floyd called me 'Pillowhead.' He thought my head was shaped like a pillow. Or he would call me 'No-eyebrows.' My eyebrows were very thin. It was mostly barking. I have a twin brother, Lawrence, and my brother and I weren't fighters. So we were scared of this guy until the fifth grade, when I realized I was bigger than he was. So when he challenged me to a fight, I said, 'Okay, let's go fight.' It was lunchtime, and as we stepped outside, and he said, 'I don't want to fight.' I said, 'I do.' I knocked him down to the ground, and he started to cry. I said to myself, 'Now he'll leave me alone.' And he did.

"My brother wasn't bullied, but he had an adversary in his class. We actually had our own separate friends. My brother had no interest in sports whatsoever. My friends were more athletic. We played baseball a lot. In 1962 the Mets began playing at the Polo Grounds, and I became a Mets fan and so did my parents. I got it right away why they were Mets fans. The Yankees were not acceptable, because of their racial policies. Elston Howard was the first black player on the team, but he wasn't treated very well. My parents were well aware of that. They grew up with the Dodgers, and when the Mets came in, it seemed like everyone who was black in New York City became a fan. I loved watching Willie Mays play. I enjoyed going to the games. My brother had no interest whatsoever.

"As we got older, my friends began to break up along racial lines. I got the distinct feeling that some of the kids who grew up as friends made a conscious decision not to be friends any longer. Some were Italians. Others were Protestants. The white friends I had who were Jewish stayed friends, until we went to separate high schools. It was disappointing to lose them as friends. I thought it was a real loss. But it was something that happened, so I just moved on and made other friends.

"Some of my friends ended up on the wrong side of the tracks. Oh yeah. Some of them died in their twenties. It was mostly drugs. Heroin. They weren't doing well in school. A lot of them dropped out of school. They had no prospects, so they got involved in the drug trade. They were dealing.

"These kids gave up on school because of race. A lot of it was race. I was a victim of tracking. I wasn't that serious about studying in elementary school. But I became a lot more serious when I entered junior high school at I.S. 211.

"My white friends were placed in 7-1 and 7-2, the best classes, and they put me in 7-19, and I was horrified. Some of the other black kids were in 7-23. First of all, just being in 7-19 bothered me, but when I was doing extremely well, it dawned on me one day in social studies class that we were going over the same material day after day. We had a white teacher, and I challenged him. I said, 'We've covered this already several times. Why don't we move on to something else?' He didn't lose his cool. Essentially, he said, 'Not everybody gets it.' I made a conscious decision to get out of this class by working extremely hard to make sure all my grades were tops.

"In the eighth grade, they put me in a better class, but I didn't make 8-1. But when I got to Canarsie High School in 1966, I was put in a very good class.

"My friends, who were going to a vocational high school, didn't want me going to Canarsie High. They wanted my brother and me to go with them. Some of them went to Westinghouse High School, studying to be dental technicians. Others went to Aviation High or Automotive High School. My close friend Lee warned me, 'By choosing to go to Canarsie High and taking academic courses, you're going to end up dropping out of high school.' That was the prejudice in the black community. They were doubting that we were going to be successful. That had been drummed into a number of black kids, by the white teachers to a degree, but also coming from the black community.

"I remember going into my social studies class. I was the only black student in the class, and the first day of class I remember sitting next to a white student who I knew in junior high school.

"The class had already started, and I heard some mumbling from a couple of kids. Then five minutes later another black kid came into class, and this white kid exploded. He said, 'What the hell is going on?' Clearly he was offended at having two black students in the class. One was bad enough, when I walked in, but when a second black walked in, he couldn't take it. As though somehow this was no longer a good class.

"I excelled in that class and did a hell of a lot better than he did."

*In February of 1967 the Brownsville Community Council was formed. For years there had been anger in the black community over how poorly the public schools were serving their children. On February 3, 1964, Bayard Rustin and the Reverend Milton Galamison had organized a boycott of the public schools. Almost 500,000 mostly black students had stayed home. Of the 43,000 mostly white teachers, only 3,500 had been sympathetic. Galamison, the head of the Brooklyn NAACP, called for busing to further integration, but he was opposed by the Anti-Defamation League and the New York Civil Liberties Union.*

*The school board made one concession in 1965, when it agreed to send 1,700 Brownsville students to a white school in Bay Ridge to ease the overcrowding. The*

Albert Shanker was the head of the United Federation of Teachers. *Library of Congress*

blacks were bused over, put in segregated classes, and treated badly by white children. To many black parents, this was further proof of the need for community control.

Thus was formed the Brownsville Community Council, which began negotiating with the New York City Board of Education to gain control of the local schools. Rhody McCoy, an acting principal in a "600" school, which was for kids who were emotionally disturbed or who presented disciplinary problems, was named superintendent of the school district. The white teachers, who were not involved in the selection of a black school superintendent, were furious. They called for a strike in September of 1967.

The strike lasted twelve days. Teachers demanded that disruptive children be removed from the classroom, and they began transferring out of the district.

By May of 1968 there was a crisis when McCoy fired thirteen white teachers and six white administrators for "incompetence." UFT president Albert Shanker said the accusations of incompetence were based on flimsy charges and that the firings were illegal. McCoy was ordered to reinstate them, but he refused. All nineteen ignored McCoy's letter and showed up for work anyway.

The United Federation of Teachers urged teachers to walk out until the nineteen were reinstated. By May 24 only a handful of teachers were at work.

**CLARENCE TAYLOR** "It was extremely emotional. I had become not only a good student, but one who was active in the antiwar movement. I joined the Peace Club. I remember when the teachers strike erupted, I made the conscious decision to go to school. I had also befriended a social studies teacher by the name of Merchant Chernoff. He was a left-wing teacher who was opposed to the strike. He was one of the seven thousand teachers who walked across the picket line and joined that group, Teachers for Community Control. I knew he was going in, and my brother and I made a conscious decision to go in and cross the picket line. I can remember all the screaming and yelling. One teacher in particular, who my brother and I became friends with, was a third-degree karate expert and a phys-ed teacher; he was very disappointed we crossed the picket line. We told him we were very disappointed he was out there picketing. He showed us an anonymous leaflet that had been circulated—an anti-Semitic leaflet—and he said, 'This is what's going to happen.' It became really emotional.

"My friend got in a fight with one of my friends from the Afro-American Student Club. He kicked this guy through a glass door. Nothing happened to the guy. Luckily, even though the glass shattered, my friend was hurt but he wasn't cut.

"Our point of view was that the strike was an affront to the blacks in the community. We were in support of community control, and we crossed the picket line because we didn't recognize the strike. We were going to school. Merchant Chernoff was actually attacked by a colleague, a big, burly phys-ed teacher by the name of Levine, thrown to the floor, and beaten up. Lots of folks were extremely upset over the issue.

"Loads of students sympathized with the strikers. There were very few students in the building. Some white students—the radicals—crossed, but for the most part the students who crossed were black students.

"There were essentially three strikes. After two weeks the teachers went back. A deal had been struck where the thirteen teachers and principals who were dismissed were able to go back, but when they went back, they were harassed, and then Albert Shanker, the head of the UFT, pulled the teachers out again. Then there was another problem. Altogether the strike lasted two and a half months.

The 1968 teachers' strike pitted Jewish teachers against black parents in a struggle for community control of the schools. *Charles Frattini,* New York Daily News

"The teachers who crossed the picket line conducted the classes. It was really strained. My brother and I were hanging out with Merchant Chernoff most of the day. If you wanted to go to a math class, there was a math teacher. It was an opportunity in many ways for us to discuss politics.

"The strike strained the relations between students and teachers. It really made people suspicious. I saw incidents in the school after the strike where black students would be called thugs. The confrontations were between the teachers who crossed the picket lines and those who were on them. When everyone went back to work, there was tension. I had a friend of mine who crossed the picket line, and for twenty, thirty years, people who struck would not talk to him.

"When I became a teacher myself—I worked in the New York City public school system—I went to the United Federation of Teachers convention, but I was involved with the teachers who crossed, the Teachers for Community Control, and this was ten years later, and Albert Shanker was yelling at them and calling them scabs.

"I once interviewed Rhody McCoy, and he told me a story of running into Shanker in Washington, DC, twenty years after the strike. Shanker wanted to push him and loudly complained, "What's he doing here in this city?" I make the argument that Shanker played a large part in the Jewish-black hostility the strike created. Others do not see it that way. But he was really heating things up, and I make the argument he changed the strike from a collective bargaining strike to one where he was accusing blacks of taking over the schools. There was a lot of craziness going on in Ocean Hill–Brownsville and elsewhere. I'd never deny that."

*Fueling the enmity between the black parents and the Jewish teachers was an anonymous, viciously anti-Semitic leaflet that was placed in the mailboxes of teachers at Junior High School 271. In it Jews were called "Middle East murderers of colored people" and "bloodsucking exploiters" who shouldn't be teaching black students because they brainwash them. UFT president Albert Shanker, certain that black separatists were behind the leaflet, made certain the leaflet was publicized.*

**CLARENCE TAYLOR** "To blame the school board for that anonymous leaflet was wrong.

"No one knows where it originated from, but Shanker got a hold of it and made half a million copies and passed it throughout the city. Then a black by the name of Les Campbell went on the air and read an anti-Semitic poem written by a junior high school student. That was insane. It was clearly a very bad time.

"During my senior year, 1969–1970, the major focus for me politically was the

Vietnam War. Lots of my close friends wound up being drafted or joining the air force so as not to be drafted. In Vietnam a lot of the soldiers were black. I knew kids from my neighborhood who went over there and were killed. My brother and I made a decision we were not going, to the disappointment of our father, who was not supportive of our decision.

"We were part of the antiwar movement. We were planning, if we got drafted, to go to Canada. We would just leave. It seemed that every weekend we went to Washington, DC, for a demonstration. We put up posters, and my father complained about it, and then we got involved in the Peace Club in school. It was very controversial, because we organized a one-day walkout. We shut the school down for a day as we called for the United States to end the war in Vietnam.

"A list circulated, of the ten greatest troublemakers in the school. I was on the list. I'm sure that my brother was not.

"I did extremely well in high school, and I got into Baruch College, but once I got in I decided I did not want to study business, so I transferred to Brooklyn College. I ended up majoring in history. I wasn't involved in any political activity. When I got to college my main concern was doing well.

"Friends of mine were surprised I wound up in college. When I decided to go to college, my father fought me on it. My father had become successful. He had the Puritan attitude. He was an inflexible, nose-to-the-grindstone kind of guy. When my brother and I turned seventeen, he signed us up to take the New York City Police Department exam. He wanted us to become cops or work for the post office.

"He said, 'Civil service. That's the way to go.'

"I said, 'No, I want to become a teacher.'

"When I went to college, tuition was free, and my father gave me the $36 for the consolidation fee that one had to pay every semester. That was it. He did not want us to go to college. Even after I became a college professor, I was talking to him, and he said, 'Well, you can still go and do something else.'

"I didn't end up in Vietnam or Canada, because they came out with the lottery, and my number was 276. The cutoff was around 150. My brother and I were extremely happy with our high numbers. We were out of that danger.

"After Brooklyn College, I started to teach. I taught as a substitute teacher at various places including my old junior high school, I.S. 211. I remember my first day of school. The rumor was that Sidney Poitier was coming into the classroom. Remember the movie *To Sir with Love*? Lulu sang the song. They were talking about me. I had a mix of kids, but I was the only black teacher in the school. Some things hadn't changed.

"I got my first full-time job teaching special ed, because the need was so great, but after a year I decided it wasn't for me. I went into social work. I went to Fordham, NYU, and other places, looking for a social work program, and when I was at NYU I got lost looking for the social work building, and I accidentally walked into the School of Education. I spoke to the director there and asked for directions. He said, 'Look, I can offer you a great deal if you want to go to school here. You can get a master's of education, and we'll pay for it and give you a stipend.' He asked me to apply.

"I have no idea how he knew I was a good student. But I said to myself, 'What the heck,' and I applied. I quit my teaching job and went to NYU full-time, and I got my master's degree in a year. I went back to teaching special ed, and I did that for eight years. I worked with students who had been certified as emotionally handicapped or learning-disabled or physically handicapped. And I always had questions about how those evaluations were determined. I felt like special ed was a dumping ground for black and Latino students.

"In the classroom I encouraged these kids to fight to get themselves into regular classes, but I did not have a great deal of success. By the time they were placed in special ed, they were pretty much done. By the time they got to me in junior high school, their skills were so bad, they could not leave. This was what Rhody McCoy was fighting against. He had been a principal of a '600' school, and he was fighting for community control so the black and Latino children would have a fairer chance. But obviously community control was defeated, and so special education courses increased dramatically.

"My take is that the school system has failed. It was failing these kids. It was so obvious, throughout the city, that these kids were moved into these classes, and these classes were relegated to some corner of the schools where they received fewer resources. They were trapped. They were doomed.

"Without community control, it's very hard to prevent this without a movement consisting of parents. Legal action has to be taken.

"The problem still exists. It may even be worse at this point. My brother is a high school teacher. We do talk about it. So is my brother's son, an intermediate school history teacher. He's only been teaching a couple years, but he realizes how kids in special ed classes are discriminated against. I think the United Federation of Teachers holds a lot of responsibility for this.

"After eight years of teaching special ed, I moved into high school, and I also was enrolled at the graduate center of City University working on my PhD. After a few years of teaching high school, I got my PhD and moved on to teach at the college level. I was at Lemoine College in Syracuse for six years. I went to Florida International in 1996. I was there eight years. There were problems there, two departments on separate campuses twenty-three miles away. And I just didn't like the political climate. But it's a nice place to visit. I left there in 2004 and went to Baruch College. I'm teaching modern American history and African-American history. I'm the acting chair of the department at Baruch."

# GOING TO SCHOOL WITH THE *MOOLIES*

CURTIS SLIWA

CURTIS SLIWA WAS A STUDENT AT PS 114 DURING THE TEACH-ers' strike of 1968. Sliwa was one of the few white students who crossed the picket lines to go to school. He went because his father, who didn't want him to grow up to be a racist and who wanted him to learn to get along with the black kids, forced him to. Sliwa, who was raised in an Italian household, got to witness the struggle between the black parents and the predominantly white Jewish teachers up close.

**CURTIS SLIWA**    "For my early education I went to Catholic school. My dad was a believer in public schools, but my mom said, 'We went to public schools. We have to do better for our kids. I want them to go to Catholic schools.' They would argue at the dinner table. Finally my dad said, 'Okay, Frances. You're with the kids most of the time. Curtis can go to Catholic school. But I am not going to let him go to OLM, Holy Family, or St. Jude's. Because I don't want him to be influenced by the *cugines*. I'll look at the archdiocese map and pick one, and that will be our compromise.'

"My dad picked St. Matthew's, which is in Crown Heights on Utica Avenue and Eastern Parkway. It couldn't have been farther away from Canarsie, particularly for a first-grader. I took the number B17 bus, the green clunker. In the winter they put chains on it when it snowed, and it would belch black smoke and you would pass out from the diesel fumes. It took forty-five minutes to get there, and forty-five back.

"It was an integrated school, which was unusual. At one time it was an Irish school, but then Cubans who fled Castro began to attend, and also black kids who were moving into the area. When I first went, it was a third, a third, and a third. And that was fine.

"By the time I was in the fourth grade, it was mostly Hispanic and black, and I was a bleach spot in an inkwell. The public school was down the block on Schenectady Avenue, and the public school kids always felt inferior to the parochial school kids, but they also knew the parochial school kids had lunch money, and they got out fifteen minutes earlier. So they'd run over to our school, and they knew I was the only one who had to make it to the B17 bus to Canarsie. Sometimes I would have to run through a gauntlet, like an Apache line, with the black kids looking to whup me. I could fight one or two, but they'd swarm me. So I had to use all kinds of chicanery to get out of there.

"Let me tell you, if you weren't a racist, after you got beat up a few times, you became a racist. You despised them.

"When I'd come home, the Italian kids would say, 'Oh, the *moolies*. What's wrong with your father? He must hate you. What the hell is he sending you up there for, into niggerland? Is he crazy?'

"I was starting to think, *Maybe my father really doesn't like me. What the hell am I doing going to school there? These kids can't wait to tear me from limb to limb.*

"I started having all kinds of stomachaches. My mother would take me to the doctor, and he'd say, 'It's psychosomatic. It's in his head.' My mother would ask me what was wrong, but I wasn't a snitch, a rat. I kept it to myself.

"I was getting all this agita, virtually ulcers, from my situation at school. I'm thinking, *Boy, I am hating black kids.*

"One of the nuns called my mom, and she comes to school and sits down with one of my fourth-grade teachers, and the nun says, 'Curtis has hit a point of no return. He's bored in his class, and I think there are other things going on he's not

Curtis Sliwa's Catholic-school class picture. *Courtesy of Curtis Sliwa*

telling me about. He's so advanced.' In the Catholic school, everyone was treated the same. There was no advanced class. The teacher said the words that horrified my mother. 'I think you need to transfer him to the public school in your neighborhood. He will do better if he can get into an advanced class at his grade level.'

"And that's when I walked into Sarah Wilson's class with the Jewish kids. I had been getting gold stars in Catholic school. When I first transferred to PS 114, I was barely staying above water, academically. So it was quite an awakening. To walk in and see all the Arista awards [Arista is a branch of the National Honor Society], and every name on the wall was Jewish. Now they are Asian and East Indian. Back then, all Jews. Could not find a name with a vowel at the end.

"Once I went to PS 114, I had the exposure to two different groups. We were surrounded by *gavones* and *shadrools*. I had my relatives, the Italian kids who were constantly told by their relatives, 'What do you have a book in your hand for? You're only going to be a carpenter or a sanitation worker. Go get a paper route. Get a job.' Discouraging them. So the three o'clock bell would ring at PS 114, and my cousins would say to me, 'Hey, come on out.' Play Johnny on the pony, buck-buck, ring-a-levio, stickball, boxball, stoopball, all different street games that would keep us entertained morning, noon, and night and keep us out of harm's way.

"Meantime, on the other side were the Jewish kids, and they were being encouraged to study. We'd say, 'Where is the Lost Tribe of Israel going at three o'clock?' They were going to the library! I was in an advanced class with them, one of the few gentiles, so you learned to do what the Jewish kids did, which was to excel in school. They taught me how to use microfilm in the fifth grade. Morning, noon, and night we did research reports. Weekends were dedicated to doing more extra-credit homework, while my cousins were trying to perfect their stickball, boxball, and Chinese handball skills. In order to survive and go back and forth across the cultural divide, I had to be good at both.

"I don't know what I aspired to. In first grade I wanted to be a sanitation man. I would drive my tricycle around and pick up garbage. Things I wanted to do were very blue-collar, working-class, because I was growing up in an Old World Roman Catholic household, and selfless service, sacrifice, and poverty were the closest things to God. So I really didn't have a desire for a lot of the things we associate with taking advantage of success in the American lifestyle. We did not put a premium on materialism. And ultimately, that's what brought me to start the Guardian Angels."

*By the mid-1960s, Canarsie was beginning to change as the rest of Brooklyn was changing. Blacks continued to flood into the borough, as whites streamed out, moving to their half-acre of paradise on Long Island, in New Jersey, or in Connecticut. By the end of the decade, New York Mayor John Lindsay had instituted forced busing as a way of integrating the public schools. The panic of the whites grew. Curtis Sliwa lived through it all. It was not pretty.*

**CURTIS SLIWA**   "When you lived in Canarsie, it fed your racism. The black kids lived in Brownsville in the projects and the tenements. The dividing line was Linden Boulevard, and the black kids would come across that line. There would be six black kids on four bicycles, two of them on the handlebars, and you didn't have to be a mathematician to figure out that their intent was to steal two bicycles and come back in a pack to Brownsville. So my older cousins, like Lenny 'Beans' Bianchino, would see them, and they'd say, 'Hey nigger, when the sun goes down, you better be out of this part of town,' and Lenny would start whistling to his friends, and the chains and bats would come out, and those kids would pedal just as fast as they could. When you look back, it was a defensive mechanism. Those kids were like sharks, ready to take a bike left outside while a kid ran inside to get a sandwich. 'Cause Canarsie was that kind of neighborhood. But it was clear racism. Al Roker, the weatherman on the *Today Show,* grew up in the Bay View projects at the end of Canarsie, and he would tell stories of how he would have to take the train to Xavier High School, and if he was spotted by the Italian kids, he would have to run quick. The Jews would leave them alone. The Jews got along with blacks. But increasingly, I was becoming more and more of a racist. All I was having were bad experiences with blacks and Hispanics.

"Then in 1966, when John Lindsay was the mayor, we had forced busing, forced integration, and Brooklyn was in an uproar.

"Lindsay was handsome, erudite, but very arrogant. He looked down on the working classes. So he would send deputies to community meetings to explain why there was going to be forced integration through busing. You'd have the Jewish and the Italian parents there, and the Jews were much better at communicating. Many of the Italians were uncouth, and the 'n' word would slip out, but they basically were saying, 'Wait a second. We moved from East New York because they moved in, and we came to Canarsie. We could have gone to Long Island or New Jersey. But we wanted to live in the city, so we came here. We want our kids to go to our local school, and now you're telling us you're going to put our kids on a yellow bus and send them back to the neighborhood we worked so hard to leave? What's the point of staying here?'

"I remember those Lindsay deputies. None of them had kids who went to integrated schools. They went to private schools, didn't even live in the city, and these guys demeaned and humiliated my uncles and their peers, made them feel as if they were uneducated, boorish, racist—in fact, there was some racism—but there also was some logic. Why are they sending kids of these hardworking men and women, people who are law-abiding, pay taxes, back to the neighborhood from which they fled because of crime and because the school no longer was effective? It wasn't their kids. It was the blue-collar, no-collar kids.

"When the Ocean Hill–Brownsville strike occurred, the white parents called for a boycott of the schools, including PS 114. I was in the fifth grade. The boycott lasted a few weeks. There weren't very many kids coming to school so they gathered up everyone in the cafeteria. And here were these black kids in the corner, practically shivering in fear because outside the Italian parents were vicious, ugly, and they kept their kids out of school. My dad was different. He made me go. He said, 'No son, you're not going to become a racist. You're not going to be like the rest of these folk. You gotta learn to get along with the blacks. If these parents are going to be so pig-headed, so backward, in not understanding that the black kid is the same as the white kid, well guess what, as long as you live in my house under my roof and I'm paying the bills, you're going to go to school whether there's a boycott or not.'

"So I was there with about eight other white kids, Jewish Trotskyites, socialists, communist kids of Jewish parents, who talked about the 'workers' paradise,' about 'black and white brotherhood.' They were singing 'Kumbaya' and Joe Hill's 'We Live Together Forever.' Civil rights. Martin Luther King. I didn't fit. You had the black kids, who I didn't like, and these Jewish kids, who felt this forced integration was the greatest thing since lox and bagels. 'This is a civil rights struggle. We'll be like Schwerner and Chaney.' And I'm thinking, *What the hell am I doing here?*

"Imagine, I'm walking past the picket line, and all these parents from the neighborhood are looking at me. My cousins and their friends say to me, 'Your father must really hate you. First he sends you up to *moolieland* where the blacks pick you apart like a carcass in the Mojave Desert, and then you come back here, and you figure you're okay at PS 114. Then they try to send the *moolies* into the school. We're all outside, screaming, protesting, calling them niggers, and you're going in?'

"I would say, 'My dad.'

"I asked him, 'What are you doing to me? Why are you sending me to school with the enemy?'

"It was a very volatile time, but again my dad said, 'You should fear no man.

They are just like you. There's good. There's bad. You have to learn to live with them.'

"But it was a great learning experience, because I actually got to see the black kids not as adversaries. They were too afraid to be angry. I began to understand they were frightened, intimidated. Because previously they had this false bravado. Now they were a pack surrounded with all these people screaming outside. Once they got on the bus, these people were throwing things at them. They were experimental guinea pigs of these white, liberal progressives. I saw that the blacks were victims of our prejudices the way we were victims of theirs. I saw you couldn't just judge all blacks as being one way, the same way you couldn't judge all Italians as being these knucklehead *shadrools, mongalooches* with muscles between their ears. So I got balanced.

Curtis and his father. *Mary Sliwa*

"My teacher that year was Allen Topal, the best teacher I ever had in my life. There were teachers who also boycotted, but not Allen. The teachers' union, which was led by Albert Shanker, was considered one of the most liberal, progressive unions. It was predominantly Jewish, and then all of a sudden decentralization came, with community control of the school boards, and the blacks began saying, 'We don't want any Jewish teachers in our school. We want to teach our kids Swahili, teach them black culture.' Now all of a sudden there was anti-Semitism, which came as a shock to these progressives, these liberals. They wanted to believe that people would live together, that blacks would not have the same prejudices as whites. Well, guess what? The moment the blacks had some community control, they were just as bad as the crazy Italian parents yelling 'nigger' at the black kids coming in.

"When it came time for me to go to high school, my mind was beginning to wander, and my grades were dropping. I wasn't paying attention, because all of a sudden I'm noticing a shot of leg. I was noticing the girls.

"My mom said, 'You need to go to an all-boys high.' I got into Brooklyn Prep because my sister's debate coach, a guy named John Sexton, who is now president of NYU, went to bat for me.

"The headmaster, Father Jack Alexander, said, 'Son, I'm going to do this as a favor to John Sexton, and to your mother, who obviously must really love you. But I think this is going to be a mistake. I think years from now I'm going to have to kick you out of the school.'

"It was as if he was a soothsayer. It's my senior year. We're two months from graduating, and I'm the student government president. The tradition of the school was to wear jackets and ties, but the students took a vote not to wear them, and I was one of the ringleaders. Father Jack Alexander told my parents, 'It's part of our tradition. You gotta convince Curtis not to push the envelope, or he'll be on the outside looking in.'

"I didn't believe him. This was 1972, when students were beginning to defy authority, and he is holding me responsible, and rightly so. Father Jack warned me as well. But I figured if they threw me out, the other students would walk out and support me. Also the Jesuits taught us in class that they were open and progressive, as long as you did your homework. You can debate any subject. Take any point of view. But outside of the classroom, the Jesuits are to the right of Ayatollah Khomeini. He gave me every notice in the world, and I ignored them.

"One day they put up a notice on the student bulletin board: 'Curtis Sliwa is no longer president of the student body.' I was defiant. I said, 'It's not going to stop me from organizing.' Great organizers like Saul Alinsky didn't have to be president to organize. A week later they put up another notice: 'Curtis Sliwa is no longer a student at Brooklyn Prep.'

"I was devastated. None of the other kids would come near me. They didn't walk out. There was no solidarity. I learned one thing: when you're gone, life goes on, and they forget you tomorrow.

"I went to Canarsie High, a relatively good public school, compared to the others.

It was a nice interracial mix, part Jewish, part Italian, part black, part Hispanic, but it was a zoo, an Animal House compared to what I was used to at Brooklyn Prep. Kids were taking acid. If you went into the boys' room, you could smell marijuana. As for the studies, I might as well have been back in junior high school.

"I was in French class, and the teacher, an older man, asks for the homework. I pass in mine, and these two kids give him a hard time. He tells them, 'Go to the dean's office.' They knock him down, and the poor old-timer falls back and hits his head on the side of the desk and passes out. The rest of the kids are frozen. Some are giggling, others are in their drug-induced state. I see the two guys, grab them in headlocks, and I bulldog them right into the blackboard. And I pound one of them.

"The dean came running in with his flying squad, his rapid-response team, and they see me pounding the guy's head into the blackboard, and it looks like I'm the troublemaker. They grab me, handcuff me, take me downstairs, and take me to the 69th Precinct. I'm thinking, *I got kicked out of Brooklyn Prep, and now I'm going to be arrested.* Luckily the teacher had been brought to Brookdale Hospital for a few butterfly stitches, and he told them, 'Oh no, Curtis came to my aid.' So they didn't arrest me. They sent me home.

"The next day I expected the keys to the city, an acknowledgment that I did good. Instead the dean read me the riot act. 'Your job is to let us know. No wonder they threw you out of that prestigious high school. I couldn't figure it out, and now I know. You're an asshole.'

"I thought, *You mean I should be apathetic and indifferent like the other kids?* For the next few days I was like a zombie, just showing up. Then in history class, the one class I had a little interest in, a kid gets up and starts doing a Richard Prior imitation. The kids are laughing, and the teacher is trying to get their attention and control the classroom. I picked up my books and walked out the door, walked out of the school.

"I told my mother what I had done and told her I wasn't going back."

# NOTHING STAYS THE SAME

PETER SPANAKOS

Peter Spanakos taught in the new york city public school system from 1964 until 1991, when he was offered early retirement and took it. Spanakos began his career during a time when blacks began moving into the city in large numbers, and he saw the animosity that developed between the whites and blacks. By the time he retired, he saw, much of the hatred had faded.

**PETER SPANAKOS**  "I went to New York Law School in 1960. By then I had three brothers practicing. One of my professors was Roy Cohn. He taught for one hour a week. He needed the title. He had a Cadillac limo, and the engine was always running. He taught criminal law techniques.

"Mario Biaggi, a very powerful man in the police force [Biaggi retired from the NYPD in 1965 as the most decorated cop in the country], was sitting next to me. When he got out, they made a special law for him saying he didn't have to go to college to get his law degree.

"The first day Cohn came into class, he said, 'Listen guys, no one fails in my class.' We all gave him a standing ovation. He said, 'Everyone starts with a B and up. And Mario, you don't have to worry about anything.'

The Verrazano Bridge changed the skyline of southwestern Brooklyn. *Library of Congress*

"Roy was gay, and he came down with AIDS. He was a very pleasant guy, but he was as fucked up as they come.

"I hated law school. I just hated the concept of a guy coming in, guilty as sin, and I have to make up lies and excuses to get him out of it. If you do something wrong, you should be punished. When later on I was a dean and a drug counselor in the public schools, kids would come to me and say, 'Get me out of this.'

"I'd say, 'I'm not getting you out of anything. Take your punishment like a man. Don't come looking for me to bail you out.'

"I started working in the schools in 1964 when I was still in law school. I was called an attendance teacher, but I worked as a truant officer, and then I was assigned to one of the '600' schools, which were the worst schools in the city. When they kicked you out of all the other schools, you went to a '600' school.

"I got married in 1966, and in 1967 I bought my home in Sea Gate. Then I started teaching at schools in Coney Island, because it was a shorter commute.

"When I was in high school in the 1950s, we didn't have racial conflict, because we had de facto segregation in the neighborhoods. But as the urban blight spread from neighborhoods, people were intimidated. I remember my neighbors were the first Jewish family to sell out, and then, within a year, the whole five- or six-block radius turned black. This happened in East New York, Brownsville, Bedford-Stuyvesant, areas that had good housing stock.

"Back in the '50s, in the school system we had a box for 'other' in the 'race' category. Which back then was for 'miscellaneous.' Over the years, 'other' turned out to be whites. As the whites left, they were replaced by Hispanics, who were primarily Puerto Rican, and blacks. Later on came the Cubans and Dominicans. The Verrazano Bridge opened in 1964, and whites went to Staten Island.

"The Brooklyn economy also played a role in the white flight. Red Hook had three going factories that paid very, very well in the 1950s. There was White Rock soda, a sugar factory, and a coffee factory. They couldn't fill up the jobs fast enough. I worked there during the summers in the 1950s. But then Red Hook started dying in the 1960s, and all the companies moved out. Once you lost that economic base in Red Hook, you lost a lot of people. As the city filled up the projects and made them bigger and bigger, you just intimidated more white people to leave.

"The Red Hook projects used to have a very good screening committee. If you wanted to live there you couldn't have a felon in the family. You had to have an intact family. Your kids couldn't have records. About 1966 John Lindsay, that *putz,* came in, and he wiped out all the committees. He was pushing to be the black man's representative, and, unfortunately, the instant exodus from the projects was devastating. Even the blacks didn't want to live with the blacks who came in there. They wanted to live in an integrated community. But it turned just the opposite.

"The parents felt intimidated sending their kids to the public schools, so if they wanted to stay in the city, the ones who could afford it sent them to private or parochial schools. They used to sell homes in the Catholic areas by the parish. If you had a good parish, a good parochial school, that was a big selling point for your house.

"In the 1970s we literally had to give away our home on 584 Court Street, a six-family home over the restaurant. The banks, the bastards, did what is called 'redlining.' Irrespective of the merits of your house or your credit, if the house fell into a certain area, they were not going to give you a mortgage, and insurance companies at the same time cut back. We had insurance for thirty years, never filed a claim, and they dropped us. So all these things were putting pressure on the whites to get out. The speculators did very well. Sea Gate had the same problem in the 1960s and 1970s. You didn't sell your house. You gave it away. This was a blight and a curse on a lot of neighborhoods.

"I can remember a famous black doctor in Crown Heights. He had a beautiful home on President Street. In fact, the orthodox Jews would throw rocks at him when he drove on the Shabbat. The doctor put the house up for sale, and a Jewish guy wanted to buy it. The other blacks told him, 'You're not respecting us. You're selling the fucking Jews your house.' So he sold it to a black guy for $35,000 less, and that black guy then took the contract, walked to the office next door, and he resold the house to the Jews.

"Everybody was hustling, wheeling and dealing.

"The Coney Island school I taught in was rough, because we had kids from the Coney Island projects and the Marlboro projects. I began at PS 288 on West 25th Street between Mermaid and Surf Avenues on Coney Island in 1971. I was impressed with a kid, Eric Marbury, the oldest brother of Stephon, the pro basketball player. Eric was a talented kid, and I loved him. I said, 'You're amazing. You remind me of this kid Cassius Clay.' But Eric was cursing a lot, so I called his parents in for a conference.

"I said, 'I like Eric a lot but every word is m-f. I can't tolerate it in my classroom.'

"The father got up and he said to me, 'That's what's wrong with you white guys. You don't understand how we talk at home.'

"I said, 'Sir, whatever you do at home is your business. When you come to school, it's my business. I'm telling you as a friend, he's got to cool it.' The mother, the class act of the family, a sweetheart, got up and she said to her husband, 'You shut up. Mr. Spanakos, you won't have that problem again.'

"Eric was a leader. One afternoon he was about to get involved in something he shouldn't, with a gang of kids who surrounded the both of us. I grabbed him, marched him through the group, and I took him in my car and took him to my home.

"The next day a male teacher came up to me.

"'You're a *schmuck*,' he said.

"'Why?'

"'You got involved in something you shouldn't have.'

"I said, 'When those kids were surrounding me, I saw you guys walk past me. No one helped me out, and I don't appreciate that.'

"My teacher friend said, 'Peter, look, you took this black kid home. What would have happened if the black kid told his parents you touched him?'

"I said, 'What are you talking about?' Then I thought about it. I had no authority to take him home. If he had said I had touched him, I would have been out on my ass. And that happens all the time today. Kids make up all sorts of stuff. Fortunately, Eric wasn't that type of a kid.

"In the mid-1970s I became a counselor at Seth Low Junior High School. The animosity between the blacks and the Irish and the Italians was really bad at the time.

"I told the black kids who went there, 'Look, this is the radius. You can't go more than two blocks past the school.'

"'What are you talking about?'

"'It's an Italian neighborhood,' I said. 'You're from Coney Island Avenue and Marlborough.'

"They didn't heed my warning. After a few months they got their courage up, and during lunch hour they went three blocks, and the Italian kids beat them with their bats. They were bleeding like pigs.

"I said to them, 'It's a sad commentary, but there are different parts of America, like Bensonhurst, when you're not in America. You can't walk down Avenue U. Hopefully this will change, but right now this is reality. It's how it's going to be.'

"This was a period when the city was trying to push integration, and kids from the projects were bused in. The buses had a two-car police escort, one in front, one in back.

"Today blacks freely walk up and down Avenue U. They come into the gym. They come into the school. You don't have as much ugliness today as we had back then.

"Things change. Back then the Puerto Rican mothers used to go nuts when their daughters were dating blacks. Today they date, and it isn't an issue.

"The Puerto Ricans and the Dominicans hate each other. We didn't have problems with Dominicans, because they didn't come into Brooklyn. Now we're getting Asian kids, Chinese and Korean kids, and they are forming their own little gangs. They are all wannabees, and that's an issue we're having, but we don't have the black-white racial problems we had in the 1960s and 1970s. By the 1990s it started to die off, because the city wouldn't tolerate it anymore. Because blacks came into prominence. Because of Martin Luther King. And because the Italian fathers told their sons, 'Listen, leave the *mulignans* alone. You get in more trouble than it's worth.'

Peter, left, and his twin brother, Nick Spanakos. *Courtesy of Peter Spanakos*

"The anti-Semitism also seems to be gone. I don't know if it's globalization, government, or good leadership. We don't have it the way we used to. And there's a lot of fallout from Middle East issues. They used to have a saying, 'Guns for the Irish, sneakers for the Jews.' But once the sabras turned out to be first-class fighters, everybody backed off. So that helped.

"Getting back to immigration, if you knew Bay Ridge, Eighth Avenue always was Scandinavians. What is Eighth Avenue now? Chinese. They are very tribal, and they took over everything. In Flushing you have Koreans. In Sunset Park, now it's the Chinese. No more Italiantown. It's Chinatown. The Chinese bought it all up. A lot of ethnic groups are going out while others come in. It's very New York, very Brooklyn."

# THE GUARDIAN ANGELS

CURTIS SLIWA

O NE OF THE LEADERS OF THE ITALIAN COMMUNITY'S FIGHT to protect itself from the incursion of the blacks was Joseph Colombo, the head of the Colombo crime family. Colombo started an organization called the Italian-American Civil Rights League. At its peak it was a force in the city. But according to Curtis Sliwa, it was just another way to extort money from the honest citizens. Colombo, however, became too high-profile for his own good. He was murdered during a Columbus Day celebration held fittingly at Columbus Circle. A rival, Carlo Gambino, ordered the hit.

Curtis Sliwa, the founder of the Guardian Angels, had his own run-ins with the Mob. After bad-mouthing John Gotti, he was beaten to a pulp. Later he was almost murdered, purportedly on the orders of Gotti's son. The outspoken Sliwa, who is nothing if not brave, fears for his safety every day.

**CURTIS SLIWA**   "The gangs used to say, 'We have to protect the neighborhood.' Then along came Joseph Colombo and his Italian-American Civil Rights League, and he was able to convince a whole bunch of top-level Italian-Americans in different fields to join his organization. Mario Biaggi, the most decorated police officer in the history of the department, was part of it. So was one of Mayor Lindsey's deputies. They organized.

They held meetings. They were vocal in opposition to integration. They gave the feeling of Italian-American pride. But it was false pride, fueled by the hate of others. They would say, 'The Jews get all the breaks. They're liberals. They want to let the blacks come and eat with them at their tables, and they don't realize the blacks are going to take a blackjack and hit them over the head and take all their money.' It was the time of *Guess Who's Coming to Dinner,* with Sidney Poitier. Because the impression was that the Jews were naive, weak, too gullible. Their attitude was, 'We'll join in partnership with them and teach them.' They [the Italians] made it a white pride thing without it being a KKK thing.

"Joseph Colombo was a very good spokesperson. He wasn't a Mustache Pete. He would constantly say, 'There is no such thing as organized crime, the Mafia, the Cosa Nostra.' He was able to convince Mario Puzo to remove all references to the Mafia and the Cosa Nostra from *The Godfather.*

"I would see his goons go to the stores, and they'd say, 'We're selling these decals to put on the front door to make sure people know you're a supporter of the Italian-American Civil Rights League, because we're protecting the neighborhood. The spiel would be, 'The *mulignans* are trying to make trouble trying to integrate our schools. The next thing, they are going to want to buy your house and rape your daughters.'

"Some merchants would say, 'No thank you. I belong to the Kiwanis,' or 'the Lions.' The representative, in his guinea tee, would say, 'You don't seem to understand what I am saying. We're the Italian-American Civil Rights League. Whether you're Italian or not, we're protecting white people's civil rights. So you're with us, or you're against us.' It was ominous. They were flexing their muscles. It was another way to extort money and bamboozle the public.

"Joseph Colombo was using it as a cover, a ruse, and continuing to operate high-profile as their big-time mob chieftain. Meanwhile, the head of the Old Guys, Carlo Gambino, a quiet guy but just as vicious, was living on Ocean Parkway in a very humble, two-family home. He's seeing Joseph Colombo all over the place, and he says, 'Hey, this is wrong. He's too high-profile. He's going to make it bad for us. We got judges in our pockets, politicians in our pockets, cops in our pockets. This is not good.'

"And he put out a contract on Joseph Colombo. He hired 'Crazy Joe' Gallo and his crew to do the job. 'Crazy Joe' had been in Attica, and he had befriended blacks and Hispanics, so he had an interracial crew.

"Each year Joe Colombo would hold an Italian-American Civil Rights Day gathering at the Columbus statue at Columbus Circle, near the entrance to Central Park. So Gallo knew where Colombo would be. He chose a black guy from his crew and got him AP credentials as a photographer, to get the guy near the stage, taking pictures.

"Joe Colombo, the keynote speaker, began talking, and this guy with the AP badge takes out his toolie and blasts Joe Colombo. Colombo's guys pull their weapons and 52,000 shots later the black guy is shredded like Swiss cheese, dead on arrival. The black guy, for whatever reason, has become a Jihadist, a suicide bomber, except this was death by Gambino.

"They took Joe Colombo to Roosevelt Hospital, which is right there, and he was on life support, and he was a vegetable for years and eventually died.

"The Colombo crime family figured out 'Crazy Joe' and his crew from Carroll Gardens did this. They set the wheels in motion for revenge.

"Meanwhile 'Crazy Joe' is all of a sudden hanging with the literati. The artsy-fartsy Hollyweird crowd can't get enough of him. He's wining and dining on Broadway, because he tells great stories at dinner parties. He's thinking of writing a play and a movie script. Jerry Orbach and his wife befriended Gallo. They loved his storytelling, so they'd have him to parties, and he'd entertain this crowd on the Great White Way.

"It was Gallo's forty-sixth birthday, and after going to the theater and the theater gin mill, everyone, including Jerry Orbach, his wife, and the other trendoids decided to go down to Umberto's Clam House to celebrate Joey's birthday.

"It's the wee hours of the morning, and they are having their scungilli, it's great, and Matty 'the Horse' Ionello spots him, and he drops a dime to the Colombo family and says, 'He's here.'

"A little while later two Colombo guys walk in. Joey Gallo's bodyguard was a Greek guy named Diopolis. He recognizes it's a hit, takes his gun out, but fumbles it. They blast him. They blast Joey Gallo multiple times. Jerry Orbach and the others dive for cover. They don't hurt anyone else. The Greek bodyguard and Gallo died. That was their revenge for shooting Joseph Colombo."

*Sliwa, who, like his grandfather, was an enemy of the Mob, became a minor celebrity in New York City when he began hosting a morning talk radio show on WABC, beginning in 1991. When John Gotti Sr. went on trial in 1992, Sliwa began talking about what he knew about Gotti and his henchmen, when the Teflon Don decided to get even.*

**CURTIS SLIWA** "I was broadcasting, ranting and raving against them. They took great umbrage. I was attacked with baseball bats in April. They broke my wrist and my elbow, cracked the back of my head, figured I would learn from that and shut up.

"I just came back and ratcheted it up, and on June 19, 1992, I was in the back of the cab on my way up to WABC, and what I didn't realize was they had stolen a yellow cab the night before, jerry-rigged it so once you got in you weren't going to get out, like a rolling coffin.

"There was a gunman stuffed under the dashboard next to the driver, and once I settled in the back, he popped up like a jack-in-the-box, and after saying, 'Take this, you son of a bitch,' he started firing hollow-point bullets at me.

"I tried bouncing around in the back, trying to break my way out, open the doors, which I wasn't able to do. Three bullets hit my lower extremities. I went to jump out the front window on the passenger side, and I got past the gunman but only made it halfway out. The gunman tried to pull me back in by my belt, and that's when the driver smashed me into parked cars. I fell out, and I guess they figured there was no way I could survive. But luckily I did."

*John Gotti Jr. was charged with kidnapping, assault, and attempted murder of Curtis Sliwa. After three hung juries, federal prosecutors gave up. Sliwa, as fearless as his grandfather, continues to speak his mind on his early morning radio show on WABC. His life's journey is one more incredible Brooklyn tale.*

*After the teenage Curtis Sliwa told his parents he wasn't returning to Canarsie High to get his diploma, his father informed him that he would have to pay them $70 a week room and* *board if he wasn't going to go to school. Sliwa would then embark on a journey taking him from Brooklyn to Manhattan to the Bronx, which would years later lead him to found the Guardian Angels, a citizens group dedicated to keeping the city safe from crime. It would take almost fifteen years from its founding for the group to gain legitimacy under the law-and-order regime of Mayor Rudy Giuliani. Today there are more than forty chapters of the Guardian Angels in seven countries around the world.*

**CURTIS SLIWA** "I didn't want to go back to school, and so I looked for work. I passed Rocky's Shell station, corner of Seaview Avenue and Rockaway Parkway in Canarsie right before you get on the Belt Parkway. It's a rough gas station because it's open all night, and it's been robbed a few times. There was a HELP WANTED sign in the window. Rocky was in the back in the mechanic's bay. He had a see-through mirror, because Rocky had done some time upstate in a federal prison for counterfeiting, and I'll bet you he was still counterfeiting back there.

"Rocky came out and said, 'What do you want, kid?' I told him I wanted to be the night manager.

"'What do you know about running a service station?' I BS-ed him, and for some reason he hired me.

"I worked seven nights a week, and after taxes I had $118. Then when an A&P supermarket opened up right next to the 69th Precinct on Foster Avenue and Rockaway Parkway, one of these huge box stores, I got a job with the night crew. It was a union job with benefits and much better pay and working conditions.

"I was a management trainee, and I eventually became the key man, the sergeant, and I had a crew of twelve guys, all my father's age, hard-core union guys, and it was our job to get the store packed out for the next day's business.

"I moved to Brownsville, which was considered totally whacked out. I moved into *moolieland*, a place you would never go. All blacks. No whites, and I married a black woman, one of my friend's sisters. After I'd been living there awhile, A&P started closing stores, and I was fired.

"I opened the Sunday *Daily News* to the want ads. An ad said, 'Nighttime managers wanted, McDonald's, the Bronx.' I got on the number 2 subway line—the

Beast—and took it to White Plains Road in the Bronx for an interview. I showed the guy hiring me my scrapbook, with all my accomplishments. The guy says to me, 'Kid, you're not competing for a Rhodes scholarship. We got a security problem in the stores. We gotta have people who can run a store in a tough neighborhood.'

"I was living in Brownsville. I said, 'This is music to my ears. Where do I sign?'

"I was trained at the store at White Plains Road, Allerton Avenue, near the Pelham Parkway, by a guy named Marvin Barnes. This guy was a great teacher. They never sent me to Hamburger University, because I would have been an embarrassment to them, so what I learned I learned from Marvin.

"'The art of being a good manager is not to be behind the grill making the hamburgers or the coffee or the Egg McMuffins. The best manager is the person who can come in the morning, put the key in the door, make sure everything is up and running, get in the car, ride around, come back, and at the very end of the night look in, ask everyone how things are going, look at the paperwork, sign off on it, lock the door, and go home,' he said. 'Then you're a good manager, because you have trained your staff.'

"I went to work at the McDonald's on White Plains Road. The guy who trained me at night was named Don Chin. At six-two, three hundred pounds, Don was massive. He was so atypical of a McDonald's manager. He had been a member of the Savage Skulls street gang. And he had a split personality. There was Don Chin the Good, the friend who I could confide in. And then there was Don Chin the Psychotic, who would stand down to no man, no group of men. He drove a Harley, had a machete, and wore steel-tipped combat boots. This guy was a warrior. But he also loved being a McDonald's manager, and he knew how to run McDonald's by the book. He also knew you couldn't run it that way, because this wasn't the neighborhood of *Leave It to Beaver* or *Father Knows Best*.

"He sat me down and he said, 'Curtis, you could do it their way, the book way. At five o'clock Marvin Barnes is out of here. He don't want to be here after five. 'Cause the only things open late at night is the all-night liquor store with the bulletproof glass with the guard who looks like he had steroids with his Wheaties. And McDonaldland.

"'We have no protection. It's me and the crew. You do not hire someone for his ability to make Macs, fries, and strawberry shakes. You hire someone for his ability to back you up when you have to jump over the counter, because you will, and if you don't jump over the counter and deal with a disturbance, they will turn on you.'

"He showed me his hiring techniques.

"'I notice you don't have a job history the last two years,' he'd say.

"'I've been away.'

"'I know you weren't at CYO summer camp,' Don would say. 'What prison were you in?'

"And the guy didn't want to say anything.

"''Fess up,' Don would say. 'What prison were you in?'

"'I was in Schuylkill.'

"'You want to work. If I jump over this counter and I have to deal with some guys, will you cover my back?'

"'I'll give it a try.' And Don'd hire him.

"McDonald's was as traditionally mainline as you can get, and he was hiring the rejects of the neighborhood for backup, and some would accommodate, and some wouldn't, and he'd get rid of those. But he'd give all these guys a chance.

"Don said to me, 'You can do it their way and you may not survive, or you can do it the Don Chin way and not only survive but have a crew that will back you up.' It was obvious what I was going to do.

"I increasingly got better and better at it.

"Meanwhile, I was still living in the Brownsville part of Brooklyn. It was 1975, and it had suddenly become Crooklyn. Brownsville was tougher than tough. We had an expression, 'From the Ville, never ran, never will.' Tenement buildings were burning down. The projects were a factory of criminal activity. There were gangs like the Jolly Stompers and the Tomahawks, vicious, bad. And the subways, the veins and arteries of the city, what everyone had to use to travel, were becoming *very* dangerous.

"I liked being futuristic, coming up with solutions. I had an idea that if private citizens banded together and patrolled the subways, everyone would be a lot safer. I bounced it off a few of my friends. They looked at me like I was *cucamonga*.

Don Chin and Curtis Sliwa in front of an A train on one of their first Guardian Angel patrols. *Courtesy of Curtis Sliwa*

"I parked my idea, and when I got up to the Bronx, it was just as bad if not worse. The number 2 train had to go through the South Bronx, and I would see the burned-out buildings, the gangbangers, and the feel of hopelessness and despair. It was worse than Brownsville, and people had tried everything, with no remedies. Jimmy Carter had shown up on a pile of rubble in the South Bronx on Charlotte Street when he was running for president. He said, 'I will rebuild the South Bronx.' And nobody believed him. And guess what, he never did. Until I met Don Chin, every person I bounced my subway patrol idea off of said the same thing, 'You're crazy, man. You'll get killed.'

"Don Chin didn't think it was crazy. He said, 'Man, this is the kind of crazy I like.' At the time the big movies were *Taxi Driver, Death Wish, Buford Pusser, Walking Tall*. Don was living vicariously through this thing. His one reservation was that if I did it, I ought to carry a weapon. Because Don always had a weapon on him.

"I was still living in Brooklyn, and so in the wee hours of the morning Don and I would take the number 4 train—what the riders called 'the Muggers' Express'—back home to Brownsville. I would sit in the rear car dressed as a McDonald's manager, with the jacket, with the M stamped all over the tie and the socks, reading a copy of the *New York Times*. I had my boom box next to me. What I was doing was baiting the thugs. This would be like throwing a chunk of meat into a sea of piranhas, because when the sun went down, there were very few cops around on the subways. These thugs would come rolling through the subway cars in posses of eight, ten, or twelve. When they saw me, it was like they had just seen an ATM and they knew the PIN number. They thought it was too good to be true. Or they thought I was a cop and it was a setup.

"They would come over to talk to me, and I would fake I was fearful or a little naive. I'd look up, and there would be three guys with one tooth in their mouths and bad breath, looking like they were about to strangle the life out of me.

"Meantime Don Chin, in another car, was dressed like a biker with a bandana around his head, and as soon as he saw these guys surround me and start to do their dance, he would come charging through the car.

"He would let out a banshee wail, and when they turned around, they would have an Ex-Lax attack. They would be so terrified they would try to run through the side of the car. I'm adept at the martial arts, and as soon as they turned their backs on me, I would start taking them out. We'd have them sucking concrete, and sometimes we would pull the emergency cord to signal the conductor to get the cops. The police would finally roll in, see me dressed as a McDonald's manager, see Don in his biker outfit, see the guys sucking concrete, and they'd figure we were undercover DTs.

Curtis Sliwa on patrol.
*Courtesy of Curtis Sliwa*

"We'd tell them, 'No, we're citizens.'

"'What the hell do you think you're doing?'

"'We just made a citizen's arrest.'

"'What the hell is that?' We would have to go to the precinct to explain it. Obviously the brass knew you could do that, but they tried to put the fear of God into us, trying to discourage us from doing that.

"The problem with the way we were doing it was that nobody knew who we were, so we weren't acting as a deterrent. Secondly, Don carried a weapon, and I knew it was only a matter of time before he would use it. We went different ways.

The Guardian Angels is an international organization today, with chapters in eleven countries and more than one hundred cities. *Brad Guice*

Then I had to retool, rethink: *How was I going to do this?* It took me months and months to come up with the visual deterrent of the red beret, the T-shirt, and the red jacket.

"The first patrol of thirteen were members of my closing crew at McDonald's. It wasn't easy to recruit them. A lot of white guys were too cool and they didn't want to do it for nothing. 'I ain't working with no black and Hispanic guys without getting paid. Are you crazy?' The black guys would look at me and say, 'Farrakhan says you white devils can't be trusted.' The Hispanic guys were the ones who glommed onto the idea, because they were into group things by nature. They formed the biggest gangs. They had the biggest car clubs, the biggest social clubs. They had ten thousand cousins. So they were into joining me, even though they were skeptical.

"'We're going to get killed. We have no weapons. We're dealing with Uzi-toting, dope-sucking psychopathic killing machines.'

"But they were men's men, and I kept testing their machismo. 'This could be your mom who's being mugged,' I'd say. 'Think of it. Maybe she's on the number 4 train right now. Who is going to stand up and protect her? Everyone else will act like they don't see what is happening to her.'

"'No one is going to do this to my mom.'

"We launched our first patrol on February 13, 1979. We were on the number

4 train, the Muggers' Express, between 161st Street, Yankee Stadium, up north to the last stop. We stood two different shifts, from eight at night to four in the morning.

"I continued to work my night job, and stand guard on patrol. I got very little sleep. Ever since I began delivering the *Daily News* when I was a teenager, I had a belief system: 'There will be plenty of time to sleep when you're dead.' Plus, when you like what you're doing, you're jazzed up and motivated.

"It wasn't until 1993 that we were accepted by City Hall and the police. Until then, I was arrested seventy-six times. I had all sorts of harassment from the cops. Sometimes I was arrested for breathing air or not being at room temperature.

"It wasn't until Rudy Giuliani was elected mayor on a law-and-order platform, where public safety was the key, that we were accepted. Giuliani rewrote the book on how the police were to work with the Guardian Angels. From then on he ordered all city agencies, including the police, to work with us the way they would with any block watch, crime watch, or any other citizens organization. And that changed the whole tone, because it had a trickle-down effect.

"Since 1979, when we first started to patrol, we easily made four thousand arrests in New York City. Some were for serious offenses, like murder, attempted murder, rape, armed robbery, and armed assault."

*Curtis Sliwa today splits his time between talk radio on WABC and his work as the guiding spirit to the Guardian Angels. After John Gotti Jr.'s first trial ended in a hung jury, in September of 2005, he became convinced Gotti would make another attempt on his life.*

**CURTIS SLIWA**    "I am a dead man walking. I fear for my safety every day. But one thing I know for sure: John Gotti Jr. will still be able to see me like George Washington on the $1 bill, my red beret on my head. It will be like I'm surrounded by neon, because these colors do not run.

"I will not go away. I will take every opportunity I get to tell him he can't run and he can't hide. The U.S. government has assured me that it is going after round two on the very same charges. I intend to be around for that trial."

G. Segal

The trial was held in September of 2006, and again there was a hung jury. There was hard evidence Gotti's men had tried to kill Sliwa all right, but to convict Gotti Jr., the government had to prove that Gotti Jr. was a member of the Mob at the time of the attempted rubout. Imagine the surprise when no one stepped forward to testify to that effect. The jurors were sure Gotti had planned it, but without any evidence they couldn't bring themselves to convict him. Curtis Sliwa continues to look behind him wherever he goes.

# KING OF THE TRA-LA-LAS

NEIL SEDAKA

**H**AVING TASTED SUCCESS AS A SONGWRITER, NEIL SEDAKA embarked on a career as a performer, and he hit it big between 1958 and 1963 until the British invasion virtually put him out of business. In the early 1970s he moved to London, where he was still extremely popular, and he was befriended by a British pop artist by the name of Elton John. The two collaborated on an album, *Sedaka's Back,* propelling the king of the tra-la-las back into the spotlight. Today he travels the world playing concerts. After fifty years in the business, Sedaka's popularity continues unabated.

Sedaka's big break as a recording artist for RCA came in 1958 with "The Diary." But Sedaka found out quickly how fickle the music business could be. His next hit was called "I Go Ape," a Jerry Lee Lewis–like piano-thumping piece that Sedaka was sure would showcase his versatility. It flopped. He recorded another song, "Crying My Heart Out for You," which also flopped. Sedaka feared that RCA would drop him if he didn't have another hit, and so he decided to study up on what made a hit record. An avid reader of *Billboard* magazine, he turned to the page that included the "Hits of the World," and he made it his business to buy the number one records from England, France, Germany, and other countries. One song was "M'Lord" by French chanteuse Edith Piaf. Another was "Little Darlin'" by The Diamonds. He analyzed the drum beat, the lyrical contents, the chords, and where the harmonies changed. He also noticed that a lot of the songs contained the names of girls. He had been enamored of Carole King while he was in high school, so he decided he and Howie Greenfield would write a song called "Oh! Carol."

*Courtesy of Neil Sedaka Music*

Sedaka wrote the tune, took it to Greenfield, and Howie Greenfield wrote the lyrics in twenty minutes. It began, "Oh Carol, I am but a fool. I love you, though you treat me cruel."

**NEIL SEDAKA** "Howie was a perfectionist. He was a polisher. He loved Lorenz Hart. When he was finished, I said to him, 'This is very home-spun. It's very layman. The lyric is very natural.'

"He said, 'I can't let it go as it is.' I took the paper away from him. I said, 'I'm going to record it like this.' Against his will. I even highlighted the lyric in the middle. I had a recitation of his lyric. He wanted to die.

"In the middle of the session, I decided I needed some kind of chorus, and we didn't have any singers in the studio. But four high school students who were friends of the producer were watching. I asked them, 'Can you carry a tune?' They said they could, and I invited them in. I taught them, and they did a good job, and behold, 3 million copies! I still have the chart where 'Oh! Carol' appeared in the top three of every country in the world.

"And RCA didn't drop me, of course. And I had ten records in a row that were in the top ten."

*One of those hits was a single called "Calendar Girl." It's so catchy that once you start singing it, you can never get it out of your head.*

**NEIL SEDAKA** "Howie and I were looking at a *TV Guide*. We saw an old movie named *Calendar Girl*. We thought it would be a great idea for a song. I was inspired by singers and their records, and there was a record at the time called 'Personality,' by Lloyd Price. It went,

"'Cause you got—ch, ch—personality . . .' I heard the beat, boom-a-chicky, boom-a-chicky, a shuffle beat, and I said, 'That's a very good beat,' and I said to Howie, 'Let's start with the months of the year.'

"I called it a sandwich song, which became a trademark of mine. It started with a piece of bread—'I love, I love, I love my calendar girl . . .' Then the meat of the song—'You start the year off fine.' And it ended with the same piece of bread—'I love, I love, I love my calendar girl.' It was a trademark for some of my other songs, including 'Stairway to Heaven' [*not* the Led Zeppelin rock anthem], 'Little Devil,' 'Breaking Up Is Hard to Do,' and 'Next Door to an Angel.'

"We were riding high. The writing was getting better and better. We wanted to write a perennial. I said to Howie, 'We're so hot we could write a birthday song, and it would be a hit.' And so we wrote 'Happy Birthday Sweet Sixteen.' Once again there was the sandwich.

"I also began recording multiple voices, because I loved listening to Patti Page and Les Paul and Mary Ford, who often had multiple voices on their songs. And loving harmony and parts singing for The Tokens, I would sing harmony with myself. I was the first in rock and roll to use multiple voices on his records. 'Happy Birthday Sweet Sixteen' was one of those songs. There were three Neils singing in 'Breaking Up Is Hard to Do.' There were three Neils in 'Next Door to an Angel.' I was becoming the king of the doo-be-doos and the tra-la-las."

*Sedaka wanted to perform live, but Al Nevins and Don Kirshner didn't think he was polished enough to tour in America. They decided he could best improve his stage act by going abroad.*

**NEIL SEDAKA** "They put me in little clubs in Brooklyn. There was the Club Elegante on Ocean Parkway, the Merrick Town and Country, another club in Sheepshead Bay. But as a performer I was a novice. I wasn't very good. So what did they do? They didn't want me flopping on the stage, for fear my record sales would stop, so they booked me in the Philippine Islands, booked me in Rio de Janeiro, booked me in Italy, so I could learn my craft singing far away and it wouldn't affect the American buying public.

"When I went to Rio, little did I know that 'Oh! Carol' was the national anthem. It had been playing number one in so many countries. My father and I went to Rio before jets. We took a propeller plane, and it took hours. When I got off the plane in Rio, I saw there were thousands of people on the airstrip. I thought, *Somebody on this plane must be very famous.* It was me.

"I learned to sing in five languages, and I became a top American singer in Australia, Japan, South America, and Italy. I came back to America a seasoned performer. I was bigger overseas than I was in America.

"In New York I became friends with all the top DJs. I grew up with Cousin Brucie at 370 Ocean Parkway. He was married to the beautiful Susan Morrow. We were social friends. We went to Palisades Park together. We had our children at the same time, and we went to Coney Island with the kids together. We were very close.

"I knew Alan Freed very well. Alan was always a little on the toughie side, a little on the greasy side, and I was a washed-face, peaches-and-cream type. I was a little intimidated by him. But he played my songs. And I knew Murray the K, who was a friend of Bobby Darin's. I played the Brooklyn Paramount, where Murray the K, Alan Freed, and Cozy Cole were the hosts. Brenda Lee and Bobby Rydell were on the bill, and I had to appear after Bo Diddley, and he was impossible to follow. Suzanne Pleshette's father was the manager of the Brooklyn Paramount, and I went to his office and I said, 'Mr. Pleshette, I can't follow Bo Diddley. He's too strong.' Bo had a homemade guitar, and he used to knock people over with his sound. I said to myself, 'Maybe he'll break his leg,' and that afternoon that's exactly what happened, and I didn't have to follow him."

*Most pop singers have short careers. Most are one-hit wonders. Five years of success is a rarity, and so when in 1964 The Beatles landed in America with their hit "I Want to Hold Your Hand," followed by The Rolling Stones, The Dave Clark Five, The Who, The Animals, Jerry and The Pacemakers, Herman's Hermits, and The Kinks—it was indeed a British invasion— Sedaka and most American recording artists discovered that their record sales had died.*

**NEIL SEDAKA**   "It was a natural five-year progression of hits. I thought that was it. It had happened to the Everly Brothers, to Brenda Lee, and to Fats Domino. My five years were about up, and then with this new English influx, I knew it was over."

The Brooklyn Paramount was the place to be in the early days of rock and roll.

*Fortunately for Sedaka, he could still write songs for other performers.*

**NEIL SEDAKA** "I was able to write for other people, which brought in $30,000 to $40,000 a year. Howie and I wrote a song called 'Amarillo' and one called 'Working on a Groovy Thing,' for The Fifth Dimension. We wrote 'Puppet Man' for Tom Jones. I also went to Australia once a year for six weeks. They held on to me and liked me, and I made $60,000 to $70,000 a year, not *schlef,* doing that. It was a good time to take stock of myself and raise a family."

*Sedaka should have been wealthy, but the music business didn't work that way.*

**NEIL SEDAKA** "Aldon Music had the publishing rights. I got the rights as the singer and composer. In those days a lot of things were going on behind my back. I was thrilled to be on the radio and have top ten records. Little did I know that Nevins and Kirshner were getting $100,000 a year as my record producers, and their publishing royalties were very healthy. So yeah, 'Stupid Cupid' brought in $40,000, and 'Calendar Girl' brought me $50,000, and that was a substantial amount, but nothing compared to what Al Nevins and Don Kirshner were making. Then they sold Aldon Music to Screen Gems for a couple million dollars."

*Sedaka, though married, was never far from the control of his mother. She decided where he would live. And then she decided that Neil should entrust his money to her lover, a guy named Benny, who, with Neil's mother's help, pissed most of it away.*

**NEIL SEDAKA** "I was a momma's boy. Yes. She wanted me near her. She picked out the apartment. We lived across the street from each other.

"And then my mother started to manage me. Should I go into this? My mother was before her time. She had a lover for thirty years with my father's full knowledge. My father, who was thrifty and cheap, accepted it, because Benny, her lover, would buy her jewels and furs. Little did I know that I was paying for them. My wife, Leba, and I were put on a small salary. We couldn't buy toilet paper without Eleanor and Ben's approval. My father was a sweet guy, but he was rather passive. And she had Benny for thirty years, until she died. And my father was fine. They were in love with each other, and he accepted it. But she had spent all my money.

"I discovered that in 1962, and in 1963 my career started to go down. Benny was an air-conditioning salesman, and my mother wanted him to be my manager. Whatever my mother said, I did. But when the English bands started taking over and my career started downhill, I said to my mother, 'I think I'm going to leave Ben.' And she was so devastated I was leaving Ben, she took an overdose of sleeping pills. I discovered her on the floor. We rushed her to the Coney Island Hospital. We didn't speak for a few months, but we got over it. Benny continued to see my mother, but he was no longer my manager. Leba and I took back control."

*By 1972 Sedaka's career was dead in the water. His agent, Dick Fox of the William Morrow Agency, suggested he go live in England, where he and other American rock pioneers like Gene Pitney and Jerry Lee Lewis were still very popular. Sedaka, along with his wife and kids, rented an apartment in London, and he started playing the small, workingmen's clubs, such as the Wookie Hollow in Liverpool and the Golden Garter in Manchester.*

*Frustrated, Sedaka determined he needed to find another lyricist, someone who was more poetic, who painted pictures, who was more evasive and elusive, and he hooked up with Phil Cody at Screen Gems. It was a perfect match. Sedaka and Cody wrote "Solitaire" (which later became a big hit by The Carpenters), "Bad Blood," and "Laughter in the Rain."*

*While in England, Sedaka discovered a group called Hotlegs. They were working a small club, and their manager came to Sedaka and asked him if he would be willing to help on an album they were making. He went to Stockport, England, and he began working with this group that changed its name to 10cc. They wound up collaborating on two full albums. Among the songs he wrote for the group was "Solitaire" and "The Tra La La Days Are Over." His new songs, including "Laughter in the Rain," "Love Will Keep Us Together," "Bad Blood," "That's Where the Music Takes Me," and "Standing on the Inside" showed a maturity that helped make 10cc a hit in England in the early 1970s.*

*Sedaka had become friendly with Maurice Gibbs of The Bee Gees, and he also met a young British rocker by the name of Elton John, a huge star and a big Sedaka fan. John asked Sedaka if he could come over and listen to the album 10cc had made with Neil.*

**NEIL SEDAKA**   "He had funny clothes on and funny glasses and high-heeled shoes. He said, 'I know all your records, and I'd love to hear them.' I played them and some of the new ones. Elton said, 'These could be a hit in America. You're as good as Carole King.' Carole had just made *Tapestry* [the biggest-selling album in history up to that time]. I just thought he was talking off the top of his head. But during that time we had a party at my flat, and he and John Reed, his manager, said, 'Would you consider us signing you to a record contract? We're starting a label in America called Rocket Records.' I said, 'Wow.' Elton John was the biggest rock singer in the world. I said, 'If you write the liner notes saying I'm a genius, yeah, I'll do it.'"

Neil and Elton John worked together with great success in the 1970s.
*Courtesy of Neil Sedaka Music*

*And that's what he did. Late in 1974 he put out a record called* Sedaka's Back. *Half the songs were recorded with 10cc in England, and half were recorded at the Santa Monica Boulevard Studio. Elton put it out, promoted it, and it became a gold album.*

*When "Laughter in the Rain" and* Sedaka's Back *hit, Sedaka was signed to a management contract by Elliot Abbott, who was also managing the Carpenters, Karen and her brother Richard. The deal was that Sedaka would open for The Carpenters on their six-month tour.*

**NEIL SEDAKA**   "It was a great show. I did the opening forty-five minutes, and The Carpenters closed, and at the end we did some duets together. The one problem was I stole the show. I got more applause. Karen was marvelous, but she sounded exactly like her records,

Neil Sedaka was honored by the borough of Brooklyn and Borough President Howard Golden.

*Courtesy of Neil Sedaka Music*

where I jumped and danced and kicked, and when I was done, the audience cheered until they were exhausted.

"In the middle of our tour in Vegas Richard came to me and said, 'You're fired.' I said, 'Why?' During one of our shows I had introduced Dick Clark, Paul Anka, and Tom Jones in the audience, and Richard said to me, 'The star attraction has the distinction of introducing celebrities in the audience.'"

*Richard Carpenter couldn't stand that Sedaka was stealing the show.*

**NEIL SEDAKA**   "Alan Carr, the publicist, may God rest his soul, said to me, 'Neil, you call a press conference and you tell them the real reason you were fired.' And I did, and six months later Elliot Abbott signed me as a headliner at the Riviera Hotel in Las Vegas. That was the start of my second career.

Neil Sedaka today. *Courtesy of Fadil Berisha*

"After 'Laughter in the Rain' and *Sedaka's Back,* I went from making $60,000 a year to making $6 million a year. That one song, the one album. Then I had a hit record with my daughter Dara, called 'Should Have Never Let You Go.' And then I started doing the talk shows on television. I was on Merv Griffin, Mike Douglas, Johnny Carson, Dinah Shore, Tony Orlando, and Sonny and Cher. People could now put a face to the voice. My goodness, they saw a little, short guy with a plump face and a beautiful voice with beautiful songs. And that did it.

"I was given an award in Los Angeles by the New York Alumni Association. Every year they honor someone, and the person they honored in 2006 was me. John Voight and Lou Gossett Jr., who went to Lincoln High School, spoke.

"We never forget where we come from, and we appreciate what happened to us. I worked very hard. It didn't happen overnight. There's something special about coming from Brooklyn, because we had to show people we could make it. If you weren't a baseball player or a football player, you had to show them how you could do it. And I had a gift, and I never forgot what I came from."

# THE NIGHT THE LIGHTS WENT OUT. AGAIN.

ABRAM HALL

AT 8:37 P.M. ON THE SWELTERING NIGHT OF JULY 13, 1977, lightning struck an electrical substation on the Hudson River, tripping two circuit breakers in Westchester County. A second bolt hit the nuclear power plant at Indian Point. Two other major transmission lines became overloaded, and Con Edison was in deep trouble. After two more lightning strikes, by nine thirty the three power lines whose job it was to supplement the city's power were overtaxed and in serious trouble. When Big Allis, the biggest generator in New York City, shut down, all the lights and energy of New York City went with it. Though Con Ed said the blackout was an act of God, Mayor Abe Beame, leading a city beset by financial woes, was scathing in his rebuke.

Air-conditioners went silent. Elevators stopped. Broadway went dark. Traffic lights went out. New Yorkers couldn't watch TV, or listen to the news unless they had a battery-powered transistor radio. Those with flashlights or candles who owned books read. Many went on a looting rampage.

This was a whole lot different from what happened on November 9, 1965, when there was a blackout of the entire Northeast. Then, an area from New York all the way north to Canada lay in darkness. During the 1965 blackout, residents milled about outside their apartments on a cool fall evening, trying to enjoy themselves for the most part. This time it was scary different. In the twelve years that followed, the City of New York had nearly gone bankrupt. Unemployment was dangerously high.

John Lindsay had been a congressman from the Silk Stocking District of Manhattan, who had helped draft the 1964 Civil Rights Act. A liberal Republican, he all but disowned his party.

He was forty-three years old, handsome, had gone to Yale, served in the navy during World War II, and graduated from Yale Law School. He was elected to Congress from Manhattan's Upper East Side in 1958.

In 1965 Lindsay won the election for mayor in an upset. It was expected he would restore pride to the city, but he turned out to be one of the more disastrous mayors in the city's history. Hours after he was sworn in, the transit workers went on strike and were out for twelve days, shutting down the subway for the first time in history. His attempt at community control of the schools led to a bitter fight between black community leaders and Jewish teachers. For two months teachers went on work stoppages. When it was over, the alliance forged by blacks and Jews in New York had ended.

Lindsay won reelection anyway, some say riding on the coattails of the 1969 Mets' unlikely World Series victory. During his second term, comptroller Abe Beame warned him that he was way over budget, but Lindsay could not bring himself to cut services. Instead, he borrowed. Bankruptcy loomed.

When his successor, the sixty-seven-year-old Beame, took office in January of 1974, Lindsay had left the city awash in $1.5 billion worth of debts. Beame, as Lindsay's comptroller, knew what he was getting into, but he stoically took the job anyway. A year later Beame was forced by the banks to freeze all municipal hiring. Then he became a villain when he laid off a couple of thousand city workers, infuriating the unions. In April 1975, Standard and Poors suspended trading in the city's bonds. In danger were city pensions, subsidized public transportation, rent-controlled apartments, and free higher education. Republican president Gerald Ford had no sympathy for the city. He refused to provide any federal aid. The headline in the New York *Daily News* read: FORD TO CITY: DROP DEAD.

Beame was in a box. During the summer of 1975 he had no choice but to fire 38,000 city workers, including 5,000 cops. New York's Finest picketed. When sanitation workers walked off the job, the city began to smell. After Beame closed twenty-six firehouses, enraged citizens protested. Thirteen thousand public school teachers were fired. A graduate of City College, Abe Beame ignominiously ended free tuition at New York's public colleges after 139 years.

Library branches and public hospitals closed. New York City was slowly dying.

After the firing of five thousand policemen, crime began to rise dramatically as the city became less and less able to deal with the growing social and economic problems of the poor. In the 1970s, arson became commonplace in poor neighborhoods, such as Bushwick, as landlords, unable to toss out deadbeat tenants, set the buildings on fire to collect the insurance. Some derogatorily called the practice "Jewish lightning." Vandals also set fires for the fun of it. Entire blocks were burned, one building at a time. As they burned, crime rose. Drug dealing became commonplace.

This time, when a blackout occurred, looters and vandals struck thirty-one neighborhoods across the city, including every poor neighborhood in the five boroughs. Stores in Alphabet City—in the East Village—in Manhattan were looted. East Harlem was pillaged. So was the Upper West Side. The Bronx was hit hard too.

The most damage occurred in Brooklyn. Areas affected included Crown Heights, Sunset Park, Williamsburg, Brownsville, and Flatbush. More than seven hundred stores in Brooklyn were looted or damaged.

Bushwick was hit worst of all. Ten years earlier it had been a middle-class white community, but between 1973 and 1976 the city had lost 340,000 jobs, and white flight to the suburbs accelerated. Black middle-class families moved in, but jobs were hard to find, and when they left, Bushwick became inundated by welfare families, some who had been "temporarily" relocated from East New York and Brownsville as part of a Model Cities program. One problem: the new housing promised was never built.

In 1976 there was more criminal activity in Bushwick's 83rd Precinct than in any other district in central Brooklyn. Meanwhile, racial tension was growing. Almost all the cops in the 83rd Precinct were white, and most of the residents Hispanic or black, although some Italians still lived along its western border.

On the night of July 13, 1977, Bushwick was populated by a lot of poor people who were angry and frustrated. Temperatures were still in the high nineties. Water levels were dangerously low.

Shortly after the lights went out that night, enveloping the entire city in darkness, the residents of Bushwick vented their anger as thousands, sensing the opportunity, rushed from their sweltering apartments toward the shops on Broadway. Because of the cutbacks, there

When New York's second blackout occurred in July 1977, many of Brooklyn's black neighborhoods were decimated by looting. Bushwick was particularly hard-hit. *AP Photo*

were exactly thirty-four police officers on duty in an area of a hundred thousand residents. Off-duty policemen rushed to the scene, but without help from other precincts, the men of the 83rd were woefully outnumbered.

Professional criminals sawed off locks or used crowbars to open steel shutters. They stole tow trucks, then used the tow hooks to pull off storefront gates. Next came the shattering of glass followed by the wholesale looting of jewelry, electronics, and furniture stores. After the professional criminals struck first, alienated adolescents and those motivated by "abject greed" followed in profusion. When many store owners heard about the looting, they rushed back to their stores toting guns—most always too late. When the cops didn't arrive on time to prevent looters from taking guns and ammo from John and Al's, a sporting goods store, the situation became even more dangerous.

That night not one single cop from another precinct was sent to help the members of the 83rd.

After the expensive shops and the shoe stores were emptied, the looters next set their sights on the grocery stores and bodegas. After five hours, there was little left to steal. What came next was the burning of Bushwick. Two blocks of Broadway were on fire at one point. When firemen came to put out the fires, residents threw rocks, bottles, and other objects at them.

When dawn timidly arrived, broken glass, mannequin parts, litter, and soot-blackened water covered the area. By the morning, thirty blocks of Broadway were damaged or destroyed, forty-five stores had been looted and torched. More than twenty fires still burned the next morning.

In all, 1,600 stores in New York City were looted or damaged and 3,776 people arrested, the largest mass arrest in the city's history.

Despite the estimated $300 million dollars in losses, Jimmy Carter, who had run for president on a platform of promising to help New York, refused to declare the city a disaster area, using the excuse that it was not a *natural* disaster. As a result, the city was denied federal funds. Mayor Beame, whose endorsement of Carter helped him win the election, was bitter. Carter never even made a token visit. The looting gave whites more ammunition to hate and fear blacks.

The power didn't come back on until 10:39 P.M. the next day.

Abram Hall was living in Bushwick at the time. The night of the blackout of 1977, he says, accelerated the downward spiral from which Bushwick is still trying to recover.

**ABRAM HALL** "I was born on March 10, 1962, in St. Mary's Hospital in Brownsville. My daddy was from Riegelwood, North Carolina, which was originally called Carver's Creek, and then it got a little bit more segregated, so they changed the part where the blacks lived to Riegelwood. My daddy died when I was only three years old. Everything I know about him was told to me by my mother and her brother and sisters.

"My daddy was a favorite son. He was the leader of the family in a lot of ways, after my grandfather, who was a bit of a patriarch. My grandfather had a farm. He started out with one wife and one bull, and he built it into a pretty big farm, and even though he had my dad and ten or twelve sisters, every one of them went to college, including my dad. He went to a community college on a basket-

Abram's father. *Courtesy of Abram Hall*

ball scholarship in 1945, and then he went into the army, and he was posted in Nuremberg, Germany, in 1945, and he stayed in Germany for five years. He didn't want to come home, because North Carolina was so racist.

"Eventually my grandfather got him to come home. He went to the Red Cross and told them he hadn't seen his boy in five years, and so they contacted the army and got him transferred back home. I didn't think Daddy was too pleased about that.

"But I guess it worked out for the best because he got transferred back home, went to Washington, DC, and met my mother. She was from Rockfish, Virginia. If you watched *The Waltons* on TV, that's where the show took place. Rockfish is a real

Abram's mother, Daisy Hall.
*Courtesy of Abram Hall*

place in Nelson County, Virginia. My mother knew Earl Hamner [author of the novel *Spencer's Mountain,* which became the basis for *The Waltons*] when they grew up. He lived on one side of the road, and she lived on the other. The thing is, back in the 1940s, there was only one high school, and only white people were allowed to go. My grandmother wanted my mother and her sisters to get an education, so she sent my mother to stay with her sister in Washington, DC. My aunt had a boardinghouse, and my mother stayed with her while she got a degree from a technical high school not far from Howard University.

"My mother became a Washington Senators fan, while my dad became a Brooklyn Dodgers fan, because my uncle still tells me all the people down there in North Carolina all became Dodger fans when Jackie Robinson joined the team. To this day most of my dad's family will root for National League teams. My aunt Ernestine, who lived in Brooklyn before retiring down there, will always root for the Dodgers, unless they are playing the Mets.

"Most of my relatives from my dad's side of the family came to New York because that's where the jobs were. My mom and daddy came to Brooklyn in 1957. They came to Brooklyn because it was more affordable than Manhattan and less racist than Queens. I'm not saying it wasn't racist. It was *less* racist. My aunt Ernestine and my

Abram's second-grade class photo shows the changing demographics of Bushwick. *Courtesy of Abram Hall*

aunt Waddy owned a house in Brownsville about two blocks off Eastern Parkway, and by the mid-1960s things had gotten so bad she moved out to Springfield Gardens, where they burned a cross on her lawn. But their attitude was, 'We're staying,' and they did. But you had to be careful.

"My parents first moved to Patchin Avenue in Bed-Stuy. I went to PS 274, the Kosciuszko School. It's on Bushwick Avenue, one block from Broadway, which served as a dividing line between Bedford-Stuyvesant and Bushwick. We eventually moved into a three-family house on Himrod Street in Bushwick. That's where I grew up.

"Bushwick was originally settled by the Dutch. And starting around Cooper Street, we had breweries, Rheingold, Shaeffer, and when we were kids we'd go on tours. Some of the large houses in Bushwick had been owned by the brewery owners.

"I went to Amsterdam a few years ago, and the construction and architecture of those houses were exactly the same as the one we were living in. We lived in what they call a railroad flat. You go in and walk straight through all the way to the back. We had a pretty backyard.

"We rented the third floor from a Mrs. Sumter. She used to keep a lot of foster kids. One of them, a guy named Gene, had a little dog, maybe two feet long, named Sputnik. He was the friendliest dog, but he would kill sparrows and rats, and my little sister Patricia was afraid of him.

"When I was growing up it was one of the most beautiful neighborhoods in Brooklyn. There were pretty tree-lined streets, a true bedroom community. Bushwick Avenue was closed to commercial traffic. Bushwick had been predominantly working-class German, Dutch, Italian, and some Irish, and we were the first black family to move in. Next door we had this one girl, Rose Marie, a little bit older than me, but younger than my sister Rita. Her grandmother loved me. She gave me candy and comic books. But I discovered as I got older and began to understand things that a lot of the people weren't so pleased to see us. My mother was deeply involved in the Bushwick Neighborhood Council, the block association—in a different lifetime she would have been a politician. Ma was a compulsive joiner. She explained to me later that after Daddy had died she needed to keep busy.

"There came a time when more and more white families moved out and more and more black and Puerto Rican families moved in. Our church, which was on the corner of Bushwick Avenue and Himrod Street, started out as a predominantly white church, and then as years went by more and more of them left, and it became more and more a predominantly black church.

"It became more dangerous. We didn't lock our doors during the day until 1970 or so. Hard crimes started coming in. Hard drugs started coming. And then in July of 1977 we had a blackout.

"I remember it so clearly. I was fifteen in 1977, and I had a summer job at the church. I had returned home and night had fallen, and I was sitting in my sister Rita's room looking out onto the street and listening to WCBS radio. I was reading *The Once and Future King* when the lights went out.

"My mother was worried because Rita was going to New York City Tech, which is in downtown Brooklyn. Mrs. Sumter was going to pick her up, but something was wrong with her car, and she couldn't go. There wasn't much she could have done, because the traffic lights were out, and there was no way to get down there really.

"And as time went on, this went from, 'Oh wow, this is fun,' to where you started saying, 'Hmmm, there's something wrong here.' It was eerie. You started hearing noises. That's what I remember most, the sounds, the noise. It was no longer pleasant. Something had gone wrong.

"People were running up and down the streets with bags and boxes, and you heard the sounds of windows being broken. At a certain point you didn't want to be outside, because this was bad. You heard the noises, and you could see the police cars racing up and down Bushwick Avenue. Around eleven, I could see these guys in a station wagon with all this stuff like box springs and mattresses strapped to the top of their car pulling a tight turn with the cops chasing after them, and the cops pulled them over, and they had a spotlight on their car, and the guys were resisting and they had guns. A lot of people started screaming and yelling. Some people threw something at the cops, and this one cop swung around, and he had his gun out, and he said, 'If you don't get back in your fucking houses right now . . .' My older sister pulled me down from the window.

"The rest of the night we heard things. I heard someone who was walking down Broadway saying, 'They've wrecked Broadway.'

"Broadway was our shopping center. It was a strip that went all the way from Jamaica Avenue to the Williamsburg Bridge. If we had to, we'd go down to Fulton Street and go to A&S or May's or Korvettes. But Broadway was our main shopping center. As the night went on, I could hear the vandalism. Looting was going on in the stores, and police were fighting with the looters.

"The next morning it was like a storm had passed. Finally I went out to take a walk on Broadway, and it was horrible, nothing but the crunching and tinkling of broken glass. Broadway had been destroyed. Lakin's Department Store was wrecked. The supermarkets had been ransacked. All the little shops too. My mother had bought a guitar from a music shop, and the store was destroyed. A toy store. The Sunset Shop. It was as though a bomb had hit them.

"To this day I don't get why there was so much vandalism. I suppose at the beginning it was, 'Ha ha ha, freebies.' And then it took on a life of its own, when the professional criminals came in. But Bushwick was in transition, and right after that a lot of arson hit Bushwick, people collecting insurance money. I also heard from one of the elders of my church, a white woman, essentially my godmother, she worked in a bank on Gates Avenue, and she told me point-blank, 'I'll never forgive the SOB in the 81st Precinct.' That was the precinct on the other side of the J train. She said when the looting started, the captain of the 83rd Precinct, in Bushwick, begged the captain of the 81st Precinct to give him some of his men, and the captain of the 81st Precinct refused to give them to him. How was it that Knickerbocker Avenue, which was predominantly white, was protected, and how come our area of commerce was just destroyed? If you do the math, you know the answer. And after that night, our neighborhood was never the same again. The blackout of 1977 was *the* dividing line. There was no going back after that. That was it. After that I felt danger walking out my front door. Not every minute of the day, not every day, but it was there often enough. Drugs began to take over, and street crime rose. I had to deal with bullies. I had to deal with people trying to rob me. Mrs. Sumter's mother was mugged I don't know how many times. She was an old woman. Houses were always being broken into. Cars were being stolen. I wondered, *How bad can it get?* Pretty bad.

"I didn't move until after my mother died in 1986. She died the day before her birthday, of a heart attack. My mother had been a teacher for a while, but she developed a heart condition, and she had to retire. Before she died, she was telling me about how she was getting strange phone calls. She'd pick up the phone, and the person at the other end of the line would hang up.

"She died on a Saturday, and her sisters came over and stayed with me. The strange phone calls continued. We went out to the funeral home on Utica Avenue on Tuesday to make arrangements for the funeral. My cousin gave my aunts a lift, and on the way home there was a traffic jam, and they got out to walk the last block, and they surprised guys who were robbing our house. I'm glad I didn't see them. They had smashed down the door, and when my sisters walked in on them, they ran across the roof. They had stolen pretty much everything of value, except for a few things they didn't have time to pack up. And I was furious, because my mother was dead, and they had stolen the last Christmas gift my mother had given me.

"Even after the robbery, the strange phone calls continued. Rita said, 'They're calling to see if anyone's home so they can break in again.' On the day of the funeral I left my uncle Bert to watch the house. He'd been a commander in Vietnam, and he and a couple of his lodge brothers kept watch. They did try to break in, and he apologized to me that he didn't catch them, but I'm glad he didn't. I was afraid of what might have happened.

"But after the funeral my sisters said, 'You have to leave.' I didn't want to go. I didn't want to leave my house. But they said, 'People are calling at strange times. They're breaking in. How can you stay?' So I moved to Manhattan to live with my sister Rita. I lived there for two years. Then I moved back to Brooklyn."

Abram Hall today in front of his old house at 48 Himrod Street.
*Courtesy of Abram Hall*

PART FIVE

# The 1980s and 1990s

# WHITES MOVE BACK

HARRY SCHWEITZER

**W**ITH THE CITY SLOWLY DYING, BROOKLYN-BORN GOVERNOR Hugh Carey, who was elected in 1974, and his banker friends came riding to the rescue. Felix Rohatyn, the managing director of the investment bank Lazard Frères, was put in charge of overseeing the city's finances. Rohatyn sold bonds through the Municipal Assistance Corporation. New York City was saved by the bankers.

When Mayor Beame ran for reelection in the fall of 1977, his opponents were two Jews, a black, and an Italian. Congressman Ed Koch and congresswoman and feminist Bella Abzug were the Jews, Manhattan Borough President Percy Sutton was the black, and New York Secretary of State Mario Cuomo was the Italian.

Koch, who had defeated longtime Democratic power broker Carmine DeSapio for the position of district leader back in the early 1960s, was backed by the *Village Voice*. Koch had marched on Washington and had performed pro bono legal work for the ACLU in Mississippi during his August 1965 vacation. In 1968 he won Mayor Lindsay's congressional seat. His ultimate goal always was to become mayor of New York.

Koch had one problem. He lived in Greenwich Village, had never married, and didn't date. He needed voters to think he wasn't gay, so David Garth, his image consultant, paired him with Bess Meyerson, the first Jewish Miss America and chairperson of the Koch campaign.

Despite the city's financial woes, Beame—the city's first Jewish mayor—might have been reelected had it not been for the rioting on the night of the blackout. After that happened, there was a backlash against blacks and Latinos, destroying any chance for Percy Sutton and for Mario Cuomo, who was campaigning against the death penalty. Koch won voters with a law-and-order approach. When talking about the riots, he would lace his speeches with the question, "Why wasn't the National Guard called out?"

During this time serial killer David Berkowitz, the Son of Sam, was caught, and Koch ran on a platform calling for the death penalty. Liberals were spitting mad, but the riots had changed the mood of the city. When Koch opposed busing, the liberals were beside themselves. With the support of Australian newspaper magnate Rupert Murdoch and his formerly liberal *New York Post,* Koch won a runoff election over Cuomo in a landslide. Koch, whose hero was Fiorello LaGuardia, became the people's mayor. He began to rebuild the city, to reshape its image. Under Koch's leadership, New York crawled back from the depths.

Between 1973 and 1975, 300,000 Jewish voters had moved out of New York City. In the 1980s they slowly began moving back, lured by housing that was cheaper than what you could get in Manhattan and was still just a subway ride away. Harry Schweitzer was one of the young professionals who moved into Brooklyn. After growing up in Bensonhurst, he had moved to Queens and then Manhattan. He settled in Park Slope in 1984, and he has lived there ever since.

**HARRY SCHWEITZER** "I had gotten married very young, at age twenty-four. I was working at Citibank, and I was married to a very nice young woman, Jeanie Goldstein, and when we got married, I moved away to Queens. I lived there until 1980.

"I got divorced, and for a brief time I moved to Forest Hills, and then I met a woman, a California girl by the name of Diane Simon. We moved to the city, and I lived in the city from 1982 to 1984, and in the interim we got married and we had my oldest daughter. We were subletting on the Upper West Side, when the person we were subletting from told us he needed the apartment for himself. At that point Diane said, 'We ought to look in Brooklyn.'

"I said to her, 'Brooklyn? Why do you want to move to Brooklyn?'

"She said, 'You know the neighborhoods.'

"I said, 'Yeeesh.'

"We started hunting for an apartment in Brooklyn, though I was not necessarily for it. She suggested we first look in Fort Greene. I said, 'Suuuuure. I'll take you to Fort Greene. I remember it very well.' We started driving around Brooklyn Tech up and down a couple of blocks, and it wasn't looking anywhere near what Spike Lee has it looking like today. It was seedy and dangerous.

"I said, 'What do you think?'

"She said, 'How about Park Slope?'

"Now Park Slope was never known as a Jewish neighborhood—ever. There was one area of Park Slope on Prospect Park West near Grand Army Plaza on the park, which was called Doctors Row, but it was never known as a Jewish neighborhood.

"Park Slope was never known as upper-class. It wasn't even middle-class. It was more of a working-class area, a lot of longshoremen, dock workers. Along Seventh Avenue there was a string of bars up and down the street.

"In the 1970s the city was on its ass, and Mayor Koch made it imperative that if you worked for the city as a teacher, a cop, a fireman, you had to live in the city. What happened, a lot of people started moving to these close-in areas of Brooklyn where the housing stock was pretty decent—nice brownstones—all SROs [single-room-occupancy hotels—basically rooming houses]. But it would take a while to see the changes.

"We drove down Seventh Avenue, and in those days it didn't look anything like what it looks like now. It looked like Dresden after the bombing.

"The apartments had gone by the by. The landlords, saddled with rent control and crime, abandoned them. The area had a heavy Latino population and was gang-infested. It was drug-infested.

"As we drove along Seventh Avenue, we came to the corner of Seventh and 12th Street, and there was this factory-looking building with a banner on a pole saying, CO-OPS AVAILABLE. My wife said, 'Stop.'

"I said, 'What?'

"She said, 'I want to go in there.'

"I said, 'Why?'

"She said, 'Let's go in.'

"Well, we went in, and inside, the building had been all rehabbed. It looked very European. It had a quadrangle courtyard, a third-of-an-acre grassy area. It had a fountain. And patio decks. It was to die for.

"We walked in, and we said, 'We need a three-bedroom.' The Realtor said, 'We have two available, and one is under contract.' We didn't want the other one, and when the contract fell through on the other, we bought it. Thirteen-foot ceilings. Hardwood floors. It wasn't cheap. We paid $151,000, which in 1984 was a lot of money.

"I came in with 10 percent down. I had $5,000 from a life insurance policy. I borrowed $5,000 from my dad, and I borrowed $5,000 from Diane's dad. And we moved in.

"The neighborhood was dead, scary dead. It was eerily quiet at night. I had to walk Diane home from her job. We were only three blocks from the subway, but it was frightening enough. You could get drugs on any corner: marijuana, heroin. Whatever you needed, you could get. We used to see drug paraphernalia on the streets. We would have a rash of car break-ins. That was endemic.

"My mother had been very proud that I had moved to the City. She would say to me, 'I can always say my son lives in the City.' It was a big thing to her. After we bought the co-op, my mother called me on the phone all upset.

"She said, 'Why did you move to Brooklyn? Why do you want to live in Brooklyn? I hated living in Brooklyn! Why are you moving back? You were so excited when you lived in the City!'

"I said, 'Ma, wait till you see this place.'

"I went to meet her at the front door, and she came in, and I gave her the treatment through the hallway into the courtyard. Her mouth dropped. This is a gorgeous place. And when she walked into the apartment—we have 1,600 square feet. 'Where do you get that in Manhattan?' I asked her. She said, 'Beautiful. But still, why in Brooklyn?'

"But it was the best move I ever made. The Park Slope neighborhood had so much going for it, and little by little the word got out that Park Slope was really where it was happening, so we started getting throngs of people.

"Park Slope had a number of things going for it that a lot of other neighborhoods didn't. At the time it had affordability. From the late 1970s through 1987, when the stock market crashed, the housing was affordable for people like myself, yuppies, boomers, who wanted to live close to the city but who couldn't afford to live there, people who couldn't swing $2,800 a month or didn't want to pay $151,000 for a one-bedroom apartment. For that money I was getting three bedrooms. It was three blocks from the subway. I could be in New York in a half an hour. And I had a neighborhood, a candy store. I could walk with a carriage. I had Prospect Park two blocks away. This was amazing.

"At first the nice thing about my building was that everybody was like me, pocket-poor. No twelve-figure bonuses. And we had one of everything. We had cross-dressers, we had black/whites, we had green/yellow, everything in the building, and it was the friendliest place. It was a co-op in the true sense of the word. And I was president of the co-op for two and a half years starting in 1985, until I separated from Diane, and that was it. She left. She was itching to move.

"I said, 'You want to move, move. I'm keeping the place.' Eventually we worked it out. She was from California. She was never much interested in staying here. My first mortgage was a variable. I had no idea I was going to stay as long as I did. The neighborhood is amazing.

"The area is no longer affordable. The Brooklyn real estate market has kept its own. We're seeing a little softening, but not much. My apartment right now is probably worth $1.2 million. Somewhere in that range.

"The co-op is still very family-oriented. We started getting people from out of town, people who had gotten jobs in the city. In our building we have a lot of people who relocated from the Midwest, the South, Texas. And the people who moved into the building in the last eight, ten years are coming in with buckets of cash. They have a certain sense of entitlement we didn't have. Young kids, very nice people, but they think the co-op should be providing. What was the Kennedy line about asking not what your country can do for you? They want to know, 'What can the co-op do for us?'"

# A MARINE GUARDS THE PEACE

RICHARD GREEN

THROUGH THE 1960S, THE ALLIANCE BETWEEN BLACKS AND Jews held strong. But with the emergence of the Black Panther movement with its assertion of Black Power, the ties that bound the two groups began to untangle. Jews had flocked to the South to help their black brethren in the Movement, but now blacks like Malcolm X and other leaders were slapping the Jews, who had supported them, in the face, telling them that their help no longer was needed or wanted.

There was a real fallout from this rejection as these Jews made the survival of Israel a more important cause than the civil rights movement. For many Jews, keeping Israel strong against Arab aggression turned Democrats into Republicans. When that happened, the old alliance crumbled.

In 1991 Crown Heights was a home to approximately 50 percent Caribbean immigrants, 40 percent African-Americans, and 10 percent Jews. A small but influential group of Jews were members of the Lubavitcher community, a sect of ultraconservatives led by the esteemed Rebbe Menachem Mendel Schneerson, whom his followers believed to be the long-promised Messiah.

In the late afternoon of August 19, 1991, a three-car motorcade bringing the rebbe back from a visit to his father-in-law's grave came driving through a Crown Heights intersection. The last car in the motorcade, a station wagon driven by twenty-two-year old Yosef Lifsh, may or may not have been speeding and may or may not have driven through a red light, but what is certain is that he had to swerve to avoid a collision at the intersection of Eastern Parkway and Utica Avenue, and he lost control and drove onto the sidewalk, where he ran over two seven-year-old black children from Guyana who were pinned under his car.

As hundreds of black onlookers gathered, a Hatzolah ambulance—part of an Orthodox Jewish volunteer ambulance corps—stopped to offer assistance, but drove off upon the appearance of the city's EMS ambulance, prompting rumors that the Jewish ambulance had refused to provide service to the black children. Lifsh got out of his car and went to see if he could help the kids, and when he did so, he was robbed and beaten by black bystanders. Police hustled him off, and false rumors began to spread that he was drunk. When the police refused to charge him with a criminal offense, word spread that he had gotten away with something, more "proof" that the Jews of Crown Heights received preferential treatment over the blacks. The death that evening of one of the children, seven-year-old Gavin Cato, fanned the flames of resentment.

That evening around eleven, black youths began throwing bottles and rocks. Someone shouted, "Let's go to Kingston Avenue and get a Jew." In some of the ugliest racial violence, let alone anti-Semitism, ever seen in Brooklyn, black youths began a three-day rampage, burning police cars, looting, beating people, and screaming "Heil Hitler!" and "Kill the Jews!"

A twenty-nine-year-old rabbinical student from Australia, Yankel Rosenbaum, was in the wrong place at the wrong time when he was accosted by several black youths. He was stabbed several times and suffered a fractured skull. He would later die in Kings County Hospital.

The anger directed at the Hasidic community burned hot. At Gavin Cato's funeral, the Reverend Al Sharpton told the mourners, "If the Jews want to get it on, tell them to pin their yarmulkes back and come over to my house."

Sharpton would go on to criticize Mayor David Dinkins, calling him an "Uncle Tom." The Hasidic community blasted Dinkins for not calling out the police immediately. Former mayor Ed Koch called the riot a pogrom, hearkening back to the czar's Cossacks burning the shtetls of Russia in the late nineteenth and early twentieth century. For three days the rioting went on unabated. The police also lashed out against him, and when Dinkins ran for reelection in 1993, he was defeated handily by law-and-order candidate Rudy Giuliani.

What Crown Heights needed badly was someone who could bridge the chasm left between the black and Hasidic communities. It fell to an ex-marine Vietnam vet by the name of Richard Green, a man who believed in the goodness of all people, who was sure if he could somehow establish communication between the blacks, the Jews, and the police, that the hatreds and resentments would lessen and perhaps even disappear. That he succeeded says a lot about the goodness found in Brooklyn.

Green, who started the Crown Heights Youth Collective in 1978, was born on February 26, 1948, in Honduras. His father was a merchant seaman, and his mother was a nurse. In 1957 she decided to move to the States, and after a short stay in San Antonio, Texas, she came to Brooklyn to live near her sister. Richard was nine years old when he arrived in Brooklyn.

**RICHARD GREEN** "We moved into an apartment at 289 Kingston Street in the heart of Crown Heights. It was right across the street from Lubavitcher headquarters. The neighborhood was primarily Jewish. If you went to the other side of St. John's, it began to become more black.

"I went to PS 167 through the fifth grade. Then we moved a little farther up to Midwood Street, and I went to PS 92 in the sixth grade. Both of the schools were predominantly black and Jewish, but very well integrated. The students pretty much got along, though in PS 92 there was a larger mix of Italian and Irish students. You had a large number of ethnics to deal with, and each one had its own spirit, and you had to learn how to get along with their spirit. But basically we got along very well.

"The Hasidim, the orthodox Jews, sent their kids to the yeshivas, private schools. The big yeshiva was at the corner of Church Avenue and Bedford. I went to Lefferts Junior High School, and from there I went to Walt Whitman High School, and I graduated from Erasmus Hall High in June 1966.

"I started Brooklyn College in the fall, and then I got my draft notice, and in December of 1966 I enlisted in the military. I went to Vietnam in April of 1968, on the day Dr. King was assassinated."

*For African-Americans of Green's generation, the assassination of Dr. King was the third in a series of assassinations that left the black community mourning the demise of inspiration and leadership. Dr. King seemed to be the key to ending Jim Crow. Now he was dead. Was there no way out from racism?*

**RICHARD GREEN**   "First came the assassination of President Kennedy, and then Malcolm, and then Dr. King. Coming out of the 1950s, John Kennedy was the best thing that ever could have happened to this world. When Kennedy ran, I was twelve years old, and I was really, really excited about him. And when he was assassinated, that was a real damper. And when Malcolm was assassinated, I said, 'Oh my goodness, that means you're not supposed to speak up, that anything you say will be held against you.' And when Dr. King was killed, that really shook me up, because Dr. King wasn't a political leader, wasn't a president. He was a real church minister.

"When we got to Vietnam, we wondered, *What's going on back home?* Dr. King had been a change factor. We asked ourselves, *Now what? When we go back home is it going to be worse than when we came? Are we going to have to leave Vietnam and go home and have to deal with home?*

"We were discriminated against in Vietnam by the Vietnamese. Yeah. They would call you a nigger in a minute. If you made them mad and they wanted to get your attention, they used the n-word. I don't think they knew the volatility of it. That was something you never wanted to hear.

"And there was still a level of racism in the military. The military was still getting over it. Remember, we had only been integrated in the military for twenty years.

"I served in the Marine Corps, a small organization. And what Vietnam did was thrust a lot of people together. It was good, because you met guys from other parts of the country—the guy who slept in the bunk above me was from Alabama. I was from New York. And he caught malaria, and I had to take care of him. He was so sick he couldn't even get out of his bunk. Before he arrived in Vietnam, he might have been a racist, but as he lay there, I was the one who would go and bring him food, and I was the one telling him, 'Man, you gotta get out of here. You have to see a corpsman.' He had lost a whole lot of weight. Finally they medevaced him out, and I never saw him again.

"That was the thing about Vietnam: you got to be close with guys, and it wasn't based on their ethnicity. If you got close to a guy, he became your friend. Sometimes white, sometimes black, sometimes Latino, sometimes Native American. They were your friends. My best friend was Bobby Farrell from Chicago, and another [white] friend was from Kentucky. No matter what race they were, your friend was your friend. Whatever preconceived notions they had about you ended then. And vice versa.

"We went on patrols together. Sometimes I would sleep, and they would stay awake. My life was in their hands, or their lives were in my hands.

"Vietnam wasn't very nice. Innocent people got killed. Anytime you have a war with civilians involved there are going to be civilian casualties. I can remember one guy who had been shot already and who didn't want to go back into the field asked me to break his trigger finger. I started to pull it back, but I just couldn't put him in that kind of pain.

"I was in Vietnam thirteen months. I still had eighteen left. I was an MP in Norfolk, Virginia. By that time I had a little rank. I was a sergeant, and there were a hundred and some guys under me. By 1969 the racism had started to loosen up. The riots were over, and people began to see after Woodstock that love would supersede all the hatred.

"I stayed in Virginia, went to school at Norfolk State College, and then my brother told me to come up to Marist College in upstate New York. He was going there, and he wanted me to check it out. One time I came home on leave, and I went up there and liked it, and I graduated from there in 1974. I then went to graduate school at New Paltz and got out in 1977 having majored in history.

"I started to look around for work as a teacher, but there had been layoffs, so I went to work at Brooklyn College as a counselor. I had always had a desire to start a youth community initiative, so after a semester I left and came out to Crown Heights to work for another youth group and after six months I started my own group called the Crown Heights Youth Collective. It was for all age groups, and it specialized in school programs, sports, job development, and counseling. The idea was to get our young people directed and redirected.

"Our first challenge came after the Michael Griffith incident in 1986. He was coming back from a job in Howard Beach, and he was chased onto the highway [by a group of white teens], and he was struck by a car and killed. White guys in Howard Beach wanted to know what he was doing out there.

"I knew the Griffith family, a really beautiful family. They didn't allow it to get too carried away. They kept it pretty much controlled. They didn't allow it to go into that continuous back and forth, tit for tat. His mother was a very conscientious person, and she managed to minimize the hatred."

*Mayor Ed Koch was jumpy. He was aware of a series of race riots in Brixton, a suburb south of London, England. Unemployment of black youths in Brixton was at about 50 percent when in 1981 two policemen stopped a black youth who had been knifed, and spontaneously hundreds of onlookers began to riot. Fueling the hatred for the police was a campaign called Operation Swamp 81. Police had swooped down on the black community and stopped and frisked large numbers of black youths. The rioting was ugly, and it would pop up sporadically again in 1985.*

**RICHARD GREEN** "Mayor Koch really took precautions to make sure that wouldn't happen in New York City. For many years I ran a youth employment agency. We had been given a summer allotment to employ five hundred youths. After Brixton, Koch brought us in for a meeting, and he gave us money for another four hundred slots. We hired them to do everything from child-care work to sports in the parks, hospital jobs, and day-care centers."

*As the 1980s came to an end, an ugly incident arose in 1989 that incited the racial passions of all of New York. Four black teenagers were beaten by twenty to thirty whites in Bensonhurst. One of the white Bensonhurst residents shot and killed a sixteen-year-old black youth by the name of Yusef Hawkins. The Reverend Al Sharpton led marches in Bensonhurst, and the whites who came to heckle were vicious in their behavior toward the black protesters. Screaming "Nigger go home," some whites held watermelons to mock the demonstrators. In May of 1990, when one of the two leaders of the white mob was acquitted of the most serious charges, Sharp-*

*ton led another protest through Bensonhurst. A resident, Michael Riccardi, tried to kill Sharpton, stabbing him in the chest. Eight months later came the Crown Heights riots.*

**RICHARD GREEN** "Mayor Dinkins realized that one of the biggest problems facing black youths was a lack of jobs. In June of 1991 he initiated a job-training program called Safe Street, Safe City. Dinkins hired five thousand new cops, and he ordered five thousand youths to be trained as leaders. He put together a serious thirty-day citywide youth leadership initiative, and those youths who hit the streets in Crown Heights were part of his new group, called Street Outreach Program.

"At that time violence was high. The streets were tough. In one of those years there were 2,400 homicides. The thinking was these trainees would go out in the neighborhood and talk to their peers in an effort to stop the shootings. And we were part of the Street Outreach Program. And when the Crown Heights riot struck, we were able to hit the streets on the very first night or two of the violence."

*By August 1991, discord between the black and Hasidic communities had been brewing for a long time. Blacks felt that the orthodox Jews received preferential treatment from the government. Housing was an issue, and blacks felt more Jews had access to it than they did. The Hasidim had started what is called the Lubavitcher Security Patrol, and while they played their role as block watchers, there were ugly incidents. The blacks saw the security patrol as racist.*

*After Gavin Cato died, blacks went looking for revenge. It wasn't but a few hours later that a group of black teens isolated a Lubavitcher student from Australia, Yankel Rosenbaum, and stabbed him to death. Richard Green, who had hoped to become a bridge between the two communities, could only stand by helplessly and watch as rioting escalated.*

**RICHARD GREEN** "There was a lack of communication that night. Gavin Cato needed a city ambulance, which provided advanced trauma care. The Hasidic ambulance only provided basic care. The cop at the scene, who was black, knew this, and he told the Hasidic ambulance corps, 'Don't even stop.' And that fed the misperception in the black community that the Jewish ambulance wouldn't stop for the young black

Crown Heights residents rioted for days in 1991 as tensions flared between blacks and Hasidic Jews.
*AP Photo/David Burns*

male. The word never got out that the reason was the Jewish ambulance crew would have done more harm than good because they lacked training.

"It was nine thirty when Yankel Rosenbaum, the rabbinical student from Australia, came down the block into trouble. This young man was just an innocent bystander. He fit the profile. He probably hadn't even heard about the Cato incident. Had he known, he would have walked the other way. But he was new to Brooklyn, and he didn't understand the dynamics of the situation, so he walked right into it.

"He was stabbed, and he was taken to Kings County Hospital, and for some reason they weren't able to recognize the wound had been much deeper than they thought, and he died.

"That very first night I was called out, and the Hasidic youths were just as animated and active and angry as the black youths. Even before word of Yankel's death, there had been minor skirmishes in the streets. Action, reaction.

"But because of the Street Outreach Program, after two or three days we were able to get the Hasidic youths and the black youths to sit around a table and talk. On the first night of the riots, Mayor Dinkins asked me, 'What would be a good place for people to meet?' I suggested PS 167, my old elementary school, because it was easily accessible to both the black and Hasidic communities. It became the headquarters for everyone, including the cops.

"Through these meetings, the tensions were defused rather quickly. One of the good things that happened, something people probably will never understand, was that Dinkins didn't send in the heavy hand of the cops the very first day. We lost some property, and there were minor injuries but no bodies. His not sending in the heavy hand of the law allowed for a compromise to settle it, and the people who were yelling and shouting the loudest soon were ignored by the people who were not. But if a couple of folks had been shot or beaten by the cops, those people would have left and gone over to the other side. So that was the best thing that could happen. By Thursday, when the cops decided to go full-force, the incident was almost over. All that remained were skirmishes."

*Dinkins lost his bid for reelection in 1993, seen by the whites as weak and ineffective. The man who replaced him, Rudolph Giuliani—a former federal prosecutor who was tough on the Mafia—brought with him a law-and-order philosophy. Richard Green, who has been a mediator between the police and the community, saw the benefits of the new philosophy for the community, as well as the negatives.*

**RICHARD GREEN** "Mayor Giuliani used the 'broken-window theory.' If there's a broken window in a building and you don't fix it, soon there will be two broken windows, and after that it will become an abandoned building. His thing was to fix the broken window right away. He went to war against graffiti and the squeegee guys. Remember the squeegee guys? And his philosophy was if I pick up enough youths causing trouble enough times and get them into my data system, when they really mess up and do the big thing, I have them in my system and I can go after them. And so under Giuliani there was a lot more interaction between the police and the community. The cops were doing a lot more stop-and-frisks. They were going after drug users. It came across that the cops were in your face, which they were, and there were a lot of arrests.

"As a result there was a lot of resentment in the black community. Everyone knew someone who was arrested, and the resentment was deep.

"The Crown Heights Youth Collective had good relationships with precinct commanders and borough commanders, and we would talk to them about what they were doing and how they were doing it. We would discuss with them issues relating to making a stop. Once the stop is over, there is a certain protocol that has to be used. A commander must be able to tell the cop that if he stops someone and finds nothing, a strong apology does not detract from his or her status. We remind the cop that he or she may never see that person again, but it's likely someone not part of the stop-and-frisk might walk away with a bad taste in their mouth about policing, and they'll react the next time they are in a situation.

"We use different methods to bring cops to our meetings, to teach them things. We would bring the cops and the members of the community together, people in the community who really cared, and the cops came to see that everyone who was being arrested wasn't riffraff, that a lot of times a cop would think he was riffraff just because he looked the part or she looked the part. In a sense, this was racism without racists, because a lot of time they were just being cops, being who they are. Like one cop said to me, 'We are a service organization. We service the criminal community.' And in an inner-city precinct, the majority of the people he services will be black or Latino."


*The relationship between the cops and the community was tested several times after reports of violence by white cops against blacks. Each time, Richard Green and his organization took steps to ease tensions.*

*On August 9, 1997, a Haitian immigrant by the name of Abner Louima was arrested outside Club Rendez-Vous, an East Flatbush nightclub. There was an altercation, and a policeman from the 70th Precinct was punched. The cops thought Louima did it, and he was arrested.*

*On the ride to the station he was beaten by fists, nightsticks, and police radios. At the station he was strip-searched. The beatings continued, and he was sodomized with the handle of a toilet plunger so badly he needed several operations. One of the cops reportedly told him,*

*"It's now Giuliani time," meaning that after four years of Mayor Dinkins keeping the police under constraint, now it was their turn. Officer Justin Volpe responsible was sentenced to thirty years in prison, and Louima won a judgment of $8.75 million against the City of New York.*

**RICHARD GREEN**   "After the Louima incident, the Haitian community wanted to march across the Brooklyn Bridge, and we were able to get that set up. Almost fifty thousand people marched down to City Hall. We were able to get the Manhattan South borough commander to sit down with the Haitian leadership. That's the kind of thing I can do. I have a good relationship with the community, and I broker marriages between the cops and the community to get them to sit down and talk. When Bill Clinton was president, he would invite me down to Washington to talk to the police chiefs around the country just to get them some methodology how to deal with the community and the cops."

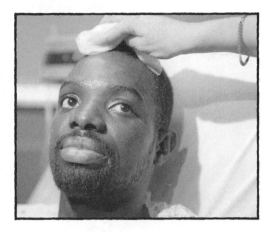

Abner Louima in the hospital after being tortured by police from the 70th Precinct.
*AP Photo/Todd Plitt, Pool*

*The next incident that caused public outrage occurred in the Bronx on February 4, 1999. A twenty-three-year-old Guinean immigrant by the name of Amadou Diallo, in the United States to study computer science, was stopped by four plainclothes policemen. He was stopped because he matched the description of a serial rapist.*

*Ordered to stop, Diallo reached into his jacket pocket to get his wallet so he could show the police his identification. As he reached into his jacket, the four policemen shot him forty-one times. His parents were paid $3 million by the City of New York, and because of the Diallo case, the Street Crime unit was disbanded in April 2002.*

*Through all of this, Crown Heights remained calm. Those who know are convinced that the work of Richard Green played an important role in keeping everything quiet.*

CORE members walking down Fort Hamilton Parkway en route to the March on Washington. *AP Photo/Bebeto Matthews*

**RICHARD GREEN**    "We had been doing a lot of things with the precinct and borough commanders, getting things back on track before an incident went any further. On the surface, if something happened it seemed that violence might break out, but we had meetings and got people together to keep everything calm.

"After the Diallo shooting, we brought in Street Crime cops to talk with members of the community. I had developed a relationship with the commanding officer of the Street Crime unit. We had met a few times to talk about how we could bring his cops, who were viewed in a real negative way, to the community to show that all the street crime cops weren't like the four cops responsible for the shooting. We also tried to impress on the community that the four cops hadn't been malicious in their actions, but more or less made unprofessional decisions."

*Meanwhile, Green's efforts to keep the black and Hasidic communities in close contact with each other have paid off handsomely.*

**RICHARD GREEN**    "Today there is much more understanding between the black and Hasidic communities than ever. We have the opportunity now to communicate. We have technology—cell phones and e-mail—so if there's an incident in Crown Heights, if something is said or something happens, I get a call on my cell phone and I get over there, and the best thing to do—I remember this from Vietnam—they always used to tell us, 'If you ever get captured, make sure you try to escape as soon as you get captured. As soon as you know you're in captivity, go all out to escape because one, you're still near your lines, and two, you're not yet in a captive mode. I use the same technique when we deal with issues. It's best to get on it right away, when it's happening. Don't wait a few hours, because if you do, people are going to have their own notions. We're not in control of it anymore. We're in the hands of the rabble-rousers and the riffraff who have beef with the cops that has nothing to do with civil or human rights. A cop might have arrested him for drugs, and this is an opportunity for him to get back at cops in general. So we want to keep it out of their hands and also the hands of the media saying what they want to say to sell the best six-o'clock headlines. We have to keep it close to our lines. So if something goes down right now,

I get out there when it first is happening. Sometimes we're out there before the police lines are even set up. And we get it rolling in our direction. If there's an allegation of someone getting beat down, we want to find out who was responsible, and if the person responsible was malicious, he's going to be as maligned as the person he beat down."

*One source of tension between the black and Hasidic communities has been the Hasidic street patrols. At times they go too far. Green is always available as a neutral advisor and mediator.*

**RICHARD GREEN** "We sit down with the Hasidic leaders and talk all the time. If something happens, I'll get a call, even late at night, and they'll ask if I can come by and check it out. Very likely I can talk to the people in the black community. They know my face. I let them know, 'We're going to make sure your rights are protected.'

"We have to make sure the [Hasidic patrol] understands the rules of engagement, that you can't just take a citizen and crack him over the head because he is alleged to have done something. You can't beat someone up for breaking into a building. That's wrong. And folks know that. When the patrol goes out, they are less likely to hurt somebody if there's an arrest being made. I've gotten a phone call: 'We know the bike is stolen. We want to grab him.' I say, 'Hang up with me and call 911. Those guys are paid to do that. Don't go out and grab him, because if he's not the right person and he reacts, and you react back, you face legal liability.' They mean well. They keep the area secure, but sometimes it gets a little heavy-handed, a little out of hand."

*Richard Green is modest about the hundreds of awards and honors he has received. He received the key to the city and was named Person of the Week by the New York Police Department. In 1992, ABC-TV national news made him their Person of the Week. But perhaps the award he cherishes most came after a visit to see Rebbe Schneerson, who died on June 12, 1994. Ordinarily, after a visit, the rebbe would present his guest with a dollar bill for good luck. When he heard about the work Green was doing, he presented Green with two dollars. "When you get two from the rebbe, that's major," says Green. In his wallet is a photo of him with Rebbe Schneerson, which serves as his passport to the Hasidic community. "The young people are mesmerized when I show them the picture," says Green. He has also been the subject of a documentary titled* Crown Heights.

**RICHARD GREEN**  "It showed how we are able to bring blacks and Hasidics together, cops and Hasidics together, and cops and blacks together. We bring in all the players. As someone said, 'In Crown Heights, you have blacks, blues, and Jews.' And we work together every day to make things happen.

"We're not at Nirvana yet, but you won't hear of this happening in Crown Heights ever again. Knock on wood when I say that.

"There's an African saying, 'Working together, ants are able to devour the elephant.' And what we've done in the city is work together with different people to devour this great elephant of chaos, the elephant of racism, and the elephant of the prejudicial attitudes that people come in with. We are devouring them."

## SHIRLEY CHISHOLM'S BOY

VICTOR ROBLES

Victor Robles grew up poor, raised by a single mom in the tenements of Williamsburg. In an era when Puerto Rican immigrants were discriminated against because of their culture and their language, Robles rose from his disadvantaged upbringing to become the second Puerto Rican member of the New York State Assembly, and for seventeen years he served on the New York City Council. All the while he demonstrated an ability to represent his entire constituency without prejudice or favor. He learned to do this, he says, after being mentored by two saintly political leaders, Gil Ramirez and Shirley Chisholm, New York's first black female legislator. He says he was influenced most by Aurea Blanco, his mother. If you look at the street signs between Manhattan Avenue and the Avenue of Puerto Rico, you will find a street named Aurea M. Blanco Way, named for her. She was a tough act to follow.

**VICTOR ROBLES** "When I was a boy, my family was poor. We were on welfare. Today it's called public assistance. My mother used to take me with her when she went to the welfare center, which today is called the Department of Social Services. I went with her, because I had to interpret and listen to all the nonsense and the accusations. One of the things you had to prove to them was that your father wasn't living with you. Believe it or not, in my day you had an investigator assigned to you, and at nine at night he would be knocking on your door to see whether the father was in the house.

"Today you get money. In my day we got coupons. On the first of the month you'd go to Sumpter Houses, and you would get a box of cheese, a box of powdered milk, and some cans of fruit, and that was your food ration. You got coupons for clothes, and you'd go to a place in Sumpter Houses, and I would choose from someone else's clothes. As my grandmother told me, 'As long as you have one suit, cleaned and pressed, you are somebody.' I have to tell you, in all my life I have never put on a T-shirt or underwear that was ripped. That's the culture. That's the family.

"After my mother began to stand on her own two feet, she became very politically involved and active. For example, there is a hospital on the corner of Flushing and Broadway called the Woodhull Hospital. Congressman Fred Richmond, a filthy-rich person, got elected, a white man in the barrio, and he built this facility, and it was supposed to be a federal prison. It's the only hospital that has three separate corridors. They don't have wards. They have individual rooms, because it was supposed to be a prison. That's when he got in a scandal with a page in Washington, and he was forced to resign. That facility was closed for almost fifteen years. Every year we would pay $20 million just to keep the boilers working and the infrastructure, and mind you, it was four city blocks of a facility that had displaced Puerto Ricans from the neighborhood, though when they built this, they didn't want to give the jobs to Puerto Ricans, and my mother and [step]father were pioneers demonstrating in front of that hospital. Ed Koch was the mayor who opened it as a hospital [in 1982]. That's why when Rudy Giuliani attempted to privatize it, I fought him tooth and nail, had him in court for four years, and I beat him. My feeling was, it's a city hospital. He cannot privatize it.

"My mother was president of the senior center that was part of the Borinquen Plaza housing complex. She was the vice president of the tenants' association. She was the president of the PTA in my elementary, intermediate school, and high school. She was always an active parent. Clearly I would not be where I am if it were not for my mother. She was a *pionero,* a pioneer.

"I used to go with my mother to the tenants meetings at the community center, and Gil Ramirez, who was also a tenant, was there. I was so impressed with him because he was blind and a Puerto Rican. When he chose to run for the state assembly in 1965, the political clubhouses were controlled either by Jews or Italians, and it was quite a feat when he won.

"He asked me to work with him on his campaign. One day we were campaigning, and he said to me, 'Victor, is there a man behind me selling pencils?' In those days blind men used to sell pencils on the street for 15¢. I said, 'Yes, Gil, how did you know?' He said, 'Let me teach you something, Victor. If I, Gil Ramirez, born with sight—God took away my sight—if I dare to run for office, then you have no excuse, with everything you have.'

"Gil was not born blind. He lived in public housing, in the Bushwick/Hylan Houses in Williamsburg. When he saw himself going blind, he was working for the City of New York as a Dictaphone operator. He was raising his family and going to school at night. It normally takes a person with normal sight three years to graduate from law school, but he did it in two. When he ran for office [the New York State Assembly], here was this blind man, the first Puerto Rican from Brooklyn to run. His opponent was a female Puerto Rican who, to embarrass him, had a motorcade of seeing-eye dogs. And this was at a time when the machine did not welcome Puerto Rican elected officials.

"Gil won, and when he got elected, he asked me to go with him to Albany. In 1965 Albany was just a state capital. It wasn't the Empire Plaza. Around the capital was the black community, which was displaced to build the Rockefeller Mall.

"Gil Ramirez was the only Puerto Rican, and after one year they redistricted and cut him out altogether, and it wasn't until 1978 when I became the second, so clearly we were the stepchildren. The point was he always motivated me, encouraged me, always made me part of what he was doing. Can you imagine—I was in rooms watching all these power people making decisions?

"And when I went to Albany, I met Shirley Chisholm, a real West Indian woman, a teacher, with the high-collar starched shirts.

"Though I didn't know it, she was watching me. Once she said, 'Victor, I always watched how you took care of Gilbert Ramirez. You were always there at his side.'

I never looked at it that way. That man gave me the opportunity. He was blind, and I was his aide. I had a responsibility.

In 1972, Congresswoman Shirley Chisholm became the first black woman to run for president. *Library of Congress*

"After I was drafted into the army, I went away for two years, and when I came back to Williamsburg, I saw a poster of Shirley Chisholm running for Congress. Oh, I was tickled pink. So I gave her a call. She wanted me to come to work for her in Washington. I said, 'No, no, no, no, no. Let me stay in my neighborhood and work the Puerto Rican community, and when you get elected, then you call me.' I worked day and night, and she got elected.

"There are people who come along once in a lifetime and who really make a difference. To me Shirley Chisholm was the greatest gift Brooklyn had. She put Brooklyn on the national map. Here's what I can say about her: she was a humble woman whose parents were from the West Indies—her father was from Guyana, mother from Barbados. Even down in Puerto Rico we read about the Statue of Liberty beckoning: Give me your tired and wretched souls, here not to destroy America but to nourish it by showing the beauty of immigrants. And Shirley Chisholm was the first black woman to graduate from Brooklyn College when in those days blacks were not admitted. So Shirley Chisholm, while speaking of the ills of America and how black America was a stepchild, how blacks were getting second-class treatment, talked to the conscience of America, reminding us all that the beauty of America is that those before us were immigrants coming here and are so grateful for what America offered, that they are part of history.

"Of course Gil Ramirez had been very supportive of Shirley Chisholm. They were like peas in a pod. One was a Puerto Rican, the other black, but they had their progressiveness in common, their opening up the door for minorities.

"They both wanted to be the voice of the downtrodden, the masses who were yearning but who were not being heard. They wanted to be judged based on their God-given attributes, and not what language they spoke or the color of their pigmentation. If you want to go back to the history of America, it was built on the sweat and backs of slaves, and Puerto Ricans were slaves too, because when America beat Spain and took over Puerto Rico, the people weren't asked whether they wanted to stay Spanish or become Americans. We had no choice. So Gil and Shirley tried to be the voice in the wilderness. They wanted to prove that one could be poor and still stand tall, that each of us was gifted even if we were poor, that if properly nourished, we all could become productive Americans. So when Shirley Chisholm spoke out about black America, she was not talking to blacks alone. When she ran for president in 1972, she also spoke about white America. She said when she became president, the first thing she would do was make the White House the Polka Dot House. She didn't say she was going to paint it black.

"Gil and Shirley were voices who paid attention to the suffering of the masses, because they had no voice or clout, because they were being ignored. America is immigrants. Come on—when the Jews from Europe came to America, they didn't know how to speak English. They learned. So you have to understand that just because they are immigrants—wait a minute—doesn't mean they are anti-American. Gilbert Ramirez and Shirley Chisholm were about saying, 'Hey, we are Americans, and we too have the right to hold a proper place in the sun, to be looked at with respect for what God has given us, not the prenotions the bigots have that all Puerto Ricans have come here to be on welfare, that all blacks make babies. So they tried to change the mentality. They taught me to stand up when right is right, and wrong is wrong.

"When Shirley ran for president, I was able to travel to twenty-five states. I was her aide and her bodyguard, because in those days the candidates didn't get Secret Service protection. That happened after the attempted assassination of George Wallace.

"In 1972 I ran for delegate of the Democratic presidential convention. Of New York State's 270 delegates, 4 were for Shirley Chisholm, and I was one of them. I went to Miami. With the exception of Hillary Clinton, I have not yet found anyone since Shirley who motivated and encouraged me to spend money to go down to the convention.

"I worked for Shirley for over ten years. Whenever she was in Washington, I was the one who was sent to all the meetings in central Brooklyn and Bedford-Stuyvesant, so a lot of people watched me grow up. When I ran for office, I used to get 90 percent of the black vote.

"One day she said to me, 'My son, I want you to run for office. But I do not want you to be a politician.' She caught me off-guard.

"I said to her, 'What do you mean, Mother dear. Aren't you a politician?'

"She said, 'Yes, we are all politicians. I want you to be a statesperson.' In those days, don't forget, women were not supposed to be in politics. They were supposed to be in the kitchen. So she didn't say 'statesman.' She said 'statesperson.' She said, 'Let me tell you the difference between a politician and a statesperson. A politician worries about winning the next election. A statesperson worries about the next generation.'

"I was very fortunate to have that kind of person around me.

"And so, when I was running for assembly, my opponent, an Italian named Peter Murdle, ran a campaign that said, 'If you elect Robles, you'll have all of them on welfare.' So I went to the Italian community, and I talked to them, and I won the election by forty-nine votes. So in all my years in public life—six years in the assembly and seventeen years in the city council—I did not play favorites. I did not go around saying, 'Puerto Rican, Puerto Rican, Puerto Rican,' but rather 'Our community. We are people. We have to come together.'

"When I was first elected to the New York State Assembly, I would sit in that chamber and see the beautiful high mahogany ceilings. I sat there for six months, staring up, saying to myself, 'Am I really here?' Of 150 members I was the only Puerto Rican from Brooklyn. I can't tell you what that meant to me.

"After Shirley left office, I was on the city council. She went to settle in Florida, and on her birthday, Christmas, and New Year's I would call her, and she would say,

'My son, you never forget me. Your card is the one I expect.'

"I'd say, 'Mother dear, you opened up the doors of opportunity.' She would say to me—and I really don't want to use her words—'Do you know how many niggers I've helped get elected, and now they don't even call me?'

"Usually I called her. One day she called me. I said, 'Mother dear, is something the matter?'

"She said, 'No no no. I just came from my lawyers. I want you to know I did my will, and of all my staff people in Washington and New York, you're the only one I put in my will.' I started crying, and I said, 'You don't have to do this.' And when she died in January 2004, I got a call from a lawyer in Florida. But forget about the money. I feel good knowing she put me in her will.

"I was elected to the state assembly in 1978, and I took my seat in 1979. I served until 1984, when the councilperson I replaced unfortunately went to jail for a scandal. The machine handpicked a young lady by the name of Nydia Velásquez, who today is a member of Congress. I was so incensed that here was a young lady not even a year after coming from Puerto Rico, she could hardly speak English, and I was an elected official, and Howard Golden, the borough president, was so arrogant he didn't even have the courtesy of reaching out to me.

"Meade Esposito [Brooklyn's Democratic boss], as bad as he was, at least would call me. In that gravelly voice, he would say, 'Hey, ya wanna run?' 'No, Meade.' 'Ya got anybody?' 'No, Meade.'

"When I called Howard about the nomination, he said, 'Well, they say you can't win.' I was in the assembly. How could they say I couldn't win? I gave up my seat, and I ran for the city council and for the district leader, and I won both seats. So Nydia Velásquez was appointed for six months, and then I beat her. I took over the seat in January 1985, and I served on the city council for seventeen years, until 2001. During the time I was in the assembly only five Puerto Ricans were elected, and I was the only one from Brooklyn. When I joined the city council in 1985, again I was the only Puerto Rican from Brooklyn. And I became the third-highest member of the council, the majority whip. I got to be in the room when the mayor met with the power brokers. And when it came to the budget, my community reaped benefits, because I was part of the leadership team. And all the time I remembered what Shirley Chisholm told me, 'A politician worries about the next election. A statesman worries about the next generation.' The bottom line was, I was able to produce for those who were the least of thee."

*Term limits ended Victor Robles's political career, but he was rewarded handsomely for his public service. In 2001 he was appointed clerk of the city council. With that honor he became the city clerk. Once appointed, he cannot be fired unless he violates his oath of office. He'll hold that office forever. As secretary of the city he attests to all legal documents involving the city, and he is the trustee of the seal of the City of New York. He is responsible for seeing that all lobbyists register. He is also responsible for all marriage licenses—seventy thousand a year, plus forty thousand marriages. Robles has so far resisted the call for him to sanction gay marriages, but who knows how long that will continue. Though it goes against his religious beliefs, he is too much of a humanist not to be compassionate. Brooklyn's Victor Robles, after all, has always been a uniter, not a divider.*

# BRIGHTON BEACH'S RUSSIAN JEWS

ALEC BROOK-KRASNY

BRIGHTON BEACH WAS ORIGINALLY SETTLED IN THE 1880s as a middle-class summer resort. The Brighton Beach Hotel and racetrack attracted tens of thousands of visitors every summer. Then in 1909, New York State outlawed horse racing, and the resort's golden age was over. When a housing shortage struck New York City at the end of World War I, people began settling in Brighton Beach year-round.

In the 1920s developers built thirty six-story apartment houses, and Brighton Beach became a diverse Jewish immigrant community. The area became a hotbed for both the Socialist and Communist Parties. When the Depression hit, Jews from other parts of Brooklyn flocked to the area, sharing apartments with friends and moving in with relatives.

After World War II and continuing through the 1960s, the children of the immigrant settlers began leaving Brighton Beach for the suburbs. Replacing them were Holocaust survivors and the elderly, who, motivated by the fear of crime, moved from older immigrant areas, including Brownsville, East Flatbush, and the Grand Concourse of the Bronx.

But a community of senior citizens must shrink, and by 1975 the vacancy rate in Brighton Beach was almost 30 percent. Stores and apartments stood empty. Then the city released thousands of nonviolent mentally ill patients from mental hospitals. A large number of these people moved to Brighton Beach. There was a real fear that Brighton Beach was dying.

The savior of the community came with *glasnost,* the thawing of the Cold War under President Ronald Reagan. The first Soviet Jews to leave Russia settled in Brighton Beach in the early 1970s because the rent was cheap and the housing decent. The settlers were taken by the fact that Brighton Beach was a seaside community. Odessa was on the Black Sea. Jews who came from there and settled in Brighton Beach were reminded of home. News traveled fast. Brighton Beach became known as Little Odessa.

By the late 1980s Brighton Beach was overcrowded. Store signs in English and Yiddish were replaced by Cyrillic letters. You could buy borscht and smoked fish, caviar and Russian pastry. Russian restaurants and nightclubs prospered. Today one is hard-pressed to find residents who speak English. Russian predominates.

Alec and Grandpa Nochim in 1972.
*Courtesy of Alec Brook-Krasny*

The Russian Jews even have a representative in the New York State Assembly. His name is Alec Brook-Krasny, a remarkable man with an improbable story. Brook-Krasny came to Brooklyn in 1989, at the age of thirty-one, knowing twenty words of English. In a little more than seventeen years, he went from an immigrant stock clerk in a shoe store in Greenwich Village to a New York State assemblyman from the 46th District.

When his second daughter was about to celebrate her first birthday, Brook-Krasny sought to find a place that would throw her a glitzy birthday party. When he discovered that no such place existed, he built one himself. His business was so innovative that in 1999 he was named Entrepreneur of the Year by *Leisure and Entertainment* magazine.

But doing well financially wasn't enough. Following in the footsteps of a philanthropic grandfather, Brook-Krasny saw the need to bring members of the Russian Jewish community together with the mainstream Jewish community, and so he founded an organization called the Council of Jewish Émigré Community Organizations. With that platform he was able to meet all the important politicians of Brooklyn, and he was encouraged by former city councilman Howard Lasher to embark on a political career. He became treasurer of Community Board 13, and after failing twice in runs for state office, in 2006 he won a seat in the New York State Assembly. More than anything, Brook-Krasny's story is further evidence of the vitality that immigrants bring to American life and culture.

Alec Brook-Krasny with Jan Krasny, his stepfather, in downtown Moscow. *Courtesy of Alec Brook-Krasny*

**ALEC BROOK-KRASNY** "I was born in Moscow in 1958. My father's name was Simon Katsnelson. He was a shoemaker in his early years, and then for many years he ran a shoemaking plant. Life was hard for him in the Soviet Union. Under the Soviet regime, it was impossible even to open a small business. He had to work for the government, and he was paid about 140 rubles a month, about $100 a month at best.

"My father, who is not with us anymore, was a very smart man but because he was Jewish, he was not able to go to college. In the '50s and '60s they wouldn't allow him to pass the test.

"My mother was a bookkeeper in a beauty salon for many, many years. Her name is Clara Brook, and she's with me now. My father and mother got divorced a long time ago, and the person who brought me up in my early years was Jan Krasny. He ran a small plant that repaired refrigerators. They [Brook and Krasny] met a long time ago, and they got separated too. For some years I used the last name Krasny, but I wanted to change it to Brook. When I came to America, I came as Krasny, and when I got my citizenship I saw I couldn't change it, because so many people knew me as Krasny, so I decided to hyphenate it and make it Brook-Krasny as a way to honor both names.

"The person who had the greatest influence on me was actually my grandfather,

Nochim Katsnelson, and I'm sitting in my office looking at his picture. My grandfather mentored me in many, many different domains, including Jewish heritage and Jewish culture. He was a religious man, and he taught me many of life's values. He was a very honest man who was ready to help others. I can remember him bringing in people virtually from the street, who needed food and clothes. There were only four little synagogues in all of the Moscow metropolitan area with its 15 million people. He was a *gaboy* in one of them, in a small village outside of the Moscow called Perlovka. The whole of Perlovka knew him, and people of virtually every nationality liked him a lot. He helped a lot of Russians, and other people, including the Tartars. He was a shoemaker all his life. He had a small store right by the Perlovka train station.

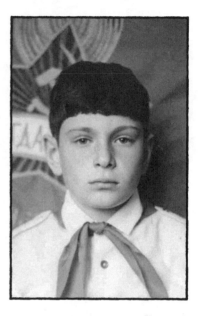

Alec in the fifth grade in Moscow.
*Courtesy of Alec Brook-Krasny*

"He was proud to be Jewish, and during the repressive '50s and '60s he dared to walk the streets of Moscow wearing a yarmulke. The state didn't like it, but they never punished him for it because he was absolutely, openly Jewish and religiously so, and I believe to some degree they were afraid to touch him. Everyone knew how helpful he was to so many, and maybe that was the reason they didn't touch him.

"He was my hero, but unfortunately, he passed away when I was fifteen. When I was a young boy, I had a bris, because of him. My mother was totally against it. Every year in school you had to take a physical exam. My mother said, 'Your first physical exam will bring you a lot of trouble.' And it turned out that way. The exam revealed my secret: that I was Jewish. And within five days, the whole school knew. So it wasn't the best experience, but I'm still very grateful to my grandfather for doing it, because I'm proud of it. And though I was always a good student, I never received any awards I might otherwise have gotten.

"Leonid Brezhnev ran the country when I was growing up. The country was regressing. It's interesting to make comparisons with life in the United States today.

Two days ago I was in the state senate, and we had to vote on a new state comptroller. Alan Hevesi had been removed from his position, and according to the Constitution, his successor is supposed to be chosen by the assembly and senate together. The governor Eliot Spitzer—who I liked very much—decided he was going to interfere with the process by using his own version of the process. Now, making parallels, I lived for thirty years in a country where the legislative branch was totally inferior to the executive branch, and that was one of the main reasons why the country collapsed.

"When I got up in front of the assembly, I told them this, and explained why I was voting against what the governor was trying to do. Because I believe in the separation of powers. That's the only way democracy can exist. It was not in place in the Soviet Union at all. We didn't have jobless people, but all of us were making what we here call welfare, or even less than that.

"Everything was lacking. Absolutely everything. There was nothing to buy. In the early 1970s there wasn't even any bread. Fortunately my mother and father were able to find things on the black market through their own connections.

"There was a bright side. The educational system was very good. I got to college, and I went to the Moscow Technological Institute. I got a degree in engineering and economics. It took me seven years to get it, because I was working for a government agency overseeing the production of refrigerators. After I graduated I became manager of a small plant with about forty people repairing refrigerators. It was what my stepfather had done, but I felt it was something I could do within the framework of the governmental system in which I was living. I was making about 200 rubles a month, which is $150.

"For the Russian people, one of the highlights was our space program. We all were proud of it. Yuri Gagarin was our first cosmonaut, and we followed him up into space. I had mixed feelings, because on the one hand you know what the government is all about, and on the other hand, you live in a country. You love the streets where you were born.

"In 1985, when I was twenty-seven years old, Mikhail Gorbachev replaced Chernenko, and Gorbachev instituted *glasnost,* and it meant a lot to me. I was aware of the practices behind the Iron Curtain, and I was aware of democracy. I was listening to the

Voice of America. I was also part of a group of about forty Jewish boys and girls who would get together every September and celebrate the festival of Simchas Torah, where everybody dances. We would gather at a Hebrew school every year.

"We weren't dissidents. We just wanted to celebrate our roots. And we would go to a hotel and spend holidays together. I'm still friends with people from that group, including Alexander Lubov and Igor Schtarkman. That was very unusual. In Moscow it's usually very hard to find a group of Jewish guys, because everyone remains hidden. But I was following in my grandfather's footsteps, and he didn't hide it, and I didn't hide it either. I would never hide it.

"And he was probably the reason my first wife was Jewish, and now my wife is Jewish. But getting back to Gorbachev and *glasnost,* in 1985 I came to the mistaken conclusion that everything can be changed in the country. By 1987 I realized that for the country to change, it would take a hundred years.

"Since I knew a lot of young Jewish people, the idea of immigration was in the air. For many years I was thinking about it, but for many years I was afraid to apply, because I knew what would happen to me. I knew people who applied and who lost their jobs, their opportunity to feed their family, the chance to make any kind of money at all. So I have to say I was afraid of the government. I was afraid my family and I would end up like them. By the end of 1987 it appeared that the climate had changed, that there would be no reprisals if I applied for an exit visa, and so I applied early in 1988, and it took me a year to get an Israeli visa, because that was the only chance to leave the former Soviet Union. I left with my wife and daughter.

"At the time, I credited Ronald Reagan with getting us out of Russia. I was sure he was the one who helped open the doors. I feel a bit differently today. I believe that Mikhail Gorbachev was the driving force, and I can say that Nancy Reagan was second, and Ronald Reagan followed her lead. But certainly you can say that the work of Gorbachev and Ronald Reagan made it possible.

"We went to Vienna, and I went to the American consulate and asked for permission to enter the United States. This process, which was supported by HIAS [Hebrew Immigrant Aid Society] and NYANA [New York Association for New Americans], took about six months, and we lived in Italy during this time, in Torvaianica, a small village about forty minutes from Rome, on the Mediterranean Sea. I worked for my landlord as a fisherman, pulling nets from five in the morning until one o'clock in the afternoon for $5 an hour. I was rich. It was a wonderful village with a real sense of camaraderie. My landlord and I became very close. He didn't want us to leave. The first month our rent was $750, and he lowered it to $370 in an attempt to keep me from leaving.

"I had it in my mind to go to the United States. My ex-wife, Elvira, had relatives in Brooklyn, and we rented an apartment on Avenue Y and East 13th Street. The first time I saw Brighton Beach, I was very disappointed. I had heard about all the big skyscrapers, and I was imagining them there in Brighton Beach, and there weren't any. But after only twelve days in this country, I was working already. I started as a stock boy in a shoe store in Greenwich Village in Manhattan on West 8th Street. Igor Schtarkman, one of my childhood friends, was friendly with the store owner.

"I worked there about two years. I spent a year as a stock boy and a salesman, and then as soon as I picked up the language I became a manager of the store. I came to this country speaking twenty words of English—hello, good-bye, please, thank you, shoes—and Greenwich Village turned out to be an excellent place to learn English, because there were no Russian speakers around.

"I lived at Avenue Y and East 13th Street for about a year. Elvira was a dentist, and she went to NYU to get her credentials. I guess she was under the impression I was going to be a stock boy for the rest of my life, and she found another dentist. Being the mild kind of person I was, I decided I would throw away all her suitcases and start over. My daughter Dina stayed with me, and my mother, realizing I was alone and struggling, making $350 a week, came over from Russia to help look after her. Dina is twenty-four years old now. She works for CBS Sports. She is absolutely great, the smartest twenty-four-year-old girl I know.

"In 1992 I decided to attend the York Institute, a business school in Manhattan, just to pick up the lexicon. I became an accountant, and in 1994 I became the manager of a trucking company in Brooklyn.

"I met my wife, Iviva. She's from Vilnius, in Lithuania, and on February 14, 1994, my second daughter, Rebecca, was born. At the beginning of 1995 I went looking for a place to celebrate her first birthday. When I couldn't find a place, I realized this was something lacking in the city. I went to my childhood friends, Alex Lubov and Igor Schtarkman and a couple others, and they became my investors, and within a year I converted an old beer warehouse on Neptune Avenue in Brooklyn into a beautiful, fourteen-thousand-square-foot space that became a kids' community, entertainment, and educational center called Fun-O-Rama.

Alec with daughter Dina, wife Iviva, daughter Rebecca, and son Jonathan. *Courtesy of Alec Brook-Krasny*

"During the six months I spent investigating the business, I discovered that a Chuck E. Cheese in Vancouver, Canada, went out of business. I bought the equipment for 15¢ on the dollar, rented three trucks, and carted it back to Brooklyn. For 15¢ on the dollar anyone would do it. So Fun-O-Rama was built, and from the second month it was profitable. It caught the attention of some people in the industry, and why, I don't know, but in 1997 I was named the Entrepreneur of the Year by *Leisure and Entertainment* magazine. And then it caught the attention of the local politicians. With the development of the place, I got acquainted with the local city councilmen, Howard Lasher and Jules Polonetsky, and they appointed me to Community Board 13 in 1997. For six months I sat there doing absolutely nothing, and then I started to get involved.

"The first issue was the building of a cultural center in Brighton Beach. It was to be a center for Russian-speakers, but, due to lack of parking, the community board rejected the proposal to build it.

"Out of curiosity, I decided to look into the matter. I saw that according to a grandfather law, the owners of the building had a right to put up a movie theater with four thousand seats in the building. I also realized it was a historical landmark. They could not demolish it. In other words, you had to do something with it.

"When I realized that their proposal was for establishing a theater with about 1,900 seats, I saw a way to get it built. I went to the community board, and they gave me three minutes to speak. And within three minutes I explained to them very simply that for 1,900 seats you need half as much parking as for 4,000 seats, and for the first time in the history of Community Board 13, five months later they reversed their decision. It was all over the newspapers.

"I didn't tell them they were wrong. I told them their lawyer was wrong.

"What was even more important, Howard Lasher and Jules Polonetsky realized what I could do. Two years later I was elected treasurer of the community board, and was the only Russian-speaker on the board.

"I was also very active in the mainstream community—I was more active in the mainstream community than in the Russian community—and in 2000 I ran for state assembly. It was Howard Lasher's idea. I was nominated by the local Democratic club, and I believed I would win, but I was removed from the ballot. They played a dirty trick on me. I was running against Adele Cohen, and she had won the previous election by 2,500 votes. You needed 500 signatures to run, and I had more than 4,000, but 12 of those 4,000 were collected by a twelve-year-old boy. I knew nothing about it. Adele Cohen went before a judge, and the judge removed me from the ballot.

"I had come from the former Soviet Union, where this sort of thing happened all the time. And in the United States it was happening to me! I was very upset, but I didn't give up. I ran a write-in campaign, and in 2000 I set a record for a write-in candidate. I got about 1,600 votes, and I came in second.

"In 2001 I ran for city council against Dominick Recchia, who became a very effective public servant. Of the seven candidates, five were American-born. And I won the *New York Times*'s endorsement over Recchia. I met with the editors for over three hours. It was 2001, and when people talked about the Russian community, they were talking about the Russian mafia. They really had to know who I was and where I came from. But I got the endorsement.

"Dominick was the choice of the Democratic machine, and he won.

"That same year I started an organization called the Council of Jewish Émigré Community Organizations (COJECO). I started with a few files in the trunk of my car right after September 11. I wanted to build a bridge between the mainstream Jewish community and the Russian Jewish community. What I was saying was that it was no accident that the Rabinowitz from New York and the Rabinowitz from Moscow had the same last names. We needed a bridge and COJECO became that bridge. I found good people for the board of directors, and we started programs for youth, for seniors, for going to Israel, for rallies in support of Israel. We had mutual programs with big Jewish institutions like the 92nd Street Y [in Manhattan]. For two years in a row our organization has been named on the list of the top fifty most innovative Jewish organizations in North America.

"After Dominick Recchia won, the council redistricted about five thousand Russian Jews out of his district just to keep me from beating him. On the other hand, the redistricting of the assembly also was taking place, and those same Russian Jews were in the 46th Assembly District, and by that time Howard Lasher was very ill with Alzheimer's, and I decided to run for his seat. I was able to convince Dominick how important the Russian-speaking community was by showing him the numbers and by its economic success, and he campaigned for me from sunup to sundown. My opponent was Ari Kagan, a journalist for a Russian-American newspaper.

"Ari was preparing himself for this race for a few years, and while he was writing about what I was doing in the community he was actually getting lessons from me. He was ready for a big fight.

"I realized by reading about elections in different ethnic communities that the first election is always about the former country. I found out that Ari had graduated from a military academy in Russia and that he had become a propagandist for the Soviets in 1988, and he was using some of those techniques. Ari, in turn, accused me of having ties to the Kremlin. Walter Ruby had written an article about me in *Jewish Week,* in which I stated I supported a meeting of Hamas leaders and the Russian leaders. You should know what the other side is thinking. It made a lot of sense. But based on that, Kagan started accusing me of supporting Putin and Hamas.

"I thought I would win by a big margin, but I won by only 140 votes out of 6,000. I ended up getting more mainstream votes than I got Russian-speaking votes. I won because of mainstream voters.

"And now that I am a member of the state assembly, I feel like I can do good for my community. I don't think I can change the world tomorrow, because Albany is probably harder to change than the whole world. But I am a fan of after-school programs. I'm a product of them in the Soviet Union; that's where you learned culture, music, and art. We don't teach these things in the American school system, and I talked to the governor about this for a couple minutes, and he was very receptive. So I think I can change things. In some areas I think my knowledge will be helpful.

"I never would have become a politician in the Soviet Union. They talk about democracy, but Russia is still a long way from democracy. And in my heart, I would not have been able to become a politician in another kind of government. Because I believe in democracy totally.

"I have lived in Sea Gate for fourteen years. It's on the western tip of Coney Island, an incredible place to raise kids and live with your family. Even though I wasn't born there, I really feel like a Brooklynite."

Courtesy of Alec Brook-Krasny

# THE BATTLE FOR SEXUAL FREEDOM

RENEE CAFIERO

**S**CIENTIFIC FACTS OUGHT TO BE ACCEPTED BY EVERYBODY BY definition, but as proponents of global warming and evolution know, Republican leaders under George W. Bush refused to recognize the former, and the religious right denied the latter. There's a third inescapable scientific fact about a segment of our citizenry: gay people are gay from birth and have no choice in the matter.

Again, the religious right disagrees, contending that gays choose to be gay and as a result are damned to rot in the afterlife. It is this bigotry that led to the annihilation of the gay population in occupied Europe during the Nazi reign of terror and to bigotry in America that until the 1970s forced most gays and lesbians to keep their sexual identity a deep, dark secret. Not even famous Americans such as Rock Hudson, Johnny Mathis, or Liberace dared reveal their sexual orientation. Hudson, who once married his secretary to keep the truth from the public, did so only after contracting the AIDS virus. Liberace was outed shortly before his death by a jilted lover.

Renee Cafiero (née Pachter) is currently the secretary of the Lambda Independent Democrats, the largest gay and lesbian political organization in Brooklyn. Born in 1943 to a Jewish father and a Christian mother two years after her parents came to New York from France to escape the Nazis, Cafiero grew up on the Upper West Side of Manhattan. Her father, a socialist who grew up in Berlin before fleeing to

France ahead of the Nazis, during World War II worked as a translator and wrote a dictionary of Nazi terms for the U.S. government. He and his wife, Hedwig, also worked for *Dissent*, a quarterly magazine of the American Socialist Party. It was, and still is, an anti-Communist publication.

Renee was apolitical until she was in her twenties. After graduating from Hunter High School, she attended Queens College, where she aspired to become an opera singer. At age eighteen she fell in love with a gay man by the name of Cafiero. Their marriage lasted a year, but she kept the name because she figured that the judges of her opera singing would favor Italians.

Renee Cafiero protesting for gay rights in Lower Manhattan in 1964. *Courtesy of Renee Cafiero*

**RENEE CAFIERO** "I was going to be an opera singer, but I didn't have the chutzpah. If you want to be an opera singer in New York City, when you go for an audition you not only have to be convinced you can do the role, you have to be convinced there is no one else in the world who can do the role, and I just never had that conviction.

"I was eighteen years old, and it was right about that time that it occurred to me that I might be bisexual or gay. My so-called husband was gay. I fell in love with this guy—including the fact he was gay. Of course, when you're a teenager, you figure you can change the world, so I figured I would make him fall in love with me and it didn't matter if he was gay. Before then, I had not known anything about that. Suddenly it dawned on me, with no previous knowledge whatsoever: *Oh, this guy likes guys.*

"The way I was raised, if you love somebody, you love them. End of story. Knowing my parents had some difficulty because they were of different religions added to my tolerance. I loved him, and he did love me. It wasn't a question of that, but he didn't love me in that all-encompassing way I wanted, and the marriage only lasted about a year."

*After the marriage ended, what was clear to Renee was that she preferred relationships with women to those with men.*

**RENEE CAFIERO** "In 1964 I was casting about for a summer job, and a friend of mine said I should look into working for the Mattachine Society. He thought it was a lesbian organization, and it wasn't. There were a few women, but it was mostly guys. They weren't hiring anyone, but they needed volunteers, so I started giving my time.

"We had monthly programs, which were lectures, discussions, or panels. We put out a newsletter every month. We did a certain amount of agitation for change.

"I was in the first gay picket in the United States. It was in '64, and we went to Whitehall Street to picket the Selective Service and protest the lack of gays in the military. Forty years later we still don't allow gays in the military.

"It was a Saturday, and there was practically no one around. The few people who passed by looked at us very strangely. There weren't any nasty comments. I don't know why we picked Saturday, except that we all worked during the week.

"That same year, I moved to Brooklyn. I was twenty-one, and I had met a lady. A friend of mine had been telling me about his friend Nancy for quite a while. He finally introduced us. She was a writer working at the time for a literary agency. Her name was Nancy Gordon, and she's now a very well-known writer. She wrote *Annie on My Mind,* one of the first lesbian novels for teenagers. Hers has survived many, many book burnings.

"Nancy lived in Brooklyn Heights, and I moved into her apartment very briefly, and then we moved into a slightly larger apartment. We were together for five years, and then she got back with her first love and has been with her ever since. They live in Massachusetts, and they got married about two years ago.

"I didn't hide the fact I was gay. I was still in college. I really didn't have anything to lose. Most of us felt the same way. Obviously, no celebrity would come out.

"I attended several more demonstrations sponsored by a coalition of gay and lesbian groups called ECHO—East Coast Homophile Organization. The New York Mattachine Society was one of the member groups.

"One of the projects of the Mattachine Society was to try and get the state liquor laws overturned, because at that time it was illegal to serve a homosexual in a bar. Some people went on 'sip-ins.' They'd go up to a bartender and say, 'We're gay. Serve us.' But the bartenders kept saying, 'Okay.' They didn't care. Finally, they went to one place where they found a bar owner who was afraid a police officer was lurking in the background, so he refused service, and they got some publicity out of it.

"I was never harassed by the police, but I have friends who were. I wasn't a drinker so I didn't go to the bars. In New York the cops did some entrapment and closed down bars, unless they got payoffs from the Mafia. All the gay bars were Mafia bars up until the 1970s. If the Mafia was paying off the cop on the block, the place didn't get raided.

"Back then not only couldn't you sell liquor to gays, but there was a law that same-sex people could not dance together. There also were masquerade laws, which said you couldn't dress as the opposite gender except on Halloween. So you had drag queens dancing and drinking, and the cops had three reasons for performing a raid. And they'd load up the paddy wagons, and if they really wanted to get people in trouble, they would jail them overnight and call their employers and say, 'Hey, your employee is in jail tonight because he was in a gay bar.' That wasn't very nice, because there were no antidiscrimination laws on the books. Outing often meant dismissal.

"New York was a much better place for gays than Los Angeles. In Los Angeles the cops really did numbers on gays. Why did the police do this? Paul Goodman, who was a philosopher of the 1960s, came to one of our dinners, and he talked about societal homophobia. He said, 'In every society you have kikes, niggers, and queers. You have somebody who is going to be the one who is stepped on, because people have to see people as lower than them. People have a need for looking down on someone else.'"

*In 1969 the gay rights movement began in earnest at a bar in Manhattan called Stonewall Inn. The police moved in, and the gay customers, instead of going meekly, fought back and staged a protest.*

**RENEE CAFIERO**   "The drag queens basically said, 'Enough is enough. They fought back. I wish I had been there, but I was on the Cape, breaking up with Nancy. When we came back, I said, 'Did anything new happen?' 'Oh yeah, something happened,' and it was a source of great pride in the gay community. It was a *big* deal. The Mattachine Society had been working quietly through the politicians to try to get these laws changed, and all of a sudden here was this civil disobedience, and everyone began to sit up and take notice.

"It was 1969, a time when other groups—Black Power and antiwar—were demanding their rights, and finally somebody reached the breaking point and said, 'I want my rights too.' And they didn't want to pursue them in a nice way anymore. The Mattachine Society had been viewed as Uncle Tomish and 'go along to get along,' and once people wanted to be more militant, the organization died a couple years later. It just petered out."

*Shortly after the Stonewall riot, militant groups formed, including the Gay Liberation Front and the Gay Activist Alliance. The chant arose, "We're out, loud, and proud." Gay Pride parades began to gain attention from the media.*

**RENEE CAFIERO**   "I didn't join either of those groups. After I split up with Nancy, I was a bit of a hermit for a while. There was a group that formed, called the Gay Alliance of Brooklyn. A guy by the name of Jim Jarman decided he wanted to form a Brooklyn group. He lived in Brooklyn Heights, which had quite a large gay population. He got himself a place to meet in a church, and he stood at a subway stop handing out flyers. I went. I thought, *I've been a hermit long enough.* Jim was expecting ten or twenty people and three hundred showed up."

*Things began changing for the gay and lesbian community in the early 1970s. Jill Johnston, an openly gay columnist in the* Village Voice, *wrote a groundbreaking book called* Lesbian Nation. *In 1973 the American Psychiatric Association broke new ground when it declared that being gay no longer was to be considered a mental illness.*

**RENEE CAFIERO**   "People say the sixties ended in 1969, but they went on until about 1973. There was black militancy and antiwar militancy, and gay people started being tired of being in the closet. The change by the American Psychiatric Association came as a direct result of pressure from a woman by the name of Barbara Giddings. Barbara lived in Philadelphia and was active there, and she was one of the movers and shakers when we did demonstrations in Washington and Philadelphia in the 1960s. She and Frank Kameny, a World War II vet, were very active in getting the psychiatric classification changed.

Renee, left, worked on the George McGovern presidential campaign in 1972. *Courtesy of Renee Cafiero*

"Barbara, who died in 2007, was also active with the American Library Association. She fought to get decent books on homosexuality out on the library shelves, because when I first started exploring the whole subject, I would go to the public library and try to take out books on homosexuality, and you had to ask the librarian for them. They were not on the open shelves.

"There was no bar to taking them out. You didn't need a note from a parent, but you had to ask for them. That was a barrier for anyone who didn't have the guts to say, 'I want this book.'

"I was mad enough to say, 'Okay, I have to find out about this, and I'm mad this barrier is being put in my way. It's not correct.' I would ask for them, but very few people checked them out because you couldn't be anonymous. Barbara worked on that.

"The Gay Alliance of Brooklyn lasted for a few years, but there were a bunch of us who wanted to be more political. The GAB was more a social thing. We had huge dances every couple of weeks. It was quite a phenomenon having all these out people—or semi-out people—at a dance. But a bunch of us wanted to be more politically active, wanted to talk to actual politicians, to get things done and not just dance, so in '72 we joined the local Democratic club, the West Brooklyn Independent Democrats, and because I was female and had an Italian name, I got to be a delegate for George McGovern. I came out in the *New York Times* and the *Daily News*. I was working in the children's book department at Harper and Row, and I warned my boss beforehand, and she approved. My boss was in the closet, but she allowed me to be out of the closet. I got a couple of weird phone calls after that from someone who read the article in the *Daily News* and was being snotty. Other than that I didn't get any flak.

"That year we tried to get a gay rights plank into the '72 Democratic platform. There were five openly gay delegates nationwide out of three thousand delegates and another two thousand alternates. We didn't have much clout, and we got to make our presentation after the abortion presentation, which also was not in prime time but was given by Shirley MacLaine, who was quite eloquent. Shirley told us she was for gay rights but she couldn't ask for both planks. She said, 'We can't get both planks, and you know which one is going to be more popular.' [New York Congresswoman] Bella Abzug said the same thing.

"I stayed active in the West Brooklyn Democratic Club for quite a while, until there were some political problems. In 1978 the Lambda Independent Democrats was founded. Today it is the largest gay and lesbian organization in Brooklyn. I decided to move my activism to Lambda. Lambda takes up a lot of issues but looks at them mostly through a lesbian and gay prism. It's a little more limiting, and I'm of two minds about that.

"Our club has become very successful. Brooklyn politicians clamor for our endorsements. Most of the local clubs are not very political—most people aren't political—and somehow we manage to get things done because we are political.

"You know, people keep voting for term limits. I don't believe in term limits. They think, *My representative is great, but all those other guys, I wish they'd go away.* So therefore they vote for term limits, and they find out their beloved leader has to be out too.

"We had a decent relationship with several mayors. Not that much with Ed Koch. He talked to everyone, but mostly he said, 'How am I doing?' We had some relationship with David Dinkins. Rudy Giuliani was elected in 1993, and we had no relationship with him, and I'm glad of that."

*One indication of the strong prejudice against homosexuality was how long it took the country to overturn the sodomy laws, which criminalized gay sex. In 1965, in the case of* Griswold v. Connecticut, *the U.S. Supreme Court struck down a law barring married couples from using contraceptives. It was the first case to recognize the right of privacy under the Constitution. The court limited its ruling to married couples, but later expanded the ruling to all heterosexual couples.*

*In 1986, in the case of* Bowers v. Hardwick, *the court explicitly refused to give this privacy protection to homosexuals. Then in 1998, in the case of* Lawrence & Garner v. Texas, *the Texas Supreme Court struck down the state's sodomy laws, and in 2003 the U.S. Supreme Court affirmed by a six-to-three vote. Gays no longer had to fear the police banging down their doors and arresting them for consensual sex.*

**RENEE CAFIERO**   "It took the *Lawrence* case to get the sodomy laws off the books. They are still fighting about that. There are still many states that have no antidiscrimination laws on the books. There are localities that have specifically voted against antidiscriminatory laws. The voters in Colorado passed a law that said no town could pass an antidiscriminatory law. I had friends who lived in Denver, and they couldn't understand how the state could pass this amendment. It went all the way to the Supreme Court, which decided you can't have a law like that on the books.

"I worked against a similar bill in Maine one year. It had been put before the voters three times—the religious right kept trying—and it was defeated three times, fortunately. But they literally stood in front of the voting booth and would not let a voter in until they found out how he was going to vote. If the voter was going to vote against the amendment, their people blocked the voting booth. The cops had to come and physically remove them, and they just kept coming back. It was horrendous. This is what they mean by Christian tolerance? Excuse me.

"How can people who believe in the goodness of Jesus be so bigoted? I wish I understood it. I truly wish I understood it. It boggles my mind. I don't get it, why someone who supposedly worships somebody who said, 'Turn the other cheek,' and 'Render unto Caesar the things which are Caesar's and unto God the things that are God's' can then go and do the opposite? I don't get it.

"But because of this opposition, Massachusetts is the only state that allows same-sex marriage. Canada has it. Holland does. Spain is about to. This is one thing we've been fighting for all along, and, interestingly, this is one fight the leaders of the movement didn't think should be fought at this time. They thought it was too soon, and apparently for a lot of people it is, but this all came up from the grass roots.

"New York State was going to have same-sex marriage. The issue went all the way to the Appellate Court, the state's top court, and the court said the legislature should deal with it. But it did not mandate that the legislature deal with it, which is what both Massachusetts and New Jersey did. Now those people who were decrying activist judges were saying, 'The courts did this terrible thing in Massachusetts, and they should have left it to the legislature.' Then you look at California. Well hey, the California legislature passed a gay-marriage law, but then the Austrian governor said, 'No, this should be left to the courts.' Schwarzenegger vetoed the legislation saying the legislature should not be doing this. At the same time everyone else is saying, 'What are the courts doing?'

"Obviously it has nothing to do with either the legislature or the courts. It has to do with 'We don't want this,' and I have yet to understand why if John and Mary Smith are living in one house, it harms their marriage if Dick and Tom live in the next house over and have their union made official by the government."

*According to Cafiero, getting married in Massachusetts doesn't necessarily give partners sanctuary. Partners who marry in Massachusetts, she says, face a potentially serious scrutiny from the IRS because of their declared union.*

**RENEE CAFIERO**  "I actually asked a friend of mine who lives in Massachusetts if he and his partner were going to get married, and he said it wasn't the right time, because what happens, when you file your state taxes, you can file jointly. But then when you file a federal return, you can't, and that automatically looks funny to the auditors, and so you get audited. So there are all kinds of roadblocks.

"New Jersey allows civil unions instead of marriage, but what they are finding is that it doesn't work, because there are too many gray areas where people don't know what their rights are.

"That may change relatively quickly. We're hoping that in New York, if we manage to elect a Democratic state senate, we should be able to push it through. At this point, the senate is Republican and the assembly is Democratic, and they hate each other. If the leadership of one says the sky is blue, the other says, 'No, it's brown.'

"New York City Mayor Bloomberg is wishy-washy. We had a New York City judge rule that a marriage could be performed, but Bloomberg overturned it. I don't know how he did that, because he can't veto a judge, but Bloomberg said no, even though he might or might not be for gay marriages. He says it should be up to the legislature, that he doesn't want the courts to deal with it. So he talks as if he's for it, and then he overturns the decision. That's not wonderful. Of course, because of term limits, he's out in 2009."

*Christine Quinn, the majority leader of the city council, will be one candidate running for mayor. Quinn, from Chelsea, is gay. One can be sure the Lambda Independent Democrats will be backing her. Meanwhile, over the years, despite the roadblocks, gays and lesbians have gained important rights. Of the top fifty Fortune 500 companies, forty-nine allow domestic-partner benefits. Only Exxon-Mobil does not.*

**RENEE CAFIERO**    "Most companies see that it's to their benefit. They get good people that way. It makes economic sense. It has nothing to do with discrimination or being tolerant. They are looking at the bottom line, and the bottom line is they are getting good people because they are opening their doors.

"Before the merger, Mobil gave domestic-partner benefits. When Exxon acquired Mobil, they cut it out. So that was a case of actively regressing."

*It was noted that recently a number of Republicans had turned out to be gay, including Idaho senator Larry Craig, who for years campaigned against gay and lesbian rights.*

**RENEE CAFIERO** "I have to tell you that I don't know any Republicans, but there is this myth that you can't be gay and have any kind of public life, so you hate yourself for what you are just because of the social ramifications, and if you are in a religious right congregation, you also can't be gay, because you'll be damned, and so they defeat themselves because they keep trying to deny it, and then they get into these pickles. Instead of being in a loving relationship, they go out and have anonymous sex, because that's all they can admit they can like.

"There's a phenomenon in a lot of AIDS literature. They don't talk about people having gay sex. They talk about men who have sex with men, and they specifically do not call them gay, because especially in the African-American and Latino communities, that's a no-no. Even if they admit they have sex with men, they aren't *gay*.

"If you remember Roy Cohn in *Angels in America,* he was the prototype of the self-loathing gay. In his

Renee with friends today. *Courtesy of Renee Cafiero*

era you might understand it, but this is 2007. Cohn and McCarthy had more gays thrown out of the State Department than Communists, because that was the way you proved you were a red-blooded, macho American.

"A couple years ago, the United Church of Christ endorsed same-sex marriage, but the Episcopal Church is being torn apart at this point, which is really too bad, because they should be happy to have people in loving, committed, monogamous relationships. But some people . . . I don't get it."

*Today Renee Cafiero lives in Park Slope, which boasted such a large lesbian population for a while that the area had taken on the nickname "Dyke Slope." Despite the greater tolerance for gays over the years, and Brooklyn's reputation for being a borough that accepts all people, Cafiero says that gays, especially gay men, still have to be careful.*

**RENEE CAFIERO**    "I had a rent-controlled apartment in Brooklyn Heights, and my landlords wanted the apartment, and my lawyer didn't know what he was doing, and I lost the apartment. My mother died right about then, so I was able to sell her apartment for a ridiculous amount of money, and I bought a tiny brownstone in Park Slope. Now I don't have a landlord who can throw me out.

"Things happen in Brooklyn. We've had a few assaults, incidents of gay-bashing. When I have people visiting, I say, 'I wouldn't worry any more than you would anywhere else.' It's a pretty open society in our neighborhoods. It doesn't happen that often, but it's still acceptable on some level, where beating on blacks or Latinos is less acceptable. I don't know why any violence is acceptable."

# PART SIX

# The Twenty-first Century

Demolition of the Thunderbolt, 2000. It last operated in 1983.
*Library of Congress*

# THE ECHOES OF 9/11

RICHARD PORTELLO

RICHARD PORTELLO WAS BORN IN BAY RIDGE HOSPITAL SIX months before the assassination of President Kennedy. His great-grandparents had come to Brooklyn in the 1880s from Italy and settled in Brooklyn. The family congregated in a one-block area by Avenue T and West 9th Street.

His relatives, born of immigrants, were hardworking, productive members of society. His dad's father worked for the A&P supermarket chain, testing olives. After he was laid off, he worked for the R. J. Reynolds tobacco company. His grandmother did beadwork on wedding dresses. His mom's dad drove a truck.

Portello's father spent most of his life as a butcher. The shop had been around the corner from their home, and Portello's father began working there as a youngster, making pennies a day. As he grew up, he was taught how to cut meat, and it became a career.

Portello, who was born in 1963, grew up in Bensonhurst on West 5th Street between Avenue O and 65th Street. He was raised Catholic. No meat was served on Friday nights. The Portellos usually ate pizza or some kind of macaroni. At two P.M. sharp, Sunday afternoons, the whole Portello clan gathered for dinner.

Tony's, a candy store, sat on one corner. To this day, says Portello, he has never tasted better malteds or egg creams. The movie theater he attended most frequently was The Marboro on Bay Parkway. It's where he saw *Jaws* and where he experienced his first kiss. [The theater was demolished in 2007.]

When Portello was in his early teens, his mother, not wanting to go alone, would wake him up in the middle of the night and drive the fifteen minutes to Nathan's in Coney Island for a hot dog.

"She would just be in a mood," he says. "Then when I was in my late teens and early twenties, every Sunday night during the summer my friends and I would go to Coney Island and ride the Cyclone and the Jumbo Jet."

From first through eighth grade Portello went to St. Athanasius Catholic School on Bay Parkway between 61st and 62nd streets. From there he went to William E. Grady Vocational High School, a vocational-technical school specializing in air-conditioning and TV repair as well as the automotive, electrical, and printing trades.

As a kid, Portello lived down the street from the corner firehouse. He spent a great deal of his time there with the men, and for years he swore that when he grew up, he was going to be a fireman. Then he entered high school, took climate control, and when he graduated in 1981, he began a career repairing and maintaining oil burners.

Richard Portello with his grandmother on the day he was promoted to lieutenant. *Courtesy of Richard Portello*

Unhappy with the way his life was going, when he heard from a friend about an upcoming fire department test, Portello decided to apply.

First came a written test. There were math questions. If a hose length is fifty feet and you need to drag the hose three hundred feet, how many lengths of hose do you need? There were questions asking in which direction a gear turns. There was a memory section, where the applicant was shown a picture, and he had to remember what he saw.

Forty thousand men and women took the test. Twenty-seven thousand made it to the second round. Portello was one of them. He scored a ninety-eight.

Next came the physical test, which was designed to separate those who would be hired from the thousands rejected. An applicant needed to get a hundred in order to get hired.

The test was strenuous. First you had to pick up a length of hose and run with it fifty feet. Then, with another length of hose, you had to run up a flight of stairs and run to a window, and then drag the length of hose into that window. You then had a hundred seconds to walk from one side of the armory building to the other, then you had just over two minutes to jump over a six-foot wall, pick up a twenty-foot ladder lying on the ground, stand it up, climb it to a platform, run back down, pick up a 15-pound dumbbell, go up three more flights of stairs, pick up an 80-pound tire, carry it twenty feet across a table, crawl through a twenty-foot tunnel two feet high by two feet wide, then carry a 180-pound dummy around the twenty-foot table.

In training for a high angle rope rescue, Portello repels from a 360-degree tower.
*Courtesy of Richard Portello*

To prepare, Portello paid to take a review course. After the course, he figured the test would be a piece of cake, but just to be sure, he decided to take a second practice course, this one run by an FDNY lieutenant by the name of Pudgy Walsh. It was a good thing he did. After being put through his paces by Walsh, Portello discovered just how difficult the test was going to be. He practiced hard, and when it was time to perform for real, he made a perfect score.

Twenty of his buddies had taken the test with him. Of the group, Portello was the only one to score a hundred and get hired.

"It was probably the happiest day of my life," says Portello. As for the others? "Everybody else became cops."

*Portello's first assignment was to Ladder 118 in Brooklyn Heights.*

**RICHARD PORTELLO** "Here's how the fire department works: there are engine companies, ladder companies, squad companies, and rescue companies. Our 118 was a ladder company. We had one of only fourteen ladder trucks left in the city, which you still drive the front and the back.

"In a [ladder or] truck company, basically what happens, there are five positions:

when you get to the fire, the ladder company forces entry into the building, the men look for the fire, they find the fire, they search for people, and they vent windows.

"Then the engine company stretches the hose and actually puts out the fire. It may not look like it, but there is a very particular order in which things are done. For instance, one of the jobs of the truck company is to go up to the roof of the building, and that guy will open up and vent the roof so the heat and smoke has someplace to go.

"First he will open up anything he can, and if the fire is on the top floor, he will cut the roof with a saw. Then what happens, the engine company pulls up, and sometimes there's just a lot of smoke. The men on the truck have to go in and locate the fire. Once they do, they let the engine men know, 'It's third down on your right.' The engine team will stretch the hose, go to the third room on the right, and once they have water, are ready to put out the fire, and are ready to move in; there's a man from the truck team outside the building who will break the window and give a place for the smoke and heat to go. It's very orchestrated."

*Portello served with Ladder 118 for three years, in the end given the important job of vent man. He then transferred to Engine 214 in Bedford-Stuyvesant.*

**RICHARD PORTELLO** "There were quite a few more fires there than my first company, and I got a chance to work with some of the guys who were in the fire department from what we call 'the heyday.' Those guys were on the job in the 1960s and 1970s during the blackout and the riots. I was fortunate to get to work with those guys. They had so much experience. And as long as you were interested and asked questions, they were very good about sharing their experiences.

"They told quite a few stories. The night of the [1977] blackout they would be putting out one fire and look up the block and see another fire, and they'd have to leave the first fire and go to that one, and there'd be two more fires burning on the next block.

"The same with the riots. They told of a Brooklyn dispatcher asking on the department radio if there were any companies available in Brooklyn. There weren't.

"Firefighting is very much a team effort. Any time you see a fireman being interviewed after a rescue, you will always hear him say, 'It was a team effort. Everyone did a great job. I just happened to be the one.' And truly we depend on each other. That's what makes the job so great: the camaraderie and the fact we would do anything for each other, and we would do anything we could for anyone trapped in a fire. You just keep going until the fire is out and you get everybody out."

*Portello wanted to return to a truck company, and in 1991, just as the citywide crack epidemic was winding down, he transferred to Ladder 103 in East New York.*

**RICHARD PORTELLO**   "It was pretty incredible to me, the devastation of the neighborhood from the crack epidemic. When I got to 103, we were the only building on an entire square city block. The *only* building. Everything else was weeds.

"In the late '50s and early '60s there were apartment houses on the block—tenements, we called them—but they all burned down during the heyday, and then it was all vacant lots except for the firehouse. It was pretty amazing. I went there recently, and all the buildings have been rebuilt. Wow, what a difference!

"But when I arrived there, East New York, like Bed-Stuy, was very busy. There were a lot of fires during the seven years I was there."

*In 1997 Portello was promoted to lieutenant, and he got the job of "covering," working at night and bouncing from company to company as needed. By September of 2001 Portello was assigned to Squad 41 in the South Bronx.*

**RICHARD PORTELLO**   "Squad 41 is part of Special Operations Command. There are only seven squads in the entire city. A squad at a fire has a pretty big response area. Squad 41 covers all of the South Bronx and Manhattan. We cover from 80th Street on the East Side and 100th Street on the West Side all the way up to the northern end of Manhattan.

"A squad can be used as an engine or as a ladder, depending on what the chief needs. We are manpower. We find out how the chief wants to use us when we arrive at the scene.

"We are veterans, and in addition to the fires, we respond to hazardous material incidents. We respond to subway derailments, car accidents when people are trapped, confined-space rescues, and building collapses."

*On September 11, 2001, Squad 41 responded to the greatest building collapse in history, the toppling of the twin towers of the World Trade Center after each was attacked by Al Qaeda terrorists who flew jetliners into the buildings. After the towers fell, trapping thousands under the debris, the body count began. Of the 2,752 men and women who died in New York on 9/11, 343 firemen lost their lives, including 12 from Squad 41. Years later, 9/11 remained a topic that Portillo found just as painful to discuss as though it had happened yesterday.*

*They say that timing is everything, and on that beautiful sunny morning in September, Richard Portello wasn't at his post. He was home in Staten Island.*

The Twin Towers on fire on 9/11, looking south on Sixth Avenue in Greenwich Village. *Doug Grad*

**RICHARD PORTELLO** "I wasn't working that day. In the squad it was change of tours, and everyone met to be given positions by the officer. Then after the first plane hit, they were relocated to Manhattan to cover Squad 18's area, after Squad 18 was sent to the Trade Center. Then after the second plane hit, Squad 41 also was sent to the Trade Center.

"So I was home and had gotten dressed to go when somebody called me to say a plane had crashed into the World Trade Center. I was going to drive, but then I said to myself, 'Who am I kidding? If I get on the Gowanus Parkway, I'm going to be stuck in traffic like being in a parking lot.'

"I was watching on TV to see what was going on, and then the second plane hit, and then I knew it was terrorism, and I got in my car to head in. By then the Verrazano Bridge was closed, so I went to Rescue 5, the firehouse on Staten Island, and a bunch of us went to the Staten Island ferry and got across on the ferry.

"By the time we got on the ferry, the first building had collapsed and the second one was still on fire. When we were halfway across to Manhattan, the second one came down.

"It was incredible to look at. I stood there, not believing what I was seeing. We landed in Manhattan, and there were thousands of people at the ferry terminal looking to leave Manhattan. There was a city bus there, and we all got on it, and we had the bus take us to the site.

"There was a division chief on the ferry boat going to Manhattan, and he assigned five firemen to a lieutenant or captain, and we wrote down on a piece of paper what we call a 'riding list.' What happens normally, the officer keeps a copy on him, and a copy goes on the fire truck with everyone who is riding that day. The chief made us fill out a 'riding list,' and he took one copy, and each officer kept a copy. Once we got to the Trade Center, we went wherever we were needed or wherever we felt we could do some good.

"As we were walking up to the site, there was this white stuff all over the place. It almost looked like snow. It was very quiet. I was assuming the white stuff muffled a lot of noise. It was very, very quiet. All you heard was the occasional voice of someone you were walking with. White stuff covered everything. Lower Manhattan was pretty empty by then.

"We got up to the site, and it was total devastation. We just went to wherever we thought there were voids, and we searched the voids to see if we could find people. All six guys from Squad 41 were missing, five firemen and a lieutenant. And this was true of companies all over the city. There were roughly four hundred men in Special Operations Command, and we lost ninety-three.

"I was there until one in the morning. We realized it was fifteen hours after the fact, and we needed to let the families know they were missing and that we were looking for them, to tell them to say your prayers and let them know we were doing everything we could.

"I notified the wife of one of the men, and I went home for two hours, and then

I went right back to the site. I spent weeks there. I can't tell you how many.

"It was a very difficult experience, but you know what? We looked at it as our job, and we also knew it wasn't nearly as difficult as what those guys did that day. So we just wanted to find as many people as we could, both civilians and firemen. And hopefully give their families closure. And in between spending all that time at the site, I went to a lot of funerals, as many as I could. It had a psychological effect on me—it did on everyone, including civilians. As time went on, I spoke to a lot of New Yorkers, and I would hear their stories."

Squad Co. 1, after a fire. Portello is fourth from left.
*Courtesy of Richard Portello*

*One result of the death of so many firefighters was that there were openings in the hierarchy. The Sunday after Tuesday's World Trade Center attack, Richard Portello was told he was being promoted to captain and that he would head Squad 1 in Park Slope, starting in late January. When he finally reported, he saw that the squad, which had lost twelve men in the disaster, including their captain, James Amato, was well on its way to being rebuilt.*

**RICHARD PORTELLO** "The guys were doing a tremendous job. They didn't need me to get them going. We started bringing in some new men, and the old guys did a great job teaching the new guys. And the new guys learned quickly. Everybody did an incredible job. It was a total team effort. We all worked hard, with the common goal of rebuilding the company. It was very important, because twelve guys got killed, and we were all determined to bring the place back to what those guys had worked so hard to build."

The front of Squad Co. 1. The 9/11 memorial is to the right. *Courtesy of Richard Portello*

*To the right of the firehouse sits a wooden memorial to the men from Squad 1 who lost their lives on 9/11. Like the soldiers at Iwo Jima, the sculpture depicts firemen hoisting an American flag amid the rubble of the fallen towers. According to Captain Portello, it was donated by an artist from Oregon and placed on the site owned by the Park Slope Food Co-op next door. On the wall of the Squad 1 firehouse the names of the men who fell on 9/11 are listed: Captain James Amato, Brian Bilcher, Gary Box, Thomas Butler, Peter Carroll, Robert Cordice, Lieutenant Edward D'Atri, Lieutenant Michael Esposito, David Fontana, Matthew Garvey, Lieutenant Michael Russo, and Stephen Siller.*

**RICHARD PORTELLO**   "When you go to a fire you depend on each other so much. This, and every other firehouse in the city is very tight. The camaraderie is amazing, and that's every firehouse in the city."

# THE MURAL PAINTER

JANET BRAUN-REINITZ

**A**T THE TENDER AGE OF TWENTY-THREE, JANET BRAUN-Reinitz already had made history when, in the fall of 1961, this well-to-do suburbanite from Rye, New York, rode a Greyhound bus from St. Louis into the heart of the racist South to test the Jim Crow practices as one of the "freedom riders." The first stop was Little Rock, and the bus was met by hundreds of screaming whites. After arrival, she and four others went to the waiting room of the bus station, where she was arrested and taken to the city jail. Unprepared, she was terrified. It was the lead story on the *Huntley-Brinkley Report.*

After spending three days in jail, the freedom riders were told they would get suspended sentences if they'd leave Little Rock. After two stops in Texas, the bus moved on to Shreveport, Louisiana, where a large gathering of angry whites and police awaited them. To avoid trouble, they left town at two in the morning. At their last stop, New Orleans, she and a black civil rights protester were served at the lunch counter. Reinitz would say later that her civil rights activity was inspired by the coming of Jackie Robinson to the Dodgers.

Upon her return to New York, her husband was accepted to graduate school at the University of Rochester. She would have to take her civil rights work with her.

Braun-Reinitz joined the Rochester CORE chapter and immediately became involved in the case of Rufus Fairwell, an attendant at a gas station. On August 23, 1962, he was closing up when the police pulled up. Sure that he was robbing the place, the police arrested him; he wound up in a wheelchair, with two cracked vertebrae and a severely damaged eye. Back in the 1960s, blacks got shot by the police all the time, and nothing ever happened. This time it was different. The civil rights movement was slowly building.

Her husband died in 1979, and in 1987, after her children were off to college, Braun-Reinitz moved to Park Slope. A mural painter, she was able to pursue her craft on a grand scale. Her work can be seen all over Brooklyn, especially in East New York.

On September 7, 2001, she moved from Park Slope to Clinton Hill, between Fort Greene and Bed-Stuy, across the street from Pratt University.

Four days later she was a tad late for an early-morning meeting at 7 World Trade Center. After watching the second plane hit a tower and explode in an orange ball, she decided it would be best to get off Manhattan island. She walked across the Brooklyn Bridge as the cloud of debris from the fallen towers rose behind her.

If she was horrified by the events of the day, she was even more upset by the actions of President George W. Bush, as she waited in vain for him to rush to New York to show New Yorkers he cared. Several days later, when the president finally did arrive, he promised money to help repair the damage and ease the pain, but his promises would prove to be empty. Then came his invasion of Iraq in 2003, a sovereign country with seemingly little or no connection to the Al Qaeda terrorists who brought down the towers. After Bush's administration spent countless billions mounting an unpopular war, the Republican Party had the nerve to hold their 2004 National Convention in New York. Braun-Reinitz once again marched in protest.

**JANET BRAUN-REINITZ** "After Rufus Fairwell was gunned down by the Rochester police, I felt very strongly that we had to do something about this, and so we had a meeting at our house, and all sorts of people came: ministers, a rabbi, a really good group of people, and we talked well into the night about what we were going to do. The people who came from the university were full of verbiage and analysis, but no action. Finally at two in the morning, I said, 'I'm sick of this. I don't know what the rest of you are going to do, but I'm going to sit in at the police station.' One of the black schoolteachers said, 'I'm coming with you.' No one else volunteered.

"The wife of one of my husband's fellow graduate students said, 'I'll stay out here and do the PR. I'll call UPI and AP and I'll check on you about seven in the morning.' She did a great job, because by nine in the morning there were a hundred people sitting in at the police station.

"What we were asking for was a police review board. Meanwhile, Malcolm X was scheduled to arrive in town to speak at the university. He was also going to be speaking at a settlement house in front of a black audience. We went. There were six white faces in the audience, and he was mesmerizing. To watch him was an experience unlike anything I had ever had. Malcolm was smart. He was powerful, and he scared the hell out of me, because he talked about the blond-haired, blue-eyed devils. And there I was: brown eyes, brown hair, but it was the same deal.

"When Malcolm spoke at the University of Rochester, it was a different kind of speech, much more intellectual and controlled, and afterward he and CORE got together for a meeting on the campus. He had bodyguards. There were about twelve of us there, and Malcolm laid it out. He said, 'Right now these people'—the city—'think you're the radicals. And they are not going to give you the right time of day. But if they perceive that we have joined the fight, *we* will be perceived as the radicals, and you will be just where you need to be, which is right in the middle ground.'

"Malcolm X spoke out about the Rufus Fairwell case, and it all worked. Rochester became the second city in the United States after Philadelphia to have a civilian review board. And Fairwell sued the city and won, a victory though the man was still in a wheelchair. How often did a black victim get compensated? Never. But we won through that very simple tactic and timing—Malcolm made his statements at a crucial moment, and I am forever in his debt in a thousand different ways.

"I also met Martin Luther King. I chatted with him a little bit. I met him through a mutual friend, a black woman who was hounded by the FBI for being active in the movement.

"Our phones were tapped. We knew that, because we could hear it. These days the FBI has all sorts of people they are after—terrorists, environmentalists, critics—so I don't suppose anyone would bother to tap my phone, but just in case, HELLO, HOW ARE YOU? But it was like that.

"I am permanently paranoid. I rarely use a credit card. I don't book my own flights. I don't have e-mail. I'm not kidding. After my husband died in 1979, I wanted to get his FBI file. I had a lawyer write to get both of our files. His came back describing his having stowed away to get to Europe when he was seventeen, which he did,

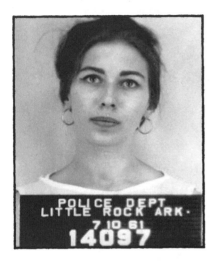

Janet Braun's mugshot.
*Courtesy of Janet Braun-Reinitz*

but everything else was blacked out because he had been in the Young Socialists League. They said they had no record of me and could I please give them some information so they could find it. My lawyer wrote me a letter. It said, 'I don't know what they're after, but I suggest you drop it immediately.' Which I did.

"For a while I used to cross the street so as not to walk past a policeman. I finally got over that, but I am of that paranoid generation. I told my daughter, 'You won't find me on Google.' She said, 'Mom, there are fourteen pages on you on Google.' That's where they found my mug shot from my booking in Little Rock. I had never seen it. I looked pretty good. The kids had the photo put on a mug. Hilarious.

"Everybody has had a moment—it's not possible now not to understand at a very early age, even if you're white and privileged, that the world is segregated and that people are discriminating against you. But you could live that way without understanding it.

"I got involved in the women's movement. I got involved in the antiwar movement, though I must say that I always felt that the antiwar people were extremely disorganized. When they were tear-gassed, they would go, 'Oh my God, we're being tear-gassed.' I kept thinking, *Doesn't anyone train anyone? Don't they know? Why aren't they disciplined?* It always made me angry when people whined when they got tear-gassed and were taken off to jail.

"After my husband graduated, he taught at Hobart and William Smith in upstate New York. After he died, I promised my children I would stay in Ithaca until the last one graduated from high school. We had brought them to Brooklyn in 1974, when my husband swapped jobs with a friend of his, and so we lived in the city for a year. But my kids were small-town kids, and they were not happy. And when the last one graduated, I came to Brooklyn, and I began painting murals. I had been to Nicaragua. I had been to Georgia in the former Soviet Union, painting murals. I had painted one in Ithaca. And I had really gotten the bug to take my art to the streets and work for a mass audience. What I liked most in life was to be out on a scaffold on the street.

"I moved to Fifth Avenue in Park Slope [in 1987], an old Italian neighborhood as well as a black and Latino neighborhood. It wasn't long before it would become the most elite place in Brooklyn, but it wasn't then.

"I lived over a butcher shop. The building was owned by the butcher. There weren't many restaurants or bars, no movie theaters, but there were good things, like cobblers. When the cobbler goes, the neighborhood is gone, as far as I'm concerned. At that point there were no Starbucks. It had a great flea market. Not much else was there, but it was close to Prospect Park, and it was pretty, not too noisy, and affordable.

"Then about five years later, about 1992, the change came. My building got sold, and the new owner, an Italian, was planning on putting in one of the first chic restaurants in Park Slope. He really wanted to put his workers in the building. Meanwhile, a homeless man moved onto our roof, and at some point I wasn't happy anymore.

"I hooked up with another artist, Rochelle Shicoff, and we rented a great, big, walk-through apartment, still in Park Slope. Each of us had our own studio and bedroom and our own sitting room. We shared the kitchen and the bathroom.

"She's a great person, and we have collaborated on painting murals. During this time I hooked up with the United Community Center, a community organizing group in East New York. Mel Grizer, the director, understood the power of murals for community organizing, and for the last ten years I have been out there during the summer, painting murals. This has been my living.

"The very first mural I did, at 999 Blake Avenue in Brooklyn, was a baseball mural. In 1988 I was asked to go out to East New York—I knew nothing of East New York—but I went out and looked at the wall in an industrial park, a very rough place. I designed a 150-foot mural called *Home Run* that wrapped around the corner of the building. It's all silhouette of someone at the plate hitting a home run. On the other side of the wall is a dugout, and there's a crowd in which I painted all my favorite baseball players. I'm a Mets fan, so Doc Gooden was pitching, Darryl Strawberry was hitting the home run. Mookie Wilson was on base. Keith Hernandez was at first, and Ozzie Smith was at shortstop. In the dugout was Henry Aaron, and then there was this huge baseball about four feet high on the wall where the baseball was autographed by Jackie Robinson, Stan Musial, and a lot of players. When people came and wanted to do graffiti, they would write their name on the baseball. The workers would come out of the factories at lunchtime while I painted, and there would be a discussion of baseball during lunch hour. It was wonderful.

"Home Run," corner of Hinsdale and Glenmore, East New York, Brooklyn. *Courtesy of Janet Braun-Reinitz*

"Then I met the people at the United Community Centers, and I did about ten murals for them. The United Community Centers was started around the idea that working-class people should be able to live together in an integrated and positive way. By the time I got there, East New York was the murder capital of the city. But UCC had gotten a building and ran a day-care center, and took up the issues that arose in the community. When private interests tried to put a sewage plant in East New York, the UCC hooked up with our assemblyman, Charles Barron, a young man with ambitions, and stopped it. The UCC has never sold out. As a result, it has been politically committed, not politically smart, and therefore very poor. But Mel Grizer understood that painting murals in a community is a sign that people care. Among the murals I've painted is one called *From Somali, West Africa, to East New York, Brooklyn.* We used traditional signs and symbols and invented others for the neighborhood, so that we have the symbol of the gun with the X through it and hot dogs and Brooklyn Bridge and headstones from old cemeteries.

"Another mural is the *Woman's Wall.* It reflects the health issues of women in the community. Another painted in Martin Luther King Park is called *Freedom Train and Interracial Journey.* We paired Thurgood Marshall and Earl Warren. We paired Jackie Robinson and Branch Rickey, Eleanor Roosevelt and Marion Anderson. Wilma Rudolph, Roberto Clemente, Maya Angelou, and Alvin Ailey, the dancer, are represented, Martin Luther King, Rosa Parks, and Louis Armstrong.

"Last summer we did the biggest one yet, in Bed-Stuy, called *When Women Pursue Justice.* It's seventy-six feet long and forty-six feet high and features ninety mostly twentieth-century women activists. Shirley Chisholm is there, of course. She stands four feet by six feet, along with Emma Goldman, Betty Friedan, Gloria Steinem, Wilma Mankiller, Fanny Lou Hamer, Dorothy Day, and Margaret Sanger, who is controversial in the black community because she believed in eugenics. When the radical money ran out, she took a lot of money from the eugenicists, and the black community never forgave her, because she didn't speak out against it. Ever.

"I moved from Park Slope to a little slice of Brooklyn called Clinton Hill. It's between Fort Greene and Bed-Stuy. I moved in in September of 2001. I like Clinton Hill very much. We have a wonderful coffee shop, just not a chain. People do not sit there all day with their computers. You can go in any direction, and there are varieties of people, and it's very nice, integrated by age, race, and by class, where Park Slope is white, upwardly mobile, double strollers and nannies. There are more nannies in Park Slope than other people. It's supposed to be a liberal place, but it was, 'You don't want to build a halfway house in our neighborhood.' Some things don't change.

"Four days after I moved to Clinton Hill, I was headed to an all-day meeting at the Deutsche Bank building at the World Trade Center. I never go to that part of

town, but it was an art meeting for an organization I work with in the public schools. It was primary day in New York, so I had stopped to vote, and I was late. I was supposed to be there at eight thirty in the morning, and I was a little late, and as I came out of the subway at Fulton Street, the first plane had already hit.

"I asked a cop what was going on, and he said they thought a private plane had hit the tower. There was a streak of orange across the building against this bright clear blue sky. I have to say—it sounds awful—that it was beautiful. I said to the cop, 'I have to get to this meeting.' He said, 'Lady, you can't go down there.' I said, 'I have to. I'm late.' I paid no attention to the gravity of the situation. None. I started on my way anyway—until I saw the second plane hit the other building. They say there wasn't a lot of noise or a lot of panic, but it depends on what you think noise is and what you think panic is. Because you could feel the noise bouncing off the buildings in those canyons. It was all around you and very personal. It sounded like explosions—all around, which you couldn't see. And it kept reverberating.

"My instinct was to get off Manhattan island. I had a little radio with me, because I was going to be in this meeting all day, and it was September, and there were ballgames I had to know the scores of. I needed to know how the Mets were doing.

"The artists who had gotten there on time were held in that building, and they evacuated just at the time the towers collapsed. No one was hurt, but they were caught in the mess, and they suffered from a lot of posttraumatic stress and a lot of inhaling of nasty things.

"I ran as far as City Hall Park, and then I tried my cell phone, and it was dead, and I listened to my radio trying to figure out what was going on, but that didn't work very well either. I decided the best thing for me to do was simply walk across the Brooklyn Bridge. It was open for traffic going out of Manhattan, and it was open for people walking out of Manhattan. Nothing was allowed in except for emergency vehicles.

"This was before the buildings had actually collapsed. I got onto the bridge, and I kept looking back, and I kept my radio on, and when I got about halfway, I could see a group of five or six guys running across the bridge, and my thought was, *They know something I don't know. This bridge is about to go.* I felt, *If it does, I've had a moderately long and interesting life, and it'll be okay.* I turned my back to the smoking towers, and I walked with some haste. By the time I got off this long, long ramp onto Tillary Street, I heard on the radio that a plane had attacked the Pentagon and a fourth plane had crashed. I have to say I didn't quite understand the gravity. I had just moved to a new apartment, and I was very busy trying to figure out where I was and how I could get home.

"The scope of it didn't really hit me until later in the day. Then I went and gave blood, which was what everybody did. The one thing I was waiting for was for Bush to come to New York. Rudy Giuliani, who was hardly my favorite mayor, was doing very well, coming on the television, saying, 'I don't have any answers, but it's okay.' You could see from where I live the cloud over Manhattan coming toward us. And I kept waiting for Bush to arrive.

After the World Trade Center fell on 9/11, the smoke blew right over Brooklyn, as seen from the Manhattan Bridge. *Doug Grad*

"If you remember the accident at the Three Mile Island nuclear plant, Jimmy Carter, a nuclear engineer who knew how dangerous it was, came immediately. Unlike Carter, Bush didn't come. And he didn't come. And he didn't come. And I had that feeling all over again that for him New Yorkers weren't really Americans, so no one in the federal government was coming to take care of us. It was dreadful.

"Aside from what happened to the city, our government's answer was not to take care of us but rather to go find a scapegoat and make war.

"During the run-up to the war, New Yorkers turned out by the hundreds of thousands to show they didn't want war. It was clear to a lot of people that Bush intended this war no matter what anybody thought. It was very interesting being in Europe and hearing people talk about Bush. They don't understand how Americans could have voted for him—twice."

*On Sunday, August 28, 2004, hundreds of thousands of protesters filled the streets of Manhattan to protest the presence of the Republican National Convention and the war in Iraq. As marchers passed Madison Square Garden, they would at times erupt into chants of "Liar, Liar." Janet Braun-Reinitz and her son were among the marchers.*

**JANET BRAUN-REINITZ** "There were hundreds of organized events around the convention. If you were a woman and wanted to march against the Republican policy of choice, you could. If you wanted to go and march to protest what was going on in Darfur, you could. You could march with labor, march on immigration, march for peace.

"My son and I marched over the Brooklyn Bridge. In one demonstration we marched in front of the Fox television headquarters. We went to the Sudanese embassy to protest the genocide in Darfur. We marched up and down Fifth Avenue [in Manhattan].

"There were a huge number of people in the streets. The cops were cordoning us off. The usual stuff. At one point I said, 'I know where we can go to rest. We can go down by Macy's, where there's a little park.' But CNN had set up their outdoor interviewing headquarters there. When we got there, it became very dicey.

Janet and friends protesting the Bush agenda.
*Courtesy of Janet Braun-Reinitz*

"One of the things about having been in the civil rights movement, you have a different antenna for crowds. We were two blocks from Madison Square Garden. I saw more police. The traffic was stopped. All the streets were cordoned off, and there were a lot of empty buses in anticipation of arrests.

"I just felt uncomfortable. I said to my son, 'Let's get out of here.' We ducked into the subway, got in through the turnstiles, just before the police blocked all the entrances. We got on the train that was on the platform—I don't remember if it was even going in our direction—but we got out of there.

"There were a lot of arrests. It wasn't Bull Connor–ugly, but it was such an insult to see the Republicans in the city. They said the convention was going to help our economy, to show solidarity with us. When you think how antithetical they are to anything about this city, it was just one more slap in the face.

"Bush never did give us the money he said he was going to give us. And whatever facilities we have in this city, we pay for. We're paying for it, and we have to do this because of the policies of Bush and the feds. If Bush had not waged war on *our* behalf, and that's the point—*on our behalf*—we wouldn't have as many potential terrorists. It seems so clear and sensible that what he has done is so irrational, and the fact it's all being done in our name—it just rubs the wrong way every day—every time there's something the city needs money for, something other than security. I get so angry. It's not something I can be completely rational about.

"We New Yorkers know we really don't have a place in Bush's government. As far as going out in the streets to protest, the truth is, at this point we know it won't make any difference in terms of federal policy. But it does make one feel better. I think there's a little less hopelessness. It was so different for civil rights, where the targets of who we were going after were so clear. Here, to be anti-Republican is very amorphous. Primarily because we really haven't a clue as to what's really going on in Iraq. Plus the amount of money that disappeared to Halliburton—you would think that alone would cause Americans to vote them out.

"I was talking to Bob Filner, a freedom rider who is now a congressman from California. He told me when he first ran, his opponent questioned the validity of it—was he really a freedom rider? And he lost. The next time he ran he won.

"We've come to expect these Republican attacks. The Swiftboat campaign against John Kerry was another example. There was no outcry, because he wouldn't stand up. That was surprising. But people are not going to protest for someone who won't protest on his own behalf.

"We'll see what they dig up this time."

# THE COUNCILMAN FOR CHANGE

CHARLES BARRON

THE RELIGIOUS RIGHT FIRST MADE ITS PRESENCE FELT IN the presidential election of 1976, when it supported Jimmy Carter, the Democratic presidential candidate. Carter, a victim of high inflation and the Iranian hostage crisis, lost the next election to the ticket of Ronald Reagan and George H. W. Bush, in large part because the evangelical Christians switched sides. They preferred Reagan's positions on social issues, taking the side against abortion, gay rights, and civil rights. Reagan aligned himself with televangelists like Jimmy Swaggart, Jerry Falwell, and Pat Robertson. Falwell especially railed against the civil rights movement, the antiapartheid movement in South Africa, and sufferers of AIDS. He went so far as to blame the spread of AIDS on the "wrath of God against homosexuals." An aghast Republican senator John McCain labeled Falwell and his ilk "agents of intolerance."

When George W. Bush ran for governor of Texas in 1993, he ran as God's disciple. He read the Bible every morning. His campaign planks included a call for religion-based drug-treatment centers and prison ministries. After attending church, Bush would tell people, "I feel as though God was talking directly to me."

When he ran for president in 2000, he wed economic and social issues. He took on the left head-on. He talked of "tough compassion" when it came to the poor and talked of his being "a uniter, not a divider." What we got was a president who turned out to be as divisive as any president in American history. Though the Constitution calls for a separation between church and state, George W. Bush acted as though Christianity was the national religion. If it had been left to this born-again dry alcoholic, we'd have returned to the age of Puritanism.

Under George W. Bush, "faith"—as in Christian faith—became a crucial test for political appointees. But admitting to being religious apparently doesn't reflect what Jesus might have done, as Bush's appointees in the Federal Emergency Management Agency turned a blind eye to the dire suffering of the citizens of New Orleans after Hurricane Katrina. For five days the survivors sat and waited in vain for federal aid. Too many died during the wait.

Bush placed appointees with right-wing Christian backgrounds, but with little experience or skill, in key government posts, including FEMA and the Justice Department. The head of FEMA, Michael Brown, had been an official in a dog-racing organization, but he was a devoted Bush supporter, and he was hired for his loyalty. When New Orleans flooded, he was helpless to do anything—or perhaps he was told by the Bush adminstration not to do anything. The country watched in horror as the poor of New Orleans had to sit for days before something as basic as water was brought to alleviate their misery. Bush ran for president on a platform of minimal government. Here was minimal government in its most disgraceful form.

When President Bush said, "You're doing a heck of a job, Brownie," he was taunting all who believe the abandonment of New Orleans was a disgrace to this presidency that will forever be one of the legacies of the Bush administration.

As for Bush's Justice Department, it was revealed that Monica Goodling, a top aide to Attorney General Alberto Gonzalez and a graduate of Pat Robertson's Regent University School of Law, with no practical experience, had the task of hiring and firing U.S. district attorneys. When nine of them either wouldn't go after Democratic candidates for vote fraud or wouldn't stop prosecuting Republicans accused of misdeeds, she fired them, replacing them with appointees dedicated not to justice but to the Republican Party. Goodling pleaded the Fifth Amendment against self-incrimination, to keep from going to jail for choosing loyalty to George W. Bush, Karl Rove, and the Republican Party over loyalty to her country.

One after another, Bush's religious-right cronies became tarred by scandal. The homophobic Ted Haggard, the head of the National Association of Evangelicals, was forced to resign when it was revealed he had a gay lover. Other Moral Majority Republicans with God-is-my-pilot credentials bit the dust in the wake of the Jack Abramoff payoff scandals. Tom DeLay, the speaker of the House, was forced to quit, kicking and screaming, in disgrace. Ralph Reed, the number two man in the Christian Coalition, was accused of having his hands in the corporate cookie jar, as was the Reverend Louis Sheldon of the American Family Association, and James Dobson of Focus on the Family, all of whom were accused of taking money to promote gambling casinos. Apparently they didn't heed the eleventh commandment: Thou Shalt Not Get Caught.

Meanwhile, in Brooklyn, the Reverend Herbert Daughtry did what any real minister who cares about his flock should have done: he protested Bush's thirst for war. Daughtry stood in front of the United Nations along with Daniel Ellsberg of Watergate fame in an attempt to make people see the folly of Bush's Iraqi invasion. He was arrested. He has even traveled to Darfur to protest the genocide there. The Reverend Daughtry, who has spent years trying to get the city's police to stop killing defenseless black citizens, has been a legendary influence in the black community.

City Councilman Charles Barron has been one of the Reverend Daughtry's most loyal parishioners. After growing up poor on the Lower East Side and becoming a Black Panther, at age twenty Barron decided to pursue a college degree. It took

Charles Barron and Rev. Daughtry. *AP Photo/Ed Bailey*

him a dozen years, but he earned his bachelor's degree in 1988 from Hunter College. While in college, he became associated with the Reverend Daughtry and his political organization, the Black United Front. Daughtry and Barron organized sit-ins and protests after every instance of what they perceived to be police brutality against African-Americans.

Once Barron began to see and understand the difference between having influence to make a difference and having the *power* to make changes, he decided to run for political office. After losing a race for the city council as an independent running against twenty-two-year incumbent Priscilla Wooten in 1999, Barron won the seat two years later against the Democratic-machine candidate Greg Jackson. Since then he has become chair of the committee overseeing the CUNY system and he has gotten millions of dollars to improve parks in East New York. Along the way he has also shaken up the establishment. He believes one day he can become mayor of New York City.

**CHARLES BARRON** "When I went to Hunter College in the CUNY system, there were a lot of student activists. It was in 1979, and I was part of a program called 'In the Spirit of the '60s.' I invited Malcolm X's daughter and the Reverend Herbert Daughtry, and Richie Perez, who was a member of the Young Lords. [The Young Lords started as a street gang in Chicago in the 1960s, split into ministries, and morphed into a Puerto Rican equivalent of the Black Panthers.] Richie was at Brooklyn College, and he and I became friends.

"Through the Reverend Daughtry, I joined the Black United Front, and we engaged in just about every issue you could think of, from police brutality and apartheid in South Africa, and that's when I really started my political action on a leadership level.

"Our movement started with the shooting of Arthur Miller. He was a black businessman who went to check on his brother who police had roughed up and who was in custody. Miller had a permit to carry a gun when he went over to them. They saw his gun around his waist and shot and killed him. We started the Arthur Miller Patrol. Three hundred people with green jackets on patrolled the streets to protect us against the police.

"Then Victor Rhodes was beaten up by Hasidic Jews. Fifty of them stomped him into a coma in Crown Heights. We protested after that incident. Then came our boycott of stores in downtown Brooklyn that wouldn't hire blacks, which led to more attention.

"Then came the Eleanor Bumpers case. She was a grandmother who was arthritic and diabetic. They said she was a couple months behind in her rent, and the police came to evict her and took the hinges off her door. They came with riot shields, riot helmets, restraining rods, and they claim she came at them with a kitchen knife. I would too if you broke down my door and came in with white police officers with all that gear on.

"They blew her hand off with a shotgun, the hand they claim the knife was in, and then they shot her in the chest and killed her.

"So we demonstrated and went to court. Our lawyer asked the judge, 'They blew her hand off. Why the second shot?' We didn't even think the first shot was justified. The answer: the timing between the two shots. The cops walked.

"Then came the Michael Stewart case. He was a young black graffiti artist who the police said was painting on the trains, and they wound up choking him to death. To death.

"By now we knew enough that the medical examiner had to tell you the manner of death and the cause of death. They can't just say, 'Cardiac arrest.' We know that. He's dead. His heart has stopped.

"The manner of death is one of four things: natural causes, homicide, accidental death, or suicide. We knew it wasn't suicide. They knew it wasn't natural causes. If he had said accidental, it could have been reckless endangerment or manslaughter. But they didn't write anything for manner of death. The police got off that time too.

"In 1980 we became the Black United Front and emerged as a national organization. We had our founding conference in Brooklyn, where over a thousand delegates came from thirty-five states and five foreign countries. I became a little more known and took more of a leadership role. I became Reverend Daughtry's assistant and the New York State coordinator.

"Then in East New York the city wanted to build an incinerator, and I fought against them. The emissions would have been horrendous in such a congested area. I found a law that said that no private company could build an incinerator in New York City, and we went to court and stopped it, an environmental victory that was unheard of. That was in 1995.

"I was getting more known, and when they [the owners of the property] wanted to build a movie theater in East New York on Linden Boulevard, we protested, saying what we really needed was a supermarket, a youth center, and a technology building. We demonstrated. I brought in Al Sharpton. Three hundred people were yelling, 'Not another brick over my dead body.'

"The next day they put up the whole wall. They still built it. I said to myself, 'How did this happen?' Come to find out that the city council member, Priscilla Wooten, who had been in office twenty years, voted for it. The city council, I discovered, passed the budget, and it passed laws over land use. We have fifty-one districts, 162,000 people in each district, and the council member has to sign off on it. That's power.

"I was demonstrating, screaming and hollering for the person in power to make a decision in your best interest. That's influence. But when you have that seat, that's power. I said to myself, 'What's missing in our movement is power. I'm going to get that seat.' That's what launched me into electoral politics.

"To get in, I had to learn how to win. When you're going up against the machine, you have to learn how to win elections. They may not know how to do anything else, but one thing they do know is how to win elections. They know how to get on the ballot, and they know how to kick you off the ballot. They know to make sure they have the high-powered lawyers, and then they are going to beat you by mailings and the election operation.

"My first run was against Priscilla Wooten in 1999. She was close to Rudolph Giuliani, the mayor, and to Peter Vallone, the speaker of the city council. Both of them campaigned for her. I had the Reverend Herbert Daughtry, the Reverend Al Sharpton, and [former mayor] David Dinkins on my side. And we went to war.

"On that first run I had five thousand signatures to get me on the ballot. I only needed nine hundred. They charged that I wasn't a U.S. citizen, and they took me to court so I could spend some of my campaign money. I had to spend $10,000 just to give the judge my birth certificate. And they said I forged most of the signatures, when no two signatures looked alike and they didn't even bring in a handwriting expert.

"First of all, they were shocked I could get five thousand signatures. They thought, *Oh, radical Charles doesn't know about this stuff. He's not even going to stay on the ballot.* We beat them in court twice.

"We went to war. They said I was a Black Panther who hates white people. They said I'd never be able to deliver anything to the district because the mayor and the speaker hate me. They said if I won, the people who were given jobs by the incumbent would lose them. They even got preachers to speak against me.

"They outspent me. If there were forty polling places, they had ten supporters in front of every site. I had two, because I couldn't afford to pay for any more. People make their decisions at the last moment. They might be familiar with the mayor, and they might not be familiar with the council race, so they say, 'Vote for Mayor Giuliani and Priscilla Wooten.' They hand you a palm card.

"Then there was the postering. I put my posters up, and they paid kids to tear them down. So you had to be ready for war. The bottom line was she had the infrastructure, the congressmen, the assemblyperson, and eight senators—that's a political machine, and even though I lost—four thousand votes to her six thousand—I was encouraged we could do so well. For a first-time run, we got 40 percent of the vote to her 60 percent, and everybody was shocked we got that close.

"I stayed organized, stayed visible, attended planning board meetings, school board meetings, and in 2001 they passed term limits in New York City, so the seat opened up. You could only spend two terms in office, eight years. This was Priscilla Wooten's last term.

"The machine selected another popular candidate, Greg Jackson, to be the Democratic machine's candidate. They didn't come to me, because they knew they couldn't control me. I'm an independent who just happens to be a registered Democrat. It's not that they dislike me. They can't control me.

"The second time around we worked hard. I went to train stations in the morning, went door-to-door, held block parties, went to churches on Sunday, and I got another 4,000 signatures on the ballot. I won by 300 votes: 4,900 for me, 4,600 for Greg Jackson. We beat the machine.

"After I won the city council seat, I did a great job in my community. I got $3.6 million to transform Linden Park from nothing to something. It's going to be named Sonny Carson Park. Sonny was a gang member who became a political leader in Ocean Hill–Brownsville. He got people jobs, fought police brutality.

"I got another $1 million for Venable Park, and I got $2 million for the Brownsville Recreation Park.

"When the Community Service Society of New York made a study saying nearly 50 percent of black men were unemployed, I went to Mayor Bloomberg and the speaker to get money for a workforce-development program. I got $34 million over three years to get people jobs now.

"After I was elected, I became the chair of the Higher Education Committee, which has oversight over CUNY. When the mayor tried to cut this and that from the CUNY budget, I led the charge and got it restored. For the first time in history, we have a five-year CUNY capital plan for $602 million to fix up the CUNY schools. I got nearly $40 million for the Peter Vallone scholarship. I got about $20 million for a safety-net program where if they raise the tuition in the community colleges, students can apply for that difference.

"I get a lot of media attention. I'm very outspoken. I speak my mind. I don't speak like a politician. When I went to City Hall, I asked why all the pictures on the walls were only of white men. Some were slaveholders. One, Thomas Jefferson, was a pedophile. And George Washington sold us for molasses. I said, 'We need to have some black people up on the wall.' Where's Harriet Tubman? Malcolm X came this way. Martin Luther King came this way. Adam Clayton Powell was the first black city councilman. Where's his picture?

"One of the issues I brought up was freeing Assata Shakur from her exile in Cuba. Before she changed it, her name was JoAnne Chesimard, and she was in the Black Panther Party. She and several other Panthers were in a car driving on the New Jersey Turnpike, and the police stopped them, pulled them over simply because they were Panthers. Once the police rolled up on the car with their guns out and they saw Zaid Shakur in the car, they opened fire. Zaid fired back, and he was killed. Assata was arrested. She didn't even have a gun. Then she was liberated from prison. They broke her out, and she went to Cuba. She's been there ever since, and I think she should be brought back and freed. [To prevent this, in 2006 the Department of Homeland Security had her designated a terrorist.]

"They rolled up on her, fired, exchanged fire. She didn't pull a weapon. I don't think she should have ever been charged with anything. I don't think she did anything.

"After I said that, the *New York Post* called me 'terminally odious.' They called me the 'execrable Charles Barron.' Words I had to look up in the dictionary to find out how bad they were. They called me everything but a child of God.

"They said I was a race-baiter and a racial arsonist. And there is another issue that really gave them some fuel to work with. I called for reparations for African people for the years of slavery. The Jews got paid. The Japanese got paid. The Africans should get paid for 246 years of free labor and 100 years of Jim Crow racism. We need reparations. We built this country, which is another issue. Come on. It would be better than spending the billions in Iraq. Why don't they spend the money to build up all the neighborhoods in New Orleans, where black people live?

AP Photo/John Marshall Mantel, File

"I spoke at a reparations rally in Washington, DC, in front of about sixty thousand people. Al Sharpton spoke. The Reverend Farrakhan spoke. It was my turn, and I noticed the crowd wasn't listening, and I said, 'You all be still. This is serious stuff.' I was doing rally talk. I said, 'They are lucky we want to talk. They are lucky we want to run for office. They murdered us. They lynched us, and they don't want to pay back. We should go to the Treasury Department and take our reparations.'

"Everyone cheered. It was just rally talk. I said, 'It makes me sick. When I get back to New York City, for my mental health I'm going to slap the first white man I see and tell him it's a black thing.'

"Everybody clapped. The whites in the crowd laughed.

"But I forgot that I was on CNN, C-SPAN, NBC, CBS, ABC, oh my God, and I got e-mails from all over the country. One said, 'I'm a white man from North Carolina. If you want to slap somebody, come slap me.' It got crazy.

"The next day I went on the radio with one of the conservative talk-show hosts. He asked me if I said that. I said I did. He asked me why. I said, 'It was a case of oratorical improvisation and black hyperbole.'

"He said, *'What?'*

"I repeated it: 'Oratorical improvisation and black hyperbole.'

"They say I'm controversial. I find interesting that the word 'controversial' has been applied to me, as has the other word, 'defiant.' Those are biased terms. Isn't it interesting that 'controversial' just means people disagree with you? Who isn't controversial? Mayor Bloomberg is also controversial.

"Mayor Bloomberg seems to be a gentleman. I call him a kinder, gentler Giuliani, though his policies are the same. Giuliani was a horror show. He's a racist man. He's power hungry, and he has a disdain for black people. He came in there and left us with a $3.3 million deficit, and nobody talks about that.

"When he first came in he put a little mask on his face and walked around the World Trade Center site so the dust didn't get in his throat, and he became America's mayor.

"But five years later the World Trade Center site is still not built. Not under Giuliani, not under Bloomberg. And one year later the same Republicans are asking, 'Why didn't Ray Nagin rebuild New Orleans?' When in fact the Republicans destroyed New Orleans. The people survived Katrina. What they didn't survive was the FEMA/Bush hurricane.

"So I think Giuliani's policies were bad. Police brutality was at an all-time high, because it was Giuliani's time, and they did what they wanted to. Housing for blacks was a major problem under Giuliani. Housing is still a problem under Bloomberg. Apartments are not affordable.

"Unemployment was high under Giuliani, and unemployment in our neighborhoods is extremely high under Bloomberg. Isn't it interesting, we have a $53 billion budget in New York City, larger than forty-eight states in the United States. Larger than every African country, larger than every Caribbean country, or any European country. And many Asian countries.

"Only the federal budget of $2.7 trillion, the California budget of $140 billion, and the New York State budget of $112 billion is larger. Having said all that, how do you now have the most impoverished congressional district in America in New York City?

"This is a tale of two cities: black and white. Rich and poor. The South Bronx has 42 percent poverty—$19,000 is the median income. Charlie Rangel's district in Harlem has 30 percent poverty. In New York City! Carol Maloney's Upper East Side district has 12 percent poverty and a median income of $72,000.

"So that's why I'm not impressed that Mayor Bloomberg isn't as racially inflammatory as Giuliani. He doesn't have the same disdain Giuliani has for black people. Bloomberg will meet with black leaders like Al Sharpton. Giuliani wouldn't meet with any black leaders, moderate or otherwise. He wouldn't even meet with Carl McCall or C. Virginia Fields, a moderate borough president. Giuliani has disdain for black people. He really does.

"He never would have made it as president because of that, though there are a lot of whites in America who like that. They thought because he was popular, he'd keep us in check. Maybe that's the kind of president they want.

"I've been asked how George W. Bush's election affected me. For me personally it didn't change much. There's a marginal difference between Bush and Clinton, who was very harmful in his own way, because he was a conservative Democrat. A lot of legislation got passed that shouldn't have, including the free trade agreement and the welfare reform bill. Clinton was weak on immigration and affirmative action.

"When Bush came in, one of the things that disheartened so many young people was the Republicans' stealing the election in Florida, and stealing it again in Ohio [in 2004]. The young people said, 'My vote doesn't matter.' That has made it difficult to convince people to be involved in electoral politics. That changed things tremendously. And of course, there's the PATRIOT Act, which makes it more difficult to organize in protest. People are more fearful. There are so many ways the government now can come down on you.

"The whole country, Republicans and Democrats, is leaning to the right so much that some of us say we have a one-party system of Republicrats. That's what we have to fight for, for there is great danger within the Democratic Party, for black people in particular, because the Democratic Party has moved so far to the right trying to win elections that our issues from the civil rights movement and the '60s are being blown apart. The Democrats no longer are strong on civil rights, the Voting Rights Act, they aren't that strong on immigration, welfare, not strong on a lot of our issues.

"And where the Democrats are losing, of course, is their lack of vision. Say what you want about Bush and the conservatives, their vision is very clear. You don't have to agree with them, but they let you know: No stem-cell research. Killing an embryo is immoral and against God. No abortions. That's death, against God. No gay marriages. That's out.

"The Democrats say, 'I may be against abortion, but I'm for choice. I'm for stem-cell research, for gay marriage. The Bible Belt thus has a belief that Bush and the Republicans are more spiritual and religiously convicted, though it's incredible you can be concerned about the unborn but murder the born with the death penalty. Or bomb the born in Iraq or Afghanistan or Palestine or anywhere in the world, but still have this concern about the unborn. That's the hypocrisy. But the Democrats have not made the case.

"The Democrats can take the country back because of the Iraq War. It's such a failure, and there is no clear exit, and even the Democrats, if they wouldn't be such cowards, should stand up and say, 'Bring the troops home immediately and let the United Nations go back in where they were from the beginning.'

"We should never have made the unilateral decision to do this in the first place. Osama Bin Laden was Ronald Reagan's freedom fighter and Clinton's terrorist. How do you figure that one out? The Taliban, you remember, was funded by America when Russia was in Afghanistan. Real international hypocrisy. But the Democrats are not calling it like that. They think the way to get elected is to go conservative, and that's their big problem. The voters say, 'Why should we go for an imitation when we can vote for the real thing?'

"I am hopeful things will change. Any leader who has no hope is not fit to lead us. And any leader who subscribes to any form of our oppression is not fit to lead us. So when you have leaders saying, 'Racism isn't going anywhere,' they are not fit to lead.

"Change is inevitable. The question is the probability of it in your lifetime. And that's what you have to work toward: the probability of the inevitable."

# THE REAL ESTATE BOOM

ABRAM HALL

W HEN ABRAM HALL LEFT WAR-TORN BUSHWICK IN 1986
after his mother died and his house was robbed, Brooklyn was in bad
shape. Hall had moved in with his sister in Manhattan, just north of
Central Park, and he wasn't happy living there, so in the fall of 1987
he returned to his Brooklyn roots, first settling in Fort Greene near the
Atlantic Yards, where Walter O'Malley had wanted to move the Dodgers, and then, after two years with a miserable landlord, moved into an
apartment that once housed students from Long Island University's
Brooklyn campus.

When he moved in, downtown Brooklyn was devoid of commerce.
Drug activity, prostitution, and other criminal behavior flourished.
But the rent was cheap, and Hall was happy to be back in Brooklyn.

Then in 1988 a company called Forest City Ratner built 1 Pierrepont Plaza, near Cadman Plaza in Brooklyn Heights. Two brokerage
firms, Morgan Stanley and Goldman Sachs, established a beachhead
there. Forest City Ratner's president, Bruce Ratner, had been the head
of the Consumer Protection Division of the Department of Consumer
Affairs under Mayor Lindsay, and after working for four years as a
professor of law at NYU, he returned to government as Mayor Koch's
commissioner of consumer affairs.

Ratner's family had owned a company that had been investing
in real estate since the 1930s, and in 1988 he made his first foray

into commercial real estate development in Brooklyn with Pierrepont Plaza. He followed that with an even bigger project, the MetroTech Center, a 6.4-million-square-foot office building and retail complex in downtown Brooklyn that broke ground in 1993. It was a project that had long been bandied about, dating back to the 1969 City Planning Commission report. The impetus for the development came partly from president of Polytechnic University George Bugliarello, who wanted to create a Silicon Valley for Brooklyn. Borough President Howard Golden was instrumental in changing the focus from research and development to back offices for the major Wall Street financial firms, only a short subway ride away. Among the MetroTech Center tenants are JP Morgan Chase, Bear Stearns, and Keyspan (formerly Brooklyn Union Gas). Ratner followed MetroTech with a retail development called Atlantic Center, a large shopping mall that opened in 1996, and that was followed up by the Atlantic Terminal Mall, with Brooklyn's first Target store, in 2004.

Ratner's next downtown project will be a gigantic twenty-two-acre project called Atlantic Yards, a complex that not only will house the New Jersey Nets, the professional basketball team he owns and which he will move from New Jersey, but it will also include sixteen skyscrapers. Designed by world-famous international architect Frank Gehry, the Atlantic Yards has been blasted by opposing groups for dwarfing everything in the immediate area. It has also been praised by community and religious leaders for agreeing to include "affordable" housing in the deal. Rent payments will be subsidized by the New York City Housing Development Corporation. Despite the vocal opposition, the project received the green light from the Public Authorities Control Board in February of 2007. At the same time, Ratner sold the naming rights of the arena to Barclays Bank for $400 million. What Ratner didn't consider was that Barclays got its start in the 1700s from the transatlantic slave trade. Black leaders wanted the deal killed. Barclays is obligated to spend $2.5 million to fix up basketball courts on Brooklyn's playgrounds, but community leaders say it is not enough. Despite any criticism, many Brooklynites are looking forward to the building of the Atlantic Yards project.

Abram Hall, whose profession is print production, graphic design, and illustration, remembers when his Prospect Heights neighborhood was a slum. He is one of those rooting for Ratner and his new project, even if it means more density and more traffic.

**ABRAM HALL**   "I lived in Manhattan with my sister for two years, and I discovered that for me Manhattan is not real. It's like Disneyland. Brooklyn is more of a living kind of place. You have a neighborhood. I moved into my apartment in Prospect Heights in 1987. I was making $21,000 a year, which was not a lot of money in 1987 and I could barely afford to live there, but I took it because it was cheap. When I first moved in, that section of Brooklyn was rough. It was down and dirty. On Fourth Avenue, right in front of the unemployment office, you had hookers hanging out all night and people shooting up their drugs right there on Dean Street. If you walked down Pacific Street, it was, 'Hey, you want a date?' One antidrug activist was murdered by drug addicts. They paid $200 to take out a hit on her, and she was killed.

"Right across the street was the *Daily News* printing plant. It was operating twenty-four hours a day, and at eleven at night you'd see this whole parade of tractor-trailers go right into the plant to deliver the newsprint. If you hung around long enough, around three, the trucks would come out with the papers. But the *Daily News* left that plant and moved to New Jersey, and the area took a big hit, because a lot of satellite stores depended on the *News* employees. For a long time there was nothing around whatsoever.

"I bought my apartment in 1996 for $50,000 and today I could sell it for $430,000. In the last ten years the LIU Brooklyn campus has improved greatly, but more important, the MetroTech Center was built. The Chase Bank headquarters is there. Ironically, Chase was the bank that wrote out the mortgage for my place, because at that time no other banks were granting mortgages for co-ops. They established that right there, and from that point the next big improvement came around 1997 when the Brooklyn Marriott went up, and for a long time the Brooklyn Marriott was the most successful Marriott in the city. It has a very low vacancy rate. For some strange reason a lot of people who come to the city don't want to stay in Manhattan, but they don't mind staying in Brooklyn. So the Brooklyn Marriott was another piece in the puzzle. Also, around that time, Pratt Institute revitalized itself. I graduated from Pratt, and while I was there it was run by Jerry Pratt, who was worth hundreds of millions of dollars in Exxon stock. His father was one of the original partners with John D. Rockefeller and Standard Oil, but I was never too impressed with him as my college president. I thought he ran the place almost into the ground, but the man they have now seems to have a vision, and now they are turning students away who want to come to Pratt. They have a big campus, big dorms. When I went there in the 1980s, you could rent a one-bedroom around there for $300 a month. It was dangerous. When I was there, a student was murdered. It was a traumatic event. Pratt has worked hard with the community and the police, and they have turned the place around, and now Pratt is a top-flight school again.

"The churches like Emmanuel Baptist Church have revitalized themselves. Emmanuel Baptist now has four or five services every Sunday, and it's open every day. A lot of things have come together, but I give the most credit to the MetroTech Center. And I am looking forward to the building of the Atlantic Yards project.

Abram Hall in front of the University Apartments.
*Doug Grad*

"If you ask me, I'd say most people in Brooklyn are for it. Atlantic Avenue goes all through Bushwick and Bedford-Stuyvesant, black and Hispanic neighborhoods, and all the people who own houses in those communities are 100 percent for it. If you go in the other direction and hit Boerum Hill, residents are less enthusiastic. If you head into Prospect Heights, it becomes a topic of hot discussion. If I had to make a bet, I'd say it's sixty-forty against, there.

"Those of us who lived here when Prospect Heights was a crime-ridden empty area remember what it was like. We knew where we wanted Brooklyn to go based on where we started. But the people who moved in just ten years ago, they liked it the way it was, and they don't want it to change. But this is a snapshot. It is not the end of the movie.

"I'm seeing high-income people moving in. My co-op, University Towers, has been predominantly black, but most of the people moving in today are white. Most of the people moving into the neighborhood are white or Asian. The blacks moving in are professionals driving Hummers. The economic status of its residents has gone up, up, up. Philip Michael Thomas lives here, because no one bothers him. Rosie Perez lives here. And other famous people as well."

*After working for Oxford Press for ten years, Hall went to work for Golden Books, which went bankrupt. He was let go during the summer of 2001. He set up his own publishing/consulting business, concentrating on printing and production, but in 2004 his sister Rita died, and the emotional hit took its toll. He now works in White Plains for the Starwood Hotel creative services department. He has had to buy a car, and that's another reason he is happy he is living in Brooklyn.*

**ABRAM HALL**   "If I lived in Manhattan, I could drive around for an hour and not find a parking spot. Most of the time in Brooklyn, I can. And Brooklyn has the character I like. When I was growing up in Bushwick, I could bike over to Shea Stadium. I could do it in twenty minutes. I would get on Myrtle Avenue until it became Cooper Avenue, and I'd cross to Queens Boulevard and go up to 108th Street and take that to Roosevelt Avenue and make a right. I'd lock up my bicycle and go to the game. I never needed a car."

# BROOKLYN'S CHEERLEADER

MARTY MARKOWITZ

IN THE 1980S THE ECONOMIC MIRAGE OF THE REAGAN ADMIN-istration changed everything, bringing in a pestilence of speculators, developers, and profiteers of all sorts. The empty apartments seemed to fill up overnight, and rents shot up. With rent control and rent stabilization cramping their profits, some of the less scrupulous landlords resorted to dirty tricks: threatening tenants, turning off heat and hot water during the winter, and disabling elevators in high-rises in order to get the tenants to move out so new, higher rent–paying tenants could move in. There were more landlord-tenant disputes and rent strikes than ever before.

Marty Markowitz grew up poor in Crown Heights. His father, Robert, who'd worked as a waiter in Sid's, a kosher deli, died when Markowitz was nine. A couple years later his mom, Dorothy, moved into subsidized housing with Marty and his two sisters. Markowitz had to work, but that didn't stop him from getting a college degree. He graduated from Brooklyn College in 1970 after taking night classes for eight long years. It was in 1971 that he decided to fight back against the tactics of the landlords. He organized the Flatbush Tenants Council, and it wasn't long before his organization grew into what became Brooklyn Housing Services, the largest tenants' association in New York and probably in the whole country. On a salary of just $10,000 a year he worked seven days a week fighting for Brooklynites who didn't have the ways and means to defend themselves.

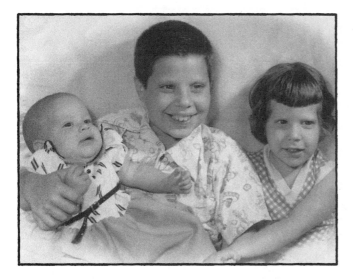

Jill, Marty, and Sherry Markowitz. *Courtesy of Marty Markowitz*

Markowitz became a public figure as a result of his championing tenants' rights, and he turned to politics as a career. He served in the New York State Senate from 1979 until 2001—eleven consecutive terms—all the while living like a transient in a threadbare hotel room in Albany, returning as often as possible to his Brooklyn home. He held on to his seat even though his constituency went from being 55 percent white to 92 percent black and Latino after being jerrymandered twice.

While he was a state senator, Markowitz coveted the post of Brooklyn borough president, long held by Howard Golden. The popular Golden, who was elected to the job in 1978, had an iron grip on the position. Golden defeated Markowitz in 1985, and Golden would have kept the job indefinitely, until term limits made him bid adieu. Even though revisions to the city's charter in 1990 stripped away the power from the borough president's office by abolishing the Board of Estimate that controlled NYC's purse strings, Markowitz quickly threw his hat in the ring. In 2001 he defeated Ken Fisher and was re-elected in a landslide four years later.

After Markowitz became the borough president in 2001, he became the face of Brooklyn. He attended every parade, every opening, every festival, and issued proclamation after proclamation, all the while promoting his beloved turf like a modern-day P. T. Barnum. If there ever was a true public servant devoted to his hometown, Marty Markowitz is it. Tommy Lasorda always bragged that he bled Dodger Blue. Lasorda has nothing on Marty Markowitz. Especially since before the word "Dodger" comes the word "Brooklyn."

Markowitz is also bound by term limits, and he is scheduled to depart in 2009. His final political decision looms: whether to run for mayor. Meanwhile, under his leadership, Brooklyn's economy is booming and Brooklyn residents are feeling very good about themselves and their borough.

"Why not?" asks Markowitz. "Why would you want to live anywhere else?"

**MARTY MARKOWITZ** "I was born on February 5, 1945, in Crown Heights. My grandparents came from Germany and Romania in 1915, and I lost them when I was very young. I was only eleven when the last of my grandparents passed, so I don't have any recollection of them except that my grandfather on my mother's side had very beautiful suits—he must have been very successful in his day. I also remember how he would pour coffee into his saucer and then drink it with a cube of sugar.

"My dad was a waiter in a kosher delicatessen on Empire Boulevard. I remember the pastrami and corned beef. He did that six days a week, and he worked another job six days a week as a shipping clerk for a company called Cardinal Place, which manufactured men's clothing.

"My dad loved the Dodgers. If the Dodgers

Young Marty rides a pony.
*Courtesy of Marty Markowitz*

won, everyone in the deli seemed to eat more. If they lost, it was a sad day for him. I can remember the Dodgers as far back as 1950, when I was five. I went to the games with my father. He didn't have that much time off, but when he did, he'd go to the games. We lived two blocks away from Ebbets Field, and we walked there. During batting practice my friends and I would hang out on Bedford Avenue, hoping Campanella or Snider would hit one over and we'd catch a ball, though I was never quick enough to get one. When I was around ten, my friend and I would sneak into Ebbets Field. We waited for the main crowd to come in, and maybe in the second inning nobody was there anymore, and other times the ticket-takers would hand us a ticket.

"I can remember one game when the Dodgers were leading the Milwaukee Braves twenty-four to three, and even though it was the eighth inning, nobody left the game. Absolutely nobody left. That's how happy we were. And I can remember the Brooklyn Symphony and Hilda Chester and her cowbell.

"The day we won the World Series in 1955 was the most glorious day of all. Brooklyn stopped. A trolley that ran on electrical wires ran in front of the building I lived in, and I remember the passengers coming off screaming and yelling, and people were going crazy in the streets. I went down with some of my friends and watched the procession, which went around Borough Hall. People hugged and kissed and jumped up and down. Looking back, to me it seemed the celebration lasted for about a month. I'm sure it didn't, but it sure seemed that way.

"To us, the Yankees were a Manhattan team, not a Bronx team. I know they were called the Bronx Bombers, but I looked upon them as being elitists from Manhattan. We were the workers, and they were the elites, the aristocracy.

"My favorite players were Duke Snider, a slugger, and Johnny Podres, who beat the Yankees in that final game in 1955. He was a great pitcher. And I loved Gil Hodges, and when I was young, Jackie Robinson certainly was my idol. He was all the kids' idol, the most popular player on the team.

"I grew up in a liberal family, and the fact that he was able to play for Brooklyn was an exciting thing. Civil rights movement was beginning—not that my father was active, but there was that sense of civil rights and equal opportunity and stopping the bigotry, even in those days.

"Our joy, of course, was short-lived. The Dodgers left after the 1957 season, leaving us with shock and anger. I was twelve years old. I didn't know about the role Robert Moses played in not letting the Dodgers build a new ballpark at the Atlantic Yards. But there is no doubt that O'Malley, as the owner of the Dodgers, was a dreaded name. There was shock and disbelief we would lose the Dodgers. It was unheard of, and after they left, we were filled with a great unhappiness, a terrible sadness. After the Dodgers left, of course we were hoping beyond hope that someone

Carl Erskine with wrecking ball as the demolition of Ebbets Field begins. *AP Photo* would come in and play at Ebbets Field. We wanted another team to come, but obviously that didn't happen.

"Another sad day came when they knocked down Ebbets Field. I was there because I lived two blocks away, and I saw this big ball knock it down. As I'm talking to you, I can see the crane out in the outfield. I must tell you, on the fiftieth anniversary of our winning the World Series, I went to speak to Little Leagues, and when I told the kids, 'The Brooklyn Dodgers defeated the other team from the Bronx,' all I heard was, 'Boo, boo, boo,' because they were Yankee fans. They were raised as Yankee fans. I said, 'God, forgive them. They know not what they do.' And their parents laughed, and they laughed. Although the parents weren't around either.

"I went to junior high school in East Flatbush, and then to Wingate High School in Crown Heights. I graduated from Wingate in 1962. I was always interested in politics. I remember when Dwight Eisenhower paid a visit to Brooklyn in 1956, we all went up to Empire Boulevard to see his motorcade. Martin Luther King was an idol of mine in the 1960s, when I became conscious and the country became conscious. I had worked in 1960 to help get John Kennedy elected president. I worked with the local Democratic committee.

"My first experience with civil rights came when I was fourteen. I was in a White Castle, which is still there on Empire Boulevard. At that time you would bring your car in, give your order, and a girl would bring it out. The kitchen staff was black, but the servers were white. Blacks could not serve you. And CORE, the Congress of Racial Equality, called for a boycott. I was the only white guy on the line that I can remember. I'm sorry to say an Italian kid swore at me, put me down. So it was in middle school that I began to see images of what was happening in the South.

"Wingate High School was about 40 percent black. I didn't have any problems. There was a lot of friction between the blacks and the Italians. There were rumbles, because part of Crown Heights was all Italian. The Jewish population picked up on Lefferts Avenue going north up the Eastern Parkway. Crown Heights was Italian, a rough section, and coming home I would have to watch myself. I don't remember any racism or name-calling in the school itself. Blacks and whites did everything together.

"One of our basketball heroes was Roger Brown, one of the greatest basketball players of all time. [Brown was a small forward with the Indiana Pacers in 1967–75, leading the Pacers to ABA titles in 1970 and 1972. He died of liver cancer in 1997.]

I used to hold his coat. I was *proud* to hold his coat. Oh yes, he was a star. And in the [New York City] finals at Madison Square Garden against Boys High, we lost by one point. Connie Hawkins was their star. There was no name-calling. None of that. Blacks obviously knew there was a significant amount of racism, even in Brooklyn, which was not integrated. It was difficult for blacks who wanted a cab ride, and they lived with poverty, and when blacks started moving into neighborhoods, people fled. Those days are gone. That doesn't happen anymore.

Assemblyman Markowitz with Coretta Scott King.
*Courtesy of Marty Markowitz*

"We lived in Crown Heights, and after my dad died of a heart attack, my mom was up against it. She tried to get into public housing, but it took a number of years.

"My mother wrote letters to politicians, and they didn't give her the time of day. But then she wrote to Jacob Javits, who was our senator, and he helped us get into the Sheepshead/Nostrand Houses. I lived in public housing for five years.

"It didn't bother me. I was young. I didn't know anything. Actually, it was a nice development. We had hot water and electricity and modest rent.

"I went to Brooklyn College at night starting in 1962, and during the day I'd work. I had to contribute to my family. My sisters were younger than me, and I had to take care of my mom.

"I had quite a few jobs. I worked at CIT as a commercial factor. It was the days before computers, and my job was reading tallies on commercial properties. I went from there to selling tobacco for May's, a department store attracting lower-income customers, where my mom regularly shopped. I was a detail salesman for P. Lorillard, makers of Kent cigarettes. In those days I smoked. Everybody smoked. I would call on candy stores, trying to get them to take a couple cartons of cigarettes. I put up posters in windows. I gave out samples to customers coming into the stores. I did it because May's gave me a company car, and I couldn't afford my own car. It was a way of having a job and a car. But I didn't know the car they gave their salesmen didn't have a backseat. It was filled with cigarettes. Nonetheless, I appreciated having the car very much. But the job only lasted a year and a half. I couldn't stand it. I gave up smoking in 1973.

"From there I went to Clairol. I called on variety stores and drugstores, selling their products, and then I left that and went into personnel placement, finding people jobs. I did that for a couple years. I was a kid. And then I got a job with a company that specialized in the placement of lawyers.

"I already knew I wanted to go into politics. By the time I was sixteen, I knew I wanted to be borough president. To me that was a bigger deal than Congress. Right after I graduated college in 1970, I took a job as head of the student government at the graduate level at Brooklyn College. And because of doing that, I didn't have to work in Manhattan. I stayed in Brooklyn, which gave me access to the neighborhood where I lived. I no longer was living at home. I had moved to Flatbush and my first apartment on the short block of Tennis Court.

"In 1969 I became a member of the Democratic Club. I became really active in the club from my neighborhood. Mel Miller was the head of the club. He later became an assemblyman, and I became his campaign manager. My job was ringing doorbells for him, canvassing. It was at that same time in 1971 that I founded a group of tenants, to fight for better conditions in the building.

"Rent regulations kept rents very low for long-standing tenants, but rent regulations also made it almost impossible for a landlord to throw out a long-standing tenant. So the landlords would deteriorate the place to make him leave. Many landlords would bring blacks in, because they knew nothing worked like that did. And it worked. There was an extensive city program that gave the landlord a bounty if they placed a low-income black family. The landlord would get a $2,000 bonus per apartment, because there wasn't enough housing for low-income people. So the landlords sometimes got a double dime. Not only did they get their bonus, but they got the long-standing tenant paying low rent out of the building. It worked. Needless to say, it's a fact that it worked. They knew what they were doing. So there was that issue and also the issue of a diminution of the quality of service.

"Even though I had a job, I helped the tenants organize, and I spent most of my life fighting for tenants' rights—because I was involved in politics. My regular job paid me $15,000 a year, not a lot of money in 1973 and 1974. The mayor then, Abraham Beame, paid me $10,000 a year more to help organize the tenants, so I lived on about $25,000 a year, and that was all right, because my interest was to develop a constituency.

Assemblyman Markowitz speaking. To his right is Howard Golden, the borough president who preceded him. *Courtesy of Marty Markowitz. Photo by Deborah Gardner*

"I know for sure thousands and thousands of residents were helped directly. No doubt about it. We went on rent strikes, and the strikes worked. I would go to two or three buildings a night. I had a secretary and a two-line phone in my little office, and I did it for years. I got grants. I worked every day of the week and often on Saturdays. The tenants lacked hot water, services in the building, there were broken windows, and roaches. Part of my job was to get the tenants organized. I inspected for the HPD, the city's Department of Housing Preservation & Development. In those days the agency had the power of making emergency repairs. And that was another incentive for the landlord to fix up the building.

"We held back rents, and the landlords would negotiate with us. We had many successes, as well as a number of failures, either because the tenants were not well organized or because the landlord bought off the tenants. Look, it happens in every walk of life. The landlords had good lawyers.

"I ran for city council in 1973 against Sam Horwitz of Coney Island. My plans didn't quite work out. The neighborhood at the time was represented by a landlord by the name of Leon Katz, who is now just a blessed memory. Leon was a landlord, owned many buildings, and although he himself was not a bad landlord, he was still a landlord, and how could the district be represented by a landlord when the majority of the people were tenants?

"There was a redistricting [creating the 33rd District of Brighton Beach, Coney Island, and a part of Staten Island], and the district no longer included where most of the apartments were. It became a large homeowner area. But I ran anyway, and the regular Democratic Party endorsed the regular candidate, and I lost by a few thousand votes. I put on a very sturdy campaign. It was the most fun campaign of my career. I came in second out of five candidates.

"So he won reelection, and he got rid of me. He became a council member and he was defeated years later by Bernard Marcus.

"The mayor appointed me to the Conciliation and Appeals Court from 1973 to the end of 1978, when State Senator Jeremiah Bloom, happily for me, wanted to run for the governorship against Hugh Carey, and he announced in the morning, and I announced I was running for his senate seat in the afternoon. Bloom put up his top person, Howard Silverman, his chief of staff, to run against me. I was part of the reform Democrats, and this time I won. I took office on January 1, 1979.

"I really did not like being a state senator in Albany. I loved being a state senator in Brooklyn. It was depressing in Albany. I lived in a hotel room. I didn't want to rent an apartment, because I never wanted to live there. I always wanted to come home.

"In the senate I was always part of the minority party, since the Democrats have not had control of the state senate since 1955. Before that, they had control from 1932 to 1934. And before that, it was in the eighteenth century. The Democrats have been out of power in the New York State senate for almost the entire creation of the state.

"And the reason for that is simple: reapportionment. The Republicans cut up the districts in a way conducive to their winning. That's how they did it. In the assembly, the Democrats do the same thing to stay in the majority. The only way the Democrats could take over the senate is if the voters get angry and vote the Republicans out.

"I stayed in the senate almost twenty-three years. I lived out of a suitcase in a motel in Albany, and as soon as the gavel went down, I picked up and raced back to Brooklyn. I knew what I really wanted to be: the borough president. I ran in 1985 against the then-incumbent Howard Golden. There were four candidates, and I came in second. After I lost, I figured I'd take one more shot at it, and when term limits kicked in, Howie had to go. Even if he didn't have to go, I would have run, because at age fifty-six, it was my last chance, and a new generation of politicians was waiting right behind me, people in their forties waiting for their opportunity.

"On December 31, 2009, I will have to leave. Unless they change the law, which is unlikely, you can serve two terms, and then you leave, and that's the end of it. Even if most of the residents of Brooklyn feel they'd like to have me stay, I can't.

"When my term is up I will either run for mayor of New York City or call it a day in my public-service career. I don't know which way I'm going to go. The good news is I will be almost sixty-five, and it's not so bad.

"What I have tried to do as borough president is make the job relevant to the lives of Brooklynites. I have tried to make people proud of being Brooklynites. I have put a smile on their faces. And I think I've done a good job of providing programs for Brooklyn, whether it's health care, affordable housing, bringing in the Nets in three years, which I believe will happen, or fixing up City Hall, which was neglected by every administration before Mayor Bloomberg. Those are my accomplishments.

"In my job I bring a little creativity. I didn't want signs that said WELCOME TO BROOKLYN. That's not Brooklyn. Brooklyn has an edge. We're a bunch of meshuggeners. We are, and I'm proud of that. And I like that. I wanted the signs to reflect what we are. One of them is HOW SWEET IT IS! If you remember, Ralph Kramden [played by Bushwick's Jackie Gleason on *The Honeymooners*] was a Brooklyn bus driver. Another is BELIEVE THE HYPE! And I also wanted to put up signs when you leave,

Marty stands besides his handiwork, the sign for motorists leaving Brooklyn, before it was hoisted onto the Belt Parkway exit for the Verrazano Bridge. *Courtesy of Marty Markowitz. Photo by Katherine Kirk*

such as OY VEY and LEAVING BROOKLYN—FUGHEDDABOUDIT. It's a way to give a Brooklyn attitude. The people who come into Brooklyn should know they aren't coming into a place that is like most other places. And it gives people a smile. They love it.

"Not everyone loves me. Many of them don't. But the great majority like the work I do. You can't please everyone. You try to please everyone, but it's impossible. Impossible. I try. I always try. But it's impossible.

"Once a Brooklynite, always a Brooklynite. In 1957 we said *sayonara* to the Dodgers. Even though we have a great little team in Brooklyn, the Brooklyn Cyclones, a minor league baseball team, the truth is that Brooklyn is a major-league city, and it will be back in the major leagues when the New Jersey Nets get rid of the NJ and replace it with BROOKLYN in a beautiful, new, sparkling arena on Atlantic Avenue in downtown Brooklyn, opposite where Walter O'Malley—who we thought was the devil—really wanted to build a new Ebbets Field, right across the street, and Robert Moses destroyed that opportunity. But the good news is, that was then, we're going to have a major league team in Brooklyn in 2010, and right now I'd say the number one sport in Brooklyn is football, second is basketball, and baseball and soccer are number three, and that's the truth. Stay tuned."

*Like most Brooklynites who can remember the halcyon days of the Brooklyn Dodgers, Markowitz suffered unspeakable heartache when Walter O'Malley hijacked his baseball heroes and fled west to Los Angeles. It was an ache that never went away. When he campaigned to become the borough president, Markowitz announced that one of his goals would be to bring major league sports back to Brooklyn. Few took him seriously. But during his first weeks in office Markowitz called Dodgers' owner Peter O'Malley and with a straight face asked if he might be interested in moving the Dodgers back to Brooklyn. His sales pitch: "Mr. O'Malley, it would be great for your family name and everything if you would consider moving the L.A. Dodgers back to Brooklyn." O'Malley, not amused, declined.*

*Markowitz, who is nothing if not persistent, determined that he would bring to Brooklyn a major league sports franchise—any franchise, regardless of the sport—and to that end he began calling around to see who might be interested in buying a pro team and moving it to Brooklyn.*

*His first thought was Donald Trump. But Trump had a casino in Atlantic City, and Markowitz felt there was too much risk The Donald would move the team there and not to Brooklyn. Markowitz then considered Bruce Ratner, whose company Forest City Ratner had jump-started Brooklyn's downtown renaissance when he built the huge MetroTech Center. By 2002 Forest City Ratner had become the largest developer in the city. Over fifteen years it had finished thirty-five commercial projects—six times the volume of all of their commercial competition combined in New York.*

*Ratner, who professed little interest in sports, told Markowitz no thanks.*

*Markowitz, convinced his idea had merit, kept calling Ratner back, two and three times a week. Eventually Ratner saw a way for both of them to fulfill their dreams. He figured out that if he could incorporate a sports arena into a plan for a truly grand development that included millions of feet of retail space and hundreds of apartments, he could own a big chunk of downtown Brooklyn and at the same time return to Brooklyn the sports glory that Markowitz envisioned.*

*The development, called Atlantic Yards, is on the site where Walter O'Malley wanted to build a new domed stadium for the Dodgers in the 1950s. It will stretch six blocks along the*

Marty cutting a cake in the shape of Borough Hall upon his election to the borough presidency. *Courtesy of Marty Markowitz*

*border of Prospect Heights and will include sixteen separate high-rise buildings, one of which was initially proposed to rise 650 feet into the air, towering over the nearby Williamsburg Savings Bank building and becoming by far the tallest building in Brooklyn. It has since been scaled back considerably.*

*Not surprisingly, Marty Markowitz is the project's loudest drum-beater. He boasts that 50 percent of the housing will be for low- and middle-income residents whose incomes are between $18,000 and a $100,000 a year. Opponents rail loudly that Markowitz gave Ratner a sweetheart deal and are outraged that Ratner will be allowed to build on such a grand scale. Markowitz is unrepentant, and the plans to build the complex proceed unabated despite a series of lawsuits. In an office that is more ceremonial than power-wielding, Markowitz's legacy is certain to be the Brooklyn Nets and the Atlantic Yards.*

# THE ATLANTIC YARDS

JIM STUCKEY

**D**OWNTOWN BROOKLYN HAD BECOME A WAR ZONE BY THE 1980s. Crime was rampant. Drug use and prostitution proliferated, and when five o'clock rolled around, you could roll a bowling ball down Fulton Street and not hit a soul.

Things began to change with the building of the MetroTech Center, the brainchild of the leadership of the Polytechnic University, who feared that if something wasn't done about the state of the area they would be forced to move to their tonier campus in White Plains. When Polytechnic University approached the Public Development Corporation, the PDC was run by a Brooklynite by the name of James Stuckey.

Immediately, Stuckey had two major problems to solve if he wanted to keep the Polytechnic University from fleeing Brooklyn. He had to find someone to build MetroTech. And he had to find companies to rent space in it after it was built. To accomplish such a feat, Stuckey would have to be a magician.

After failing to attract a single New York City developer in the project, he made a deal with Forest City Developers of Cleveland to construct the ten-building project. Getting tenants to move in proved far more difficult.

Jim Stuckey, who today is the president and CEO of Verdant Properties, LLC, a real estate development, ownership, acquisitions,

Jim Stuckey in 1989 at the start of construction of the Metrotech Center. *Courtesy of Jim Stuckey*

and consulting limited-liability corporation, is a self-admitted "mutt." He was born in Sunset Park, an immigrant neighborhood, on February 15, 1954, at Sister Elizabeth Hospital on Fourth Avenue and 51st Street. His father was Scottish, Swiss, and a little bit English and Irish, and his mother Norwegian and German. While he was growing up in the late '60s and early '70s, the neighborhood began to change, as blacks and Hispanics moved in.

**JIM STUCKEY**   "During the years when I was growing up there were all sorts of fights between the Puerto Rican gangs and the white gangs. It was very much a *West Side Story* kind of situation. Unfortunately, I was not always a spectator, but I don't want to glorify it. You would find yourself where a gang of kids would be roaming the neighborhood. There were the Savages, a Puerto Rican gang, another gang called the Young Savages, kids who were younger, and I remember the Flying Dutchmen, a white gang from Bensonhurst. There was a lot of real serious fighting, knives, ripping antennas off cars, throwing bottles, tough stuff.

"I went to grammar school at PS 94 on Sixth Avenue and 51st Street, and I rarely saw African-Americans, but when I got to junior high school—I went to Pershing Junior High, JHS 220, on 49th Street and Ninth Avenue—there was a lot of busing, and interestingly enough, I made a lot of friends from neighborhoods like Fort Greene and other downtown Brooklyn neighborhoods, and the same was true when I began Fort Hamilton High School in 1970. In part to escape being around the gangs in my neighborhood, I began hanging out with a couple friends from the black neighborhood down near Fort Greene, areas close to the Atlantic Yards, which we are now developing. You're talking about how the world positions you.

"It's interesting, because these are the things that shape your life. I had a great friend, Maurice Skipper. We went to Pershing and then Fort Hamilton High. Maurice had an older brother, Ben, who was a fabulous basketball player. He preceded Bernard King at Fort Hamilton. I don't know why he never went further. I heard later on he died. I don't know if that's true or not. Maurice and I were super, super friends. That whole friendship came about as a result of busing and the integration efforts of the time. He and I always would hang out. It caused me to come down to some of the downtown neighborhoods and explore the city. He would come into my neighborhood, and we had a great friendship. We lost touch when I went to college at St. John's. It was unfortunate, because he was almost a soulmate.

At age nine on the L Dees baseball team.

*Courtesy of Jim Stuckey*

"But busing further added to the tensions existing between certain communities. You were adding another party to the mix, the African-Americans.

"In retrospect I think about how close-knit the city is today and how many friends I have of all nationalities and ethnicities, and to think in the '60s and '70s you had in many ways a more insidious and deeper type of discrimination than you did in the South, where people openly practiced it. Here you had cities like New York and Boston where people acted as if it was okay to live alongside minorities, but really didn't. I think how insane those times were.

"I took the lead on negotiating for our office, community benefits agreement for the Atlantic Yards project. I think deep down inside, how my empathy for the less well-off led me to make sure some of the local groups—predominantly African-

At age eighteen at his prom with his future wife, Debbie. *Courtesy of Jim Stuckey*

American and Caribbean-American groups, will be involved in the job growth and the development of the Atlantic Yards project. Minority- and women-owned contractors will get health care in communities that unfortunately don't get appropriate health care, educational initiatives. I look back and wonder how maybe those years were very formative in my understanding how important it is today to do a community benefit. It's not because you read about it being socially correct but because you lived through the eyes of other people.

"When I was in high school, my family worried I would never go to college because I almost always failed my first and last class, because I always cut them. It wasn't because I couldn't do chemistry or trigonometry, but in the morning my friends and I would go have breakfast. In the afternoon we'd go hang out someplace. Sometimes it was because I had a job. When I was a kid, I loved sports, and I made the varsity baseball team, but I decided there was no way in the world I was going to play, because it was much more important to go work at a delicatessen stacking boxes so I could make some money. That was indeed what was important at the time.

"My dad was an accountant. Ultimately he worked his way up to having a very good comptroller's job, but when we were young, honestly, we lived in a very small, three-room apartment. We didn't have much. My brother and I, going to bed, would roll out the Castro Convertible. It was a very modest, humble setting, but I had a wonderful family.

"I went to St. John's, and I managed to get through it in three years. I graduated college magna cum laude, and I went to graduate school at St. John's. They offered me an assistantship, and I did a master's in experimental and physiological psychology. Twenty-five years later, in 2002, I got a second graduate degree, in sacred scripture and theology from St. Joseph's seminary.

"My first job, which is kind of perverse, was as a social worker at the Mount Loretta Home on Staten Island. The job was an intake worker, and what was perverse about it, I would have to go to people's homes and make recommendations to the family court in Brooklyn about whether or not kids should be permitted to stay in their homes, either because of abuse or drug situations. It was a terrible job. Twenty-five years later, working for Forest City Ratner, I had the good experience of being able to rebuild that court. When I went there, I would walk in, and because it was so antiquated, you'd have families fighting in hallways, find guns hidden in the hedges, and lawyers had to interview their clients in bathrooms. It was really bad. As I said, you never know how those experiences shape something you can touch later.

"That job lasted about six months, and in October 1977, I was offered an opportunity to work in the city, doing personnel work in something called the Office of Economic Development. Doing personnel work seemed obvious for someone with degrees in psychology and a bachelor in business, and right at that time Ed Koch became mayor and a new team of people came in, and to my benefit they saw I was capable of doing more than personnel work, and as time went on with the Office of Economic Development, they began to expose me to other opportunities, one of which was getting involved in real estate development for the city.

"The first project I got exposed to was the South Street Seaport. I worked really hard on that, and within a short period of time, around 1980, we got the project approved and began moving into construction. It was clear I had discovered a job that was both fun and that I was good at and enjoyed, and ultimately something I could make a career of, because at that time I also had my first child and also was working on getting my doctorate in psychology.

"As I continued working for the city in development, I got more and more exposure and particularly began to get more exposure to the mayor, who I didn't know. I was not political in any way.

"I thought Ed Koch was absolutely terrific. He was an incredibly talented and smart man. I'm impressed with the current mayor [Mike Bloomberg], and I think Ed Koch was a great mayor, and fortunately he got to see what I was able to do—I worked for some really good people who were not shy about letting me shine a little bit—and by 1986 I was asked by the mayor to become president of what is now called the Economic Development Corporation, what was then called the Public Development Corporation. In that capacity I stayed president for three and a half years, until 1990, and during that time I oversaw $15 billion in projects for the city.

A press conference in 1987 with Mayor Koch, left, and UDC President Vince Tese, right. *Courtesy of Jim Stuckey*

"Among those projects were MetroTech; Times Square redevelopment; 42nd Street redevelopment; the Brooklyn Army Terminal, a major industrial facility; the retention of what was then called Shearson-Lehman-Hutton; the Citicorp Center in Long Island City, which you see when you drive down the BQE; a number of the city's industrial parks; the heliport—projects that helped to create or retain about a hundred thousand jobs in New York City. Most of these projects were brought by developers, and it was primarily the Public Development Corporation's responsibility to oversee and negotiate on behalf of the city.

"I would negotiate the business deal whether it was negotiating a lease, bringing it to a public approval process, or handling the environmental side.

"When I began working for the city, Bruce Ratner was working at Consumer Affairs. He was its commissioner in the early '80s. I didn't know him well, but I knew who he was. When the MetroTech project began, I was not dealing with Bruce. I was predominantly dealing with Bruce's cousins from Cleveland—Albert Ratner, our current chairman, and Jimmy Ratner, the head of the commercial arm of the company out of Cleveland. Forest City had not yet opened an office in New York City.

"It was mainly the people from Cleveland I was working with in the early stages of MetroTech. A year or two later, Bruce joined the company when he merged his company with Forest City, and then I indeed began meeting more with Bruce."

*When Ed Koch lost the Democratic nomination for mayor to David Dinkins in 1990, Jim Stuckey, knowing that Dinkins would want his own man to head the Office of Economic Development, resigned. He had worked with a lot of different developers, so he knew he wouldn't have much trouble finding a job in the private sector, but he had spent the last thirteen years working in government, and he didn't want to rush into a decision.*

*He became a consultant, and the first job he accepted was with Forest City Developers to build a project in the South Loop area of Chicago, near Soldier Field, called Central Station. For six months he commuted to the Windy City to help the Ratners get through the approval process. He also helped them put together tax increment financing with the city and the state of Illinois. They had other plans: an office building and an international trade center, and he worked with Forest City on those projects as well.*

*When he finished in Chicago, he returned to New York.*

**JIM STUCKEY**  "I joined Forest City Ratner in 1994. The first buildings we did were the 330 Jay Street courthouse, the headquarters for the fire department, the Times Square/Madame Tussaud AMC project, the Hilton Hotel, the Mercantile Exchange in Battery Park City, the Embassy Suites Hotel.

"Then Bruce got a call from Marty Markowitz. If you go back to when Marty became borough president in 2002, one of his platforms was to bring a professional sports team to Brooklyn. When he first called, he wasn't partial to whether it was baseball, basketball, hockey, or soccer. He was just pushing for a professional sports team. Some sports were more logical than others; basketball always being the most logical. Marty believed there should be a professional team, and along with it was the question: Where should it be located? Should it be in Coney Island? The Brooklyn Navy Yard? The idea of doing it at the Atlantic Yards was not necessarily a front-burner idea on anyone's plate. And then, as much as Marty pushed, Bruce agreed that we would look into this.

"We had redeveloped Times Square, so the idea of doing an entertainment facility was not a crazy idea for us. So we began to look, and before we knew it, we learned that the New Jersey Devils hockey team was for sale. We looked at it seriously and put in a bid, but our goal, quite honestly, wasn't to buy the Devils for the sake of buying the Devils, but to buy the Devils so we could also buy the Nets, because we realized that basketball was much more important, was a much better economic gamble, a better fit for Brooklyn than hockey.

"The owners of the Devils, a company called the YankeeNets, was made up of Ray Chambers of the Nets and George Steinbrenner of the Yankees. They had formed a company because they felt there was going to be real synergy in having a basketball team, a hockey team, and the Yankees, as well as the YES network. Put it all together, and you'd be able to get something greater than the sum of its parts. But it didn't work out. The partnership didn't work, despite the fact that they tried, and it became clear they had to break this whole thing up.

"They began by trying to sell the Devils, but ultimately Ray Chambers decided to keep it. He really wanted the hockey team for an arena he wanted to build in Newark, so he kept the Devils, and to our surprise he then put the Nets up for sale. Which was what we wanted in the first place.

"There was competition to buy the Nets. We were competing against one group, which included now-Governor Corzine, that wanted to keep the team in New Jersey. We were also competing against a team out in Long Island that owned the Islanders [Charles Wang and Sanjay Kumar, who sold his shares to Wang in 2006 after pleading guilty to securities fraud]. So we did have real competition.

"The winner would have to satisfy the NBA, but the problem for the New Jersey group was that the past ownership had teams going to the finals but they could not get the arena filled. We had to show we could get the project built. We were able to show we had a business plan that went beyond a simple arena, because sports economics are not always the best in the world, and this would be a larger development that made the economics work better.

"As we began pursuing the team, part of the process was picking a site, and when we looked at it closely, it became clear that the only place in Brooklyn a real good sports facility worked would be at the Atlantic Yards, predominantly because of the public transportation—the ability to move people using public transportation is huge.

"When it came time to put in a bid, there was a lot of drama and a lot of hard work. You're bidding and putting together your economics, figuring out the right purchase price and how you're going to put together your equity and financing.

"We won the bidding by a fair margin. Our bid was $300 million. It wasn't leaps and bounds above the other competitors. The bid was better, but the other factor was that the team would come to Brooklyn. That played a big role in the old ownership selling the team, because the deal had to be approved by the NBA, and I think the NBA was excited we were bringing the team to Brooklyn. I think all of this contributed to that success.

"And once we bought the team, our next steps were very, very complicated."

*Ratner, Stuckey, and company would have an endless row of hoops they would have to jump through—approval from the state and the governor, approval from the mayor, from councils, boards, environmental tests, and on and on. I asked Stuckey whether there was a possibility that after they bought the team, the NBA wouldn't allow them to move it to Brooklyn, whether there was a possibility the government would halt the project.*

**JIM STUCKEY** "That was always a risk, because one can never assume that just because we thought it was a good idea that the government would. Some people like to think we have that kind of magic wand we can wave, but the truth of the matter is that government acts very independently, and there were multiple levels of government that had to be involved. Ultimately we had to be approved in the state process, but we had to have the city planning people help us with design. We had to negotiate a business deal with both the state and the city. We had to get approved by the Public Authorities Control Board, the governor, the legislature—assembly and senate.

"And in the course of the last two or three years I have gone to over two hundred community meetings and had to go before the city council twice. We've had to complete full environmental impact statements on this project. We have three or four lawsuits still hanging around, concerning eminent domain. We made a calculated decision to try to limit the issues of eminent domain by going out and assembling 85 percent of the site, particularly focusing on assembling people's homes and businesses first, because we realized that they were going to be most sensitive, and we didn't want to have to worry about where they were going to live. We worked diligently to make fair deals, buy people's homes and businesses so what's left, predominantly, that has to be condemned are vacant lots and abandoned buildings, chop shops, places like that.

"All this had to be coordinated. While Bruce and other people were spending their time on the acquisition of the team, I was working with the real estate team trying to figure out if we were to win it, how we were going to get this through the approvals, through the litigation, and ultimately to build. I've been at this around three and a half years now, and it has been a long, Herculean effort.

"We have been approved. We have begun to do some of the infrastructure work on the Long Island Rail Road. We have begun some of the demolition work, and we are now fighting the litigation, but the fact is in the fall of this year [2007] we could very well be in a position where we could start to see the arena coming out of the ground, or at least the excavation for it. In the meantime there's a bunch of infrastructure work that needs to be done, and this would have to be done with or without lawsuits, and we're doing that so we can try to keep this thing on schedule."

*In addition to the basketball arena, the plan calls for sixteen high-rise buildings. As with the MetroTech Center, the Atlantic Yards will be built in phases.*

**JIM STUCKEY**    "First we are going to build what we call the 'arena block,' which is the arena and four buildings around it, as well as one other building, which we refer to as Site Five, a building across the street, technically outside of the Atlantic Yards but part of the approval. That phase of the development is scheduled to be completed by 2010, and that will include rental units and office development, some retail space, and possibly a hotel. Then the second phase, all the buildings east of Sixth Avenue and Vanderbilt Avenue, will all be residential buildings. When it's all done, there will be a total of 4,500 rental units, half of which will be affordable. There will be about 1,930 condo units. There will be a half a million feet of office space. Plus the arena itself, and up to 180 hotel rooms."

*While researching Jim Stuckey's interview, I saw that the opposition to the Atlantic Yards project was fierce and constant. I read Stuckey a laundry list of the major complaints: the project is too big; it will bring too many people to the area; there isn't enough low-income housing in the project; the character of downtown Brooklyn will change too dramatically; the area will become too much like Manhattan; Bruce Ratner will make too much profit; the project tears down too many landmarks; the public schools will become too crowded; Ratner has tricked everyone using sleight of hand; the tax giveaways are too great; the centerpiece of the project, Frank Gehry's sixty-five-story building, is ugly; the residents were never consulted; blacks will be driven out of central Brooklyn; who wants a basketball team anyway?; and finally, the only reason Ratner is doing this is for the money. I could hear Stuckey let out a long sigh when my recitation was completed.*

An artist's rendering of part of the Atlantic Yards—the Frank Gehry–designed arena and "Miss Brooklyn" tower at the intersection of 4th, Flatbush, and Atlantic avenues. *Forest City Ratner*

**JIM STUCKEY** "I've heard all of those too. And we obviously have responded. Let's step back from the specifics of all those criticisms for a second, and let's look at what we're doing and why we're doing it. In my mind, the beauty of working here at Forest City, and I think it's also true of Bruce and many others, is that we can involve ourselves in a great business where we can also make a difference for other people from a social, moral, and economic point of view. All the goals and good things Bruce and I have felt when we were in government, all the things that motivated me at one point in my life to go to school for psychology and to get a second degree in theology, all those things we can live for and do in the job, we do here. We don't build monuments. People will live in, shop in, recreate in, and work in the buildings we are building. You have to start from the basic premise that we wouldn't go bankrupt building it, that people are going to use and occupy these buildings. That takes you to your next step, which is that we are building in a city that needs to grow. Like any other organism, if a city doesn't grow, it dies. Your cells constantly need replenishing and need to grow, and that's true with a city as well. And if it grows too quickly, you have cancer and you die.

"You're looking at a situation where this city has an incredible housing crisis, where the vacancy rate stands at almost 1 percent. At the same time if you look at the next ten to fifteen years, we're going to have a million more people living in New York. Of those, 300,000 to 400,000 are expected to settle in Brooklyn.

"It's already not affordable. You have less middle class in New York City than you have in any other major city in the country. And so how do you reconcile the fact that you don't have growth in this city? You can't. You can't possibly reconcile it.

"And then you have to also look at the fact that the ones who get hurt traditionally are the poorer people, the minority populations. In fact, if you were to look at the demographics in Brooklyn, and if you were looking at the people lobbing the criticism, largely they are the wealthier people who have lived in the neighborhood less than ten years—most less than five years. Most of them have advanced degrees, and if you look at what's happening over time in these neighborhoods, the poorer, predominantly African- and Caribbean-American population is being forced out. So now you say, where do you build? Well, in Brooklyn, less than 4 percent of the land is vacant. The question then is, if you recognize you must build, where do you build, especially when less than 4 percent of the land is vacant? Doesn't it make implicit sense to build densely where you have mass transportation?

"I will answer my own question. Every major planning agency in the world, and more specifically the regional planning agencies, will tell you that the perfect planning scenario is to put density where there is mass transportation. Which is exactly what we are doing. Now layer on top of that the fact that in order to build this, we've had to spend a tremendous amount of money to acquire properties, to acquire condemnation, and on top of that we have had to spend about $600 million on infrastructure, building platforms, relocating rail yards, doing subway connections, doing new sewer and water mains, rebuilding bridges over Sixth Avenue and Carlton Avenue—it's going to cost $50 million alone just to clean up the dirty soil there. So before you put a shovel in the ground, you have close to a billion dollars in cost between the infrastructure and the land. So the basic economics demands you do a certain density if you're going to build there at all.

Jim Stuckey and wife Debbie celebrate their thirty-third wedding anniversary.
*Courtesy of Jim Stuckey*

"So I will submit to you that while it's very easy to be critical and to stick one's head in the sand and just make believe these problems are going to go away—don't put it in my backyard—there is an absolute responsibility, not just the government, but every one of us who lives in New York City, to make sure we do things to solve these problems.

"Now for better or worse, our job is to be a developer. For better or worse. And I come full circle and say if it weren't going to be occupied by somebody, we wouldn't build it. So while it's easy to make the developer the target—it's a TV storyline: corrupt officials, big developer, overdevelopment—we can all write that script. We've seen it on TV a million times. But when you peel back the onion, there's not a shred of truth to it. Everyone knows the hundreds of meetings I've been to. They can't dispute that I've gone out into the community more than two hundred times. They can't dispute the fact I've made two city council presentations, the first one in 2004 and the second in 2005. The project only got approved at the end of 2006. Those are matters of record. I've gone to community board meetings where we had support from more than nine hundred people from three community boards. But the opposition to this project hopes if they say something enough times, people will believe it.

"Well, the fact is, it's not true. Unless the city steps up, unless the people step up and do this, then this city is a goner, it's dead. It will become the next Detroit or Pittsburgh or Buffalo or other cities where people see there is no growth and decide to leave. If companies don't have workers who can live in the city they are going to go to cities where they can get cheap labor. This is not rocket science. You can see how strongly I feel about this.

"These criticisms are not the community view. Polling shows that close to 70 percent of the people in both Brooklyn and New York City as a whole support this project."

*With the recent downturn in the real estate market and the economy, it seems as though the ambitious Atlantic Yards project has hit some roadblocks. Although construction may be delayed, Jim Stuckey is confident it will be built.*

# REMAKING CONEY ISLAND

JOSEPH SITT

**N**ATHAN'S FAMOUS STILL SITS IN THE SAME PROMINENT SPOT it has taken for most of the last century: on Surf Avenue, a gateway to Coney Island. Behind it and to the west stands the majestic, iconic Parachute Jump, a symbol of the days before jet flight, computers, and cell phones, when large, glitzy amusement parks attracted millions of visitors a year.

In 2006, more than 10 million visitors walked the beach, ate the hot dogs, and experienced Coney Island's quirky charms. Nearby, there are signs the area won't be quirky much longer. One indication is the remodeled, solar-paneled Stillwell Avenue subway terminal. Another is Keyspan Park, home of the Mets' Single A minor league Brooklyn Cyclones, one of the country's most successful minor league franchises. But Keyspan's fans race home right after games, and during the six months between baseball seasons, Coney Island is desolate. The experts say Coney Island is destined to be a blighted area. One contrarian Coney Islander disagrees, and he has put his money where his mouth is.

Joseph Sitt, who grew up in Gravesend, one of Brooklyn's tougher neighborhoods, intends to build a glitzy billion-dollar hotel/mall/Las Vegas attraction on the boardwalk. His grandiose plan is to make Coney Island a year-round resort. A lot of people think he is overreaching, but Sitt's remarkable track record makes it hard to bet against him.

The tangle of overhead wires leads to the light towers for Coney Island's Keyspan Park and the parachute jump. *Doug Grad*

Sitt, a comic-book collector from childhood, named his now-huge real estate company Thor Equities, after the Norse god and comic-book character that protected Earth from the bad guys. Sitt, who built his fortune by daring to cater to inner-city customers, saw himself as a protector of cities, and he felt the image was perfect.

Thor Equities today controls more than 14 million square feet of property in cities all over the country. In recent years he has quietly spent more than $100 million buying up properties that cover over twelve acres of Coney Island real estate near the boardwalk. Residents, slowly catching on to what Thor Equities was doing, worried he was planning to build a Wal-Mart, but Sitt, who lives in Coney Island in baronial splendor, would never do anything so pedestrian. Instead he intends to remake Coney Island into a Bellagio-like attraction with a five-hundred-room four-star hotel, an *indoor* water park, and a retail-and-entertainment colossus to rival anything Las Vegas has to offer. He even intends to have a dirigible take off from the roof and carry tourists on joyrides. Of course the blimp will advertise the name of his complex: THE BOARDWALK AT CONEY ISLAND. But Sitt will not ignore the past, kitschy Coney Island. He intends to salute the old days with a merry-go-round and water fountain topped by an elephant shooting pyrotechnics. Will casinos be far behind? Will Joseph Sitt be able to attract the 13 million customers a year he needs to break even? Will Sitt be the latter-day George Tilyou?

Lady Deborah, no stranger to risk-taking when she founded Coney Island, would have approved, but unlike Bruce Ratner, who hired Brooklynites that could navigate the political landscape, Joseph Sitt finds himself at loggerheads with Mayor Bloomberg and Amanda Burden, the director of the New York City Department of City Planning and chair of the City Planning Commission, who question the wisdom of building time shares and condos around an amusement park. Never mind that people have bought condos adjacent to the Lowe's Motor Speedway in Charlotte, North Carolina, but when the politically powerful say no, there's not a whole lot you can do, even if you're as wealthy as Joseph Sitt.

Sitt professes not to know what he has done to make such powerful enemies, but it is clear that without the support of Bloomberg and Burden, his grand plans will remain in limbo. He is going to have to hope that he gets more cooperation from the next mayor, whoever it may be. In the meantime, he says, he is willing to wait it out.

The rise of Joseph Sitt is a story of America. He was born in Brooklyn in 1964. Sitt's grandparents on his father's side came from the Middle East to the United States around 1900. His mother's side of the family came from Colombia.

His father, who grew up in Bensonhurst, sold higher-end children's clothing for a living. A member of a family business, he was a salesman who spent a lot of time in his car on the road. During the summer of 1975, when Joseph was eleven, he accompanied his father on one of his trips.

Joseph Sitt and his father. *Courtesy of Joseph Sitt*

**JOSEPH SITT** "That was hard work for him trying to make a living, and I traveled with him as a young kid during summers and vacations because it was the only way I could see him. As a boy, I went with him to Detroit to visit S. S. Kresge, which became Kmart. When I was eleven, we flew to Bentonville, Arkansas, to visit Wal-Mart. Having someone come from New York City to visit was a big deal for the town of Bentonville.

"We got up at four thirty in the morning before we got on the flight, and we went to a bagel store and loaded up a garment bag full of bagels. We brought them poppy, sesame, everything bagels. They were a real novelty. There was no such thing as Lender's bagels back then.

"We'd arrive at one in the afternoon with our bagels, and the employees would come out of every cubicle of that home office, hoping to be one of the lucky ones to get a Brooklyn bagel. Dad once offered them sushi, but they got afraid because of the name.

"During those trips I would often talk to him about business. I loved to learn, and I was inquisitive. One day my dad told me that Wal-Mart was going to be the biggest company in America and maybe the world. That was a big statement back then, because Wal-Mart only did about a hundred million in sales then, and they were competing against Kresge, Sears Roebuck, McCrory's, and Woolworth's.

"I asked him why. He said, 'Everybody overanalyzes and overcompensates life and business. Companies like Kresge and Sears Roebuck and Woolworth's have gotten so analytical about this business that they have lost sight of the forest from the trees. Sometimes you just have to make it simple.'

"That was one of the concepts he brought up to me: keep things simple. Go to the simplest form. Go to the root. Cut out all the baloney. And the second thing he said, 'Wal-Mart is so honest with their customers. Everyone else says they are a discounter, but they work on 60 percent margins. Wal-Mart from the get-go works on less than a 40 percent markup.' They are true to the customer, and as a result they get rewarded with a tremendous amount of volume. He said, 'As a smart person once told me, "At the end of the day you don't deposit percentages into the bank. You deposit dollars."' So Wal-Mart's formula for working on short percentages and giving value worked. And then they also have the other common-sense things, like a greeter at the front door to make you feel welcome. My dad used to point out that Wal-Mart was one chain where the stores always changed their lightbulbs. Back then we'd go into Kmart, and 20 percent of their lightbulbs would be out, and the manager's attitude was, 'We'll get to it one day.'

"My mother's name is Louise Chera, and she also grew up in Brooklyn, in Bensonhurst. She went to Lincoln High School, and she and my dad met at a local dance. They settled between Bensonhurst and Coney Island, and that's where I grew up, a neighborhood that was a mix between Italians and African-Americans. It was an interesting mix. They didn't get along, and there were often gang fights and rivalries, depending on your ethnic background. I did some fighting. You didn't have a choice. I was Jewish, so I hung with the Jewish kids. Somehow you defended yourself. That was a great part of growing up in New York. The diversity of people and cultures really helped me. I had African-American friends. I had Italian friends. Maybe when you're a young kid, you fight a little bit more, but as I got older and matured, it turned into bonding and close relationships."

*When Joseph Sitt was twelve, two events affected him so deeply they would ultimately color his adulthood and lead to his business success. On both occasions, there were items he wanted. But he lived in the inner city, and in both cases there were no retail stores in his neighborhood for him to shop for those items.*

**JOSEPH SITT** "One time I asked for a parrot, and at another point I asked for a video game, and I remember them not being available. I went with my grandmother. I remember how frustrating it was. We didn't have those basic kinds of stores in our neighborhood, and we had to take the train into Manhattan to get them.

"No big companies would open stores in Brooklyn. They were afraid of New York. To them, any neighborhood in New York was a neighborhood to avoid. They were afraid of crime, afraid of cost, afraid of race, afraid of a culture in a town that was so different from other markets around the United States of America. It's amazing to think that Brooklyn got its first discount store in the year 2004. Target opened that August [in Bruce Ratner's Atlantic Terminal mall], and by the way, it is now among the top two or three stores in the nation. Manhattan didn't have a home-improvement store until a year and a half ago. Home Depot opened two stores in Manhattan. Some of these retailers come either because they want to experiment or because of a sense of social responsibility, and the store quickly becomes the number one store for them in the country. Just because the market is so underserved, because there's such a gap between supply and demand. And I made a career out of filling that void.

"Because when I wanted that parrot, and I couldn't find a store to sell me one, that had an impact on me. We had nothing available to buy where we lived. Small towns across America had so many more basic goods and services than we had in New York. It was a terrible shame. A few years back they opened the first Starbucks a couple neighborhoods over from me. You'd have thought it was manna from heaven!"

*Through his entire educational career, Sitt went to Jewish parochial schools. Where exactly, he doesn't want to say. His kids go there now, and he doesn't want to put them in jeopardy. "There are a lot of crazy people out there," he says.*

*He went to New York University because that had been his father's dream. His dad had started there but he couldn't afford to stay, so he was hoping his boy could do what he couldn't. His first year in college he lived in the International Dorm. He lived with students from around the world.*

**JOSEPH SITT** "That showed me my susceptibility to diversity. It made you more receptive, especially when you traveled the globe. After college, for a short period, I worked for a manufacturing company, and I did some oveseas travel for them, buying products from Asia. I'd come home, and I could see I should be just as welcoming and receptive to all kinds of people right here in my own hometown."

*It was at NYU that he devised his plan to buy retail space in minority areas, fix it up, and go into business.*

**JOSEPH SITT** "Everybody who's got a dollar has a dream. That's my motto: A dollar and a dream is all you need. People like to make money, and I approached the parents of my college roommates, knocked on doors of family members, friends of family, parents of friends, so they knew what I was trying to do. It's the same thing with my Coney Island project. People get it. They know the history. They know what was there, and having known that, people, especially the older folks who know what the waterfront means, can imagine what can be. It was the same way with my early syndications. When I went knocking on people's doors to raise money, people were able to understand the concept of bringing quality retail into areas that don't have any."

*Sitt raised close to $40,000. Then he studied the lists of tax auctions looking for properties that risked foreclosure. The first one he bought was on East Tremont Avenue in the Bronx.*

**JOSEPH SITT** "What I liked about it was that it had vacant land with green grass. The rest of the neighborhood was a lot of blight. It was almost suburban-looking, in what was really a tough part of the Bronx. I was able to envision what could be there. It was a burned-out building that the city demolished, but it had a green patch of grass that allowed someone like myself with vision to make something good out of it.

"It was tough. I remember my second visit to the site. I saw a handmade sign on the corner dedicated to people who had died. But growing up in Brooklyn, I was used to that.

"I had to build the building, and inside I put in a ladies clothing retailer and a shoe repair shop, and we had a drugstore. And I have to say it was a very successful property."

*Most people would have been satisfied to see their plan come to fruition. Sitt had grander plans If he could make one retail center profitable, why couldn't he build a chain of a hundred of these? I asked him what made him think he could do that?*

**JOSEPH SITT**   "What makes someone think that they can't? It only takes one beacon in the night to bring in a thousand ships. I had a concept. I didn't want to get too far ahead of myself, but I just went with it. I wanted a more exciting project, and then from there I opened a half dozen locations, and by then I became frustrated by the fact that I couldn't get a national chain to move into one of my retail centers. The tenants who were there, local merchants, were doing very well. It was very, very frustrating getting turned down over and over.

"I'd rather not say [which national retailers said no], because many of them now are starving for inner-city locations, and I don't want to burn any relationships. These were some of the largest businesses and retailers in the United States. They constantly turned me down, laughed at me. They said, 'Are you crazy? In those neighborhoods?' And getting turned down so many times made me think, *There's a real void here.*"

*For a man like Joseph Sitt, there was nothing to do but fill it.*

**JOSEPH SITT**   "I started a business called Ashley Stewart. The Ashley is from Laura Ashley and the Stewart is from Martha Stewart. The concept was, I was going to swim upstream. I was going to build the first upscale retail chain in the neighborhoods to cater to the needs of minority customers. My stores had beautiful carpeting, clean marble-granite floors, mahogany trim, couches so husbands could sit down and be occupied while the women shopped. We served coffee and had great customer service—all designed to give respect to the African-American consumer.

"We didn't check their bags at the front like most inner-city stores did. We treated them with respect. We became famous for our hiring practices. We had 98 percent African-American employees. Today the president of Ashley Stewart is African-American. We held hundreds of fund-raisers for various community events. We recruited for our board of directors so the majority is African-American. All with the concept of 'Do the right thing.' We really built the business the right way, and we did the same thing with a Hispanic-oriented company called Marianne, with stores mostly in South Florida and Puerto Rico."

*How successful was the Ashley Stewart chain? Before he sold it, Sitt had built 308 Ashley Stewart stores across the inner cities of America. He even had stores in St. Thomas and St. Croix in the Virgin Islands.*

*Sitt also bought a chain of stores that catered to inner-city children, called Children's Place. He sold it because he needed the money to start his own chain, which he called Kid's Spot, low-priced stores where African-American and Hispanic women could buy good-quality brands of children's clothing at low prices. Eventually he sold this chain as well.*

Joseph Sitt at the opening of one of his Ashley Stewart stores. *Courtesy of Joseph Sitt. Photo by Doug Grad*

**JOSEPH SITT** "By the end of the 1990s I noticed that potential started to show. What do I mean by that? I was invited to investment conferences, and all of a sudden the CEOs from big companies wanted to meet me. I was particularly impressed by a fellow by the name of Mickey Drexler, who was working for Banana Republic and Old Navy, for the Gap. He started tapping my brain on where to open Old Navy stores. He wanted to go into the inner cities and open Gap stores. He was looking at 125th Street in Harlem.

"I honestly was honored, and I started tapping his brain for merchandising and resource advice but what struck me was the pendulum finally was shifting. Retailers for the first time had interest in these markets because the traditional markets were saturated, or they woke up and discovered the 'socially responsible' stores in the inner cities were quickly rising to become the number one store in the chain. I now realized that the void shifted from retailers interested in the market to having a developer out there to provide a platform for all these retailers so they could grow their businesses in inner-city locations in the United States."

*Another void to fill, and Sitt changed direction just that quickly. He began buying run-down malls and vacant land for new malls in the inner cities.*

**JOSEPH SITT**   "The same way I executed my concept by giving respect with the shopping experience, I took it to another level by doing it in shopping malls. I changed the floors, ripped up the linoleum, put in granite floors, and opened up the ceilings with skylights for natural light. Instead of having a big burly guy with a gun at the door, scaring the customers half out of their wits, I took that same burly guy and put him in a spanking-new tuxedo. He still carried a gun, but he greeted people when they came in, and not just that, we gave every woman who came in a rose. 'Welcome to the Galleria so-and-so.'"

*He was so successful, his holdings had made him very, very wealthy. And then came his crazy dream to revitalize Coney Island.*

**JOSEPH SITT**   "As a kid, a lot of times I liked to play hookey, and I used to go to Coney Island, so they used to tease me and call me 'Joey Coney Island.'"

*When the other executives in his company learned he wanted to spend $500 million to build a Las Vegas–like edifice on the boardwalk, they called him something else: out of his mind.*

**JOSEPH SITT** "At first, they looked at me a little funny. They said, 'It's a big undertaking. Are you sure Coney Island can come back?' But when everyone started to get closer to it, they started to buy into my dream, my vision. I said, 'It's waterfront. The infrastructure is in place for it.' Because if I'm developing in New York City, the places I develop have to have a history. It's not like I'm buying a farm in Oklahoma.

Doug Grad

"For example, I own the Palmer House in Chicago. It's the oldest operating hotel in the United States, 140-something years old. It's a hot, hot hotel. When I bought that property, I thought the owners were undervaluing the Palmer House brand, with the beautiful ceilings and the statues, the solid-gold flatware. It's the same thing with Coney Island. I saw a brand name and a rich history and I saw waterfront, and I saw the infrastructure was there. If you buy land in Oklahoma, you have to bring water, electricity, and transportation. All of that is in place in Coney Island. You have the Aquarium, which draws multi-multi millions of people. You have the baseball team that Rudy Giuliani built, bringing some life and comeback, and the city started to invest in the boardwalk. The boardwalk has started to become fashionable again. It was always a scary place, and all of a sudden people started to want to come back and walk that boardwalk, and they started to fix the beach, and they put volleyball courts in and bathrooms for the first time. Coney Island has soft, soft sand. It's one of the prettiest beaches I've ever seen in the world. I've seen the beaches in Greece, on the French and Italian Rivieras. The Coney Island sand is beautiful. We even have a state-of-the-art train station. The city spent hundreds of millions of dollars building the first solar-powered train station. And right in the heart of Coney Island, on Stillwell Avenue, is the bus depot. Hundreds and hundreds of buses pour between the boardwalk and Surf Avenue in the heart of Coney Island. I said, as I have so many times in my life, 'Pinch me. This looks too good to be true.'

"When I was catering to Hispanics and African-Americans, they went from 18 million to 36 million people in 1990, my early days. I thought to myself, *How can it be that I'm the only one realizing their population has just doubled?* By the way, the population has doubled again in the last ten years, to 76 million in 2000. The same way with Coney Island. So many people tell me it's impossible. They ask, 'How can it be that you can buy Coney Island?' I say, 'It isn't going to be easy.'

"There were about forty different people who owned that property, but you know what? I think everybody gave up. Those owners had given up. Plans would come and go, and nothing really happened. And what I did, instead of coming in with fake companies with Japanese names, I came in up front and center. I said, 'I'm Joseph Sitt, and I want to buy your property. You should sell it to me for two reasons, because nothing is going to happen here if you don't, and because I have a dream.'

"Some of those properties have been in the family for a hundred years. I bought land from the Tilyou family. Do you know the famous George Tilyou? I bought another tract from the Handwerkers, the family that founded Nathan's Famous hot dogs. I bought Astroland from the Alberts, who had purchased the land from the Feltmans, the family that actually invented the hot dog. Nathan copied this guy. My pitch to them was this: 'Wouldn't you like to see Coney Island reborn?' Many of them were true to form. They wanted me to present my plan before they would sell. I was afraid they would charge me a fortune when they found out what I was doing, but that didn't happen. They wanted to make sure the family's crown jewels went into the right hands."

*If Sitt ever gets to build his dream, it will be a destination to match those of Las Vegas and Atlantic City. Instead of Coney Island being a summer-only spot, the Boardwalk at Coney Island will bring life to the area year-round. Sitt is chomping at the bit. Only the recalcitrance of city officials is stopping him.*

**JOSEPH SITT**   "Our goal is to create the modern version of Coney Island the way it was many years ago, when it was a very dense, very active, very busy destination. Unlike the way it is today. In addition to the area going down from a safety, security point of view, a quality point of view, it's also gone down in terms of the physical improvements and the physical build-up there.

"As an example of my challenges dealing with the city, when I went to the city with my plan, they said they wanted *no* restaurants. They said, 'Coney Island has no restaurants.' I said, 'Are you crazy? You don't know what burned down.' If you look at the history of Coney Island, there used to be 230 restaurants. But the problem is you're dealing with young folks in government who don't know history, never picked up a book, so it's all within their own instincts what they *think* was there. This is just one example.

"Our goal is to tap the entertainment aspect in terms of restaurants, movie theaters, of course keeping the amusements that are there, putting in more modern, more vertical rides that go up and down, a water park, which was something Coney Island had years ago. We want to put in hotels and build condos. We want residents. We want people who are physically there. We want to create density, which creates security and hustle and bustle that makes New York so special. That's another challenge I am going through. I have to convince the city to let me build hotels and to build time shares for residents. The city is fighting me. But the ultimate goal is a mixed-use project that includes amusement, entertainment, hotel, and residents. We want to action-pack this place so it is thought of as a number one destination by people who want to be entertained, be it at a restaurant, a ride, a water park, a hotel, or otherwise.

"I'm in the hands of the City of New York now, and the City of New York tends to move rather slowly. Everybody has to go through the education process, and right now we're walking a bit of a tightrope with the City of New York, trying to convince them of the importance of having all of this. One aspect is financial. Today's amusement doesn't make money. It's very expensive, especially with the land values we're paying. We need hotels and rentals to pay for it, but that's only half. The other half is having people see this as a destination, and the challenge is convincing the government of the need.

An early rendering showing a new Coney Island amusement area as well as hotels and condos. *Thor Equities*

"The government says there are people who live in the apartments across the street from the Cyclone who complain once in a while about the noise. My answer is twofold. Number one, how many complaints can there be? The Cyclone has been there eighty years. You've never seen an article calling for them to turn off the Cyclone. And number two, anyone who is buying a condo within the amusement district is doing so knowing it's the amusement district. That's *why* they are buying the apartment. They know what they're getting into. This is brought up to me by people in government like I should have my head examined.

"My problem is that I don't know if I'm in a two-year process, a five-year process, or a fifteen-year process. This administration has three years left to go. If they don't approve, it'll take the next administration a year to gear up, and then we start the process all over again. It'll be anywhere from one to three years if it's this administration, four to seven years with another one.

"Atlantic Yards is a residential community, and there the opposition is the community against the developer and the government. In my case it's the community and the developer against the government. We did polls, and the polls show that 80 percent of the people support us. The community is with us.

"My problem is that the low-level city administrators have their own vision of what they want in Coney Island, and if it isn't what they want, they're content to let it sit as a vacant site.

"I have to think positively. There is no Plan B. Plan B is just to keep fighting for Plan A. A lot of Coney Island got turned into parking lots. I'm hoping that one day the government wants to see Coney Island happen. Bobby Kennedy had a saying: 'There's a no, there's a no, there's a no, until one day, hopefully, comes a yes.'"

## ACKNOWLEDGMENTS

**T**HIS IS ONE OF THOSE MAGICAL BOOKS WHERE AT THE BEGINNING OF THE PRO-cess you wonder if any publisher will be savvy enough to understand exactly what it is you're trying to do, and at the end of the process you say to yourself, "How in the world did I accomplish this?"

Let me start at the beginning. When I wrote the book *Bums* back in 1984, my superb editor Phyllis Grann cut two chapters from my manuscript. One was about the Irish enclave of Windsor Terrace. The other was poet Donald Hall's reminiscence of what it was like for him to root for the Brooklyn Dodgers. For years I wondered if I could come up with another book about Brooklyn that would allow me to incorporate those two chapters.

Then one morning the idea came to me while I was taking a shower. Bud Selig had announced that every April 15 would be Jackie Robinson Day in every major league ballpark, and I got to wondering, *Why was it that when Jackie came up to the Dodgers in 1947, he was beloved in Brooklyn but hated just about every place else?* That became a key focus, and that led to explorations of broader subjects, including racism, bigotry, immigration, and assimilation. My goal was to try to do for Brooklyn what John Dos Passos did for America: let the people involved tell the stories of their lives and at the same time reveal the history of Brooklyn and also of America.

To do that, I knew the man to call. Ten years ago I had been invited by Professor Joseph Dorinson to visit the Brooklyn campus of Long Island University to take part in a symposium celebrating the life of Jackie Robinson. Professor Dorinson invited dozens of fascinating speakers. I listened to Lester Rodney, whose rants against racism in the *Daily Worker* had helped pave the way for Robinson. I had lunch with Howard Fast, the author of *Spartacus* and dozens of other best-sellers. Fast had been jailed for refusing to name names in front of the House Un-American Activities Committee. I asked Mr. Fast whether he had been scared to go to jail. He said, "Oh no, I looked at it as an opportunity." I thought to myself, *This country sometimes has a strange notion of who's a hero and who's not.* Well, there are a lot of unsung heroes in this book.

I knew that I needed to interview Rodney. It was too late for me to talk to Fast, who had passed away in the interim. I was hoping when I told Professor Dorinson what I was planning, he could provide me with important leads. He came through like the champ he is. Through him, I was able to interview Rodney, Henry Foner, Dorothy Burnham, Stan Kanter, Ted Rosenbaum, Abe Smorodin, and Peter Spanakos, important figures in the early chapters of this book. Professor Dorinson was also kind enough to read some of the chapters and give his helpful comments. I owe him a lot, and it is to him that I dedicate this book.

My close friend and neighbor, Professor Ray Arcenault, also provided me with invaluable contacts. It was through him that I was able to interview John Hope Franklin, Justus Doenecke, Si Dresner, Ira Glasser, and Janet Braun-Reinitz.

My fine, supportive, Brooklyn-dwelling editor, Doug Grad, did yeoman's work. A third-generation Brooklynite, he was captivated by the concept, and he provided inspiration and editorial guidance throughout. A great editor, he is also a prince of a guy. He led me to his father, Ian, and through his friend—PR man Howie Greene—to Neil Sedaka and Bruce Morrow, and to Curtis Sliwa, Abram Hall, Harry Schweitzer, Robert Crosson, and John Mackie. Peter Meinke and Dave Radens I met through tennis here in St. Pete, and I play softball with John Ford. Thanks for your stories. I wish to thank Mike Walsh, whose font of knowledge is encyclopedic, for his advice and suggestions. The Brooklyn politicians—Marty Markowitz, Charles Barron, Alec Brook-Krasny, and Victor Robles—graciously made themselves available to me. Through the efforts of Barry Baum of Forest City Ratner I was able to interview Jim Stuckey and Bruce Bender. Through Gersh Kuntzman I was able to interview Richard Green and Renee Cafiero.

I want to thank my dear friends from *Bums:* Joe Flaherty, Joel Oppenheimer, Irving Rudd, Bill Reddy, and Bobby McCarthy. To them and the other interviewees—Pete Hamill, Clarence Taylor, Joseph Boskin, Charlotte Phillips, Marvin Miller, Joseph Sitt, Gene Brock, and Monte Irvin—I owe a deep sense of gratitude. Your heart and soul are what makes Brooklyn, and this great country, so special.

# BIBLIOGRAPHY

Michael Barkum, *Religion and the Racist Right: The Origins of the Christian Identity Movement* (University of North Carolina Press: Chapel Hill, 1997).

John Barry, *Rising Tide: The Great Mississippi Flood of 1927 and How It Changed America* (Simon and Schuster: New York, 1997).

Taylor Branch, *At Canaan's Edge: America in the King Years 1965–1968* (Simon and Schuster: New York, 2006).

Committee on Un-American Activites, *Guide to Subversive Organizations and Publications (and Appendixes),* revised and published December 1, 1961 (U.S. House of Representatives, Washington, DC).

Frank J. Coppa and Thomas J. Curran, *The Immigrant Experience in America* (Twayne Publishers: Boston, 1976).

Roger Daniels, *Guarding the Golden Door: American Immigration Policy and Immigrants Since 1882* (Hill and Wang: New York, 2004).

Joseph Dorinson and William Pencak, eds., *Paul Robeson: Essays on His Life and Legacy* (McFarland: Jefferson, NC, 2004).

Michael Dorman, *Witch Hunt: The Underside of American Democracy* (Delacorte Press: New York, 1976).

Mary L. Dudziak, *Cold War Civil Rights: Race and the Image of American Democracy* (Princeton University Press: Princeton, NJ, 2000).

Edward Robb Ellis, *The Epic of New York City* (Kondansha International: New York, 1997).

Jack D. Foner, *Blacks in the Military in American History* (Praeger: New York, 1974).

Philip Foner, *American Socialism and Black Americans* (Greenwood Press: Westport, CT, 1977).

Diane Garey, *Defending Everybody: A History of the American Civil Liberties Union* (TV Books: New York, 1998).

Peter Golenbock, *Bums* (G. P. Putnam Sons: New York, 1984).

James R. Grossman, *Land of Hope: Chicago, Black Southerners and the Great Migration* (University of Chicago Press: Chicago, 1987).

Pete Hamill, *Forever* (Little, Brown: Boston, 2003).

Thom Hartmann, *Screwed: The Undeclared War against the Middle Class—and What We Can Do about It* (Barrett-Koehler: New York, 2007).

Florette Henri, *Black Migration: Movement North 1900–1920* (Anchor Press/Doubleday: New York, 1975).

Burton Hersh, *Bobby and Edgar* (Carroll and Graf: New York, 2007).

John Higham, *Strangers in the Land, Patterns of American Nativism 1860–1925* (Rutgers University Press: New Brunswick, NJ, 1988).

Luciano Iorizzo and Salvatore Mondello, *The Italian-Americans* (Twayne: New York, 1971).

Julius Jacobson, ed., *The Negro and the American Labor Movement* (Doubleday/Anchor: Garden City, NY, 1968).

Daniel M. Johnson and Rex R Campbell, *Black Migration in America: A Social Demographic History* (Duke University Press: Durham, NC, 1981).

Jonathan Kaufman, *Broken Alliance: The Turbulent Times between Blacks and Jews in America* (Touchstone: New York, 1995).

Joel Kovel, *Red Hunting in the Promised Land: Anti-Communism and the Making of America* (Basic Books: New York, 1994).

Nicholas Lemann, *The Promised Land: The Great Black Migration and How It Changed America* (Alfred A. Knopf: New York, 1991).

Peter Levine, *Ellis Island to Ebbets Field: Sport and the American Jewish Experience* (Oxford University Press: New York, 1992).

George Lewis, *The White South and the Red Menace: Segregationists, Anticommunism, and Massive Resistance, 1945–1965* (University of Florida Press: Gainesville, 2004).

Leon Litwack, *The American Labor Movement* (Prentice-Hall: Englewood Cliffs, NJ, 1962).

Max Lowenthal, *The Federal Bureau of Investigation* (Harcourt, Brace: New York, 1950).

Jonathan Mahler, *Ladies and Gentlemen, The Bronx Is Burning: 1977, Baseball, Politics, and the Battle for the Soul of the City* (Picador: New York, 2007).

John Barlow Martin, *The Deep South Says Never* (Ballantine Books: New York, 1957).

Edo McCullough, *Good Old Coney Island* (Charles Scribner's Sons: New York, 1957).

Seymour Martin Lipset and Earl Raab, *Politics of Unreason: Right-Wing Extremism in America* (Harper & Row: New York, 1970).

Douglas Miller and Marion Nowack, *The Fifties: The Way We Really Were* (Doubleday: New York, 1977).

Elizabeth Mitchell, *W., Revenge of the Bush Dynasty* (Hyperion: New York, 2000).

Michael Moore, *Dude, Where's My Country?* (Warner Books: New York, 2003).

Mark Naison, *Communists in Harlem During the Depression* (University of Illinois Press: Urbana, 1983).

David M. Oshinsky, *A Conspiracy So Immense: The World of Joe McCarthy* (Free Press: New York, 1983).

Richard Gid Powers, *Secrecy and Power: The Life of J. Edgar Hoover* (Free Press: New York, 1987).

Richard Reeves, *The Reagan Detour* (Simon and Schuster: New York, 1985).

Richard Rovere, *Senator Joe McCarthy* (Harper/Colophon Books: New York, 1973).

Luc Sante, *Low Life* (Vintage Books: New York, 1992).

Arthur Schlesinger Jr., *The Crisis of the Old Order 1919–1933* (Little, Brown: Boston, 1957).

Ellen Schrecker, *The Age of McCarthyism: A Brief History with Documents* (Bedford/St. Martin's: New York, 1994).

Peter and Rochelle Schweitzer, *The Bushes—Portrait of a Dynasty* (Doubleday: New York, 2004).

Maxine Seller, *To Seek America: A History of Ethnic Life in the United States* (Jerome S. Ozer: New York, 1977).

Robert Sherrill, *First Amendment Felon: The Story of Frank Wilkinson, His 132,000-page FBI File, and His Epic Fight for Civil Rights and Liberties* (Nation Books: New York, 2005).

Russell Shorto, *The Island at the Center of the World* (Vintage Books: New York, 2005).

Clarence Taylor, *Knocking at Our Own Door: Milton A. Galamison and the Struggle to Integrate New York City Schools* (Columbia University Press: New York, 1997).

Wye Craig Wade, *The Fiery Cross* (Simon and Schuster: New York, 1987).

Jeff Woods, *Black Struggle, Red Scare: Segregation and Anti-Communism in the South 1949–1968* (Louisiana State University Press: Baton Rouge, 2004).

William Workman, *The Case for the South* (Devin-Adair: New York, 1960).

# NOTES

## Chapter 1: Coney Island's Conscience—LADY DEBORAH AND GEORGE TILYOU

*Interview with John Manbeck, former official historian of Brooklyn for eight years under Borough President Howard Golden.*

*See* A Dangerous 1600s Woman, *by George Dewan,* Newsday *community guide.*

*Some of the material in this chapter was researched from Jeffrey Stanton's unpublished book on Coney Island.*

*Also see* Good Old Coney Island, *by Edo McCullough (Charles Scribner's Sons: New York, 1957).*

*p. 2*   *Columbus first called them Indians. Another explanation was that the word derives from "una gente in Dios"—a people in God—which was Columbus's description of the people of the New World.*

*p, 3*   *In 1649, nine years after Lady Deborah left for New England, the Puritan Oliver Cromwell murdered Charles I and changed England into a fundamentalist, terrorist state. He murdered Catholics with impunity, initiating a reign of terror.*

*p. 4*   *"She is a dangerous woeman." Russell Shorto,* The Island at the Center of the World *(Vintage Books: New York, 2005), p. 160.*

*p. 4*   *The witch test. Joseph McCarthy in the 1950s came up with a similar witch test for subversives. According to his logic, if you once belonged to the Communist Party, you were a subversive. No one was ever proved innocent under either test.*

*p. 5*   *The Illuminati. Lipset and Raab,* The Politics of the Unknown, *pp. 36–37.*

*p. 7*   *August Belmont's real name was August Schoenberg. A Jew who had converted to Protestantism, he was one of the founders of the Metropolitan Museum of Art.*

*p. 7*   *"My Mariooch-Maha-Da-Hoocha-Ma-Coocha," McCullough, p. 257.*

*p. 8*   *With no competition, McKane and his construction company got rich in the nineteenth century the way Vice President Dick Cheney and his Halliburton construction company did more than a hundred years later in Iraq.*

*p. 9*   *Anthony Comstock had a huge influence both in Brooklyn and Manhattan. He was one of the first great reformers in New York City's political history.*

*p. 11*   *"The people of Gravesend must not be interfered with . . ."* Good Old Coney Island, *p. 89.*

*p. 11*   *William Gaynor later became mayor of New York City. He was a rare reform Democrat (most reformers of the time were Republicans), and after he double-crossed Tammany Hall, they refused to renominate him. He was nearly assassinated in 1910.*

p. 11    *"They're all drunk." Ibid., p. 94.*

p. 12    *"Don't you bet he'd change places with me now." Ibid., p. 110.*

p. 12    *The Pan-American Exposition in Buffalo was where President William McKinley was assassinated.*

p. 14    *Hell Gate refers to the dangerous waters near the northeast tip of Manhattan. A few years earlier, the ship General Slocum burned and sank with the loss of more than two thousand lives.*

p. 15    *The Thunderbolt rollercoaster. In the movie* Annie Hall, *Woody Allen's character, Alvie Singer, lived in a house under the Thunderbolt.*

## Chapter 2: Here Come the Jews

p. 17    *. . . only five thousand Jews in the United States until 1830. Coppa and Curran,* The Immigrant Experience in America *(Twayne Publishers: Boston, 1976), p. 148.*

p. 18    *. . . nine Jews were brought up for trial.* Brooklyn Eagle, *May 14, 1879.*

p. 19    *A hundred thousand Jewish families were reduced to "homeless beggary." Ibid.*

p. 19    *The captives were turned loose.* Brooklyn Eagle, *May 15, 1891.*

p. 20    *Very few ever went back. Maxine Seller,* To Seek America: A History of Ethnic Life in the United States *(Jerome S. Ozer: New York, 1977), p. 108.*

p. 20    *. . . the figure had risen to 3,388,951 by 1917. Coppa and Curran, p. 149.*

p. 20    *The Jewish community grew from 250,000 to 3,500,000. Ibid., p. 147.*

p. 20    *At its height, a million Jews plied their skills in the garment trade. Ibid., p. 154.*

p. 21    *The German Jews noted that the names of many Russian Jews ended in "ki." Edward Robb Ellis,* The Epic of New York City *(Kondansha International, New York, 1997).*

p. 21    *"It cannot be denied these Jews are a species of social nuisance."* Brooklyn Eagle, *May 7, 1870.*

p. 23    *"Is America the Jews' Promised Land?"* Brooklyn Eagle, *February 24, 1901.*

p. 23    *By 1910 there were 1,252,000 Jews living in New York City. Ellis, p. 417.*

## Chapter 3: Crushing the Jewish Toublemakers—THE PERSECUTION OF EMMA GOLDMAN

p. 27    *Goldman believed in peaceful means to accomplish the annihilation of law and government.* Brooklyn Eagle, *September 9, 1901.*

p. 27    *. . . her reaction was, "You fool."* Brooklyn Eagle, *September 10, 1901.*

p. 27    *"There is no anarchist ring that would help him." Ibid.*

p. 27    *"To them we must look for the accused inspiration that struck down the President."* Brooklyn Eagle, *September 14, 1901.*

p. 29    *Landis, who was also a racist, sentenced Wisconsin Congressman Victor Berger and several others to twenty years in prison for sedition. John Barry,* Rising Tide: The Great Mississippi Flood of 1927 and How It Changed America *(Simon and Schuster: New York, 1997), p. 138.*

p. 30  The elites transmitted fear to the populace . . . Joel Kovel, Red Hunting in the Promised Land: Anti-Communism and the Making of America *(Basic Books: New York, 1994), p. 16.*

p. 30  In his book The Age of Surveillance *(Alfred Knopf: New York, 1980), Frank Donner argued that intelligence agents were often chasing scapegoats and pursuing critics of the status quo in order to undermine social change.*

p. 30  *. . . bringing the demonizing mentality up to full speed." Ibid.*

p. 30  *"They were going to 'slaughter the bourgeoisie . . .'" Ibid., p. 17.*

p. 30  *"[Nothing] will save the life of this free Republic . . ."* John Higham, Strangers in the Land, Patterns of American Nativism 1860–1925 *(Rutgers University Press: New Brunswick, NJ, 1988), p. 227.*

p. 31  *. . . racists were sure the blacks were incapable of raising their voices against injustice. Kovel, p. 19.*

p. 31  *. . . undermining the loyalty of the Negroes. Ibid.*

p. 31  *Wilson had Colonel House spy on Baruch.* Edward Robb Ellis, The Epic of New York City *(Kondansha International, New York, 1997). p. 508.*

p. 31  *"Palmer, do not let this country see Red."* Arthur Schlesinger Jr., The Crisis of the Old Order 1919–1933 *(Little, Brown: Boston, 1957), p. 42.*

p. 32  *Henry Ford accused the Jews of trying to corrupt baseball.* Daniel A. Nathan, *"Anti-Semitism and the Black Sox Scandal,"* Nine . . . 4 *(Fall 1995), pp. 96–98.*

p. 32  *Jews were enemies of all that Anglo-Saxons mean by civilization.* Higham, pp. 280–284.

p. 33  *Proof the Jews were intending world conquest. Kovel, p. 26.*

p. 35  *. . . most were innocent of any crime and were not connected to radical politics. Kopel and Olsen.*

p. 35  *". . . the unmistakable criminal type."* Burton Hersh, Bobby and Edgar *(Carroll and Graf: New York, 2007), chapter 2.*

p. 36  *They were arrested, held incommunicado . . . Kovel, p. 21.*

p. 36  *Hoover told Stone he would comply with all new policies.* Diane Garey, Defending Everybody: A History of the American Civil Liberties Union *(TV Books: New York, 1998), p. 75.*

p. 37  *". . . and the howling savage at the gates." Ibid., p. 22.*

p. 37  *filthy, un-American, and often dangerous in their habits."* Maxine Seller, To Seek America: A History of Ethnic Life in the United States *(Jerome S. Ozer: New York, 1977).*

p. 37  *"a solution to this immigration business."* Roosevelt to Joseph Gurney Cannon, January 12, 1907, in Elting E. Morison, ed., The Letters of Theodore Roosevelt, vol. 5 *(Harvard University Press: Cambridge, MA, 1952), p. 550.*

p. 38  *Dillingham ordered a study of the 2 million public school children in 1908.* New York Times, *Sam Dillon, "In Schools Across America, the Melting Pot Overflows," August 26, 2006.*

p. 38  *The least retarded were those children of British ancestry.* John M. Lund, *"Boundaries of Restriction: The Dillingham Commission,"* University of Vermont History Review, *col. 6, December 1994.*

p. 38  *Congress virtually cut off the entry of Eastern European Jews and Italian Catholics in 1924.* Higham, p. 285.

p. 38   . . . that rationality against the entire U.S. population. Seller, p. 218.

p. 39   "The day of indiscriminate acceptance of all races has definitely ended." Roger Daniels, Guarding the Golden Door: American Immigration Policy and Immigrants since 1882 (Hill and Wang: New York, 2004), p. 55.

p. 39   More than 300,000 Jews who applied for visas were turned away. Ibid., p. 78.

p. 40   987 refugees, mostly Jewish, from camps in Italy, were helped. Ibid., p. 86.

p. 40   twenty thousand charming children would all too soon grow into twenty thousand ugly adults." From the manuscript diary of State Department official Jay Moffat, May 25, 1939, as cited ibid., p. 79.

## Chapter 4: Growing Up Jewish—IRA GLASSER

p. 41   Jews were accused of profiteering, smuggling, and draft-dodging. Frank J. Coppa and Thomas J. Curran, The Immigrant Experience in America (Twayne Publishers: Boston, 1976), p. 160.

p. 41   Grant's position was clear. Ibid.

p. 41   Resorts, social clubs, and private schools excluded Jews. As a result, there arose in the Catskills the development of the so-called Jewish Alps.

p. 41   The Jews were climbing too fast and had to be kept in their place. Coppa and Curran, p. 160.

p. 42   In 1944 a poll showed that 24 percent of Americans believed Jews to be a menace to American society. Ibid., p. 163.

p. 43   To the fathers, they were lost souls. Ibid., p. 132.

p. 44   Vincent Impelliteri, the New York City Council president, took over as mayor on August 31, 1950, when mayor Paul O'Dwyer was appointed ambassador to Mexico by President Harry Truman. O'Dwyer was facing indictment for fiscal improprieties. Impelliteri ran and won as a third-party candidate. He was defeated in 1953 by Robert Wagner.

p. 45   Jimmy Wechsler, a member of the Communist Party during his Columbia days, was for more than forty years a liberal columnist for the New York Post. He stood up to J. Edgar Hoover and later was on Richard Nixon's enemies list.

p. 45   P.M. was succeeded by the Star and then by the Daily Compass. Dr. Seuss, aka Theodore Geisel, started there.

p. 46   Brooklyn Catholics were fed anti-Semitic rhetoric by the notoriously right-wing Tablet, a shrill tabloid.

Interview with Ira Glasser.

## Chapter 5: A "One Hundred Percent Jewish" Childhood—SY DRESNER

p. 51   By 1976 four out of five Jewish high schoolers went to college. Frank J. Coppa and Thomas J. Curran, The Immigrant Experience in America (Twayne Publishers: Boston, 1976), p. 157.

Interview with Israel Dresner.

## Chapter 6: The Lincoln Brigade—ABE SMORODIN

Interview with Abe Smorodin.

## Chapter 7: Victims of Rapp-Coudert—HENRY FONER

p. 73   *The American Communists by the mid-1920s had no interest in violence or regime change. Ellen Schrecker,* The Age of McCarthyism: A Brief History with Documents *(Bedford/St. Martin's: New York, 1994), p. 2.*

p. 80   *The conservatives considered Bertrand Russell an advocate of free love. It is also what the conservatives said about Emma Goldman.*

p. 81   *The Co-ops in the Bronx were apartments built in 1927 by the Amalgamated Clothing Workers Union.*

p. 82   *The Peekskill Riots were set off by an announced concert by Paul Robeson, who had expressed his extreme displeasure with the way blacks were treated in America. It was organized to benefit the Civil Rights Congress. It was held on September 4, 1949; twenty thousand people attended. After it was over, veterans and hate groups threw rocks and bottles at the cars of the attendees. Over 140 people were injured as the police stood by and watched.*

*Interview with Henry Foner.*

## Chapter 8: On the Side of Labor—MARVIN MILLER

p. 88   *The Rochester company that locked its faucets and sent home workers who were a minute late . . . Leon Litwack,* The American Labor Movement *(Prentice-Hall: Englewood Cliffs, NJ, 1962), pp. 15–16.*

p. 89   *Strikers were called Communists as far back as 1877. Ibid., p. 53.*

p. 89   *DO IT NOW!* John Barry, Rising Tide: The Great Mississippi Flood of 1927 and How It Changed America *(Simon and Schuster: New York, 1997), p. 139.*

p. 89   The Call *was ransacked. Ibid.*

p. 90   *ten thousand strikes involving 5,600,000 workers. Litwack, p. 119.*

p. 92   *At a rally at Madison Square Garden, Avery Brundage praised the Nazis, and in 1941 he was expelled from the America First Committee for his Nazi leanings.*

p. 98   *Robert Taft was a Republican U.S. senator from Ohio, who was a leading opponent to FDR's New Deal. He ran and lost in a bid for the presidency in 1940, 1948, and 1952.*

*Interview with Marvin Miller.*

## Chapter 9: The Roots of Racism—DOROTHY CHALLENOR BURNHAM

p. 105   *The poor white Southerners didn't know it, but they were being sold a bill of goods. Taylor Branch,* At Canaan's Edge: America in the King Years 1965–1968 *(Simon and Schuster: New York, 2006), p. 166.*

p. 107   *In 1872 President Grant spelled out the aims of the Klan.* Freakonomics, *p. 50.*

p. 107   *Klansmen had to believe in three tenets, including the virgin birth of Jesus; the literal infallibility of the Bible; and the bodily resurrection of Christ. This was explained to me by Fred Lamar, who was pastor of Bynum (Alabama) Methodist Church in the years 1959–1961. Lamar protested the burning of the bus on which the first freedom riders traveled. By 1965 he was ordered out of Alabama under the penalty of death.*

p. 107   *Jesse Max Barber fled to Chicago. James R. Grossman,* Land of Hope: Chicago, Black Southerners and the Great Migration *(University of Chicago Press: Chicago, 1987).*

p. 108    Wilson said, "My only regret is that it is all so terribly true." Wye Craig Wade, The Fiery Cross (Simon and Schuster: New York, 1987), p. 124

p. 108    Colonel William Joseph Simmons announced the rebirth of the Klan. John Barry, Rising Tide: The Great Mississippi Flood of 1927 and How It Changed America (Simon and Schuster: New York, 1997), p. 141.

p. 108    By 1920 the Klan had eight million members. Steven Leavitt and Stephen Dubner, Freakonomics (New York: HarperCollins, 2005), p. 50.

p. 108    ". . . the rank and file of the Baptist and Methodist ministry has either acquiesced in it or actively espoused it." Barry, p. 154.

p. 108    In the 1920s the enemy below was Catholics, immigrants, blacks, and political radicals. Ibid.

p. 109    Forty years later segregationists in Congress read the Communist Party's platform into the Congressional Record in an attempt to undermine civil rights reform. Congressional Record, January 23, 1964, p. 1249.

p. 109    To show how little sway the Communists had with the black community, Moore garnered exactly 296 votes. Mark Naison, Communists in Harlem during the Depression (University of Illinois Press: Urbana, 1983), p. 17.

p. 110    Adam Clayton Powell threw his support to the Communists. Ibid., p. 87.

p. 120    Henry Wallace was elected vice president to FDR in 1940. He ran for president on the Progressive Party ticket in 1948. His platform advocated the end of segregation, full voting rights for blacks, and universal government health care.

Interview with Dorothy Burnham.

## Chapter 10: Sports Editor of the *Daily Worker*—LESTER RODNEY

p. 130    Once the "Red Scare" era began, Wendell Smith distanced himself from Lester Rodney.

p. 131    In 1943 Benjamin Davis took the council seat of Adam Clayton Powell, when Powell was elected to the U.S. Congress. In 1949 Davis was indicted under the Smith Act and sentenced to five years in prison. After getting out of prison he resumed his role as black leader and social critic. He died on August 22, 1964.

p. 140    After Stalin's war crimes were revealed, Rodney and editor John Gates attempted to open up the pages of the Daily Worker to debate. The CPUSA leaders suppressed the effort and suspended publication of the paper. Rodney resigned after twenty-two years and moved to Torrance, California, where he worked as the religion editor for the Long Beach Press-Telegram. On April 17, 2008, he celebrated his ninety-seventh birthday.

Interview with Lester Rodney.

## Chapter 11: The Negro Soldier Returns from the War—MONTE IRVIN

p. 141    "The war provided a fascinating social laboratory in which to observe a nation's schizophrenic behavior . . ." Jack D. Foner, Blacks in the Military in American History (Praeger: New York, 1974), p. 135.

p. 142    "Negroes cannot help but feel that their country does not want them to defend it." Ibid., p. 136.

p. 142    The Red Cross even refused to take blood from blacks . . . Ibid., p. 140.

p. 143    "It looks, smells, and tastes like Fascism." Ibid., p. 148.

p. 143    They were considered "bad Negroes" . . . Ibid., p. 149.

p. 144    *"In that so many blacks were poorly educated . . ." Ibid., p. 159.*

p. 144    *"I have never seen any soldiers who have performed better in combat than you." Ibid., p. 162.*

p. 145    *"We certainly are not fighting for the Four Freedoms." Ibid., p. 155.*

p. 146    *"Segregation was an egregious error . . . " Ibid., p. 172.*

p. 146    *". . . a certain hope died, a certain respect for white Americans faded." Ibid., p. 175.*

*Monte Irvin served as assistant to baseball commissioner Bowie Kuhn from 1968 until 1984, when he retired. It was Irvin who pushed to open the doors of the baseball Hall of Fame to former members of the Negro Leagues.*

*Interview with Monte Irvin.*

### Chapter 12: The Jews Love Jackie—JOSEPH BOSKIN AND JOEL OPPENHEIMER

p. 156    *Woody Guthrie was born in Okremah, Oklahoma. After he was discharged from the army in 1945, he moved into a house on Mermaid Avenue in Coney Island. He had four children, including Arlo. By the late 1940s his health deteriorated. He left Brooklyn to briefly live in California and Florida, but he returned to Brooklyn and lived there at the time of his death in 1967.*

*The Oppenheimer material is the only section I borrowed from* Bums, *my oral history of the Brooklyn Dodgers. It's evocative and fits perfectly.*

*Interviews with Joseph Boskin and Joel Oppenheimer.*

### Chapter 13: Jackie Robinson's Place in History—IRA GLASSER

*Interview with Ira Glasser.*

### Chapter 14: The Accidental Rabbi—SY DRESNER

*Interview with Israel Dresner.*

### Chapter 15: Victims of the Smith Act—STAN KANTER

p. 179    *Dies sought an investigative committee in an attempt to become more visible.* Michael Dorman, Witch Hunt: The Underside of American Democracy *(Delacorte Press: New York, 1976), p. 18.*

p. 180    *Hearst called the president Franklin Stalino Roosevelt.* Joel Kovel, Red Hunting in the Promised Land: Anti-Communism and the Making of America *(Basic Books: New York, 1994), p. 37.*

p. 182    *"Every organization in Negro life which was attacking segregation per se was put on the subversive list."* Cheng, Cold War and the Black Liberation, *p. 189.*

p. 183    *Hoover used hearsay, rumor, snitching, backbiting, and innuendo.* Kovel, *p. 89.*

p. 183    *Congress turned down the request because it felt such a unit would create a "blow to freedom and to free institutions." Ibid., p. 90.*

p. 183    *"All the institutions young Hoover joined—Sunday school, church, Central High—regarded themselves as defense against the immigrant threat to the nation . . ."* Richard Gid Powers, Secrecy and Power: The Life of J. Edgar Hoover *(Free Press: New York, 1987), p. 33.*

p. 183    *For Hoover, the immigrant and the radical were part of what he saw as a larger pattern of lawlessness belonging to the modern world. Ibid., p. 91.*

p. 184    Hoover's justification. Ibid., p. 96.

p. 184    ". . . he was not going to rest until America's cities were 'completely cleaned up.'" Max Lowenthal, The Federal Bureau of Investigation (Harcourt, Brace: New York, 1950), pp. 18–19.

p. 184    Viola Liuzzo's husband was a Teamster Union official, which is what put Teamster boss Jimmy Hoffa on the side of Martin Luther King Jr. and the civil rights movement.

p. 184    He could turn on Communism everything that wracked his twisted soul. Powers, p. 97.

p. 185    McCarthy was discussing how he could revive his flagging political fortunes. Kovel, p. 112.

p. 185    Hunt said Communism began in this country when the government took over the distribution of the mail. Ibid.

p. 187    The Red hunt gave the appearance that the government was riddled with spies. Douglas Miller and Marion Nowack, The Fifties: The Way We Really Were (Doubleday: New York, 1977).

p. 188    Howard Fast, who was a member of the Communist Party, was jailed for contempt of Congress for three months in 1950. When I asked Fast whether going to jail scared him, he said, "No, quite the contrary. I looked on it as a challenge." While in jail, he began writing his most famous work, Spartacus, about an uprising among Roman slaves. He wrote dozens of books, including Citizen Tom Paine, Freedom Road, and The Immigrant's Daughter.

p. 194    The Giants stole the signs from the opposing team during their pennant run in 1951. According to Giants catcher Sal Yvars, infielder Henry Schenz and coach Herman Franks relayed signals from the Giants center-field clubhouse to the bullpen with a buzzer system created by electrician Abe Chadwick. Yvars then relayed the signals to the hitters, who knew what pitch was coming. The Associated Press, February 2, 2001.

Interview with Stan Kanter.

## Chapter 16: Victims of McCarthy—TERRY (TED) ROSENBAUM

See Ellen Schrecker, The Age of McCarthyism: A Brief History with Documents (Bedford/St. Martin's: New York, 1994).

p. 203    McCarthy undermined the findings. Richard Rovere, Senator Joe McCarthy (Harper/Colophon Books: New York, 1973), p. 156.

p. 210    Alfred Lama won the election. He served as a member of the New York State Assembly from 1943 to 1972.

Interview with Ted Rosenbaum.

## Chapter 17: The Absurdity of McCarthyism—JOSEPH BOSKIN

p. 284    Erich Fromm, a psychoanalyst, extolled the virtues of humans taking independent action and using reason to establish moral values, rather than adhering to authoritarian moral values.

p. 223    "Good night—and good luck." David M. Oshinsky, A Conspiracy So Immense: The World of Joe McCarthy (Free Press: New York, 1983), p. 399.

p. 224    "Have you no sense of decency left?" Ibid., p. 463.

p. 224    ". . . one of the most disgraceful episodes in the history of our government." Ibid., p. 471.

p. 224    Editorial in the Fort Worth Southern Conservative. *Richard Rovere,* Senator Joe McCarthy *(Harper/ Colophon Books: New York, 1973), p. 252.*

p. 224    McCarthy never uncovered one single Communist. *Oshinsky, p. 507.*

p. 224    *"He understood that force, action, and virility were essential for a Red-hunting crusade." Ibid., p. 507.*

p. 224    Ann Coulter to this day stoutly defends McCarthy.

*Interview with Joseph Boskin.*

## Chapter 18: Fearing the Unknown—PETER MEINKE

p. 234    *The poem comes from the book* Underneath the Lantern, *1986.*

*Interview with Peter Meinke.*

## Chapter 19: The Protestants Blend In—JUSTUS DOENECKE

p. 236    *A mob stripped him naked, wrapped him in the American flag, dragged him through the streets, and lynched him. John Barry,* Rising Tide: The Great Mississippi Flood of 1927 and How It Changed America *(Simon and Schuster: New York, 1997), p. 137.*

*Interview with Justus Doenecke.*

## Chapter 20: Muslim Immigrants—DAVE RADENS

*Interview with Dave Radens.*

## Chapter 21: Growing Up Greek in Red Hook—PETER SPANAKOS

*Interview with Peter Spanakos.*

## Chapter 22: Here Come the Italians—CURTIS SLIWA

p. 277    *Four million Italians came to America between 1890 and 1920. Frank J. Coppa and Thomas J. Curran,* The Immigrant Experience in America *(Twayne Publishers: Boston, 1976), p. 128.*

p. 277    *Some towns in Calabria lost as much as 20 percent of their population. Ibid., p. 124.*

p. 278    *The Irish were prejudiced against the Italians because they weren't orthodox enough. Ibid., p. 132.*

p. 279    *"Don't make your children better than we were." Ibid., p. 142.*

p. 279    *Only 6 percent of students at City College had Italian names. Ibid.*

*Interview with Curtis Sliwa.*

## Chapter 23: Here Come the Irish—Pete Hamill

p. 297    *Cromwell drove out the "treasonous, idol-worshiping, priest-ridden . . ." Pete Hamill,* Forever *(Little, Brown: Boston, 2003), p. 21.*

p. 298    *". . . the intention was clear: to humiliate Catholic men and break their hearts." Ibid., p. 58.*

p. 298    *Protestants were convinced Catholics were conspiring to undermine the American Revolution. Maxine Seller,* To Seek America: A History of Ethnic Life in the United States *(Jerome S. Ozer: New York, 1977), p. 95.*

p. 298    "Can one throw mud into pure water and not disturb its clearness?" Ibid.

p. 299    It was a secret Protestant fraternal organization . . . Roger Daniels, Guarding the Golden Door: American Immigration Policy and Immigrants since 1882 (Hill and Wang: New York, 2004).

Interview with Pete Hamill.

### Chapter 24: Windsor Terrace Memories—JOE FLAHERTY, BOBBY MCCARTHY, AND BILL REDDY

Interviews with Joe Flaherty, Bill Reddy, and Bobby McCarthy. These interviews were conducted in 1983 for my book Bums but were not used in the published book.

### Chapter 25: A Wild Child—JOHN FORD

p. 323    English laws prevented Catholics from owning land. Frank J. Coppa and Thomas J. Curran, The Immigrant Experience in America (Twayne Publishers: Boston, 1976), p. 95.

p. 323    The Irish were accepted after hostility shifted to the newer immigrants. Ibid., p. 109.

Interview with John Ford.

### Chapter 26: Son of Holocaust Survivors—HARRY SCHWEITZER

Interview with Harry Schweitzer.

### Chapter 27: For the Love of Billy Cox—JOHN MACKIE

Interview with John Mackie.

### Chapter 28: The Musical Genius of Lincoln High—NEIL SEDAKA

Among the early groups who recorded Sedaka-Greenfield songs were Laverne Baker, Clyde McFadder, The Clovers, The Cardinals, and The Cookies, who later went on to join Ray Charles as The Raylettes.

Interview with Neil Sedaka.

### Chapter 29: The End of Race Music—BRUCE MORROW

Interview with Bruce Morrow.

### Chapter 30: The Whites Discriminate—JOHN HOPE FRANKLIN

p. 392    White working-class homeowners viewed the prospect of Negro neighbors as a catastrophe equal to the loss of their homes. James R. Grossman, Land of Hope: Chicago, Black Southerners and the Great Migration (University of Chicago Press: Chicago, 1987), p. 175.

p. 392    Results of the 1921 public opinion poll. Ibid., p. 168.

Interview with John Hope Franklin.

### Chapter 31: The Move to the Burbs—IAN GRAD

Interview with Ian Grad.

### Chapter 32: The Dodgers Flee West—BILL REDDY, IRVING RUDD, STAN KANTER, AND PETE HAMILL

*p. 417*    *The editor of one L.A. paper vowed that the phrase "Dem Bums" would never appear in his newspaper. Edo McCullough,* Good Old Coney Island *(Charles Scribner's Sons: New York, 1957), p. 181.*

*See my book* Bums: An Oral History of the Brooklyn Dodgers *for more on the subject.*

*Interviews with Bill Reddy, Irving Rudd, and Pete Hamill.*

### Chapter 33: Growing Up Black in the Hood—ROBERT CROSSON

*p. 424*    *Loans became scarce, and times became hard. James R. Grossman,* Land of Hope: Chicago, Black Southerners and the Great Migration *(University of Chicago Press: Chicago, 1987), p. 28.*

*p. 424*    *In 1917, 2,500 blacks were forced out of two Georgia counties. Ibid., p. 17.*

*p. 425*    *Booker T. Washington's advice was to "stick to the farm," Ibid., p. 33.*

*p. 425*    *New York City's black population only rose from 91,709 in 1910 to 152,467 in 1920. Ibid., p. 4.*

*p. 425*    *In Macon, police evicted several hundred migrating blacks after they entered the railroad station. Ibid., p. 48.*

*p. 425*    *At Summit, Mississippi, police closed the railroad station. Ibid.*

*p. 425*    *The police of Greenville, Mississippi, would go into trains and drag out blacks trying to leave. Ibid., p. 108.*

*p. 426*    *Employers argued if they raised wages, blacks would use the extra money to buy a train ticket out of town. Ibid., p. 53.*

*p. 426*    *By 1899 reformer Jacob Riis declared Brownsville to be "a nasty little slum." Edo McCullough,* Good Old Coney Island *(Charles Scribner's Sons: New York, 1957), p. 201.*

*Interview with Robert Crosson.*

### Chapter 34: Cop on the Beat—JOHN MACKIE

*p. 438*    *By 1980, 656,000 whites had left, and 67,000 new blacks arrived. Edo McCullough,* Good Old Coney Island *(Charles Scribner's Sons: New York, 1957), p. 212.*

*Interview with John Mackie.*

### Chapter 35: The Black Panther—CHARLES BARRON

*p. 453*    *Marcus Garvey, the founder of the Universal Negro Improvement Association, like Martin Luther King forty years later, was targeted by J. Edgar Hoover for persecution. Hoover badly wanted to deport Garvey, but he didn't have grounds to do so. In November of 1919 the Bureau of Investigation hired five African-American agents to infiltrate his organization. A charge of mail fraud was brought against him in connection with the sale of stock of a shipping line he owned. Brochures that Garvey mailed bore the picture of the ship* Phyllis Wheatley, *before Garvey had the chance to change the name from the* Orion. *Hoover, calling the brochures "fraudulent," pushed for a conviction and got one. Garvey was sentenced to five years in prison. His sentence was commuted by President Calvin Coolidge. Since he was convicted of a felony and was not a U.S. citizen, he was deported to Jamaica, where a large crowd cheered his arrival. Garvey died in London in 1940, after a stroke. Garvey is lionized in a number of rap songs by black artists, including Ludacris, the Wu-Tang Clan, and Nas. A branch of the New York Public Library in Harlem is dedicated to him.*

p. 446    *Malcolm focused on the problems of the ghetto and black self-denial.* Nicholas Lemann, The Promised Land: The Great Black Migration and How It Changed America *(Alfred A. Knopf: New York, 1991), p. 163.*

p. 446    *The IRS collected dossiers on ten thousand individuals.* Michael Dorman, Witch Hunt: The Underside of American Democracy *(Delacorte Press: New York, 1976), p. 256.*

*Interview with Charles Barron.*

## Chapter 36: Here Come the Puerto Ricans—VICTOR ROBLES

*Interview with Victor Robles.*

## Chapter 37: Ocean Hill–Brownsville—CLARENCE TAYLOR

p. 468    *Clark's studies.* Clarence Taylor, Knocking at Our Own Door: Milton A. Galamison and the Struggle to Integrate New York City Schools *(Columbia University Press: New York, 1997), p. 53.*

p. 474    *Albert Shanker called the firings illegal. Ibid., p. 198.*

*Interview with Clarence Taylor.*

## Chapter 38: Going to School with the *Moolies*—CURTIS SLIWA

Mulignon *is a corrupt form of Italian for "eggplant."*
*Interview with Curtis Sliwa.*

## Chapter 39: Nothing Stays the Same—PETER SPANAKOS

*Interview with Peter Spanakos.*

## Chapter 40: The Guardian Angels—CURTIS SLIWA

*Interview with Curtis Sliwa.*

## Chapter 41: The King of the Tra-la-las—NEIL SEDAKA

*Interview with Neil Sedaka.*

## Chapter 42: The Night the Lights Went Out. Again.—ABRAM HALL

p. 519    *The city lost 340,000 jobs.* Jonathan Mahler, Ladies and Gentlemen, The Bronx Is Burning: 1977, Baseball, Politics, and the Battle for the Soul of the City *(Picador: New York, 2007), p. 224.*

p. 520    *There was more crime in Bushwick than any other district. Ibid., p. 189.*

p. 520    *There were thirty-four police officers. Ibid.*

p. 520    *First the professionals, then the alienated adolescents, then those motivated by "abject greed."* Robert Curvin and Bruce Porter, Blackout Looting! Report of the Ford Foundation.

p. 520    *Not one single cop from another precinct was sent to help. Mahler, p. 195.*

p. 521    *Forty-five stores had been looted and burned. Ibid., p. 205.*

p. 521   *3,776 people were arrested. Ibid., p. 218.*
*Interview with Abram Hall.*

## Chapter 43: Whites Move Back—HARRY SCHWEITZER

*Interview with Harry Schweitzer.*

## Chapter 44: A Marine Guards the Peace—RICHARD GREEN

*Interview with Richard Green.*

## Chapter 45: Shirley Chisholm's Boy—VICTOR ROBLES

*Interview with Victor Robles.*

## Chapter 46: Brighton Beach's Russian Jew—ALEC BROOK-KRASNY

p. 558   *Replacing them were Holocaust survivors . . . Nancy Foner,* New Immigrants in New York, *p. 278.*
*Interview with Alec Brook-Krasny.*

## Chapter 47: The Battle for Sexual Freedom—RENEE CAFIERO

p. 571   *Whitehall Street in Lower Manhattan was the location of New York's Army induction center. Lower Manhattan was a ghost town on the weekends, as there were no hotels or apartments at the time, and Battery Park City had not yet been built.*
*Interview with Renee Cafiero.*

## Chapter 48: The Echoes of 9/11—RICHARD PORTELLO

*Interview with Captain Richard Portello.*
*On June 22, 2007, Richard Portello was promoted to battalion chief.*

## Chapter 49: The Mural Painter—JANET BRAUN-REINITZ

*Interview with Janet Braun-Reinitz.*

## Chapter 50: The Councilman for Change—CHARLES BARRON

*Interview with Charles Barron.*

## Chapter 51: The Real Estate Boom—ABRAM HALL

*Interview with Abram Hall.*

## Chapter 52: Brooklyn's Cheerleader—MARTY MARKOWITZ

p. 622   *His constituency went from being 55 percent white to 92 percent black and Latino. Rebecca Mead,* The New Yorker, *April 25, 2005.*
*Interview with Marty Markowitz.*

## Chapter 53: The Atlantic Yards—JIM STUCKEY

*Interview with Jim Stuckey. On June 12, 2007, two weeks after my interview, Jim Stuckey resigned as executive vice president of Forest City Ratner.*

## Chapter 54: Remaking Coney Island—JOSEPH SITT

*Interview with Joe Sitt.*